As the Witnesses Fall Silent: 21st Century Holocaust Education in Curriculum, Policy and Practice

Zehavit Gross • E. Doyle Stevick
Editors

As the Witnesses Fall Silent: 21st Century Holocaust Education in Curriculum, Policy and Practice

United Nations
Educational, Scientific and
Cultural Organization

International Bureau
of Education

Editors
Zehavit Gross
School of Education
Bar-Ilan University
Ramat-Gan, Israel

E. Doyle Stevick
College of Education
University of South Carolina
Columbia, SC, USA

ISBN 978-3-319-15418-3   ISBN 978-3-319-15419-0   (eBook)
DOI 10.1007/978-3-319-15419-0

Library of Congress Control Number: 2015932960

Springer Cham Heidelberg New York Dordrecht London
© Springer International Publishing Switzerland 2015
This work is subject to copyright. All rights are reserved by the Publisher, whether the whole or part of the material is concerned, specifically the rights of translation, reprinting, reuse of illustrations, recitation, broadcasting, reproduction on microfilms or in any other physical way, and transmission or information storage and retrieval, electronic adaptation, computer software, or by similar or dissimilar methodology now known or hereafter developed.
The use of general descriptive names, registered names, trademarks, service marks, etc. in this publication does not imply, even in the absence of a specific statement, that such names are exempt from the relevant protective laws and regulations and therefore free for general use.
The publisher, the authors and the editors are safe to assume that the advice and information in this book are believed to be true and accurate at the date of publication. Neither the publisher nor the authors or the editors give a warranty, express or implied, with respect to the material contained herein or for any errors or omissions that may have been made.

Printed on acid-free paper

Springer International Publishing AG Switzerland is part of Springer Science+Business Media (www.springer.com)

I dedicate this book to my father Zvi Brenner, a Holocaust survivor from the Transnistria camp. I also thank him for choosing to live, and for choosing to lead a meaningful, spiritual, religious life.

–Zehavit Gross

This book is for Lucia, whose light always dispels the darkness.

–E. Doyle Stevick

Preface

In 2005, the United Nations passed a resolution on Holocaust Remembrance, encouraging all member states to "develop programmes that will inculcate future generations with the lessons of the Holocaust in order to help to prevent future acts of genocide". It was clear that Holocaust education would be at the centre of this effort, and, in 2007, UNESCO resolved to take leadership in making this vision a reality. As UNESCO Director-General, Irina Bokova, later explained, "Holocaust education is a responsibility—to face the reality of crimes perpetrated, to commemorate the victims and to sustain a meaningful dialogue between history and memory" (Bokova 2014, p. 5).

This dialogue is necessary not because the Holocaust is unique, but because we too often hear its echoes, in Bosnia, in Rwanda, in Syria and beyond. If we are to learn the lessons of the Holocaust, we must learn its history, and to do so it must be a meaningful part of the curriculum for students around the world. Its complexity requires time and engagement. Its depth is suffused with systematic violations of human rights of almost every imaginable kind, and can thus sensitize us to problematic and threatening trends both near and far. But just because Holocaust education can do these things does not mean that it will.

It is not enough to do what we believe we must; we need also to assess whether we are accomplishing what we intend. Research, policy and evaluation are indispensable elements of educational efforts to further humanize the world, to empower citizens, to break down prejudice, to address the extent of human suffering that is still inflicted by others. We must be driven by our moral convictions and seek evidence to guide our efforts. This book constitutes another step in this journey, and continues the commitment of UNESCO's International Bureau of Education (IBE) to promote up-to-date, high-quality research and good practice and policy in the field of curriculum and learning.

This journey takes teaching and learning about the Holocaust to parts of the world far removed from the sites where Nazis and their collaborators attempted to eliminate Jews—and many others they deemed inferior—from the face of the earth. But too many of these destinations know trauma all too well; they find parallels and similarities with aspects of the Holocaust in their own histories. It is these connections that make the Holocaust simultaneously particular and universal, a shared reference, a lens for understanding atrocities, and a warning for generations to come.

The Holocaust's broad relevance derives in part from its position in the broader global history of racialized thinking. Antisemitism's close cousin, racism, blighted the trans-Atlantic world for centuries, fueling the trade in human beings and the institution of slavery, thriving on exploitation and oppression. Patterns of racialized thinking moved easily between European and American cultures, manifested in a shared heritage of scientific racism that was discredited only with the advent of the Holocaust. If scientific racism was discredited, cultural racism and antisemitism lived on. However, a new commitment to non-violence flourished as well. Inspired partly by Gandhi's philosophy, African-Americans and Jews in the United States often stood side by side as they confronted racism. Gandhi had himself witnessed in both India and South Africa the racism that accompanied colonialism and in which laid the seeds of apartheid. The global roots of such struggles for justice and peace flowed together with lessons from the Holocaust, inspiring people across the world to begin to dismantle some of the institutional legacies of racism.

The spread of Holocaust education around the world inevitably entails a re-examination of curriculum, of the social and political processes that inform it, and of the policies, teacher training, and instruction that support and give expression to it. The Holocaust's complexity and deep connections with difficult histories require not a simple new addition or insertion into a set curriculum, or a few more hours squeezed into an already packed schedule, but a careful examination of its purposes, its fit and the complementary nature of the studies around it. In raising these important issues, this book makes a profound contribution to the work that lies ahead.

Our shared global commitment to end genocide and mass atrocities requires a multifaceted effort, with education at its heart. The lessons of history cannot be learned without effective history lessons, and each child's views should be shaped by a respect for Universal Human Rights. It is a task of constructing shared cultures of peace. It is a shared responsibility of universal importance.

Mmantsetsa Marope
Director
UNESCO International Bureau of Education
Geneva, Switzerland

References

Bokova, I. (2014). Foreword. In K. Fracapane & M. Haß (Eds.), *Holocaust education in a global context*. Paris: UNESCO.

Editors' Notes and Acknowledgements

Zehavit Gross In 2007, I was invited to join the official Israeli delegation to the United Nations and attend sessions held by the UN Commission on the Status of Women (CSW). I was also honored with the responsibility of presenting the State of Israel's official declaration at the UN General Assembly. While visiting the Foreign Ministry in Jerusalem to be briefed about the occasion, an official named Adam Ron asked if I was excited about the opportunity. I replied that I found it thrilling to represent the state, mainly, and perhaps paradoxically, because, as a second-generation Holocaust survivor, it presented me with a special opportunity to close one personal circle and open a new one. It was the United Nations that formally recognised Israel as a state. The same official told me that as one of the second generation, I should meet with Kimberley Mann, manager of the Holocaust and United Nations Outreach Programme. She was involved in implementing UN resolution 60/7, which designated 27 January—the anniversary of the liberation of the Auschwitz death camp—as an annual International Day of Commemoration in memory of the victims of the Holocaust.

My meeting with Kimberly Mann was among the most significant in my life. Ms. Mann, who is not Jewish, described the numerous endeavors of the United Nations to commemorate the Holocaust. Particularly impressive was her professional approach, the empathy she showed, and most of all her personal commitment to remembrance of the Holocaust. Her eyes gleamed as she described her work and dedication to the subject. When I left the meeting with her, I looked up at the sky—a moment I cannot forget—and wondered, "Zehavit, where are you in this story?"

As a second-generation Holocaust survivor whose field of research is Jewish identity, I had never dealt with the question of educating about the Holocaust. I had simply kept my distance from the subject. As a child and schoolgirl, I had central roles in plays and ceremonies at elementary and high school, but I always refused to take part as a representative on the platform at Holocaust memorial ceremonies. Though the ceremonies are considered highly important for the second generation, I simply lacked the psychological strength to deal with the ceremonies and the terrible sights described there. I ran away. I used to say cynically, "I've got the Holocaust at home"—a tough sentence, I know, and one that only the children of Holocaust survivors can understand.

My father came from "there" (the death camps, which one survivor described as another planet). That is what they called it when I was little. No one specifically said "camps", to avoid hurting the survivors. When they said "from there" everyone knew what they meant and a heavy silence would fall. We—who saw our parents coping daily with the loss, and with serious medical and psychological problems—were unable to speak. We are the generation of silence: a generation that absorbed the unease and the post-traumatic reactions of our beloved parents, and most of all, the loss of extensive parts of our family. It was only when I gave birth to my first son that I grasped how huge the loss was. My mother, who was born in Israel, immediately phoned her relatives to announce the new grandson, while my father, whose entire family was killed in the Holocaust, had no one to phone. There was no one he could invite to the *brith milah* ceremony. Having witnessed their terrible loss, we know why we stayed silent. How could we talk about it? And if we did, what would we say?

The Holocaust ruined the lives of many in my generation, and this has had numerous implications, though this is not the place to discuss them. But after that wonderful meeting with Kimberly Mann at the UN, I realized I could no longer seek refuge in the privilege of saying "I can't do it". Like the Biblical Jonah who fled from the mission that ultimately caught up with him, I now felt it was time to enlist special mental powers and use them in my mission.

My research on Holocaust education will continue as I focus on a Culture of Remembrance as a conceptual construct and systematically analyze how to implement its principles in practice. I intend to use the typology (denial—recognition—construction—deconstruction) I presented in this book as a conceptual device to conduct meta-analyses and comparative studies between countries around the world. My main focus will be distinguishing between research and advocacy by fostering new theoretical directions we can use to better navigate these uncharted waters.

E. Doyle Stevick Just months after the tragedy at Columbine High School exploded Americans' perception of schools as safe places, I learned from CNN that the police wanted to speak with a former student of mine about a string of shootings targeting Jews, blacks and Asians around Chicago. Had I read the student newspaper when he was in my course, I would have recognized his picture at once. An outspoken white supremacist, distributing hate literature around town, he had not shied away from the lens.

The day after his television appearance, this boy who once sat in my classroom took his own life in a gun battle with police, leaving his victims' families with questions impossible to answer.

I, too, had questions. How was it possible for an intelligent young man from good schools to embrace such an insane and hateful doctrine? His profile was scarcely different from my own. We were both straight, white, young American males from prosperous, high-achieving, and yet largely segregated Northern suburban schools and good public universities. What made us so different? Our views were learned, but apparently not in school. Nothing in my education would have changed, or even challenged, the perspective I brought with me to school. America had dismantled the legal segregation of schools and society, but there never was a national effort to use education to combat racism directly and systematically. I wondered what such an effort would look like.

In order to find out, I studied Estonian and researched how a highly successful post-Soviet country was attempting to shape the civic attitudes and dispositions of its young people through education. While I was conducting my research, a great backlash rose up against a group of foreign institutions that wanted Estonians to address the history of the Holocaust. I could not imagine that any sincere person could think differently from me about the killing of the Jews. I felt I needed to understand the backlash from their point of view. Foreigners rarely understood their language or knew anything about their country's tragic history, the devastation they experienced during World War II, and the constriction of life under Soviet rule. The same outsiders who stood by when their country was invaded from east and west now wanted to tell Estonians what they should think and do. Membership in the community of European nations was made contingent on adopting the western view of the Holocaust. What would it be? Would they take the carrot of funding or the stick of exclusion from joint security and western markets that are fundamental to the very existence of a tiny country on Russia's borders?

I presented my research about this controversy at the Comparative and International Education Society conference in Baltimore in 2007. Zehavit Gross approached me and proposed that we work together to plan a special issue of a journal dedicated to research on Holocaust education. That vision resulted in a double special issue of the comparative education journal *Prospects*, published by UNESCO's International Bureau of Education (IBE) in 2010.

Readers wanted more. Why should we teach about the Holocaust and subject young people to these painful revelations? And what should we teach them—is there agreement about that? And do our students have anything to tell us about their lives that can spark the dialogue between the present and the past? A hidden community of disparate inquirers was asking the same questions. In response to this grassroots search for answers, we were invited to develop this book. We couldn't be happier with the emerging community of scholars that is represented in this book. Great research not only answers questions, but raises new ones. These outstanding contributions multiply our questions and deepen the mystery of ultimate answers.

Sometimes it takes a global village. This book is the product of such an effort. We thank both Mmantsetsa Marope and Clementina Acedo for their support of this crucial project. We also thank all the contributors to this volume for their patience, persistence, and commitment. We owe a special debt to Simona Popa, for her extraordinary dedication and persistence; without her, the book could not have happened. Helen Snively did remarkable work with manuscripts, and with great spirit. Aaron Anthony, a student at the University of Pittsburgh, also contributed to the process.

–Zehavit Gross and E. Doyle Stevick

From the bottom of my heart, I want to thank Simona Popa of UNESCO IBE, who invited us to edit the two special issues of *Prospects*, and later the book, and also Doyle Stevick, who, with immense sensitivity and persistence, helped me free myself from that personal discomfort about the Holocaust. Then, together, we could develop conceptual systems to assist Holocaust education research internationally, along with methods of teaching the Holocaust—but most of all could contribute to shaping a Culture of Remembrance in the schooling systems of many countries.

–Zehavit Gross

Sometimes, the right person hears your work at the right time. When Zehavit Gross came to listen to my paper at the 2007 Comparative and International Education Society (CIES) conference in Baltimore, I could never have imagined where it would lead. But in the 8 years since we began working on the special issues of *Prospects*, many doors have opened; many great colleagues have contributed to this journey, and this volume, and have enriched my life as colleagues and friends. Wolfgang Meseth and Matthias Proske brought me to Germany; en route I met Dienke Hondius, and, from there, the remarkable community at the Anne Frank House: Jan Erik Dubbelman, Barry van Driel, Karen Polak, and so many more. The journal introduced me to Monique Eckmann and through her the members of the IHRA and the great team she assembled there. The opportunity to work closely for years with Magdalena Gross and Deborah Michaels has been invaluable. Karel Fracapane has been as steadfast in his commitment to research as he has been to the field. Closer to home, the Rosengartens, Ted and Dale, have been great friends, travel companions, editors, and raconteurs. Ted's advice always serves me well.

I also thank my family. I thank Calvin and Lucia for your patience—now let's spend more time building with Legos and getting out on the ice rink. Kara Brown, your boundless energy helped to sustain my own. And Eugene and Emily Stevick are still helping make everything possible. Thank you, everyone!

–E. Doyle Stevick

Contents

Part I Introduction

**Holocaust Education in the 21st Century:
Curriculum, Policy and Practice** 3
E. Doyle Stevick and Zehavit Gross

Part II Framing the Issues for a New Millennium

**Address to the German Bundestag: Holocaust Remembrance Day
(Berlin, 27 January, 2000)** 19
Elie Wiesel

**"Why Does the Way of the Wicked Prosper?":
Teaching the Holocaust in the Land of Jim Crow** 25
Theodore Rosengarten

**Is Teaching and Learning about the Holocaust Relevant
for Human Rights Education?** 53
Monique Eckmann

Shoah, Antisemitism, War and Genocide: Text and Context 67
Yehuda Bauer

**Learning from Eyewitnesses: Examining the History
and Future of Personal Encounters with Holocaust
Survivors and Resistance Fighters** 81
Dienke Hondius

**Teaching about and Teaching through the Holocaust:
Insights from (Social) Psychology** 95
Barry van Driel

Part III Reckoning with the Holocaust in Israel, Germany and Poland

Between Involuntary and Voluntary Memories: A Case Study of Holocaust Education in Israel 111
Zehavit Gross

Domesticating the Difficult Past: Polish Students Narrate the Second World War 137
Magdalena H. Gross

Mind the Gap: Holocaust Education in Germany, between Pedagogical Intentions and Classroom Interactions 159
Wolfgang Meseth and Matthias Proske

Part IV Holocaust Education in Diverse Classrooms

Holocaust Education and Critical Citizenship in an American Fifth Grade: Expanding Repertoires of Meanings, Language and Action 185
Louise B. Jennings

"They Think It Is Funny to Call Us Nazis": Holocaust Education and Multicultural Education in a Diverse Germany 209
Debora Hinderliter Ortloff

Genocide or Holocaust Education: Exploring Different Australian Approaches for Muslim School Children 225
Suzanne D. Rutland

Part V International Dynamics, Global Trends and Comparative Research in Holocaust Education

A Global Mapping of the Holocaust in Textbooks and Curricula 245
Peter Carrier, Eckhardt Fuchs, and Torben Messinger

International Organisations in the Globalisation of Holocaust Education 263
Karel Fracapane

Compliant Policy and Multiple Meanings: Conflicting Holocaust Discourses in Estonia 277
E. Doyle Stevick

The Holocaust as History and Human Rights: A Cross-National Analysis of Holocaust Education in Social Science Textbooks, 1970–2008 299
Patricia Bromley and Susan Garnett Russell

**Measuring Holocaust Knowledge and Its Relationship
to Attitudes towards Diversity in Spain, Canada, Germany,
and the United States** 321
Jack Jedwab

Part VI   Holocaust Education in National and Regional Contexts

**Holocaust History, Memory and Citizenship Education:
The Case of Latvia** 337
Thomas Misco

**Mastering the Past? Nazism and the Holocaust in West German
History Textbooks of the 1960s** 357
Brian M. Puaca

**Informed Pedagogy of the Holocaust: A Survey of Teachers Trained
by Leading Holocaust Organisations in the United States** 375
Corey L. Harbaugh

**"Unless They Have To": Power, Politics and Institutional
Hierarchy in Lithuanian Holocaust Education** 391
Christine Beresniova

**Holocaust Education in Austria: A (Hi)story of Complexity
and Prospects for the Future** 407
Heribert Bastel, Christian Matzka, and Helene Miklas

**"Thanks to Scandinavia" and Beyond: Nordic Holocaust
Education in the 21st Century** 427
Fred Dervin

**Holocaust Education in Scotland: Taking the Lead
or Falling Behind?** 439
Paula Cowan and Henry Maitles

Part VII   To Know, to Remember, to Act

Failing to Learn from the Holocaust 455
Geoffrey Short

**Towards a New Theory of Holocaust Remembrance
in Germany: Education, Preventing Antisemitism,
and Advancing Human Rights** 469
Reinhold Boschki, Bettina Reichmann, and Wilhelm Schwendemann

**Epistemological Aspects of Holocaust Education:
Between Ideologies and Interpretations** 489
Zehavit Gross and E. Doyle Stevick

Notes on Contributors 505

Part I
Introduction

Holocaust Education in the 21st Century: Curriculum, Policy and Practice

E. Doyle Stevick and Zehavit Gross

In 2005, the United Nations encouraged its member states "to develop educational programmes that will inculcate future generations with the lessons of the Holocaust in order to help to prevent future acts of genocide" (UN 2005). But the bold dream of preventing genocide has run up against the reality of state-sponsored mass murder in different parts of the globe by perpetrators who were fully aware of Nazi aims and atrocities. Former United Nations Secretary General Kofi Annan (2010) expressed frustration: "it is surprisingly hard to find education programmes that have clearly succeeded in linking the history of the Holocaust with the prevention of ethnic conflict and genocide in today's world" (Stevick and Michaels 2013 discuss and critique his argument). The failure of the noble purposes that animate Holocaust educators to avert the most dreaded outcome of hate-driven conflict threatens to disillusion supporters of these efforts and undercut their real successes.

We share the conviction that teaching the Shoah effectively can contribute to making a better world, to protecting human rights and strengthening democracy, and even to preventing genocide. Yet, this conviction derives more from anecdotal evidence, eloquent as it is, than from empirical research. That foundation does not yet exist, but we hope this volume establishes a cornerstone.

This darkest of chapters in human history poses a formidable test for educators, many of whom rise to the challenge with passion and creativity. At their best, this union of purpose and ingenuity can produce extraordinary lessons. But educators

---

E.D. Stevick (✉)
College of Education, University of South Carolina,
318 Wardlaw Hall, Columbia, SC 29208, USA
e-mail: stevick@mailbox.sc.edu

Z. Gross
School of Education, Bar-Ilan University, Ramat-Gan, Israel
e-mail: grossz@mail.biu.ac.il

are burdened not only by the need to get the content right, to tell the true story, but also by expectations that teaching about the Holocaust will transform attitudes and character, and change future behavior. Holocaust education may or may not be able to deliver on these changes; we simply do not have enough research to draw this conclusion definitively. Furthermore, firsthand experience makes us skeptical that Holocaust education as currently conceived in most places could have such measurable, long-term impacts on behavior. Learning about the Holocaust is simply too rich, complex, and culturally specific for simple cause-and-effect studies to establish universal best practices.

How do teachers and students make sense of the Holocaust from one country to another? Conscientious studies of what teachers believe, what students understand, and how these meanings are debated in the classroom reveal worldviews and cultural assumptions, a dazzling variety and disparity of educational tools, teaching built on memories and personal encounters, and lessons driven by textbooks. Such studies, rooted in particular institutional and cultural contexts, cannot be integrated into a clean, comprehensive synthesis, but they do have a broader relevance whose boundaries we cannot yet discern.

For example, a rich set of observations in a Bavarian classroom may offer fascinating insights, but begs the question of whether those qualities hold true, e.g., across Germany, among immigrant students everywhere, only in Catholic countries, or just in that particular community. An investigator's local expertise allows her to emphasise those apparently meaningful characteristics of the milieu that may be present in other contexts, but until the research base into Holocaust education expands, we will be unable to establish the parameters of broader trends or the common circumstances that are conducive to them. This much is certain: we are nearer to the beginning of what there is to know about the trends and limits of Holocaust education and its potential for transforming individuals and societies than to the end.

The need for high-quality research is particularly urgent today. Holocaust education is expanding rapidly around the world, and we have much to learn about how peoples far from Europe make sense of its history and its meaning for today. In societies more directly affected by the Holocaust, opportunities for personal encounters with Holocaust survivors are diminishing, disappearing all too soon. We cannot predict how new generations will relate to this terrible past and what it means for us all going forward.

Research is also needed to explore both the efforts of organisations dedicated to Holocaust education and work occurring in other language contexts. Institutions including Yad Vashem, the International Holocaust Remembrance Alliance (IHRA), the United States Holocaust Memorial Museum (USHMM), the Anne Frank House, and many others promote Holocaust education all over the world. Unfortunately, they seldom conduct or commission high-quality research or evaluations of their projects and make them public, a missed opportunity to refine their own practice while sharing successes. Fortunately, this trend may be reversing. Representatives and affiliates of many of these institutions (Bauer, Fracapane, Harbaugh, Hondius, and van Driel, all in this volume) are strongly represented here, and the future of the field will benefit greatly from their ongoing and expanded participation in it. The gulf between what is occurring in the field and what is researched remains exceptionally large.

The field also needs richer exchanges across language contexts. Countries such as Israel and Germany have both extensive Holocaust education programmes and multiple scholars who regularly publish in English as well as their domestic languages. This volume represents an effort to bring together in one place a diverse range of high-quality research about Holocaust education from across the globe. It includes empirical research by scholars from English-speaking countries who work in other languages or language contexts (including Beresniova, M. Gross, Misco, Ortloff, Puaca, and Stevick). Conducting and writing up high-quality empirical research in Holocaust education is daunting enough for native speakers. We are particularly appreciative of the contributors to this volume who crossed the language barrier into English (Bastel, Matzka, and Miklas; Boschki, Reichmann, and Schwendemann; Eckmann; Fracapane; Z. Gross; Hondius; and Meseth and Proske). This volume, which significantly extends these exchanges, builds upon the 2010 publication of two special issues (volume 40, issues 1 and 2) of *Prospects*, the comparative education journal published by UNESCO's International Bureau of Education. Other special issues soon followed: *European Education*, volume 44, issue 3, dedicated to Central and Eastern Europe; and *Intercultural Education*; volume 24, issues 1 and 2.

Much remains to be done. Such research is often expensive, and a combination of building scholars' and institutions' capacity to do research, developing cooperative and comparative multilingual projects, and making grants contingent on external, public evaluations can all help to advance the field in the future. The field will certainly be enriched when more voices join a dialogue already rich with English-, German-, and Hebrew-speaking scholars.

Our belief that Holocaust education has profound potential is shared by many, educators and researchers alike. Indeed, scholars have explored the affinities between Holocaust education and anti-racism (e.g., Carrington and Short 1997), particularly struggles against antisemitism (Gordon et al. 2004) and homophobia (van Dijk 2010), democratic education (Kavadias 2004), education for human rights (Eckmann, this volume), citizenship education (Maitles 2008; Maitles and Cowan 2004), intercultural education (van Driel 2003), including intergroup encounters (Bekerman and Zembylas 2010), remembrance (Boschki, Reichmann, and Schwendemann, this volume; Von Der Dunk 2002), and transformative learning (Boyd 2009; Carlberg 2008; Tinning 2014). Similar explorations are warranted for the fields of comparative genocide, global citizenship education, multicultural education, and peace education (Powers 2007). These largely (but not exclusively) theoretical explorations are often rooted in optimal or maximal approaches to Holocaust education.

The expanding corpus of empirical research is particularly rich with studies of educational materials, particularly textbooks, thanks in no small part to the resources of the Georg Eckert Institute. For language contexts whose Holocaust education is not extensively documented in English, textbook analyses are among the first studies to appear (e.g., Bărbulescu et al. 2013; Beresniova 2014; Dietsch 2012; Frankl 2003; Michaels 2013). Used creatively, they can open a window on the past (Puaca, this volume), reveal global trends (Bromley and Russell, this volume), and show patterns of local adaptation (Carrier, Fuchs, and Messinger, this volume).

Studies of how such materials are employed in the classroom are comparatively rare, as are studies of teaching methods and student-teacher exchanges generally. Teachers may answer surveys about their methods, pointing to broader trends (Harbaugh, this volume), or researchers can conduct direct observations of individual class sessions, recording, transcribing, and analyzing what happens there (for example, Meseth and Proske, this volume). This approach reveals fine-grained exchanges and raises issues of broader concern, even when the methods are not designed for generalisation.

In practice, not only are materials bound up with teaching methods, and methods integral to the shared construction of meaning in the classroom; they also become increasingly difficult to research and uncommon in the literature. The same trend holds for studies of knowledge, skills, and attitudes or dispositions. The field is almost completely devoid of such experimental studies. Surveys of knowledge can provide useful baselines and point to correlations with desirable traits such as tolerant attitudes (Jedwab, this volume), but studies of skills are less common, and attitudes and dispositions are particularly difficult to research. The field could benefit greatly from free access to validated instruments for affective learning, for example.

The moral vision of Holocaust survivors and the expertise of leading historians play central roles in the field of Holocaust education. Although distinguishing the moral and empirical bases for Holocaust education approaches is important, these voices orient the field and guide research as well. To advance the dialogue between advocacy and research, this volume features Elie Wiesel, Theodore Rosengarten, and Yehuda Bauer. The production of knowledge, never a morally neutral activity, unfolds within the broader moral discourse in the field. Perhaps no individual has been a more vocal advocate for Holocaust education over the past half century than Elie Wiesel. On 27 January, 2000, he addressed the German Bundestag, speaking in the same city where he and his people "were condemned to isolation, distress, despair and death". His quest to fight hate could not be conducted with bitterness, and his own lifelong struggle to understand the universal human tragedies of his times provides a natural starting point for considering the educational imperative for the 21st century. Wiesel is a master storyteller, and starting with shattering memoir *Night*, which opened the floodgates for Holocaust remembrance, his stories have been among the most powerful and enduring tools teachers have used to communicate the visceral realities of the Holocaust. Survivor and witness, a Hungarian Jew born in Romania, Wiesel does not accuse, but empathizes: "The children of killers are not killers, but children". He sees what we are attempting to sort out: "I am not sure that I have the answer to the Holocaust, but surely education is a major component of that answer".

Theodore Rosengarten offers a memoir of a lifelong journey into Holocaust education. From the first celebrations of Hitler's demise in Brooklyn and the influx of "refs", victims of a horror for which the world still lacked a name, to the arrival of Jackie Robinson on the baseball diamond, the stories of Americans of African descent and of the country's established and newly arriving Jews unfolded in tandem. His journey spans research into slavery and the Holocaust, the intellectual ferment of Harvard, and the strange pull of the American South on historians from Brooklyn. His biography of an Alabama tenant farmer, *All God's Dangers*, won the 1974 National Book Award for Contemporary Affairs. When his southern college offered the opportunity to teach the Holocaust, he planned to proceed, "by comparing the policies and results of radical racism in two different environments". Ted and his wife Dale travel frequently with students from the South to Holocaust and Jewish cultural sites in Eastern Europe. Each place has its own story, each student her own motivation, her own insight, which Rosengarten reports, thus extending the circle of fellow travelers from Brooklyn to Bialystok, from 1945 to 2014.

Monique Eckmann observes that the Holocaust can play three roles in relation to human rights education: education about human rights, for human rights, or within the framework of human rights. Risks exist, of course, such as moving towards simplistic moralising before students have had sufficient time with the material to acquire foundational knowledge and to develop historical understanding. Eckmann believes we can be attentive to history and memory without setting them at odds, but notes the importance of maintaining a clear distinction between commemorative and educational activities.

Dienke Hondius uses eyewitness testimony to bring World War II and the Holocaust in the Netherlands into sharp focus. Holland lost 75% of its Jews, the highest rate of Jewish mortality of any occupied country in western Europe. These terrible losses were followed by a post-war wave of antisemitism and by a general avoidance of discussions about this national calamity. Public discussion confined itself to the war and the victimisation of all Dutch citizens, studiously dodging the special plight of the Jews. Change came slowly, and in the 1970s the Holocaust began to merit more attention. Emphasis shifted to witnesses' experiences, and by the 1990s, an awareness that the Dutch could have done more to save Jews converged with NATO's failure to intervene in Srebrenica, where thousands of Muslim boys and men were killed while Dutch forces stood on the sidelines. Combined with increased understanding of Dutch conduct in Indonesia, the self-image of the nation suffered. Hondius attests to the trend of demystification, as the first generation to grow up hearing about the Holocaust from a young age confronts its parents and grandparents as they look to revise the Dutch historical narrative to incorporate individual acts of heroism and collective crimes toward the Jews in wartime Holland.

Yehuda Bauer reminds us that antisemitisim was at the heart of Nazi ideology, and that the Nazis started World War II, using the war as a cover for tracking down and killing Europe's Jews. Bauer cites a 1936 memo and a more famous speech to the Reichstag in 1931, in which Hitler loudly anticipated the end of either Germans or Jews in the event of a war with Bolshevism. Though seemingly a paradox, this racial ideology saw Jews behind both capitalism and communism, both perceived to be grave threats. Noting that neither Germans nor German industry wanted war, Bauer critiques traditional structural-functionalist and internationalist explanations for the Holocaust. He is concerned that understanding "what actually happened and why" too often gets eclipsed by peripheral considerations.

If Yehuda Bauer takes a primarily historical approach, Barry van Driel sees his two decades of work in Holocaust education at the Anne Frank House and around the world through the lens of social psychology. In "teaching about and teaching through the Holocaust", van Driel draws on a passage from Anne Frank's journal about the spread of antisemitism. When a group begins to suffer, that suffering does not necessarily lead to increased empathy and support from others; too often what happens is the opposite. A circular logic can ensue, in which outsiders adopt a "blame the victim" posture, and attribute the group's suffering to its own conduct or character. The examples he cites of attitudes hardening towards Jews in the 1930s, despite an awareness of what was being inflicted upon them, are striking. Anne Frank's observation thus supports an entry point to a broader examination of prejudice and racism and shows how the dynamics of prejudice can be taught in schools, an action van Driel hopes can contribute to the design of more effective educational programmes to combat prejudice.

Holocaust education poses different challenges for the countries most directly connected to the history of the Holocaust. Here, Zehavit Gross, Magdalena Gross (no relation), and Wolfgang Meseth and Matthias Proske explore some of the dynamics of Holocaust education in Israel, Poland, and Germany. Zehavit Gross reviews the history of Holocaust education in Israel, placing it into periods to capture the major turning points in public attitudes about the Holocaust. She employs the distinction between voluntary and involuntary memory to guide the discussion. She explores the increasingly prominent role of the Holocaust in Israeli national identity, and the major turning points, from the Eichmann trial, through the Six-Day War, to Likud's election. To characterise these shifting periods, Gross employs the concepts of epistemology and ontology. Seeing "a flow from the collective to the individual, the emotional to the cognitive, the particularistic to the universalistic, the Jewish to the civic", Gross proceeds to explore ongoing dilemmas in Israel's relationship to the Holocaust and education about it.

Magdalena Gross examines the ways in which Polish students narrated World War II. By analysing 53 student responses, she is able to discern patterns across student narratives, grouping them into three major categories: ruin, resistance, and victimhood. These students tamed or schematised the difficult past. However, amidst these variations, which generally reflect Poland's broader national narrative on the Holocaust, Gross finds that a few students produced a counter-narrative. This counter-narrative not only better reflects the reality of the Holocaust in World War II Poland; it also presents an enormous opportunity for teachers. If used effectively, teachers could build upon students' counter-narratives to break down schematic, or well accepted, versions of the Holocaust past. In other words, teachers could use students to teach other students about wartime realities.

Wolfgang Meseth and Matthias Proske analyze how the organisational framework of instruction in Germany shapes the treatment of National Socialism as a topic and gives it a specific pedagogical form; it gives rise to a tension between the need to provide an adequate representation of National Socialism's crimes and to fulfill the goals of moral education. This dilemma is illustrated across four cases, each of which demonstrates the challenges that can arise—and how they are handled in the classroom—from the moral implications of certain teaching materials, such as an interview with a contemporary witness, an excerpt from Hitler's *Mein Kampf*, and a documentary on Hitler's seizure of power. The authors draw attention to a paradox: how can teachers develop students' autonomous judgment while directing the moral outcomes to be achieved? They reveal a line that can be hard to navigate, between the frequent over-moralisation and under-moralisation of German Holocaust education in practice. Meseth and Proske also refocus the reader on a critical but under-attended issue: the diverse pre-existing knowledge and understandings that students bring to the classroom, and their implications for the process and the group as a whole.

Meseth and Proske raise the issue of teaching the Holocaust in diverse classrooms, a circumstance rife with its own challenges, risks, and opportunities. Louise Jennings' analysis brings the tools of qualitative research to bear on classroom interactions surrounding the Holocaust; her fully ethnographic work elaborates the issues at play in four critical instances. She explores the benefits and possibilities of Holocaust studies for fifth grade bilingual children in the United States. She examines how this classroom context and use of particular academic practices supported these young students in grappling with the very difficult questions and content of the Holocaust, from genocide, racism, and discrimination to organised resistance and social responsibility. She brings to these data a framework of critical citizenship, asking how the Tolerance Focus supported students in developing a capacity for sociopolitical critique and action.

Among Jennings' critical contributions is the placement of effective Holocaust education within broader academic contexts. Holocaust education is often treated as a unit, discrete from what comes before or after, and preparation for it is too often absent; when deliberate preparation and anticipation is present, it generally is limited to addressing the historical roots and antecedent events. Jennings spent a year working with Irene Pattenaude, who with her colleagues constructed a year-long focus on community, tolerance, and rights. The Holocaust was a focus of study for the second half of that year, but the students had been primed for it through four months of careful work on rights, respect, and community, establishing the patterns of thought and intellectual tools for their engagement with the complexity and horrors of the Holocaust. The project proved so compelling that Jennings spent the following year with the group, effectively locating an intensive Holocaust study within a broader two-year learning environment. The powerful ways in which their Holocaust study is conceptualised within this broader context make it one of the most valuable qualitative studies we yet have in the field.

Debora Hinterliter Ortloff reveals how efforts to link Holocaust education with anti-violence education and multicultural education in Bavaria too often have exclusionary if paradoxical effects. Textbooks intending to send a pro-tolerance message inadvertently adopt a perpetrator perspective—don't be a neo-Nazi—which makes little sense to students not of ethnic German backgrounds, even if they are citizens. Teachers reflect this view: they believe students with a migrant background cannot really understand what it is like to be German, because only ethnic Germans can bear the shame of the Holocaust.

Suzanne Rutland grapples with one of the most challenging situations documented in the Holocaust education literature: students' open expression of anti-Jewish sentiments, in this case by Muslim children in Sydney. She explores the possibility of reframing Jewish-Muslim relations in the context of their common heritage as Abrahamic faiths, with a focus on the shared values in both traditions. Rutland applies her data to consider whether a focus on the Holocaust alone can succeed in such a context, or whether a comparative genocide approach might be more effective.

From diverse classrooms, we turn to international and comparative research about Holocaust education. Peter Carrier, Eckhardt Fuchs, and Torben Messinger provide an overview of their cutting-edge comparative work on Holocaust education curricula and textbook research. The Georg Eckert Institute for International Textbook Research, together with UNESCO, examined 272 active curricula from 135 countries, including national curricula in centralised education systems and curricula from states and regions in decentralised systems like the United States and Germany. From 26 countries across the inhabited continents they also examined 89 textbooks, and were supported and informed by the cultural and linguistic insights of local educators and researchers. Their work reveals patterns of convergence and localisation in how the Holocaust is understood and presented around the world. This work is particularly critical as reference and study of the Holocaust spread through parts of the world less directly connected to its history, and unsurprisingly, it often occurs in problematic ways. The Holocaust may be used instrumentally, not to illuminate the history of the Holocaust per se, but to accomplish other aims, such as teaching about human rights, or drawing explicit or implicit comparisons with episodes of other nations' suffering.

The authors find that roughly half of the countries examined formally stipulate teaching about the Holocaust, while curricula from others refer to the context alone, and others make no reference at all. Those countries that refer only to context, or make no reference, may in fact address the Holocaust, but one may suppose that its treatment is inconsistent without clear policy and curriculum guidance. In such cases, textbook treatments may provide some sense of its possible presence, but textbook and curriculum treatments of the Holocaust are not always fully consistent either, particularly as one or the other is revised.

Despite some convergent trends, the variations are substantial enough, not just regionally but even from one textbook to another, that the authors felt they were often witnessing not just different representations of the Holocaust, but the construction of multiple Holocausts in educational materials. This chapter, read in tandem with that by Bromley and Russell, gives a complementary sense of the patterns of convergence and localisation that have provoked scholars of globalisation and proponents of institutional isomorphism: the idea that educational systems, policies, practices, and curricula are becoming more and more similar.

Carrier, Fuchs, and Messinger find potential models in many places, suggesting that it would be a mistake to envision a linear model of delivering appropriate approaches from exemplar countries to others. Instead, they see potential mutual influence in many directions. Argentina is notable for presenting different interpretations of the Holocaust, including Arendt, Goldhagen, and Baumann, to be examined critically. South Africa provides a compelling historical approach to racism that others might emulate. Yet, common challenges remain. There is little, if any, discussion of Jews outside the period of 1933–1945. The "Great Man" theory of history is manifested in frequent Hitler-centric representations of the period, as if his individual hatred and ideology were sufficient to explain the Holocaust. By portraying Jews mostly as voiceless victims, textbooks remain centred on the perpetrators, sometimes using their language and even perspective, and focusing more on the crime than on the people and cultures that were devastated.

Karel Fracapane has played a leading role in UNESCO and the International Holocaust Remembrance Alliance (IHRA) (formerly the International Task Force for International Cooperation on Holocaust Education, Remembrance and Research), an organisation launched at the turn of the century following an effort by Swedish Prime Minister Göran Persson. Fracapane's *Holocaust Education in a Global Context* (2014), which he edited with Matthias Haß, includes the perspectives of many leading figures in the field. In his contribution to this volume, Fracapane examines the role of international organisations in expanding education and knowledge about the Holocaust around the world.

Doyle Stevick applies a socio-cultural analysis to Estonia's Holocaust Day policy, established in 2002. He investigates the multi-level development of the policy in light of external pressure (from foreign advocates and transnational groups including NATO and the Council of Europe) and the ways in which policy as normative discourse was constructed and its meanings negotiated between international sources, the national government, and educators. It draws attention to the multifaceted nature of discourse in a post-authoritarian context in which the disparities of power between people at different policy levels (international, national, school) are quite large.

Patricia Bromley and Susan Garnett Russell examine Holocaust education in secondary school social science textbooks around the world since 1970, using data coded from 465 textbooks from 69 countries. They find that the books and countries that are more likely to discuss the Holocaust are those that are more connected to world society, with an accompanying emphasis on human rights, diversity in society and a depiction of international, rather than national, society. They also find a shift in the nature of discussion, from seeing the Holocaust as a historical event to seeing it as a violation of human rights or a crime against humanity. These findings broadly support the arguments of neo-institutional theories that the social and cultural realms of the contemporary world are increasingly globalised and that notions of human rights are a central feature of world society.

For researchers of Holocaust education, an important task is to tease out the implicit theories of Holocaust education policy and practice, and to examine these theories in light of the empirical evidence. Jack Jedwab does precisely this. Advocates and practitioners of Holocaust education hope that a better understanding of the Holocaust will result in a deeper multicultural perspective or impulse, yet, in his examination of survey data, Jedwab can detect no clear causal or correlational relationship between knowledge of the Holocaust and, for example, attitudes about immigration.

Following the comparative and international studies are a collection of national and regional studies. Tom Misco has worked in Holocaust education intensively in Latvia and Romania. His work (Misco 2006) has documented how an open and dialogic process can facilitate a critical engagement with difficult history among peoples who often feel accused when the topic is raised. Conceptualising Holocaust education as a powerful component of democratic citizenship education and arguing for the value of engaging directly with controversial issues, Misco deals in depth with the particular challenges Latvia faced as it began to grapple with this difficult history.

Brian Puaca overturns the conventional picture of German textbooks and their treatment of the Holocaust and its antecedents during the 1960s. He draws attention to changes, too often overlooked by scholars, in the narrative, design, and pedagogy of the books, and particularly their inclusion of primary sources, photographs, and probing questions. Notably, he shows how they encourage students to confront not just the predominant societal discourses around the Holocaust and treatment of Jews, but even their own parents and grandparents. The dynamics he reveals complement the work of Proske (2012) in Germany and Z. Gross (2010) in Israel, both of whom emphasise the importance of generational shifts in their countries' approach to and interpretation of the Holocaust.

Corey Harbaugh, whose work in the field drew the attention of President Obama, surveyed American teachers who had completed training from at least one of three major American institutions dedicated to Holocaust education, in order to understand the influences on their practice and their approaches to teaching. These are alumni of programmes run by the United States Holocaust Memoriam Museum, where Harbaugh is a fellow, the University of Southern California Shoah Foundation, and the Memorial Library. Harbaugh developed a useful template of ten approaches to teaching the Holocaust, and shed important light on the opportunities to teach about the Holocaust in American schools and the practices of extensively trained teachers. Particularly notable are the flexibility of language and literature teachers to engage Holocaust issues in their courses, whether through novels, memoirs, or graphic novels, and the extremely high percentage of these well-prepared educators who still desired further professional development about the Holocaust.

Christine Beresniova spent more than 2 years conducting ethnographic research around Holocaust education in Lithuania. Because the degree of local collaboration in Holocaust atrocities in Lithuania makes the climate particularly contentious, teachers who do wish to teach the subject face considerable peer pressure. Somewhat paradoxically, the support available from different powerful hierarchies is not equally helpful. The teachers were found to strongly desire the support of their direct supervisors, the school directors, to create space for them to teach the subject; meanwhile the advocacy of foreign authorities complicated their efforts, because it often generated a backlash and helped to frame Holocaust education not as something intrinsically linked to Lithuanian history but rather as a specifically foreign or Jewish endeavor that does not belong in the country.

Heribert Bastel, Christian Matzka, and Helene Miklas analyze Holocaust education in Austria, tackling the ambivalence, complexity, and sensitivities involved within this issue. They point to the lack of serious research concerning memorials in Austria as compared with Germany, especially because of the antisemitism and Nazi background of Austria. With a focus on the Heldenplatz and its place in the culture of remembrance in Vienna, the authors find that, despite some ongoing challenges and troubles, Holocaust education has made important strides after a slow start after the war. Unfortunately, the nationalistic tendencies that did little to inhibit the spread of National Socialism can still be found in the negative attitudes towards Turks and Slavs, attitudes that are too often stoked by right-wing parties.

Shifting from a national to a regional perspective, Fred Dervin examines the state of Holocaust education in the Nordic countries, which span the three countries of Scandinavia plus Iceland and Finland. Although strikingly right-wing parties have gained power in the Scandinavian countries, it is also the home to efforts to counteract racism, particularly the influential Declaration of the Stockholm International Forum on the Holocaust, which gave rise to today's International Holocaust Remembrance Alliance. Although many of these states had quite distinct experiences during the war as victims or allies or ostensibly neutral onlookers, a prominent self-image in the region derived from efforts to protect Jews, such as the October, 1943 evacuation of 7,000 Jews by Danish fishermen. Unfortunately, this is not a complete picture. Dervin helpfully gathers sources showing the range of informal and local efforts to support Holocaust education in the region, a common but under-documented phenomenon in the field. Among these efforts of note is the campaign against antisemitism by a young Swedish Muslim, Siavosh Derakhti.

Paula Cowan and Henry Maitles, who for years have helped to make Scotland one of the best researched countries in the field of Holocaust education, explore the ways in which a country outside the direct impact of the Holocaust begins to make connections with this history and think about its local meanings. By exploring the emergence of Holocaust education in a context more peripheral to the Holocaust, Cowan and Maitles help the field to conceptualise the emergence of Holocaust education in more distant non-European locales.

The final section examines thematic concerns, including the possibility of failure, the role of remembrance, and the importance of epistemology. Geoffrey Short draws on a long career of conducting Holocaust education research in several countries to argue that the subject can contribute important lessons about the nature of racism and thus aid the fight to prevent genocide. These outcomes, however, are not inevitable. Poor pedagogy can entrench stereotypes rather than dismantling them. In particular, students may bring with them preconceptions or stereotypes about

Jews that are neither addressed nor engaged. If teachers miss this opportunity, the outcomes could be adverse.

Reinhold Boschki, Bettina Reichmann, and Wilhelm Schwendemann take seriously the possibility that Holocaust education can fail in their chapter on remembrance in Germany. Drawing on research about antisemitism, they seek to use education about the Holocaust to attack antisemitism directly. Doing so, they say, can also advance broader aims of supporting human rights. Their explorations of research and concepts about the Holocaust and antisemitism lead them to develop a theory of remembrance and the potential of Holocaust education to cultivate it.

References

Annan, K. (2010, 17 June). The myth of never again. *The New York Times*. http://www.nytimes.com/2010/06/18/opinion/18iht-edannan.html

Bărbulescu, A., Degeratu, L., & Guşu, C. (2013). The Holocaust as reflected in communist and post-communist Romanian textbooks. *Intercultural Education, 24*(1–2), 41–60.

Bekerman, Z., & Zembylas, M. (2010). Fearful symmetry: Palestinian and Jewish teachers confront contested narratives in integrated bilingual education. *Teaching and Teacher Education, 26*(3), 507–515.

Beresniova, C. (2014). An unimagined community? In J. H. Wiliams (Ed.), *(Re)constructing memory: School textbooks and the imagination of the nation* (pp. 269–292). Rotterdam: Sense Publishers.

Boyd, B. L. (2009). Using a case study to develop the transformational teaching theory. *Journal of Leadership Education, 7*(3), 50–59.

Carlberg, C. (2008). *Making connections between transformative learning and teaching of the Holocaust in the high school classroom*. Unpublished doctoral dissertation, St. Louis University.

Carrington, B., & Short, G. (1997). Holocaust education, anti-racism and citizenship. *Educational Review, 49*(3), 271–282.

Dietsch, J. (2012). Textbooks and the Holocaust in Independent Ukraine. *European Education, 44*(3), 67–94. doi:10.2753/EUE1056-4934440303.

Fracapane, K., & Haß, M. (2014). *Holocaust education in a global context*. Paris: UNESCO. http://unesdoc.unesco.org/images/0022/002259/225973e.pdf

Frankl, M. (2003). Holocaust education in the Czech Republic, 1989–2002. *Intercultural Education, 14*(2), 177–189.

Gordon, S. B., Simon, C. A., & Weinberg, L. (2004). The effects of Holocaust education on students' level of anti-semitism. *Educational Research Quarterly, 27*(3), 58–71.

Gross, Z. (2010). Holocaust education in Jewish schools in Israel: Goals, dilemmas, challenges. *Prospects, 40*(1), 93–113.

Kavadias, D. (2004). Past perfect tense? The link between knowledge of Nazi-genocide and democratic attitudes of adolescents in Brussels. *Res Publica, 46*(4), 535–554.

Maitles, H. (2008). "Why are we learning this?": Does studying the Holocaust encourage better citizenship values? *Genocide Studies and Prevention: An International Journal, 3*(3). http://scholarcommons.usf.edu/gsp/vol3/iss3/7

Maitles, H., & Cowan, P. (2004, 25–27 November). *One country, many cultures!: Does Holocaust education have an impact on pupils' citizenship values and attitudes?* Paper presented at the Scottish Educational Research Association conference, Perth.

Michaels, D. L. (2013). Holocaust education in the 'black hole of Europe': Slovakia's identity politics and history textbooks pre- and post-1989. *Intercultural Education, 24*(1–2), 19–40.

Misco, T. J. (2006). *Breaking historical silences through cross-cultural curriculum deliberation: Teaching the Holocaust in Latvian schools*. Unpublished doctoral dissertation, University of Iowa, Iowa City, IA.
Powers, J. M. (2007). Teaching war literature, teaching peace. *Journal of Peace Education, 4*(2), 181–191.
Proske, M. (2012). Why do we always have to say we're sorry? *European Education, 44*(3), 39–66.
Stevick, E. D., & Michaels, D. L. (2013). Empirical and normative foundations of Holocaust education: Bringing research and advocacy into dialogue. *Intercultural Education, 24*(1–2), 1–18.
Tinning, K. (2014). *Embodied responsiveness to the survivor: Museum exhibitions, traumatic life stories, and transformative learning experience*. Freeland, Oxfordshire: Interdisciplinary.net. http://www.inter-disciplinary.net/at-the-interface/wp-content/uploads/2014/02/Tinningtirpaper.pdf
UN [United Nations] (2005, 1 November). *Resolution adopted by the General Assembly on the Holocaust Remembrance*. A/RES/60/7. New York: UN. http://www.un.org/en/holocaustremembrance/docs/res607.shtml
van Dijk, L. (2010). Examples of best practice 3. Holocaust education and sexual diversity: A positive link between teaching about the persecution of Jews and sexual minorities. *Intercultural Education, 21*(1467–5986, 1467–5986), 81–84.
van Driel, B. (2003). Some reflections on the connection between Holocaust education and intercultural education. *Intercultural Education, 14*(2), 125–137.
Von der Dunk, H. (2002). The Holocaust: Remembrance and education. *European Review, 10*(1), 53–61.

Part II
Framing the Issues for a New Millennium

Address to the German Bundestag: Holocaust Remembrance Day (Berlin, 27 January, 2000)

Elie Wiesel

President Rau,
President of the Bundestag,
President of the Bundesrat,
My dear Chancellor Schröder,
Members of the Cabinet,
Distinguished Members of the Bundestag,
Excellencies,
Friends,

Allow me to tell you a story. But, first, I hope you understand that I speak to you as a witness. When a witness speaks, he or she must take a vow to tell the truth. The Jew that I am feels that he ought to make a prayer. Fifty five years ago the Russians came a bit too late for me and those who are close to me. Do not look at me and see the man that I am now. Please try and see in me the person I was 55 years ago. Today, I am here with my wife, Marion, and two very close friends, Inga and Ira, and so I will say a prayer. The prayer is from the Book of Baruch: "Blessed be the Lord for enabling me to be here at this day".

And now a story.

Once upon a time in a faraway land, there lived a benevolent king. One day, he was told by his astrologists that the next harvest would be cursed and that whosoever would eat from it would go mad. And so he ordered an enormous granary built and stored there all that remained from the previous year's crop. He then entrusted the granary's key to his closest friend and this is what he told him: "When my subjects and their king will have been struck with madness, you and you alone will have the right to enter the storehouse and eat uncontaminated food. Thus, you will

---

E. Wiesel (✉)
The Elie Wiesel Foundation for Humanity, 555 Madison Avenue,
New York, NY 10022, USA
e-mail: marissa@eliewieselfoundation.org

escape the malediction. But in exchange, my poor friend, you will be dutybound to fulfill a vital and impossible task. Your mission will be to crisscross the earth, going from country to country, from town to town, from marketplace to marketplace, from person to person, shouting with all your might: 'Good people, do not forget that you are mad! Men and women, do not forget, do not forget that you are mad!'"

This tale, told by the very great Rabbi Nahman of Bratzlav, who was a forerunner of Franz Kafka, surely applies to this century which has just ended, a century in which madness erupted in history and turned it often into a nightmare. And so the witnesses that we are, some of us, we, too, go around the world simply to say: "Don't forget that you were mad, don't forget that history has carried madness in it". And so the man you so kindly invited to take part in this solemn and moving session devoted to the memory of the victims of what we so inadequately call Shoa or Holocaust—there are no words for it—is a son of an ancient people whose mission over the centuries has been to teach the oneness of God and the sacredness of human life. Some 60 years ago, in this very metropolis, in this city, this man that I am and his community, were condemned to isolation, distress, despair and death. And yet, I hope you believe me, I am a witness and I speak to you today with neither bitterness nor hate. All my adult life I have tried to use language to fight hate, to denounce it, to disarm it, not to spread it.

Will my words hurt you? That is not my intention. But please understand, when I entered this chamber, I did not leave my memories behind. In fact, here, because of you, they are more vivid than ever. All I wish to do in this short time is to evoke in a few words an unprecedented event which will, for generations to come, continue to weigh on the destiny of my people and yours.

And this event, I still don't understand it. I go on trying and trying. Since my liberation, on 11 April, 1945, I have read everything I could lay my hands on that deals with its implications. Historical essays, psychological analyses, testimonies and testaments, poems and prayers, assassins' diaries and victims' meditations, even children's letters to God. But though I managed to assimilate the facts, the numbers and the technical aspects of the "Aktionen", the implacable significance which transcends them continues to elude me. The Nuremberg Laws, the anti-Jewish decrees, the Kristallnacht, the public humiliation of proud Jewish citizens, including brave World War I veterans, the first concentration camps, the euthanasia of German citizens, the Wannsee conference, where the highest officials of the land simply met to discuss the validity, the legality and the ways of killing an entire people. And then of course Dachau, Auschwitz, Majdanek, Sobibor—the capitals of this century. Yes, these names... flags, black flags, reminding a world that will come, of a world that has been. What made them possible? How is one to comprehend the cult of hatred and death that flourished in this country? How could bright young men, many superbly educated, from fine families, with diplomas from Germany's best universities, which then were the best in the world, how could they allow themselves to be seduced by Evil to the point of devoting their genius, the genius of Evil, to the torture and the killing of Jewish men, women and children whom they had never seen? They didn't do it because these Jews were rich or poor, believers or non-believers, political adversaries, patriots or universalists, but simply because they had been born Jewish. Their birth certificate had become a de facto death sentence. But did it really make these killers feel strong and heroic to murder defenceless children? Could they really have been so afraid of old and sick people, of small children as to make them their priority targets? What was it about them that was frightening? Their weakness, their innocence perhaps? Were the killers still human? That is the question which is my obsession. At what point does humanity end? Is there a limit beyond which humanity doesn't deserve its name anymore?

While preparing myself for today's encounter with you—an encounter of course which is symbolic on more than one level, as you put it very well, President of the Bundestag—I reread certain chronicles by survivors and witnesses, both living and dead. And I was struck again by how similar the scenes of cruelty were. It is as though one German, always the same, tortured and killed one Jew, forever the same, six million times. Yet, each episode is unique, for every human being, created in God's image, is unique.

Since I am not a historian, rather than discuss history I tell stories. And here is one, just one: it takes place in September 1941 in Babi-Yar, in Kiev, as reported by an eyewitness, a certain B.A. Liebmann.

He tells of a Jewish family which has spent several days hiding in a cave. The mother decides to seek help in a nearby village with her two small children. They are intercepted by a group of drunken Germans who, in front of the mother, behead one child, then the second. As the distraught mother clutches the bodies of her dead children, the Germans, obviously delighted with the spectacle, kill the mother as well. And when the father appears on the scene, they murder him too. I don't understand.

One could tell you more stories, six million more. Of all the crimes committed against my people, the Jewish people, the murder of its children is the worst. They were always the first to be taken and sent off to death. A million and a half Jewish children perished, Ladies and Gentlemen. If I were to begin reciting their names, the Moischeles, the Jankeles, the Sodeles, here and now, I would have to stand here for months and years.

Haven't the peoples of the world lost so much, too, not only my own, through what was done? How many benefactors of humanity perished when they were a month old, or a year? There could have been among them scientists who would have discovered a remedy for AIDS, a cure for cancer. They could have written great poems to inspire everybody, to renounce violence and war, a few words perhaps or a song to bring people together at last.

There is a picture that shows laughing soldiers surrounding a Jewish boy in a ghetto, I think probably in the Warsaw ghetto. I look at it often. What was it about that sad and frightened Jewish child with his hands up in the air that amused the German soldiers so? Why was tormenting him so funny? Were these soldiers, who likely were good husbands and fathers, not conscious of what they were doing? Weren't they thinking of their own children and grandchildren, who one day would have to carry the burden of their crimes although, as I shall say later, they are innocent? Ivan Karamazov believed that "cruel people are sometimes very fond of children". Yes, but not of Jewish children.

Of course, for us Jews in occupied Europe, it soon became clear that the free world was aware of and therefore responsible, though to a much different degree, for what was happening to us. The Allies seemed not to care very much; they did not open their borders to us when there was still time. And so Berlin became convinced that our fate was of no real concern to anyone. Not even God, the God of Israel, seemed to care. More than anyone else's, his silence was a mystery that continues to puzzle and distress many of us to this day. But that is another matter, one we debate mostly when we are among ourselves. Today, we shall speak only of Jews and Germans, then and now. My people has had innumerable enemies since it appeared on the world stage. We remember them all. But none had wounded us as deeply as Hitler's Germany. Over time, we endured discrimination, persecution, many forms of isolation, we survived the Crusades, the Inquisition, the pogroms, the various results of ingrained antisemitism. But the Holocaust went much farther indeed. I say it with pain: no nation, no ideology, no system has ever inflicted brutality, suffering and humiliation on such a scale on any people as yours has on mine in such a short period.

The sentence the Third Reich imposed upon us was deadly and irrevocable. The Final Solution, precisely outlined, was eschatological in nature; its goal was to annihilate every Jew, down to the last one on the surface of the earth. That was actually a kind of principal objective; the deportation of Hungarian Jews, and I am one of them as you know, had priority over the military convoys taking much-needed soldiers to the front.

I know, there were Germans who did not comply. And we must remember them, you and I. Those who had the courage to oppose the official racist ideology. Those who resisted the Nazi totalitarian regime. Those who tried to topple it and paid with their lives. And you are right in honouring their bravery. Only, sadly, they were few. And those who rescued Jewish friends and neighbours even fewer.

Now, many in Germany and elsewhere choose to put all the blame on the Nazis. "The Nazis did this or that", is the accepted formula. The Nazis, not the Germans.

Does it mean that there were two parallel histories of Germany, a Nazi history and a German history? Of course, all Germans were not Nazis. But I can tell you again as a witness, I remember in those times that the word German inspired fears; we were afraid when we heard that the Germans were coming.

Here, in this very place, the new leaders of the German people are so valiantly and honourably trying to build a new destiny, a more human philosophy of living. And we are here to tell you that we appreciate this. In those times, the decision to kill the Jews was taken at the highest level of government but was implemented down below. And for the victims, everything was German: the Zyklon gas was German, those who built the crematoriums were German, those who built the gas chambers were German, the orders given were German. As Paul Celan put it: "Der Tod ist ein Meister aus Deutschland". And Celan committed suicide because he felt probably that his words could not communicate this essential truth of his or our experience. Until the end of times, Ladies and Gentleman, Auschwitz will remain a part of your history, just as it will continue to be a part of mine.

I know, it is difficult and painful for you to think in these terms. Yours is a new generation, none of you have had to swear allegiance to Hitler. Of course, none of you have committed any crime or any sin. But I am sure that, in moments of anguish, you wonder where your parents were then, were did they stand then?

I feel compelled to tell you what I repeat everywhere I go, not only here: I do not believe in collective guilt; only the guilty and their accomplices are guilty, but surely not those who were not yet born, surely not their children. The children of killers are not killers, but children. And your children, many of them are so good. I know some of them; a few have been my students. They are so marvellous, so highly motivated, and at the same time tormented, understandably so. They somehow feel guilty, although they should not feel guilty at all. And what they are doing to somehow redeem your country, your people, is extraordinary. Whatever touches the spirit is of concern to them. They go to Israel to build, and they help any cause that deals with violation of human rights because they feel, your children feel, that it is important not to forget this dark period.

So what is what we call the Holocaust? Was it the consequence of history, an aberration of history? This is not the time, nor the place, to speak about that. There are other times, in school, when education is important. The Chancellor and I yesterday participated in a meeting in Stockholm about education on the Holocaust. And your words were very highly appreciated there. I am not sure that I have the answer to the Holocaust, but surely education is a major component of that answer. So emphasise education, increase the budget, do whatever you can so that the children, your children, who want to know, are able to know.

I am here, and I remember 55 years ago. I remember, and if I were to tell you what I remember, you would, like me, tremble. So, let us speak rather of what has to be done. I as a Jew, of course, speak of the Jewish victims, my people. Their tragedy was unique, but I do not forget other victims. When, as a Jew, I evoke the Jewish victims, I honour the others as well. As I like to put it: not all victims were Jewish but all Jews were victims.

And it is to remember them, Mr. President, Mr. Chancellor, President of the Bundestag, that this Parliament is marking the 27th of January as a day for commemorating the victims of the Nazi regime or, as I would call it, National Holocaust Remembrance Day. And this decision does you honour. And my presence here is meant, of course, to highlight your willingness to open the gates of memory and to declare together our conviction and resolution that it is high time for Cain to stop murdering his brother Abel.

Surely, there will be those who will say that it is too easy for you to devote one day a year just to pay a kind of homage and then go back to your normal business. Some will say it is a mockery. I don't agree. I take your move very seriously. I don't believe that it is to forget Auschwitz that you wish to remember its liberation. On the contrary, I believe that you wish to recall its liberation so as to condemn what preceded it, and to know more about it. I also believe that you will not listen to the indecent voices here in this land urging you to "turn the page" because you allegedly are "fed up with those stories". Those who want to turn the page have done so already. Not only have they turned the page, they have ripped it out of their consciousness. But by conspiring to obliterate the victims' memory, those who want to turn the page are killing them a second time, and that will be their burden.

After the war, some of us expected a defeated and humiliated Germany to deliver a more powerful message of remorse and contrition, one that would be linked to morality; instead, in those years it was related more to politics. But, since Chancellor Konrad Adenauer's time, you have become a democracy, worthy of taking its place in the family of nations. You have consistently supported Israel, and your record of financial reparations to the victims, mainly to the Jewish victims, but also to all slave labourers, as the law you are introducing in Parliament stipulates, is positive. But I believe that perhaps the time has come for you to make a gesture that would have world-wide repercussions.

President Rau, you met a group of Auschwitz survivors few weeks ago. And one of them told me that you expressed something very moving. You asked for forgiveness for what the German people had done to them. Why shouldn't you do it here? In the spirit of this solemn occasion. Why shouldn't the Bundestag simply let this be known to Germany and its allies and its friends, and especially to young people? Have you asked the Jewish people to forgive Germany for what the Third Reich did in Germany's name to so many of us? Do it, and it will have extraordinary repercussions in the world. Do it, and the significance of this day will acquire a higher dimension. Do it, and the world will know that its faith in this Germany is justified. For, beyond national, ethnic or religious considerations, it was mankind itself that was threatened then, in those darkest of days. And in some ways, it still is. Whatever this new century holds in store, and we desperately want to have hope for the new century and its new generation, Auschwitz will continue to force men to explore the deepest recesses of his and her being so as to confront their fragile truth.

I told you before that I prefer stories. I would like to conclude with the story of a little Jewish girl who died with her mother the night they arrived in Birkenau in May 1944. She was 8 years old, and believe me, she had done nothing to hurt or harm your people—why did she have to die such an atrocious death? If her brother lives to be as old as the world itself, he will never understand. And so, he will simply quote another great Hasidic master: Rabbi Moshe Leib of Sassov. He was known for his great compassion and he said: "My friends, do you wish to find the spark? Look for it in the ashes".

"Why Does the Way of the Wicked Prosper?": Teaching the Holocaust in the Land of Jim Crow

Theodore Rosengarten

Hitler's dead! The war's over! We won! The Jews of Brooklyn can come out of hiding now, only it takes my parents about 10 years to get the message, and even then they don't quite believe it's safe to be a Jew. These are great times to grow up in Brooklyn, home of Ebinger's Bakery and its incomparable chocolate blackout cake. Three blocks from our apartment, at old Ebbets Field, Jackie Robinson is playing baseball for the Brooklyn Dodgers. Each time he puts on his uniform and runs onto the diamond he is smashing the color line and transforming the United States. The country is fixated on everything he does. Every hit, every run he scores, every base he steals, every insult he shoulders, every fight he avoids. We are watching and we feel we are present at the beginning of a new world.

That isn't all that's happening. I can still hear my parents talking in low voices about the influx of certain people into the community, into our very building. My father called them "refs", for refugees, and he didn't say it with affection. The poor souls had come from displaced persons camps in Europe. They arrived in the United States penniless and disoriented. Many couldn't ask for directions in English and others didn't want to speak in any language. Amazingly, many of these immigrants made a great success of life in America. Today we honour them and call them survivors. But not then. Then they were refugees from a calamity that had no name but somehow had something to do with my family. Lots of refs had numbers tattooed on their forearms. There were some who kept their tattoos covered at all times and others who liked to show them off. On Friday nights, in summer, a great roar would invade the building through open windows—it was the Sabbath but it

---

T. Rosengarten (✉)
Zucker-Goldberg Chair in Holocaust Education, College of Charleston,
66 George Street, Charleston, South Carolina 29424, USA

Associate Scholar in Jewish Studies, University of South Carolina, USA
e-mail: tedrsc@gmail.com

was noisy as hell. Had Jackie Robinson stolen home or were the refs who lived on the lower floors reliving their nightmares?

For me, the narratives of black people and Jews in America were emerging simultaneously. At Amherst College in the early 1960s, I never heard the word "Holocaust", and not because I wasn't listening. The word and the concept behind it were just beginning to creep into our vocabulary and into the classroom. For some of my teachers the Holocaust was the elephant in the room, but no one spoke of it.

The American Studies programme at Amherst was built around a method of debate. Two professors would defend opposing views of a troublesome question in front of the whole sophomore class. The format owed more to the Lincoln-Douglass debates than to Socrates. Most moving of all was to see the orators enthralled by the intellectual combat. Three topics contested with great gusto were the nature of American democracy, now that our system had shown its resilience by weathering Joe McCarthy; the justice of removing the Cherokee Indians from the southeastern states to reservations in the inhospitable West; and slavery as a cause of the American Civil War. Was slavery merely one cause among causes, along with taxes on imports, a state's right to nullify a federal law, and western expansion policies that favored the North? Or had slavery become a moral outrage that the non-slave states could no longer countenance?

We all read Stanley Elkins' (1959) *Slavery: A Problem in American Institutional and Intellectual Life*, a book that had introduced post–World War II America to the reality of racial slavery in the nation's past. Elkins dared to compare the totalitarian environment of the southern plantation to Nazi concentration camps. Though he would later downplay the analogy, it was too late; the genie was out of the bottle. A person defined as a Negro in the pre–Civil War South, or as a Jew in the German Reich and Nazi-occupied Europe, was stripped of a citizen's rights, personal property, and control over his or her identity and fate. Total domination, we have learned in the decades since, was less pervasive on the plantations and more encompassing in the camps than we imagined.

In 1961, the year before I started college, Raul Hilberg had published *The Destruction of the European Jews*, a three-volume account of the machinery of mass murder to which every major German industry and institution had enthusiastically contributed manpower and expertise. But who knew? Who knew about the books and who knew about their contents? Publication had come only at the end of a great struggle. No one wants to hear about this, said the rejections that had showered down on Hilberg. Elie Wiesel's *Night*, his "deposition" of his year and a half in the camps, had come out in English in 1960, and it took three years to sell 3,000 copies. The first of Primo Levi's Auschwitz memoirs, published in Italy in 1948 under the title *Se Questo È un Uomo,* was made available to English readers only in 1958, as *If This Is a Man*, and to American readers as the more saleable *Survival in Auschwitz* two years later. In June 1963, nearly two years after East Germany put up a wall in Berlin to stop its citizens from defecting to the West, President John F. Kennedy visited the city and declared his solidarity with freedom-loving Germans: *"Ich bin ein Berliner"*. Really? Did that make me a Berliner too? I don't think so.

By that time, I was captivated by black history and the Civil Rights Movement. The bombing of 16th Street Baptist Church in Birmingham, on 15 September, 1963, one week after Alabama Governor George Wallace tried to block four black children from entering elementary school, sealed me to the struggle for black freedom. In 1964, Wallace came shaking the bushes for votes in the hills and valleys of western Massachusetts before the state's Democratic presidential primary, with the goal of toppling President Lyndon Baines Johnson. Wallace was formidable and ridiculous, a character out of fiction yet dangerously real. I heard him speak, coding his message of white superiority in a feeble populism that pitched the "people" against the educated "elite".

You don't have to go far in Massachusetts to find the elite. Just follow your nose east to Boston and Cambridge. I did. In graduate school, it was my good fortune to take Harvard University's last seminar on the history of American agriculture and its first on American slavery. The latter was taught by Oscar Handlin, eminent, brilliant, stout of mind and body, a driving force behind the rise of social and ethnic history. Handlin (1951) had won the Pulitzer Prize fifteen years earlier for *The Uprooted: The Epic Story of the Great Migrations That Made the American People*. Like me, he was from Brooklyn, which by this time was known as a breeding ground for regional historians—of the South.

Professor Handlin blew the lid off the kettle when he asked, "How do we know that the slaves wanted to be free?" The room was packed with student activists who sensed that intellectual life was on the cusp of change. Three hours was not enough to allow everyone to speak. The answer to Handlin's question seemed obvious in an era that was witnessing the violent death of colonialism in Africa and the overthrow of segregation in America. It was becoming known that tens of thousands of former slaves had joined the Union Army in 1863 and '64 when the objective of the war became clear. A hundred years later, the 40-plus volumes of ex-slave narratives collected by the WPA in the 1930s were awaiting historian George Rawick (1972, 1979) to make them accessible to us all. They are a chronicle of unremitting horror and spiritual resistance. But the motivation for resisting may not be the same as the desire or hope for freedom, and there is still the question of evidence, which Professor Handlin demanded we evaluate dispassionately.

In 1968, I followed my girlfriend, Dale, to Alabama in pursuit of the story of the Sharecroppers Union, an association of sharecroppers, tenant farmers, and small landowners organised by the American Communist Party in the early 1930s to fight for farmers' rights to sell their own crops and deal directly with creditors rather than go through their landlords. Rosen (1969) and Kelley (1990) offer detailed accounts of this struggle. Though many poor farmers across the South were white, in the counties where we were looking the union locals were entirely black. In 1971, I returned to Alabama to record the life story of Dale's chief informant, Ned Cobb. Ned Cobb is the real name of Nate Shaw, the hero of *All God's Dangers*, which I published three years later (Rosengarten 1974). In 1976, Dale and I moved to South Carolina. We settled near a neglected river delta that once produced the finest staple crops in the New World. Rice and cotton had moved long ago to the Southwest and the West, and many of the people who cultivated these crops had moved away too.

But many stayed on, choosing the freedom of living on "heirs' property" acquired by their families after the Civil War and traveling distances for paid work. The ancestors of our African-American neighbors may have arrived on these shores when Shakespeare was yet writing but no one lifted a finger to educate them until 60 years ago. In the 1950s, a young historian named Louis R. Harlan (1958) published his doctoral thesis on the crisis in Negro education in the seaboard South at the turn of the 20th century. The destitution of black schools, he observed, held "a special significance as a symbol of inferior personal status" (p. 20). Laws that forbade educating black people before the Civil War had materialised in the built environment in the post-Reconstruction era of Jim Crow. The situation was bad from state to state, but South Carolina, our adopted home, took the cake. Harlan conveyed the principle that governed the thinking of South Carolina's ruling class in a chapter title: "Inequality as a Higher Law". We discovered that this law was still in effect in 1976.

About 15 years ago, the professor who was teaching a course on the history of the Holocaust at the College of Charleston became ill and could not continue. Born in Russia, raised in Romania, Beatrice Stiglitz was brilliant and beautiful. She spoke at least six languages and taught French and Italian. She was a keen observer and an eloquent listener, and she faced death laughing at life's absurdities. When at last she had to stop teaching, the director of the College's Jewish Studies Programme, Marty Perlmutter, asked me if I would stand in for her. I told him I had never taken a course on the Holocaust, but I'd been collecting material for 50 years. He smiled because we both knew there were no such courses when we came along. Our teachers were the people who had survived the era of annihilation. We knew their stories and I thought I could integrate them into a syllabus. Yes, it would mean a change of direction. For the time being I would set aside my courses in southern studies and race relations and concentrate on teaching the history of the Jews in Europe during World War II. I'd use my knowledge of one to illuminate the other by comparing the policies and results of radical racism in two different environments.

Every other year, Dale and I lead a study abroad trip to Poland and Germany. The core group consists of 20 undergraduates from the College of Charleston and University of South Carolina who want to see for themselves the places where Hitler's final solution was planned and carried out. Some want to walk the ground that members of their families had walked on their way to being murdered; some go to test their faith in a God who lets terrible things happen to His children. Some come along to tour a part of the world less celebrated than London and Paris but the place to go if you want to experience Europe's cultural renewal. Some hope to learn lessons that will help them promote human rights at home. I lecture on the fly, with help from Polish and German friends, in Krakow, Łodz, Warsaw, Bialystok, at the sites of former Nazi death camps and in the streets of Berlin, where memorials to the murdered Jews of Europe are part of the fiber of the city, storing memories that would otherwise be a burden to conscience and make ordinary life impossible.

One of my aims in arranging these trips is to expose students to the history that I confronted growing up around the remnant of persecuted Jews who populated the Brooklyn of my childhood. I want these privileged young people to meet the descendants of perpetrators and compliant populations and to discover the many other histories—Polish, Ukrainian, German, etc.—in which the Jewish tragedy is embedded. I want them to come face to face with the dialectic of remembering and forgetting and to grasp the struggle of people then and now to live normal lives on soils saturated by blood (Meng 2011).

Flying low over western Poland, the first thing that surprises the students—who, like all adventurous travelers are hoping to be surprised—is the deep green countryside. Their mental image of Poland comes from black and white newsreels. Having grown up in small cities and towns, they can understand why empires to the east and west have coveted this fertile country and gone to war to get it. They can see why Poles have cause to call their country "the Christ of nations", because it was dismembered and sacked for generations by German and Russian conquerors. But they come armed with a second story too, one that's been reinforced by several controversial books, starting with Jan Gross's (2001) exposé of the wartime murder of the Jews of Jedwabne, a village north of Warsaw, at the hands of their Catholic neighbors. This second story, one that curiously echoes old Soviet propaganda, paints Poles as a nation of blackmailers and informers, antisemites all, who cooperated with the German occupiers, informed on their Jewish neighbors, and killed on their own initiative when they thought they could get away with it.

My mother's father was born in Tarnow, a city of small garment factories in southeastern Poland. The Jews who made up half the population were deported to Auschwitz and Belzec. About one in thirty was alive in 1945. My grandfather had immigrated to America before World War I, so he was unharmed. His cousins who stayed behind were "burned"—he never used the word "gassed"—in the camps. Dale's family, on her mother's side, came from the town of Kryvitsh in a part of eastern Poland that is now in Belarus. A *Yizkor*, or memorial book produced in Israel in 1977 tells the story of the town's destruction. It came suddenly, without warning, on a sunny Tuesday in April 1942, some 10 months after the murders in Jedwabne, 60 km to the west. The SS, goaded and aided by non-Jewish collaborators, herded the Jewish people into a large wooden building at the edge of the village. Jews who survived in hiding described Polish women and children clapping their hands and throwing rocks at their neighbors who were taking their last walk. "Where is your God, you filthy Jews?" shouted the Poles. Local police and volunteers doused the building with kerosene and set it on fire. Some 370 people were killed; no one escaped. The full story has been seeping out over the past decade as the last surviving Polish eyewitnesses recall the grisly details. Death by fire was preceded by shootings in the streets. Young women—their names are recorded in the *Yizkor* book—were raped before being burned alive.

When the last surviving onlookers disappear, who will be left to tell their stories? One answer is the people who guide visitors through Auschwitz. This band of docents is like no other on earth, because there is no place like Auschwitz on earth. They seem driven by an inner need to explain. They are constantly sharing ideas and findings with one another, and adapting their commentary to new discoveries. They seem to be in a rush, not because they have to be somewhere else but because there is so much to tell. They are determined themselves to remember everything. They let you know some of what they know, but not all.

There's nothing mystical here, and during the years of extermination you might expect to find the rule of lawlessness. Yet, we learn that the bidding on contracts to build the gas chambers and crematoria, for example, was strictly regulated, and blueprints had to be drawn to specification. Germans who served the Reich here, including many medical doctors and PhDs, believed in a future that excluded Jews from the human family. They were helped in pursuit of this mad utopia by a bureaucracy and resourceful technology that supplied them with everything they needed, at precisely the right moment, as if all of Europe were an assembly line for Auschwitz.

I tell my students not to be upset that the parking lot at Auschwitz looks like the parking lot at Disneyworld. The giant tour buses come from every country in Europe, just as the Jews had arrived here 70 years ago from all corners of Nazi-occupied Europe and North Africa. It's a different story at Treblinka, about an hour and a half drive north of Warsaw, off the main road to Bialystok. Here there is never a crush of people; indeed, some days no one comes. Treblinka was built to murder the Jews of Warsaw. Trains brought people from distant countries as well, to the astonishment of the Christian farmers who seldom saw strangers even from the nearby capital, never mind the bourgeoisie of western Europe. Treblinka boasted the first stationary gas chambers. There are no structures left standing and the field the Jews would have crossed to reach the *himmel way*—the road to heaven as the "worker Jews" called the path to the gas chambers—is covered with large broken stones carved with the names of Jewish settlements in Poland that were eradicated by the Nazis. The stones were put there in the 1960s to recognise the victims at Treblinka and to deter people from digging in the wretched earth for gold rings and gold teeth.

Treblinka is a very sad place, and people without a direct connection to someone who was murdered there tend to stay away. To my Polish friends, Treblinka is a dagger in Poland's heart. Here God and man failed. A force so evil, a racism so pernicious, drove otherwise reasonable men and women to try to eliminate every person in the world whom they identified as Jewish. Auschwitz made sense to someone, somewhere, and served a host of evil purposes, from human selection to the production of synthetic rubber, but Treblinka had no strategic value whatsoever. It was a crude unstoppable machine for killing Jews. Auschwitz commandant Rudolf Hess scoffed at Treblinka's inefficiencies, including the small gas chambers and the loud diesel engines used to produce carbon monoxide when the more reliable death-dealer, Zyklon B, was available. Yet, in the space of a year and a half, nearly a million people were murdered at Treblinka, second only to the total at Auschwitz, which was 50 times its size and manned by 50 times more Germans, and in operation 3 additional years. Once, I came here with a student group that included four Native Canadians from British Columbia. Off the bus, they separated themselves from everyone else and walked to an open space on the far side of the camp, laid down their blankets, and began dancing and chanting. These people had studied at universities in Europe, but they had not forgotten the traditional way of mourning. They recognised an apocalypse when they saw one. The rest of us were numb with wonder and envy.

At the hotel in Bialystok—10 years and three visits later—our group met after dinner to discuss what we were seeing and doing. Jared started the debriefing by saying that coming to Treblinka "has shown me that nothing is ever truly erased.

Everything leaves traces". (The names of students quoted in the essay have been changed; the words are their own.)

Treblinka was on our minds because we had just left there a few hours ago, and because it is unforgettable. In between visits to Auschwitz and Treblinka, we had made stops at Chelmno and Majdanek. Majdanek had the distinction of being the only death camp overrun while the gas chambers were still operating, and the only one in a suburb of a city. At Chelmno, the method of killing was poisoning by engine exhaust in the sealed compartments of large vans specially fitted for the job, with red crosses painted on the roof and sides to deceive. The Jews of Łodz, pre-war Poland's second largest city, with more Jews than all of Germany, and the Jews of the western part of the country annexed into the Reich, were murdered there, starting on 8 December, 1941. So were Roma and even a group of nearly a hundred Christian children from Czechoslovakia sent to Chelmno to revenge the assassination by Czech partisans of Reinhard Heydrich, a vicious antisemite who was being groomed to succeed Hitler.[1]

Allison held up some bullets and casings she found in the bed of the train tracks leading to Treblinka. (Later, once we were back in the States, the ammunition would be identified as standard German issue in 1942.) The tracks had been pulled up and removed by the authorities 5 years before, but the bed itself was not disturbed.

"We need more narratives", said Nina. "In times and conditions that destroy a sense of reality, what matters is what you remember. Memories are just as real".

"The scariest time", said Charles, "would have been getting off the train and seeing there were no barracks to put you up in. No one would be staying here but no one would be leaving either".

"It was a non-stop site of execution", added Deanna.

"Even the Jews who were kept alive to do the dirty work knew they were going to be killed", said Sasha. "Two hundred people broke out. The amazing thing", she said, "is that 20 of them were alive when the war ended".

Nina could hold back no longer. "They had to be helped. Someone had to hide them and give them food. And it had to start here. I wish I could go to the church in Treblinka, and I would ask the priest to announce after mass on Sunday that a young American wants to meet people who can tell her about the farmers who helped the prisoners in their hour of need".

"Do you believe that", asked Jared, "or are you saying that just to get people to talk? You need to find people who will talk about what they didn't do to help the Jews".

"We shouldn't be so ready to judge", snapped Sasha.

---

[1] One of the iconic villains of modern times, Reinhard Heydrich was a terrifying figure even to his Nazi colleagues. He held the posts of Chief of the Nazi Criminal Police, the SS Security Service, and the Gestapo, and overlord of the Nazi-occupied Czech provinces, Bohemia and Moravia. He was a leading planner of the "Final Solution" and would not have stopped at the murder of the Jews if he had the chance. On his assassination, see MacDonald (1989). For an incisive sketch of his character and his vision of a new Europe arrived at through systematic genocide, see Deak (2011).

But Jared was having none of it: "Withholding judgment just lets the killers off the hook".

"The commanders in Berlin knew what they were doing putting Treblinka out here", added Jared's ally Dan. "Treblinka was their dream. It was an optimised death camp. Optimised to kill and deceive. It was different from other places".

Of course, Auschwitz was also designed to kill and deceive, with such things as signs announcing that "after showering" every person would get a cup of tea. If that didn't help move people fast enough into the gas chambers, there was always beating and clubbing to accomplish the goal.

"Chelmno was the most coercive", said Andrew, a new voice. "Nothing like it had ever been done before".

"Chelmno was shocking", observed Holden, the group's unofficial photographer and self-appointed protector. In fact, when we got to the town, which is just off the east-west freeway that connects Warsaw to West Europe, on a hill above the Narew River, the sun was already setting and thunderstorms were moving in. When the bus stopped we heard the choir practicing in the church—the very church where 70 years before the Nazis had piled the luggage of the Jews as they got off the trucks and trains that brought them. It was as if we had just stepped into the filming of Claude's Lanzmann's *Shoah*, almost 40 years ago. The same church, the same choir, the same obliviousness to history.

"Did they ever purify that church?" asked Jaime. "The Jews would purify their synagogues after the Nazis had used them for stables and latrines".

"Well, I'm sure they cleaned it", ventured Sasha.

"To me the church is *treyf*", said Jaime, a term normally applied to unkosher food.

"It's the singing that gets me", said Holden, "it drowns out the screams of the people".

If Auschwitz and Treblinka were kingdoms of deception, and Chelmno a shock to the system, Majdanek was a vast stage-set on the outskirts of Lublin, a commercial centre in eastern Poland that once was home to the largest Talmudic school in the world. Today Lublin is a city without Jews. The ovens at Majdanek look brand new and in fact had been installed just before the Russians pounced in July 1944. With the Soviet Army came a team of expert filmmakers to record the arrest and trial of SS men who were caught before they could flee. Most of the students had seen the footage prior to coming to Europe. In one highlight the Polish prosecutor pleads passionately for the death sentence for all six defendants, and the film ends with their hanging. But not before an SS lieutenant implores his captors to spare him because he only killed Jews, never Soviet prisoners of war.

We got out at the city centre which during the camp era was near enough for the Germans to take their dirty laundry to the Jewish-owned cleaners and shop in the bakeries and liquor stores. On a street of old houses that once had stores on the first floors and living quarters above, one student noticed a gouge on the right side of a doorframe looking in, about face-high. She had grown up in New Jersey and was used to crossing the threshold into Jewish homes past a *mezuzah* on the doorpost. A *mezuzah* is a piece of parchment with verses from the Torah contained in a small decorative case the size of your index finger. Someone had chiseled or pried the *mezuzah* off the house in Lublin and sundry coats of paint could not fill the gash. One student alerted another and an impromptu crew of urban archeologists started photographing the indentations.

"You're photographing nothing", said Zach.

"No, it's something", said Holden. It was the mark left by the Jewish people of Lublin.

In northeastern Poland, Bialystok fell under Soviet occupation in 1939 by the terms of the Hitler-Stalin pact that divided Poland between its two ancient foes, delayed war in the East, and gave Hitler a free hand in the West. Pre-war Bialystok had a higher proportion of Jews than any city in the world, numbers swollen by people who fled the German occupation. When the Germans launched their long-planned invasion of the Soviet Union and seized the city in June 1941, mobile killing units wasted no time rounding up and shooting thousands of Jews. Some 50,000 were spared execution and moved into a ghetto. In 1943, the ghetto was emptied and the inmates deported to Treblinka, Majdenek, Auschwitz, and even to Theresienstadt, near far-away Prague. Knowing that deportation meant death, hundreds of Jews took up arms and attacked German troops at the ghetto fence, holding off their killers for 5 days. More than a hundred men and women managed to escape and make it to the forests where they joined partisan groups that harassed the Germans with remarkable success.

As in Lublin, today there are virtually no Jews in Bialystok. The old Jewish cemetery, which shares a wall with the Catholic cemetery, is looked after by the small Jewish community of Warsaw. We had been invited to visit Bialystok and work in the burial grounds by its caretaker, Lucy Lisowska. The place was overgrown with weeds, shrubs, and stunted trees, and only the graves nearest to the entrance showed signs of upkeep. The rest was in high disorder. We plunged into the task, picking up trash, cutting grass, washing headstones and setting them upright. We had to bring our own buckets and equipment, and our bus driver found a source of water for cleaning. Smoking one cigarette after another, Lucy told us about some of Bialystok's famous Jewish sons, including the cubist painter Max Weber, Dr. Albert Sabin, developer of the oral polio vaccine, and L. L. Zamenhof, inventor of Esperanto, an international language whose name alludes to hope—the hope, in his mind, of healing the "anguish" of a world divided into enemies who could not understand one another. Growing up in multi-ethnic Bialystok in the late 19th century, his parents had taught him that all people were brothers, while "outside in the street at every step" he felt "there were no people, only Russians, Poles, Germans, Jews, and so on" (Wheeler 2013, p. 136).

The babel of languages that so alarmed Zamenhof is etched on the faces of the tombstones. As the students bent to their labours, and names, dates, and fragments of inscriptions shone on washed stones, Lucy rolled her eyes and looked to heaven. All very good, she said, but when we leave thieves will come and steal the marble slabs. They make paving stones in patios and gardens. At that very moment, three young men emerged from the woods at the back of the graveyard and strolled past us. They did not say a word but were content to make mental notes of the scene.

"What did I say?" said Lucy. "They will be back". I had a different thought. "No, Lucy, they're not looking at the stones. They're checking out the girls".

An elderly man and woman entered the cemetery through the front gate and approached us for help. They said they live in Israel and had come here looking for the grave of his grandfather. But the anarchy of the cemetery disheartened them they were about to give up. We fanned out looking for a stone with the name of his ancestor, but given the size of the cemetery and our ignorance of languages, it was hopeless. Determined not to go away defeated, the man picked out an anonymous headstone, put a glass with a *yahrzeit* candle on its smooth top, lit it and recited the mourner's kaddish. We gathered around him and a few who knew the words joined in.

Every November, on All Saints Day, Poles fill the well-groomed cemetery on the other side of the wall and remember the dead by saying prayers and lighting candles. In 1988, during the heyday of Solidarity, the anti-communist movement that transformed Poland using the methods of civil disobedience, Catholics in Bialystok placed candles on the Jewish graves. Hearing Lucy tell the story gave us goose bumps. For a fleeting moment, the citizens of Bialystok had welcomed the departed Jews into the fold of Polish history. They showed up their Soviet masters by acting out a forbidden narrative. They told the world, which wasn't listening, that in post-communist Poland it would be safe to say I am a Jew.

Hastily packing our pails and scrub-brushes, we boarded the bus for Warsaw to catch the overnight train to Berlin. We had time to follow Marek Edelman's historic walk in 1983 to the bunker where ghetto fighter Mordechai Anielewicz died in the last days of the ghetto revolt. Edelman, a prominent cardiologist and the last surviving leader of the uprising, had refused to take part in the Communist regime's official celebration of the fortieth anniversary of the uprising. To do so, he explained, "would be an act of cynicism and contempt" in a country "where social life is dominated throughout by humiliation and coercion" (Kaufman 2009). Five years later, in the park in front of the monument to the Ghetto fighters, one of the few open spaces in Warsaw where people could freely assemble, Solidarity leader Lech Walesa addressed the workers' movement. "The history of Poland is a history of uprisings", he said. "And the uprising of the Jewish ghetto was the most Polish of all". Or so my friends in Warsaw told me. Lech Walesa, revolutionary lion and distinguished mourner at Edelman's funeral, future President of Poland, did you really say this? I can almost forgive you for pandering for votes by mocking your opponents' Jewish ancestry.

In 2012, President Obama, while awarding a posthumous Medal of Freedom to Jan Karski, a resistance fighter who had snuck behind German lines to witness first-hand the atrocities being committed against the Jews, referred to "Polish death camps", a term that is anathema to Poles. Though a spokesman for the National Security Council offered a clarification, the president's reluctance to take back the remark angered everyone in Poland. Right, left, and centre reject the notion of Polish involvement in planning or facilitating the Holocaust. The death camps were conceived by the Germans—the architects were German luminaries—while the workers, the enslaved carpenters and bricklayers and all of their helpers were a cross-section of camp humanity, including prisoners of war, political foes, Jews, Catholic dissenters, communists. Many Germans today acknowledge Germany's crimes against humanity by surrounding themselves with reminders of the people persecuted and murdered by Hitler's henchmen. While they maintain that Germans too were victimised, programmed to do the work of an evil elite, they admit the unique suffering of the Jews and the exceptional guilt of the German people.

In Berlin, the rise of state terror and social conformity in the service of mass murder is the subject of the Topography of Terror Documentation Centre, a museum that opened in 2010 and quickly became one of the city's most visited remembrance sites. *Stolpersteins* or stumbling blocks laid flush with the sidewalks identify individuals and families who lived in the adjacent buildings before they were deported into the night. These cobblestone-sized memorials are overlaid with brass plates stamped with a person's name, year of birth, date of deportation and death. In the Bavarian Quarter, brightly printed signs with colorful images of familiar domestic objects such as hats and clocks, goblets and jewelry, cats and bird cages on one side, and black-and-white texts on the other, adorn the lampposts. Behind the cat we learn the date that Jews were no longer allowed to keep pets; the reverse side of the goblet announces the date that Jews were forbidden to enter theaters and concert halls. A railroad car on a fragment of track on the broad sidewalk of a busy Berlin street is a reminder of the trains that took the Jews and other condemned people from this spot to the East. Cut in a wall of metal next to the car, the facsimile of a train schedule is in fact a timetable of deportation, complete with the destinations that, unknown to the frightened travelers, spelled death.

Richard L. Rubenstein (1976) lectured us 40 years ago in *The Cunning of History: The Holocaust and the American Future,* a concise meditation on the lessons of Auschwitz, that "one of the least helpful ways of understanding" the mass murder of Jews is to see it as "the work of a small group of irresponsible criminals" who forced an unwilling nation to pursue "a barbaric and retrograde policy" that was at odds with their own longings or with "some of the most profound tendencies" of western civilisation (p. 21). The project of ruling the world and annihilating the Jews occupied Germans from every walk of life: architects, engineers, scientists, doctors and nurses, businessmen, factory owners, industrial managers, legislators and lawyers, teachers, blueprint makers, paper suppliers, church leaders, philosophers. How could they? At Treblinka we didn't ask, "How could it have gone on for so long without someone stopping it?" But in Berlin we do. Should we throw up our hands and concede that in trying to understand the Holocaust we come up against what Israeli novelist Aharon Appelfeld (in Roth 2001, p. 25), himself a child survivor in Ukraine, calls "archaic mythical forces" that normal kinds of historical analysis don't seem to get? Or should we go home and try harder? Should we students from the American South pause and ask if knowing what has happened in our own backyard can help us fathom the tragedy of Europe and the Jews?

When I was a kid, fights would break out on the subway platforms beneath the streets of Brooklyn. Jewish boys, some wearing *yarmulkas* and sporting the sidelocks of yeshiva students, and others, like me, in secular garb, were sent out by their rabbis to hustle coins for charity from scurrying passengers. We were taught to shake our cans of nickels, dimes, and quarters like Purim noisemakers in the faces of people getting on and off the trains. The competition was brutal and pious boys would occasionally snatch the cans of *gelt* from their rivals who would chase after them and give them a pounding if they caught them. Woe to the boys who were not fleet of foot, because once we emerged from the depths we had to run the gauntlet of Polish and Irish gangs who taunted us for being Christ killers and tried to take our money.

And what were the charities for which we risked our dignity, if not our lives? Orphanages in Israel, schools under the wing of immigrant rabbis trying to rebuild their pre-annihilation congregations in America, Zionists making the deserts bloom, anti-Zionists who rejected a Jewish political state. They shared an orientation to the future, and a fierce embrace of hope. They wanted to show the world that despite the recent catastrophe human destiny was still bound up with the fate of the Jews. I think of my father who dared not miss a day of work or even show up late, lest the planet stop spinning and tumble from its orbit.

Returning from Europe, several of our rising seniors started plotting the essays they needed to write to graduate. One young woman planned to investigate "the contingencies of faith". She wanted to read survivors' memoirs and conduct interviews on her own of men and women who kept their belief in God through what they suffered and witnessed, or who lost and regained their faith—"faith interrupted", she called it. Another girl set up interviews with American GIs who in 1945 had liberated Dachau concentration camp, outside of Munich, Germany, the very first camp built by the Nazis when they came to power in 1933. She planned to ask the war vets how they had been prepared for the horrible things they discovered. A third girl made sketches for a series of oil paintings depicting the killing of animals raised for meat, each death experienced by an individual sentient creature. She called the series *Eternal Treblinka*, after a line from "The Letter Writer", a short story by Isaac Bashevis Singer, the Polish-born winner of the Nobel Prize who lived the last 56 years of his life in the United States. "In relation to them, all people are Nazis; for the animals it is an eternal Treblinka". Jared, who has gone on to pursue a PhD in genocide studies, hoped to uncover links between the great textile factories of 19th-century Łodz, which were built with capital from Germany and France, and slave plantations in the Carolina low country, producers of the world's finest long-staple cotton.

About ten students formed a discussion group, each receiving credit from me for Independent Study. Our class compared racial controls in the United States, particularly the rise of Jim Crow law after Reconstruction, and racially inspired persecution of Jews in Europe, going back to the formation of the transnational Antisemites League in 1880 and pogroms in the last decades of Czarist Russia. At home and abroad we were astonished by the tenacity of the idea of race and the division of human beings into racial groups. Inequality, we found, dresses from the same closet of disguises. Dehumanisation was written into law and enforced with an iron hand. It was painted on doors and windows too. Like the indelible scars of *mezuzahs* on the old houses in Jew-free Lublin, blunt messages of hierarchy and exclusion poke through layers of pigment on the lintels of old Charleston stores and public buildings. "Whites only". "Maids in white uniforms permitted". "We cater to white trade only". "Whites only beyond this point". "Colored waiting room".

"The whole South was a colored waiting room", said Holden. "Let's not kid ourselves".

"We're past that now. We've made real progress", countered Sasha.

"I don't buy it", Holden held out. "It goes deep. It goes deep".

I take Holden's side. Indeed, the language of white officials who tried to prevent black people from voting and keep them from learning to read and write, 40 years after the end of slavery, was candid and venomous. "If we force the negro into the schools, we will be sharpening weapons with which to cut our own throats", warned "Pitchfork Ben" Tillman who, as governor of South Carolina and a US senator, raised demagoguery to an art (quoted in Harlan 1958, p. 194). "Compulsory education is a rattlesnake that can warm into being" (p. 193) was one of his typical rhetorical pearls. Desks, blackboards, maps, and books were some of the weapons that a succession of lawmakers promised to keep out of black hands.

It was the rickety school house, more than the weather-beaten dwelling house or the substandard hospital, that stamped a person and a community with inferiority. Every social institution reflected and supported the tyranny of whites over blacks. And if some black people learned to read in spite of the state's best efforts to keep that from happening, local libraries, the pride of every town, were charged to "fit up and maintain a separate place for the use of the colored people who may come to the library for the purpose of reading books or periodicals".[2] In an era of rationed education, libraries were battlegrounds.

Reading a collection of Jim Crow laws tested my students' ability to keep a straight face: The blind shall be housed separately from the blind, white from black. Black and white workers shall not look out of the same windows in the mill—but no problem, the drinking fountains are clearly marked. A black person and a white person may not fish with pole and line from the same boat....

"I mean", said Deanna, "someone had to sit there and think this stuff up".

"And someone else wrote it down", said Andrew, picking up the thread. "And they held a big debate about it". It was hearsay that Hitler had used the Jim Crow laws as a model for Nazi laws restricting the liberty of Jews.

"He wouldn't have had to", offered Jared, "it was the spirit of the age. They copied us and we copied them. We exiled people who went on living right in the middle of us".

I like the concept of "exile". It has many meanings and they all seem to apply. Seventy-five years after their respective emancipations, the Jews of Germany and people of color in the American South found themselves exiled from the rights of citizens and the sympathies of their countrymen. This was old hat for blacks. For the Jews in Europe, particularly in the West, it happened all at once. Yesterday you looked and acted like everyone else, today you have to wear a yellow star on your

---

[2] Often cited as an example of a Jim Crow law suggesting a realm of separate and equal facilities for blacks and whites, this particular ruling comes from North Carolina. See, for example, AFT (2014) and NPS (2014).

dress or your jacket, you've been turned away at your job or from your school, you have to give up your bicycle and your radio. Surely this was a stage in the long social compact between German Christians and Jews, to which Jews could adapt as they had done for centuries. There was no precedent to tell the Jews that this regime of separation and dispossession was a prerequisite to the final aim, an exile from which very few would return.

The story has a happier outcome for people of color in America. Here, exile from education, property, wealth, and power appears to have been a stage—a cruel plateau—on the long road to freedom. For many, the Jim Crow statutes have come and gone, and life hasn't changed very much. For others, the change has been astonishing. Like antisemitism, overt racism in America has lost its respectability. Witness the high regard across all social boundaries in which students hold Anne Frank and Martin Luther King, Jr. Coincidentally, both Frank and King were born in 1929, on the eve of economic collapse, and both were murdered by racism. Both were precocious and displayed their gifts at a young age—for Anne Frank it was literary naturalness and moral passion; for King it was merging his voice with the voices of his prophetic forerunners and sounding as though he spoke for history. I was 20 when King was 35, so our lives overlapped for many years. My life also overlapped briefly with Anne Frank's, and the thought that she and I were alive at the same time disturbs and excites me.

Frank comes to us as someone fully formed at a tender age. King went through a period of trial and error, doubt and reluctance, before he accepted his place on the world stage. Like Moses talking back to the Lord when He bid him go to Pharaoh and threaten him with plagues, King pleaded, "Pardon your servant, Lord. Please send someone else" (Exodus 4:13). Privately he had to struggle against his fears and against the hatred he felt for white people. Jews felt camaraderie with him. Marching with him filled a great need—for justice in this world and for a story with a happy ending. By answering the call, many American Jews felt that their own historical journey had not reached its end. The Reverend King never made you think he wanted to convert you to his religion. His Christ was the teacher who had led the gentiles to the God of Israel.

King's death on the balcony of a seamy motel in Memphis, Tennessee, where he'd gone to support striking sanitation workers, struck some observers as a sign that he had come down in life and that his movement had lost its relevance.

"The reverse is true", said Charles. "The more time that passes, the more relevant his final act now seems".

King was 39 when he was murdered.[3] Anne Frank was 14 when she was betrayed and sent to Auschwitz, on the last train carrying Jews from the Netherlands, and 15 when she perished in Bergen-Belsen. Until the moment of her arrest she had believed she would live, and she counted on her captivity to make her career as a writer. Emboldened by news of the allied landing in Normandy and by Free Dutch radio broadcasts from London, she had begun revising her diary for its post-war readership.

---

[3] The late Nigerian novelist Chinua Achebe discussed King's youth and universal appeal in a *Paris Review* interview (Brooks 1994).

Both the original and edited versions were found in her hiding place hours after her arrest. After the war, the hand-written pages were returned to her father, the only one of her companions in hiding to survive.

Otto Frank tried to smooth his daughter's rough edges by witholding her hard feelings toward her mother and her awakening sexuality from the first published version of the diary. But he left her message intact, and you can hear its echo in the letter King wrote from the Birmingham jail in 1963. King addressed his words to a group of white clergymen who had sent a letter of their own to the newspaper saying the fight against injustice should be carried on in the courts and not in the streets, and calling him an outsider and a troublemaker. King wore the badge proudly, and like Anne Frank before him, he proclaimed his belief in the goodness of people and his disgust with the philosophy of moderation. Both martyrs challenged their readers to act from bottled-up goodness.

In September 2012, I left my classes in good hands—turning them over to Dale, now curator of the Jewish Heritage Collection at the College of Charleston—and travelled to Ukraine to present a paper at a conference on the Polish-Jewish writer Bruno Schulz, in Schulz's hometown, Drohobych. I met my friend Jerzy Pytko in Warsaw and we took the one-hour flight to Lviv, formerly Lwów, and its new spic-and-span airport built to impress travelers to the 2010 World Cup and now waiting mostly empty for the city to grow to justify the expense. Jerzy has been our guide in Poland for several of our student trips. There is a Yiddish expression about a scholar who possesses "the learning of twelve-in-one", a person for whom no question is too simple or too difficult, no problem that cannot be solved, and that description fits Jerzy. He grew up in the rubble of Warsaw, a city leveled by the Nazis like ancient Carthage, and starved of investment by its post-war Soviet masters. His background in photo journalism, his pride in his country and its culture, his knowledge of languages and history, and his romantic attitude toward life make him an ideal tour leader. A vigorous walker, he has a knack for making you think that he is alongside you, whether you are in the front, back, or middle of the pack.

Jerzy had his own reason for going to Ukraine. He wanted to search in Lviv for the house his grandfather had lived in when the Nazis arrested him in 1942 as a political enemy and sent him to his death at a labor camp outside the city.

On the southern border of the old Austro-Hungarian province of Galicia, in the piedmont of the Carpathian Mountains, Drohobych once belonged to Poland and over the past century many different flags have flown over the town. Soviet Ukraine, Reich Ukraine, Poland, the short-lived Republic of Western Ukraine, and Austria-Hungary have come and gone, each change of rule accompanied by demographic upheaval. Jews had lived in the region for hundreds of years when the Nazis showed up.

Bruno Schulz wrote in Polish, never Yiddish. He was an anomaly, admired and despised by the gatekeepers of Polish literature. He had a German-Jewish name and wrote in a language they thought alien to him—their language—but which was as natural to Schulz as French was to Proust and German to Kafka. Not only Poles, but Jewish writers were ambivalent about Schulz. Isaac Bashevis Singer, who wrote in Yiddish even during his long exile in the United States, marveled at Schulz's mastery of Polish but berated Schulz for abandoning the language of the Jewish masses and depriving his fellow Jews of his art. Aharon Appelfeld, the incomparable novelist of the Holocaust, had Schulz in mind when he said he "always loved assimilated Jews because that was where the Jewish character, and also perhaps Jewish fate, was concentrated with the greatest force" (cited in Roth 2001, p. 36). And what was this fate? They were blinded by their own humanistic values to think that the world no longer saw them as Jews. It was easy to fool them. "With the simplest, almost childish tricks they were gathered up in ghettos, starved for months, encouraged with false hopes, and finally sent to their deaths by train" (Roth, p. 26).

In addition to writing, Schulz was a draftsman, printmaker, illustrator, and painter. He made a living teaching drawing and woodworking in the Drohobych high school. Frescoes he had created as a slave artist in the home of the Gestapo boss of Drohobych in 1942 were found in 2000 under layers of paint in the kitchen pantry. Recognising a cultural treasure and a potential cash cow, authorities in Ukraine, Poland, and Israel asserted competing claims to the work. Appelfeld leapt to Israel's defense. Pointing to the deplorable conditions for preserving works of art in the Ukrainian backwater, sneering at Poland's newfound respect for its former Jewish citizens, assessing Schulz's work as evidence from a crime scene, and noting that the enduring value of the frescoes is as artifacts of the Holocaust, Appelfeld declared in a public letter with many renowned signees that Israel is the legal inheritor of the property of the murdered Jews.[4]

The winners of this battle were Israel and Ukraine, the losers were Poland and anyone who might want to be able to study or simply appreciate Schulz's frescoes in one place. Israel, when it learned about the frescoes, sent agents to the house in Drohobych to strip the murals off the walls and spirit them out of the country. They managed to scrape five frescoes or fragments of frescoes and left, like thieves in the night, with half of the work. Ukraine demanded Israel return the "kidnapped" Schulz paintings; Ukrainian Jews accused Yad Vashem, which received the purloined paintings, of erasing Jewish history in Ukraine, the very nourishment Jews there need in order to survive. Ukrainian academics quoted Schulz (1988; Davis 2010) on his attachment to Drohobych—"this town and land became a self-sufficient microcosm"—to make the point that his work was inseparable from its environment. What made his writing and graphic art unique were their local character and roots, without which "he would be deprived in death of true greatness". Polish intellectuals charged Yad Vashem with "predatory collecting". They were angry and aggrieved. "I can hardly begin to describe how much outrage and how much pain we feel", said the Polish Jewish journalist Konstanty Gebert at a New York forum on the contested paintings (Smith 2001). "I have never before seen such a unanimity of public opinion, Polish, Jewish, and non-Jewish Ukrainian".

But Israel held the trump cards: the mutilated frescoes themselves. It took about 8 years to work out a deal. Israel would recognise Ukrainian ownership of the

---

[4] This response to an earlier letter by 24 American scholars calling for Israel to return the frescoes to Ukraine appeared under the heading "Bruno Schulz's Wall Paintings" in *The New York Review of Books*, 23 May, 2002.

paintings and Ukraine would make them available to Israel on open-ended loan. Poland was left out in the cold. But that wasn't the last word—is there ever a last word to conflict in this part of the world? The Bruno Schulz Conference, a week-long feast of films, classical and rock concerts, art shows and street events has become an annual event designed "to emphasize Schulz's role in interwar Polish letters" and to illuminate the cultural legacy of Galicia, a region of history and imagination shared by Poland and Ukraine. Co-sponsoring the conference is Poland's way of saying that Poles are worthy stewards of the Polish-Jewish heritage. Ukraine and Poland, two of the three repository nations for Bruno Schulz's drawings, prints, paintings, letters, and manuscripts, show that they can work together, though they regularly keep each other's citizens waiting for six hours to cross the border.

The list of conference speakers in 2012 was dominated by Ukrainians, Poles, and Russians, with a sprinkling of scholars from the four corners of earth. I was one of a handful of Americans on the programme, and one of two, the day I spoke, to present in English. My paper posed the question: who reads Bruno Schulz in America and what do readers get from his fiction? I included examples of my students' responses to Schulz's novels—we read both *Street of Crocodiles* and *Sanatorium under the Sign of the Hourglass*. One young man summed up Schulz as "Proust on acid in pre–Nazi-occupied Poland". The Russian scholars in the room did not appear to be amused, while the crew of the Polish national television station who were filming the event gave me a thumbs-up.

Another student reader was put off by the frequently made comparison of Schulz to Kafka—exploitation of the Czech genius, he grumbled. The writer Schulz really made him think of was William Faulkner, from Mississippi. Both Schulz and Faulkner wrote about a "postage stamp" of the world where they found something infinite. Both, Jared said, sampled mythologies and put them in a new pattern, like DJs who take clips of recordings and paste them into their unique compositions. Jared compared Schulz's sensitivity to seasons in *The Street of Crocodiles* to Faulkner's treatment of late summer light pouring into Mississippi parlors in *Light in August*, a novel about missing fathers and the men who try to take their places. Faulkner's book came out in 1932, which goes to show, Jared said, that the great minds of any one generation have more in common with each other than they do with people of their own cultures who come before or after. I had told Jared that I find Addie Bundren's transformation into a fish in *As I Lay Dying* no more or less credible than Joseph's father's transformation into "a monstrous, hairy, steel blue horsefly" in Schulz's *Sanatorium*. Death was the great transformer, though in Schulz's Drohobych death did not mean the end. Father merely resumes his life in the evening.

I told the audience how a young woman had surprised me by saying she was moved by *Sanatorium's* "boundless optimism". The narrator's father defeated death, she said, just as Christ had promised. He may have died in one place, but that did not stop him from carrying on with his life in another, where the dead mingle with the living and no one can tell them apart. My student, Claire, is an evangelical Christian. When Joseph's father sensed the presence of the black-bearded stranger outside his shop and announced, with a radiant face, "He is coming … open the door", Claire heard the fulfillment of prophecy, the arrival of a savior. And indeed it was so. After wrestling physically and metaphysically night and day with Joseph's father, the stranger took his leave, and "seven long years of prosperity began for the shop" (Schulz 1977, p. 111).

I heard something else. I heard, "Ehr Kumt. Yidn Farlawst ayer shtetl"—"He is coming, Jews abandon your city". This was the warning delivered to the Jews of Vilna in 1938 by the Zionist seer from Odessa, Vladimir Jabotinsky.[5] Schulz's story was written probably 10 years earlier, in 1928, so of course this was not something he could have heard. But nothing was beyond his imagination, and isn't that what great artists do? "The artist", wrote Berlin sculptor and painter Otto Freundlich, "is a barometer of transformations. He senses them in his acts and his thoughts before they are realised in the world. When he detaches himself from the generally admitted forms and truths, he is executing the edicts of a new reality".[6]

My Jewish students are unhappy to learn that Schulz renounced his membership in the Jewish community. He did it for love of a woman, I tell them, but that's as far as he went, he did not take the next step, baptism. Philip Roth's literary creations, Alexander Portnoy and Nathan Zuckerman, try to abandon Judaism, Zuckerman wanting to "shed his American Jewish writer's skin". But skin does not come off easily. Aharon Appelfeld wrote a novel about a resort, a sanatorium, if you will, for Jews who want to lose their Jewish posture, Jewish voice, Jewish mannerisms. The discussion turned electric when I revealed that my niece had just returned from a semester at a school in Egypt where she had to pretend she wasn't Jewish. She, too, did it for love. She erased everything on her Facebook page that might give away her secret.

During a break in the Drohobych conference I walked a few blocks to an Internet café that was more café than Internet, and part bakery too. It was staffed by students from the teachers' college, lovely young women and men—just like coffee bars in every American college town, only there were more workers here per customer than you'd find at home. I sat down at a small but conspicuous table and when the waitress came over I started to order in Polish thinking, well, it's geographically close at least. She looked at me and put her finger to her lips and said, "No Polish, English please". She would like to practice her English with an American, and so would some of her co-workers. She came back with my tea and a biscuit, and several young people walked over and stood between the mostly empty tables. I told them

---

[5] "Few figures in 20th-century Jewish life were quite so admired and loathed" as the mercurial Jabotinsky, according to the overview of Hillel Halkin's (2014) welcome new biography of him. The forebear of Israel's most militant territorialists and defenders of the vision of a Greater Israel, Jabotinsky was also an avid "believer in democracy". He died in New York in August 1940, while visiting a Jewish self-defense camp run by *Betar*, a Zionist Youth group that he had founded in Latvia in 1923.

[6] This quote appeared in 1930 in the second issue of *Cercle et Carré* (Circle and Square), a manifesto printed periodically by a group of painters and sculptors in Paris who called themselves Constructivists. Classified as a "degenerate artist" by the Nazi regime, Freundlich was deported to Majdanek death camp in Poland in 1943 and murdered upon arrival.

who I was and where I was from and why I had come to Ukraine—to take part in the Schulz festival and give a talk about American reader and Bruno Schulz.

"Bruno Schulz, yes, we read him in Ukrainian", said a tall blond boy, wearing a waiter's black and white.

"And you know", I said, pointing to the front door, "he was killed across the street".

"Yes, there is a sign", he responded, throwing his head in the right direction. The young women were happy to let him do the talking.

"I know the sign". It's a plaque on the level of the sidewalk with script in Ukrainian and Polish, and the Polish reads,

Here in this place
19 November 1942
Was killed, shot by Gestapo man
great artist, citizen of Drohobych
Bruno Schulz

"Did you know", I asked, "that Schulz was Jewish?"

"No, a Jew, well…" the young man answered.

"Yes", I said, "and on the day he died more than 200 Jewish people were shot in the streets. Did you know", I said, drawing them into my tale, "when the Germans invaded Ukraine thousands of Jewish people were living in Drohobych. Fifteen thousand. Maybe more".

"No, really?" the young man ventured, with gentle skepticism, as if the story were contrary to reason. It certainly was contrary to anything he'd ever heard. "What happened to them? Where did they go?"

How could I be the bearer of that news? What kind of devil walks into your shop and tells you such terrible things? I felt like reaching out and sweeping up these big children and protecting them from the world they so eagerly want to join. If there'd been time—what an idiot I was not to make time—I would have offered to take them on a walk in Bronica Forest, the site of the mass murder and burial of thousands of Drohobych Jews. A modest stone monument marks the site. You can't help but think of the people buried beneath, who would burst out of the earth like a new chain of mountains if they could.

Or we could load up a van and drive west 80 km to the site of the Belzec death camp, between Ukrainian Lviv and Polish Zamosc. Thousands of Drohobych Jews who escaped shooting were sent there to be gassed, along with half a million more Jews from eastern Poland. Schulz probably would have wound up there if he'd stayed alive a little longer. My grandfather, too, if he hadn't emigrated. If we went as far as Zamosc, in beautiful hops country, we would find the handsome restored synagogue on Zamenhofa Street (formerly ul. Żydowska—"Jewish Street"). Built in 1610 by Sephardim from the Ottoman Empire and Venice, it was the northernmost Sephardi community in Eastern Europe, a fact that tied it to the Atlantic world—the dream destination of these students. The German occupiers used the building, of Polish-Italian design, as a woodshop, and thus it was saved. But the people who once worshipped here were not. No new worshippers have come to take their place and, for all of its charm and outward brightness, the interior feels like a stage set. What a contrast to the ogre of a building in Drohobych that once was a mighty synagogue and has been given over to vandals and graffiti artists. But on second thought, perhaps the decaying hulk is a necessary reminder of the void left by the annihilation of the Jews and the impossibility of genuine restoration.

My impromptu Ukrainian students look just like my American students and want the same things for themselves. Love, good music, high times, community, privacy, a job that lets them fantasise about getting ahead. I don't detect any anti-semitism in them. They are the first Ukrainians in modern times to grow up free of foreign occupation, free to think for themselves, free to venture outside of the narrow pathways traditionally laid down for them. If I could give them anything to help them on their way it would be a new story, or even better, the tools and will to find that story and to tell it themselves. To paraphrase one of Ukraine's favorite western writers, James Joyce, I wish them an encounter with "the reality of experience" and the drive "to forge in the smithy" of their souls "the uncreated conscience" of their nation.

Now is the moment for revision, for turning inside-out and upside-down narratives that were composed to serve obsolete political dogmas. But the task is immense. Around the school desks and café tables in Drohobych were young people who had not previously reflected on whether Jewish identity and Ukrainian identity could occupy the same geographic space. How easy it is to forget the Jews when they're gone! Will the new Ukrainian story have room for the history of Ukraine's Jews, skilled settlers who first appeared in these lands a thousand years ago? They were neighbors of these students' grandparents. They shared the vicissitudes of numerous foreign occupations, famine, and civil war. There were so many Jews that the Nazis and their accomplices couldn't shoot them all, though they tried. If the Jewish past is indeed restored to respectability, will it happen because Ukraine has been pressured by its western partners to adhere to the European narrative or because young Ukrainians are open to the truth and free to pursue the full story?

I've seen and heard it done. The results are life changing and paradigm shifting. It happened when my friend Rudy Herz spoke to students at a Catholic high school in his home town of Stommeln, Germany, then came to my class at the College of Charleston to report on his trip. Rudy was born in 1925 and had a normal childhood until Hitler came to power in 1933. Warned that it was not safe for Jews to stay in Stommeln, his father moved the family to the nearby city of Cologne. In 1942, the Herzes were deported, first to Theresienstadt and from there to Auschwitz. From Auschwitz, Rudy embarked on a cruel odyssey from one Nazi labor camp to another, seven or eight in all. In May 1945, he was liberated by the Americans at Gusen, in Austria, a satellite of Mauthausen, famous for a deadly stone quarry and underground armaments plant. At Mauthausen-Gusen, the Nazis murdered Jews and political opponents of all faiths by working them to death.

Rudy had been living in South Carolina for 40 years when, in 2011, he was invited to Stommeln by a young teacher and 19 students from the upper grades at Papst-Johannes XXIII.-Schule. The group had been working with their teacher, Carsten Mayer, on a year-long project called *Judische Kinder im Nationalsozialismus:*

Untergrund, Emigration und Verfolgung (Jewish Children during National Socialism; Underground, Emigration and Persecution). Rudy spoke to them about growing up in Stommeln among Christians and Jews and feeling as German as the next person. "We Jewish children pictured ourselves among the brave German Fighters in the Tuetonberg Forest", vanquishing the Roman invaders and sealing their German identity.

"If Prime Minister Merkl had asked me to come, I wouldn't have come, but because you asked me I am here", he told his hosts. Indeed, he was curious to see if Germany had changed since his last visit in 1986, when former perpetrators were living out their lives in opulence and people were telling him he should feel happy to be alive. He did not think much better of audiences in America and, in fact, he never volunteered to speak to my classes. He had to be tempted by a small stipend and the promise of a meal in a fine restaurant. His wife, Ursula, didn't want him to speak at all. She complained that he would lose a day of work which they could ill afford—they owned a nursery and landscaping business—and the pain of talking about the massacre of his family put him in a sour mood.

In the hours we would spend driving to Charleston and Columbia from his home in Myrtle Beach, Rudy would tell me things he had never told anyone. About the horrors of the camps, about his narrow escapes as a GI in Korea where he came closer to dying than he did at Auschwitz, about the free-and-easy time he spent bumming around the Mediterranean after the war, failing at one preposterous scheme after another, posing as a prince, gambling away fortunes in Monaco and Nice, lecturing on existentialism, conducting an orchestra of vagrant musicians, selling counterfeit watches to tourists and soldiers, smuggling cheese into Italy. After marrying Ursula in 1964, his adventures continued. They bought land on the French Riviera near the Italian border; the terraces produced fine cut flowers, apricots, and, recalls Ursula, "the best cherries in the world" (Herz 2013). To make a living, they put up tourist cabanas; when that flopped they tried raising rabbits. Rudy and I laughed so hard that by the time we got to school our eyes would be as red as beets. Before getting out of the car, Rudy patted down his hair and said, "If this was a movie, as soon as they see my face they know I'm not going to get the girl".

Two months after visiting Stommeln, he was in my classroom in Charleston, beaming and full of energy. I asked him to tell us what he had told the German students about growing up in Stommeln and how life changed when the Nazis came to power. He began by contrasting his recent visit with the one he'd made 25 years earlier, before any of the current group of students was born. He had taken part in a radio panel show with people his own age—that is, Germans who had lived "on the outside", while he clung to life with his animal instincts inside the camps. The moderator lampooned every point the locals made. "They made no room for their fellow citizens who spoke the same language, loved the same food and wine, listened to the same music".

One panelist was the son of a man who had bought Stommeln's small synagogue after the Jews were chased out of town and turned it into a pig sty. On the night of 9 November, 1938, the night we call Kristallnacht, men "came with gasoline", intending to set the building on fire. "Don't do it", shouted the father. "It's changed ownership". So the arsonists left it alone.

"Can you recall the Herz family?" asked the moderator, passing around a photograph of the mother with her four sons. "Two of them survived, Karl-Otto and Rudy. Alfred and Walter were gassed with their mother, Lilli". Her two daughters, Rudy's sisters, were not in the picture. They were the babies. And gassed, too, of course.

"Lilli", a woman piped up. "Gassed! Oh my!"

"The first deportations occurred after we were all told to wear the Jewish star", Rudy interjected. "A big yellow Star of David with 'Jew' imprinted in Jewish letters". He felt degraded as a Jew and as a German. For people "who knew Goethe, Schiller, Kleist, and Lessing, such a humiliation was going way beyond..."

"You were not able to foresee what would happen to those Jews?" asked the moderator, ready to scoff at any answer that wasn't "we should have known".

"Who knew that? I ask you in return", demanded one woman, throwing back the question: "Who knew what happened with the Jews? We didn't know. We knew only they had to leave".

"They went to work camps—yes, that was the term familiar to us", recalled the son of the synagogue-buyer.

Only after the war, they agreed, did they learn about the death camps and the gassings. No rudeness meant to Mr. Herz, but, "we partially consider it to be exaggerated".

"Was there no solidarity among the village population?" persisted the moderator.

"Those are all illusionary questions", protested the woman. "No one was able to strike back. They would have been put up against the wall".

The moderator wasn't buying it. "How could this have happened in Stommeln, this Catholic village?"

"Hitler, the stupid dog", said the elderly man. "At first he was great, he eliminated unemployment. Then came the Jewish persecution. He was obsessed with power".

A local historian read from a diary that had been kept by the town's priests since 1873—80% of the people of Stommeln were Catholics. For the year 1942, the diary reports unusually large snowfalls and elaborate preparations for the celebration of Saint Christina's birthday, in June. On that very day, the town's last remaining Jews, Helena and Jacob Stock and their daughter, were deported. The diary makes no mention of this.

The elderly man denied he had any bad feelings toward the Jews. He did not see then, and he does not see now, how it would have been possible to help them. "When they were picked up, my mother was standing at the gate. We couldn't watch it any more. We were friends with the Jews, the whole house over there were our friends. We interacted with one another as family. If my mother was baking, the Stocks received goods, and vice versa. We always went there in the morning to get firewood to light up the stove".

"We could smell the burned human flesh", Rudy broke in. "It was daily in the air. Auschwitz was the end for us. Hell. The Abyss, the atrium of death. And we thought: Does no one know in Stommeln? Does no one know our fate in Cologne? Are we completely deserted? That was when we knew: we were abandoned for death. They will kill us when they deem it the right time" (Herz 1986).

In 25 years a lot had changed in quiet Stommeln. The generation that was alive when Hitler came to power had died away. In Stommeln and Charleston, Rudy sensed the solidarity students feel with people their own age, an identity of interests that crosses all borders. He could unburden himself and give these young people the gift of knowledge. The children of Stommeln gave *him* the biggest gift of all. They turned the town into a laboratory of investigation and a theater of living history. The stars of their play were his sisters and brothers who had disappeared many years ago into the furnaces of Auschwitz. Carsten Mayer's students had designed and printed posters and hung them on storefronts all over town. Close up they read, "We remind you of the Jewish children of Stommeln". One broadside featured the names of Rudy's 2-year-old sister Jona, 6-year-old sister Johanna, and 12-year-old brother Walter, the date of their deportation to Theresienstadt, and their ages, in bold, at the time they were murdered at Auschwitz. For Walter a precise date of death is given as 11 July 1944. The name of 12-year-old Ilse Moses also appears on this poster, with the drab-sounding news that she was deported to Riga, the Latvian capital, where executioners waited with clubs and knives to do in the Jews.

A second poster called on people to remember 15-year-old Wolfgang Stock and his 13-year-old sister, Susi, children of the respected Jacob and Helene Stock. The Stocks met their deaths in the ghetto of Minsk, in faraway Belorussia. Young, up-to-date, and happy to disturb their elders, the students filmed people in the streets reacting to the signs. "No, I haven't seen them", said several old men and women, not stopping to read and mistaking the names for runaways.

"Yes, it is true they are missing children", the students would answer. "Do you remember the Jews?"

Ahhhhhh, a trap! They knew they were in for it now.

Some said yes, a few said no, some thought that more attention should be paid to Germans—by which they meant non-Jews—who lost sons and brothers during the war. The Stock family were recalled as "good, honest people. Better than some Christians". One man said solemnly, "Every dictatorship creates an enemy".

"Now all the children are the enemy", said another, under his breath.

Rudy felt he had come home. The militant young scholars had turned him back toward life by focusing not on the anomalous condition of survival but on the dead, restoring names and even personalities to the lost Jewish children of Stommeln. They had created an afterlife for his brothers and sisters, one that did not depend on his existence. He could die but they would live, in a manner of speaking, in memory and in history. Back in 1942, Rudy recalled to the students, "No German could be found who said, 'Listen, you can't do this to these people. They are our fellow citizens'". It took nearly 70 years, but now he'd found one, and more than one: they were everywhere. They embraced him and asked him several times to move back to Stommeln.

My Charleston class listened to Rudy's story and watched the film of the German high school students who looked, sounded, and acted like them. They asked some of the same questions, as if hoping for different answers. They wanted to know why the Herz family stayed in Germany, while the majority of Jews got out in time. Rudy told them how instead of following through on plans to immigrate to Argentina, or take refuge with cousins in Holland, his father tried to adapt to the new conditions. When his grain business was confiscated he used his two pick-up trucks to haul cargo until that was forbidden too and the trucks were seized. Still, Rudy's grandmother refused to leave and his mother would not go without her. In 1941, "the settlement orders began coming. All our relatives were taken away".

Rudy's family was sent to Theresienstadt, the model ghetto that was a holding pen for Auschwitz. The move delayed their destiny for 2 years. Perhaps they owed this good luck to the fact that his father had served in the German army during World War I, on the staff of General Hindenberg, and that he had been imprisoned by the French. The Herzes reached Theresienstadt after a 3-day ride in a sealed railroad car, but one with seats. Already 18, Rudy was assigned the job of gravedigger. Making the best of their new lives, the brothers read everything they could get their hands on. Rudy recalled his younger brother Walter had hidden a book by the poet Goethe. "We read it twice", he said proudly. "We memorised it. We quoted from it".

Feeling German to his core, and unwilling to believe that Germans would kill their own kind, Rudy was easily deceived. Even in Auschwitz. "We did not know that Auschwitz was an extermination camp or that we could be put to death", he told my class. Could it be true that by the summer of 1944, when the heinous death factory had been in full swing for more than 2 years, literate, curious people, with access to clandestine radios and to an occasional newspaper smuggled into the ghetto, did not know what was going on at Auschwitz? My students do not want to believe it. At their trials, the perpetrators claimed they were ignorant, too. Even the ones who dropped Zyklon B pellets into the gas chambers could say they were not present when the gas had finished its work.

From the "family camp" at Birkenau where the Theresienstadt deportees were kept, "We saw a large chimney belching smoke 24 hours a day", Rudy reported. "We saw German military ambulances"—those consummate vehicles of deception—with a Red Cross symbol on them going back and forth". Only "much later" did he learn that "these ambulances were carrying the cyanide poison canisters". And in the morning, "when the cart came to collect the bodies" of people who had died in the barracks during the night, even then "we knew they were taken to the crematory to be incinerated but we still had no knowledge of the gas chambers, and that people were killed in such numbers as they were".

But they were, and soon after he was transferred to another camp, his mother and three siblings were gassed.

"Do you expect to meet them again in heaven?" one girl asked.

"No, I do not", Rudy replied. "At Auschwitz we called out to God but He did not answer. His silence shattered our ear drums".

Rudy was not in a forgiving mood.

"I was old enough to be responsible for my sins", he continued. "My little sisters were not".

"Can you tell us about the last time you saw your mother?" asked a young man who had prepared the question in advance.

Rudy explained that in the family "lager" at Birkenau, though the men were separated from the women and children, they could approach each other at a fence that was not electrified. Informed that he would be departing at any moment for another camp and a better chance to live, he went to the fence to say goodbye to his mother. They knew it was unlikely they would see each other again. If only she had overruled her mother and exhorted her husband to take the family out of Germany while there was yet time. Rudy wanted more than life to relieve her pain. He still wanted it. He told us about a ditch that ran through the women's camp; prisoners had laid sod on the ditch banks to keep them from collapsing. At the time, the children were starving. They dreamed about food and it was all they talked about. "My mother remembered seeing in Stommeln the geese eating the wild grasses. She knew there were plants growing in the sod that we could eat. She gathered them when she could and we ate them". She saved her children for whatever came next.

Rudy Herz died, at the age of 86, at the VA hospital in Charleston, South Carolina. His death was a great loss to humane studies. Rudy left this world never having heard adequate answers to the questions posed by the prophet Jeremiah. "Why does the way of the wicked prosper? Why do all the faithless live at ease?" In private, Rudy carried on a relentless interrogation. Like Jeremiah he was not afraid to say to the Lord, "I would speak about your justice". Over the years that he visited my classes, Rudy addressed about a thousand students. In the beginning, I felt that he was coming because he thought it was a help to me and because we would get to spend a day together. He was willing to be "Exhibit 'A' of the Holocaust", as he called himself. At the end he was coming for the students. Rudy indeed may have lost his faith in a God that acts in history, and even in the idea of a Creator, but his last visit to Stommeln restored his faith in man, or more precisely, in children.

The lesson of Rudy's encounter with the students at Stommeln is that the Holocaust cannot do for us all that we ask it to do.[7] We Jews remember the Holocaust and teach it as a way to defend our humanity and to give the gift of vigilance to a conflict-ridden world. And for less noble reasons. We bank on it to fill classrooms and appeal to investors in Jewish education. We use it lazily in place of theology—and thoughtfully as a challenge to theology. For some it is irrelevant to theology. Most of the time we can't get it off our minds. Philosopher and novelist Charles Johnson (2008) observes that the "black American narrative" of oppression sits "quietly in the background of every conversation we have about black people". Likewise, the Holocaust occupies a place in the room whenever the conversation turns to Jews. Among Jews themselves, it is an unspoken bond, wanted or unwanted; talking about the destruction, however, is generally unpleasant. There was nothing redeeming about it.

---

[7] A paraphrase of Anthony Kwame Appiah's (1992) observation about the impossible demands placed on the word "race". "There is nothing in the world that can do all we ask race to do for us", he wrote, quoted in Charles Johnson's (2008) luminous essay on why the inherited racial and ethnic stories we tell ourselves are out of date and in need of revision.

In my mind's eye I see Rudy behind the wheel of his pick-up. He is driving by himself from Myrtle Beach to speak to my class at the university. He's late and I'm anxious. Even if he gets here at this instant he won't have time for a cup of coffee. Then, I hear him before I can see him, his old truck clamoring up the hill, loaded to the gills with composted goat manure destined for a customer, spreading a fine mist of fertilizer over the campus.

Rudy, the children are waiting for you, somewhere very near, just up the road and around the corner. All is well.

References

AFT [American Federation of Teachers] (2014). *Legislating Jim Crow*. Washington, DC: AFT. http://www.aft.org/newspubs/periodicals/ae/summer2004/brownsb1.cfm
Appiah, K. (1992). *In my father's house: Africa in the philosophy of culture*. Oxford: Oxford University Press.
Brooks, J. (1994, Winter). The art of fiction, no. 139. Interview with Chinua Achebe. *Paris Review*.
Davis, J. C. (2010, 3 August). *Translation of The Republic of Dreams*, by Bruno Schulz. Wordpress.com. http://oldearthisdying.wordpress.com/2010/08/03/the-republic-of-dreams-by-bruno-schulz/
Deak, I. (2011, 3 November). Review of Robert Gerwarth biography, *Hitler's hangman: The life of Heydrich*. The New Republic. http://www.newrepublic.com/book/review/hitler-hangman-reinhard-heydrich-robert-gerwarth
Elkins, S. (1959). *Slavery: A problem in American institutional and intellectual life*. Chicago: University of Chicago Press.
Gross, J. T. (2001). *Neighbors: The destruction of the Jewish community in Jedwabne, Poland*. Princeton: Princeton University Press.
Halkin, H. (2014). *Jabotinsky: A life*. New Haven: Yale University Press.
Handlin, O. (1951). *The uprooted: The epic story of the great migrations that made the American people*. New York: Grosset and Dunlap.
Harlan, L. J. (1958). *Separate and unequal*. Chapel Hill: University of North Carolina Press.
Herz, R. (1986). *The Jews of Stommeln*. Talk on *Here and today report*, on West German Broadcasting. Transcription in Rudolf Herz papers, 1944–2011, Mss 1065-050, Special Collections, College of Charleston Library.
Herz, U. S. (2013, September). Telephone conversation with Dale Rosengarten. Notes available from Jewish Heritage Collection, College of Charleston Library.
Johnson, C. (2008, June). The end of the Black American narrative. *The American Scholar*. http://www.freerepublic.com/focus/news/2052493/posts
Kaufman, M. T. (2009, 3 October). Marek Edelman, commander in Warsaw Ghetto Uprising, dies at 90. *The New York Times*. http://www.nytimes.com/2009/10/03/world/europe/03edelman.html?pagewanted=all&_r=1&
Kelley, R. D. G. (1990). *Hammer and hoe: Alabama communists during the Great Depression*. Durham: University of North Carolina Press.
MacDonald, C. (1989). *The killing of SS Obergruppenfuhrer Reinhard Heydrich*. New York: The Free Press.
Meng, M. (2011). *Shattered spaces: Encountering Jewish ruins in postwar Germany and Poland*. Cambridge, MA: Harvard University Press.
NPS [National Park Service] (2014). *Jim Crow laws*. Washington, DC: NPS. http://www.nps.gov/malu/forteachers/jim_crow_laws.htm
Rawick, G. (1972, 1979). *The American slave: A composite autobiography* (Vols. 18 and 19). Westport: Greenwood.

Rosen, D. (1969). *The Alabama Share Croppers Union*. Senior honors essay. Cambridge, MA: Radcliffe College.
Rosengarten, T. (1974). *All God's dangers: The life of Nate Shaw*. New York: Knopf.
Roth, P. (2001). *Shop talk: A writer and his colleagues and their work*. New York: Houghton Mifflin.
Rubenstein, R. L. (1976). *The cunning of history: The Holocaust and the American future*. New York: Harper & Row.
Schulz, B. (1977). *Sanatorium under the sign of the hourglass* (C. Wieniewska, Trans.). Middlesex: Penguin.
Schulz, B. (1988). Republic of dreams. In J. Ficowski (Ed.), (W. Arndt, Trans.), *Letters and drawings of Bruno Schulz* (pp. 217–223). New York: Harper & Row.
Smith, D. (2001, 18 July). Debating who controls Holocaust artifacts. *The New York Times*. http://www.nytimes.com/2001/07/18/arts/debating-who-controls-holocaust-artifacts.html
Wheeler, G. (2013). *Language teaching through the ages*. London: Routledge Educational Research.

Is Teaching and Learning about the Holocaust Relevant for Human Rights Education?

Monique Eckmann

Introduction

Is Holocaust education a tool for teaching about human rights? Should it be? Can it be? Over the last decade, as a member of such organisations as the Education Working Group (EWG) of the International Holocaust Remembrance Alliance (IHRA), the former Task Force for International Cooperation on Holocaust Education, Remembrance and Research (ITF), I have observed these questions being discussed widely, and seen how much the answers differ depending on the national and regional contexts. These questions point out the need to consider how history can be relevant today and in the future, and to consider questions of rights, of dignity, and of access to full citizenship.

The expression Holocaust education is ambiguous; in fact I believe we should not use it, for several reasons. First, the word Holocaust has become an institutionalised expression, but only in an Anglo-Saxon context, and cannot be easily transposed to other languages and other socio-historical contexts. The term is not universally employed. French speakers, for example, prefer to say Shoah, as do Israelis, as long as they speak in Hebrew, and others such as German speakers use more complex expressions such as *Völkermord an den Juden* (the Destruction of the Jews). Second, because the term Holocaust has theological connotations and lacks analytical meaning, it can sometimes mystify rather than clarify. "Shoah" may not be much more analytical, but at least it comes from the language of the murdered group and does not have the Christian connotation of a burnt sacrifice/offering. Both Holocaust and Shoah have religious or mystical connotations and tend to put

M. Eckmann (✉)
School for Social Work, University of Applied Sciences Western Switzerland,
28, rue Prévost-Martin, 1211, Geneva 4, Switzerland
e-mail: monique.eckmann@hesge.ch

the emphasis on the uniqueness of the event. Even if we fully acknowledge that uniqueness, simply using these expressions raises the risk of taking this genocide out of history and sacralising it, thus making it a historical. This does not really make it more understandable.

And third, the term Holocaust is used with different meanings in different contexts: for many, it designates the murder of the Jews and includes only Jews. Others, however, including states, historians, and NGOs, officially use the term Roma Holocaust, and for some that term also includes other victims of Nazi crimes, mainly Roma, and sometimes homosexuals and people with disabilities. In fact, the word Holocaust is used in contexts far beyond the Nazi crimes, for any kind of genocide or mass crime, or even for the killing of animals. This context of competition and claims for strict or wide definitions makes the term even more difficult to employ. An option could be to use Hilberg's (1961/1985) expression, "the Destruction of the European Jews", but as we cannot avoid using the shorter and more common expression, at least let us be aware of its complexity. Having discussed all these possibilities, in this chapter I choose to use the two terms—Holocaust and Destruction of the European Jews—interchangeably.

The wider expression, Holocaust education, is even more problematic, and those outside the field are often amazed at it. Indeed, it does not indicate whether it involves learning about history, literature, moral issues, the Jews, the Nazis, or other victims of Nazi politics. Does it focus on history or on the lessons of history? But it is used in recognition of a field and it has an institutional dimension, even if the term does not explain exactly what it addresses. However, it is difficult to find an alternative expression, and the challenge to redefine the expression, and the field, remains.

Often, the words of politicians, educational planners, and ministries in charge of memorials make it seem obvious that whatever the term may means in a given context, Holocaust education should be a tool for human rights education. Society places a certain pressure on memorials, educational programmes, and memorial days: they should not only be opportunities to learn about the past, but should also have an impact on the future, i.e. through human rights education and education for democratic citizenship. Educators who deal with such issues on a daily basis find that they, and their students, have strong expectations in this regard. Nevertheless, they often say it is very difficult to teach about both the Holocaust and human rights in one school programme, during one visit, or within one project.

Teaching and Learning about the Holocaust Today

Before we can begin to connect Holocaust education to human rights education, we must first understand the need to teach about the Holocaust, and what is being done today. To begin, I report some findings from a study I co-conducted in Western Switzerland, interviewing history teachers about their experiences teaching about the Holocaust (Eckmann and Heimberg 2011). Our research question was linked less to human rights education than to citizenship education; it explored how these teachers felt, and what their experiences had been in teaching the topic of the Destruction of the Jews. They declared that to them it is one of the most important topics to teach, if not the most important. One said that "it is important to show that it is an unavoidable topic, something difficult but decisive, something that shows a turning point in the reflection of human beings and history". The Shoah is the culminating point of the programme and some of the teachers said it was the reason they had studied history.

But they are also quite aware that this strong conviction could weigh too heavily on the students: "For me it is not a topic like the others, and that is the danger, so I am careful not to focus all of my teaching on this point". They are also aware of the risk that students may identify too strongly with the victims: "I am afraid of overdoing it in the direction of the victims… I don't want to depress the students, so I also show the aspect of resistance, to provide some hope".

These and other testimonies show that for history teachers the Holocaust is a crucial topic in the curriculum. They are concerned that students might object to studying the Holocaust, though in fact that seldom happens. Most of the overt objections arose in 2005, the 60th anniversary of the liberation of Auschwitz-Birkenau, when the topic received considerable media coverage. They also think very carefully about pedagogical approaches, and about how to teach this topic. Although they are deeply convinced of its importance, they feel it is difficult to explain why it is so important to teach about the Holocaust.

The EWG (2014) developed guidelines/recommendations on why to teach about the Holocaust, what to teach about the Holocaust, and how to teach about the Holocaust. It appears clear—and other studies show similar results—that the most difficult part is articulating *why* to teach about the Holocaust.

Teachers also find it difficult to answer questions such as "Why are you always speaking about Jews?" and "Why not speak about Rwanda, about slavery, or about the Roma?" Or, in post-Soviet countries they might ask, "Why not speak about the Gulag?". In Western European contexts, we observed that such questions lead teachers to adopt new strategies. Usually in the lower grades the Holocaust is taught within the context of World War II and the rise of Nazism. But more and more educators, especially in the upper grades, tend to teach it within the context of comparing genocides, or within the context of topics like racism and totalitarianism, and in a post-colonial perspective.

Focusing on History or on Memory?

In Latin countries, scholars often emphasise the distinction between history and memory. I believe this is essential. Learning about the Destruction of the Jews should be a matter of history, not of memory, as the primary aim is historical knowledge and remembrance, rather than commemoration. Memory is certainly part of the experience when one is visiting a memorial, exploring a local area, or interviewing witnesses. Of course, to a certain extent, the teachers want to create in their students a sense of empathy with the victims—which is a basic requirement. But to ensure that students gain an understanding that spans the experience of individuals or families and their own country's role in the larger event, and that they grasp the Destruction of the Jews in its entirety, Holocaust educators often discuss a focus that includes three elements: These are the overall picture or historical framework; the specific history of one's own national context; and detailed knowledge about a place, person, or memorial, linked to a specific territory or to a community.

Each element offers different benefits. Students need the overall picture so they can locate the isolated event or place in the frame of the history of World War II, Nazism, and the Destruction of the Jews. A more general framework also helps students establish relationships, for example between war and genocide. The specific national context gives students the opportunity to reflect self-critically about the history of their own society and its involvement in this part of history. Detailed knowledge of a place or a person facilitates access for students, and helps teachers make it concrete and tangible. But learning about the Destruction of the Jews also means dealing with the perspectives of all the other groups—victims, perpetrators, bystanders, rescuers, and opponents—as well as with their memories. Often this means dealing with competing memories, and even with denial of memory.

This leads to the question of memory. A community of memories keeps alive the memory of its own members, and promotes the commemoration of its own people. In Europe, however, the various national or social narratives differ. Ours is a Europe of divided memories—divided along the lines of different historical experiences. Even within each national memory the narratives of specific groups may differ. But to address divided memories, we educators must share memories and listen to all the various stories. We have to build a complex, multi-perspective vision of the past based on a dialogue of memories, between communities of remembrance, and we must mutually recognise victimhood and suffering, all while refraining from any kind of denial. Achieving this combination is not easy in groups with a diversity of narratives.

In this context, it is important to counter a common misinterpretation: that Holocaust education is above all a duty of memory. In fact, it is first and foremost a duty of history: the duty to transmit and to teach and learn the history. Teachers can place too much emphasis on the duties of memory and of commemoration, and some students react negatively to this. We must indeed distinguish between remembrance and commemoration: one of the aims of teaching and learning about the Holocaust is to keep alive the memory of the victims. This is remembrance; it does not mean one must organise a commemoration ceremony. Commemoration does not have the same meaning for everyone; to one community it means mourning its own members and preserving its group identity, while for others it means taking responsibility for its own history. My intent is not to oppose memory and history, nor to choose between them, but rather to emphasise the need to distinguish between history, remembrance, and commemoration, and the need for educators to focus on the first and the second, but not necessarily on the third, depending, of course, on the educational context.

Moreover, the *history of memory* must be studied. It is important to understand what has been told at which moment of history, during and after the Cold War, for example. What is told in small countries that were not occupied during World War II? When did people discuss the banks and the refugee policy, and why didn't they do that earlier? What is the context and the history of the decision to create a memorial or a commemoration day? Which advocacy groups took the initiative to propose a memorial place or a commemoration date, and when, and for whom? What groups were involved in memorialisation politics? What victims are named? Who is mentioned in the official memory, and who is not included?

Focusing on History or on the Lessons of History?

Another misinterpretation is what the French describe as *"trop de morale, pas assez d'histoire"*: too much moralising and not enough history, or putting the lessons of history before the knowledge of the history itself. Precisely because it is such a crucial topic, many educators want to draw out moral lessons, and these lessons are not always correct. A moralising approach anticipates what has to be learnt, and leaves no space for the students to discover by themselves in a constructivist approach.

Also, history cannot be transposed to the present in a linear way. For example, in connection with learning about Nazism and the Destruction of the Jews, students may think about contemporary stereotyping and conclude that they can now see where stereotyping leads. But such a conclusion may be too simple, because stereotyping alone does not necessarily lead to genocide. In this example, students draw on their personal feelings, and then move too rapidly to parallels with the mechanisms of state-sanctioned murder.

Another risk lies in trying to draw lessons without knowing the history, or in attempting to compare and conclude without precise, concrete historical elements. Of course it is impossible to know everything about the Destruction of the Jews, but lessons must be taught carefully and based on historical sources wherever possible. Then students can compare, once they are clear about what, how, and why to compare. Comparison is, per se, a scientific method that requires knowledge and tools in order to be conducted properly. And comparing is not equating. It is also important to know what to compare. For example, compare facts such as legal dispositions against targeted groups, or ideological settings, or ways of defining and excluding targeted groups.

Let's add two more challenges. The first is the dilemma of whether to focus on emotion or on cognition when teaching and learning about the Holocaust. Empathy with the victims is certainly a desirable aim for any educator. But can we request empathy from the students? I doubt it. I heard a teacher say that when a student is moved to tears, the goal of education is reached. This again contains the risk of sacralising the Holocaust and turning it into an ahistorical event, putting it into the field of emotion rather than cognition. Rather than empathy based on emotions, we should refer to the concept of historical empathy, dealing with the understanding of the circumstances, in which people in the past acted or reacted. The second challenge is the question of which teachers or disciplines have to teach the topic of the Destruction of the Jews. It is actually taught in at least four fields: history, philosophy, literature, and religion. This creates the risk of repetition in the curricula, as the topic could be introduced in several uncoordinated ways, without offering students any academic progression. Coordinating lessons, and building an advancing spiral, are crucial to avoid any feeling of redundancy.

What Does Human Rights Education in Holocaust Education Mean?

Having considered this background, and keeping in mind that learning about the Holocaust is a very complex field in and of itself, I now ask: Can Holocaust education be human rights education?

Human rights education is also a complex topic. It includes the history of the idea of human rights and of the Universal Declaration of Human Rights, along with the more legal and institutional dimensions of the various conventions and their implementation, as well as the philosophy and culture of human rights. Finally, a pedagogical and motivational dimension includes understanding and standing up for human rights and against their violation.

Scholars usually distinguish two main options in human rights education (Lohrenscheit 2002): learning *about* human rights and learning *for* human rights. Recently a third dimension has been added, which I see as equally crucial: learning *with (or within)* the framework of human rights.

What does it mean, then, to learn *about, for,* and *within* the framework of human rights?

These three dimensions deserve to be considered in more detail. First, learning *about* human rights involves the cognitive dimension. It includes knowledge about the history and the philosophy of human rights. It can also include the institutional dimensions of the Human Rights Council, along with other aspects such as the various conventions, states' reports and responsibilities, and reports and possible interventions by civil society, as well as lobbying and media work. It includes awareness of both the legal and institutional systems and the violations of human rights. In this dimension the emphasis is on knowing, understanding, and valuing.

Second, learning *for* human rights includes a motivational aspect and the development of competencies to act, as advocates within our own communities or cities. Learning for human rights implies knowing about such rights, recognising violations of them, and learning to protect and reestablish these rights. It also means knowing about one's own rights; as part of knowing about, respecting, and defending the rights of others, it requires an attitude of dignity and solidarity. Thus, the motivation to act is part of education for human rights, but not all of it. Education for human rights also means developing competencies to act and learning about strategies like lobbying and advocacy. The emphasis is on respect, responsibility, and solidarity.

Third, learning *within a framework* of human rights includes not only the content, but also the learning process and the learning conditions that must be framed by human rights considerations. The learning process must be coherent, connecting the content and the pedagogical methods of the process to the students' learning situation. Pedagogically, this requires that teachers use active methods such as learning by experience and peer education. This educational process must guarantee respect for human rights and for the rights of the child as a frame for learning, for all children or students. This includes, for example, ensuring that all students and children have the right of access to all sectors of higher education, a right not everywhere guaranteed to the children of undocumented workers.

What are the possibilities for, and limitations to, implementing these dimensions within Holocaust education? I consider each one separately.

Learning about Human Rights in the Context of Holocaust Education

The first dimension, learning *about* human rights in the context of Holocaust education, offers many possibilities, including three I outline here. First, the link between World War II and the UN decision regarding the Universal Declaration of Human Rights (UDHR) and the Convention on the Prevention and Punishment of the Crime of Genocide offer students the chance to learn about the history of the UDHR and the discussions about a Genocide Convention, as well as their institutional, judicial, and philosophical aspects. Students can also learn about violations of children's rights and actions to protect them. For example, the associations founded in the memory of Janus Korczak deal extensively with children in the Holocaust and with children's rights, by describing life in the ghetto, and not only the deportation but also the way the orphanage dealt with children's rights. Korczak, a Polish-Jewish pediatrician and pedagogue, developed an educational perspective in his orphanage in the Warsaw Ghetto, based on respect for children and their rights. Although people offered to rescue him, he refused to abandon the children and they were taken together to Treblinka, where they were probably all murdered.

As a second possibility, students can consider the philosophical and historical dimensions of the Destruction of the Jews in the context of discussions about what is usually called the three generations of rights referring to the UDHR; thus they can deal with the differences in individual, social, and cultural rights.

Third, the study of the Destruction of the Jews provides many examples of the Nazis' extreme violations of human rights and can help develop awareness of such violations: the violation of such rights as owning property, moving freely, and being protected by or from one's own state—and even the right to live. The history also includes violations by bystander countries. These include refusing to grant asylum or protection, failing to protect human dignity, denying access to citizenship, and failing to protect individuals from persecution by other states. Of course, Holocaust education also helps students see the need to protect human rights. The connection between the Destruction of the Jews and human rights should not be seen as overly linear, because the debate on human rights started far earlier, and includes previous efforts such as the French *Déclaration des droits de l'homme et du citoyen* and the United States *Bill of Rights*. However, the historical experience and the knowledge of the Holocaust have led people to fundamentally reconceptualise human rights, and have favoured the embrace of human rights worldwide and the broad adoption of the universal declaration. This strong bridge between the two is mainly shown through the extreme violations of human rights. But in fact, as already mentioned, the *Convention on the Prevention and Punishment of the Crime of Genocide*, adopted just a day before the UDHR, on 9 December, 1948, can also be considered an important outcome of World War II and of the Holocaust.

We could sum up this dimension of learning about human rights with Hannah Arendt's expression regarding the recognition of a crucial right: *the right to have rights*. Indeed the destiny of the Jews reveals the extreme vulnerability of stateless persons who are denied any rights at all. Only states can ensure the right to have rights and to protect people, along with their rights and dignity. This points to the necessity for all people to hold full citizenship.

A limitation here is that all these topics require a certain amount of resources and mostly can only be touched upon within learning about the Holocaust. It is often difficult to delve into them more deeply within the timeframe available to teach about the Holocaust or while visiting a memorial.

Learning for Human Rights in the Context of Holocaust Education

The second dimension, learning *for* human rights in Holocaust education, would suggest learning and exercising advocacy and intervention to protect human rights, and establishing or reestablishing rights that have been denied. This requires that students understand that states are accountable for human rights violations, that to learn this way they have to experience attitudes and patterns of acting, and that to do so they work on specific cases, document violations, create networks, learn to lobby, etc. These activities recall the words of the well-known Swiss educator, Johann Pestalozzi, whose concept was learning by "head, heart, and hand"; learning by hand also means learning by doing.

But this dimension of learning *for* the protection or the reestablishment of human rights seems limited and difficult to fulfill within lessons on the Holocaust, for several reasons. First, as the worst violation of human rights, the Holocaust provides us lessons not merely in learning how to prevent discrimination or how to fight against human rights violations or how to protect human rights. Also, Holocaust education does not directly provide opportunities to experiment with the various competencies required for action and intervention, such as lobbying or advocacy. Of course, students can consider examples of resistance and opposition, but those examples must be placed in the context of the political situation, including the rise of state violence and state terror. Also, some teachers address the dilemmas of human rights, or situations in which human rights dilemmas arise, based on events during the era of National Socialism, promoting reflections on acting for human rights. Confronting different perspectives on such dilemmas—such as the perspectives of perpetrators, victims, bystanders, and rescuers and resisters—is one way to deal with moral judgment and a first step toward considering action.

Learning within Human Rights in the Context of Holocaust Education

The third dimension, learning within human rights in the context of Holocaust education, refers to the process, the atmosphere, and the pedagogical framework, but also to the legal and civic framework that must be established in accordance with human rights principles. The rights of children and students must be protected, access to education for every child must be guaranteed, and the educational system must be constructed according to human rights principles so it can ensure equal opportunities and a democratic structure.

On the other hand, learning within a framework of human rights also means including human rights attitudes in learning systems, active learning settings, and a democratic pedagogical approach. Also, peer education is a basic tool for human rights education: as Jean Piaget pointed out, it is our peers, rather than our parents or teachers, who most influence us as we develop moral judgment. These pedagogical approaches must give students the space to deal with their personal or family experiences with rights and discrimination. Building on personal experiences is a powerful motivation for learning, whether those are personal experiences of discrimination, or experiences of witnessing discrimination against others. Such incidents and experiences often emerge during lessons about the Destruction of the Jews, or while visiting a memorial or watching a movie about it, and they enable students to establish links between past and present kinds of discrimination.

Can, and Should, Teaching about the Holocaust be a Tool for Human Rights Education?

Overall, my answer is nuanced and skeptical. First, *can* teaching and learning about the Holocaust be a tool for human rights education? I suggest that it cannot fulfill all the requirements of human rights education, but that it represents a powerful symbol for (the violation of) human rights and it can contribute significantly to opening minds. However, human rights education can be present when people are teaching and learning about the Holocaust, mainly through the dimension of learning *about* human rights and learning *within the frame* of human rights.

Teaching about the Holocaust offers opportunities and is a starting point to confront human rights issues. But even if it seems difficult to really learn *for* human rights in the context of the Holocaust, it is nevertheless crucial to learn a few things *about* human rights and learn *within a framework* of human rights. Most teaching about the Holocaust addresses the human rights dimensions only marginally, but they should be examined more closely, either before dealing with the Holocaust or later on, or in another setting. So learning about the Holocaust constitutes a motivation and a starting point for an interest in human rights, as a tool for building awareness; it can also include several valuable elements of human rights education, but it cannot be considered as its true core.

Still, this combination offers several possibilities to explore and new approaches to experience. Several recently initiated studies and projects in Europe are addressing this question and should bring us new insights. One example is the recent study by the EU Agency for Fundamental Rights (FRA 2011) on the role of Holocaust commemoration sites and memorials for human rights education. Another is in Germany: an action-research study, led by a group of *Gedenkstättenpädagogen* or educators working in memorial sites and museums, has developed new training modules for guides at such sites (Thimm et al. 2010). And a programme of the EVZ Foundation (2014) supports projects linking history and human rights education. The evaluation of these projects (Engelhardt et al. 2012) has shown that this connection is not easy to handle in an integrated way: one topic or the other tends to dominate, as the institutions are not equally committed to both fields. This reveals the need to promote cooperation, but mainly to develop concepts, and engage in further research and experimentation, in order to link these topics in a clearly articulated way.

Second, *should* Holocaust education be a tool for human rights education? Some people take it for granted that Holocaust education is human rights education—perhaps too much for granted. Both are challenging tasks, but they do not represent the same kind of challenge. Moreover, the links that are established vary in each context, depending on the learning context as well as on the context of national history and experience. In Switzerland, for example, some teachers link teaching about the Shoah to citizenship education, especially when they organise memorial days. Moreover, it is history teachers who mostly address the aims of human rights education or citizenship education. But human rights education aims not to deal mainly with the past, but instead to clearly address human rights violations today in one's own national and social context.

At memorial sites, however, this link might be more difficult to achieve: some memorial places are cemeteries, places to mourn, places of memory. We must remember that even the best educational programme cannot repair the Holocaust, cannot undo what has happened, and cannot bring back to life those who were murdered. Educators may be tempted to try to forge this link, but such a goal may be too ambitious for human rights education.

I suggest that we consider Holocaust education and human rights education as elements of a triangle where we again find Pestalozzi's head, heart, and hand.

Learning about the history of the Holocaust is a mainly cognitive experience, and thus involves the head. Memory and commemoration involve the heart, and human rights education, including the dimension of acting *for* human rights, involves the hands. These three cardinal points stand in a complex tension to each other. They can be placed on a continuum and we can draw various connections between them, depending on the combinations found in each learning setting. Each teaching module, each project or programme dealing with the Destruction of the Jews, each memorial place or museum, has a specific potential and deals in a specific way with a specific combination of these three dimensions: closer to or farther away from history, commemoration, or human rights, according to its specific context. But no educational approach can fully address all three of them at once, so teachers must make some choices.

Further Challenges

Within the possibilities and limits sketched above, I see several further challenges and new projects and experiences that should be promoted in the future.

Reinforce Links to Neighbouring Topics

Because the Destruction of the Jews is an important topic in the teaching of history, it is linked to the European history curriculum. But it can also be placed under the umbrella of other frameworks or allied topics, which would benefit from closer links. Examples of such frameworks are intercultural education, antiracist education, and education for democratic citizenship, or citizenship education. In this chapter I have addressed human rights education, but those working in other fields should also reinforce their linkages to the question of the Holocaust, as a dialogue between colleagues in distinct fields who can learn from each other before they try to include their own work in the other's. For example, it is impossible to carry out antiracist education without any attention to the Holocaust; on the other hand, antiracist education is not limited to the topic of the Holocaust, as it includes present-day forms of racism. Intercultural education targets the question of how people can live together when they come from diverse cultural, national, or religious groups, and even bigger questions that underlie relationships between minorities and majorities, as well as the protections of minority rights. Of course, it can also include aspects of the processes that led to the Destruction of the Jews. Citizenship education deals with the rights of every person living in a given territory and thus addresses the active participation of all members of the society. These fields evolved quite separately, and they would benefit by being brought together.

Reach out to New Target Groups

Holocaust education as human rights education is particularly promising when it is used to address target groups of professionals, such as police, social workers, and medical staff, in their professional training or in service training. It is also important not to limit it to formal or school education, but to address informal education as well, including municipal or community initiatives, community work, and neighbourhood initiatives.

Yet, even if we want to focus mainly on schools, we could reinforce our action not only by addressing in-service training for teachers, but by focusing on teacher training institutes, and on pre-service training, reinforcing cooperation with the teachers and specialists responsible for training history and citizenship teachers in universities or professional colleges.

Develop Experimental Joint Projects to Bring Together Both Fields

Human rights and the history of the Destruction of the Jews are both wide and complex fields requiring very competent educators. It is difficult for one person to master both fields, so actors from both fields need to come together in person to exchange their knowledge and experiences. We need to experience models and methods that can bring the two topics closer together; this also means bringing together both the persons and the organisations involved in the two fields. Here I can imagine several concrete approaches:

- Promote collaboration by organising conferences or joint seminars, activating networks of the two fields and building coalitions.
- Sponsor experimental projects and research studies, in order to develop new pedagogical concepts and materials, as we do not know enough about the methods and outcomes of joint learning.
- Promote experimental projects and actions in school, and in municipalities, neighbourhoods, and communities.

Conclusions

Using Holocaust education as a tool for human rights education offers some possibilities, but it also has many limits. It seems crucial, however, for teachers to keep in mind four fundamental elements of teaching about the Holocaust and about human rights education, in order to meet the basic requirements of both fields. First, it is important to learn the historical facts, and know about the process leading to the

Destruction of the Jews. Second, attention must be paid not only to what happened during the era of National Socialism, but also to what happened afterwards, to the history of memory, and to the diversity of historical narratives. Third, it is important to address current violations of human rights, especially those occurring in our own society and in our own national contexts. Finally, we must challenge and deconstruct national myths about this history that are present in our own countries, and reflect on how to come to terms with each country's own past.

Note This chapter draws on Eckmann (2010) and is based on a paper presented at the Holocaust Era Assets Conference, Prague, June 2009.

References

Eckmann, M. (2010). Exploring the relevance of Holocaust education for human rights education. *Prospects, 40*(1), 7–16.
Eckmann, M., & Heimberg, C. (2011). *Mémoire et pédagogie. Autour de la transmission de la destruction des Juifs d'Europe* [Memory and pedagogy: About transmitting the Destruction of the European Jews]. Genève: ies éditions.
Engelhardt, K., Jah, A., & Knoth, A. (2012). Inhaltliche Komplexität und vielfältiges Entwicklungspotential in europäischer Perspektive. Ergebnisse der Evaluation von "Menschen Rechte Bilden—Förderprogramm für Menschenrechtsbildung durch historisches Lernen" der Stiftung 'Erinnerung, Verantwortung und Zukunft' [Evaluation of the programme on history and human rights, run by the Foundation Remembrance, Responsibility, and Future]. *Politisches Lernen, 30*(3–4), 19–22.
EVZ Foundation [Stiftung Erinnerung, Verantwortung und Zukunft] (2014). Organisational website. http://www.stiftung-evz.de/eng/home.html
EWG [Education Working Group] (2014). *Teaching guidelines*. EWG. https://www.holocaustremembrance.com/educate/teaching-guidelines
FRA [Fundamental Rights Agency] (2011). *Discover the past for the future:. The role of historical sites and museums in Holocaust education and human rights education in the EU*. Luxembourg: European Union Agency for Fundamental Rights. http://fra.europa.eu/sites/default/files/fra_uploads/1791-FRA-2011-Holocaust-Education-Main-report_EN.pdf
Hilberg, R. ([1961]1985). *The destruction of the European Jews*. New York: Holmes & Meier.
Lohrenscheit, C. (2002). International approaches in human rights education. *International Review of Education, 48*(3–4), 173–185.
Thimm, B., Kößler, G., & Ulrich, S. (Eds.) (2010). *Verunsichernde Orte. Selbstverständnis und Weiterbildung in der Gedenkstättenpädagogik* [Uncertain places: Self-understanding and further education in the teaching at memorial places]. Frankfurt am Main: Brandes und Apsel Verlag.

Shoah, Antisemitism, War and Genocide: Text and Context

Yehuda Bauer

In this chapter, I argue that educators must deal first and foremost with the core issues of the Holocaust before they deal with its broader contexts. This core includes my argument that the Nazis bear the primary responsibility for World War II, and that their motivation was primarily ideological; in addition, that ideology centred on their antisemitism, which nearly extinguished Jewish life in Europe, while claiming the lives of 29 million non-Jews. Thus, antisemitism was (and is) a common threat. Students must understand the ways in which the Holocaust was unprecedented, but not unique: genocides often share common features. A critical contextual issue, which too often obscures the core, is the failure to make the proper distinctions between the Nazi and Stalinist regimes.

In August, 1936, Adolf Hitler wrote a very private and secret memorandum to his number two, Hermann Göring. It was the only memorandum he ever wrote himself, and it obviously was not intended for publication and propaganda. The purpose was to explain to Göring that Germany had to rearm in order to be ready for war within four years; this was later reduced to three. Hitler stated the reason for this:

> Since the beginning of the French Revolution the world has been drifting with increasing speed towards a new conflict, whose most extreme solution is named Bolshevism, but whose content and aim is only the removal of those strata of society which gave the leadership to humanity up to the present, and their replacement by international Jewry... a victory of Bolshevism over Germany would not lead to a Versailles Treaty, but to the final destruction, even the extermination of the German people.[1]

And on 30 January, 1939, in a speech to the Reichstag which we can actually see because it was filmed, he added: "If the international Jewish financiers in and

---

[1] *Documents on German Foreign Policy, 1918–1945*, series E, vol. V, 2, 1977, pp. 793–795.

Y. Bauer (✉)
Yad Vashem, The Holocaust Martyrs' and Heroes' Remembrance Authority,
P.O.B. 3477, 9103401 Jerusalem, Israel
e-mail: bauer1926@yahoo.com

outside Europe should succeed in plunging the nations once more into a world war, then the result will not be the bolshevisation of the earth, and thus the victory of Jewry, but the annihilation of the Jewish race in Europe". His reason, then, why Germany should start the war was that otherwise international Jewry, which includes both the Bolsheviks and Western capitalism which is controlled by the Jews, would destroy or even annihilate the German people. In order to prevent that and assert German hegemony in Europe, the Germans had to obtain living space in the East so that Ukrainian agriculture, coal, and steel, as well as oil and raw materials from the Caucasus, could make German supremacy a reality. The enemy preventing the realisation of this policy was the Jewish World Conspiracy.

Of course, Germany was in no need of a war to get these materials. It could have obtained them easily enough by normal trade with the Soviet Union, which was eager to receive German industrial goods in return for its raw materials. Stalin was willing to sell every mother in Russia, if he could prevent a war for which the Soviets were not prepared—because his brutal purges in 1937 had killed most of the Soviet military leadership.

In Germany, who wanted a war? It is clear, from quite unanimous reports of the many foreign journalists and diplomats in Germany in 1938–1939, that the German population did not want a war. That is not surprising, as the last war, with its millions of casualties, had ended in 1918, only 21 years earlier. It is equally clear, from archives of the great companies in the fields of industry, communications, trade, banking, and so on, that the captains of the German economy overwhelmingly did not want a war, because they were doing quite well in an economy that had risen out of the Great Depression. The top military leaders, with the chief of staff, General Ludwig Beck, at their head, planned a putsch against Hitler in September, 1938, because they were afraid that Germany would lose a two-front war. The putsch did not come about, because at Munich, in September–October 1938, Britain and France yielded to Hitler and handed over Czechoslovakia to the Germans. No military opposition would rebel against a successful government. But the leadership of the Nazi Party, with Hitler as the radicalising factor, wanted a war. They wanted it in order to assure German hegemony in Europe, and that could only be achieved by defeating the great threat to such hegemony: the Jews. As a result, in the war that ensued 35 million people died in Europe alone, close to six million of them Jews. Twenty-nine million were non-Jews, who died in large part because of the murderous antisemitism of the Nazis, which was a central part of the ideology that led to the war. Antisemitism kills Jews, but it also kills huge numbers of others. It is a universal danger. It was also, of course, the central motive for the genocide of the Jews.

It becomes clear, then, that the German policy of expansion to the East, which on its face seems to have been dictated by economic interests, was in fact the result of an ideological imperative. The economic argument was subordinated to it. The overall conclusion is obvious: World War II was initiated by Nazi Germany for reasons that were primarily ideological, and within that antisemitism played a central role.

Many, probably most, of you are aware of the historiographical debate around the Holocaust, which places two basic trends against each other. There are those who explain the Holocaust as a reaction to impasses of a socioeconomic character in a crisis-ridden German society. They say that these crisis-ridden structures and the attempts to solve structural issues led to a radicalisation of Nazi politics which led to the genocide of the Jews. This is the functionalist or structuralist interpretation. The other trend argues that the genocide was the result of an ideology imposed by a leadership of the Nazi Party headed and radicalised by an all-powerful dictator. This is the intentionalist view. It is hard to find anyone today who will still defend these extreme positions. As to intentionalism, it is clear that Hitler did not plan the Holocaust, and that in fact it was not pre-planned at all. When he made the statement I quoted above, in which he threatened the Jews with annihilation, there was no planning behind it. Not even in 1940 was there any planning, as we know from a memorandum by Himmler, of 25 May, 1940, in which he presented the Jewish "problem" as something that would be solved by deporting the European Jews to Africa. In that memorandum Himmler stated, explicitly, that the physical annihilation of a people was a Bolshevik method, un-German, and out of the question. Hitler approved of the memorandum. Later, there was indeed planning, but that happened parallel to the actual murder campaign, from mid-1941 on. By 1942, plans were developed for the total murder of European Jews, and intentions were made clear regarding the extension of the murder campaign to wherever in the world German influence would reach. While no planning occurred until 1941 at the earliest, there was a murderous ideology and, given the lack of other practical solutions, the genocide was inherent in it as an option that became actualised when the situation demanded it. Thus, the Holocaust was not pre-planned, but it was pre-figured.

The structuralist or functionalist interpretation is not convincing either. Structures don't kill; people do. And people have views and attitudes, as they act in a certain social environment. If they have strong views, it is likely that, given the chance, they will try to translate their ideologies into practical reality. The perpetrators murdered because they were convinced it was the right thing to do. There was a consensus to commit murder, and that consensus arose through the acceptance of an ideology, even if most people would not have been able to define what the ideology was saying. A major element in that ideology was the absolute belief in the charismatic Leader, elevating him to a divine status. It was he who, in most Germans' eyes, could do no wrong, and if he initiated or approved of the annihilation of the Jews, that was the right thing to do. I therefore think that the Holocaust was, primarily, the result of an ideology, and the structural elements, while undoubtedly important, were secondary.

This combination of an ideological genocide committed during a war fought, by the perpetrators, for ideological reasons, is unprecedented.

To be sure, the genocide of the Jews at the hands of National-Socialist Germany and its collaborators has to be seen in its various contexts. However, the first thing is to deal with the core, or if you like, the text, not the contexts. By core, I mean, among other things, the rise of Nazism and its ideology, the type of war it fought, the situation of the Jews in various European countries, the persecutions of the 1930s and the Jewish reactions to them, Jewish emigration, and the attitudes of the various outside powers and of Jewish communities to what was happening.

Then come, among others, the developing Nazi plans regarding the Jews, ghettoisation in Poland and later in other countries, forced labor and concentration camps, mass murder after Germany's invasion of the Soviet Union, the death camps, Jewish unarmed and armed reactions, the problem of the Jewish Councils, and the death marches at the war's end. The war itself, and its aftermath, the fate of the survivors until their final emigration either to Palestine/Israel or to the West, primarily the United States, are also part of the core.

There has been, of late, a tendency to prefer dealing with the more remote contexts, instead of looking first of all at the Holocaust itself: at the core. It is my view, to the contrary, that one must deal with the core first. Having done that, one can then deal with remote causes, comparisons with other genocides, human rights and their denial, psychological traumas that appear in the wake of the tragedy, the aftermath, memory and its institutionalisation, and so on. But, if you really want to deal with the Holocaust, you first of all have to learn what actually happened and why. For teachers especially, this methodological approach would seem to be crucial.

When we begin to know what actually happened, when, by whom, and what the victims' reactions were, we are ready for the first question, still within the core: why should we deal with the Holocaust at all? Why should we have special memorial days for that event? Why should we devote valuable schooling time to deal with it? The answer is that we deal with it because it was the most extreme form of genocidal killing until then, and arguably until today. Extreme, not because of the suffering of the victims; the suffering of victims of mass atrocities is always the same. There is no gradation of suffering, and Jews did not suffer more or less than Tutsi in Rwanda, Fur in Darfur, Khmer in Cambodia, or Russians, American Indians, or anyone else in situations of mass murder. Why then talk about the Holocaust as an extreme case? Let me put it this way: when you examine the elements that went into any genocidal situation at any time in history, you will always find similar elements in some other genocide, including the Holocaust.

Take Rwanda as an example. Hutu and Tutsi are actually not ethnic groups. Originally, in pre-modern times, they were different social classes, with the Tutsi minority ruling the majority, the Hutus. They speak the same language, and they shared the same religious beliefs. Today, they belong to the same Christian denominations. The German, and later, the Belgian colonialists supported the aristocratic, wealthier, better educated Tutsis, as against the peasant Hutu majority. Towards the end of their rule, in 1958, the Belgians switched to support the Hutus, and when independence came, the Hutu majority came to rule. Enmity erupted, on the basis of the previously Tutsi-imposed inequality, and between 1958 and 1994, there were several massacres of Tutsis. A Hutu dictatorship assumed power, led by descendants of Hutu groups that had never been part of the Tutsi-dominated pre-modern monarchy. A large number of Tutsis fled into neighboring countries, especially to Uganda. They organised there, and in 1990 invaded Rwanda from the north. International pressure forced the Hutu dictator to agree to a power-sharing compromise, but he was killed; radicals, who were supported by France and called themselves Hutu Power, launched their pre-planned genocidal massacre against the Tutsis.

Against the background of these tensions between Hutus and Tutsis, the motivations were the fear of an advance of the Tutsi Army from the north and the attendant loss of power, and a desire to inherit the possessions of the Tutsi landowners and middle class. This is of course an oversimplification, because there were many poor Tutsis and many wealthy Hutus, but there was nevertheless some substance to the accepted stereotypes. The elements that went into the genocide were the employment of special militias to commit most of the actual murders; the elimination of moderate and democratic Hutus opposed to genocidal killings; use of a bureaucratic system that had been developed by the Belgian colonialists; massive genocidal propaganda; the use of a radio station to incite the Hutu population, and a trumped-up ideology that served to rationalise the killings, which saw the Tutsis as foreigners who were endangering the survival of the Hutus.

Every one of these elements can be found in other genocides. Consider prior mass murders leading up to the genocide in the Armenian case, or in the cases of American Indians. Consider special militias: such militias were used against the Armenians, during the Holocaust, etc. Consider developed bureaucratic structures: these were present in Nazi Germany, in the genocide of the Herrero in Namibia in 1904, and in the annihilation of American Indians in North America. We also find massive propaganda utilising up-to-date technology in the Holocaust, against the kulaks in the Soviet Union in the early thirties of the 20th century, in Nazi Germany, etc. And so on.

However, the Holocaust includes some elements that one simply cannot find in genocides that preceded it. There are quite a number of these, but let me mention just a few. To start with, there was no precedent for a state-organised genocide where every single person of the targeted group—as defined not by the individuals concerned but by the perpetrators—was to be identified, marked, humiliated, dispossessed, concentrated, transported, and killed, everywhere on earth. Furthermore, the ideology that served as a motivation for the Holocaust had nothing at all to do with the real Jews. In all other genocides that I am aware of, behind the ideological rationalisations there always was the economic, social, political, and/or military background.

Not so with the genocide of the Jews. Nazi ideology spoke of a world Jewish conspiracy, of the control by Jews of both capitalism and Bolshevism, a conspiracy out to control the world: a mirror image of what the Nazis themselves wanted to do, and a nightmarish fabrication. It spoke of Jews killing non-Jewish children to use their blood for ritual purposes—a continuation of the notorious blood libel accusations of the Middle Ages. It declared that the Jews were a satanic force corrupting civilisations, and therefore had to be annihilated, and that they were the sworn enemies of Germany. In fact, 12,000 Jews had died for Germany on the battlefields of World War I, out of the 100,000 Jews who served in the German forces. Given that the whole Jewish population in Germany numbered only about 500,000, or 0.7% of the total population of Germany, this was a disproportionately high number; the Jews were what one might call "desperately patriotic" German citizens.

All the accusations were fabricated, nightmarish concoctions. They had nothing at all to do with real Jews and their communities. They were totally non-pragmatic.

The Jews did not have a territory that could be coveted, and contrary to some legends, Jewish individuals did not control any major German industry. Nor did Jewish people control German banks. And, even more important, at the time there was no Jewish political collectivity or Jewish state that could pose a threat. There were German Jews, but there was no German Jewry: there was no public body that would represent all German Jews, or any body that represented all Jews worldwide; the Zionist Organisation and various social welfare bodies represented sections of the Jewish people, but never all or even most of them. A body representing most (not all) German Jews was set up for the first time some 8 months after the Nazis came to power, as a necessary reaction to the Nazi persecutions. It is also important to note that very few bodies represented all Jews in a given country. For instance, the Board of Deputies of British Jews, founded in the 18th century, never included all Jews. Some were always outside of it. Today, it represents only a certain percentage of British Jews, probably not even a majority.

In some ways, Nazi antisemitic ideology was similar to other such rationalisations of murderous actions, but in some ways it totally deviated from them. Like other such ideologies, for instance Marxism-Leninism and Radical Islam, it promised a utopia, in which a world society based on racism would be an earthly paradise for those who deserved it, namely the pick of the Aryan race. The struggle for everlasting happiness would be conducted against Satan and his minions, and Satan was the stereotypical Jew. There is a parallel here between Nazism and Stalinism, which saw the Jewish bourgeoisie supposedly controlling the capitalist West as the spearhead of the enemy that had to be defeated. Radical Islam today portrays the Jews ("Zionists", but often they simply say "Jews") as the element that controls the world they want to conquer, and therefore the Jews become the arch-enemy that prevents the establishment of the Islamist utopia.

The Nazi version, with the Jews as the implacable, corrupt, and devious foe standing in the way of the realisation of the racist utopia, was easily understood by the German masses, as it derived from Christian antisemitism. Christian antisemitism had never planned or advocated a genocide of the Jews, but it had advocated persecution, discrimination, eviction of Jews, humiliation, and dispossession. Christian antisemitism had formed the necessary (though not the sufficient) background for the Nazi variety, contrary to the statements of the Catholic Church. Christian antisemitism saw the Jew as possessed by Satan. The accusation that the Jews had killed Christ was based on the belief that Satan wanted to control the world against God and the Jews were his tool.

More than that: the way I read it, the desire to force the emigration of Jews from Germany in the 1930s, deportation to Poland in late 1939, the plans to deport them to Madagascar in 1940, or the Soviet Arctic in early 1941, and then the genocide itself, were also part of the wish to exorcise the devil from the midst of the Chosen People, namely the Nordic peoples of the Aryan race. The Nazi genocide of the Jews was thus totally devoid of any pragmatic basis. Certainly, the methods, the timing, the stages in which these policies developed were determined by pragmatic considerations. Yet, whenever there was a clash between the purely ideological aim and practical economic or other considerations, the ideology always prevailed.

Thus, the existence of major Polish ghettos, for instance in Bialystok and Lodz, was very important for the German war machine because they produced goods for the German Army, and their survival was supported by local Nazi officials. Contrary to all modern capitalistic logic of cost-effectiveness, these ghettoes were annihilated by orders from the Berlin centre, in pursuance of ideological aims. Examples of this kind are legion.

The Nazis, as I said, wanted to exorcise the Jews out of the German people. In the Middle Ages, Jews were sometimes burned at the stake, when they refused to convert to Christianity or when they wanted to return to Judaism after they had been converted, often by force. The emotional basis behind that appears to have been that Satan, or people possessed by Satan, were being burned. The fire would exorcise the Devil, and the community would expiate its sins by burning the offending devilish creature that had polluted it. The same applied to Christian heretics, of course, such as the Waldensians in Southern France, and to witches. When the Nazis gassed and burned their Jewish victims, is it possible that they were unconsciously repeating a type of action that had been part of European civilisation all along? Jewish bodies had to be totally consumed, by fire, and the Nazis set up a special SS unit, called Unit 2005, headed by a sadistic Nazi by the name of Paul Blobel, that tried to eliminate all traces of mass killings of Jews outside of the camps by digging up the bodies of murdered Jews at the hundreds of sites in Eastern Europe where these murders had taken place. These bodies were then burned. Is there then a link between the *auto-da-fes* of the Spanish Inquisition and the actions of the Nazis? It is, I think, worth examining.

The Holocaust was the most extreme form of genocide to date, for the reasons outlined above. It was not unique, because if that had been so, we would not have to bother about it, as it would have been a singular case never to be repeated. But everything that humans do can be repeated, though never in exactly the same way; and the Holocaust was committed by humans, not by some God or Satan. It was unprecedented, not unique, which means that it can be repeated in some way, and that answers the original question I posed, namely why we should teach it. We live in a world where something like that not only can happen again, but where things that are somewhat similar, though not quite parallel, are indeed happening all around us. The Holocaust happened in the midst of the most advanced civilisation of its time, and came out of a country which had rightly been proud of its liberalism, of its tremendous achievements in arts, in music, in literature and philosophy. It presents a tremendous problem and a challenge to civilisation. The people who committed the crimes, the people who supported the murderers in some way or another, the people who knew and looked away and refused to react, were all baptised into Christianity. To quote Franklin H. Littell, a Methodist minister and a Holocaust scholar, they were "baptised heathen". This goes far beyond the controversy over whether the wartime pope, Pius XII, did whatever he could to help or whether he kept silent and is therefore, in part at east, culpable. It concerns the roots of Christianity, in that 1,900 years after the appearance of the Christian Messiah, his people were murdered by people who had been raised believing in his message. It raises the question—to quote Littell again—of the credibility of Christianity.

It also raises the credibility of Judaism, with the question of where was the God of the Covenant when millions of Jews were being slaughtered, but that is a different story.

In World War II, Nazi Germany wanted to destroy liberalism, democracy, pacifism, socialism, conservatism, Christianity—all those things that we inaccurately call Western civilisation. Germany's war was to clear the way for the conquest of Europe as a whole, and then, with allies, of the whole world. A new system of values was to be imposed on humanity, a racist hierarchy, with the Nordic peoples of the Aryan race on top, and everyone else in a hierarchical order under them. No Jews, because all Jews would by then be annihilated. This racist world was a completely new utopia. Mankind has experienced uncounted attempts to substitute one religion for another, destroy one nation or empire by another, or one social class by another. But Nazism was new; the establishment of a racial hierarchy was utterly novel—especially as we know today that races do not exist, because we all come, as DNA research has shown, from East Africa, where the first humans developed about 150,000–200,000 years ago.

The idea of a racially defined world was therefore truly revolutionary, possibly the only really revolutionary attempt in the last 200 years. It was directed against "Western civilisation". More specifically, it was directed against the legacy of the French and American revolutions, and the traditions of British democracy. All these had been based on older cultures, deriving their legitimacy from Greece for aesthetics, literature, and philosophy; from Rome for law and order, the state, architecture, literature and the arts; and from Jerusalem, for the ethics of the biblical prophets. The people who now live in Greece or Italy speak languages that are derivatives from the ancient forms, but they are different; they pray to different gods and they write different literatures. But the Jews are still there, speaking and writing the same language, writing literature that is directly connected to the biblical forms. The Nazis, as I said, wanted to destroy these legacies, and that civilisation. The Jews were a symbol of what the Nazis wanted to destroy, because of the moral teachings their culture had produced. Also, the ideological, religious basis for all of modern Western civilisation was the Bible, and for Christians, or people like the German Nazis who had been raised in that culture before they abandoned it, it had two parts: the Old and the New Testament, and both were written largely by Jews. There was a certain logic in the Nazi ideology: if you want to destroy the Western tradition, you start with the annihilation of one of its founders, namely the Jews.

The direct connection between World War II, the Shoah, and present-day genocidal events and threats is more than obvious. There are repetitions today that hark back to the genocide of the Jews. The Shoah was unprecedented. But it was a precedent, and that precedent is unfortunately being followed, in the Middle East, the Balkans, in Darfur, and elsewhere.

Now, having dealt with some of the problems of the core, let us come to some of the contexts. One of them is connected to present international politics. The after-effects of the Shoah and of World War II are very much with us—this is a past that is present, a past that still has a future, and there is a major issue that is beginning to be addressed, but that needs to be explored much more seriously, namely the comparison between the two totalitarian regimes, National Socialism and Stalinist Communism, and the comparison between both of these and present-day Radical Islam. I have no time here to discuss Radical Islam. The parallels between the two totalitarian regimes of the 20th century are obvious: a one-party dictatorship with a half-mythical dictator at the top, the existence of a massive terror machine of a well-organised police state, an ideology that became the substitute for an exclusivist religion, and so on. The differences have not been properly explored, and all I can do here is to hint at some of the issues. The Soviet Union was a centralised state with a centralised economy, with an inbuilt tendency to massive corruption and economic inefficiency.

Conversely, Nazi Germany was a basically polycratic regime, where vassal fiefdoms competed for the attention of the all-powerful dictator, but which was built on a combination of powerful private enterprise and a clever manipulation by central fiscal authorities. Private property, especially that of big industrial, agricultural, and banking enterprises, flourished. Inefficiency was the result not of the economic structure, but of the intervention in the economy of an ideology-motivated political dictatorship. During the war, ideology-driven political inefficiency decisively influenced military planning and execution as well. These were faulty, as we now know; German efficiency was partial and was attended by a catastrophic lack of proper oversight. Nevertheless, both regimes could overcome their deficiencies in the short and medium term by tremendous efforts emanating from the centre.

Stalinism has rightly been accused of many acts of politicide, a term coined by Barbara Harff, meaning the destruction of groups of humans for political, ideological, economic, or social reasons. Thus, huge numbers of so-called kulaks, i.e. peasants who refused to collaborate with the collectivisation of agriculture, were starved, deported, or killed. Real and imagined political opponents were annihilated in huge numbers, too. There can hardly be any doubt that the number of victims of Soviet oppression far surpasses the number of dead in Nazi concentration camps, even if you include the victims of the genocide of the Jews. But there can equally be no doubt that the number of victims of a world war that was initiated, willed, and prosecuted by Nazi Germany far surpasses the number of victims of the gulag and the Soviet oppression. The numbers game here, as elsewhere, does not lead us anywhere.

Germany, with the help of many collaborators, engaged in what the 1948 United Nations Convention would call genocide: against the Roma, the Poles and, primarily, totally unpragmatically and purely ideologically, against all Jews. The Soviets did nothing of the kind.

Had the Germans not attacked the Soviet Union in June, 1941, after almost two years of a fairly close alliance, would there have been a permanent collusion between the two totalitarianisms? I don't think so. It was quite clear to both elites that the alliance was temporary, and that sooner or later they would clash. When they did, the Germans almost overwhelmed the Soviet state. Many people think that the alliance forged between the West and the Soviets was an unnatural one in terms of political cultures and far-reaching aims. But in actual fact it was, in many ways, not unnatural that a regime that threatened all of the achievements of "Western civilisation" should be opposed by all of those who, in their different and contradictory ways, wanted to continue that civilisation, even in a very distorted form, as the Soviets did. The war was, in the end, won mainly by the Soviets. The West helped by supplying them with crucially important armaments, and its help shortened the war. The invasion of Western Europe contributed markedly to the final victory. But the war was won by the Red Army, which defeated the main German forces, at tremendous cost. The Soviet Union liberated the world from the threat of another long period of the darkest ages imaginable. This is the perception of recent history prevalent in many quarters, indeed in the world, and it determines Western historical memory. It is true even in, say, the Ukraine, where originally the Germans were enthusiastically welcomed by most people, including in the areas that had been part of the Soviet Union prior to 1939, areas where the Soviet regime had caused massive death by starvation in the 1930s. But even there, there was an important though unquantifiable pro-Soviet minority as early as 1941, when the Germans invaded. Ukrainians in large numbers participated in the murder of the Jews, volunteered for pro-German police, and collaborated with the German administration—but soon deep disenchantment took over. The Germans did not permit any kind of Ukrainian autonomy, treated Ukrainians as lesser beings, and then deported hundreds of thousands of them as forced laborers. The mood changed rapidly.

Both many Ukrainians and many of the peoples in the Baltic areas collaborated in the destruction and deportation of the Jews, while hoping to gain autonomy from Germany. But it did not work as they had hoped.

After the war, the further west one went from the real Soviet Union, the greater the enthusiasm for the Soviet liberators. For the Jews, it was even simpler. German rule meant certain death. Soviet rule meant ethnic oppression, and later on, between 1947 and Stalin's death in 1953, violent and murderous antisemitism as well. But the only hope for survival was Soviet victory. All Jewish survivors owed their lives to the Red Army. After the war, the majority of these survivors were concentrated in displaced persons camps in Central Europe, and they were a major factor in the establishment of Israel. The Soviet victory made that possible. The Soviets really did liberate Europe, however problematic that liberation was.

In the Baltic States the perception is different. There, the view is that there were three occupations: a Soviet one, between 1940 and 1941; a German one, between 1941 and 1944; and a second Soviet one between 1944 and 1989/1990. The second Soviet one lasted for decades and in the eyes of many Baltic people was worse than the German one. The choice, it is felt there, was between two totalitarian regimes, but people thought— mistakenly—that the German variety did not endanger the basic fabric of society. On the other hand, the Soviet regime, represented at least in part by Baltic communists, violently oppressed the Baltic nationalities, in part also by introducing people from other Soviet nationalities, especially Russians, threatening to overwhelm the local ethnic groups.

Did the Soviets commit genocide, or something approaching that, during their two occupations of the Baltic countries? Let me take Latvia as an example; other nations in Eastern Europe are not that much different. I rely here on the results of the admirable work of the Latvian Historical Commission, that is, those parts of the work that I could read in English. There were close to two million people in Latvia in 1939, about 75% of whom were ethnic Latvians; the rest were mainly Russians, Germans, and close to 95,000, or about 5%, were Jews. The Soviets repressed and persecuted some 3,000 persons during the first occupation, and deported 15,400 more, together less than 1% of the population. Many of the deportees survived, under terrible conditions, suffering great physical and mental anguish. But of these 15,400 deportees, 11.7% were Jews, so the percentage of persecuted and deported Jews was more than twice their proportion of the population.

The Soviets did not abolish the Latvian language, and they more often transformed than abolished local cultural institutions. But they forbade Hebrew, and in time effectively suppressed Yiddish; they dissolved all specifically Jewish institutions, though they did not formally abolish Jewish religious worship. Jewish communities were not transformed, but eradicated. During the second occupation, in the late 1940s, the Soviets deported 43,000 Latvian citizens, and again, an unknown proportion of these were non-ethnic inhabitants of Latvia. Together with the first wave in 1941, the total amounted to roughly 3.3% of the population or, say, 2.5% of the Latvian people. And though the Germans, with local help, had by then murdered almost all Latvian Jews, there were quite a number of Jews even among the deportees of the second wave. One can hardly talk of an anti-Latvian genocide. If there was anything approaching cultural elimination at Soviet hands, it was that of the Jews, not of the Latvians, although Latvian culture was diminished and attacked. Latvian historians have also deconstructed the myth about significant Jewish participation in Soviet governmental and police organs. That turns out to have been another antisemitic legend: while it is true that there were Jews in the Soviet organs of repression, they were relatively few. The vast majority were Russians, Ukrainians, and local Latvian communists.

The same picture emerges, for instance, in the formerly Polish territories of western Belarus and the western Ukraine. There, according to Polish figures, of the roughly 800,000 deportees to Siberia in 1939–1941, 30% were Jews, though Jews were only 10% of the population. All this amounts to oppression and persecution. In addition, in the occupied Baltic areas, because of the relatively higher economic and social standards, there was mass immigration of non-Baltic peoples from inside the Soviet Union. The question is still open whether this was intentional or not; probably it was a mixture of both. All this was very bad, but it was certainly not genocide, not even of the Jews. Had there been a genocide of the Baltic peoples, there could have been no independence movement, and it was finally victorious, between 1987 and 1991. It was then that the regime collapsed under its own weight of inefficiency and political and moral corruption. Apart from the murder of several thousand wandering Roma, the only genocide that happened in the Baltic States was that of the Jews, at the hands of Nazi Germany and its local collaborators.

Two major problems emerge: one, the collaboration of the majority of Baltic and Ukrainian peoples with the Germans, not necessarily because of any sympathy with Germany or with Nazism, but as a result of the political, ethnic, and economic situation determined by geography and history. This again resulted in the collaboration of large numbers of them, actively or by silent agreement, in the annihilation of the

Jews. This history is also the reason for a disconnect between some East European perceptions of the past and those of the rest of Europe, and indeed the world, namely different perceptions of the historical role of the Soviet Union in the war against Nazi Germany. This is not to be taken lightly. People forget that good and evil can seldom be painted in black and white. And yet, the Nazi regime, with its near-absolute evil, is an exception. Today, many people in the world see World War II as a very central point of historical and political reference, and the Shoah as the pivotal event in it. They see the Soviet Union, historically, as a crucial partner, a liberator, though an extremely problematic one, in the rescue of the world from a potential threat to its very existence at Nazi hands. A continued disconnect between the historical consciousness of the Baltic States and that of the rest of the Western world would be a tragedy, mainly for the Baltic peoples themselves.

Why is this important for teaching the Holocaust? Because quite recently, on 2 April, 2009, the European Parliament passed a resolution to commemorate 23 August; on that day in 1939 the Molotov-Ribbentrop Pact was signed, which enabled Nazi Germany to start World War II. The purpose, the resolution said, is to commemorate, properly and equally, the victims of the two totalitarian regimes. The Holocaust, it says, has to be remembered as a special case. Victims of German Nazism are equated with victims of Soviet oppression. But this is a travesty of historical truth. World War II was initiated and pursued by Nazi Germany, not the Soviet Union. If the Soviet Union, through its pact with Nazi Germany, is guilty as an accessory to the crime, then so are Britain and France, who at Munich sacrificed Czechoslovakia, in clear contradiction both to their treaty obligations and to elementary political morality, and enabled Nazi Germany to embark on the warpath. Nazi Germany committed genocides, not only against Jews, but against Poles and Roma as well.

Moreover, they concocted a plan, called *Generalplan Ost*, which provided for the elimination of the three Baltic nationalities as such. These nationalities would be absorbed into the German people, and any opponents killed or exiled beyond the Urals. Poles would become a population of slaves, without any education. The Czech people were to be eliminated in much the same way as the Baltic nations. The Soviets never planned anything like that. The Soviet dictatorship, brutal and oppressive as it was, was a deadly mutation of an ideology, Marxism, that had emerged from the legacy of the French Revolution, and was eager to acknowledge that. Nazism was diametrically opposed to that revolution's legacy. To equate Stalinist oppression with Nazi genocide is understandable, from the point of view of nationalities that had to suffer from Soviet oppression for decades, but it cannot be accepted.

Finally, I want to discuss an issue that lies somewhere between core and context, that is especially important, I think, for teachers: the relationship between human rights and their denial, and the Holocaust. There is a tendency to argue that denial of human rights is a first step towards mass destruction, the Holocaust, and Holocaust-like events. There can be no doubt that human rights and teaching about the Holocaust are related issues. The persecution of German Jews did indeed begin with a denial of their civic and human rights. But there was no necessary linear development between that persecution and the Holocaust. If the major powers of the day, Britain, France, and the Soviet Union, had come to an agreement to stop German expansionism—and negotiations took place as late as in June 1939 to perhaps reach such an agreement—then the Holocaust would most likely have been avoided. In that case, the denial of rights of the small Jewish minority in Germany would have remained another case of oppression, but not of a necessary preamble to a genocide. Denial of human rights is bad in itself, but not necessarily connected to genocide. Moreover, once the Holocaust was enacted, it was no longer a matter of denial of human rights. The victims no longer had any rights that could be denied, and killing them was not a denial of rights but a matter of murder. You cannot start teaching the Holocaust from a basis of argument about human rights, because this is simply not true. What is true is that denial of human rights preceded the murder, and was one of the preparatory steps, though it did not necessarily lead to the genocide of the Jews. What you can do is to say that the Holocaust teaches us that observation of human rights is and should be a basic obligation that can do much to prevent a development towards a genocide. In other words, don't start from human rights to teach the Holocaust, but use the Holocaust story to emphasise that when human rights are successfully defended, that creates an almost insurmountable obstacle against mass murder. So, do not start with humans rights. End with them.

I draw seven conclusions from all this. First of all, the realisation that World War II was conducted by Nazi Germany for mainly ideological reasons: that was the context for the Shoah—the ideologically motivated annihilation of the Jews—which was an end in itself. Second, that antisemitism was the basic motivation, and has deep historical roots; and that it did and does endanger the life of huge numbers of non-Jews. Third, that both parallels and also very considerable differences emerge between that genocide and other genocides. Fourth, that this cannot be done without a comparison between Nazi Germany and the Soviet empire. Fifth, that it was the Soviet Union, an oppressive and murderous dictatorship, that defeated Germany, that quite unintentionally rescued the remnant of the Jews of Europe, prevented the horror of decades of Nazi rule over large parts of the world, while instituting a totalitarian reign of terror in large parts of the continent. Sixth, that a simplistic equation between Nazism and Stalinism is wrong, and that one of the proofs of that is the Holocaust. Seventh, and most important, when you teach the Holocaust, you have to start from the core, from the text, before you can approach the context.

Learning from Eyewitnesses: Examining the History and Future of Personal Encounters with Holocaust Survivors and Resistance Fighters

Dienke Hondius

Introduction

Everyone who attended school in Western Europe grew up with lessons about the history of World War II and the Holocaust. After the liberation, the generation that was alive during the war years was determined to tell the youth what had happened, and soon engaged young people in commemoration activities. Now, almost seven decades later, we can write a history of these lessons, about their ideals, expectations, and practices. In this chapter I summarise the main findings of my study on these developments, *Oorlogslessen*, or Lessons of War (Hondius 2010), a study of what I call the educational culture of memory, with many examples from the Netherlands.

I have been directly involved in scholarship about the Holocaust through my work for the Anne Frank House and in higher education from the early 1980s onwards. I developed exhibitions, books, and educational projects that have travelled in many different countries across Europe, in the United States, Central and Latin America, Asia, the Middle East, Australia, and Southern Africa. Among my first projects at the Anne Frank House was the international exhibition, *Anne Frank in the World, 1929–1945* (Hondius 1985). It was the starting point for numerous translations as well as local educational projects and temporary local exhibitions and public programmes in many countries. New editions of the travelling exhibitions were made in the 1990s and after. The archives of the Anne Frank House, International Department, contain many files by country and city where these exhibitions were shown, and the local organisations that were involved, as well as the reactions by local press, visitors, school groups, etc.

D. Hondius (✉)
Faculty of Humanities, History Department, VU University Amsterdam,
De Boelelaan 1105, 1081 HV Amsterdam, The Netherlands
e-mail: d.g.hondius@vu.nl

The core of this article is an analysis of the role and the potential of eyewitnesses as teachers. As the opportunity to discuss this period directly with members of this generation slowly disappears, it is important to reconstruct what they have tried to convey to youth, and to what effect. One of my first findings is that the practice of teaching lessons from the war began not in 1945, but in fact immediately, during the war, as teachers and students continued to meet each other in the classroom. Even in hiding places and in concentration camps, a lot of educational activity, sometimes improvised but equally determined, continued. Learning took varying forms, from individual parents teaching their children to read and write, to academic lectures and debates in the camps, to lessons given by teachers in hiding to students in hiding. These activities are striking because they document expressions of hope for a future in freedom.

One specific characteristic of teaching is that it is immediate, and improvisation is crucial, as we hear from memories of teaching about the war during the war. In my study of the Jewish Lyceum in Amsterdam (Hondius with Gompes-Lobatto 2001), I interviewed many surviving teachers and students, who mention and remember this continuity and the attempts to maintain a sense of normality. An example of such teachers is David Koker, then a 19-year-old Jewish law student who was in the camp of Vught. He wrote in his diary (Koker 2012) about trying to get a group of young children to listen in order to explain things, to reassure them; this diary is now available in a new English edition. What happens outside the classroom then takes place inside the classroom, entering the discussion. In every camp, people took the initiative to do some teaching; there were also impressive academic encounters and initiatives. In Westerbork, Bergen Belsen, and especially in Theresienstadt, groups of inmates improvised lectures, exchanges of ideas, and insights, according to my friends Jaap Polak, who shared his memories of teaching in Westerbork, and Frank Diamand, who described his mother's first language lessons in Bergen Belsen. For an impressive collection of the lectures held in Theresienstadt, see Makarova et al. (2004). For the prisoners it was a way to encourage each other with knowledge, to encourage self-respect, trust, and spiritual balance. It appears that encouragement is a fundamental function of education, particularly in difficult circumstances.

Soon after 1945, teaching continued in the more orderly forms again, although during the first years schools were improvised in many countries and places where the war had brought a lot of damage. Coming to terms with what had happened took place in classrooms at first without specific teaching materials, but in a more informal way. The war years were still fresh in the memories of everyone, students and teachers alike. In the decades that followed, World War II and the Holocaust became more formalised as a topic. Teachers transmit knowledge, experience, memory, and insight to young people in the classroom, in textbooks, and in guided tours at memorial places, in museums and in exhibitions. A clear shift took place around 1980, when the first war generation retired and then became much more involved in these educational activities than before. From the 1980s onward, their voices were newly recognised as valuable first-person accounts and incorporated into a multitude of testimony projects.

The development of an educational memorial culture has local and national aspects, while taking place in an international context. A new interdisciplinary field of research is emerging here, linking historical, educational, pedagogical, social science, and memory studies. Early German pioneers in this field are Matthias Heyl (1997) and Micha Brumlik (1995, 2004). Other new inspiration comes from Germany, Austria, and the United States, and international comparative studies have been conducted in several other countries (Meseth 2005, 2007; Meseth and Proske, in this volume).

One of the challenges is finding a balance between the description of local, national, and international projects and developments. My study of this educational culture of memory shows that one of its key elements is an intense coherence between the lessons of war and national identity, pride, and shame. This coherence is the outcome of political historical developments that are partially specific, partially comparative. One common element I observe is a longing for national pride in commemoration and education about World War II, which can be found across and beyond Europe. Although one article cannot do justice to all international developments, trends in historiography in the Netherlands and a critical analysis of educational projects there have relevance for experts in other countries. One useful approach would be to publish an international study of the educational memorial culture about World War II and the Holocaust, with a focus on trends and historical developments, based on lessons about Anne Frank and her diary. Across Europe I found examples of work that is conducted with good intentions, but results in similar intriguing misunderstandings and frictions. The unintended consequences of these developments allow several clear-cut conclusions and recommendations for lessons about World War II and the Holocaust in the near future, when the generation that lived through this will no longer be with us.

Another common element in commemoration policy across Western Europe is that national consensus building was and still is an important element. Lack of consensus creates a sense of uneasiness, and in Holocaust education and commemoration, a strong desire for national consensus can be found. In the Netherlands, for example, a commemorative event has to be supported as broadly as possible, and it has to also be intensive, relevant, and impressive. Not only in the Netherlands' history of remembrance but all over, consensus has been very important for decades, and several elements have been used to create an intensive atmosphere: silence, cut with short musical elements, reflective speeches, and poetry. Very often these events include a combination of elements, such as standing still in silence after a short march or walking together to a monument, or standing next to a flag, or several flags. A ceremonial element can involve flowers, wreaths, or single flowers, often presented by children.

Pride and Shame

Authorities look for ways to incorporate accounts of the past into a national narrative about the nation's history. Every nation has its own history of education, and in every nation we can find two elements in the politics of memory: pride and shame.

They are opposites and so there is a continuous tension. Especially in a national context, and in the context of nationalism, pride and shame are uneasy categories. What is there to be proud of, and what is there to be ashamed of? A history of shame and pride develops in uneven steps, growing and shrinking, acknowledging and denying, remembering and forgetting. The international comparison is intriguing and shows that these elements can also be easily found for example in China, as Rana Mitter (2000, 2008, 2013), a professor of modern Chinese history at Oxford, describes. In China, Chinese national memory is framed similarly, as the war of Chinese resistance against the Japanese. National memory prefers a simple scheme, presenting a nation of victims and heroic resistance fighters against a brutal enemy, a history with little ambivalence. In this respect, China has many elements that are comparable to Dutch, European, and American history.

For decades, World War II has been one of the most broadly shared educational subjects. The war is considered important, weighty, serious. The national consensus requires that it should remain important, impressive, special, fascinating, gripping. A lesson about the war may not be dull. It should speak to the learners, and there is a certain fierceness in this transmission. This national consensus varies from nation to nation, and is defended vigorously.

In the Netherlands, we can see that immediately after liberation, the country was in need of some encouragement. There was a need for national pride, unity, and the idea of courage: these qualities were most directly evident in the resistance movements against the Nazis. To be proud of the Netherlands, to be proud of being Dutch, was—and is, still, and again—apparently a strong need. For several decades after the war, Dutch pride was created indirectly by maintaining an image of the German as the enemy. The anti-German message was fostered, and the unity of the Dutch people, the *volksgemeenschap,* the community of the people, was underlined. The resistance fighters who were particularly anti-German became the moral winners of the war. Until recently the anti-German and the non-German image of the Dutch has remained an important element of Dutch identity. What the Dutch were was not always so clear, but they were convinced and reassured that they were not Germans. Recently, the German historians Michael Wildt and Frank Bajohr have offered a German perspective on *Volksgemeinschaft* as a crucial theme in Nazi and post-Nazi history.

Jewish Voices

In the first period after 1945, there was no audience and no voice for minorities such as the Jews: they could not claim participation in this national resistance community. More than 75% of the Jews in the Netherlands were murdered. A very small minority returned from the camps and from hiding places, and they were not generally given a warm welcome. On the contrary, as I have written elsewhere (Hondius 2003), an upsurge of antisemitism was noted in the summer of 1945. The Jews were left to themselves. In the public sphere, the Jews were told that they should now be thankful. Their duty was to be grateful.

In the Netherlands, the national ideal images were formulated most explicitly in 1955, when the tenth anniversary of liberation was commemorated nationally. The idea was for children to gather early in the morning in a central square of the city or village where they lived. There they were addressed by people of authority—the mayor, a school director, a politician—around the flag, and together they sang national songs. It was called the *Youth Appèl*, the Call for Youth. Such events occurred from the second half of the 1950s until the end of the 1960s, and after that only in small provincial towns.

The 1960s brought enormous cultural change and criticism, but the schoolbooks did not change so rapidly. Continuity and repetition are major characteristics of education: what is found acceptable endures for years. A more critical tone entered the atmosphere around commemorations and, slowly, a new generation began to criticise memorial culture as old-fashioned and nationalistic. Several confrontations took place between 1962 and 1977. On the whole, confrontations were avoided and what emerged was a landscape with two streams in memorial culture: one more nationalist and militarist, one more critical and progressive. Youth culture was much more visible and independent than before, and particularly in the large cities youth were more involved in commemorative activities. The history of militarism and anti-militarism plays a role in this as well. It was the time of the Cold War, and the Netherlands invested heavily in arms and military systems. In many parts of the country, the commemoration of World War II was also an arms show.

And it was also often an occasion for walking and marching. Especially in the east and south of the country, this element was strong during the annual events. The schoolbooks in this period were still quite traditional in their clear-cut division of who was right and who was wrong during the war: simply put, the Germans were wrong, the Dutch were all good, and every schoolbook continued to show this division clearly.

Another major change in this period is the greater attention paid to the history of the Holocaust and the persecution of the Jews. In the second half of the 1970s, this trend became more accepted, which can be seen from the new monuments. In particular, in 1977, the sculptor and writer Jan Wolkers created the Auschwitz monument, made of glass plates that were broken to represent the broken sky. It included the text: *Nooit Meer Auschwitz* (Never Again Auschwitz).

An important phenomenon in the educational culture of memory was a series of exhibitions. The first exhibition directed at a young audience was made in 1946, organised by former resistance fighters of the organisation Expogé. With it was also an exhibition with large paintings made by Amsterdam artists who were said to have been "good", that is anti-Nazi, during the war. In these exhibitions, former resistance fighters showed young people around and spoke of their experiences. During that walking, conversations began. This phenomenon of eyewitnesses who tell young people about the war is an important and lasting element, repeated over and over again. From the late 1970s, a new element entered educational commemorative culture: the effort to connect past and present. An active connection was made between remembering the past and warning for the future while reflecting on the present. This approach found broad acceptance and initiated a long tradition that continues to this day.

Ido Abram, a pioneer in Holocaust education in the Netherlands, developed the first educational programmes about the Holocaust in 1979, with a television series simply called *Holocaust*. Educators began to take new initiatives to deepen and to refresh knowledge about the Holocaust. A generation of critical young men who resisted the draft and refused to join the army became involved in the practical organisation of this educational work by dedicating their alternative social service years to nongovernmental organisations. The Anne Frank House, for example, set up a system to link schools and teachers to organisations of survivors and resistance fighters as well as individual eyewitnesses of the war, to arrange their visits to schools and exhibitions as guest speakers and guides. This effort established a new trend that continues to influence commemorative culture today. Indeed, the evolving and various rules and regulations and guidelines for these guest speakers over the last 30 years reflect changes in attitudes and approach to this issue.

From Avoiding Emotion to Embracing Emotion

One clear trend is the change from avoiding emotion to embracing emotion. In 1980, for example, there was significant hesitancy towards anything involving emotion around commemoration in the classroom. Guest speakers were instructed to tell a school group the complete history of World War II, and to somehow squeeze their own personal history into it. How they were supposed to do this was not clear; there was a much greater emphasis on providing a complete and balanced account, mentioning many different aspects of the history of the war. This trend continued in the 1980s, but changed significantly from the 1990s onwards.

This period ushered in what has been called the era of testimony, the period of the eyewitness, and with it came a greater acceptance of emotions in education, even a welcoming of emotional presentations. Today we find ourselves in what could be called an overemotional culture. The Israeli historian Amos Goldberg (2009) has warned about this current trend in a recent inspiring article; he sees a danger in melodramatic memory. Twenty years ago, it was still new to interview an eyewitness on film or on television; now we are used to witness testimony and to emotions on television, with quick shots of edited films in which the emotional element comes almost immediately.

Emotions have become an expected element, and we need to find out how this has affected education. I am not opposed to emotional elements in education, but there are risks, for example in the emphasis that is laid on identifying with victims or persecuted groups. In order to stimulate children's identifications, to get students to imagine themselves in a war situation, some teachers come up with weird ideas. One teacher in the Netherlands had his class of primary school children eat tulip bulbs in the classroom. This was to imagine the last winter of the war, the so-called hunger winter. While it was well intended, to create empathy and identification, the whole class became ill, angering parents. A British primary school teacher sought a way to have her class imagine the experience of exclusion and oppression. She divided the class in two and told one half that from now on they were prisoners in a camp and that they would never see their parents again. Again, this was well intended, in order to create empathy, understanding, and identification, but the children broke out in tears, making their parents quite angry with the teacher as well. These stories were exceptions; there is a great deal of commitment and dedication in the lessons about the war, and in general there is also much care, reflection, and careful planning.

Guest Speakers in Schools

In the Netherlands, in contrast to the early 1980s, the idea that a guest speaker has to tell the complete history of World War II and the Holocaust has now been abandoned. This is significant. Today, the guest speaker is asked to tell about his or her own wartime experience in the form of a story, and to place this story in a timeframe of the war. Also apparently abandoned are the need for relevant facts and figures and context and the correct representation of history. These are now considered more the task of the history teacher; it appears that facts have lost a lot of their earlier weight and value. Another element that has become much less prominent is the awareness of World War II as an international event. The turn to lessons of war that are more emotional, local, and individual; and the turn to testimony, have had more unexpected effects. World War II appears to be much less a *world* war, and more a series of events in a national and even local frame. Of course this focus can speak to students when local issues are addressed, as they discover who lived in their own area, what happened there. The possibilities for finding out more about local history have increased and have resulted in impressive results. However, an unexpected consequence is that the international history of the war is no longer a prominent part of the history lesson; in Dutch history books, the treatment of international developments in World War II has shrunk to just a few pages.

A third trend I observe is the rise and fall of the war as a required subject in school exams. In the Netherlands, the war was a focus of examinations for the first time in 1974. That focus continued, and became self-evident. But, in 1991, to my surprise, it stopped. Since 1991, the war has not been a separate topic in the national history exams. Thus, two decades of attention to personal history has had the effect of leaving behind national norms for exams, and the loss of knowledge about the big picture and broader historical context. This loss appears to be an unintended consequence of these developments.

Collaborators and Perpetrators

The trend towards more personal and individual history has remained restricted to several groups, especially the victims and the resistance fighters. Much less attention has been given to other groups; in particular, the attention paid to collaboration remained frozen for decades. Recently, several new studies about collaboration have appeared, explaining what it was like to join the National Socialist movement in the Netherlands, or to grow up in a family where the parents were active in Nazi organisations. There is also a new trend in perpetrator history. This has taken a long time and it raises an important question: how can perpetrator history and the history of Nazis, the NSB (Nationaal-Socialistische Beweging, National Socialist Movement) and the SS find a way into the history schoolbooks?

I see a dilemma here in the current trend of emotional history, as well as the trend toward identification and imagination and empathy. To what extent would teachers be prepared to teach students to empathise with the collaborationists, the Nazis, the perpetrators? What would introducing these new elements mean for the balance of attention to the victims?

There are examples of giving attention to perpetrators. In Ravensbrück, for example, the visitor learns about many aspects of this complicated place. Like many memorial places, Ravensbrück is itself a museum of the history of memory, which has left visible markers from several decades that are quite diverse. One of the latest trends at Ravensbrück is to show more of the ordinary lives of the female guards, the camp's other personnel, and the SS families who lived in special family villas just outside the camp. I welcome this historical research and the many striking facts it shows. However, I have to admit that seeing these exhibitions about perpetrators, about guards, also provoked immense anger in me. I was especially shocked by the short biographies of the camp guards, many of whom were able to escape prosecution after the war. Reading and hearing about perpetrators on location in a former camp had a powerful effect.

The 1990s: War Returns to Europe

Halfway through the 1990s, important new developments in education took place in the context of new military conflicts, first in the former Yugoslavia and later in Iraq and Afghanistan. In the Netherlands, direct involvement in a war close to home had been virtually impossible to imagine until then, but that changed, thoroughly. This new time of war and the period of peace missions and attacks continued longer than World War II lasted. Without much explicit discussion, these new developments are taking their place in history books, and they inform and influence the writers of these books and the teachers in the classrooms. These developments seem to be occurring without much reflection.

The next new development is of course the digital era. In education, this has quickly led to new individual work forms, with students looking for information on the Internet for presentations and papers in a way that was unimaginable 15 years ago. This development presents both opportunities and risks. The reader, the learner, the student, and the user of information increasingly are irritated about forms of paternalism: "I can do this myself", we think, "let me do this myself". However, searching and finding and critically filtering and interpreting digital information is a skill and an art in itself. As e-learning and e-humanities are developing, one specific risk with regard to information about World War II and the Holocaust is the amount of misinformation, myths, and denial online. This provides an opportunity for teaching general Internet research skills.

Next to this new world of online self-search education, we find the world of entertainment. For young people, computer games and films form a parallel universe in which entertainment and interaction come together. Many computer games are about war and conflict situations, and game researchers have found that a significant number are about World War II (Nieborg 2005, 2010), including *Killzone, Mortal Combat, Airborne*, and *Call of Duty: World at War*. Gamers are encouraged to imagine themselves as soldiers and fighters. This is a multi-million dollar industry that directly involves military advisors from real armies. A debate about the impact of games on players' lives and the interaction between game and reality is emerging. There are opportunities to connect these worlds; "serious games" offer opportunities to enhance historical understanding.

National Self-Image and the Shoah

In the memory of war in all countries, shame and pride remain important issues and questions. The Dutch national self-image as a small but courageous country struggling against the big and evil German occupation remained strong for decades; however, starting in the 1960s, this image eroded more and more, through the knowledge and insight in the history of the Shoah. In the 1980s and 1990s, the new educational approach led to new questions: Could the Netherlands have done more for the Jews during the war? National pride and the self-image of a nation of victims began to shrink. It led to emerging shame about the lack of active help to Jews, to an increasing awareness of the loss of the Jewish community, and to some extent also to forms of public mourning about the brutal consequences of the lack of alertness and lack of solidarity towards the Jews. The knowledge that the Jews were so quickly segregated, registered, and isolated, and that resistance was late, rare, and not very widespread: this all created forms of uneasiness that include shame. In education this insight is interpreted as a warning for the present and the future, and as a lesson to recognise injustice, discrimination, and exclusion in an early phase, before it is too late.

In 1995, a television documentary was made about the people who lived in the immediate surroundings of Camp Westerbork during the war. One of them, a farmer, who had seen a lot, said it simply: "We could have done more" (Vuijsje 1995). In the same year, Queen Beatrix gave a speech in the Israeli parliament, the Knesset, and she said the same thing: "More should have been done". This same year, 1995, was also the year of Srebrenica. More than 8,000 Muslim men in Bosnia were murdered while our soldiers, sent there to keep the fighters separated, became and remained bystanders, some would say accomplices. Again the feeling: we could have done more. We should have done more. The national self-image of a nation that knows what right and wrong is and that is active in the field of human rights and minority rights was eroding. There did not remain much to be proud of.

The second half of the 1990s revealed more shameful episodes. We found out more about the robbing of the Jews, and what had been done with Jewish possessions during and after the Shoah. The Swiss banks had kept Jewish assets, owners of paintings and other goods that had belonged to Jewish families had kept silent, but many forms of profit were addressed and reparations followed. Here the United States was leading the way. Jewish survivors and their children were now interviewed again and their voices were significantly stronger than before. In the Netherlands, Jews had been regarded and treated politically as patients and traumatised victims—spoken about by others on their behalf. Now for the first time angry Jews took the microphone and spoke out for justice. This was effective; new research and reparations followed for the Jewish community as well as for the Dutch Indonesian community, as acknowledgment of the lack of support and solidarity during and after the liberation. Between 2000 and 2002 these developments led to new publications and reports, and the Srebrenica report lead to the fall of the Dutch government of Prime Minister Wim Kok, a Social Democrat, in 2002. Meanwhile, in the Netherlands, a large historical research project called SOTO (Stichting Onderzoek Terugkeer en Opvang Oorlogsslachtoffers) resulted in three major volumes as well as a series of restitution and reparation decisions; the archive is housed at NIOD, the Netherlands Institute for War Documentation in Amsterdam.

In Germany, this awareness of loss, the public shame, and the idea of not having done enough for the Jews have been around much longer and my impression is that they became influential in education earlier than in the Netherlands. Directly after the liberation, this shame was very actively forced upon the German population by programmes of re-education with American educational material about democracy, as well as by forced visits to former concentration camps and mass graves in German towns and villages (see Dorn 2005; Tent 1984; van Vree 2010). Only during the last few years are we seeing more public expressions of German pride; it was clear during more recent football matches that there is now more room for German national pride. In my view, these developments are linked: the broader recognition and acknowledgement of failure during the Shoah in the Netherlands and France for example, meant that a new form of relaxation could grow within Germany.

The last 14 years have been an unstable period. Soon after the terrorist attacks of 11 September, 2001 in the United States, the Netherlands found itself in an atmosphere of crisis, fear, uncertainty, tension. The loss of national pride quickly became a political opportunity. The pride and national self-consciousness that had been lost were felt as something that is needed, necessary. New political parties have filled the gap and addressed this loss. There is an active search for pride about being Dutch, even a short-lived nationalist conservative political party called *Trots op Nederland* (Proud of the Netherlands). We also see a focus on pride in Dutch national history, and a search for courage, heroes, and heroism. How all this will end up in the history books is an open question.

Less Lecture, More Discussion

The study of educational cultures of memory is a broad and virtually new field of research with many possible connections, where the main source materials are texts and the memories of those who have been involved in this work for the last several decades.

Contacts with eyewitnesses of the war, and with survivors of the Shoah, remain possible and inspiring. I plead for continued activity in this field, and for arranging meetings, encounters with war witnesses in education. Many very special meetings are taking place, but there is also miscommunication, friction, and tension in these meetings that I find very interesting to study in more detail. What happens between the generations, what happens in encounters? Which questions come up, how are they addressed, what is said, and what remains unsaid? Some results from international research, particularly in the United States and Germany, are intriguing for the Dutch situation as well. One clear outcome of this research is the crucial advice to create conversations with war witnesses instead of lectures. Having a guest speaker in one's classroom or at an exhibition becomes a much more engaging experience when students prepare their own questions and the speaker can improvise answers and connect with spontaneous associations.

One explanation for the success of the meetings between generations is the distance in age and experience. For young people, it can be an eye-opener to see, and speak with, someone who has been directly involved in something. For the older eyewitness, finding a willing ear and audience among young people is usually a rewarding and positive experience—also because that audience is harder to find elsewhere, among peers and people of the same age group. In their own circle of friends, family, and others, people experience significantly more tension, rivalry, mistrust, competition, and hierarchy. But this falls away in an encounter across the generations. I have observed this phenomenon at meetings between Jewish survivors and youth groups, but also for other groups like veterans, resistance fighters, and political prisoners. It is important to invite only one witness at a time. Bringing in groups of witnesses will quickly lead to difficult situations where rivalry, dissent, and competition begin to play a role. Right now I notice that as the generation of guides and speakers, aged 85 and older, are retiring from their active involvement in Holocaust education, a new generation is ready to be more involved in teaching: the just-retired 60- to 65-year olds who have kept their involvement limited until now. While they were babies or very young children in the immediate post-war period, the memory of World War II and the Holocaust had a huge influence on their youth and their lives. They are also the first generation to be told the war lessons from a young age onwards.

For the teacher or facilitator, it is instructive to study the reactions of the students and the interaction between the guest and the students. I am convinced that documentary makers and journalists must still have a wealth of information about what has worked and what has been tried, and how these experiments have changed and continue to evolve. Therefore, I also advise participants to collect rough film of question-and-answer sessions, to post these online, and to study and compare them.

The speeches of survivors and other guides and witnesses are important sources for reconstructing and analyzing the changing discourse of lessons about war. Speeches given at commemorative events are good sources as well, to study the more official and formal elements in commemorative culture. Film clips of interactions between speakers and their audiences promise to provide more insight into the practice of Holocaust education during recent decades. Another abundant source is the so-called reaction books kept for visitors of memorial places and exhibitions. I have initiated a research project studying the reaction books at the Anne Frank House, with students at VU University Amsterdam and Amsterdam University College. Can we imagine more diversity in approaches, and more contrasting views? Some people welcome polarisation and dissent; contested and competing memories are a new field of study within memory studies, and it is clear that conflicting views exist of most historical events. However, for policy makers and in matters of national commemorative cultures, explicit conflicts are still unfamiliar territory. Therefore, a crucial question in Holocaust education is how passive bystanders can be motivated to act. The Israeli historian Yehuda Bauer (1998) stated that for him, the major lesson of the Holocaust was a reminder: "Never, but never, be a bystander". In classroom discussions and other meetings between generations as well as among peers, Bauer's commandment can be used as a question and starting point for self-reflection about moments of choice in our own lives and those of our parents and grandparents. The time that Holocaust education was only about celebrating heroes and martyrs, or about mourning victims, is not entirely over, but a present-day approach requires personal involvement from anyone who shares a lesson of war.

Perhaps one of the most valuable elements of Holocaust education is exactly this: the opportunity to provoke and facilitate honest self-reflection about our own choices in life, our points of view, attitudes, and actions, and our independence or dependence on others. How impressionable, how compliant and passive are we, and how independent and active would we like to be or to have been?

This gives a deeper dimension to the old terminology of immunisation and vaccination that can be found in Holocaust education from the first instances onward. In every European language, one can find recorded the hope that Holocaust education, a lesson about the war, or a visit to an exhibition or to a former concentration camp would have the effect of a vaccination for students and children. This hope can easily lead to disappointments, given the fact that antisemitism still exists and that Holocaust denial and racism have not vanished either. A much more direct approach is possible, as Wolfgang Meseth and Matthias Proske, in this volume, show in their example of one classroom discussion in Germany. There, the question about being an impressionable follower of Hitler's propaganda became very personal and individual when students began to question themselves and each other, asking, would I—would you, would we—have been immune to Nazi propaganda or would it have pulled us in too? (See also Heyl 2013).

An honest and focused discussion can address all involved, including grandparents, authorities, politicians, teachers, survivors, former collaborators, resistance fighters, and their children and grandchildren and other learners. This may lead to new insights and, hopefully, to a new decision or resolution to try to stand up and act whenever the situation requires action. Honest self-reflection can be facilitated by interaction with eyewitnesses of history in person as well as in short film clips, making this an option for discussion across borders or across generations and nations.

The study of a developing educational culture of memory shows that intergenerational conversations about World War II and the Holocaust started during the events and continued after the liberation. New generations renewed and refreshed these conversations, and aging and retiring eyewitnesses found new roles as educators within and outside classrooms. These findings enable a comparative study of developing educational memorial cultures after war, armed conflict, genocide, and mass violence elsewhere.

Acknowledgements This chapter is based on Hondius (2010). I thank Doyle Stevick for his help in transforming the texts of speeches given at teacher conferences in Amsterdam, Amersfoort, New York, and Berlin into an article. I am grateful for earlier comments from my colleagues and friends Karen Polak, Inger Schaap, Jan Erik Dubbelman, and Jaap Tanja.

References

Bauer, Y. (1998). *Speech to the German Bundestag*, Berlin, 27 January. Frequent Question no. 16 at the website of the United States Holocaust Memorial Museum. http://www.ushmm.org/research/library/faq/details.php?topic=06
Brumlik, M. (1995). *Gerechtigkeit zwischen den Generationen* [Justice between the generations]. Berlin: Berlin Verlag.
Brumlik, M. (2004). *Aus Katastrophen lernen? Grundlagen zeitgeschichtlicher Bildung in menschenrechtlicher Absicht* [Learning from catastrophes? The foundation of contemporary education in the perspective of human rights]. Berlin: Philo Verlag.
Dorn, C. (2005). Evaluating democracy: The 1946 US Education Mission to Germany. *American Journal of Evaluation, 26*, 267–277.
Goldberg, A. (2009). The victim's voice and melodramatic aesthetics in history. *History and Theory, 48*, 220–237.
Heyl, M. (1997). *Erziehung nach Auschwitz. Eine Bestandsaufnahme. Deutschland, Niederlande, Israel, USA* [Education after Auschwitz. A picture of the state of the art. Germany, Netherlands, Israel, USA]. Hamburg: Kraemer.
Heyl, M. (2013). *Mit Überwältigendem überwältigen? Emotionen in KZ-Gedenkstätten* [Overwhelming with something overwhelming? Emotions in concentration camp memorial centres]. In J. Brauer & M. Lücke (Eds.), *Emotionen, Geschichte und historisches Lernen. Geschichtsdidaktische und geschichtskulturelle Perspektiven* (pp. 239–260). Göttingen: V&R Unipress.
Hondius, D. (1985). *Anne Frank in the world, 1929–1945*. Exhibition catalog. Amsterdam: Bert Bakker.
Hondius, D. (2003). *Return: Holocaust survivors and Dutch anti-semitism*. Westport: Praeger/Greenwood.
Hondius, D. (2010). *Oorlogslessen: Onderwijs over de oorlog sinds 1945* [Lessons of war: Education about the war since 1945]. Amsterdam: Bert Bakker.

Hondius, D., with Gompes-Lobatto, M. (2001). *Absent: Herinneringen aan het Joods Lyceum Amsterdam, 1941–1943* [Absent: Memories of the Jewish Lyceum in Amsterdam, 1941–1943]. Amsterdam: Vassallucci.

Koker, D. (2012). *At the edge of the abyss: A concentration camp diary, 1943–1944.* Evanston: Northwestern University Press.

Makarova, E., Makarov, S., & Kuperman, V. (Eds.) (2004). *University over the abyss: The story behind 520 lecturers and 2,430 lectures in KZ Theresienstadt 1942–1944* (2nd ed.). Jerusalem: Verba Publishers.

Meseth, M. (2005). *Aus der Geschichte lernen: Über die Rolle der Erziehung in der bundesdeutschen Erinnerungskultur* [Learning from history: About the role of education in the German commemoration culture]. Frankfurt am Main: Frankfurt University Press.

Meseth, W. (2007). Die Pedagogisierung der Erinnerungskultur. Erziehungswissenschaftliche Beobachtungen eines bisher kaum beobachteten Phänomens [Educationalising the commemoration culture: Pedagogical scientific observations of a thus far rarely observed phenomenon]. *Zeitschrift für Genozidforschung, 2*, 96–117.

Mitter, R. (2000). *The Manchurian myth: Nationalism, resistance and collaboration in modern China.* Berkeley/Los Angeles: University of California Press.

Mitter, R. (2008). *Modern China: A very short introduction.* Oxford: Oxford University Press.

Mitter, R. (2013). *China's war with Japan 1937–1945: The struggle for survival.* London/New York: Penguin.

Nieborg, D. B. (2005). *Changing the rules of engagement: Tapping into the popular culture of America's Army, the official US Army computer game.* Master's thesis, University of Amsterdam.

Nieborg, D. B. (2010). Wargames. In C. van der Heijden (Ed.), *Voorbij maar niet vergeten. Oorlog 65 jaar na de Tweede Wereldoorlog. Tijdschrift ter gelegenheid van 65 jaar bevrijding* [Over but not forgotten: War 65 years after the Second World War. Magazine on the occasion of 65 years since liberation] (pp. 27–28). Den Haag: Ministeris van VWS.

Tent, J. F. (1984). *Mission on the Rhine: "Reeducation" and denazification in American-occupied Germany.* Chicago: University of Chicago Press.

van Vree, F. (2010). Indigestible images: On the ethics and limits of representation. In K. Tilmans, F. van Vree, & J. Winter (Eds.), *Performing the past: Memory, history, and identity in Modern Europe* (pp. 257–286). Amsterdam: Amsterdam University Press.

Vuijsje, H. (1995). *Opdat wij niet vergeten: Buren van Westerbork* [Lest we forget: The neighbours of Westerbork]. Documentary on KRO television, 28 April 1995.

Teaching about and Teaching through the Holocaust: Insights from (Social) Psychology

Barry van Driel

Monday, 22 May, 1944

Dearest Kitty,
    To our great sorrow and dismay, we've heard that many people have changed their attitude towards us Jews. We've been told that antisemitism has cropped up in circles where once it would have been unthinkable. This fact has affected us all very, very deeply. The reason for the hatred is understandable, maybe even human, but that doesn't make it right. According to the Christians, the Jews are blabbing their secrets to the Germans, denouncing their helpers and causing them to suffer the dreadful fate and punishments which have already been meted out to so many. All of this is true. But as with everything, they should look at the matter from both sides: would Christians act any differently if they were in our place? Could anyone, regardless of whether they're Jews or Christians, remain silent in the face of German pressure?

This less well known passage from the *Diary of Anne Frank* will serve as the starting point for my reflections in this chapter. Writing in the relative comfort of their hiding place on the Prinsengracht in Amsterdam, Anne Frank put her finger on something quite non-intuitive: that as the suffering of a particular minority community worsens, even though people are aware of it, their response is not necessarily empathy or a growing sense of injustice. Too often the opposite happens. Those suffering injustice meet with negative reactions from the outside world. Such dynamics tend to be part of human nature, irrespective of one's cultural or religious background. Why would this be the case and how can we best explain such a phenomenon to young people in our schools? Can it help us to better understand the pervasive nature of prejudice and discrimination in the past and present?

B. van Driel (✉)
Anne Frank House, P.O.B. 730, 1000 AS Amsterdam, The Netherlands
e-mail: barry@iaie.org

Introduction

In this chapter, I share some of the insights gained in 20 years of experience in the field and address some issues I have encountered that have been largely ignored by the field of Holocaust education. I endeavor to hold these experiences and my reflections up to a social and cognitive psychology light. Generally speaking, cognitive psychology focuses on our mental processes: how do people think, remember, perceive, and learn? Social psychology focuses more on the situational influences of behavior than, for instance, on personality characteristics. Scholars in the field generally examine the impact of social norms, peer pressure, propaganda, etc. In short, they devote considerable attention to the power of the situation. Elliot Aronson (2000) summarises the social psychological perspective as follows: "each of us is greatly influenced by the power of the social situation—we tend to underestimate the degree of influence the situation exerts on other people and to overestimate the impact of their personalities as determinants of their behavior". (p. 22)

It is my sense that such an analysis can help educators in the field design richer activities that can have more impact for contemporary youth, helping them gain some insight into how human beings can blame individuals and communities when those defined as the "other" suffer discrimination and persecution. In short, in this chapter I focus more on the challenges of teaching young people today about the past and present, rather than on events in the past alone.

Teaching about and through the History of the Holocaust

There are many reasons to teach about the Holocaust in contemporary society, whether or not a society was directly and deeply impacted by this history. These reasons will vary depending on the educational aims identified by governments, educational authorities, and teachers for educating youth about this topic. The reasons will also depend partially on the particular histories of countries and communities.

From a historical perspective, we might identify at least eight reasons (though this list is by no means complete):

1. To further our understanding of what happened in Germany, Europe, and globally during this period in history—including one's own country and community—and which institutions collaborated with, resisted, or remained silent in the face of, Nazi atrocities.
2. To gain insight into the impact of the Treaty of Versailles before World War II and the way the Holocaust led to the creation of the United Nations, the Universal Declaration of Human Rights, and the creation of the state of Israel.
3. To understand how modern communication and propaganda have been influenced by insights derived from Nazi propaganda towards Jews and others.
4. To advance insight into Jewish life and Jewish history in Germany and Europe, as well as globally, and in one's country before the Holocaust.

5. To commemorate the many innocent (mostly Jewish) victims in Europe and lost Jewish culture.
6. To understand the impact of Nazi policies on other minority communities such as the Roma and blacks, as well as the disabled.
7. To understand that the Holocaust was a global tragedy that can to some extent be connected to the histories of countries across the globe.
8. To understand how the Nuremberg trials represent the origins of modern international law relating to genocide and crimes against humanity.

The pure focus on history and more macro events has often been criticised and complementary reasons and their concomitant aims have been identified. For instance, teachers have long complained that it is difficult to interest young people in historical events that took place long before their parents were born.

In their reflections on the aims of Holocaust education, Gross and Stevick (2010) state:

> Linked to vigilance, action and prevention, Holocaust education is self-consciously instrumental, eager to transform individual attitudes and dispositions, aspiring to change broader cultures and cultivate better citizens. The underlying philosophies that animate the sustenance and dissemination of Holocaust education may vary, but they share a vision of the world that embraces human rights and cultural differences. (p. 18)

In a *New York Times* opinion piece, Kofi Annan (2010), the former Secretary General of the United Nations, went much further than this, and directly confronted the expert community involved in teaching about the Holocaust. He lamented what he regarded as the failure of Holocaust education programmes to prevent genocide end ethnic conflict:

> …if we want to prevent future genocides, is it not equally important to understand the psychology of the perpetrators and bystanders—to comprehend what it is that leads large numbers of people, often "normal" and decent, in the company of their own family and friends, to suppress their natural human empathy with people belonging to other groups and to join in, or stand by and witness, their systematic extermination? Do we not need to focus more on the social and psychological factors that lead to these acts of brutality and indifference, so that we know the warning signs to look out for in ourselves and our societies? Do current education programs do enough to reveal the dangers inherent in racial or religious stereotypes and prejudices, and inoculate students against them? Does the teaching of the history of the Holocaust at classroom level sufficiently link it to the root causes of contemporary racism or ethnic conflict?

I would certainly agree with Doyle Stevick and Deborah Michaels (2013), who have criticised such goals as too ambitious for a subject that tends to occupy, at most, several hours of study and reflection in most classrooms across the globe. Still, parts of Annan's opinion piece challenge educators to reflect on the way they teach about the Holocaust and the lessons they draw from this history. In a recent study, Stuart Foster (2013) and his colleagues at the Institute of Education in London found that many teachers do exactly what Kofi Annan has called for. They not only teach "about the Holocaust" for historical reasons. In addition, they tend to focus on this tragedy for more contemporary reasons:

> …the research findings demonstrate that the majority of teachers (across a range of subject areas) teach about the Holocaust as a "universal warning" with the aim of addressing broader trans-disciplinary goals such as "understanding the ramifications of racism and

prejudice", "transforming society" and/or "learning the lessons of the Holocaust to ensure that it never happens again". For example, across all survey respondents, "to develop an understanding of the roots and ramifications of prejudice, racism and stereotyping in any society" was the most popularly prioritised teaching aim, chosen by 71%. (p. 137)

Such teachers tend to teach *through* the Holocaust. Foster and his colleagues found that, at least in the United Kingdom, this approach was quite pronounced.

If we as Holocaust educators accept the challenge voiced in Annan's statements above, and if we want teachers to have the necessary insights and competencies to help students "make sense" of the world around them, then we need to look carefully at some of the other aims that have been identified in relation to Holocaust education. Listed in random order, I suggest eleven other topics of what I will now refer to as "learning through the Holocaust":

1. How in even relatively advanced and modern societies, historical prejudices can be transformed into lethal ideologies with a total disrespect for human rights and human dignity
2. The fragility of democracy and "civilisation"
3. The nature of human behaviour we putatively define as "evil"
4. How ordinary people are capable of becoming involved in and justifying the persecution and murder of innocent people
5. How certain societies can be seduced by a demagogic leader and populist causes
6. The human potential for, and the conditions that promote, caring for others, or courageous risk taking on behalf of fellow humans who may be in peril
7. How prejudice, discrimination, racism, and the human capacity for harming others can lead to mass murder if not addressed
8. The importance of standing up for the rights of others if we hope to have our own rights respected
9. How we as humans have our interpretations of reality shaped by the influence of the media, propaganda, and the opinions of others
10. An understanding of the mechanisms of peer pressure, group conformity, and social norms
11. The conditions that can promote indifference to oppression or suffering.

In this chapter I focus on the last three aims.

Anne Frank's Insight

It is critical to note for educational purposes what Anne Frank was referring to in her diary entry I quoted at the beginning of this chapter. It was a dislike of Jews as a category—of growing antisemitism—and not of one particular Jewish person. With very few Jewish people around to counter any misconceptions and prejudices, and building on centuries of antisemitism, the propaganda and mythology about Jews as a category went unchallenged in Germany and surrounding countries.

But propaganda and the Nazis' complete control of all the media in Germany and occupied Europe cannot fully explain the widespread phenomenon that anti-

Semitism grew among the general population as Jewish men, women, and children were being humiliated, beaten, and killed. Antisemitism was also rampant in countries where the media were *not* controlled by the Nazis.

Though newspapers in the United States like *The New York Times* reported on the increasing persecution of Jews in Germany and later in occupied Europe, antisemitism among the general public in the United States remained strong and by some accounts even increased.

We know today what the general public at that time thought, especially in the United States, because the rise of the Nazis coincided with the emergence of the social sciences and empirical research methods. Starting in the mid-1930s, polling companies in the United States surveyed the US public on a monthly basis about numerous social issues. Some 400 national surveys were conducted between 1936 and 1945 by Elmo Roper's polling firm, George Gallup's American Institute of Public Opinion (AIPO), Hadley Cantril's Office of Public Opinion Research (OPOR), and the National Opinion Research Council (NORC). It was the first time in history that attitudes could be measured as a genocide unfolded.

Several years into the Nazi persecution of Jews, but a few months before *Kristallnacht,* the pogrom of November, 1938, a poll by AIPO showed that 58% of Americans agreed that Jews were at least partially responsible for their own persecution (see Figure 1).

Half a year later, shortly after *Kristallnacht*, in which close to 100 Jews were murdered, 30,000 arrested, and more than 250 synagogues torched in Germany, Austria, and the Sudetenland (USHMM 2013), a Gallup poll revealed that only

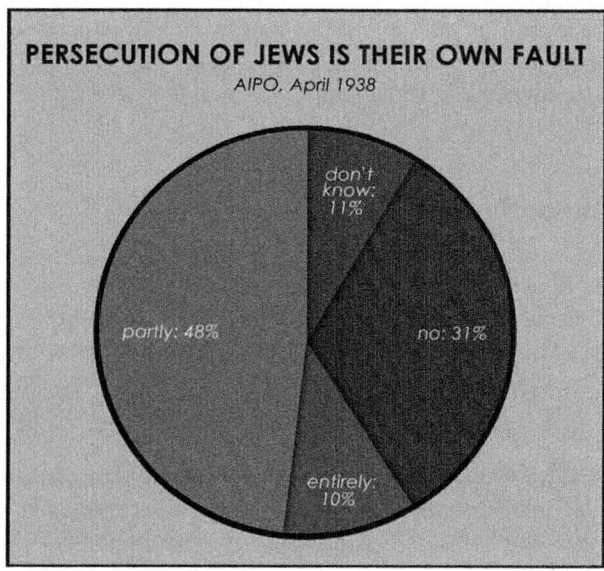

Fig. 1 Percentage of US respondents holding that Jews are responsible for their own persecution, 1938

21.2% of Americans thought their government should allow more Jews to immigrate. At this time, according to such surveys, majorities of respondents agreed with statements that labeled Jews as "greedy", "dishonest", and "pushy". The percentages that agreed that Jews had "too much power in the United States" rose from to 41% in 1938 to 58% by 1945.

A 1939 Roper poll sheds further light on the existing antisemitism among the American public. Only 39% agreed that Jews should be treated like other people. Some 53% expressed the belief that "Jews are different and should be restricted" and no less than 10% of the public believed that Jews should be deported (see, e.g., Mazzenga 2009).

At face value, it seems quite shocking that attitudes towards Jews would harden and become less tolerant in a place like the United States during a period of severe persecution. One might argue that the American public was unaware of what was happening to the Jews in Germany and elsewhere. However, information was regularly being communicated to the American public. Influential newspapers and local papers across the country covered the events in Germany and Europe. *The New York Times* reported on the events associated with the November Pogrom in several articles at the time. On 11 November, 1938, the following text was splashed across the front page: "Nazis smash, loot and burn Jewish shops and temples until Goebbels calls halt". The same day, *The Cincinnati Enquirer* led with an article on the front page, entitled "Nazis burn property, loot stores of Jews" (USHMM 2013). *The News and Courier* in Charleston, South Carolina also devoted extensive front-page attention to those events. On the same date it led with the caption "Frenzied Nazi Terrorists Flout Government Orders and Continue Destruction", using words and phrases such as "orgy of looting", "hysteria", and "terror". The paper also mentioned multiple murders (of Jews) and suicides. These are just a few examples of newspaper coverage at the time. Interestingly, the coverage in such papers, like so many others at the time, echoed the myth that the pogrom was spontaneous and that the German government had attempted to stop the violence.

Failing to Empathise

Given this awareness of great suffering, how is it possible that so many people held on to their antisemitic attitudes and that surveys showed that antisemitic sentiment grew? The growth in antisemitic sentiment is perhaps even more surprising when one realizes that the Jews were being persecuted by a country at war with the United States. One would expect empathy towards Jews to increase if only for that reason.

Arguments with a strong commonsense dimension that would help explain growing antisemitism include those that would point to already existing antisemitic, racist, and other intolerant beliefs. These certainly had an impact. However, more mundane psychological mechanisms also explain part of the picture.

Gordon Allport (1954), in his classic study of prejudice, alluded to the process where humans fail to have empathy for the suffering of others:

> There is a good reason why out-groups are often chosen as the object of hate and aggression rather than individuals. One human being is, after all, pretty much like another—like oneself. One can scarcely sympathize with the victim. To attack him would be to arouse some pain in ourselves. Our own "body image" would be involved, for his body is like our own body. But there is no body image of a group. It is more abstract, more impersonal. (p. 363)

Melvin Lerner (1980) offers some insight into why individuals might not emphathise with those who are the targets of persecution. Heavily influenced by Milgram's work on obedience, Lerner arrived at what he called the just world hypothesis. Lerner wanted to understand how individuals could accept social norms that justified the harming of others. He also wanted to know why oppressive regimes could survive and also attract popular support. During his clinical training he had seen how educated and caring people—health care practitioners—had the tendency to blame mentally ill patients for their own suffering. The just world hypothesis asserts that people have an intuitive belief in justice and that the world is fair. Seen from this perspective, people and groups get what they deserve. To put it simply: good people are rewarded and bad people are punished. If a particular community suffers, then this community is perceived as in some way having caused or provoked that suffering (see also Major et al. 2000).

The phenomenon of blaming the victim when reflecting on the causes of Jewish (and perhaps other groups') suffering before and during the Holocaust can be concretely illustrated by a question I pose after asking teachers and their students what they know about the Holocaust. Generally speaking, teachers and their students, at least those in Europe and North America, are somewhat familiar with the Holocaust (or *Shoah*). The number of six million Jews murdered does not come as a shock. But when I ask both history teachers and their students what percentage of the German population was Jewish in the early 1930s, their responses are almost always completely off target.

The study I mentioned earlier by Stuart Foster (2013) and his colleagues at the University of London confirms what I have found in dozens of countries. Foster comments on their study as follows:

> One question, for example, asked teachers what, in percentage terms, was the Jewish population in Germany in 1933. Teachers were offered 5 choices: more than 30%; approximately 15%; approximately 5%; less than 1%; not sure. Of note, the correct answer (i.e., less than 1%) was provided by a relatively small number of teachers in all subject areas. In fact, just under a third of history teachers answered correctly and less than one-in-five citizenship, English and religious education teachers provided an accurate response. Many teachers significantly overestimated the pre-war Jewish population in Germany, with 40% of citizenship teachers, for example, claiming that the answer was approximately 15% or more than 30% of the population… it is arguably very important that teachers and their students are aware of the very small numbers of Jews living in pre-war Germany. If teachers commonly over-estimate the size of the German Jewish population (in some cases by 15 or 30 times), then it might be that myths and stereotypes about their power, wealth and control are inappropriately and unwittingly reinforced. (p. 140)

A valid question here is *why* so many teachers and students overestimate the number of Jews living in Germany in 1933. The answer might be partly explained by the fact that most teachers and their students initially believe that it was primarily German Jews who were murdered. But I believe that another psychological mechanism plays a role, one that is largely subconscious, yet can have negative repercussions for minority groups. It also points to a challenge for educators when they attempt to explain the Nazis' persecution of the European Jews.

Given that individuals tend to seek the causes of persecution—at least to a certain extent—in the social characteristics or behavior of targeted groups, it is perhaps not surprising that public opinion in the United States towards Jews worsened in the late 1930s and 1940s. It is perhaps also not surprising that teachers and students today overestimate the number of Jews living in Germany in 1933. In both cases the reasoning goes something like this: If the Nazis hated the Jews so much and were willing to go to such lengths to persecute them, then the Jews must have done something to deserve or provoke this.

During my work in countries such as Lithuania and Hungary, people sometimes expressed this reasoning overtly when we were delving more deeply into this issue. When I posed the question about the number of Jews in Germany to 15 museum guides who were being trained to become guides for the traveling *Anne Frank in the World Exhibition* in Lithuania, I got responses between 30 and 70%. When I then gave the participants the correct percentage (under 1%) and asked *why* they thought the Jews, a small minority, had been targeted for persecution, they argued that the Jews had certainly provoked societal anger and envy because they were "so rich". When I asked them what evidence they had for this, the informal leader of the group reiterated that it was obvious because they were targeted for persecution. I then asked the group if they all agreed with this and their verbal and non-verbal behavior indicated that they did, though the group could sense that I was hoping for a different kind of response.

The phenomenon of vastly overestimating the size of oppressed minority groups can also be found today. For instance, Navarro and Arechavaleta (2010) conducted research in 2007–2008 among secondary school students in the Basque Country of Spain. The students were asked what percentage of the population of the Basque Country they thought were foreigners (viewed negatively by the majority of the population). While the actual percentage at the time was 4.6%, the estimates were generally much higher. More than 66% thought the percentage was over 13% of the population (this was the anchor the researchers used). More than 20% thought the percentage exceeded 25%. In 2012, the independent think tank British Future (2010) conducted a poll in the United Kingdom in which they asked respondents what percentage of their population they thought were refugees. The actual percentage is 0.4% but some 40% of those surveyed though it was more than 10%. Finally, in a comparative international study, the Transatlantic Trends Immigration survey (Topline Data 2011), respondents were asked the following question: "In your opinion, what percentage of the total (COUNTRY) population were born in another country?" While the foreign-born population in the United States at the time was approximately 13%, the mean estimate was 37.8%. The study found similar exaggerated estimates in the United Kingdom, Spain, France, Germany, and Italy (p. 54, question 28a).

The overestimates regarding the size of minority groups in society feed neatly into discourses that see such groups as a threat to tradition, nation, and culture. Throughout Europe, overtly nationalist and far-right groups, like Jobbik in Hungary, the English Defence League in the United Kingdom, and Golden Dawn in Greece, attempt to reinforce notions that minority groups such as the Roma (pejoratively known as gypsies) and immigrants are "flooding into the country", taking over the nation, and need to be stopped.

Social Conformity and Social Norms

Exaggerating the size and power of minority groups is not uncommon and can serve as a core rationale for attempts to "protect" the majority from the minority. Such exaggerations can also lead to justifications for denying minority groups certain rights. Individuals, as social beings, rarely arrive at their opinions about social groups in a social vacuum. When majority opinion holds that a persecuted group must have deserved its fate and can be blamed in some way for its suffering, social norms to accept such a definition of the situation can be strong. This tendency has also been referred to as social conformity.

Two classic social conformity experiments were conducted by Stanley Milgram (1965) and Solomon Asch (1955). Both arrived at very non-intuitive results. Few people predicted how strong normative pressure could be on the judgments of individuals. While Milgram looked at obedience to authority figures, Asch attempted to show that people did not fall in line "like sheep"; he looked at how a person's opinion is influenced by majority opinion. In the traditional Asch experiment, an unsuspecting subject is asked to make a fairly simple judgment about physical reality, like the length of a line. The subject is placed with a group of confederates who all disagree with the subject, although it is very clear that the subject's perception of the situation is correct. Contrary to what Asch had anticipated, instead of disagreeing with the others, the subjects in these experiments strongly tended to go along with the group consensus. Asked later why they did this, the subjects frequently pointed out that the others must have had a better view or had information the subject did not have. In an extensive review of social norms and social conformity, Cialdini and Trost (1998) summarise what happens to the kind of dramatic and unexpected conformity found in the Asch experiment and validated more recently. They say this conformity becomes "more understandable when one considers three powerful personal goals that conformity can serve". This kind of "shift toward a group consensus can allow an individual (1) to believe that he or she now sees things more accurately, (2) to gain the approval and acceptance of desirable others, (3) to avoid a self-conception as different, deviant or intransigent" (p. 168).

Individuals do differ in the extent to which they are influenced by others when forming an opinion about social issues. The concepts of field dependence and field independence have been used to distinguish the extent to which individuals are influenced by their outside impulses and the social environment when learning, forming opinions, etc. Wooldridge (1995) summarises the difference as follows: "field dependent individuals are interpersonally oriented and rely heavily on external stimuli. This motivates them to look toward others for reinforcement of opinions and attitudes" (p. 51).

To such observations, Cialdini and Trost (1998) add that the evidence collected over the past few decades has shown that conformity to majority opinion is more pronounced in collectivist societies than in individualistic ones. Because most research conducted on social conformity has taken place in North America (which is highly individualistic) and it demonstrates how powerful this psychological mechanism is in that particular context, we can expect the educational challenges to be even greater elsewhere.

In sum, individuals—to different degrees—will consciously and also subconsciously look for environmental cues when trying to form an opinion about ambiguous situations, but even in rather non-ambiguous situations such normative pressure is present. It is difficult to go against majority opinion, especially when the majority is respected. Following majority opinion brings a number of social rewards, such as praise, inclusion, and approval by others. It also prevents social punishment.

Conclusions and Discussion

In this chapter I have attempted to apply some insights from the fields of cognitive psychology and social psychology to learning about and learning through the Holocaust. It is my belief that these academic fields can shed some light on why some—both in the past and present—might not feel empathetic towards the Jewish (and perhaps other) victims of the Holocaust or communities persecuted more recently.

A key question we can ask ourselves is this: What are the implications of such insights from cognitive and social psychology for our teaching of students—mostly teens at an age when peer influence is quite strong? To address this question, I would like to finish by discussing two activities I have personally found to lead participants to a better understanding of the processes and mechanisms I have mentioned here. The first is relatively simple and already touched upon; the second is somewhat more complicated to implement.

As mentioned earlier, Foster's (2013) question can serve as a potentially effective and fairly simple activity—early in teaching about the Holocaust—to help young people understand how the process of blaming the victim functions and how the just world hypothesis can negatively impact our opinion of minorities. The question he asked was: "How many Jews do you think lived in Germany in 1933?" The teacher can first have students write down the question individually, to have a record and to avoid students being influenced by others; it can also be done in a plenary session. In my experience, students (and too often teachers) are very surprised by the correct answer. The obvious follow-up question is why they think this is the case. Most will most likely give rather vague answers.

But a confrontation with the actual percentage can provide just enough cognitive discomfort for students to want to know more. They will be motivated to resolve what has been referred to as a certain level of cognitive dissonance. This is the feeling of discomfort that results from holding two conflicting beliefs simultaneously. Individuals, the evidence points out, will be motivated to remove this discomfort (referred to as dissonance reduction) and restore equilibrium. The dissonance will manifest itself cognitively something like this: "Jews were innocent and there is no reason to persecute innocent people—but they were the victims of one of the most destructive campaigns of mass murder in history". This is a direct confrontation with people's sense that good things happen to good people—that there is a just world. This discovery in itself can be slightly unsettling for some youth.

A discussion of the processes of blaming the victim (without blaming the students for getting the percentage wrong), based on their own answers, can lead to learning about themselves and about human cognition. Mentioning that less than 1% of the German population was Jewish does something else that can have a motivational impact. This information is non-intuitive and providing non-intuitive information is more powerful as a learning tool than providing information that students expect to receive. Simmons and Nelson (2006) found that "intuitive biases are particularly pervasive, occurring even when all relevant information in the immediate decision context is processed and understood" (p. 423), but also that "decreasing confidence in the intuition will decrease, or even eliminate, such biases" (p. 426). I would argue further that an important first step is understanding that one's intuitions regarding why individuals and groups tend to face discrimination can be faulty. In a similar vein, according to Cialdini and Trost (1998), identifying the social norms of important referent people and one's willingness to comply with those expectations can be an important intervention tool.

Learning is always more effective when students are pulled slightly out of their comfort zone and are challenged to address their own biases, especially when the challenge is non-threatening to their self-esteem or social status. Other examples of non-intuitive information relating to the history of the Holocaust—for many youth—are that the Jews were not the only victims and that propaganda was directed at other groups as well, that Adolf Hitler was elected into power, that even some Nazis helped Jews, that the Jews were not passively led to the slaughter, that in many countries local populations led the killing campaigns, that antisemitism and persecution of the Jews is centuries old, and that many Jewish Germans had a strong Jewish identity and even fought for Germany in World War I.

A few years ago, at a seminar for the New Mexico Human Rights projects, facilitator Daena Giardella also went beyond the comfort zone of many participants. After I had done a relatively impersonal yet interactive activity that focused on the concepts of perpetrator, helper, bystander, and victim/target, Deana asked the participants to reflect on conflicts that they had experienced in their families when they were young, and the primary role they had played in those conflicts. She then asked the approximately 30 teachers to stand in one of four corners of the room.

They could choose between corners labeled "victim/target", "perpetrator", "helper", or "bystander". Though Deana focused on having people from the different corners enter into a discussion with each other—mostly about feelings—I was also interested to observe how those who saw themselves as perpetrators (a few were willing to admit this) or as bystanders perceived the situation and their siblings who had been victimised in some way. Though all my evidence was gathered unsystematically in the hallway and during lunch, it was telling. Several who admitted they had been perpetrators or bystanders mentioned that at the time they felt that the victim had in some way "deserved" the negative treatment he or she received (though they now had a different view). Those who had been bystanders also mentioned issues such as fear of reprisal, not wanting to get involved, not feeling responsible, and feeling helpless to intervene. The activity had a powerful impact and provoked rather emotional responses from some participants. Not all teachers will feel comfortable with such an activity.

Nevertheless, it is precisely activities like the two above that can generate the kind of reflection that can help students gain more insight into why we as human beings might blame the victim rather than empathise with the victim.

References

Allport, G. (1954). *The nature of prejudice*. Cambridge, MA: Perseus Books.

Annan, K. (2010, 17 June). The myth of "never again". *The New York Times*. http://www.nytimes.com/2010/06/18/opinion/18iht-edannan.html?_r=0

Aronson, E. (2000). *Nobody left to hate: Teaching compassion after Columbine*. New York: Henry Holt.

Asch, S. E. (1955). Opinions and social pressure. *Scientific American, 193*, 31–35.

British Future (2010). *Hopes and fears: The British future state of the nation report 2012*. http://www.britishfuture.org/publication/hopes-and-fears-the-british-future-state-of-the-nation-report-2012-2/

Cialdini, R., & Trost, M. (1998). Social norms, conformity and compliance. In D. T. Gilbert, S. T. Fiske, & G. Lindzey (Eds.), *Handbook of social psychology* (Vol. 2, pp. 151–192). New York: McGraw-Hill.

Foster, S. (2013). Teaching about the Holocaust in English schools: Challenges and possibilities. *Intercultural Education, 24*(1–2), 133–148.

Gross, Z., & Stevick, E. D. (2010). Holocaust education: International perspectives. Challenges, opportunities and research. *Prospects, 40*(1), 17–33.

Lerner, M. (1980). *The belief in a just world: A fundamental delusion*. New York: Plenum Press.

Major, B., Quinto, W. J., McCoy, S. K., & Schmader, T. (2000). Reducing prejudice: The target's perspective. In S. Oskamp (Ed.), *Reducing prejudice and discrimination* (pp. 211–237). Hillsdale: Lawrence Erlbaum.

Mazzenga, M. (2009). *American religious responses to Kristallnacht*. New York: Palgrave Macmillan.

Milgram, S. (1965). Some conditions of obedience and disobedience to authority. *Human Relations, 18*(1), 57–76.

Navarro, S. P., & Arechavaleta, B. O. L. (2010). Heuristic reasoning and beliefs on immigration: An approach to an intercultural education program. *Intercultural Education, 21*(4), 351–364.

Simmons, J. P., & Nelson, L. D. (2006). Intuitive confidence: Choosing between intuitive and non-intuitive alternatives. *Journal of Experimental Psychology, 135*(3), 409–428.

Stevick, E. D., & Michaels, D. L. (2013). Empirical and normative foundations of Holocaust education: Bringing research and advocacy into dialogue. *Intercultural Education, 24*(1–2), 1–19.

Topline Data (2011). *Transatlantic trends: Immigration.* http://trends.gmfus.org/files/2011/12/TTI2011_Topline_final1.pdf

USHMM [United States Holocaust Memorial Museum] (2013). *Kristallnacht: A nationwide pogrom, November 9–10, 1938.* http://www.ushmm.org/wlc/en/article.php?ModuleId=10005201

Wooldridge, B. (1995). Increasing the effectiveness of university/college instruction: Integrating the results of learning style research into course design and delivery. In R. R. Sims & S. J. Sims (Eds.), *The importance of learning styles: Understanding the implications for learning, course design and education* (pp. 49–67). Westport: Greenwood Press.

Part III
Reckoning with the Holocaust in Israel, Germany and Poland

Between Involuntary and Voluntary Memories: A Case Study of Holocaust Education in Israel

Zehavit Gross

The Personal, the Public and the Private in Israeli Holocaust Education and Commemoration

In December 2010, my family celebrated the Bat-Mitzva (lit. daughter of commandment; confirmation) of my daughter, Oriya. In Jewish tradition, when a girl reaches the age of 12, she is Bat-Mitzva, meaning that she is obliged to practice the Jewish commandments. The ceremony marks the entrance of a girl into the adult community. A special religious ceremony, a rite of passage, is held to allow her to declare publicly that she is now an adult. The role of the past is a fundamental constituent in the content of this ceremony, connecting the participant to her parents and ancestors. However, Oriya had two small requests regarding this ceremony: that I not mention the word *Shoa* (Holocaust) in my blessing to her, and that she not mention it in her address at the party. After long hesitation, I decided to comply with her request, but I was very upset about it. Because her grandfathers are both Holocaust survivors, I felt it would be not only inappropriate but impossible to talk about our family history without mentioning the Holocaust. We decided to be creative and say that her grandfathers experienced persecutions and oppression. In her eyes, this was a compromise, enabling us not to say the horrible word "Holocaust". Given the tragedy of the Jewish experience, I asked myself, how do we honour and keep faith with the past and with our ancestors without inflicting trauma on our children?

After a conversation with her, I understood that the gap between us was not merely semantic; it was basic. For her, the Holocaust is a historical event that she would like to ignore and delete from the family consciousness, an event like any other *pogrom*; for me, as the daughter of a Holocaust survivor, it is an experience I

Z. Gross (✉)
School of Education, Bar-Ilan University, Ramat-Gan, Israel
e-mail: grossz@mail.biu.ac.il

would like to analyse. What does it mean for me to be the mother of a Jewish adolescent, one who socialises her daughter into private and public Jewish history? In other words, what do I feel as I create this generational chain stretching from my father to my daughter? Is it a chain of despair or of hope?

For me, it was important to explain to the guests at the party about the impact of the Holocaust on my life. But my daughter told me that the minute I mention the word "Holocaust", nightmarish scenes pop into her mind, and she would have to deny it in order to survive and enjoy her party. What she taught me is that remembering is a kind of choice, though I had thought of it as an obligation. She helped me to distinguish between two forms of memories: voluntary memories and involuntary memories. Mace (2004) posits that voluntary memories are willed, intended, and searched for, whereas involuntary memories come to mind spontaneously, unintentionally, automatically, without effort (2008). While a voluntary memory is a conscious action, involuntary memories may be triggered by sensory cues (2008, p. 7). My daughter was afraid that one memory would lead to another and indeed, Mace (2008) asserts that involuntary memories appear to trigger other related involuntary memories, thus producing "memory chaining" (p. 7). Crucially, it is clear that what constitutes a voluntary memory for some can be an involuntary memory—even a traumatic one—for others.

The process of remembrance does not occur in a vacuum; it does not always have a pure motive, but can be instead a vehicle to reach instrumental goals. Following Linton (1986), I viewed memories as "precious fragments of the past which illuminate the future". However, my daughter taught me that sometimes we need to negotiate remembrance. Forgetting—what my daughter wanted to do—is a form of Holocaust denial. Denial may be too strong a word; perhaps I should use the word Holocaust repression. Still, denial does denote that an integral part of my daughter's initiation process as a third-generation of Holocaust survivors is her attempt to establish parameters for when it is appropriate to remember and when it is appropriate to ignore or avoid or repress. I struggled with her request, because to me, it felt like an attempt to deny, ignore, or erase. On the other hand my daughter can be perceived as a child who feels traumatised, and perhaps, with my power as author, I am accusing her of denial on top of it all. If memory is pervasive and all-consuming, it offers no relief from the nightmare. Her argument was that the ceremony is focused on her, which may have been appropriate to some extent. Not having to be confronted with the horrors of the Holocaust as a child is, perhaps, a reasonable request, which points the way to a balance in life as well. Yet, I thought that for her, this was a psychological defense mechanism (Conway 2005): she could accept the pogroms as voluntary memories, but the Holocaust was in her stage of development an involuntary memory—like a ghost that springs up and needs to be rejected if one is to survive.

Following this distinction, memory can be seen as a kind of covenant. According to terms offered by the eminent 20th-century rabbinical figure, Rabbi Joseph Soloveitchik, the involuntary memory is like a covenant of fate (*brit goral*), which brings out those moments of grief and persecution that unite the Jews as a nation by default: they share the same fate because they were chosen by God to fulfill a religious mission. Meanwhile, the voluntary memory is like a covenant of destiny (*brit yi'ud*): we construct our memories through a conscious process leading us to achieve our goals as a nation. From another perspective, we can say that involuntary memory is a living memory, whereas voluntary memory may, in many ways, be a dead memory, which we try to resurrect through articulation. We need to be able to move from the state of memory to the act of remembrance, through our ability to store and access information (Berntsen and Hall 2004). Though the expression "dead memory" is very strong and might be misleading and misinterpreted and might have connotations we do not wish to evoke, it denotes basically a passive mode as opposed to an active memory. On the other hand we can suggest an alternative terminology like self-sustaining memories and cultivated memories—those we have no choice but to recall, and those we deliberately sustain for a greater purpose such as to honour people and to have a culture of remembrance. This is not a semantic matter but rather an open-ended discussion in uncharted waters; it shows that this issue is very complicated and has far-reaching implications that lie beyond the scope of this chapter.

There is a debate among Holocaust researchers in Israel as to whether the Holocaust issue was silenced during the first years of the state. The *Zeitgeist* in that period was to ignore the personal experiences of the Holocaust survivors for the sake of constructing a coherent Zionist collective. The anonymous public memory of the Holocaust in those days was based on voluntary memories, whereas involuntary memory, which was personal and specific, was ignored. Human beings tend to perpetuate the voluntary memory and suppress the involuntary, which is more authentic and exposes the depth of personal suffering. Thus, we can say that in the period of voluntary memory, the state organised and institutionalised the memory through laws, institutions, monuments, and restitution agreements. Involuntary memory arose through the Eichmann trial, when witnesses spoke publicly, often for the first time, about their terrible experiences.

From the story of my daughter I learned several things. First, people hold a range of different attitudes to the Holocaust. Even those of us who honour the memory of the Holocaust find different conceptions of where and when it is appropriate to do so. Second, the issue of Holocaust concealment or Holocaust denial is much more complicated than was thought initially and cultivated/deliberate memories, which we can affirm at selected times and places and settings, can be very challenging, but as I discovered in this case study, the negotiation over when this is appropriate to invoke or not is an integral part of the educational process. The fact that my daughter perceives the Holocaust as an involuntary memory while I view it as a voluntary memory reveals a paradox. She sees deeper layers of suffering, to which I, having internalised the process and engaged in cold cognitive academic analysis, have become indifferent. This is my adaptive mechanism, which is due to my experience and age. While she is still caught in the memory stage, I have gone on to remembrance: simplifying history through analysis and articulation. This indicates that coping with a national trauma, and the transition from memory as a state of mind to remembrance (action), means starting the journey with the voluntary memory and only allowing the involuntary memory to arise when the public is able to handle it.

There is a connection between the processes that an individual undergoes in the private micro-sphere and the macro processes that a society at large experiences. In other words, the analysis that occurred as my daughter and I interacted over the question epitomises similar processes that Israeli society and Holocaust education in Israel have undergone. Since its inception Holocaust education in Israel has grappled with the issue of involuntary and voluntary memory. At the beginning, the involuntary memories were very strong and powerful. Then, gradually, through legislation and systematic educational processes, the voluntary memories were constructed, enabling a gradual transition from ontology to epistemology, as I will analyse below.

The Holocaust in Israeli Education

In Israeli high schools, 77% of students and 96% of teachers consider the Holocaust to be a basic constituent of their worldview (E. Cohen 2009). The term comes from the Greek *holokauston*, a translation of the Hebrew words *korbam olah,* and means a burnt sacrifice offered whole to God (Encyclopedia Britannica 2009). It refers to the systematic murder of six million Jews by the Nazis and their collaborators between 1941 and 1945. In addition to the word Holocaust, several other terms are used: destruction (*hurban* in Hebrew and Yiddish), *Shoah* (the Hebrew word for catastrophe), and genocide. The poet Uri Zvi Greenberg uses the word destruction; he views the Holocaust as part of a continuum of Jewish disasters. The use of the term *Shoah* emphasises the unique nature of the Holocaust. The use of the term genocide lumps the Holocaust together with other mass killings that fit its criteria, and thus makes it comparable to many other events.

Though the Holocaust is a central event in Jewish history, education about it is mandatory in Israel's state education system, and some research has investigated the impact of this education; still the field has not been conceptualised in a systematic way (Blatman 1995; Feldman 1995; Ofer 2004b; Schatzker 1982). In response, in this chapter I attempt to organise existing knowledge on the subject by conducting a meta-analysis of the foundations and basic premises of Holocaust education in Israel based on the major literature in the area. I begin by suggesting a conceptual framework, organising by period the changing attitudes toward the Holocaust in general and Holocaust education in particular. I then describe how Holocaust education has developed over the years, and finally, I analyse the major dilemmas and challenges facing Holocaust education.

Methodology

This article draws on two basic types of analysis. First, I conducted a literature review to elicit etic (theory-based) categories; I then reread the literature and elicited emic (internal) categories. Given the nature of the available literature, I mainly use etic categories in my analysis of the periods and dilemmas; in the other sections I use mainly emic categories. Both types of categories extended the scope of my scholarship and made it possible to navigate toward new horizons. Shapira (1997) posits that when events are fresh, it is difficult to conduct an accurate and comprehensive analysis, "not because of the lack of perspective but rather because of the richness of information we have" (p. 89).

Attitudes toward the Holocaust and Holocaust Education: Seeing Them Chronologically

Two main frameworks have been used to divide the literature on the Holocaust into periods. One sees it as part of a general period in Jewish history (Liebman and Don-Yehiya 1983; Dror 2002) and the other sees it as a period with distinct sub-divisions (Dror 1996; Porat 2004). I will divide the history of Holocaust education into more periods in order to provide a clearer analysis of this specific event, acknowledging its complexity. This is both a methodological decision and a conceptual historical consideration (see also Porat 2004), one that perceives the Holocaust as a unique event in Jewish history that should be investigated separately.

Most systems that divide Holocaust education into periods begin in 1948 with the establishment of the state of Israel (Firer 1989; Ofer 2004a, 2004b) to show how the state officially presents the Holocaust to subsequent generations through systematic socialisation processes in which voluntary memories are dominant. However, Dror (1996) posits that, in some of the Labor movement schools, Holocaust education began as early as 1943. In addressing the educational response to the Holocaust, he distinguishes two main periods. The first was from 1943 to 1948, when the *Yishuv* (the Jewish community in Mandatory Palestine) dealt with the Holocaust indirectly; this period was based mainly on involuntary memories, as the voluntary memories were avoided and denied. The second period began 20 years later, when conditions had ripened for writing curricula on the Holocaust (Dror 1996, p. 127); these were based mainly on voluntary memories. Dror divides the first period into three stages: the initial shock (from the end of 1942 until 1944), the lack of response (1945–1946), and the beginning of proportion in the educational response to the Holocaust (1947–1948).

Chaim Schatzker (1992, pp. 167–168) identifies three periods. The period of *demonisation and psychological repression* (by survivors who repressed the painful memories of the Holocaust) in the shadow of the Eichmann trial (1961) was dominated by emotional instruction. During the *instrumental* period (the 1970s and 1980s), the Holocaust was explained, through a universal interdisciplinary approach, as social behaviour. The *existential* period, in the 1990s, required people to identify directly with the Holocaust through media, art, testimonies of survivors, and visits to concentration camps. Whereas the two first stages (the demonisation and instrumental) were based mainly on involuntary memories, the third period (the existential) was based on voluntary memories. Involuntary memories were prominent in the demonisation period. They were like "the ghost" that everyone wanted to escape.

Voluntary memory became the *raison d'etre* of educational endeavours and had a visible manifestation through media, art, and survivors' testimonies.

Porat (2004) claims that "until 1954 Israeli students did not study the Holocaust at all" (p. 621). She analyses how the Holocaust shifted in the educational system, "from a marginal event better forgotten in the 1950s and 1960s to an event that from the late 1970s on defines Israelis' identity". She notes how, in light of *mamlachtyut* (statism) and in order to overcome the feeling of "national humiliation", the textbooks moved from concentrating on the Jewish revolt and heroism against the Nazis to a more realistic approach. In practical terms, we see a shift from enhancing involuntary memories to systematically enhancing voluntary memories. The core of the heroic message was based on concrete voluntary memories. The shift from involuntary to voluntary made the heroic stance more feasible. Firer (1989) identifies two periods in the way the Holocaust appeared in history textbooks: the period of shock (1945–1961) and the period of insight (1961–1988). Her focus is on the continuum between passivity and activity. In analysing attitudes toward the diaspora, she identifies a passive period, from 1900 to 1930, and a second period, from 1930 until the end of the 1940s, when textbooks emphasised Jewish political and military activism. Hence, in her analysis, Firer emphasises the juxtaposition between the "old Jew" of the diaspora, who was passive, servile, and humiliated in the host countries, and the "new Jew" in Israel who represented an activist-evolutionary approach and described the transition from the Holocaust to rebirth. Involuntary memories were the core of the passive period as they sprang up while people were being passive; the voluntary memories shaped the active period as the use and employment of active memories is, in essence, a conscious and a voluntary act.

The historiographies mentioned above revolve around various dichotomies, including active-passive, rejecting-accepting, marginal-central, and instrumental-existential. Though formulated by different scholars and different in content, they are similar in their structure. They are important for understanding the changing attitudes toward the Holocaust over the years and its impact on Holocaust education. One major landmark that most scholars use is 1961: the Eichmann trial. This was a turning point because it pushed people to discuss the Holocaust openly, though some time passed before it had an impact on Holocaust education. All these efforts to define periods reflect a diachronic description of historical changes from an Israeli socio-political perspective, but they need to be updated because they do not take into account changes affecting the field in the last 15 years.

Don-Yehiya (1993, p. 160) posits that "cultural values and concepts are shaped among other things by historical events, but these in turn, influence the interpretation and patterns of response to those events". Resnik (1999) notes that the attitude toward the Holocaust and Holocaust education was influenced by changing ideologies and national visions, from a socialist secular universalistic vision to a more Jewish particularistic approach. The change of ideologies and visions denotes a major change in perceptions that was accompanied by a change in the way memories were utilised. Hence, during those periods of transition, the concept of involuntary and voluntary memories is very valuable as it denotes the process through which the memory becomes institutionalised, from an involuntary abstract memory to a more structured memory that becomes a cultural asset. Shapira (1997, pp. 86–87) summarises this issue by saying that after the initial shock and silencing concerning the Holocaust, the main question is which historical event most intensified Holocaust consciousness. Was it the Eichmann trial, the eve of the Six-Day War that aroused collective anxiety about the annihilation of Israel, the 1973 war that exposed Israelis' vulnerability and weakness, or the Likud's coming to power in 1977? The latter is also considered a turning point: the secular socialist elite lost much of its power, leading to a fundamental change in the identity symbols of the state of Israel. In addition, Begin was the first Israeli leader to have experienced the Holocaust and include references to it in his rhetoric.

To this list should be added the two Gulf wars, which took place after Shapira wrote her book. They again intensified Holocaust consciousness as Israel was threatened with gas and chemical weapons that evoked memories of the gas chambers. In addition, for some segments of the Israeli population, each time Israel engaged in a peace process (the 1978 peace agreement with Egypt, the 1993 Oslo accords, and the 2005 disengagement plan), it did so in the context of a perceived threat to the state's existence, and hence that experience reminded many of the Holocaust (Gross 2006). Over the past few years (since 2005), Mahmoud Ahmadinejad's threats to destroy Israel, while denying the existence of the Holocaust, have also aroused Holocaust consciousness.

In addition to the need to update the descriptions of periods for educational purposes, there is a need for a broader and more abstract conceptualisation that will allow us to analyse the fundamental changes that Holocaust education has undergone as scholarship, from the point of view of knowledge processing and knowledge acquisition, and the mental processes that preceded each period of rising consciousness about the Holocaust. Hence, I would like to suggest another typology in which the main axis of discussion is ontological vs. epistemological. As I describe below, I believe it has potential educational value and can perhaps be replicated in other educational settings around the world.

Analysing Knowledge

One of the basic questions in the literature on knowledge is how we know what we know. There are two basic ways to analyse knowledge-based systems: ontology and epistemology. Ontology involves efforts to understand the nature of being or existence: What is the nature of reality? It addresses questions like what entities exist and what are their characteristics. That is, what are the contents and structure of reality? It also considers the kind of knowledge available to us (subjective or objective). Epistemology deals with questions of what knowledge is, what counts as knowledge, the sources of knowledge, the different kinds of knowledge, and what we can know about things: the borders and boundaries of knowledge (Wiersma and Jurs 2009).

When we apply the ontological-epistemological axes, we discover four distinct stages in the attitudes toward the Holocaust and Holocaust education. On the initial, ontological level, are questions of structure and content: What was the Holocaust? What were its characteristics? This level can be divided into stages of public denial and public acknowledgement. The next level, epistemological, addresses knowledge about the Holocaust: What counts as knowledge of the Holocaust? What kind of knowledge is available to us, and what are the boundaries of this knowledge? This level can also be divided into two stages: constructing knowledge, and then deconstructing it, by revisiting the Holocaust and performing a critical analysis. From the beginning, Holocaust education has grappled with both ontology and epistemology. In the following pages, I describe these four stages, two at each level.

The Ontological Level

Public Rejection: 1943–1961

The Holocaust played a substantial role in the public debate triggered by the German restitution payments, the Kastner affair, and the Kapo trials, but the *Yishuv* and later the Israeli public initially ignored the Holocaust. Denial occurred in two modes: (1) actual silence, an inability to convey anything concerning this issue, and (2) a selective attitude that referred only to the heroic aspects of the Holocaust. The brave *sabra* (a Hebrew nickname for the Israeli-born) who had just established a sovereign state, who served in the army and was willing to sacrifice his life for the state, was unwilling to relate to survivors of the Holocaust who came to Israel from the displaced persons camps in Europe. The passive victims of the Holocaust were viewed as having gone to the gas chambers like "lambs to the slaughter" (e.g., Shapira 1997, p. 97). This was considered shameful and contrary to the *zeitgeist* of the period, a climate enhanced by Ben-Gurion's vision of a new Jew who is secular and takes his fate into his own hands. Hence, Holocaust survivors were ignored. Only the partisans and those active in the Warsaw ghetto uprising were considered heroes. On the other hand, those who survived the camps were unable to talk about their trauma; thus they remained invisible and anonymous. In this period, commemoration ceremonies were private and held only by those who were directly connected to the Holocaust.

Don-Yehiya (1993) claims that Ben-Gurion's attempt to construct the new Jew stemmed from his conception of *mamlachtiyut* (statism), which incorporated Holocaust denial and negated the reality of exile. According to this conception, the Holocaust was proof that Israel was the only place where Jews could materialise their national aspirations. Unlike the passive exilic Jew and the Holocaust Jew who went like a lamb to the slaughter, the new Jew takes his fate into his hands and resists his enemies. Hence, for instance, Ben-Gurion never mentioned the Holocaust in his public addresses.

In contrast, following Medding's (1989) definition of statism, Shapira (1997) claims that *mamlachtiyut* did not refer to the cultural aspect of the state but rather to the procedural relationships between the individual and the government system: the citizen and the state. She and Dror (2001) believe that Ben-Gurion had to cope with many pressing security and governmental issues after the state was established, and thus he had no time to deal with Holocaust remembrance. Dror (1996, 2001) also added a psychological explanation: in order to cope emotionally with the stories of the Holocaust, the *Yishuv* initially needed to use the basic defense mechanisms of denial and repression. In their view, these historical events and psychological problems were directly reflected in the school curriculum.

In the first years after the state of Israel was established, textbooks tended to over-emphasise the armed resistance against the Nazis (see Altshuler 1987; Avidor and Spivak 1958; Riger 1958), exaggerating its actual role in the Holocaust (Dror 1996; Firer 1989; Porat 2004; Shapira 1997). Having examined Israeli textbooks, Firer (1987) defines the early period as the Zionist stage: materials were emotional and ideologically biased. These textbooks were mainly based on diaries written by survivors, such as Abraham Sotzkover's diary, published in Yiddish and describing life in the Vilna ghetto, and books by Chaim Yalin and Dimitri Gelpern on the partisans in the Kovno ghetto (Firer 1987). These texts were also used by youth movement counselors (see Dror 1996; Shapira 1997) and helped people to overcome the national "humiliation" caused by the Holocaust.

In the public sphere, the attitude of the government was similar. Don-Yehiya (2000) reports that Prime Minister David Ben-Gurion opposed the establishment of a Holocaust memorial day and referred to the survivors as the "dust of human beings". However, in March 1950, the Israeli Knesset decided to establish an annual day of commemoration: Holocaust Day. In 1953, Yad Vashem (literally, "a memorial and a name") was established as the world centre for documentation, research, education, and commemoration of the Holocaust. Stauber (2007) found that during the 1950s, Ben-Gurion did not participate in the commemoration events organised by Yad Vashem and did not send messages to the commemoration ceremonies. Despite Ben-Gurion's attitude, since 1959, a minute of silence has been observed on Holocaust Day, and all restaurants and places of entertainment are closed. These official acts represented a first step toward recognition, though emphasis was still on the heroic aspect, with which the public could identify more easily. This may partly explain Ben-Gurion's approval, in 1957, of the plan to capture Adolf Eichmann, and the decision to bring him to trial in Israel.

Public Recognition: 1961–1980

Public acknowledgment and recognition that the Holocaust actually happened, and that it had a tragic and humiliating facet, came during the Eichmann trial in 1961. The trial was broadcast live on Israeli radio; the country did not yet have television. When Israelis heard the first testimonies of survivors, they began to acknowledge the information and a new trend evolved of wanting to hear the testimonies. As they listened, they gradually developed solidarity with and compassion toward the survivors, and appreciated their personal achievements. Once the survivors were publicly legitimised, they became more willing to share their suffering and bitter experiences publicly.

During this period, ceremonies were organised around specific texts, including poems and songs by well-known poets, which Yad Vashem published in memory of the victims of the Holocaust. The general form of the ceremony was preserved from year to year; it was very formal and some found it cold (Balf 1998, p. 58). The focus was on the national aspect: constructing the collective memory of the Jewish nation, emphasising the impact of the Holocaust on the establishment of the state, and still glorifying the Warsaw ghetto and the activity of the partisans. People also needed tangible artifacts; they sought a place where they could "put a flower or a stone" (Ofer 2004a, p. 402). Community cemeteries were established on kibbutzim, monuments and statues were erected in public gardens, and remembrance halls and walls were constructed (Keren 2008).

Yad Vashem, which was charged by law with commemorating the Holocaust, saw its main purpose as fully documenting the factual aspects of the Holocaust through documents and personal testimonies. One way to transmit historical facts is to visualise them and thus enable the public to touch them as a way to understand them. Thus, the museum tried to document the horror through visualisation and concentrated mainly on aspects that were expected to cause emotional turmoil, thus increasing the "traumatising" aspect of the Holocaust. The fact that Holocaust survivors were still alive and able to provide authentic testimonies to the horror intensified this aspect. Though a museum is an educational site, it is unusual for a museum to take the lead in a national educational process (Keren 1998). In this case, through the museum's activities, the state took responsibility for informal education in order to commemorate an event that was inconceivable and beyond imagination, because the formal educational system was not prepared to do so in terms of either content or methodology.

Another phase in the stage of recognition was reflected in the trips to Poland by high school students, at first mostly kibbutz youth. These trips, which represent a quest to understand the Holocaust, began immediately after the Eichmann trial, and were interrupted in the period when Israelis were denied entry to Poland. They began again in 1987, and intensified in the 1990s when the Ministry of Education strongly endorsed them. They culminate in the annual "march of the living", when adolescents from Israel and the Diaspora march together from the death camp Birkenau to the main Auschwitz complex.

Boaz Cohen (1999) refers to the 1970s as the period when the Holocaust became an academic subject, beginning under the influence of the Eichmann trial. What was unique in this period was the extension of Holocaust education and the involvement of researchers who were not Holocaust survivors. Holocaust education became mandatory under a law enacted in 1963, though the changing attitude toward the Holocaust in Israeli society affected the way Holocaust education was constructed; to this day, it continues to be modified.

From the time the state of Israel was established until the 1970s, students acquired most of their information about the Holocaust through memorial ceremonies and symbols rather than instruction (Schatzker 1982, pp. 76–77). These ceremonies were loaded with phrases and clichés that aroused identification with the traumatic experience. They were "neither systematic nor coherent, and completely divorced from any historical context" (Ofer 2004a, p. 407). Their focus was mainly emotional: "to make the unthinkable events of the Holocaust emotionally accessible to students" (Ben-Peretz 2003, p. 195).

The Eichmann trial revealed the need to include the Holocaust in high school history books. Porat (2004) points out that the trial brought the Holocaust to the centre of public attention and "invigorated the handful of voices that called to enhance Holocaust memory in Israel", but "none of the textbooks published 10 years after the trial had changed" (p. 624). This shows that educational changes need time to ripen. Porat notes that in the period between 1967 and 1977, which included the 1967 and 1973 wars, the Holocaust became one event among many others in the history curriculum (p. 630).

Initially, the main problem in understanding the Holocaust was the lack of basic information on the scope of the incomprehensible events that occurred in that period. Yablonka (1997) asserts that in the early years, no one knew anything. Then came the personal testimonies of survivors, but people could not believe that such monstrous things had actually happened. As Yablonka puts it, "in a situation where information on the Holocaust was in many cases biased, it was difficult to construct a systematic and credible picture and impossible to deal with the issue in a rational and 'objective' manner. This created a tendency toward a stereotyped mode of thought about the Jewish experience of the Holocaust" (1997, p. 121). Later, other forms of documentation were provided, making it possible to assess and understand what actually happened by acknowledging the existence of diverse voices. This was crucial to developing this field of research (Yablonka 1997).

The major change came after the Likud came to power in 1977 (Kimmerling 2004; Porat 2004), bringing about a cultural change in the perception and the symbols of identity, from secular to more traditional-religious symbols in which the Holocaust played a major role.

Construction: 1980–2000

Schatzker (1982) criticised the absence of any systematic conceptual framework of historical knowledge, especially the lack of a historical context for the Holocaust and its detachment from its universal meaning. He said that the process of mythologising the Holocaust had constructed a traumatised Jewish identity, and left students anxious and unable to cope with the Holocaust and its consequences within a historical context. As a result, they demonised the perpetrators and did not know how to cope with the victims. Moreover, the teaching could be irrational. Hence, he recommended that Israeli teachers set regular educational goals for the Holocaust, basing the study on knowledge, information, and historical analysis from both a synchronic and diachronic point of view, and ignoring some of the synergetic effects of historical circumstances.

In 1980, the Knesset amended the State Education Law to include as one of its goals "awareness of the memory of the Holocaust and the heroes". In addition, the Ministry of Education decided that the Holocaust would be a topic on the high school matriculation examination in history (Segev 2000), and Holocaust education was included in the literature curriculum. Classes in history would introduce students to the Holocaust cognitively, and by studying it through literature they could address it emotionally.

In the two decades after 1980, Holocaust education became a separate, compulsory subject. Once a very emotional topic, it began to be taught and analysed more rationally. In their 1983 textbook, *The Holocaust and its Significance*, Gutman and Schatzker (1984) analysed the Holocaust as a unique chapter in Jewish and world history. The book exposed students to more documents, gave a richer and more balanced picture of Jewish resistance, and emphasised the spiritual revolt, the struggle to preserve human dignity; meanwhile it reduced the emphasis on armed resistance, and included the complications of and obstacles to the revolt. Nevertheless, the first edition was criticised severely, especially by Firer (1983) and Keren (1984). They based their criticism on the knowledge that had been accumulated in the field of Holocaust education, a perspective developed in this period that includes both criticism and the historical circumstances, especially the anxiety about the existence of the state of Israel on the eve of the Six-Day War and during the 1973 War. The second edition, published in 1987, attempted to cope with this criticism, for example by adding a chapter on the issue of the *Yudenrat*, which most books had ignored (Shapira 1997). The *Yudenrat* was a Jewish council appointed by the Nazis. Its members served as mediators between the German authorities and the Jewish communities in the German occupied territories and played an important role in the Jews' daily lives.

Research on the Holocaust and Holocaust education involved a process of redefining the terms heroism and survival (Ofer 2004a, p. 400). The stories and testimonies of ordinary Jews—not national heroes but rather the simple persons who struggled to preserve human dignity and survived—became more legitimised. In 1989, Yad Vashem initiated a project called *Lekol ish yesh shem* ("Each person has a name"), in which people read aloud the names of family members who died in the Holocaust and lit candles in their memory. Yad Vashem also created a special area where the many memorial candles represented the different stories. This was a change from the earlier ceremonies, during which six large torches were lit to denote the six million Jews killed. Families and individuals produced films based on testimonies of family members who were Holocaust survivors, and the film director Steven Spielberg initiated a project documenting the stories of individuals.

Another change involved the culture of the Holocaust, which had been seen as an experience of European Jewry. The early ceremonies had a very Ashkenazi European nature that often excluded the Mizrahi cultural heritage and thus did not appeal to Sephardic Jews—those from Arab and Asian countries. As a result, Holocaust education raised ethnic tensions (Porat 2004). In response, in the second edition of their book, Gutman and Schatzker added a new chapter addressing the final solution for "the entire Jewish people"; it explicitly stated that the Nazis applied the final solution to all Jews: assimilated, religious, and secular, men and women, Ashkenazi and Sephardic. Porat (2004) claims that the new edition gave greater prominence to the systematic killing of Oriental Jews (beyond their actual proportions) in order to make Sephardic Jewry part of this collective memory. At the same time, a new trend in ceremonies also related to the persecution of North African Jews in Morocco and Tunis, and commemorating the Sephardic Jews who were sent to concentration camps, such as those from Thessaloniki. Indeed, one researcher (Farago 1989) found that Sephardic students identified more with the Holocaust than they had previously. Twenty years later, Erik Cohen (2009) confirmed this, finding no difference between Ashkenazi and Sephardic students in their relatively high levels of identification with the Holocaust.

In the 1990s, in what is known as post-Zionist criticism, some scholars began to condemn the cynical political use of the Holocaust by the Zionist movement, which viewed the Holocaust as justifying the expulsion of the Arabs from Palestine (Segev 2000; Zertal 2002). They also noted that the *Yishuv*—the Jewish community in Palestine—had not done enough to rescue the Jews from the concentration camps.

Deconstruction: 2000–Present

The emphasis on the individual Jew's feelings and memories was the basis for constructing a new agenda in Holocaust education. In 1999, two new textbooks were introduced, written by Yisrael Gutman (1999) and Nili Keren (1999). These texts emphasised the importance of combining individual memory and thorough historical knowledge. The books analysed the Holocaust from the personal perspective of individual Jews alongside a description of the genocide the Nazis committed against others, including Poles and Roma people. Ofer (2004a) views these two books as landmarks in Holocaust education, especially because they locate the Holocaust within both Jewish and universal modern history. "The two books considered the role of the Holocaust in the self understanding of Israelis, but in addition stressed the importance of knowledge and a critical reading of memoires and documents" (Ofer 2004a, p. 409).

Using the enquiry-based approach to develop students' analytical capacity, these books gave students both primary and secondary historical sources and asked them to interpret them and create their own narratives. According to Porat (2004, p. 628), this meant that "no consistent account of the Holocaust would be communicated to students and that one could not formulate a single authoritative Holocaust account among all the students".

Following the public criticism and development of the post-Zionist discourse (Michman 1997), Danny Ya'akobi (1999) published a new history textbook entitled *A World of Changes*. Because it de-emphasised the Holocaust, Zionism, and the state of Israel, it aroused a huge public debate and was the subject of a discussion in the Knesset. The textbook was rejected "because it didn't draw the appropriate historical lessons from the Holocaust" (Porat 2004, p. 619). In addition, in the spirit of the critical tradition, an academic controversy developed in the journal *Alpayim* over the subversive meanings in Holocaust research (Don-Yehiya 2000; Grodzinsky 2000; Shapira 1999). For example, Grodzinsky (2000) addressed what he calls "the cosmetics of the Holocaust" and thus exposed the tacit narratives behind the well-known official narrative of the Holocaust. This kind of public discussion suited the critical *Zeitgeist*.

At the same time, Holocaust survivors began to criticise the commemoration process. Students began to reflect on and criticise the trips to Poland and the over-politicisation of the Holocaust and its occasional use for nationalistic rightist political ends (Segev 2000; Shapira 1990, 1999). This public criticism led to the development of alternative ceremonies that related to other minorities persecuted in the Holocaust (e.g., the Roma) and to other genocides. It also raised criticism of a civic nature about discrimination against minorities in Israel, and concentrated on the lessons one should draw from the Holocaust. These ceremonies criticised the institutional commemoration ceremonies that emphasised the symbols of the Holocaust and its general context (the Nazi and Fascist regimes), instead of concentrating on the meaning of atrocity and hatred, and where they might lead. The alternative ceremonies highlighted the notion that if the Holocaust happened once, it could happen again. Everyone could then find himself in one of the following roles: perpetrator, collaborator, victim, rescuer, or bystander. Leftist groups also tried to connect the Holocaust with the Israeli-Palestinian conflict, but many agreed that this kind of connection did more harm than good because the Holocaust was a unique event, not comparable to events in the Middle East. However, as the peace process in the Middle East advanced, it has resulted in an emphasis on more humanistic and democratic values in Holocaust education, rather than militant messages, in order to change the educational message towards peace education (Dror 2001, 2002; Porat 2004).

At this stage, the contents of the official ceremonies also changed. Alongside the traditional texts were new texts of a more universalistic-civic nature that concentrated on human rights and on abolishing racism and discrimination. This change reflects what Shapira (1997) describes as an attitude toward the memory of the Holocaust that strives to present the Holocaust as the anti-narrative of the state. This attitude attempts to remove the state's right to represent the Jewish nation and the survivors; instead it represents the Holocaust as the source of an alternative identity not connected to territory, whose realm is the memory of the exilic Jew, a transnational who is connected to global rather than national citizenship (Shapira 1997, pp. 101–102). Eyal Naveh (2009) published a new book entitled *Totalitarianism and Holocaust*, which also attempts to make the educational message more universalistic, and will become part of the 11th grade curriculum. He believes that to make the educational message more universal and to achieve a better understanding of the Holocaust, that message should be located within the literature on totalitarianism and on attitudes towards minorities. In his opinion, this will provide a balance between the emotional and cognitive aspects involved in teaching this subject.

Recently, Erik Cohen (2009) wrote that Holocaust education is a stable element in the state education curriculum. The topic is considered to be inspiring and teachers reported fewer discipline problems than during other lessons. In addition, Cohen says, high school pupils consider the school to be the most meaningful agent for exposing them to information on the Holocaust, more than youth movements or their families. Very few teachers use lectures in their lessons on the topic: 66% use diverse teaching methods. Among the 307 principals that Cohen surveyed, 83% stated that they were satisfied with the quality of teaching.

Most schools hold extracurricular activities related to the topic, especially around Holocaust Day. For many years, the educational system was deeply committed to transmitting the heritage of the Holocaust to the next generation, to ensure that the memory of it would not disappear after the survivors died, but educators were concerned about the potential emotional damage to adolescents exposed to stories of such traumatic events. Despite this fear, Cohen (2009) found that 95% of students participated in ceremonies and 82% saw shows and visited commemoration sites. Teachers and students still see the trips to Poland as the best educational intervention for fostering Holocaust remembrance and Jewish identity, in spite of criticism of them (Feldman 1995; Romi and Lev 2007).

From the Ontological Level to the Epistemological

It should be noted that the stages I have delineated above are not pure; some developments proceeded more quickly in some places, like kibbutz schools, than in other segments of Israeli society. The general transition, however, was from the national to the personal, from the particularistic to the universalistic, and from the solely Jewish aspect to the more civic, Israeli point of view. Ceremonies relate to the subjective rather than the objective perspective in order to make learning more meaningful. Whereas the core of the ontological level was the involuntary memories that "sprang up" and came back and forth, denied or recognised, the epistemological level was characterised mainly by the systematic employment of voluntary memories, which were the core of the construction and deconstruction stages.

The ontological level concentrated mainly on the past while the epistemological dealt with the present and the future. The constructive stage concentrated mainly on the particularistic Jewish present while the deconstructive stage concentrated on a universalist civic message and its connotations for the future. There is no longer just one way to relate to the Holocaust: there is a flow from the collective to the individual, the emotional to the cognitive, the particularistic to the universalistic, the Jewish to the civic—and sometimes these intermingle. As it addresses the Holocaust, each group in Israeli society can reflect on the dilemmas and values of its own subculture. The general trend also reflects the changing ideologies and circumstances of Israeli society: from war to small, gradual steps toward a peace process with its enemies.

During the ontological stages, the Holocaust was a unifying and integrating factor that strengthened social cohesion and solidarity, but during the epistemological stages, it became more of a dividing factor, one that intensifies the cleavages between the diverse sectors and subcultures in Israeli society. Each sector constructs and deconstructs the Holocaust as an ideological concept while enlisting it to serve its specific needs.

Foucault (1981) believes that knowledge is connected to power, and therefore that different forms of power produce different kinds of knowledge. He asserts that governing implies structuring the knowledge that affects action. Following Foucault, Resnik (1999) posits that different ideologies and national images (e.g., "a nation with a right to a state", "a state for a persecuted people") influenced the way people understood the Holocaust. As people constructed personal dimensions and personal meanings, each person could draw an individual lesson from the narrative of the Holocaust. This is also connected to the development of different patterns of commemoration—the move toward the personal and individual narrative in commemoration ceremonies. Students who visited Poland shaped the commemoration using new texts and poems they wrote and journals they kept during the trip. Some debated whether the trip should only be experiential, focusing on the emotional level, or should also achieve cognitive goals (Romi and Lev 2007). In a postmodern world, pupils search for meaning and can acquire it through the journey to Poland, which strengthens their sense of belonging to the Jewish nation.

Beyond its conceptual and heuristic value, the effort to create ontological and epistemological periods has educational value. It enables us to trace the linear process of knowledge development that created Holocaust consciousness, from the actual experience of the Holocaust to the stage of constructing, deconstructing, and reflecting; thus, it hints at the potential relationship between knowledge and attitude. Moreover, it may reflect the stages of awareness of a national trauma, but this idea deserves further elaboration.

In the initial epistemological stage, students were mainly exposed to study materials provided by teachers, which helped them construct knowledge. In the stage of deconstruction, students were more able to access knowledge and to compare and contrast facts, thanks to intensified processes of globalisation and advanced technologies, especially the Internet. This made it possible to deconstruct premises and former assumptions in a nonlinear way, and to construct and deconstruct new premises in a sequential way. At the same time, the Holocaust moved from a marginal place to a more central one in Israeli consciousness (Auron 1993; E. Cohen 2009; Herman 1977; Ofer 2004a). Before turning to the goals of Holocaust education, it is important to consider the Holocaust as a component in Jewish identity.

The Holocaust and Jewish Identity

Levy et al. (2004) posit three main components that determine an ethnic group's identity: national-historical, religious-cultural, and biological (p. 274). The Holocaust is perceived as one of the most important components contributing to

Israelis' feelings of being part of the Jewish people. Indeed, some researchers have found that the Holocaust was the major component of Jewish identity (Farago 1989; Gross 2000; Herman 1977; Levy et al. 1993).

Liebman and Don-Yehiya (1983) view the Holocaust as the main component of civic religion in Israel. For the religious population in Israel, the Holocaust is indeed the most important component in the construction of Jewish identity. It strengthens the connections between the state of Israel, the Jewish nation, and Jewish tradition, as the victims were killed because they were Jewish.

The current identification of the Holocaust as an important historical event indicates that more importance is attributed to it even compared to events like the establishment of the state of Israel (Auron 1993; Herman 1977). Farago (1989) noted that in 1985, the Holocaust was the first event that Israeli youth mentioned spontaneously as an influence on their Jewish identity. Among traditional and secular Jews, the Holocaust ranked second, after the Zionist-Israeli component, as the most influential component in their Jewish identity, whereas among the first generation of Ashkenazi Israelis, the Holocaust ranked as high as the Israeli experience (Levy et al. 2004). Herman (1977) found a similar pattern: when youth were asked to indicate what historical event influenced them the most, the majority mentioned the establishment of Israel together with the Holocaust. Among those in the Diaspora, the Holocaust remains the major factor in Jewish identity (Herman 1977; Levy et al. 2004). Recent surveys show that a majority of Israeli students rate the Holocaust as the most influential historical event—even more than the establishment of the state—and identify with the victims (E. Cohen 2009; Farago 2007).

Dilemmas Accompanying Holocaust Education

In constructing a special ceremony for a Jewish rite of passage, one usually asks how he or she is connected to the Jewish chain. The process involves what Kahane (1968) calls four major identity dilemmas, all of them connected directly to the Holocaust in general and to Holocaust education more specifically. They are (1) particularism versus universalism; (2) selectivity versus a holistic approach to Jewish history; (3) a religious versus a secular interpretation; and (4) the centrality of the state of Israel versus that of the diaspora. These are also the four main dilemmas in the literature on Holocaust education.

Particularism versus Universalism

A prominent theme in research about Holocaust education is the extent to which it is represented or interpreted as a particularistic Jewish event, rather than being seen as universal. In open interviews, Boaz Cohen (2009) found this to be one of the most controversial issues among teachers and principals. Most research presents it as a polarised issue, "either tempting us to regard the Holocaust as no more than the worst pogrom in Jewish history, or to declare it unique in human history because it is unique in Jewish history" (Clendinnen 1999, p. 11).

Schatzker (1992) posits that the universalistic approach is dangerous because of the "danger that the Holocaust will lose its unique significance instead of making students sensitive to the abnormalities of the Holocaust" (p. 169). However, he and others opposed efforts to present the Holocaust as a uniquely Jewish event; they claimed that the Holocaust can be understood only if the Jewish and the universal context complement each other (Ofer 2004b; Schatzker 1992). Schweber (2003a) rejects the "binary posed by this debate" and locates herself "along its contested continuum". Within this school of thought, "all historical events are both unique and universal: unique in the constellations of events that produce, perpetuate, and constitute them, and yet universal in their implications, or at least potentially so" (p. 203). Clendinnen rejects the unique stance, as "the only possible and proper stance for the observer is one of awed incomprehension" (1999, p. 21). Keren (1999), in her history of the Holocaust, describes the genocide committed by the Nazis against other nations as well as the mass murder of Poles during the Nazi occupation of Poland.

Auron (2003) and Naveh (2009) perceive the Holocaust as an example of genocide. Auron does not view it as an integral part of the history of antisemitism. Indeed, he criticises the trips to Poland that emphasise the Zionist aspect of the Holocaust and ignore or marginalise its moral and humanistic message. This approach denies that the history of antisemitism is "a key explanatory framework for understanding the Holocaust", as the historical understanding cannot be achieved without what Ben-Peretz called basic "knowledge about the historical context" (2003, p. 195). It is important to teach about the historical context of the Holocaust, but what is this context? Is it the history of antisemitism or is it the context of totalitarianism and the persecution of minorities? Do the lessons of the Holocaust justify fostering democracy in Israel or discussing the importance of democracy to the individual?

Selectivity versus a Holistic Approach to Jewish History

Several questions arise in this context. When does Jewish history begin—in lessons about the Holocaust? Do teachers start in the biblical period, or in the period when Jews first faced discrimination, or only with the Nazi regime? Can teachers omit the history of antisemitism as one of the major causes of the Holocaust? Presenting only the Holocaust itself and the establishment of the state of Israel limits Jewish history to a very short period.

Religious versus Secular

The attempt to build a national subjectivity after the Holocaust has two conflicting facets: the Jewish and the Zionist. Some see these two narratives as polarised. National unity in Israel is based on religious values. Are we Israelis or are we Jews? Will Holocaust ceremonies revolve around religious traditional texts like *kadish* (a prayer for the dead offered during Jewish prayer services and commemoration ceremonies), *yizkor* ("he shall remember", a prayer in commemoration of the dead) and psalms, or be based on secular texts and poems? What will be the proportion? What will be the emphasis? The Holocaust is a mediator and connector between Israeli and Jewish existentiality. If the educational system emphasises the Israeli aspects, it strengthens the secular-civic aspects. If it emphasises the nation's Jewishness, it strengthens the religious aspects.

Israel versus the Diaspora

Once the Jewish state was established, Zionist ideology expected that all Jews would immigrate to Israel (Resnik 1999, p. 494) but that did not happen. Therefore, what is the context, if any, in which schools in Israel have to educate students to feel solidarity with the Jewish people as a whole? Can teachers expect students to identify with Jews from the diaspora who do not live in Israel as part of the lesson of the Holocaust and perhaps as a direct consequence of the Holocaust? Resnik (1999) asserts that one of the educational-ideological messages of the Holocaust is that "only a Jewish state can ensure a Jew's physical existence" (p. 501). Moreover, the Holocaust has become "the core of the new national image" (Resnik 1999, p. 501). Thus, affiliation with the state of Israel is perceived as obligatory for Jews. As a result, some Israeli teachers tend to denigrate diaspora Jewish history in general (Ofer 2004a), especially those secular teachers who view parts of diaspora Jewish history as humiliating. Many of their students hold negative stereotypes of the exilic Jew because Jewish life in exile is perceived as an everlasting cycle of pogroms. The diaspora Jew is viewed as passive, the opposite of the "new Jew" created when the state of Israel was established. It is difficult for adolescents raised in a sovereign state with a sophisticated army to identify with diaspora Jewry. In this context, several questions arise: Are the Jews of the diaspora part of the Israeli national collective? And which is in the centre: the state of Israel or the Jewish nation that is spread throughout the diaspora?

In addition to the dilemmas that face Holocaust education as a whole, some unique methodological challenges face educators.

Major Educational and Methodological Challenges

The literature describes several challenges concerning Holocaust education. Here I briefly review four of them.

Emotional Identification with the Victims

Some researchers have compared the value of instruction based on emotion and on cognition. Romi and Lev (2007) found that employing cognitive knowledge within the educational process was effective mainly in the short run. Emotional impact was the most influential, but again mainly effective in the short run. Schatzker (1982) suggests three modes of Holocaust education: commemorative; instructional, using sacral-ritualistic teaching methods; and existential, forging connections with the existential dilemmas posed by horrifying conditions and attempting to identify with the traumatic experience of the survivors. He prefers the third, as it seems more meaningful in the long run and has the capacity to intensify the depth and breadth of students' learning. However, Ben-Peretz (2003) claims that "identifying emotionally with the suffering cannot be considered a sufficient outcome of teaching the Holocaust if it does not lead to total active rejection of all kinds of racism and discrimination" (p. 195).

Mimetic versus Transformative Learning

Another distinction is between mimetic and transformative learning. Jackson (1986) argues that mimetic learning is associated with informational instruction—the transmission of knowledge— while transformative learning is mainly associated with character development and moral education. Holocaust education should cause students to "change their attitudes, reactions and personality and be better prepared to face the future" (Schatzker 1982, p. 80). That is, instruction should be transformative. However, Ben-Peretz (2003) says most instruction is mimetic; most instruction is structured and students are provided with little "space to raise their own questions, to search for diverse sources of knowledge, and to create and share with others their constructed understanding" (p. 191). She believes that teaching about the Holocaust is seen as an end rather than as an instrument for education (p. 196). She criticises the use of vicarious learning in Holocaust education, and raises doubts as to "whether vicarious experience is at all transformative" (p. 193). She and other researchers imply that educators should be cautious; simulation games, role-playing, and vicarious experiences in Holocaust education can sometimes be problematic and cause a backlash (Auron 2005; Feldman 1995; Naveh and Yogev 2002).

The Combination of the Symbolic and the Consequential

Ben-Peretz (2003) asserts that a major problem in Holocaust education is teachers' tendency to combine the categories of symbolic, representational, and consequential. Schweber (2003b), for example, notes that students perceive the use of simulation in Holocaust education as "a close replica of the historical reality rather than a distant, distorted echo, only partially intelligible" (p. 141). That is, students view the Holocaust as a flat and simplistic issue rather than perceiving the gap between the symbolic and consequential and thus grasping the complexities. Following Sutton's (1992) notion of "negotiated learning", Ben-Peretz (2003) claims that interactive negotiated learning involves students taking more responsibility for their learning.

She encourages those involved in Holocaust education to provide students "with opportunities to interact with a variety of sources and artifacts of the period and shape their own learning path" (p. 192).

The Socio-Demographic Component

How can Holocaust education be made more meaningful for students who do not have a European background? Those from a European background have a more favourable attitude toward Holocaust education than those from a Sephardic one (Farago 1984; Sabar and Guri 1980). Bar-On and Sela (1991) found that adolescents whose relatives were survivors have more empathy and understanding, and a broader and deeper knowledge of the Holocaust than those who do not. Ofer (2004a) suggests concentrating on the universalistic aspects of the Holocaust (e.g., human rights, civic education) so that it can have meaning for more students. Although intermarriage has narrowed the ethnic cleavage, this issue deserves further investigation.

Conclusions

Since the 1950s, the Holocaust has been transformed from a marginal issue to a central one and Holocaust education in Israel has changed significantly, because of various sociological, political, and historical changes. The major change was from a highly structured uniform approach to a more pluralistic one that acknowledges diverse voices and interpretations. In Ofer's (2004b) terminology, Holocaust education has moved from studies based mainly on "memory, involuntary and voluntary" with a more heroic approach, to studies based on history that involve critical thinking, require "mastery of disciplinary knowledge", and follow "the rules of scholarship" (p. 105). Overall, the approach changed from a collective orientation to an individual one, from a more universalistic view to a more particularistic one, and from a more structured educational agenda to a more personalised one. In spite of these changes, the official education programmes continued to concentrate mainly on the voluntary memories and ignore the involuntary memories. It seems to me that the more personalised stance to the attitude of the Holocaust enabled the arousal of the involuntary memories, which were suppressed in the era where only collective memories were legitimised and enhanced. This stems, perhaps, from the fact that people had little knowledge of, or experience handling, this unique kind of memory.

The case described above should be understood in a broader perspective. It highlights the need to be more attentive to nuanced variations of memory, especially among the third and fourth generation who were exposed to the Holocaust in a way that sometimes evoked traumatised reactions rather than educational ones. The ways in which our deliberate attempts to make meaning of the Holocaust do not always work as we would wish, the ways the next generation may relate to it differently, and crucially, the ways we attempt to support a culture of peace through remembrance: all these may inflict emotional trauma on children.

It seems that the transition from the ontological to the epistemological phase reflects the most meaningful change. Although this needs to be examined further, the transition to the epistemological stage clearly shows an eclectic tendency to combine conflicting memories (involuntary and voluntary), goals, and dilemmas, thus challenging students and teachers to find educational mechanisms and methodologies that can contain these differences and make the teaching process more subtle and sophisticated. Finally, it should be noted that though the findings here refer to Israeli historiography, the ontological-epistemological levels and the stages within them (rejection, recognition, construction, deconstruction) may be universal. A comparative study could be carried out to map where each country is located on the two scales, and the implications of this location for Holocaust education in each place.

Note This chapter draws on Gross (2010).

References

Altshuler, M. (1987). Hitnagdut Yehudit Bebrit Hamoatzot Betkufat Hashoa. Betoch: Hshoa Behistoriographia: Hartzaot Vediyunim Bkenes Habein Leumi Hchamishi Al Mechkar Shoa [Jewish resistance in the USSR during the Holocaust]. In *The Holocaust in historiography: Lectures and discussions at the Fifth International Conference of Holocaust Research* (pp. 167–185). Jerusalem: Yad Vashem.

Auron, Y. (1993). *Zehut Yehudit Israelit* [Jewish-Israeli identity]. Tel Aviv: Sifriat Poalim.

Auron, Y. (2003). *The banality of denial: Israel and the Armenian genocide*. New Brunswick: Transaction Publishers.

Auron, Y. (2005). *The pain of knowledge: Holocaust and genocide issues in education*. New Brunswick: Transaction Publishers.

Avidor, M., & Spivak, Y. (1958). *Am yisra'el be-artso uva-nekhar* [The people of Israel in their land and in the diaspora]. Tel Aviv: Masada.

Balf, M. (1998). *Bein Har Karmel Lamizrach Hatichon Hahitpatchut Shel Hahanzaha Shel Hahanzaha shel Hahanzaha shel Kibbutz Magan Michael* [Between Mt. Carmel and the Mediterranean: The development of public commemoration of the Holocaust in Kibbutz Maagan Michael and Maayan Tzvi]. Unpublished master's thesis, Hebrew University, Jerusalem.

Bar-On, D., & Sela, A. (1991). Maagal Bein Hahityahasut Lametziut Vehhaityasut L'a Shoa Bekerv Tzeirim Israelim [The magic circle: Between relating to reality and relating to the Holocaust in Israeli youth]. *Psychologia, 2*, 126–138.

Ben-Peretz, M. (2003). Identifying with horror: Teaching about the Holocaust: A response to Simone Schweber's "Simulating Survival". *Curriculum Inquiry, 33*(2), 189–198.

Berntsen, D., & Hall, N. M. (2004). The episodic nature of involuntary autobiographical memories. *Memory & Cognition, 32*(5), 789–803.

Blatman, D. (1995). Al Post Tziyonut Vetishtush Hazikaron [On post-Zionism and blurring of memory]. *Bishvil Hazikaron, 7*, 15–16.

Clendinnen, I. (1999). *Reading the Holocaust*. New York: Cambridge University Press.

Cohen, B. (1999). Hahistoryographia Hayisraelit Shel Hashoa: Megamot Ikariyot [Israeli historiography of the Holocaust: Major trends]. *Bishvi Hazikron, 34,* 14–19.
Cohen, E. H. (2009). *Mehkar Al Horaat Shoa Bevatei Hasefer Hatichonim Beyisrael* [Research on teaching the Holocaust in Israeli high schools]. Ramat-Gan: Bar-Ilan University.
Conway, M. A. (2005). Memory and the self. *Journal of Memory and Language, 53*(4), 594–628.
Don-Yehiya, E. (1993). Memory and political culture: Israeli society and the Holocaust. *Studies in Contemporary Jewry, 9,* 139–162.
Don-Yehiya, E. (2000). Mamlactiyut, Shoa "Umesarim Hatraniyim" [Statehood, Holocaust and "subversive messages"]. *Alpayim, 20,* 81–106.
Dror, Y. (1996). National denial, splitting, and narcissism: Group defence mechanisms of teachers and students in Palestine in response to the Holocaust. *Mediterranean Journal of Educational Studies, 1,* 107–137.
Dror, Y. (2001). Holocaust curricula in Israeli secondary schools, 1960s–1990s: Historical evaluation from the moral education perspective. *The Journal of Holocaust Education, 10,* 29–39.
Dror, Y. (2002). From "Negation of the diaspora" to "Jewish consciousness": The Israeli educational system, 1920–2000. *Israel Studies Forum, 18,* 58–82.
Encyclopedia Britannica Online (2009). Holocaust. http://www.britannica.com/EBchecked/topic/269548/Holocaust
Farago, U. (1984). Todat Hashoa Bekerv Noar Lomed Beyisrael [Attitudes toward the Holocaust among Israeli high school students, 1983]. *Dapim Lecheker Hashoah* [Studies on the Holocaust Period], *3,* 159–178.
Farago, U. (1989). Hazehut Hayehudit shel Noar Israeli 1985–1965 Yahadut Zmanenu [Jewish identity of Israeli youth, 1965–1985]. *Yahadut Zmanenu* [Contemporary Judaism], *5,* 259–285.
Farago, U. (2007). Yoter Yehudim Pahot Yisraelim [More Jewish less Israeli]. *Panim, 40,* 4–11.
Feldman, J. (1995). Aliya Laregel Leatarei Hashmada Bepolin [The pilgrimage to the death camps in Poland]. *Bishvilei haZikaron* [In the Paths of Memory], *7,* 8–11.
Firer, R. (1983). Al Hasefer Hashoa Umashmauta [About the book *The Holocaust and its Significance*]. *History Teachers' Discourse, 21,* 13–20.
Firer, R. (1987). The Holocaust in textbooks in Israel. In R. L. Braham (Ed.), *The treatment of the Holocaust in textbooks* (pp. 178–188). New York: Columbia University Press.
Firer, R. (1989). *Sochnim Shel Lekah* [Agents of the Holocaust lesson]. Tel-Aviv: Hakibbutz haMeuhad.
Foucault, M. (1981). The order of discourse. In R. Young (Ed.), *Untying the text: A post-structuralist reader* (pp. 48–78). London: Routledge.
Grodzinsky, Y. (2000). Kosmetikat ha-shoah [The cosmetics of the Holocaust: A footnote to the narrative of the labor movement]. *Alpayim, 20,* 107–116.
Gross, T. (2000). *Influence of the trip to Poland within the framework of the Ministry of Education on the working through of the Holocaust.* Unpublished MA thesis, Ben-Gurion University, Beer Sheva.
Gross, Z. (2006). Voices among the religious Zionists in Israel regarding the peace process and the disengagement plan. In Y. Iram, H. Wahrman, & Z. Gross (Eds.), *Educating toward a culture of peace* (pp. 259–279). Greenwich: Information Age Publishing.
Gross, Z. (2010). Holocaust education in Jewish schools in Israel: Goals, dilemmas, challenges. *Prospects, 40*(1), 93–113.
Gutman, Y. (1999). *Shoa Vezikaron* [Holocaust and memory]. Jerusalem: Shazar Centre and Yad Vashem.
Gutman, I., & Schatzker, C. (1984). *The Holocaust and its significance.* Jerusalem: Zalman Shazar Centre, Historical Society of Israel.
Herman, S. N. (1977). *Jewish identity: A socio-psychological perspective.* Beverly Hills: Sage.
Jackson, P. W. (1986). *The practice of teaching.* New York: Teachers College Press.
Kahane, R. (1968). Patterns of national identity in Israel. In S. N. Eisenstadt et al. (Eds.), *Education and society in Israel: A reader* (pp. 296–313). Jerusalem: Akademon.

Keren, N. (1984). Hashoa Vemashmauta: Tguvot Nosafot [The Holocaust and its significance: Additional reaction]. *History Teachers' Discourse*, 15–17.

Keren, N. (1998). Museonim Vemosadot Lehanzahat Hashoa Vehashpaatam Al Horat Hashoa Beyisrael [Museums and institutions commemorating the Holocaust and their influence on the teaching of the Holocaust]. In A. Ben-Amos (Ed.), *History, identity, and memory: Images of the past in Israeli education* (pp. 155–171). Tel-Aviv: Ramot.

Keren, N. (1999). *Shoa: Masa Leitzuv Hazikaron* [Shoah: A journey to memory]. Tel Aviv: Tel Aviv Books.

Keren, N. (2008). Eich Leatzev Zikaron? [How to construct memory?]. *Masuah, 35*, 9–21.

Kimmerling, B. (2004). *Mehagrim. Mityashvim Yelidim* [Immigrants, settlers, natives: The Israeli state and society between cultural pluralism and cultural wars]. Tel-Aviv: Am Oved.

Levy, S., Levinsohn, H., & Katz, E. (1993). *Emunot, Shmirat Mitzvot Veinteraktzya Chevratit Bekerev Yehudm Israelim* [Beliefs, observations and social interaction among Israeli Jews]. Jerusalem: Louis Guttman Israel Institute of Applied Social Research.

Levy, S., Levinsohn, H., & Katz, E. (2004). The many faces of Jewishness in Israel. In U. Rebhun & C. I. Waxman (Eds.), *Jews in Israel: Contemporary social and cultural patterns* (pp. 265–284). Hanover/London: Brandeis University Press/University Press of New England.

Liebman, C. S., & Don-Yehiya, E. (1983). *Civil religion in Israel: Traditional Judaism and political culture in the Jewish state*. Berkeley: University of California Press.

Linton, M. (1986). Ways of searching and the contents of memory. In D. C. Rubin (Ed.), *Autobiographical memory* (pp. 50–68). Cambridge: Cambridge University Press.

Mace, J. H. (2004). Involuntary autobiographical memories are highly dependent on abstract cuing: The Proustian view is incorrect. *Applied Cognitive Psychology, 18*(7), 893–899.

Mace, J. H. (2008). Involuntary memory: Concept and theory. In J. H. Mace (Ed.), *Involuntary memory* (pp. 1–19). Oxford: Blackwell.

Medding, P. (1989). Ben Gurion Kemodel Lemanhigut Politit [Ben-Gurion as a model of democratic political leadership]. *Contemporary Judaism, 5*, 25–49.

Michman, D. (Ed.) (1997). *Post-ziyonut ve-shoa* (Vol. 1) [Post-Zionism and the Holocaust. The role of the Holocaust in the public debate on post-Zionism in Israel (1993–1996)]. Ramat Gan: Finkler Institute of Holocaust Research, Bar-Ilan University.

Naveh, E. (2009). *Totalitariyut Veshoa: Eiropa, Hamizrach Hatichon Ve hayehudim Bhetzi Harishon she Hameah Hesrim* [Totalitarianism and Holocaust: Europe, the Mediterranean and the Jews in the first half of the 20th century]. Tel-Aviv: Reches.

Naveh, E., & Yogev, E. (2002). *Historiot: Likrat Dialogue Im Haetmol* [Histories: Toward a dialogue with yesterday]. Tel Aviv: Babel.

Ofer, D. (2004a). History, memory and identity: Perceptions of the Holocaust in Israel. In U. Rebhun & C. Waxman (Eds.), *Jews in Israel: Contemporary social and cultural patterns* (pp. 394–417). Hanover/London: Brandeis University Press.

Ofer, D. (2004b). Holocaust education: Between history and memory. *Jewish Education, 10*, 87–108.

Porat, D. A. (2004). From the scandal to the Holocaust in Israeli education. *Journal of Contemporary History, 39*, 619–636.

Resnik, J. (1999). Particularistic vs. universalistic content in the Israeli education system. *Curriculum Inquiry, 29*(4), 485–511.

Riger, E. (1958). *The history of Israel in the new era*, Part 3. Tel Aviv: Dvir.

Romi, S., & Lev, M. (2007). Experiential learning of history through youth journeys to Poland: Israeli Jewish youth and the Holocaust. *Research in Education, 78*, 88–102.

Sabar, N., & Guri, S. (1980). The effect of teaching a special Holocaust curriculum. *Jewish Education, 48*(3), 27–39.

Schatzker, C. (1982). The Holocaust in Israeli education. *International Journal of Political Education, 5*(1), 75–82.

Schatzker, C. (1992). Teaching the Holocaust in changing times. *Moreshet, 52*, 165–171.

Schweber, S. A. (2003a). Rejoinder to Miriam Ben-Peretz. *Curriculum Inquiry, 33*(2), 199–206.

Schweber, S. A. (2003b). Simulating survival. *Curriculum Inquiry, 33*(2), 139–188.
Segev, T. (2000). *The seventh million: The Israelis and the Holocaust* (H. Watzman, Trans.). New York: Macmillan.
Shapira, A. (1990). Dor baaretz [Native sons]. *Alpayim, 2*, 178–203.
Shapira, A. (1997). *Yehudim hadashim, yehudim yeshanim* [New Jews, old Jews]. Tel Aviv: Am Oved.
Shapira, A. (1999). Toldotav shel mitos: Kavim la-historiographya odot ben-gurion ve-ha-shoa [The history of mythology: Outlines of historiography on Ben-Gurion and the Holocaust]. *Alpayim, 18*, 24–53.
Stauber, R. (2007). *The Holocaust in Israeli public debate in the 1950s: Ideology and memory.* Edgware: Vallentine-Mitchell.
Sutton, C. (1992). *Words, science and learning.* Buckingham: Open University Press.
Wiersma, W., & Jurs, S. A. (2009). *Research methods in education: An introduction* (9th ed.). Boston: Allyn and Bacon.
Ya'akobi, D. (Ed.) (1999). *A world of changes: History for ninth grade.* Jerusalem: Curriculum Division, Ministry of Education.
Yablonka, H. T. (1997). The formation of Holocaust consciousness in the state of Israel: The early days. In E. Sicher (Ed.), *Breaking crystal: Writing and memory after Auschwitz* (pp. 119–136). Champaign: University of Illinois Press.
Zertal, I. (2002). *Hauma Vehamavet: Historya, Zikaron Vepolitica* [The nation and death: History, memory and politics]. Tel-Aviv: Dvir.

Domesticating the Difficult Past: Polish Students Narrate the Second World War

Magdalena H. Gross

Introduction

The 20th century brought the experience of mass violence and totalitarian rule to many parts of the world. In Europe, Nazi Germany and Stalinist Russia imposed suffering upon innumerable victims. The consequences of such calamities continue long after societies have shed oppressive regimes and transitioned to democratic politics. The process of transition after war is always complex and difficult. Often, post-war institutions attempt to legitimise wartime repressions to build a compelling future for their constituents. In various ways, national communities attempt to domesticate their histories by downplaying or simply ignoring the difficult ones. For example, governments may attempt to smooth over the chaotic past through education, by communicating unifying and uplifting national narratives to post-war generations through textbooks, curriculum, and field trips.

In this chapter I focus on the influence of educational practices and media attention on student imagination with regard to Poland's history during World War II. I conducted my study at a specific moment in time, when the canon of accepted knowledge about the nation's traumatic past is rapidly changing. Although knowledge about World War II is common in Poland, some aspects are hotly and publicly debated. In many ways, Polish society is divided into two: those who cling to established narratives about the past, and those who are open to a revisionist version of war history. In this study, I asked nearly 60 Polish high school students to write about World War II in order to understand their relationship with this troubled and much debated history.

M.H. Gross (✉)
Program in Writing and Rhetoric, Stanford University,
485 Lasuen Mall, Stanford, CA, USA
e-mail: mgross1@stanford.edu

Previous research has contributed to our understanding of how students interact with history. Scholars have found that children interpret the past through the lens of family, religious, and ethnic affiliations (Epstein 1998; Porat 2004; Seixas 1997). Researchers have established that generational differences sometimes outweigh cultural ones in understanding the past, and that history can be learned as much from the streets and from television as from sitting in a classroom (Wineburg, Mosborg, Porat, and Duncan 2007; see also Wertsch 2002). Still, some questions have been overlooked. For example, how have students from counties that were ravaged during World War II come to understand and narrate difficult and traumatic national histories? More specifically, I look at how students interpret difficult histories that may be changing in the face of new information, debate, and media attention.

I am not alone in my interest in young people's understanding of the Polish wartime past. During the week of 19 April, 2013, the Institute for Public Opinion Research (*Instytut Badania Opinii Homo Homini*) in Poland released the results from a survey administered to 1,250 Polish middle school students. The survey focused on students' historical understanding of the 1943 Warsaw Ghetto uprising, a striking moment of resistance by Polish Jews against their Nazi occupiers. Media outlets cherry-picked results of the survey, arguing that Polish students' historical understanding about the uprising was "weak", because 44% of students surveyed believed that Poles and Jews suffered equally during World War II, or that 60% would be disappointed if they found out their significant other were Jewish. The public presentation of results overstated the significance of some answers and overlooked the importance of others. For example, 55% of the same students identified the leader of the Warsaw Ghetto uprising by name, and 70% knew the date of the uprising.

That survey clearly demonstrated that Polish children engage with difficult aspects of the country's past. I argue that students are historicised in many ways and that their knowledge about the past is a reflection of contemporary cultural attitudes towards that history. Here, I look at high school student narratives about World War II in Poland in order to answer two questions: What kinds of narratives do students craft about World War II? And what can these narratives tell us about how young people deal with a well-known but controversial past?

Many societies have experienced traumatic events pivotal to the development of their national narratives. The manner in which the young remember histories has the potential to divide or unite communities emerging from conflict, war, or repression. Given our increasingly interconnected global community, where war and strife are streamed into our homes via the Internet and smartphones, it is more important than ever to understand the relationship between a brutal past and the way children think about it. Such knowledge can help educators teach difficult historical episodes with clarity and relevance.

Background

Poles were the first victims of the 1939 Molotov-Ribbentrop Pact between Hitler and Stalin. The two dictators divided Poland in two. Each leader imposed a brutal regime of occupation. In eastern Poland, where the Soviets ruled from September 1939 through June 1941 (when Germany attacked the Soviet Union), private property was taken from the local population, 400,000 people were arrested and deported into the Soviet interior, and many were killed, including over 20,000 prisoners of war. The sufferings of Polish citizens under Soviet rule remained a taboo subject in Polish schools for the next 50 years until 1989, when the Communist Party finally yielded power.

The violence of German occupation, on the other hand, has been widely publicised and systematically taught in schools during the post-war era. The Communist authorities promoted a heroic interpretation of wartime resistance, downplaying the role of a patriotic (Polish nationalist) anti-Nazi (and simultaneously anti-Soviet) underground, including particular events such as the Warsaw Ghetto Uprising of April 1943, when some 250,000 Polish civilians and resistance fighters were killed. The Communist regime's educational programme also downplayed the Holocaust as a central element of the wartime experience, even though over 3,000,000 Polish Jews were murdered or died of war-related causes (Steinlauf 1997).

In May 2000, a book by Jan Gross (2001) entitled *Neighbors: The Destruction of the Jewish Community in Jedwabne, Poland* was published in Poland. Gross describes an episode in the summer of 1941: approximately 1,600 Jewish residents of a small town were murdered by their Polish neighbors. A debate exploded in the media that reintroduced the subject of the Holocaust with an unexpected twist: it included the Polish people's complicity in the Nazis' extermination of Jews. Since then, the historiography of the Holocaust in Poland has grown, thanks in part to further publications by the Centre for Holocaust Research, established in 2003 at the Polish Academy of Sciences in Warsaw.

The story of Jedwabne has also become an inspiration to artists and film makers. A leading dramatist, Tadeusz Slobodzianek, wrote the play *Our Class*, which received the *Nike,* Poland's most prestigious literary prize. *Our Class* has been produced throughout Poland, translated into foreign languages, and performed to critical acclaim in London, Philadelphia, Washington, Toronto, Budapest, and Stockholm, among other cities. The well-known movie director, Wladyslaw Pasikowski, directed a powerful feature entitled *Aftermath (2013)*, set in a contemporary small Polish town that confronts its history of anti-Jewish violence during the war. As a result, young Poles have been exposed to alternative narratives about the war, not only through scholarly volumes, but through a whole spectrum of media and artistic genres. The debates that rage about World War II in Poland reflect the chaotic and untamed complexities of the war itself. All this makes Poland a ripe case study for examining how students of history interpret and understand difficult national histories.

The Case Study

The students who participated in this study came of age during an intense climate of debate surrounding the history of World War II. "Every Pole is brought up to believe that his country is one of history's victims: the generally innocent and righteous victim of the predatory nationalism of more powerful neighbors", wrote the journalist and historian Timothy Garton Ash (1989, p. 135). However, over the last ten years historians, filmmakers, and artists have offered the Polish public a different picture, one in which Poles were often complicit in the murder and plunder of their Jewish neighbors (Bikont 2004; Engelking 2012; Grabowski 2011; J. Gross 2001). This information has the potential to challenge the previously accepted stories of the Polish wartime experience as being exclusively about martyrdom and victimisation. Because history and memory are in dialogue in Poland, there is the potential for a change in the nation's collective memory (Zerubavel 1997). That possibility guided my analysis of these students' narratives.

Sample

This study was part of a 3-year data collection effort that included interviews and surveys with 60 educators and 188 public school students across three regions of Poland. All of the sampled schools were public, and catered to an economically diverse population. Participants reflected the ethnic makeup of Poland: 99% Catholic, Polish-born and Polish-speaking. For this chapter, I analyzed 53 student narrative responses from a region in Poland I call Sarnow (all these locations and participant names are pseudonyms). Of the respondents 61% were female; their average age was 17. Although the sample of students was small, it was representative of a typical Polish population in terms of the region's economic status and the school type (public). With a current population of about 8,000, Sarnow is an economically depressed region in Poland's northwest. Most of the students have family members who are miners, of either coal or silver. During World War II, this predominantly rural region contained a large German population. The town had approximately 300 Jewish residents before the war. The synagogue was burned down by Nazi occupying forces.

Methodology

In January 2012 I mailed a set of student worksheets to the participating teacher at Sarnow's high school (see Appendix A). She administered the task to three groups of students and then taught a unit on World War II. These worksheets had one essay question on Side A and a ranking activity on Side B. Students were asked to "write the story of World War II in Poland for a foreigner, from start to finish". They were given 20 min and not allowed to use outside sources. The prompt was designed to be as open-ended as possible, allowing students to draw on their imagination and experience to craft the essay. Students were told to include whatever people and events came to mind. After completing the essay, they were asked to turn to Side B and rank the sources of historical information (such as history class, family stories, or documentary films) from most to least important (1–10), and most to least credible (1–10). I wanted to create an authentic essay task that privileged student voice and narrative without making students feel there was a right or a wrong answer. Most students wrote brief essays, ranging from 20 to 273 words with an average length of 122 words and a standard deviation of 64.33.

Analysis

I transcribed all the surveys from the handwritten student versions into Microsoft Word documents. I completed all communication and survey analysis in Polish, which I speak fluently. Before I conducted the analysis, I read the responses multiple times. After familiarising myself with the content, on my own and in conversation with colleagues, I began to consider a coding scheme, building on "grounded theory coding" or "open coding" (Corbin and Strauss 1990; Merriam 2002; Strauss and Corbin 1994).

During the initial round of coding I focused on student knowledge of names, places, and dates. This analysis, which was intended to capture certain words, phrases, or dates as they appeared in student responses, allowed me to construct my descriptor set. I then created an Excel document in which I summarised the descriptive statistical information about the narratives and compared the content of the narratives to student-ranked sources of historical information. Next, I developed theoretical and interpretive coding, looking for patterns, themes, and outliers among student narratives. Employing the concepts of schematic narrative (Wertsch 2002), I interpreted how and if students drew upon culturally accepted narratives about the past. I focused on the use of cultural resources or symbolic language used to describe World War II (Riessman 1993). I also analysed specific narratives that strayed from the norm. Throughout the process I wrote memos and theoretical notes when I saw patterns in the data or when I detected relationships among codes, items, and data sources (Glaser 1978; Miles and Huberman 1994; Strauss and Corbin 1994).

The following questions frame the presentation of my findings:

1. What is the content of student narratives about World War II, what are notable omissions, and do any types or patterns emerge?
2. What do these narratives tell us about the relationship of young people to a publicly debated past?

Results

The student narratives shared references to common events, dates, characters, and ethnic groups. A typical account began with the invasion of Poland (74%) with specific reference to 1 September, 1939. When students evoked specific names of events, they most commonly mentioned the defense of Westerplatte (13%), Katyn (11%), Hiroshima (9%), and the Warsaw Uprising (7%). One student mentioned the Polish 303 squadron which distinguished itself in the Battle of Britain and two students cited the Molotow-Ribbentrop Pact and the Holocaust. None of the students cited events more common to student narratives in other countries, such as D-Day, Pearl Harbor, or the liberation of the concentration camps. Figure 1 presents a summary of descriptive statistics from these student narratives.

Students drew on a stock set of terms. Some used such terms as *obozy*, concentration camps (64%), resistance (35%), and *zaglada,* the general term for genocide (30%). Their responses commonly cited Germans (74%), Jews (58%), and Russians (51%). While 62% of them invoked Hitler, few (11%) mentioned Stalin. Essays with a paucity of concrete information in the narrative still reflected a constructed common cultural account of the war. Although each narrative was to some degree unique, certain patterns emerged.

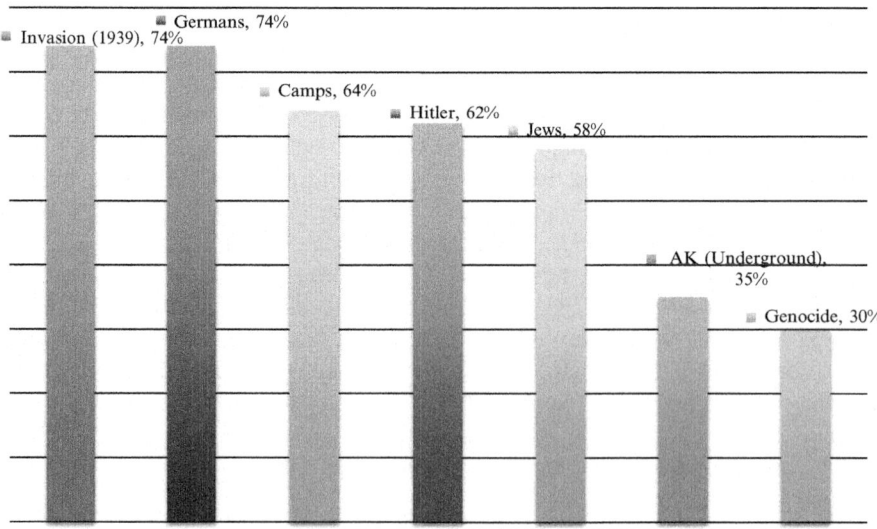

Fig. 1 Terms or events students mentioned most often (%)

The Prototypical Narrative

The tendency across the sample was to recount the war beginning in 1939 and to give an endpoint in 1945. This chronological presentation indicates a distance from the event, with children no longer telling a story in relation to their family or individual lives, but as a packaged chronological version of the past. Most narratives mentioned Polish losses, Polish bravery, bad Germans, and occasionally an ethnic minority. A typical narrative is this response by Ania, who was 18 at the time of the study:

> About the history of World War II in Poland one could say so much.... It started in 1939. Poland was attacked. A very negative figure was Adolf Hitler. He was convinced that Germans were superior to other nations, and because of him, the war broke out. Innocent people were sent to camps of genocide (*zaglada*) where they first lived in awful conditions and then were murdered. Very, very few people were able to escape death. The human losses and other losses that Poles endured were enormous.... I know that Poles fought really well in the defense of their country...I think that it is fair and rather obvious to say that World War II was something awful, inhuman, there were so many casualties, children lost their parents, mothers their children. If it weren't for him [Hitler], the world would not have suffered so, but also Poles wouldn't have a reason to be as proud as they now are. I don't know what more I can write.

This essay is typical of those from this group of Polish students. It begins with the attack on Poland in 1939. The initial focus is Hitler, emblematic of wartime destruction and the source of human and Polish loss. When Ania mentions concentration camps, she uses the term *zaglada*, which has come to mean genocide, translated literally as "annihilation" or "doom". In those camps, "many, many" people died. There is no strong evidence she is referring to death camps built specifically for Jews, as she mentions the camps only after citing Polish losses and bravery, and never refers to Jews specifically. She finishes her essay noting that the war was destructive, but if it were not for Hitler, Poles would have no reason to "be as proud as they now are". The devastation of the past provides a foundation for national pride: Poles suffered at the hands of bad Germans (personified by Hitler), but were very brave and can be proud of their wartime behaviour. This narrative is bounded by Polish cultural expectations, sufficiently vague so that the past is tamed, domesticated, and comprehensible. The complexity of war has receded along with personal or familial details.

Sources and Content

Students wrote their narratives on Side A of the worksheet. On Side B, they were asked to rank their sources of historical information (see Appendix A), such as history class, parents, and museums, in order of importance and credibility. The importance and credibility rankings that students marked on their worksheets are related to the content of their narratives. In other words, choices about which avenues constitute important or credible sources of historical information affected which events they included in, or omitted from, their essays.

An equal number of students cited history class (26%) and parents/grandparents (26%) as the most *important* sources of historical information regarding World War II. Fewer marked museums (19%) and the Internet (9%). Students were given the opportunity to check a different set of categories as the most *credible* source of historical information, and many did so. Nearly half (46%) cited museums as the most credible source, but those who cited parents also marked them as most credible (22%). In decreasing order, students ranked documentary films (19%) and public ceremonies (15%) as the most credible sources of historical information.

Although it is impossible to know the degree of veracity regarding the students' sources of information (an obvious drawback of self reports), I was able to discern that overall, the narratives changed depending on the sources students reported. As Figure 2 shows, students who selected history class as their most important source of historical information were twice as likely to mention Jews in their narratives, three times more likely to cite the Polish resistance by name, and three times as likely to give the precise date of the invasion of Poland and the 1944 Warsaw Uprising. On the other hand, students who cited their family as the most important source were less likely to mention Jews or the Holocaust in their responses. Specifically, students who cited parents as the most important source of historical information only mentioned one specific date: the end of the war. Although the

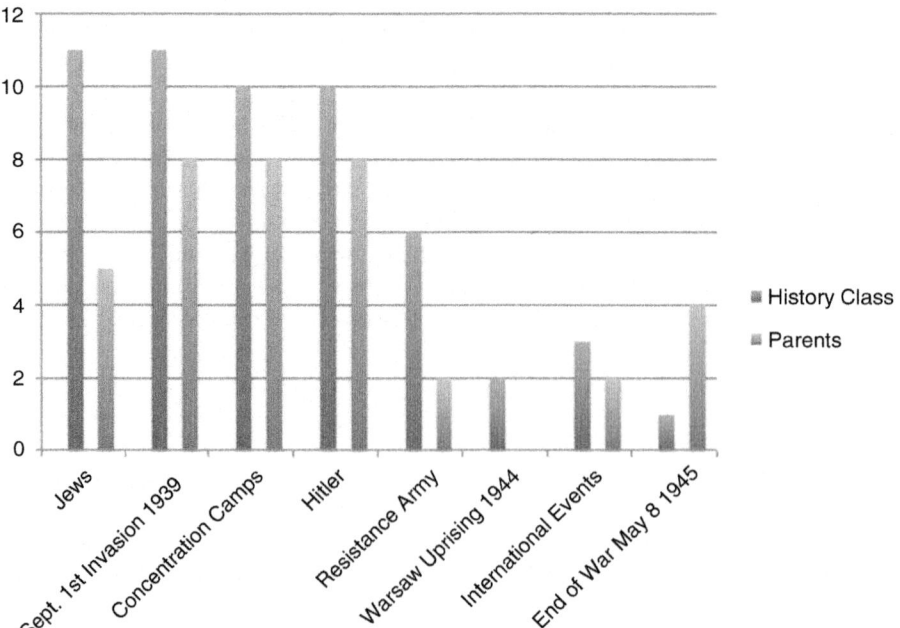

Fig. 2 Content of student responses, and most important sources

subset of students analyzed is small (see Figure 2), under 20 in each category, this finding is important because it suggests that students who think school is an important source of historical information are more likely to include concrete historical information as well as include Jews in their narratives.

Above and beyond frequencies, deeper patterns emerged in the data. Specifically, three types of essays were characteristic of the ways these students narrated the difficult past, such as Poland's role in World War II. When I analysed the narrative accounts more closely, related and overlapping, yet still distinct, types emerged: 29 essays (55%) followed what I call the *Ruin* narrative, the more general story of destruction. Another 17 (32%) exemplified the *Resistance* narrative, where the focus is on Poles fighting bravely against the occupiers. Five narratives (10%) revolve around Polish victimisation, and the remaining two were outliers that did not fall into any category.

The Ruin Narrative

The response by Lania, 17, illustrates an emblematic Ruin response, focusing on death and destruction, rather than bravery or victimhood:

> In September of 1939 the Germans and then Russia attacked Poland. The war started and engulfed many nations around the world. The fighting lasted until 1945. In these years many millions died, many of them civilians. The Germans, who saw themselves as better, started to kill off national groups, Jews, Poles, Roma. There were many concentration camps where many died.

This account is mundane on the surface. The plot is extremely general and chronological, and cites many national groups (Germans, Russians, Jews, followed by Poles and even the Roma). She mentions no concrete events other than the September invasion of Poland. Once more, the idea of German ethnic superiority is invoked as the cause of destruction during the war. Germans and Russians are the villains and Jews are listed with other nationalities.

Table 1 provides three additional typical Ruin narratives written by students. Selection A is characterised by an overarching trajectory: the war was the worst thing that ever happened to Polish civilisation. Student A mentions Germany's attack on Poland, indicating World War II was not provoked by the Poles and thus implying wartime Polish innocence. This selection was one of only two in the sample to use the term Holocaust to denote destruction of the Jews. It also refers to "amazing people" who perished, and civilians who rebuilt Polish cities after the war. The rebuilding seems to evoke once more pride in the Polish nation. These details give the narrative a personal touch.

Selection B is more tragic in tone. It talks about men buried on top of each other, the inhumane conditions of war, and the loss of personal liberty. Indeed, this excerpt is characterised by tropes of power and powerlessness: the Germans and Russians, powerful, destructive nations who enslaved and destroyed the powerless Polish masses.

Table 1 Samples of ruin narratives

Narrative	Excerpt
A	The Second World War was one of the most tragic moments in our civilisation. The attack of Germany on Poland, the Holocaust and the number of victims, the millions that will stay in our memory forever. It changed the course of history. In this war many people died. It destroyed cultural artifacts, and even whole cities, that thanks to the will of the citizens, were rebuilt.
B	The Second World War was a very brutal and bloody war. During this war, nations were competing to perfect technology to take away human lives even more. In this war there were two nations that doled out extraordinary cruelty—Germany and Russia. People were killed en masse, they were buried on top of each other in mass graves. During this war people were often forced to live in inhuman conditions. They were taken advantage of, manipulated, they were marionettes in the hands of the powers. During this war, a man was denied his rights and was so scared…
C	The Second World War—the start of the war, 1 September, 1939. It is the date of the attack of Germany on Poland. The end of the war was the 2nd of September 1945…. This was the greatest armed conflict in history, nearly 50 million people died. It ended with the victory of the allied forces.

In Selection C, the war is characterised as the most destructive war in history—which is certainly true from a Polono-centric perspective. The student notes that over 50 million people died in the war (this number includes victims of Stalin's repression), caused by Germany's attack on Poland. The narrative is chronological, giving specific beginning and ending dates for the war, although the date ascribed to the end of the war is incorrect.

Polish children who used this type of narrative painted a picture of war using broad strokes. The narrative is chronological: Poland attacked mercilessly by villainous Germans, sometimes Russians, resulting in great suffering and destruction. Occasionally they refer to German ideas of racial hierarchy, but in the main, Jews and the Holocaust are hardly mentioned, and Allied forces make only rare appearances. The Ruin narrative is largely devoid of detail; the story is remarkably Polish and domesticated, with the complexities of war glossed over.

The Resistance Narrative

The second most common story emphasises Polish resistance during the war, featuring Poles who acted bravely defending against the occupiers. Such narratives are more specific, offering a concrete classification of national ethnic groups. During the post-war years, the resistance played a role in the way European nations portrayed their wartime activities (Judt 2005). As historian Eric Hobsbawm (1994) stated, "The legitimacy of post-war regimes and governments essentially rests on their resistance record" (p. 164). The Polish underground state and its Home Army (the AK, *Armia Krajowa*) were the strongest, most robust resistance movements in occupied countries. At its peak, the AK had over 300,000 members, and there were

Table 2 Tomek's account: resistance

Line number	Excerpt
1	World War II in Poland started the 1st of September, 1939 with the attack of the
2	armies of the Third Reich on Westerplatte.
3	Then started the heroic defense of the Polish armies, and next, on the 17th of
4	September, attack by Russia against Poland was added.
5	During World War II, many cities were destroyed, including Warsaw.
6	The hatred that Hitler had towards others led to the building of concentration
7	camps, for example, Auschwitz where Jews and Poles mostly were sent.
8	They lived in horrible conditions, not for long, because they died quickly, and
9	testimonies from witnesses were falsified and said that people were dying of
10	other things [while in fact they were killed by the Germans].
11	There were also experiments done on people. Supposedly the Polish conspiracy
12	[resistance] was the best in the world, and led the nation by clandestine work.
13	Even Hitler noticed the potential of the Polish soldiers, saying that with them
14	he could take over the world. They were that good. At least… in my opinion, it
15	is because they fought for freedom, for family, and basically for themselves.

also other resistance organisations such as the Polish Communist underground organisation with its People's Army or Guard (*Armia Ludowa, Gwardia Ludowa*), and the right-wing NSZ (*Narodowe Siły Zbrojne*), National Armed Forces.

A typical version of the Polish resistance narrative can be seen in Tomek's response, in Table 2. What stands out is the sheer level of detail the student has included: names of places, people, and events. His starting point resembles other responses, with 1 September, 1939, the German invasion of Poland (lines 1–2). He immediately mentions the "heroic defense" (line 3) of the Polish armies in response to the initial attack on the nation. Notably, he includes the Russian invasion of Poland on 17 September (lines 3–4). Then he immediately makes reference to Hitler's hatred as a way of explaining the concentration camps, as well as the destruction of Poland's Jews. He then cites Jews and Poles as victims at Auschwitz, narratively placing them on equal footing in their suffering at the camps (line 7).

This type of parallel martyrdom is commonly taught in Polish schools (M. Gross 2010), as many textbooks emphasise the fact that Polish prisoners were sent to Auschwitz. Such a description gives children the impression that the death camps were places of imprisonment for both Jews and Poles. Often overlooked are the nuances of different camp types and the dissimilar treatment meted out to those with presumed Jewish background versus non-Jews. Jews were marked for death. Poles, while they were treated brutally and often died as a result of brutal treatment, were not marked for systematic elimination.

Tomek ends his essay with a series of statements about the bravery of Polish soldiers during the war and makes reference to the "Polish conspiracy", a colloquial reference to the AK and the underground state. He claims the AK was the greatest in the world (lines 11–12). This student believes Poles fought for freedom and family, a stereotypical interpretation of the Polish resistance.

Uncharacteristically, Tomek cites inhumane experiments done on prisoners in the camps. He closes the essay by stating that even Hitler considered the Poles to be such brave soldiers that with their assistance he could take over the world. This statement is one of hyperbole, and is not repeated in any other essay in the sample. In fact, startled by this hyperbole, I searched online for this notion, and found multiple Polish nationalist sites rife with quotations from Hitler and other Nazi officials, purportedly stating how bravely the Polish armies performed in combat. To some degree, then, a subset of Polish speakers have chosen to ignore the fact that Hitler saw Poles as subhuman, and have instead revised history in order to fit in this characterisation of Polish bravery.

Table 3 contains some of Gosia's response, which mirrors Tomek's in important ways. Both students begin chronologically, centring on the German and Russian invasions, as well as the establishment of concentration camps, listing Poles alongside the Jews and Roma ("gypsies") as victims. Gosia's response is slightly more dramatic, and offers information that suggests she has more knowledge about the war in general. For example, she mentions leaders by name (line 4), and their desire to split up Poland, presumably linking the Soviet invasion of eastern Poland on 17 September, 1939 to the secret protocol of the Ribbentrop-Molotov Pact (lines 3–4). She frames the Polish resistance in terms of heroism and bravery, noting that the Poles were outnumbered (line 5), abandoned by allies (line 2), or stood their ground against de-Polonising forces (line 8). She notes that the Poles were tricked

Table 3 Gosia's account: Resistance

Line number	Excerpt
1	On the 1st of September 1939, the Germans attacked Poland from the side of the sea
2	(Westerplatte) and the 3rd, then, started World War II (the allied forces stopped
3	helping Poland). Poles were weaker and weaker. The Germans took over Warsaw.
4	On the 17th of September the Russians attacked Poland. Jozef Stalin and Adolf
5	Hitler wanted to split up Poland…
6	The Poles, even though outnumbered by the enemy, did not give up…
7	On Polish terrain there started to be concentration camps for Poles, Jews, Roma….
8	The Poles showed incredible heroism during the Warsaw Uprising when they stood
9	ground against the German occupiers because they were trying to Germanise the
10	Poles…. The Poles were convinced that the Russians were their allies and were
11	happy when they freed them [from the German occupation], not knowing what was
12	waiting for them. The war ended on the 8th of May, 1945.

by their Russian neighbors, continuing the notion that neighbors, friends, and allies all abandoned Poland. The essence of the narrative is one of heroism and resistance couched in a theme of abandonment. For Gosia, Polish bravery has become the essence of Polishness during the war, and perhaps brave Polishness becomes the overall lesson from the war as well.

Although some of these responses mention Jews, many others only cite Jews as part of a list of victims. At the same time, a small subset (seven responses) stood out for providing more detailed treatment of Polish Jews within the World War II narrative. In Table 4, Student A begins with the premise that the Poles fought bravely. As is common in such narratives, the student cites German ideas of racial superiority to explain the erection of concentration camps on Polish soil. Poles are described as victims of oppression who, despite their vulnerablity, hid "sought-after Jews". This student characterises Poles' behaviour toward their Jewish neighbors as one of self-sacrifice and mutual aid, a narrative that runs counter to recent information and historical fact. While it is true some Poles did help their Jewish neighbors during World War II, historical evidence does not support the idea that this was a common practice. Selection A ends with the Katyn Massacre of 1940, where nearly 5,000 Polish officers were killed by Soviet secret police, a fact that serves to underscore the themes of Polish victimisation, bravery, and selflessness.

Table 4 Excerpts from a selection of student responses within the resistance narrative

Student	Reference to Poles	Reference to Jews
A	The Germans started the war with us. Poles defended themselves but they couldn't do much to the Third Reich.	The Germans hated the Jews and they built, in Poland, concentration camps with the goal to liquidate the Jews.
	Poles were spied on, made fun of, frightened.... this is a hurtful time in our history...The Katyn Massacre is well known... Lives of Polish officers and intelligentsia were taken.	[Poles'] lives and freedom were lost, those who hid the sought-after Jews and gave them hiding places.
B	The threats to Poland were the Russian and German armies. Poland stopped existing, and there was Russification and Germanisation...people [Poles] were treated like beasts.	The leader of the Germans was Hitler. He thought the Aryan race was superhuman and that the Jews were not people and that they need to be exterminated.
		Many Poles hid Jewish families even though they could be killed for this.
C	World War II started in 1939 when the Germans under Adolf Hitler attacked Poland. The Polish armies bravely defended against the German armies, even though the Germans had more soldiers and this didn't allow Poland to truly defend herself. At this time we have to single out how brave the soldiers at Westerplatte were, they defended Poland from the Baltic side....	Hitler was especially cruel and with hatred he targeted the Jews, and as his goal, he chose to exterminate their nation.

Similar patterns emerged in Selection B, where Poles were brutally victimised by the occupying forces; the reference to Germanisation implies de-Polonisation, a relatively sophisticated understanding of what the occupation was like for Poles, particularly in the western (Germanised) part of Poland, where this student lives. Hitler's ideas of racial superiority are again used to frame the destruction of the Jews, and Poles are lauded for having hidden their Jewish neighbors. In this narrative, Jews are instrumentalised. Although they are also victims, their role in the resistance narrative proves that Poles were brave for saving them, despite the harrowing conditions of war. The Jewish presence in this narrative thus upholds the main theme of resistance and bravery.

Selection C provides a counterpoint where the main focus is on Polish bravery, and Hitler is seen as the architect of Jewish destruction. The relationship between Poles and Jews is not mentioned.

Victimisation

Five of the responses focused almost exclusively on Polish victimhood. They typically included descriptions of hopelessness, of Poles' tragic heroism in the face of certain defeat. Although these responses also reflect ruin and resistance, they focused more broadly on the victimisation of the entire Polish nation. These responses likely reflect the ideas that pervaded the literature and poetry of the 19th century (cf. Davies 1982) that students have studied in school. In this literary canon, Poland is portrayed as the all-suffering "Christ-of-Nations" (Garton Ash 1989). Poles commonly embrace this identity, as it helps them to frame and understand their centuries of human loss during a series of wars and uprisings. Wojtek's response, shown in Table 5, is emblematic of the victimhood narrative.

The overall tone is one of frustration, but also a belief that Poland was abandoned and tricked by her neighbors and allies (lines 6–7, 12), and attacked or betrayed by Germans, Allies, and Russians (or Reds, as he calls them). All the while, Poles sacrificed their lives for the freedom of Europe (lines 1–2, 9). In this response Poland stands alone, defending the honour of the country and the European continent, reflecting what Garton Ash (1989, p, 3) describes as the "messianic allegory in which Poland, the 'Christ among nations,' suffered, was crucified, but would rise again for Europe's redemption"; see also Davies 1982; Zubrzycki 2006). In Wojtek's essay, the Poles offer assistance to the Jews during the war (line 8), but he offers scant explanation. And even though Poles helped Jews survive (line 8), they died by going "to the gas". The idea that Poles helped Jews is often stressed in Polish collective memory, most recently with the decision to create a monument to Poles who saved Jews during the war; it is to be erected in front of Warsaw's newly constructed Museum of Polish Jews (Kulish 2013).

Wojtek's narrative of World War II retains the general flow of many student responses: like other responses, it contains few specific dates, proper names, or specific events, but his essay stands out by focusing more acutely on victimisation

Domesticating the Difficult Past

Table 5 Wojtek's account: Poles as victims

Line number	Excerpt
1	I am going to start from the fact that Poland defended Europe from Communism.
2	We were weakened and hardly got back our freedom…
3	During this time, the Germans created an army.
4	In 1939, Hitler wanted to occupy Poland similarly to other countries,
5	but we (even though we had about 10% what the enemy had—not counting their
6	allies),
7	we did not give up. Poles lost quickly; we didn't have help from any side.
8	England and France betrayed us, only Romania didn't let Hitler march across it.
9	We had so many Jews who went "to the gas" first even though Poles helped them.
10	We were in a hopeless situation, no one helped us and we helped everyone. Then
11	there was a switch of the takeover and the Reds took over Poland. Poles started
12	fighting even more against Hitler. And then USSR tricked us and we stayed
13	communist until 1989.

than most. In an anomaly worth noting, this response ends later than any other narrative I analysed, mentioning Poland's transition to liberal democracy in 1989 (line 12). Conscious or not, Wojtek depicts a sense of historical continuity, as though he saw the war as another struggle of many that Poland has endured to obtain its freedom. This particular template of martyrdom and victimisation provides flexibility in explaining World War II as an historical event, showing the brave Polish population engaged in a defensive struggle, and upholding the depiction of Poland as a non-threatening (and consistent) victim of history.

Outliers

Outlier essays help to illuminate the broader trends in these essays. In this regard, two narratives stood out in particular. At first glance Darek's essay seems rather typical:

> 1 Sept 1939 around 4 a.m., the first bombs fell. That is how World War II started. On one side of the conflict were the Allied forces, on the other were the Axis powers. The war lasted 6 years. Tens of millions of people died, and there were concentration camps where 6 million Jews died. In this war, the first time the atomic bomb was used. The end was 2 September 1945.

At the same time, in subtle ways, this narrative strayed from the norm. It is atypical in naming Allied and Axis powers. It is more precise in its reference to Jewish victims: the numbers and references to Jewish deaths in the concentration camps. Furthermore, the student mentions the atom bomb; he is the only one to use that term, though two others mention Hiroshima by name. The words Poland or Poles are not used. This response seems more global in character; Poland is not mentioned, throwing into bold relief the deeply national character of the other responses.

Another narrative, by Martynia, 18, stands out for its richness and personal touch:

> War is such a hard time for everyone…Poland in World War II was attacked first. When I hear about this war, I am reminded of an interview… with an older woman…. She placed a great emphasis on human lives, and their worth. She told a moving and sad story about a soldier who left the front and wanted to hide in one of the nearby houses. But the threat of death was imminent for the families, the one he found [to hide in]. Of course they helped this man, and when there was an inspection he fled. Unfortunately, the [enemy soldiers] saw him and shot him in front of the eyes of all these people and left the body. During the war, so many people died. Many children lost their parents, grandparents, siblings. I can't even think about it, what would happen if I lived then. I don't know the answer to this question. Going back to the interview, this lady I interviewed spoke of difficult times, of suffering of her children that didn't know what a happy childhood was—they saw fighting, guns, blood…the media shows the war from the historical side, it doesn't focus on the suffering of people, the greatest for those in the war. No one deserves such a death.

This narrative begins like others: with the invasion of Poland. But immediately Martynia brings us the story of a survivor she met. The myths of heroism fall away as she tells the story through the eyes of a witness. Martynia breaks the narrative by occasionally breaking into the story to editorialise. This is one of the few accounts that ends on a moral note: "No one deserves such a death". She underscores the unfairness, the destruction and death, the blood and tragedy that war brings, and laments that "the media" do not focus on the human losses that accompany it. She does not attempt to downplay the bloodshed and confusion that war brings.

This narrative demonstrates how contact with a survivor—a person who has experienced war firsthand—can change an abstract story into something particular, understandable, and, for Martynia, empathetically relatable.

Discussion and Conclusions

During World War II, Polish civilian and military behaviour rarely fit a neat category of bystander, perpetrator, or victim; Poles faced multiple difficult challenges, among them the question of whether to help people outside their own community, such as Jewish neighbors. The war was messy and untamed, and people found themselves in contradictory predicaments (Deák, Gross, and Judt 2000). Poles lost immeasurable wealth at the hands of destructive oppressors while also profiting by looting the homes of their Jewish neighbors (Gross and Grudzinska-Gross 2012). In other words, Poles were at the same time brutally oppressed and opportunistic oppressors. They were victims of merciless Nazi occupiers and complicit perpetrators of inhumane crimes, and everything in between.

Just as the reality of war was complex, so too is the present-day memory of World War II in Poland. In his analysis of Holocaust memorials around the world, James Young (1993) begins the section on Poland with a quote from a young traveler. Poland, the traveler says, is "an odd country which never forgets its past, but more often than not does not understand it" (p. 113). World War II is taught in schools, and memorialised in the city streets and on television. Over time, certain events and heroes have come to the fore, while others have faded. Monuments adorn city parks, avenues are named after heroes, war movies and television series are released with every passing year, and commemorative parades shut down traffic during the summer. Those who witnessed the Holocaust or fought in the underground are either gone or are elderly and infirm. In the schools, children are systematically taught about World War II in 6th grade and again in 10th. In 2012, the subject was taken out of the high school history classroom, but continues to be taught in classes on Polish language and literature.

Even so, despite public debate about Polish collaboration and complicity, and international efforts to introduce a Holocaust curriculum in Poland, students continue to fashion the type of unifying history they might wish their forefathers had experienced.

Contrary to a complicated narrative in which students would learn that Poles were both an oppressed and an oppressor group, the students in this sample paint Polish wartime behaviour in broad, traditional archetypes. Their narratives suggest there is still an idealised image of Poland, which becomes a source of pride; this wartime Poland is idealised and the war is at once a defining moment of ruin, resistance, and victimhood. Students gloss over the complexity of war. Most of those surveyed created a neat chronological narrative that frames the war's bloodbath as being about ruin, resistance, or occasionally about victimisation. Their narratives are steeped in destruction, and populated by people good and bad: heroes, resisters, martyrs, and victims.

The data presented here show that Polish students feel patriotic and positive about their country. Their narratives are heroic and at times tragic, but in general, they uphold a "positive dominant myth" (Weiner 2001; Wertsch 2002). Those who feel pride view Polish deeds during the war as exemplary of bravery. The students feel that the past embodies Polishness; a reflection of something deep in the Polish national character linking wartime behaviour to the nature of being Polish today lends itself to selective remembrance.

Though these students were asked to narrate World War II, they never witnessed the horrors depicted. They could not, properly speaking, have "remembered" them. Instead, the act of writing a narrative essay for this project jogged recall of previously learned stories, and students drew upon common cultural understandings. Susan Sontag (2003, p. 115), describing the effect of iconic photographs on cultural remembrance of horrific events, states:

> Strictly speaking…there is collective instruction. All memory is individual, irreproducible— it dies with each person. What is called collective memory is not a remembering but a stipulating: that this is important, and this is the story about how it happened…common ideas of significance and trigger predictable thoughts, feelings.

Her distinction between memory (which she believes to be individual), and instruction (a social act) is important because it implies that collective memory is akin to social schooling. If we apply what Sontag is saying to the students in this sample, these children were collectively instructed to remember World War II as a narrative of victimisation, heroism, or resistance. Most students shared what was important (the invasion of Poland), and some even shared feelings about the war, such as bravery, pride, or frustration. Wartime national histories were transformed into common legends and myths that students consume and recite in patterned and similar ways. This allows generations to bond through a common narrative of collective trauma.

For this group of students, their narratives of war were tidy pictures that, in many instances, reflected what suggested an essence of Polishness. As one student stated, "If it weren't for [Hitler], the world would not have suffered so, but also the Poles wouldn't have a reason to be as proud as they are now". Past injustices help this student justify her pride in Polish bravery. How Poles behaved is more emblematic of who Poles are now than what actually happened during the war, in which Poles extorted Jews, looted their property, and, after the war, dug up mass graves looking for their gold teeth (Gross and Grudzinska-Gross 2012). This is a classic use of collective historical accounts to make sense of present circumstances.

Such tidy pictures are not unique to Poland. Nations often create neat narratives of past wars. Winston Churchill called World War II "our finest hour", while in the United States it is known as "the Good War". This rhetoric glosses over Allied plans to "eradicate" German cities, overlooks the illegal imprisonment of American citizens of Japanese descent in internment camps, and fails to consider the killing of thousands at Hiroshima through the use of nuclear weapons. The findings of this study are consistent with evidence that in the teaching, learning, and remembering of complex and brutal wars, the past is packaged in a way that exemplifies contemporary feelings about a nation. In this way, students, teachers, and politicians domesticate a brutal past. It is not surprising that they have inherited a story that begins with ruin and ends with resistance. To introduce wartime Polish-Jewish relations into this narrative threatens the positive feelings the official culture associates with World War II. In particular for nations recovering from war (Poland only regained full sovereignty in 1989) and in nations where national identity is tied to struggle, it is often deemed unpatriotic to disseminate counter-narratives about the past. As a result, it may be hard for students to learn, and even harder for them to accept, that Polish Jews perished at the hands of both Nazis and their own Polish neighbors. While such a tidy picture of the past absolves Catholic Poland of misdeeds against her Jewish neighbors, it also obscures the experience of Jews and the Holocaust.

From Ernest Renan's (1882) classic formulation we know the crucial role that exclusion plays in maintaining a national narrative and bolstering historical legitimacy: "Forgetting…is a crucial factor in the creation of a nation…. The essence of a nation is that all individuals have many things in common; and also that they have forgotten many things". This quote emphasises the place that forgotten or obstructed memories hold in the creation of a unified national identity.

However, organised exclusion is brought into focus differently when we consider the phenomenon of "European collective memory" surrounding the globalisation of the Holocaust. Levy and Sznaider (2006) write that the Holocaust is not only taught around the world, but has become a universal symbol for the evil against which we measure all crimes against humanity. According to Tony Judt (2005), the Holocaust is the mainstay of the common European identity. Given the international focus on teaching the Holocaust, as evidenced by resolutions made by the European Parliament, the Stockholm Declaration of 2000, and by the statements required from countries aiming to join the European Union (FRA 2009), one could imagine that Polish students would produce narratives that reflect local Polish responses to the Holocaust, while also reflecting global changes in the widespread and mandated adoption of Holocuast education.

Research has shown that education about the Holocaust has increased, and the teaching of the Holocaust has changed over time. The Holocaust is no longer presented in textbooks as a unique historical event but rather as an event representing the loss of human rights and the depravity of humanity (Bromley and Russell 2010), and it provides a benchmark for teaching about human rights and other genocides. But contrary to the emerging international consensus and pedagogical practices, when it comes to World War II and the Jewish experience within it, Polish students continue to emphasise a homogeneous and national story.

One small group of these students offered hints of counternarratives in their stories. In this subset of responses, knowledge of the Holocaust and of the Jewish-Polish experience during World War II appeared in its nascent stages. These children were beginning to embark on a narrative or an interpretation that ran counter to what is commonly believed in Polish society. Interestingly, the students in this subset were more likely to cite history class as the most important source of historical information. They were also twice as likely to mention Jews in their written narratives. Although this sample is small, social frameworks of memory around World War II may indeed be changing in the nation, as evidenced by children inserting Jews and the Holocaust into the overall Polish narrative. These students believed they learned this narrative in school, which may or may not be the case, but it points to the idea that school, for them, was a source of new ideas, and therefore of open-mindedness.

As a subject, history must arm children with the mental faculties to make clear and conscientious decisions about the future, using the past as a foundation. Teachers must learn to prepare children to weigh evidence, search for truth, and work toward the good of society. If we tidy up our past, and relegate messy and chaotic events to oblivion, we rob society of the ability to raise a generation of conscientious objectors to evil. In ignoring national misdeeds, we teach false myths and legends and we create an ignorant community where those who stand up to injustice must do so alone.

Appendix

Questionnaire

To the best of your ability, please tell me the history of World War II from the beginning.
Where does your understanding of World War II come from?

Rank the following sources in order of importance. Only rank the sources you used. (1 = most important)		Indicate how credible you believe each source to be (1 = Most credible, to 10 = not credible):
_____	History class	_____
_____	Family discussions (with parents or grandparents)	_____
_____	Personal reading	_____
_____	Church/Sunday School	_____
_____	History textbooks (school books)	_____
_____	Participation in historical or cultural events	_____
_____	Television	_____
_____	Newspapers	_____
_____	Visits to historical sites	_____
_____	Documentaries	_____
_____	Movies with historical content	_____
_____	Others:_____	_____

Please tell us a bit about you.

Name of school	
Number of years in school	
Place of birth	
Religious background	
Age	
Gender	

Anything you would like to add that I have not asked?
Thank you!

References

Bikont, A. (2004). *My z Jedwabnego* [Us, from Jedwabne]. Warsaw: Proszynski i S-ka.
Bromley, P., & Russell, S. G. (2010). The Holocaust as history and human rights: a cross-national analysis of Holocaust education in social science textbooks, 1970–2008. *Prospects, 40*(1), 153–173.

Corbin, J., & Strauss, A. (1990). Grounded theory research: procedures, canons, and evaluative criteria. *Qualitative Sociology, 13*(1), 3–21.
Davies, N. (1982). *God's playground, a history of Poland: The origins to 1795* (Vol. 1). New York: Columbia University Press.
Deák, I., Gross, J. T., & Judt, T. (2000). *The politics of retribution in Europe: World War II and its aftermath.* Princeton, NJ: Princeton University Press.
Engelking, B. (2012). *Jest taki piekny sloneczny dzien. Losy Zydow szukajacych ratunku na wsi polskiej, 1942–1945* [It is a beautiful, sunny day. Losses of Jews searching for salvation in the Polish countryside, 1942–1945]. Warsaw: Stowarzyszenie Centrum Badan nad Zaglada Zydow.
Epstein, T. (1998). Deconstructing differences in African-American and European-American adolescents' perspectives on US history. *Curriculum Inquiry, 28*(4), 397–423.
FRA [European Union Agency for Fundamental Rights] (2009). *Excursion to the past: Teaching for the future*. Handbook for teachers. Vienna: FRA. http://fra.europa.eu/en/publication/2010/excursion-past-teaching-future-handbook-teachers
Garton Ash, T. (1989). *The uses of adversity: Essays on the fate of Central Europe*. New York: Penguin Books/Granta.
Glaser, B. G. (1978). *Theoretical sensitivity: Advances in the methodology of grounded theory* (Vol. 2). Mill Valley, CA: Sociology Press.
Grabowski, J. (2011). *Judenjagd. Polowanie na Zydow, 1942–1945* [Judenjagd: Hunting for Jews, 1942–1945]. Warsaw: Stowarzyszenie Centrum Badan nad Zaglada Zydow.
Gross, J. T. (2001). *Neighbors: The destruction of the Jewish community in Jedwabne, Poland*. Princeton: Princeton University Press.
Gross, M. (2010). Rewriting the nation: World War II narratives in Polish history textbooks. *International Perspectives on Education and Society, 14*, 213–245.
Gross, J. T., & Grudzinska-Gross, I. G. (2012). *Golden harvest: Events at the periphery of the Holocaust*. New York: Oxford University Press.
Hobsbawm, E. J. (1994). *The age of extremes: A history of the world, 1914–1991*. New York: Pantheon.
Judt, T. (2005). *Postwar: A history of Europe since 1945*. New York: Penguin Press.
Kulish, N. (2013, 18 April). Polish museum repairs tie to a Jewish past. *The New York Times*. http://www.nytimes.com/2013/04/19/world/europe/poland-reconnects-to-jewish-past-with-museum.html?pagewanted=all&_r=0
Levy, D., & Sznaider, N. (2006). *The Holocaust and memory in the global age*. Philadelphia: Temple University Press.
Merriam, S. B. (2002). Introduction to qualitative research. In S. B. Merriam et al. (Eds.), *Qualitative research in practice: Examples for discussion and analysis* (pp. 3–17). San Francisco, CA: Jossey-Bass.
Miles, M. B., & Huberman, A. M. (1994). *Qualitative data analysis: An expanded sourcebook*. Thousand Oaks, CA: Sage Publications.
Porat, D. A. (2004). It's not written here, but this is what happened: Students' cultural comprehension of textbook narratives on the Israeli-Arab conflict. *American Educational Research Journal, 41*(4), 963–996.
Renan, E. (1882, 11 March). *What is a nation?* Lecture given at the Sorbonne, Paris.
Riessman, C. K. (Ed.) (1993). *Narrative analysis*. London: Sage.
Seixas, P. (1997). Mapping the terrain of historical significance. *Social Education, 61*(1), 22–27.
Sontag, S. (2003). *Regarding the pain of others*. New York: Farrar, Strauss Giroux.
Steinlauf, M. C. (1997). *Bondage to the dead: Poland and the memory of the Holocaust*. Syracuse, NY: Syracuse University Press.
Strauss, A., & Corbin, J. (1994). Grounded theory methodology: An overview. In N. Denzin & Y. Lincoln (Eds.), *Handbook of qualitative research* (pp. 273–285). Thousand Oaks, CA: Sage.
Weiner, A. (2001). *Making sense of war: The Second World War and the fate of the Bolshevik revolution*. Princeton, NJ: Princeton University Press.
Wertsch, J. V. (2002). *Voices of collective remembering*. Cambridge, UK: Cambridge University Press.

Wineburg, S., Mosborg, S., Porat, D., & Duncan, A. (2007). Common belief and the cultural curriculum: An intergenerational study of historical consciousness. *American Educational Research Journal, 44*(1), 40–76.

Young, J. E. (1993). *The texture of memory: Holocaust memorials and meaning*. New Haven: Yale University Press.

Zerubavel, Y. (1997). *Recovered roots: Collective memory and the making of Israeli national tradition*. Chicago: University of Chicago Press.

Zubrzycki, G. (2006). *The crosses of Auschwitz: Nationalism and religion in post-Communist Poland*. Chicago/London: University of Chicago Press.

Mind the Gap: Holocaust Education in Germany, between Pedagogical Intentions and Classroom Interactions

Wolfgang Meseth and Matthias Proske

Introduction

The injunction to learn from history is a key feature of German debates over the politics of memory and history, and since the end of World War II has been seen as primarily a task for educators. This educational impetus has marked the remembrance of the Holocaust as early as the original re-education policies of the Allies immediately after the war. Moreover, it has gone on to inform the modernisation and reforms of education from the 1960s and 1970s through to the present. These reforms have often connected to the famous admonition of Theodor W. Adorno (1971), the co-founder of critical theory, that the "very first demand on education is that there not be another Auschwitz" to a human-rights-focused education of tolerance, to the courage to stand up for one's beliefs, and for democratic values (Meseth 2005, 2007).

Thus state schools in Germany were asked to serve as society's central location for memory and learning. In particular, history curricula have a central function both in transmitting historical knowledge and in socialising subsequent generations both morally and politically. Analyses of Holocaust education curricula show that strong demands are placed on schools to address the history of National Socialism

---

W. Meseth
Philipps Universität Marburg, Fachbereich Erziehungswissenschaften,
Institut für Schulpädagogik, Arbeitsbereich Bildung und Heterogenität
Pilgrimstein 2, 35032 Marburg, Germany
e-mail: meseth@staff.uni-marburg.de

M. Proske (✉)
Institut für Allgemeine Didaktik und Schulforschung, Universität zu Köln,
Innere Kanalstr. 15, 50823 Köln, Germany
e-mail: M.Proske@uni-koeln.de

(NS). Students must learn about the extraordinary historical responsibility that the Federal Republic of Germany must accept as the successor state to the Third Reich. The memory of Holocaust victims must be kept alive. And a framework must be developed in order to derive lessons for the future from the NS past (Brumlik 2004; Heyl 1997; Meseth et al. 2004; Meseth 2005). On the other hand, Henke-Bockschatz (2004) offers a vigorous counterargument to the overly ambitious expectations for moral education in history lessons on NS and the Holocaust.

Research on history education has rarely addressed questions about how instruction on the history of NS plays out in practice, about how ambitious educational goals are implemented at the level of actual instruction, or about the challenges that teachers and students face when they are asked to address such a morally fraught topic within the organisational context of the school. In this chapter we present findings from a qualitative study that explored these issues using analyses of concrete classroom experience. Our pilot study, conducted in 2000–2001, was funded by the American Jewish Committee (AJC), and the main study, conducted from 2005 to 2007, was funded by the Deutsche Forschungsgemeinschaft (DFG).

This chapter is rooted in an overview of research on historical pedagogy for teaching about NS, and contains three sections. We first lay out the theoretical and methodological framework of our investigation and then use carefully selected case studies to illustrate our central findings. We show how the organisational framework of instruction shapes the treatment of NS as a topic and gives it a specific pedagogical form, which gives rise to a tension between the need to provide an adequate representation of the crimes of NS, and to fulfill the goals of moral education. We illustrate this tension across four cases. Each case demonstrates the challenges that can arise—and the ways these challenges are handled in the classroom—from the moral implications of certain teaching materials (such as an interview with an eyewitness, an excerpt from Hitler's *Mein Kampf,* or a television documentary on Hitler's seizure of power). Finally, we discuss our findings systematically in relation to our initial questions.

National Socialism in History Classes: Stages in Germany's Debate about Historical Pedagogy

The Historical Consciousness of Successive Generations and the Crisis in Teaching about National Socialism

Given the high political expectations that teaching about the history of NS will have enlightening effects, it is not surprising that the opinion polls documenting a lack of historical knowledge and unsettling moral attitudes among German adolescents have been taken as a sure sign of social disintegration and have led consistently, and reflexively, to calls for better history education. "Auschwitz: Never heard of it?" is the title of a widely debated study by Silbermann and Stoffers (2000) of German adolescents' knowledge about the history of NS. The study's thesis shocked the public: young people's knowledge about NS "approaches zero" (p. 47) and "we", as it reads ominously in the text, "are on the road to ignorance". But the study's supposed representativeness, and the dramatic interpretation of its findings, have come under scrutiny (Meseth 2005, p. 207; von Borries 2002, p. 14ff). Analysis of the sample shows that the number of younger respondents was under 100. Moreover, over 95%, etc. of them did understand the significance of Auschwitz; only 4.3% did not know "who or what Auschwitz is or was", which can be read as a very acceptable outcome (von Borries 2002). The study's resonance with the public, however, suggests that the question of what each new generation is learning from the history of National Socialism—or not learning—is deeply intertwined with the politics of memory in Germany.

The quality of history education is often scrutinised in light of findings such as those of Silbermann and Stoffers—and this trend is not new. For example, in 1977 Germany's largest weekly magazine, *Der Spiegel*, quoted German President Walter Scheel in the context of a widely cited study on education (1977, p. 44): "We are in danger of becoming a country without a history". Dieter Boßmann (1977) asked approximately 3,000 students to write an essay on the topic "What I have heard about Adolf Hitler…" Most of the students' writing differed greatly from contemporary research on the subject; to Boßmann this suggested a failure to clearly condemn Nazi crimes. Based on these findings, he and the political class publicly questioned the quality of history education in Germany and demanded improvements. They also argued that the lack of historical knowledge among young people posed a threat to the democratic culture of Germany. "History education" was "in critical condition", the president feared, because young people "no longer understood the meaning of this liberal democratic political order" (Der Spiegel 1977, p. 44).

Pedagogical Responses to the Crisis in Teaching History: Research on Historical Consciousness and Education

Referred to as the "Boßmann shock", the study created lasting confusion among history teachers and researchers about the goals and efficacy of German history teaching. Also, it drew attention to the apparent ineffectiveness of history education in Germany. The study exposed a state of student knowledge—shaped by family and the mass media—that was so at odds with scientific and scholarly views of history that reversing it seemed to be beyond the power of education. These tidbits of knowledge, sometimes dismissed as "historical consciousness through trivia" (Schörken 1979, p. 74), led to a new orientation in history teaching that defines the discipline to this day. The impression of a glaring discrepancy between what is taught in history class and what is learned challenged the idea of a direct transfer of historical knowledge (Knigge 1988; von Borries 1980) and led educators to abandon the simple broadcaster-receiver model: the idea that students functioned as a kind of fact machine, where a given input would inevitably produce a predictable output. Instead, research into the teaching of history shifted its focus toward a better understanding of the conditions that fostered learning. The selective appropriation of knowledge— influenced by the mass media and by personal experience—as well as the role of historical consciousness in the construction of meaning and identity, were advanced as a "key category of historical pedagogy" (Rüsen 1994, p. 3). The aim was to develop a theoretically informed explanation for the development of historical consciousness in order to clarify the objectives and methods of history teaching.

Parallel to theoretical considerations of historical consciousness and learning, a new line of empirical research on historical consciousness emerged (von Borries 1995). This new research included the administration of regular student surveys to measure historical knowledge and moral understanding, as well as subjective learning styles and interests. Only recently has history—and vocational—pedagogy in the German-speaking world pursued a strand of empirical research on teaching and learning that is focused on the possibilities and limits of acquiring historical knowledge and the formation of historical awareness (Gautschi et al. 2007). A cursory analysis of German history teaching reveals, however, that until early in this decade, most analyses of history teaching have been based primarily on historical, rather than educational, criteria (Günther-Arndt and Sauer 2006; von Borries 2009, pp. 312ff). The narrative competence and construction of historical meaning by adolescents is the focus of cognitive interest (Barricelli 2005; Kölbl 2004; Wilson 2001; Wineburg 2000; Zülsdorf-Kersting 2007). Also of interest, to the extent it is explored, is how history is constructed through communication: "how adolescents create historical contexts for their existence" (Wineburg 2000, p. 309). Thus we conclude that research on history teaching has marginalised the analysis of actual classroom interactions, i.e., the question of how teachers handle the history of NS in real-world teaching situations.

This is the aim with which our investigation begins. We want to look inside the black box of classroom interaction and—from the perspective of educational science—investigate the conditions and challenges under which the history of NS and the Holocaust are taught in school.

Methodology, Theoretical Framework and Road Map of the Study

In designing empirical studies of teaching, researchers face three closely interrelated methodological problems. First, they must set out their assumptions about how they will assess the object to be studied. That is, how is instruction conceptualised theoretically? Second, from these assumptions they must provide information about the cognitive interest they pursue and how this interest leads to concrete research questions. And third, they must clarify the methodological questions about the kinds of data needed to address the problem and how they will be collected and interpreted.

Theoretical Perspectives on Quantitative and Qualitative Research on Teaching

Various schools of thought within the research community have reached a broad consensus that education and instruction are best conceptualised as social practices that have unknown outcomes and are loaded with conflicting expectations. The question of how teaching can be described in ways appropriate to theory and investigated empirically is addressed very differently in the two main approaches to research on teaching: hypothesis-testing research on instructional effectiveness, and meaning-interpretative research. The latter best describes the perspective we present here.

The insight of instructional effectiveness, that classroom instruction is "indeterminate and uncertain", leads to the juxtaposition of cause and effect, as in the "process-product model", and probabilistic relationships, as in the "opportunity to learn model" (Baumert and Kunter 2006, p. 477). Instructional effectiveness is based on an explanatory model that assumes a probabilistic relationship between certain aspects of education (factors) and the performance of students, measured ex-post facto (Helmke 2003; Klieme 2006; Klieme and Reusser 2003). It reduces the complexity of classroom instruction to a few independent variables (or variable clusters) and can thus use the hypothesis-testing of "normal science" in its research design and ameliorate instruction's problem of uncertainty and the complexity of social interaction. These problems are dealt with as probabilistic phenomena that can be modeled using multivariate regression. It also looks for patterned regularities in the processes of teaching and learning to help make instruction more focused and effective.

In contrast, "meaning-interpretive research"—known in the international discussion as "interpretive research on teaching" (Erickson 1986, p. 122)—tries to address the issue of uncertainty in teaching, both theoretically and empirically. The aim is to reconstruct how processes of instructional communication construct meaning, to understand how instruction can overcome structural uncertainties to stabilise itself socially and to pursue its pedagogical goals. Following Clifford Geertz, Shulman (1986) has argued that the aim of qualitative research is not a "search of law" but "an interpretive one in a search of meaning" (p. 18). The goal is to study "a concrete[,] particular case in detail, aiming to develop as full a model as possible of the situation and the contexts in which it is nested" (p. 21).

This means that an account of classroom instruction is needed that allows a high-definition reconstruction of complex interactions. The concept of "instruction as a system of interaction" has been developed from Erving Goffman's work in interpretive research on teaching (Cobb and Bauersfeld 1995; Naujok et al. 2004).

Teaching as a System of Interaction and the Problem of Contingency in Education

For Goffman (1983), interaction is a *sui generis*, emergent social process whose course is neither determined by organisational requirements nor clearly controlled or coordinated by its participants. Interaction patterns are influenced, but not determined, by the organisation in which they are embedded and by the people involved. Unforeseen, unintended incidents can arise from the interaction of those taking part in the process. How a certain course of interaction develops, what paths it takes, and how it concludes, cannot be determined through a priori planning. Rather, they are best understood as discrete and contingent structuring outputs within the interaction. The emphasis on contingency in this understanding of interaction reveals a major structural problem in education by sharpening the focus on the uncertain efficacy of educational interventions. From the perspective of educational science, this uncertainty stems from the fundamental difference between teaching and learning, between intended effects and the individual appropriation of knowledge (Kade 1997; Prange 2003). During the course of interaction, instruction is realised as a form of pedagogical communication (Proske 2003a) through a sequence of transmission and acquisition operations. The transmissions, however, do not have a direct causal effect on learning itself.

Legal and organisational frames play a major role in the structuring of transmission and acquisition operations in the interaction. They stabilise the instructional system of interaction by providing objective, social, and temporal rules and order. The framing, however, does not determine the actual course of a lesson or close the gap between intended transmission and individual appropriations of knowledge. On the one hand, these legal and organisational frames underwrite the possibility of classroom instruction as an institutionalised form of state education. On the other hand they present a specific set of challenges for instruction, particularly with regard to its pedagogical-normative objectives.

What constitutes this framing of instructional interaction? In factual terms, instruction is about the expectation that classroom discussion and activities address the topic of the day, what will be "gone over". During instruction, given curricular topics are brought into a specific pedagogical form. Considering the myriad possibilities for developing themes, however, the topic could always have been addressed much differently. Moreover, through the process of negotiating a topic communicatively, i.e., under the conditions of interaction, the topic takes a specific shape that does not necessarily reflect any given lesson plan. Therefore, the specific factual challenge is to do justice to the professional and pedagogical demands of the topic within the given organisational—i.e., social and temporal—context.

In social terms, instruction's interactions are ordered in a specific, asymmetric way, where expectations are distributed relatively clearly among the roles of teacher and student. Its asymmetric character issues from the institutionalised mandate to educate and evaluate, which structures the relationship between the teacher and students as one of differences in power and knowledge. Teachers create the conditions for learning and then initiate it by formulating tasks and assignments and by evaluating student contributions. Students oscillate between the practical expectations that they participate actively or passively in the lesson and that they share interesting experiences with their peers at school.

Student attendance is mandatory, but this does not automatically translate into students being committed to participate or learn. Role expectations can always be sabotaged. Attention can be focused behind the scenes of the class, where what happens is different from the official proceedings on the "main stage". It thus follows that the specific challenge for instruction in this social dimension is to facilitate the motivation required to treat the topic appropriately under conditions of compulsory attendance. In the time dimension, the specific challenge is to coordinate and to synchronise individual learning and organisational-curricular requirements (required number of class meetings, at 45 minutes each). A certain number of hours are devoted to the treatment of a topic. This does not necessarily match the learning pace of the entire class or individual students. Moreover, the expectation that instruction meet its goals within the factual and temporal timeframe must anticipate that the lesson will evolve differently than planned. Contingent events can demand so much attention that any teleological script of a given class is in constant jeopardy.

Freedom and Coercion: Education's Paradoxical Goal Structure Between over-Moralisation and under-Moralisation

The structural problem of teaching's contingent effects also becomes a normative problem when it comes to teaching the history of National Socialism. Moral expectations linked to the treatment of this subject "in the land of perpetrators" are very high. In addition to the goal of learning historical facts, history lessons about the Nazi era, especially in Germany, face a special demand that teachers transmit moral positions, such as identification with victims of the Holocaust, empathy for persecuted minorities, and the rejection of violence and discrimination. But the attempt to use education to influence students' moral bearings poses a central normative problem for pedagogy. The conceptualisation of the moral subject as a free and autonomous being—an idea heavily influenced by German idealism and neo-humanism—leads education to what Wimmer (2006) calls a self-contradiction, expressed famously by Immanuel Kant (1803/1966): "How do I cultivate freedom through coercion?" In the context of the pedagogical treatment of National Socialism and the Holocaust this means that, on the one hand, history instruction is obligated to respect a student's freedom in service to her individual self-development. Students must reach independent historical judgments about the history of NS.

On the other hand, history instruction should ensure that the students take on the socially expected conclusions about the moral depravity of NS. They should be taught to learn from history, in the sense that they internalise socially desirable values such as tolerance and equality—of course not by coercion and indoctrination, but out of conviction and of their own free will. In this sense, the paradoxical goal structure means that education should exert influence on the students without compromising their self-determination (Luhmann 1996). It is likely, though by no means inevitable, that students will adopt the desired moral attitudes through mere exposure to the enormity of Nazi war crimes during the Holocaust. The difference between pedagogical intent and the individual appropriation of knowledge— i.e., the problem that what is taught is not always what is learned—applies even to subject areas characterised by overwhelming moral clarity, such as the Holocaust. The contingency of education's efficacy remains a structural problem in pedagogy.

This paradox links the teaching of NS to a key problem, that of avoiding both "under-moralisation" and "over-moralisation" (Schneider 2004). Under-moralisation refers to forms of communication in which the moral condemnation of Nazi crimes is not clearly identifiable, or in which the socially accepted modes of speech (political correctness) about the history of NS are not maintained. In contrast, over-moralisation refers to communication where moral judgments about individuals are reached, i.e., decisions are made about the regard or disdain of the students, but the expectations that students will appropriate those judgments are exaggerated and redundant. Thus a tension arises in history instruction: over-moralising threatens to cross the ethical boundaries of the teaching profession, but in avoiding it, teachers run the risk of not doing justice to the moral dimension of the issue and the broader educational mission.

Research Questions and Design

Based on this model of instruction as an interaction system and the specific challenge of moral expectation in the pedagogical treatment of the history of NS, we specified our research questions as follows. First, how does instruction come to terms with its uncertain efficacy and the tension between over- and under-moralising? Second, what impact does the organisational framework of schools have on processes of transmission and learning for the topic of NS?

To answer these questions, we developed a two-stage interpretation process. We first analysed the teaching concepts that teachers used in terms of their instructional intentions and learning expectations. Teaching concepts are accessible empirically primarily through the teaching materials that teachers select (textbooks, worksheets, videos, slide shows, etc.). The central question is about the pedagogical intentions that might attach to certain teaching materials (such as a video of an eyewitness account or an excerpt from Hitler's *Mein Kampf*). Furthermore, we examined the teaching approaches in terms of their implicit construction of addressees. We consider the type of learner assumed by a given pedagogical-methodical arrangement, e.g., a student who is knowledgeable or uniformed, impressionable or enlightened. The analysis of educational expectations and the construction of addressees provide an interpretive lens that can give insights into the intended student learning processes and the expected development of the lesson.

In the second step, we interpreted the factual proceedings of the classroom lessons. For this purpose we created detailed protocols of the interactions (transcripts) within the instructional units we studied. As opposed to other forms for representing social reality (codings, ethnographic recordings, etc.), transcripts document the sequential nature of the verbal contributions in detail (Deppermann 2001, p. 41) and are therefore particularly suitable for reconstructing the conversation's structure and the negotiation of meaning. We interpreted the transcribed interactions with the help of sequence analysis as it is applied in the context of conversation analysis, and elsewhere (Bergmann 1981; Hammersley 1990; Mehan 1979; Soeffner 1989). Sequence analyses are an appropriate method for our purposes, as they create "the idea of a social order that reproduces itself in the execution of its interactions" (Bergmann 1981, p. 313). They seek to make intelligible the sequential nature of events and the constructed meaning that comes to expression in the course of an interaction.

Both analytical perspectives—the reconstruction of key teaching concepts and of the course of interaction—were triangulated in the data analysis. We used our analysis of the teaching materials and the learning arrangements they created as a contrasting lens to interpret the classroom interaction and to address our research questions.

Database, Data Collection and Case Selection

We used two history classes in the pilot study and four in the main study. In most cases, two observers attended each class and made audio recordings over a period of several weeks. A selection of the recorded lessons was then transcribed. In addition to the transcriptions, we developed ethnographic reports of extraordinary classroom events, which we selected based primarily on subjective perceptions beyond the audio recordings. This process provided criteria according to which we could select relevant passages for more extensive interpretation. We selected these four cases based on an observed "intensification" of the teaching communication in a given set of lessons. "Intensification" is related to the well-known concept within qualitative research on teaching, "interactional compression" (Krummheuer 2002). We take the concept out of its original, narrower, learning context, however. In our study, communicative intensification is meant to draw attention to passages that deal with the specificity of the topic and the form of teaching so they meet three criteria. First, the subjects of NS and the Holocaust are addressed effectively, and not just communicated through formal questions. Second, we could observe that both students and teacher were interacting with each other in an active way. Third, the communication goes beyond a purely factual and cognitive form of interaction and thus makes clear that these sequences are also about moral education.

The following presentation is a condensed summary of four representative cases, prepared in the context of a detailed qualitative analysis of the transcripts (for more details, see Hollstein et al. 2002, p. 37; Meseth et al. 2004; Proske 2003b; Proske and Meseth 2006). For the purposes of illustration, the summaries should allow at least a cursory look at instructional communication on the topic of NS and the Holocaust. In the first case a teacher handles a contemporary account of the issue and its moral implications in the classroom. The second case examines the consequences for classroom discussion of a discrepancy between teacher expectations and student interpretations of an excerpt from Hitler's *Mein Kampf*. The third case also addresses a discrepancy, this time focusing particularly on the institutionalised generation gap in school. Finally, the fourth case shows how instructional communication benefits when participants assume a reciprocal, though not always articulated, consensus opinion on NS.

Integrating Authentic Contemporary Accounts in the Classroom

The reference problem in the first case is the question of how the form of instruction shapes pedagogical work on NS. What happens when this topic is dealt with in the classroom? This case examines an episode in a lesson in which the topic of (Everyday) Life in Nazi Germany from 1933 to 1938 is introduced through a video recording of a contemporary "eyewitness" account. The question is how a video documentation of a contemporary witness's account is used in the classroom, where the pedagogical intent of the video is primarily to expose students to authentic and multi-perspective approaches to NS as personally remembered history.

The video contains an excerpt from a story by Franz Wagner, who was able to emigrate in time, in 1939. Wagner talks about friendships from his childhood and youth in Nazi Germany. In one case he tells of a friend's parents and the assistance they provided to his parents when they were threatened with deportation. In another he describes an incident in which he was threatened by two members of the Hitler Youth. A friend of his, Günther Stumm—also in a Hitler Youth uniform—happens to pass by. He ignores Franz's cries for help and turns his back on him. Finally, he tells of an encounter with this same childhood friend many decades later: after a little "help with his memory" he apologises for his actions. The video ends with Wagner remarking, "better late than never".

What is the pedagogical intentionality that can be reconstructed from the use of videos featuring eyewitness accounts? Clearly evident in the diversity of the incidents in the video—one featuring a follower of the National Socialist system, another featuring a victim of everyday discrimination—is the desire to target the interpretive struggle for students with different historical experiences. The use of such authentic biographical evidence creates a pedagogical setting that is wide open to independent student interpretations. Students' empathies are not determined ahead of time, and no one can predict how intensely they will process individual aspects of the accounts. The questions that students have after experiencing Wagner's story might range from "What was this threatening experience like for Franz Wagner?" to "How would I have acted if I were in the position of Franz Wagner's friend?" to "Is it fair for Franz Wagner to demand an apology from his former friend?" No lesson plan can determine ex ante which of these questions the students will make their own. That the narrative evokes questions whose answers are not known in advance—a somewhat atypical constellation for the classroom—is more evidence of the openness of the pedagogical setting.

But what actually happens in the classroom when the videotape of Franz Wagner's story ends? One student, Svenja, reacts to the story with an awkward interjection, referring to Wagner as a "smart ass" (Note that all names of students and teachers are pseudonyms). Although the comment and the meager willingness for reconciliation it suggests come nowhere near meeting the expectations for students dealing with the testimony of a Holocaust survivor, the teacher reserves comment. The criticism was voiced in a lower than usual tone of voice, suggesting an informal mode of communication. Therefore, a response from the group, and especially from the teacher, is not likely to be either necessary or desired. Informal comments from "backstage" may be acknowledged, but need not be. The moral nonchalance (in the sense that identification with the victims of antisemitic persecution and abuse is expected) contained in Svenja's remark is not made the subject of conversation. Rather, the teacher steers the lesson toward his intended goals through a well-defined exercise in which he asks students to jot down key words to describe what went through their minds as they watched the video. He then signals that they will be looking to formulate some general topics. To develop a clear, formal goal for the lesson—to articulate and deal with a set of issues—the teacher resists allowing the spontaneous comment to steer the lesson. He could have used Svenja's comment, for example, to explore an unusual and undesired interpretation as the object of the lesson. The teacher passes on this opportunity.

Something similar happens after a later small-group discussion among three students. The conversation shows the individual responses each student has to the video; disagreements even approach the level of argument. The students disagree about Günther Stumm's moral culpability for his behaviour. Sebastian criticises the childhood friend: "What he did was shameful". But Leon finds Sebastian's conclusion unpersuasive ("What are you talking about?"). The teacher interrupts the students' discussion with a request that they write down their thoughts quietly, on their own. Again, the teacher narrows the communicative space in which the students learn, evinced here in his focused question: what do they think of Günthers's behaviour? This helps the teacher to achieve what appears to be his goal for the lesson: identify issues by consolidating concrete knowledge. This goal is even more explicit in the way the teacher reopens class discussion after the quiet work phase. He asks the students to formulate topics that systematically reflect the content of Franz Wagner's account. The teacher limits the number of topics he would like to keep on the blackboard to a maximum of four. He also signals to the students that he wants to deal with a specific set of issues, and that he will assign them if the students cannot identify them on their own.

The teacher's goal at this point seems to be to transmit a certain type of knowledge to the students: knowledge in the form of topics. Topics organise knowledge through classification and abstraction. As he collects and formulates topics, he does not seek out details, open questions, feelings, opinions, peculiarities, etc. It is hard to overlook the differences between the kinds of knowledge derived through the pedagogical medium of the eyewitness account and from the development of a clear set of topics. The knowledge conveyed in a biographical narrative is a detailed, case-specific kind of knowledge. It is characterised in the classroom setting by an openness to what students are learning. But the teacher's expectations have shifted from this case-specific kind of knowledge. The "topical" form of knowledge appropriation he now expects is tied closely to a teleological model for the lesson that structures the time available for the lesson in a specific way. This is emphasised by his announcement that later the class will work with the topics in conjunction with the textbook; he had announced this plan at the start of the class, assuming that the discussion would generally fit with the presentation in the text. Thus, the search for topics functions to help advance the instructor's lesson plans.

The teacher's announcement that he will provide the topics if the students do not come up with them on their own suggests just how narrow the scope is for students to draw independent conclusions in this teleological model. An independent student discussion about the eyewitness's story is not only unnecessary, it would disturb the development of the planned lesson; it would only be useful if it happened to correspond to the "topics". The class discussion that followed the presentation of Wagner's story displays a peculiar ambivalence toward openness and closure. On the one hand, the students are amenable to an open discussion of his story. In this sense it is reasonable to conclude that the eyewitness video offers an effective initiation for students' independent learning. On the other hand we can reconstruct a teaching strategy in which the teacher attempts to close the conversation once it is opened. This helps to attain the ultimate goal of outlining "topics" that will be discussed later in the lesson with the help of the textbook. Overall, this suggests a three-stage teleology within the teacher's approach: (1) the presentation of the eyewitness account in the video was (2) intended primarily to generate topics for discussion that will in turn (3) match up systematically to subsequent work in the lesson.

This case makes clear that the fit between eyewitness accounts and instruction cannot be assumed. On the contrary, the teacher's intentions seem to have been, ultimately, to use the eyewitness account instrumentally for the purpose of advancing his lesson plan. The students, however, focus on the details of the narrative itself. The problem of fit between the medium of instruction, the teleological temporal ordering, and the learning processes of individual students is a major structural problem in teaching NS history. Although the teacher chose to show the eyewitness account, which is one of the most authentic and open approaches possible, his pedagogical approach—whether or not he explicitly intended it—is adapted to the larger lesson plan. The temporal ordering of instruction, i.e. the management of a given topic within a limited period of time, suggests a preference for a certain kind of knowledge. The instructional transmission of knowledge cannot be given over entirely to the event-like nature of classroom interaction, especially the openness of the internal logic of the learning processes. By the end of the lesson, instructional knowledge is meant to have taken on a shape so firm that unique keywords and topics remain on the blackboard. These keywords and topics will help continue the instruction in the next class meeting and may be reviewed and evaluated.

If we try to highlight, at least provisionally, the facets of this case that characterise the relationship between the topic and the setting in which it is treated, two significant findings seem to emerge. First, instruction is shaped by the event-like, and hence unpredictable, nature of the interaction with and among students. Second, goal-oriented class discussion can only pursue a vanishing fraction of the meanings students may generate as they engage with the lesson's material.

In pedagogical terms, we can describe students' autonomous and individualistic forms of appropriating knowledge as an essential feature of the event-like nature of instruction. Teaching, however, is a mode dedicated to the targeted treatment of a topic within a limited period of time. In cases where some conflict exists between the medium of instruction, the students' individual learning processes, and the organisation of the lesson, instruction appears to ensure that the teleological script of the lesson is not lost completely. As we see in the example of the teacher using the eyewitness account to help select topics, open learning arrangements interfere with the pedagogical objectives of lesson plans. Such calculations do not mean, however, that open instructional offerings such as the eyewitness videos do not resonate communicatively with the students. The issue is whether or not this resonance always meets the expected pedagogical objectives. The autonomous and creative nature of learning may even find expression in non-conforming contributions like Svenja's "smart ass" remark.

The Treatment of Primary Historical Documents: From Distanced Textual Hermeneutics to Dedicated Educational Mission

The second case study illustrates the challenges history instruction faces when students work with material that carries with it very clear moral expectations (in this case, an excerpt from Hitler's *Mein Kampf*), and are taught and encouraged to adopt socially acceptable ways of speaking about a topic. The focus of the 12th-grade history class we observed was a presentation by a working group on Hitler's racial theories. In the previous class meeting, the group had handed out a worksheet with an excerpt from *Mein Kampf* for review; during this class session, the students were to present the results.

In Germany, Hitler's *Mein Kampf* is placed in the "dangerous for minors" category by the Federal Department for Media Harmful to Young Persons. The use of excerpts from a primary historical document such as this carries with it extraordinary pedagogical expectations. These expectations are based on a treatment of the text with a critical distance that should confirm the condemnation of Hitler's "racial theories" and thus also the moral integrity of the reader. The text is "known and notorious" enough that 12th-grade students are likely to be familiar with its incendiary character. Although the students are expected to have prior knowledge of the text, the way the teacher uses it suggests he has constructed his students as not knowledgeable, and impressionable, and thus still needing to learn about the inhumane ideology presented in the text. The exercise therefore has a kind of cathartic effect. It is intended to provoke moral outrage on the part of the students, to lead them to condemn the crimes, and to immunise them against the seductive power such ideologies may possess.

In the lessons we observed, the teacher asked the students to summarise the text. Their responses prompted harsh criticism from the teacher. The exercise, as given, is meant to be factual and to avoid the moral evaluation of the text; students are not asked to take a moral position. The subsequent student responses, for the most part, use the terminology used by Hitler himself ("Aryans", "the races")—with no apparent communicative critical distance or outrage. Once the students were finished sharing their responses, the teacher announced his dissatisfaction with the summaries, but gave no reasons for his reaction. Instead, he tried to enlist students from another working group to criticise their fellow students' work, but to no avail.

Those students were silent and seemed puzzled by the teacher's response. This prompted the teacher to let loose a barrage of explicit moral judgments about the students ("that's a bunch of garbage..."). Because they lacked critical distance from the text and used Hitler's language uncritically, he accused them of being potential victims of Nazi propaganda ("whoever makes a contribution like that...is ripe for Hitler's poison"). From the teacher's perspective, the students' summaries evince not only politically incorrect ways of speaking about NS and the Holocaust, but also a kind of ideological predisposition—whether out of naiveté or political conviction. To him, they seem to be morally compromised. What the teacher is trying to get across clearly differs from what the students are learning. The teacher recognises that the students' independent work with the text has failed to evoke a moral condemnation of National Socialism's racial doctrine. He thus switches to a mode of explicit instruction, which ends in a quasi-political, utterly unpedagogical lecture, nearly a tirade. This kind of over-moralisation tends toward indoctrination. The problem with his assessment of the students' work is that it disparages them as moral agents, and thus as whole individuals. While respect for students' freedom to form their own judgments is both pedagogically useful and a part of teaching's professional code of ethics, the disparate opinions issuing from engagement with a primary historical document as morally fraught as *Mein Kampf* pressure the teacher to address students not only from his functional role but also as an individual. Unlike physics class, where students' learning can be evaluated as right or wrong, and the failure to learn might make one a bad student, in history class the failure to learn the evils of NS can turn a "bad student" into a "bad person".

Especially in the classroom, such a moralising mode of addressing students endangers the viability of the lesson, because the failure to respect students' freedom to reach their own judgments can erode the safety that is otherwise present in this familiar role-based interaction.

We should note that at the end of class the teacher offered a lengthy monologue detailing his expectations for the lesson. The text is meant to rattle the students, he said, to wake them up and to make them aware of the seductive power of Nazi ideology:

> But in my opinion, uh, dealing with such material, as we have been work working with it, is really something so important, I realise now, where even if you are tired, physically and mentally, at a real low, then, uh, yeah, it has a visceral kind of effect, kind of like 'whoa, what's going on here?' It really makes your hair stand on end, and you're attentive, and it's enough of a spark to generate the motivation you need to keep working.

The "Ns-Traumatik": Pre-existing Knowledge as a Confounding Factor for Classroom Communication

The third case study also focuses on the teacher's response to student contributions. Unlike in the previous case, however, the object of teacher evaluation is not substantive responses to an assignment, but a spontaneous question and side comment.

The situation occurred at the end of a lesson, part of the larger unit on the racist ideology and propaganda of the Nazi regime. Following the work with primary source material and secondary literature featured in the previous class, the teacher next wanted to present a slideshow about the concentration camp at Dachau to illustrate the implementation and consequences of Nazi ideology. The slides would be shown in the next class meeting the following week. The students were to present the slideshow themselves, so the teacher summarised the current topic so they could use the remaining time to prepare for the next class. During the transition, a student named Mathias asked the teacher what they would be doing in the next week and how long they would continue working with the topic of National Socialism ("Mr. P., what is class going to be like now? How long are we going to be dealing with the, uh … you know, the, NS, NS-state and what are we doing afterwards?").

Examining this, we realise that Mathias' questions did not refer to the content of the lesson. He changed perspective to a formal-organisational consideration of the teaching plan for the remainder of the semester, asking when they would complete the current unit and what they would study next. Thus, he incorporated the current topic, Nazi concentration camps, into a question about the rest of the year's lessons, which gave it the status of a typical classroom subject. The teacher responded by estimating the time frame for the unit ("We'll be spending the whole semester on the NS state"), a long stretch for the treatment of a single topic. The subject of National Socialism has a special status in the German curriculum (Zülsdorf-Kersting 2004), but a half-year of instruction is not required.

The teacher's answer sparked a number of comments by the students. First, two students expressed their frustration at what they apparently feel is an overly long treatment of NS history ("Puuhh!" and "Uhuu!"); then another student, Brigit, responded with the remark, "the NS-traumatik!" It is not entirely clear why the students were so unsettled. They may have been displeased at having to cover NS—or any topic—for so long. They might have reacted similarly if a math teacher, or a German teacher, had announced several months' focus on exponential functions, or on *Faust*.

The word "traumatic", as Brigit uses it, is not a standard expression in the context of Germany's culture of memory, but rather a neologism. However, the theme of trauma, which the comment suggests, does aptly characterise the relationship of the Federal Republic to its "negative property" (Améry 1966/1989). Colloquially, the word "trauma" refers to events that leave psychological traces, or scars, and shape one's life and experience into the present. Trauma embeds the past into the present as an involuntary memory that appears over and over again; it cannot be forgotten. The term is a psychological category for individuals, but it is used in public debates on the history of National Socialism to describe the collective process of dealing with the past. In this sense, we can expect to encounter the term not only in reference to the victims of Nazi crimes and their descendants. In speaking of Germany's "collective trauma", the term is extended to the perpetrators and their descendants, whose experience of guilt and shame is also referred to as a trauma (Assmann and Frevert 1999, p. 112). We do not have to credit Birgit with a profound knowledge of the discourse of cultural memory to see her comment as expressing—however abruptly and briefly—an implicit and relatively sophisticated knowledge of the particular significance that NS has in Germany's history.

The comment, however, is less of a serious contribution to the discussion than a commentary on the teacher's plan to cover the subject for so long. Birgit distances herself from the importance the teacher attaches to the history of NS.

If we think of the school organisation as an institutionalised space in which older and younger generations interact and where the teacher's norms and values are a symbolic representation of the adult generation, then in the case of NS history the teacher is faced with the task of conveying a topic that has a critical moral message and expectations of high educational standards. The moral demands of the subject are provocatively juxtaposed to the students' comments, which the teacher answers with a lengthy monologue.

In his answer, the teacher ignores the side comments and addresses Mathias directly. He emphasises that the topic cannot be treated exhaustively in class ("Oh, Mathias, even if we spent the whole semester working on National Socialism and fascism, you'd only, uh, become familiar with a few individual elements, points of emphasis, with certain themes"). Addressing Mathias directly is a pedagogical act in a strict sense of the term. The teacher emphasises the general importance of dealing with the history of Nazism when he points out the limits to treating the subject in the classroom (they can only cover "a few individual elements", "points of emphasis"); thus he makes the argument that given the dimensions of the subject, even six months is not long enough to treat the subject fully. Later, he suggests to the students that they dedicate time to the topic outside of school, as well. He places special educational value on the authentic quality of visiting a concentration camp memorial, and stresses that the "direct" experience offered by the "atmosphere" of such places makes visiting them very interesting.

Although the lesson's content evokes different perceptions of the problem in the teacher and in the students, the differing attitudes toward history do not result in open conflict or reflexively become the focus of the lesson. Instead, the exchange proves to be a brief interruption, rather than a major disruption of class. It leads neither to a lecture by the teacher nor to a major protest by the students. How can we interpret this circumnavigation of conflict? In the context of school, where attendance is compulsory and the teacher has a monopoly on grading and evaluation, it is nearly impossible for students to refuse to participate in lessons that cover topics both prescribed by the curriculum and developed by the teacher. Sarcasm is a subtle, yet effective form of protest that students can use to express reluctance without igniting direct confrontation. An offhand sarcastic comment does not carry enough weight to invite serious disciplinary action, and an explicit judgment of the students' comments would be an exaggerated response. At the same time, the unequivocal immorality of NS and the Holocaust also makes it inappropriate for the teacher to allow such comments to pass unnoticed. The teacher's public duty toward memory and his desire to avoid a major conflict with his students leave him only the option of a declamatory but almost casual explanation of the topic's importance.

Can We Learn from History? Students' Pre-existing Knowledge and Its Stabilising Function for Classroom Communication

The final case study illustrates how students' pre-existing knowledge can have a stabilising effect on classroom communication—as long as it is brought to the discussion in the form of reasoned argument rather than a provocative side-comment, as we saw in the previous example. At the end of the next lesson we observed, the teacher thanked the class for a good discussion, and said he was satisfied with the lesson. His positive assessment led us to ask what it was about the lesson that he believes made it successful.

As we reconstructed the interaction, we found that the level of student participation in the lesson was very high. Over long stretches of the class period, the discussion between the teacher and the students—and especially among the students themselves—was relatively equal, as it would be among adults. The discussion focused on a problem suggested in a documentary film they watched (*Machtergreifung*, by Peter Hartl and Sebastian Dehnhardt) on the subject of seizing power versus stealing it. The material in the film pulls on key arguments in the public and historiographical debates over the question of how Hitler was able to seize power in Germany. It shows historical images alongside various interpretive perspectives: historical research, on the one hand, and subjective accounts from contemporary witnesses, some of whose stories appear in their original language, on the other. Overall, the documentary offers a diversity of perspectives on historical events, and ultimately provides no clear explanation for Hitler's success in seizing power.

After the film, the students engaged in a lively debate about Hitler's ability to persuade and the question of whether the safety of the present and hindsight can help us to identify current anti-democratic tendencies and to prevent the return of a national socialist regime. The question is whether we can learn lessons from the past and apply those lessons to the present and the future. Like the film, the classroom discussion was inconclusive. The teacher moderated the discussion by asking brief questions and calling on students, which allowed him to recede from the conversation entirely at times. In the discussion phase, students participated freely, and even competed for a chance to take part in the conversation.

In the centre of the discussion is the question of whether Hitler's electoral success was due primarily to his individual, mostly rhetorical skills, or rather a result of the socially precarious conditions of the time, i.e., an outgrowth of the history of the Weimar Republic. The student Mathias argues that Hitler's electoral success cannot be reduced to his rhetorical skills. He supports his argument with his subjective impression that Hitler seems pretty ridiculous to him and not credible at all. He cites the social and economic conditions of the Weimar Republic, and not the personal characteristics of Hitler, as a central cause for the dictator's rise. Mathias argues that Hitler's success as a demagogue makes sense only in the context of such social instability. He is trying to take an "objective" position and interpret the events of the time mainly from the safety of the present. He thus shows himself to be historically informed. He shows that he can see through Hitler's demagoguery and has a kind of immunity to such "ridiculous" and "dubious" attempts at persuasion.

Mathias's classmates, Janet and Wolfgang, counter that Mathias does not take sufficient account of the necessarily limited knowledge people had at that time. They do not trust the "objective" position Mathias claims to take, and they reject the premise that historical events can be explained in great detail from the security of the present. Janet points out that we approach historical events today with a completely different set of knowledge about history. She is supported by her classmate, Wolfgang, who suggests that although we now know what happened back then, and where it led, we still cannot evaluate with certainty the effectiveness of Hitler's rhetorical skill.

Matthias responds to the objections with a question, rather than a substantive defense of his own position. He asks Wolfgang if he would have been a follower of Hitler, given his relativistic view of historical analyses' objectivity. Wolfgang's dismissive or relativising take on the objectivity of historical analysis suggests to Matthias that Wolfgang may be vulnerable to the seductive power of a demagogue like Hitler. He addresses Wolfgang as a moral subject who must prove his moral character. His question does not support his own explanation for Hitler's success, but it does focus the discussion on the normative question of what we can learn from history. He thus takes on a role that is traditionally held by the teacher and tests his classmate's moral standing. The question adds moral tension to the discussion; the moral integrity of a participant is placed under scrutiny.

Wolfgang's reaction to this question is defensive at first. He declares that he would have been immune to Hitler's demagogic power and that "of course" he "wouldn't have followed Hitler". But in the same sentence he relativises his position, when he considers that back then, he might have been a follower of Hitler, after all ("maybe, I mean maybe I would have"). Wolfgang's response eases some of the tension in the contentious exchange. Rather than disagree with Mathias, he confirms the latter's fear that he might have been vulnerable to demagoguery. Wolfgang apparently envisions himself as a person acting in history. Despite all that we know, for him, the lived moment remains a blind spot that can never be completely illuminated. In the absence of a position of true objectivity, Wolfgang does not absolve himself of his own vulnerability, despite his vigilance against it.

This case study suggests that the lesson had a systematic resilience to the twin dangers of over-moralisation and under-moralisation. It even seems to have allowed for serious debate about the moral terrain of the subject. The discussion at least touched on current academic debates about the reasons for Hitler's successful seizure of power. The students brought to it not only their pre-existing knowledge about the topic, but also themselves—as complete individuals—as when Wolfgang reflected on his own potential waywardness in front of the class. The communicative interaction, sparked by the documentary film, turned into a kind of discussion among equals that succeeded without direct instructional intervention by the teacher. It is precisely this outcome that most likely led the teacher to call the discussion a success. It was open enough for broad participation and learning from the class and was conducted over long stretches of time at an appropriately serious level.

Summary and Outlook

The central questions of this study focused on the ways that classroom instruction deals, in practice, with the uncertainty of its efficacy and the tension between over-moralisation and under-moralisation. In this context, we further investigated how the organisational framework of school shapes the transmission and appropriation of knowledge for the topic of National Socialism.

In terms of these research questions, one of the most salient findings from the four case studies is just how strongly classroom interactions are influenced by the quirky, often unexpected, ways in which students appropriate knowledge. These appropriations frequently conflict with the intended content of the lesson and with public expectations for the treatment of Germany's NS past. Empirically observable differences between the operations of teaching and learning infuse the interaction with constant uncertainty, which can be circumscribed through various communicative patterns but can never be completely attenuated.

The first case, which features the treatment of a videotaped interview with a contemporary witness, shows the interplay of produced contingency and the integration of heterogeneous student contributions within the allotted timeframe for instruction and the cognitive structure of classroom learning. The spontaneous outbursts in reaction to the video featuring contemporary testimonials ("smart ass" and "what he did was shameful") are not dealt with in their affective-moral sense. Instead, the teacher uses the testimonials to generate a list of general themes that he already had in mind as the expected outcome of the lesson. By reconnecting the classroom discussion to these issues and visualising them on the blackboard, he did provide a symbolic confirmation of what was learned; however, he missed the opportunity to incorporate the students' offhand comments in a way that reflected the historical interests they expressed and thus could have served as a point of reference throughout the learning process. In addition, the lesson faced the risk of under-moralising on two levels: first, because the teacher failed to pick up on the provocative "smart-ass" comment and, second, because he used the historical testimonials instrumentally, raising the question of how representative such biographical testimony can be in the classroom.

The second case study documents a very different approach to the contingency problem. The teacher interpreted the student summary of the excerpt from Hitler's *Mein Kampf* not only as factually inadequate work, but also as an indication of moral failing. He turned the students' appropriation of knowledge into an explicit object of discussion and addressed it as an example of under-moralisation. This set the stage for his harsh evaluation of their work and then a lecture; i.e., he over-moralised and departed from the framework of legitimate pedagogical intercession. A comparison of the first two cases shows systematically that the moral implications of the history of NS preclude amoral treatment (Proske 2009). Even when, as in the first case, the teacher avoided an explicit moral treatment of the issue and did not intend to evaluate the moral content of students' contributions, the moral valence of the Holocaust as an integral part of Germany's culture of memory entered the interaction through students' comments.

The third case supports these interpretations. Negative attitudes toward the long treatment of the subject, as reflected in the student comments "Puuhh!", "Uhuu", and "The NS-traumatik!" placed the teacher in a position where he felt a response was necessary. And, as a representative of the adult generation, he could not ignore or let pass the nonchalance and ambivalence that this younger generation shows toward the topic's treatment in school. Here, too, the teacher passed on the opportunity to make the comments a subject of discussion and thus part of the learning process. Unlike the second case, he did respond to the threat of under-moralisation, but not with over-moralisation. Instead of lecturing his students, he suggested that a visit to a concentration camp memorial might be an enriching and powerful personal experience. Instead of either over or under-moralising, he found a compromise, in a form of motivation that manages to avoid harsh criticism. It may be an inappropriate representation of the Holocaust, however, to the extent that he portrayed a visit to a former concentration camp as an experiential exercise rather than an act of pure reflection on the memory of Holocaust victims (Brumlik 1995).

Compared to the first three cases, the fourth is something of an exception. The problem of under- or over-moralisation emerges differently than in the other cases. The diversity of perspectives in the documentary film does not facilitate clear answers to the question of what we can learn from the history of National Socialism. It sparks a heated debate among the students, and the teacher recedes to a role of neutral facilitator. He does not evaluate any of the students' contributions explicitly. The conversation takes the form of a debate among equals about problems that are unresolved, even among historians. The conversation escapes the asymmetric roles that typify classroom instruction. The students act like adults and are treated as fully socialised, morally competent individuals who are, for the moment at least, not in need of any direct instruction.

A comparison of the case studies suggests that this fourth instance was very successful in meeting the demands to treat the history of NS appropriately in the classroom. We see three reasons for this success. First, the typically asymmetric roles of teacher and student were for the most part set aside; second, the lesson was allowed to come to a "natural" conclusion, without time pressure; and third, the topic was presented as an exciting and open-ended problem, not as pre-determined material for instruction.

In pedagogical terms, this finding suggests that we present the topic of National Socialism to history classes in ways that allow for controversial discussion. If the special didactic quality of teaching in this manner sparks a factually-informed dialogue among students, then one might argue that this can reduce the negative impact that the school's organisational structure has on classroom instruction. Although it may be plausible to infer educational recommendations from the empirical findings of this case, it is important to note that these proposals must also address the problem of contingency in pedagogical communication. A provocative student comment that sabotages the openness of the discussion, for example, or conducting the lesson at an inopportune time in the school year (like just before exams) could trigger an entirely different outcome. In this sense, the contingencies of teaching suggest a link between the quality of history teaching and the ability to take advantage of opportunities as they present themselves in specific classroom situations. This could function as a kind of challenge and aspiration for practicing teachers: keep in mind the difference between pedagogical intentions and classroom interaction!

Note This chapter draws on Meseth and Proske (2010).

References

Adorno, T. W. (1971). Erziehung nach Auschwitz [Education after Auschwitz]. In T. W. Adorno (Ed.), *Erziehung zur Mündigkeit* (pp. 88–104). Frankfurt am Main: Suhrkamp.

Améry, J. (1966/1989). *Jenseits von Schuld und Sühne: Bewältigungsversuche eines Überwältigten* [Beyond guilt and atonement: A Victor's attempts to overcome]. Stuttgart: Klett-Kotta.

Assmann, A., & Frevert, U. (1999). *Geschichtsvergessenheit—Geschichtsversessenheit: Vom Umgang mit deutschen Vergangenheiten nach 1945* [Historical oblivion—Historical awareness: On dealing with the German past after 1945]. Stuttgart: DVA Deutsche Verlagsanstalt.

Barricelli, M. (2005). *Schüler erzählen Geschichte: Narrative Kompetenz im Geschichtsunterricht* [Students explain history: Narrative competence in history class]. Schwalbach: Wochenschau Verlag.

Baumert, J., & Kunter, M. (2006). Stichwort: Professionelle Kompetenz von Lehrkräften [Keyword: The professional competence of teachers]. *Zeitschrift für Erziehungswissenschaft, 9*(4), 469–520.

Bergmann, J. (1981). Ethnomethodologische Konversationsanalyse [Ethnomethodological conversational analysis]. In P. Schröder & H. Steger (Eds.), *Dialogforschung. Jahrbuch 1980 des Instituts für deutsche Sprache. Sprache der Gegenwart* (Vol. 54, pp. 9–51). Düsseldorf: Pädagogischer Verlag Schwann.

Boßmann, D. (Ed.) (1977). *"Was ich über Adolf Hitler gehört habe…". Folgen eines Tabus: Auszüge aus Schüler-Aufsätzen von heute* ["What I have heard about Adolf Hitler…" The consequences of a taboo: Excerpts from student essays today]. Frankfurt am Main: Fischer Verlag.

Brumlik, M. (1995). *Gerechtigkeit zwischen den Generationen* [Intergenerational justice]. Berlin: Berlin Verlag.

Brumlik, M. (2004). *Aus Katastrophen lernen? Grundlagen zeitgeschichtlicher Bildung in menschenrech- tlicher Absicht* [Learning from catastrophes? Foundations of contemporary historical education from a human rights perspective]. Berlin: Philo.

Cobb, J., & Bauersfeld, H. (Eds.) (1995). *The emergence of mathematical meaning: Interaction in classroom cultures*. Hillsdale: Erlbaum.

Deppermann, A. (2001). *Gespräche analysieren: Eine Einfuührung* [Analyzing conversations: An introduction]. Opladen: Leske & Budrich.

Der Spiegel (1977, 15 August). "Hitler kam von ganz alleine an die Macht" ["Hitler came to power all by himself"].
Erickson, F. (1986). Qualitative methods in research on teaching. In M. C. Wittrock (Ed.), *Handbook of research on teaching* (3rd ed., pp. 119–161). New York/London: Macmillan.
Gautschi, P., Moser, D., Reusser, K., & Wiher, P. (Eds.) (2007). *Geschichtsunterricht heute: Eine empirische Analyse ausgewaählter Aspekte* [History teaching today: An empirical analysis of selected aspects]. Bern: h.e.p Verlag.
Goffman, E. (1983). The interaction order. *American Sociological Review, 48*, 1–17.
Guünther-Arndt, H., & Sauer, M. (Eds.) (2006). *Geschichtsdidaktik empirisch: Untersuchungen zum historischen Denken und Lernen* [Historical pedagogy: Empirical analysis of historical thinking and learning]. Münster: Lit Verlag.
Hammersley, M. (1990). *Classroom ethnography: Empirical and methodological essays.* Philadelphia: Open University Press.
Helmke, A. (2003). *Unterrichtsqualität erfassen, bewerten, verbessern* [Measuring, evaluating and improving the quality of instruction]. Seelze: Kallmeyer.
Henke-Bockschatz, G. (2004). Der "Holocaust" als Thema im Geschichtsunterricht: Kritische Anmerkungen [The "Holocaust" as a topic of history instruction: Critical remarks]. In W. Meseth, M. Proske, & F.-O. Radtke (Eds.), *Schule und Nationalsozialismus: Anspruch und Grenzen des Geschichtsunterrichts* (pp. 298–322). Frankfurt/New York: Campus.
Heyl, M. (1997). *Erziehung nach Auschwitz: Eine Bestandsaufnahme. Deutschland, Niederlande, Israel, USA* [Education after Auschwitz: An appraisal. Germany, the Netherlands, Israel, USA]. Hamburg: Kraemer Verlag.
Hollstein, O., Meseth, W., Müller-Mahnkopp, C., Proske, M., & Radtke, F. (2002). *Nationalsozialismus im Geschichtsunterricht. Beobachtungen unterrichtlicher Kommunikation. Bericht zu einer Pilotstudie* [National Socialism in history class: Observations of classroom instruction. Report from a pilot study]. Reihe: Frankfurter Beiträge zur Erziehungswissenschaft. Forschungsberichte, 3. Frankfurt am Main: Frankfurt University Press.
Kade, J. (1997). Vermittelbar/nicht-vermittelbar: Vermitteln: Aneignen Im Prozeß der Systembildung des Pädagogischen [What can/cannot be taught: Instruction: Appropriation. The process of system formation in education]. In D. Lenzen & N. Luhmann (Eds.), *Bildung und Weiterbildung im Erziehungssystem: Lebenslauf und Humanontogenese als Medium und Form* (pp. 30–70). Frankfurt am Main: Suhrkamp.
Kant, I. (1803/1966). Über Pädagogik [On pedagogy]. In Wilhelm von Weichedel (Ed.), *Werkausgabe* [Working edition] (Vol. 11, pp. 697–712). Darmstadt: Wissenschaftliche Buchgesellschaft.
Klieme, E. (2006). Empirische Unterrichtsforschung: Aktuelle Entwicklungen, theoretische Grundlagen und fachspezifische Befunde. Einleitung in den Thementeil [Empirical research on teaching: Contemporary developments, theoretical foundations and field-specific findings. Introduction to the topic]. *Zeitschrift fuür Pädagogik, 52*(6), 765–773.
Klieme, E., & Reusser, K. (2003). Unterrichtsqualität und mathematisches Verständnis im internationalen Vergleich: Ein Forschungsprojekt und erste Schritte zur Realisierung [The quality of instruction and mathematical understanding in international comparison: A research project and first steps toward its realization]. *Unterrichtswissenschaft, 31*(3), 194–205.
Knigge, V. (1988). *"Triviales" Geschichtsbewußtsein und verstehender Geschichtsunterricht* ["Trivial" historical consciousness and interpretive historical instruction]. Pfaffenweiler: Centaurus.
Kölbl, C. (2004). *Geschichtsbewusstsein im Jugendalter: Grundzüge einer Entwicklungspsychologie historischer Sinnbildung* [Historical awareness in adolescence: Outline of a developmental psychology of historical meaning]. Bielefeld: Transcript.
Krummheuer, G. (2002). Eine interaktionistische Modellierung des Unterrichtsalltags, Entwickelt in interpretativen Studien zum mathematischen Grundschulunterricht [An interactive modeling of everyday instruction, developed in interpretive studies of elementary school math class]. In G. Breidenstein, A. Combe, W. Helsper, & B. Stelmaszyk (Eds.), *Forum qualitative Schulforschung 2. Interpretative Unterrichts- und Schulbegleitforschung* (pp. 29–59). Opladen: Leske & Budrich.

Luhmann, N. (1996). Takt und Zensur im Erziehungssystem [Tact and evaluation in the educational system]. In N. Luhmann & K. E. Schorr (Eds.), *Zwischen System und Umwelt: Fragen an die Pädagogik* (pp. 279–294). Frankfurt am Main: Suhrkamp.

Mehan, H. (1979). *Learning lessons: Social organization in the classroom.* Cambridge/London: Harvard University Press.

Meseth, W. (2005). *Aus der Geschichte lernen: Über die Rolle der Erziehung in der bundesdeutschen Erinnerungskultur* [Learning from history: On the role of education in the national culture of memory in Germany]. Frankfurt am Main: Frankfurt University Press.

Meseth, W. (2007). Die Pädagogisierung der Erinnerungskultur: Erziehungswissenschaftliche Beobachtungen eines bisher kaum beachteten Phänomens [The pedagogification of the culture of memory: Pedagogical observations of a hitherto underexplored phenomenon]. *Zeitschrift für Genozidforschung, 2,* 96–117.

Meseth, W., & Proske, M. (2010). Mind the gap: Holocaust education in Germany, between pedagogical intentions and classroom interactions. *Prospects, 40*(2), 201–222.

Meseth, W., Proske, M., & Radtke, F.-O. (Eds.) (2004). *Schule und Nationalsozialismus: Anspruch und Grenzen des Geschichtsunterrichts* [National socialism in school: The demands and limits of historical instruction]. Frankfurt am Main: Campus.

Naujok, N., Brandt, B., & Krummheuer, G. (2004). Interaktion im Unterricht [Interaction in teaching]. In W. Helsper & J. Böhme (Eds.), *Handbuch der Schulforschung* (pp. 753–773). Wiesbaden: VS Verlag.

Prange, K. (2003). Die Form erzieht [The form teaches]. In H.-E. Tenorth (Ed.), *Form der Bildung—Bildung der Form* (pp. 23–34). Weinheim/Munich: Beltz.

Proske, M. (2003a). Pädagogische Kommunikation in der Form Schulunterricht [Educational communication in classroom lessons]. In D. Nittel & W. Seitter (Eds.), *Die Bildung des Erwachsenen: Erziehungs- und sozialwissenschaftliche Zugänge* (pp. 143–164). Bielefeld: Bertelsmann.

Proske, M. (2003b). Kann man in der Schule aus der Geschichte lernen? Eine qualitative Analyse der Leistungsfähigkeit der Form Unterricht für die Vermittlung des Nationalsozialismus und Holocaust [Can one learn from history in school? A qualitative analysis of the ability of classroom instruction to teach National Socialism and the Holocaust]. *Sozialer Sinn: Zeitschrift für hermeneutische Sozialforschung, 3*(2), 205–235.

Proske, M. (2009). Moralerziehung im Geschichtsunterricht: Zwischen expliziter Vermeidung und impliziter Unvermeidlichkeit [Moral education in history teaching: Between explicit avoidance and implicit inevitability]. In J. Hodel & B. Ziegler (Eds.), *Forschungswerkstatt Geschichtsdidaktik 07* (pp. 44–53). Bern: h.e.p. Verlag.

Proske, M., & Meseth, W. (2006). Nationalsozialismus und Holocaust als Thema des Geschichtsunterrichts: Erziehungswissenschaftliche Beobachtungen zum Umgang mit Kontingenz [National Socialism and the Holocaust as a topic of history teaching: Pedagogical observations of handling contingency]. In H. Günther-Arndt & M. Sauer (Eds.), *Geschichtsdidaktik empirisch: Untersuchungen zum historischen Denken und Lernen* (pp. 127–154). Münster: Lit Verlag.

Rüsen, J. (1994). *Historische Orientierung: Über die Arbeit des Geschichtsbewußtseins, sich in der Zeit zurechtzufinden* [Historical orientation: On the work of historical consciousness]. Cologne: Böhlau.

Schneider, W.-L. (2004). Die Unwahrscheinlichkeit der Moral: Strukturen moralischer Kommunikation im Schulunterricht über Nationalsozialismus und Holocaust [The improbability of morality: Structures of moral communication in classroom instruction on National Socialism and the Holocaust]. In W. Meseth, M. Proske, & F.-O. Radtke (Eds.), *Schule und Nationalsozialismus: Anspruch und Grenzen des Geschichtsunterrichts* (pp. 205–234). Frankfurt am Main/New York: Campus.

Schörken, R. (1979). Geschichte im Alltag: Über einige Funktionen des trivialen Geschichtsbewußtseins [History in everyday life: On several functions of trivial historical consciousness]. *Geschichte in Wissenschaft und Unterricht, 30*(2), 73–88.

Shulman, L. S. (1986). Paradigms and research programs in the study of teaching: A contemporary perspective. In M. C. Wittrock (Ed.), *Handbook of research on teaching* (3rd ed., pp. 3–36). New York/London: Macmillan.

Silbermann, A., & Stoffers, M. (2000). *Auschwitz: nie davon gehört? Erinnern und Vergessen in Deutschland* [Auschwitz: Never heard of it? Remembering and forgetting in Germany]. Berlin: Rowohlt.

Soeffner, H. -G. (1989). *Auslegung des Alltags—Der Alltag der Auslegung* [Interpreting the everyday—The everyday of interpretation]. Frankfurt am Main: Suhrkamp.

von Borries, B. (1980). Unkenntnis des Nationalsozialismus: Versagen des Geschichtsunterrichts? Bemerkungen zu alten und neuen empirischen Studien [Ignorance of National Socialism: A failure of history instruction? Notes on old and new empirical studies]. *Geschichtsdidaktik*, 5(2), 109–126.

von Borries, B. (1995). *Das Geschichtsbewußtsein Jugendlicher: Eine repräsentative Untersuchung über Vergangenheitsdeutungen, Gegenwartswahrnehmungen und Zukunftserwartungen von Schülerinnen und Schülern in Ost- und Westdeutschland* [The historical consciousness of youth: A representative study of the historical interpretations, contemporary perceptions, and future expectations of students in East and West Germany]. Weinheim/Munich: Juventa Verlag.

von Borries, B. (2002). Forschungen über die Einstellungen Jugendlicher zum Holocaust: Empirische Befunde und sozialpsychologische Bedingungen [Analyses of youth attitudes toward the Holocaust: Empirical findings and socio-psychological connections]. In B. Kammerer & A. Prölß-Kammerer (Eds.), *Recht extrem: Auseinandersetzung mit Nationalsozialismus und Rechtsextremismus—Konzepte und Projekte der politischen und historischen Bildung* (pp. 14–36). Nuremberg: emwe Verlag.

von Borries, B. (2009). Rückblick und Ausblick [Looking back and looking forward]. In J. Hodel & B. Ziegler (Eds.), *Forschungswerkstatt Geschichtsdidaktik 07* (pp. 305–320). Bern: h.e.p. Verlag.

Wilson, S. (2001). Research on history teaching. In V. Richardson (Ed.), *Handbook of research on teaching* (4th ed., pp. 527–544). Washington, DC: American Educational Research Association.

Wimmer, M. (2006). *Dekonstruktion und Erziehung: Studien zum Paradoxieproblem in der Pädagogik* [Deconstruction and education: Studies on the problem of paradox in pedagogy]. Bielefeld: Transcript.

Wineburg, S. (2000). Making historical sense. In P. N. Stearns, P. Seixas, & S. Wineburg (Eds.), *Knowing, teaching, and learning history: National and international perspectives* (pp. 306–325). New York/London: New York University Press.

Zülsdorf-Kersting, M. (2004). Zwischen normativer Setzung und ergebnisoffenem Diskurs: Das Thema "Nationalsozialismus" in den Richtlinien und Lehrplänen für das Fach Geschichte in der Sekundarstufe I [Between normative setting and open discourse: The topic of "National Socialism" in the guidelines and lesson plans for the subject of history in secondary school level I]. In S. Handro & B. Schönemann (Eds.), *Geschichtsdidaktische Lehrplanforschung. Methoden—Analysen—Perspektiven* (pp. 165–174). Münster: Lit Verlag.

Zülsdorf-Kersting, M. (2007). *Sechzig Jahre danach: Jugendliche und Holocaust. Eine Studie zur geschichtskulturellen Sozialization* [Sixty years later: Youth and the Holocaust. A study of historical-cultural socialization]. Münster: Lit Verlag.

Part IV
Holocaust Education in Diverse Classrooms

Holocaust Education and Critical Citizenship in an American Fifth Grade: Expanding Repertoires of Meanings, Language and Action

Louise B. Jennings

Introduction

Maxine Greene (1988) challenged educators to develop educational practices that "empower students to create spaces of dialogue in their classrooms, spaces where they can take initiatives and uncover humanizing possibilities" (p. 13). In the 1990s, I collaborated with Irene Pattenaude as she sought to create such spaces with her bilingual fifth-grade class through a year-long study of social justice and responsible citizenship that included an in-depth focus on the Holocaust. Our collaboration revealed both challenges and possibilities for education regarding the Holocaust, (in)tolerance, and social responsibility in the upper elementary grades. The resource book for educators from the United States Holocaust Memorial Museum (USHMM 2001) claims that "Structured inquiry into Holocaust history yields critical lessons for an investigation of human behaviour… [and] addresses one of the central tenets of education in the USA, which is to examine what it means to be a responsible citizen" (p. 1). Teaching effectively about the Holocaust, and the important lessons it offers regarding humanity and responsible citizenship (Schwag and Wackerlig 2010; Stevick and Gross 2010: Supple 1998a, 1998b), is challenging for teachers of any grade (Cowan and Maitles 2010; Schweber 2008; Totten 1999). High school teachers are often limited to a two-week unit in a crowded curriculum with multiple classes of students (Short 2000). Elementary grades offer the opportunity, throughout the school year, to build a strong community of learners that can support thoughtful and thorough learning engagements regarding topics as challenging as the Holocaust.

Irene worked with her grade-level colleagues, Beth Yeager and Phoebe Hirsche-Dubin, to develop a fifth-grade learning environment that immersed students in

---

L.B. Jennings (✉)
School of Education, Colorado State University, Fort Collins, CO 80521, USA
e-mail: louise.jennings@colostate.edu

reflecting and acting upon what it means to be human and to be a community member. Across the school year, the study of the Holocaust was embedded within the larger classroom context constructed by Irene and her students in Room 18 that explicitly emphasised these "3Rs": rights, respect, and responsibility. They began the school year by brainstorming students' ideas about community, rights, respect, and responsibility and then developing a classroom Bill of Rights and Responsibilities in English and Spanish, languages that were equally valued in Room 18. Throughout the year, students examined their responsibilities to themselves as individuals, to their classmates, and to members of the school, neighbourhood, and world communities. In January through May, this experience culminated in a study of the nature of tolerance and intolerance through a range of texts about the Holocaust, known as the Tolerance Focus Study. (The term "tolerance education" was commonly used when Irene and her colleagues originated this curriculum. Although the term tolerance can signify passive and even reluctant acceptance of others' differences, the teachers used the term to indicate a proactive stance of acting responsibly to contribute to justice and equity). The Tolerance Focus closed with a set of action steps taken by all fifth graders.

Our earlier publications describe and analyze the 3Rs curriculum and the Tolerance Focus (Jennings 1996; Jennings and Pattenaude 1998, 1999; Yeager, Pattenaude, Fránquiz, and Jennings 1999). I revisit these data from two new perspectives. First, I consider the possibilities of Holocaust studies for fifth-grade learners. I examine how the classroom context of the 3 Rs and layering of particular academic practices supported these young students in grappling with the difficult questions and content of the Holocaust, from genocide, racism, and discrimination to organised resistance and social responsibility. Second, I bring to these data a framework of critical citizenship, asking how the Tolerance Focus supported students in developing a capacity for sociopolitical critique and action.

Expanding Repertoires of Meaning, Language and Action

This ethnographic study is grounded in a sociocultural perspective (Berger and Luckmann 1966; Collins and Green 1992; Edwards and Mercer, 1987; Santa Barbara Classroom Discourse Group 1992b, 1993) that members of a class co-construct learning opportunities for themselves and each other through their actions and practices over extended periods of time (Heras 1993; Tuyay, Jennings, and Dixon 1995). This perspective conceptualises learning as expanding repertoires of meanings, language, and action (Jennings and Pattenaude 1998), a point that is particularly important when considering learning regarding (in)tolerance and social responsibility and relates to Paulo Freire's (1970, 2005) notion of praxis. Freire's liberating pedagogy centres on people developing social/critical consciousness (*conscientização*) through engaging in dialogue grounded in their lived experiences, reflecting on the social and political conditions that produce oppression and inequity, and taking action to break the reproductive cycles that maintain the status quo.

Thus, praxis involves developing critical understandings and *meanings* regarding social conditions through talk and *language* in order to take informed *actions* for justice and equity.

Given the layered nature of Irene's curriculum, it is helpful to examine how students made meaning of the Holocaust by making connections among written, visual, and spoken texts—a process of intertextuality (Kristeva 1986; Santa Barbara Classroom Discourse Group 1992a; Short 1992). Lemke (1992) underscores the transformative power of intertextuality by suggesting that, when juxtaposed and connected, one text can multiply the meaning potential of the other, particularly when texts are presented through different sign system modalities. This study illustrates how intertextuality can also multiply language and action potential. When children are learning about topics as complex as the Holocaust, it is particularly important to provide them with opportunities to make connections among texts and to their own experiences.

Holocaust Education and Critical Citizenship

Beth Yeager originally developed the 3R's curriculum in the late 1980s, then refined it with Irene and Phoebe (Yeager et al. 1999). Since then, educators (e.g., Burtonwood 2002; Short 2000) have published and examined curricular frameworks for Holocaust education programmes that emphasise important features, such as including stories of individual experience, building empathy, building a knowledge base about the Holocaust and Judaism, making connections to other genocides and racism, and studying the bystander response countered with stories of resistance and rescue. Gallant and Hartman (2001) recommend approaches that address cognitive, attitudinal, and action outcomes. In terms of cognitive and attitudinal development, Totten (2002) describes an in-depth curriculum that provokes critical thought and personal growth, in part by posing "gnawing" questions. From an affective perspective, empathy-building is critical (Short 2000), and is supported by literature that offers first-person experiences of the Holocaust. When we reviewed the Tolerance Focus Study, we discovered that the majority of these curricular and pedagogical elements were woven into it, with an emphasis on empathy, respect for human life and human rights (Bromley and Russell 2010), the effects of racism and oppression, and the critical role of social responsibility in a democracy.

The USHMM (2001) posits that, for children 11 and older, the Holocaust is one of the most effective subjects for understanding the dynamic nature of democratic institutions. In this study I focus on how Irene's curriculum supported developing students as critical citizens (Jennings and Green 1999; Jennings, Parra-Medina, Messias, and McLoughlin 2006), or what Westheimer and Kahne (2004) refer to as social justice-oriented citizens. Critical citizens participate conscientiously, compassionately, and actively in the day-to-day building of more equitable communities, be they classroom, neighbourhood, national, or global communities. Westheimer and Kahne (2004) argue that many programmes do not address a balanced view of citizenship, but "privilege individual acts of compassion and kindness over social action" (p. 243). They add that "personal responsibility, voluntarism and character education must be considered in a broader social context or they risk advancing civility or docility instead of democracy" (p. 244).

This final point connects sharply with central tenets of Holocaust education. Through studying the Holocaust, students learn that "even unintentional indifference and silence to the sufferings and human rights infringements of others perpetuate their victimisation, and that the Holocaust was not inevitable but rather occurred because people made choices that legitimised prejudice, hatred and mass murder" (Shoemaker 2003, p. 191). Critical citizens are not passive bystanders, but critically conscious upstanders (Power 2002) who recognise our culpability in allowing injustice to stand and the vital importance of judiciously taking action to alter the status quo.

In this chapter, I examine the challenges and possibilities of bridging Holocaust education with education for critical citizenship. Two overarching questions guide this analysis. What meanings, language, and actions regarding (in)tolerance did students in Room 18 construct over time? And what academic and social practices in Room 18 supported learning regarding the Holocaust and critical citizenship?

Methodology

This article grew out of a larger research effort. Irene and I became a research team as members of a school-university research collaborative, the Santa Barbara Classroom Discourse Group (Dixon and Green 2009). In 1994–1995, I was a participant-observer in Irene's bilingual class, examining with her the role of social, academic, and literate practices in helping students to make meaning of tolerance and social justice (Jennings 1996). Here, I examine the data with a larger set of questions about the development of the Tolerance Focus.

Room 18 was situated in a bilingual school in Santa Barbara that served a large Latino population, largely of Mexican origin. Of the 520 students in the school, 80% were eligible for free lunch. In Room 18, 19 students were Latino/a, six were European-American, and one was Native American. As a bilingual class, members of Room 18 spoke Spanish, English, or both throughout the school day. Twenty-two students read the core literature in English as their primary language or as "transition" students, where English was their second language. The remaining four students were "Spanish readers", who were learning English, but concentrating on developing literate fluency in their primary language. Four students received special education resource services, meeting a resource specialist outside of the classroom.

As a participant-observer, I videotaped and took field notes all day for the first 3 weeks of each school year and during selected events. Data also include videotaped interviews with the teacher and students and student artifacts (e.g., essays, art). I examined learning in the moment and over time through an interactional ethnographic approach (Castanheira, Crawford, Green, and Dixon 2001). Using field notes, I constructed an event map (Green and Meyer 1991; Green and Wallat 1979) of the Tolerance Focus to represent the flow of activity through time. Each event was marked with types of literate actions, source texts and class-constructed texts, and connections among these texts. I engaged Spradley's (1980) cultural domain, taxonomic, and thematic analyses to uncover patterns of meanings that members were co-constructing through these events and in student-produced texts. From these analyses, I selected key events (Gumperz 1986) for transcription and analysis of discourse to investigate how learners were constructing particular meanings of the Holocaust and critical citizenship. After analysing each set of student texts, I selected examples as "telling cases" (Mitchell 1984) that represent features found across students' texts and provide a clear illustration of the theoretical construct(s) being examined.

Findings

It is important to emphasise that the Tolerance Focus Study grew out of a broader curriculum that stressed rights, respect, and responsibility from the first day of school (see Jennings 1996; and Yeager et al. 1999 for a full examination of the 3 R's curriculum). Also, the activities in the Tolerance Focus drew upon a range of academic practices that students engaged in throughout the preceding months of school. For example, from day one, children engaged in academic practices such as constructing Venn diagrams that compared features of two texts, writing diary entries from the perspective of a fictional character, and responding to poetry by writing selected lines from a poem in one column and responding to those lines in the other column (Jennings 1996; Jennings and Pattenaude 1998; Yeager et al. 1999).

The Tolerance Focus Study was organised around a range of texts (see Table 1) and strategies for examining texts that helped students make meaning of the Holocaust and take actions that promote tolerance and justice; it was organised in four overlapping phases from January through mid-May. Phase 1 introduced and framed the cycle as a study of tolerance and intolerance. Phase 2 focused on making meaning of (in)tolerance by interacting with a large variety of texts about the Holocaust. Phases 3 and 4 involved constructing personal and grade-wide action steps for promoting tolerance and justice.

My findings are organised in three sections, through the rest of this chapter. In the first section I describe engagements with texts that introduced the Holocaust to students and examine their initial responses. In the next section I examine how students constructed an expanded repertoire of meanings and language regarding the Holocaust, society, and critical citizenship throughout the second phase of the Tolerance Focus. In the final section I examine how meanings and language were integrated with action in Phases 3 and 4.

Table 1 Source texts used in the tolerance-focused study

Text type	Genre	Texts
Print	Novels	*Number the Stars/¿Quién cuenta las estrellas?* (Lowry 1989a, b)
		Jacob's Rescue (Drucker and Halperin 1993)
	Picture books	*The Terrible Things* (Bunting 1980)
		The Children we Remember (Abells 1986)
		Rosa Blanca/Rose Blanche (Innocenti 1985, 1987)
		Let the Celebrations Begin! (Wild 1991)
	Short stories	"Letter from a Concentration Camp" (Uchida 1990)
	Poems	"I am a Star"/Yo soy una estrella"
		"I wish I Were a Little Bird"
		"Why?/¿Por qué?"
	Letters	A fellow teacher's letters from his Jewish grandfather (written in Spanish)
	Newspaper articles	Editorial on response to hate crimes in Billings, MT
		Article on antisemitism in Santa Barbara
Oral	Lecture/discussion	Irene's lecture on historical background of the Holocaust
Graphic	Maps	Europe
		Axis invasions/occupations
	Statistical table	Table reporting number of deaths resulting from the Holocaust
Audio-visual	Fiction	"Miracle at Moreaux"
	Non-fiction	20/20 journalistic piece on childhood survivors "Treblinka"
		"Lodz Ghetto"
		"Purple Triangle"
Multi-media	Museum displays	Simon Wiesenthal Centre: Museum of Tolerance (Los Angeles)
	Radio/TV	Oklahoma Federal Building bombing (current event)

Initial Responses to the Holocaust

Irene thoughtfully considered how to introduce her young students to the Holocaust, scaffolding children's texts that unfolded the horrors with an informative lecture that provided historical context. She created ample opportunities to reflect on and respond to this difficult information through writing, drawing, and talking. Phase 1 introduced students to the study of (in)tolerance and social justice through the reading of two picture books, a lecture that provided an historical context of World War II, and work with maps.

The Tolerance Focus opened with two picture books. On the first day, the class read *The Terrible Things*, by Eve Bunting (1980). This allegory of the Holocaust is told through the fate of animals in a forest, which are taken away by the Terrible Things, group by group, while the other animals look away, until a single rabbit remains.

Students drew their images of the Terrible Things as pencil sketches, the medium used to illustrate the story. *The Children we Remember* (Abells 1986) is a photo essay written for elementary students that documents the lives of Jewish children who both did and did not survive the Holocaust. Irene first read aloud *The Children we Remember* before providing historical information on the Holocaust because she wanted them to see the children in the photographs as children like them, not as more distant "children of war". The students looked and listened with rapt attention as Irene read aloud. Closing the book, she told the students that this event really happened, that it is something students needed to think about, and that "as human beings we need to know about things like this so that we can make decisions so that these kind of things don't happen". Thus, from the first days of the Tolerance Focus Study, Irene stressed the individual and social responsibility to make informed decisions. Students drew their immediate responses with black marker on white paper. Their responses were deeply emotional and visceral. Several drawings represented Holocaust events, such as Cynthia's depiction of a person being shot by a Nazi soldier (Figure 1). Most of the drawings represent affective themes of sorrow or retaliation.

Sorrow

Many of the drawings illustrated sorrow, as expressed by José, a bilingual resource student (Figure 2). José made intertextual links to the Star of David and fire, both of which were presented in the book through photographs and the sentences, "they made Jews sew patches on their clothes" and "they burned synagogues". José composed these symbols in a way that multiplies their individual meaning, by placing the Star of David on a crying man, who stands before a large fire. This image, which never appears in the book, evokes much meaning and emotion with a few simple strokes of black marker. Researchers (Clyde 1994; Smagorinsky and Coppock 1994; Whitin 1994) have emphasised the role of visual arts in providing opportunities for students to express and construct meanings that would be difficult to accomplish through writing alone. Thus, opportunities to respond through visual media are recommended for secondary students as well.

Although it was important for José and his peers to be able to express their immediate reactions to this introductory text, Irene wanted them to revisit it from a broader, more informed perspective. Thus, a few days later, she provided historical information through a 45-min lecture and discussion regarding the buildup of the Nazi regime, antisemitic laws established by Hitler, the Allied and Axis powers, and general events of World War II. The students then revisited *The Children we Remember* from this historically situated perspective and responded through quick-write responses. These written responses helped them to expand upon original understandings, examine them from a different perspective, and articulate meanings through a different sign system. Thus, whereas José could express his immediate

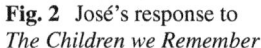

Fig. 1 Cynthia's drawing, a response to *The Children we Remember* (Abells 1986)

Fig. 2 José's response to *The Children we Remember*

emotional response in his drawing, his written response provided an opportunity to re-examine, explain, and expand upon his first response:

> I feel that it wasn't fair because they [Jewish people] didn't do anything and [they were persecuted] only because they were of another religion. Because of this their schools were burned and they closed their stores and took them away to other places and all because they were from another religion. I really feel something for them because I feel for them…it's pure sadness. [translated from Spanish]

José's illustration effectively expressed his "pure" feelings of sadness; after gaining historical information and encountering the book anew, he connected this sadness to antisemitism, discrimination, and human rights abuses in this written response. He explained his understanding of antisemitism by referring to the systematic oppression of the Jewish people, even though "they didn't do anything" and "all because they were from another religion". José named specific human rights violations, such as burning schools and forced removal, and underscored his empathy and deep sorrow.

Retaliation

Several other students responded with outrage and a desire to retaliate. After the first reading of *The Children we Remember*, Matthew, an American Indian boy, struggled for over 20 min with how to represent his feelings. At other tables, students were discussing and drawing weeping figures, but at Matthew's table a retaliation theme began to emerge. Matthew agreed with his tablemate, Alán, that he felt bad for the children and wanted the Nazis to suffer. Rather than try to steer them in another direction, Irene encouraged them to explore their "gut" feelings and how to represent them visually.

Matthew and his tablemates continued to discuss their ideas and collaborated to accurately draw symbols such as the Star of David. Matthew's drawing (Figure 3) incorporates these symbols to represent retaliation for the starvation and murder of Jewish people. Like other educators (e.g., Gregory 2000), Irene recognised how important it was for Matthew and his peers to express their sincere reactions and feelings about the Holocaust, even violent ones, and therefore she did not censor the students' expressions unless they were clearly inappropriate in a classroom setting. She also knew that they would have many more opportunities during the Tolerance Focus to expand their repertoire of responses to violence and injustice.

Matthew's written response, developed after the lecture and the second reading of the book, suggests a more complex understanding:

> I feel sad that the kids got shot and that some people were forced out of there houses. I think that that is mean that they burned schools and that they burned cinagods [synagogues]. I think that people should kill the nazis.

Fig. 3 Matthew's drawing, in response to *The Children we Remember*

Matthew's writing bridges cognitive and affective responses, expressing several reasons for his retaliatory feelings. First, he directly stated that he felt sad, a sentiment not visible in his drawing. He articulated explicit human rights violations and atrocities that led to his view that "people should kill the Nazis", which is the focus of his drawing. With additional knowledge offered by the lecture, Matthew had the opportunity to present in writing a more complex "picture" of his initial feelings and views represented by his drawing.

Totten (1998) stressed the importance of developing an effective opening to the study of the Holocaust and Irene and her colleagues thought deeply about how to best introduce the topic to their young learners. Through her choice of texts, her decisions on how to position them, and her explicit discourse, Irene facilitated the shaping of a particular context for examining the Holocaust, one that focused on humanity, human rights, and responsible social action.

A range of intertextual strategies supported students in expressing their feelings and understandings in learning about the Holocaust and the social and moral questions it raises about humanity. The children had many opportunities to share their responses and thinking; they could help each other grapple with and articulate their emotions and ideas about the perplexing and troubling events of the Holocaust. Additionally, drawing and writing responses together provided students with opportunities to extend their thinking (Clyde 1994; Smagorinsky and Coppock 1994) and to look at and respond to the texts from different perspectives. In the next section, I examine strategies that helped José, Matthew, and their classmates to move beyond these initial responses to more expanded meanings and language related to critical citizenship.

Expanding Repertoires

During Phase 2, the class studied the Holocaust through a large selection of texts. This phase was organised around the core literature the class was reading in four heterogeneous reading groups, *Number the Stars*, by Lois Lowry (1989a); Spanish readers read the translation, *Quien Cuenta las Estrellas* (Lowry 1989b). This children's novel is told from the perspective of Annemarie, a Christian girl in Norway whose family helps her Jewish friend Ellen escape to Sweden. Students interacted with over fifteen other visual and mixed media texts during this phase, as depicted in Table 1.

We cannot assume that interacting with the same text set will produce uniform understandings among different classrooms of students. Each class constructs its own referential system for interpreting texts based on how they jointly interact with the texts. Analysis of student writings in Room 18 indicated that they co-constructed knowledge around three prominent themes as they interacted with texts and each other. The first was intergroup conflict and cooperation focused on the abuse of power and social organisation against powerful oppressors. The second was rescue and resistance: individuals' need to act by resisting oppressive forces and rescuing those being oppressed rather than simply looking out for oneself. The third was action, emphasised in the theme of agency of Jewish and other people. For example, in interpreting various texts, class members often focused on the sacrifices that many Jewish people made to save their children and siblings.

All these themes centred on actions and interactions: actions of intergroup conflict and cooperation, intolerant actions, and responsible actions. In other words, these themes centred around the Holocaust as a vehicle for making meaning of the consequences of intolerant actions as well as responsible actions to create and maintain a just and equitable society. I examine how these themes were constructed as students responded to texts in Phase 2, drawing upon samples from different genres of student writing: Venn diagrams, students' letters to Anne Frank (1995), diary entries, and double-entry notes.

Venn Diagrams

Once the students had a larger historical context, Irene wanted them to revisit *The Terrible Things* and its allegorical message. Over one circle of a Venn diagram, she placed a quote from the text:

> The rabbits scampered in every direction. "Help!" they screamed. "Somebody help!" But there was no one left to help. And the big circling nets dropped over them and the Terrible Things carried them away.

Over the second intersecting circle, she placed a modification of Pastor Martin Niemöller's famous quote:

> In Germany they first came for the Communists and I didn't speak up because I wasn't a Communist. Then they came for the Jews, and I didn't speak up because I wasn't a Jew. Then they came for the trade unionists and I didn't speak up because I wasn't a trade unionist. Then they came for the Catholics, and I didn't speak up because I was a Protestant. Then they came for me—and by that time no one was left to speak up. (USHMM 2014)

The graphic strategy of the Venn diagram helped students make connections between the allegorical story and the pastor's real experience of the Holocaust. In their heterogeneous reading groups, students read and discussed both quotes before filling in the diagram with similarities and differences. Irene met with each reading group to read and discuss each quote, the commonalties and differences they saw, and how the quotes related to students' own lives. Irene asked one group, "what do you think this is saying about responsibility, about individual responsibility, your responsibility?" Sergio responded, suggesting that it was a responsibility to "stick up for other people". Matthew added that you would feel mad at yourself "because you didn't say nothing". Sergio continued, "Then you start wondering what would've happened if we had sticken up for 'em".

Irene raised similar questions with each group regarding the dangers of remaining a bystander and the possibility of making a difference in the face of injustice. Throughout the discussion, Irene's questions helped students to make personal connections to the text by focusing them on their feelings of choosing to remain a bystander. Irene helped students make additional text-to-life connections by asking them to consider situations they have encountered in their own lives, such as witnessing a playground fight and being a bystander to bullying. Thus, the class explored tensions involving the risks of action and consequences of inaction in two contexts: one more severe, complex, and distant, and another more immediate to their own everyday lives. Teachers need to tread carefully, however, when comparing playground fights to brutal genocide (Lipstadt 1995).

The students then worked in pairs to fill in the diagram. The diagrams of Sergio and Matthew, like those of many of their peers, recorded differences between the texts but still recognised a fundamental similarity of inaction: both the animals and humans, as "living things", did not "stick up for each other" and thus were taken away. While a few students wrote about this inaction in their quick-write responses to *The Terrible Things* on Day 2, most students identified this shared message of social responsibility and uniting against larger, oppressive forces in the Venn diagram on Day 6.

Diary Entries

In interpreting the story from the core literature, *Number the Stars*, students wrote a diary entry for each chapter from one character's perspective. Trinetta, a European-American girl, chose the perspective of Ellen, the Jewish friend whom Annemarie's family helped to escape to Sweden. In one entry, Trinetta managed to take Ellen's point of view even though Ellen was not "present" in the chapter, which centred on Annemarie delivering a package to the Danish resistance movement. The chapter only indicated that Ellen was hiding on a fishing boat, and Trinetta imagined her experience:

> Dear Tazzy, 3/28/95
>
> I'm in the boat. I just heard something, so I snuggled up to my mom, because I thought that it could be a soldier. Then I heard Annemarie's voice. I wanted to jump up and hug her. I looked at mama but I knew mama knew what I was thinking. She shoke her head and whispered to me, "stay down". So I obeyed. I think that Annemarie was brave to come here.
> Sincerely,
> Ellen

Trinetta recognised the danger people faced when they sought to escape the Nazi regime as well as the risk Annemarie took by participating in the Resistance. These diary entries personally engaged Trinetta and her peers in the risks, triumphs, and challenges of resistance and rescue, helping them to grapple further with the moral dilemmas of social responsibility.

Double-Entry Notes

Students used a double-entry format to record their notes and interpretations of videos, lectures, and poetry. For example, on Day 39, the class read aloud several poems written by children in concentration camps. They then wrote selected lines from the poems on the left with their interpretations of these lines on the right. The selected poems were heart-rending cries of despair and abandonment. The students' responses related to these children's dire and senseless imprisonment while also orienting to the possibility of rescue. Ben, a European-American boy whose father is Jewish, wrote the verse of one poem on the left and his interpretation on the right:

I wish I were a little bird, up in the bright blue sky, that sings and flies just where he will and no one will ask Why.	I think if I wasn't Jewish I would try to save this poor little girl so she can do what she wants and not be trapped and die. I would want her to be free!

Ben called attention to the inhumanity of imprisoning innocent children and expressed his desire for the girl to be free. He inserted himself in his response, noting that he wanted to rescue the girl, recognising her anguish and threat of death. Like Ben, many students responded to the poems by pondering the senselessness of the Holocaust and basic human rights violations, and calling for some type of action to change the situation.

Cynthia, a Mexican-American girl, recognised the possibility of rescue in a different way, responding to two lines from another poem:

Maybe from there the world will hear my cry… why?	Some people will hear but can't do any thing. and some don't do any thing.

Cynthia succinctly captured the dilemmas facing bystanders who are either powerless to insert themselves or choose not to. These students' double-entry notes responded to the atrocities of the concentration camp by empathising with and taking up the poets' point of view.

The Venn diagrams, diary entries, and double-entry responses provided students with entry points for experiencing the events themselves and grappling with their complexity (Spalding, Savage, and Garcia 2007). Because these were all practices familiar to the students from activities they had engaged in from the first days of fifth grade, they did not have to concentrate on learning the academic practice, but instead could focus on engaging in it to relate and respond to their study of intolerance and the Holocaust. Furthermore, they continued to expand their understanding of the 3R's by considering how rights and responsibilities were much more complex and life-threatening factors during the Holocaust.

Through these academic engagements, these young learners were, in the words of Alfie Kohn (1997, p. 435) "invited to reflect on complex issues, cast them in light of their own experiences and questions", and, individually and with each other, sort out important issues regarding humanity, power, and responsible citizenship. Over time, this particular class community constructed a referential system for interpreting the texts in particular ways—ways that acknowledged the incomprehensible horrors of the Holocaust while also bringing to light agency, responsible action, and intergroup cooperation. Similarly, intolerance and injustice were framed as abrogation of responsibility and abuse of power.

Personal and Social Actions

These analyses illustrate how various types of academic engagement provided the students with opportunities to construct meanings and language for tolerance and responsible social action through a range of texts and modes of expression in the first half of the Tolerance Focus. While actions were emphasised through the themes and orientations in Phases 1 and 2, they were largely related to those of the characters and people in the texts. In Phase 3, the focus shifted towards actions that the students could take themselves, through engagements that helped further multiply meaning, language, and actions regarding genocide and critical citizenship.

Personal Action Steps

Phase 3 opened with a field trip to the Museum of Tolerance in Los Angeles. Importantly, the fifth-grade classes raised the funds required to support this trip through a mathematics project that culminated in a school spaghetti dinner; in other words, students learned the necessity of collaborative work and responsibility for funding the privilege and opportunity of visiting the museum. The museum contained several sections, one focusing on the Holocaust of World War II and another containing interactive displays regarding tolerance and prejudice in general. The Holocaust section included poignant and graphic videos that illustrate human suffering and courage. In the tolerance section, signs that ask "who is responsible?" are found throughout the interactive displays. The museum staff was reluctant to permit fifth graders, but after the first visit, made the previous year, they wrote to Irene and Beth indicating that they were impressed with the maturity the students had displayed and their preparation for the museum. The students responded powerfully to the museum and were given the opportunity to express their feelings and impressions with two personal action steps: constructing a Wall of Remembrance and writing what came to be called "tolerance essays".

After discussing the Wall of Remembrance at the USHMM in Washington, DC, made from children's ceramic tiles, all the fifth graders in the school constructed their own laminated paper tiles, which were hung at the school's entrance to create a fifth-grade Wall of Remembrance (Jennings and Pattenaude 1999). Various processes allowed students to extend the meanings and language of earlier texts. First, as they created their own tiles, they could again share their knowledge and consider ideas represented in their tablemates' tiles. Second, many tiles elaborated on features from earlier text constructions, including Stars of David, crossed-out swastikas, and some peace signs, which were readily in evidence on the tiles. These tiles extended these meanings with a larger global message of peace and caring through additional images. Like many students, Matthew drew the Earth at the centre with the word "LOVE" written in big bold letters across the globe. While other students surrounded their globes with people holding hands, Matthew wrote around Earth: "Never give up hope! 1939–1945 Six years of torture! No food", showing a continued struggle with the suffering faced by so many during the Holocaust. In this drawing, however, he put these incomprehensible realities in the context of the possibility of our world uniting in love and hope.

It was important for students to be able to integrate what they had learned about the Holocaust with a view toward future possibilities as well as past and present realities. The construction of the Wall of Remembrance provided that opportunity, as well as a chance for students to give public voice to their understandings through both words and illustrations. The Wall of Remembrance became an important topic of discussion among school members and families and served as a first step in publicly speaking out for social justice and nonviolence.

The construction of the tiles helped students to envision a more tolerant and just world; they then wrote essays that helped them to think about actions they could take toward their vision. The essays thus provided an opportunity to reflect on the museum displays in relationship to all the other texts, stories, and experiences they had encountered throughout the Tolerance Focus. All students read their essays aloud to the class, an action that both enabled them to take a public stand and provided them with access to each other's understandings. Overall, the essays convey deep emotion, penetrating questions, and thoughtful reflection on the Holocaust, humanity, and social responsibility. Most of the essays grappled with the painful realities of the Holocaust; all of them brought in one of the themes of intergroup conflict and cooperation, agency of individuals, and rescue and resistance.

In her essay, Rebecca, an Anglo-American girl, reflected all three themes as well as a mature understanding of the nature of and consequences of intolerance and racism:

> At the Museum of Tolerance I learned that people went through massive suffering, massive pain, and massive heartache. The Jewish people were slaughtered and tortured. The Jews were put in concentration camps and gas chambers. They were shot at and they had everything they ever had taken away from them. This was because one group didn't like their religion and that one group wanted power. Racism goes on every day, everywhere. I learned that I should be more tolerant and respectful to anyone and everyone, no matter what their religion and no matter what they look like.
>
> The visit has and will continue to affect me for the better. Before the trip I knew racism went on. And I knew it was wrong but now I've seen what racism can do. Racism hurts. People are still getting hurt and people are still getting killed because of racism. The visit has helped me see that I need to be tolerant of everyone. I need to help and share with any human being that is in need. I know that I can't stop everyone from being racist, but I can show people how much being racist hurts others.
>
> When I came out of the museum, I knew that I had changed. I knew I wanted everyone to live in peace. I knew I need to be responsible for my actions. I knew I needed to help.

In the first paragraph, Rebecca described the suffering brought on by the Holocaust and discussed the nature of the Holocaust in terms of abuse of power, intolerance, antisemitism, and racism. She did not turn away from the stark brutality inflicted on Jewish people. (Multiple texts, including the museum displays, also referred to other groups of people victimised during the Holocaust, but students tended to focus on the Jewish people). She took the perspective of the people targeted and also articulated responsible actions that she can take against racism, particularly by showing people "how much being racist hurts others". Like many of her peers in Room 18, Rebecca underscored how she felt changed by the visit to the museum, a visit made more meaningful through the activities of the Tolerance Focus.

Irene also asked students to add a paragraph about what responsibility means to them at the end of their essays. Rebecca addressed both individual and social responsibilities to speak out against racism and discrimination, alluding to the consequences of remaining silent:

> We, as the people of this earth, are responsible for our actions. I am responsible for my actions and everyone else is responsible for theirs. People do have choices. You can choose to be a racist person who is mean and cruel to other races or you can choose to be a person who is nice and caring to everyone, no matter what they look like. If something is wrong, it is your responsibility to try and set it right. We should all unite as one big family and help each other when we are in need. If someone says something about someone or about a certain race in a racist way, it's our responsibility to speak out and say, "that's wrong".

Mayra, a Mexican-American Spanish reader, reflected profoundly on humanity and inhumanity, and the loss we all suffer through discrimination and genocide:

> This trip made me think that we all have the right to live because we are all human, and not animals. In the museum I almost wanted to cry because of all the poor people the Nazi's had killed...

> This trip changed my view and allowed me to understand the things that happen in this world. The world is different because at times there is peace and times there are wars where a lot of people die. Sometimes I stop and think that I and everyone else can change the world, by making sure there is peace and love. If no one among us were Jewish, this world would be a lonely place, because we are all part of this world. When I saw the pictures of the numbers of Jewish people that had been killed, I felt guilty for not knowing sooner so that I could have given them love and caring. Respect is what we need to give one another and we should also ask for forgiveness from one another for the evil that we have done. [translated from Spanish]

Mayra's essay demonstrates the hope expressed by Dan Napolitano, of the USHMM: "that exposure to this kind of discipline, this kind of information, will foster intelligent reflection on what it means to be a human being, what it means to live in society" (cited by Shoemaker 2003, p. 194). Mayra expressed a young girl's desire for a world united in peace and love; she also expressed deep insight into the beauty and social exigency of cultural diversity while demonstrating a maturing understanding of the culpability we each share for having allowed human atrocities to be committed by the Nazis in their quest for Jewish extinction.

These two essays represent, through the voices and eyes of fifth graders, an ability to empathise, a more complex understanding of the nature of intolerance, and the recognition of our individual and collective responsibility for creating and maintaining a just and humane society. While each essay is unique, varying in length and sophistication, they all refer to the rights to life, dignity, and equality; the need for mutual respect among all groups of people; and the need for people to uphold these rights and respect through responsible actions. The taxonomy in Figure 4 represents how all students in the class discussed responsibility throughout their essays, including, but not limited to, the final paragraph that focused on responsibility. Foremost, students referred to responsibility in terms of "taking action", "being tolerant", and "stopping violence". While many students focused on local actions and responsibilities, some had a larger social view, and suggested the need to take action to prevent the Holocaust from recurring. Patti wrote, "I think that we should treat people better because if we don't take care of our world, this is going to happen again". Similarly, many wrote about the responsibility to stay informed, a critical quality of political literacy. Angela stated, "I learned at the Museum of Tolerance to listen to the world better and to know what is happening in the world". José L. exclaimed, "!No cerran tus ojos, no!" (Don't close your eyes, no!)

The tolerance essays reflect an expanded repertoire of meanings and language for understanding (in)tolerance and social responsibility. On the second day of school, the class conceptualised responsibility as caring for people, for one's siblings, and for the streets as well as the responsibility to make decisions. In April, they added several more concepts, such as staying informed, protesting racism, uniting for change, being tolerant, stopping violence, and taking action. The difference is a more proactive voice and set of actions that are both personal and collective actions. Through the tolerance essays, students positioned themselves as thoughtful, compassionate, contributing members of various communities who pondered the capacity of humans to both hurt and kill others and to love, help, and step out for others.

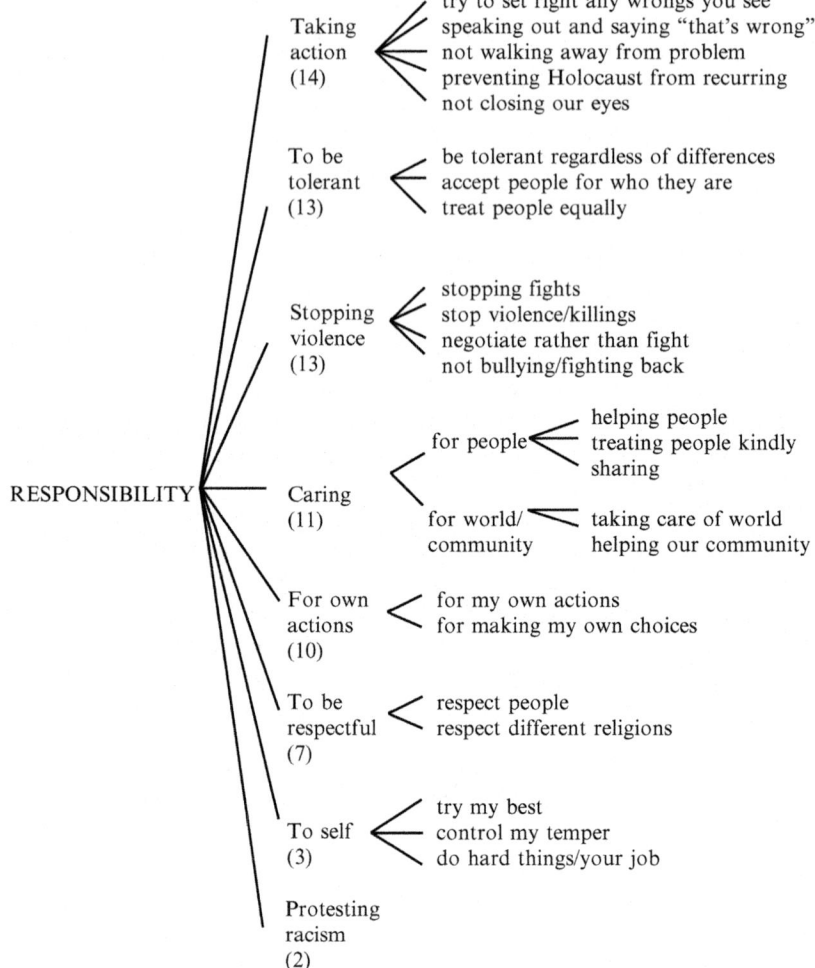

Fig. 4 Taxonomy of responsibility attributes articulated in students' tolerance essays

Community Action Step

By early May, the three fifth-grade classes were ready to take an action to support tolerance and justice in their community. Each class brainstormed ideas and then took a vote. They agreed to make a video that captured what they learned about tolerance in an interview "talk show" format to send to the city council. The process involved all students in writing questions regarding what they had learned. They practised conducting a broadcast interview in small groups; then groups of volunteers from each class carried out the actual taped interview.

In the action video, students made connections to prior texts and to their own lives, most of their comments centring on actions. For example, when Irene asked students why they think Lois Lowry wrote *Number the Stars*, Susana, a Mexican-American girl, replied, "So people could speak up and tell the people what could happen in this world now and um to see maybe what happened before and how people got threatened". Like Susana, other students connected knowledge and action, speaking about the importance of learning about the Holocaust and intolerance so that they could take actions to promote tolerance and justice.

This action video provided students with several opportunities to take action by making public statements, verbally and in writing, about strategies for stopping violence and racism and for promoting respect. Even students who did not speak during the video wrote questions and answered each other's questions in writing and during practice interviews. By hearing each other's ideas about actions they could take individually and collectively, and by extending and re-envisioning their own thinking each time they wrote, asked, and answered questions about intolerance and justice, they multiplied potential meanings, language, and actions regarding (in)tolerance. The video also created a space and time for members of Room 18 to practise and experience social action with other classes.

In the final days of the school year, the children initiated their own authentic action step, refusing to look on as bystanders at the middle school orientation facilitated by the middle school staff. During the orientation, Spanish-dominant children were separated from their English-dominant peers and brought to a room to take a language test. Room 18 students spoke up, pointing out that the Spanish-speaking children missed out on part of the orientation. When they returned to the classroom, many very upset, they told Irene that they needed to discuss it further. They pointed out how unfair it was to provide an informative school tour to the English-dominant students that partially excluded the Spanish-dominant students. These upstanding students brainstormed actions that they could take to inform the middle school about the injustice of this segregation. Although they were not able to take this action themselves on the last day of school, Irene did carry their message to the middle school orientation team. The students in Room 18 had grown in their capacity to recognise acts of injustice, to articulate and deliberate the issues, and to take collective action to make a difference.

Discussion

This ethnographic study demonstrated the possibilities of Holocaust studies and education for critical citizenship in one fifth-grade class. Irene and her students had time to establish and maintain a safe class community for exploring difficult social, political, and moral questions throughout the course of an entire school year, an opportunity rarely available at middle and secondary levels. With support from her school and classroom families, Irene and her colleagues carefully constructed a long-term approach to education about (in)tolerance and social responsibility that included an in-depth study of the Holocaust. Throughout the Tolerance Focus, students were building on social and academic practices that they had constructed together from the first day of school. By making personal connections to events in the texts, students could better see the significance of the Holocaust and examine tolerance and intolerance in their own lives. Students were provided with many resources, including each other's knowledge, as they grappled with these complex issues. Through a variety of artistic, written, and spoken responses, they could each find their own voice in articulating these understandings and further develop that voice and language over time. These multiple responses also provided many avenues for expressing empathy and compassion, essential components of learning tolerance and respect (McCall 1996).

Irene constructed with the students a framework for interpreting texts about the Holocaust that supported them in expanding their repertoires beyond sorrow and retaliation to a more comprehensive set of understandings. As they encountered and responded to a range of texts, the class constructed a common view of tolerance that emphasised action and compassion for others' points of view and circumstances. Writing, drawing, and speaking were interwoven as tools for social action in this fifth-grade class. The authentic action that they took on the last day of school suggests that the class, in general, applied the lessons of the Tolerance Focus to their own lived experience when they were segregated during the middle school orientation. Cowan and Maitles (2007) argue for the power of Holocaust education to contribute to students' development of political literacy, which includes the exercise of power in local contexts as well as national and global contexts. The students in Room 18 demonstrated not only political literacy, but also what Freire (1970, 2005) refers to as *conscientizacão*, or critical consciousness, which lies at the heart of critical citizenship: when they saw their classmates being segregated, these young learners demonstrated the capacity to locate and name an injustice occurring in their lives, then dialogue and deliberate about the nature of this injustice and take some action to address it (Jennings and Da Matta 2009; Jennings, Jewett, Laman, Souto-Manning, and Wilson 2010; Laman, Jewett, Jennings, Wilson, and Souto-Manning 2012).

The approach taken by Irene and her colleagues highlights the importance of long-term engagements, a layered curriculum that supports children in building understandings over time, and multiple opportunities for making meaning together. This approach includes many features highlighted in recently published frameworks, including empathy-building, a focus on rescue and resistance, a study of the bystander response, building a knowledge base about the Holocaust, and stories of individual experience (Burtonwood 2002). A central feature of several frameworks that is less evident in the Tolerance Focus is an examination of Judaism or a historical frame regarding antisemitism, elements found lacking across many secondary curricula in the United States and Britain (Gallant and Hartman 2001; Short 1994; Short and Carrington 1992). As upper elementary teachers develop their curricula, it is important for them to consider how to incorporate this context and knowledge, as Irene, Beth, and Phoebe did in the following years.

The purpose of this study was to examine the complexity of integrating Holocaust education into a larger study of human rights, social responsibility, and critical citizenship in one fifth-grade bilingual class. When Irene, Beth, and Phoebe have presented their work at professional conferences, teachers have asked them to package this "curriculum" in a book. However, their classroom work is not prescriptive and cannot simply be lifted from one classroom or school and placed into another. These teachers constructed the curriculum with the students, building on the students' knowledge, questions, and life experiences. They developed and continuously revised their approaches based on their own inquiry-based and student-centred pedagogical knowledge, personal convictions, humanistic values, and commitment to gaining the knowledge and insight needed to integrate this curriculum into their classrooms. They had the support of their administrators and each other, along with trust from the parents and families. The question remains how we best prepare and support teachers to engage effectively in critical pedagogy and antiracist education (Nieto and Bode 2011) that enables them to walk the delicate line between moral sensitivity and intellectual rigor in Holocaust education.

Acknowledgements This chapter draws on Jennings (2010). I am grateful to Irene Pattenaude and the children of Room 18 for the privilege of this collaborative inquiry and to Beth Yeager and Phoebe Hirsch-Dubin for their insights and continuing contributions to social justice education. The Santa Barbara Classroom Discourse Group was fundamental to the development of this study, and the support of Judith Green and Carol Dixon was invaluable. Thanks to anonymous reviewers of earlier drafts.

References

Abells, C. B. (1986). *The children we remember*. New York: Greenwillow Books.
Berger, P. L., & Luckmann, T. (1966). *The social construction of reality: A treatise in the sociology of knowledge*. New York: Doubleday.
Bromley, P., & Russell, S. G. (2010). The Holocaust as history and human rights: A cross-national analysis of Holocaust education in social science textbooks, 1970–2008. *Prospects, 40*(1), 153–173.
Bunting, E. (1980). *The terrible things*. New York: Harper and Row.
Burtonwood, N. (2002). Holocaust Memorial Day in schools: Context, process and content. A review of research into Holocaust education. *Educational Research, 44*, 29–82.
Castanheira, M. L., Crawford, T., Green, J., & Dixon, C. (2001). Interactional ethnography: An approach to studying the social construction of literate practices. *Linguistics and Education, 11*, 353–400.
Clyde, J. A. (1994). Lessons from Douglas: Expanding our visions of what it means to "know". *Language Arts, 71*, 22–33.
Collins, E., & Green, J. L. (1992). Learning in classrooms: Making or breaking a culture. In H. Marshall (Ed.), *Redefining student learning: Roots of educational change* (pp. 59–86). Norwood: Ablex.
Cowan, P., & Maitles, H. (2007). Does addressing prejudice and discrimination through Holocaust education produce better citizens? *Educational Review, 59*(2), 115–130.

Cowan, P., & Maitles, H. (2010). Policy and practice of Holocaust education in Scotland. *Prospects, 40*(2), 257–272.
Dixon, C. N., & Green, J. L. (2009). How a community of inquiry shapes and is shaped by policies: The Santa Barbara classroom discourse group experience as a telling case. *Language Arts, 86,* 280–289.
Drucker, M., & Halperin, M. (1993). *Jacob's rescue: A Holocaust story.* New York: Dell Publishing.
Edwards, D., & Mercer, N. (1987). *Common knowledge: The development of understanding in the classroom.* New York: Methuen.
Frank, A. (1995). *The diary of a young girl: The definitive edition.* O.H. Frank & M. Pressler (Eds.). New York: Doubleday.
Freire, P. (1970). *The pedagogy of the oppressed.* New York: Seabury Press.
Freire, P. (2005). *Education for critical consciousness.* New York: Continuum.
Gallant, M. J., & Hartman, H. (2001). Holocaust education for the new millennium: Assessing our progress. *Journal of Holocaust Education, 10*(2), 1–28.
Green, J. L., & Meyer, L. A. (1991). The embeddedness of reading in classroom life: Reading as a situated process. In C. Baker & A. Luke (Eds.), *Towards a critical sociology of reading pedagogy* (pp. 141–160). Philadelphia: John Benjamins.
Green, J. L., & Wallat, C. (1979). What is an instructional context? An exploratory analysis of conversational shifts over time. In O. Garnica & M. King (Eds.), *Language, children and society* (pp. 159–188). New York: Pergamon.
Greene, M. (1988). *The dialectic of freedom.* New York: Teacher's College Press.
Gregory, I. (2000). Teaching about the Holocaust: Perspectives, issues, and suggestions. In I. Davies (Ed.), *Teaching the Holocaust* (pp. 49–60). London: Continuum.
Gumperz, J. J. (1986). Interactional sociolinguistics in the study of schooling. In J. Cook-Gumperz (Ed.), *The social construction of literacy* (pp. 45–68). New York: Cambridge University Press.
Heras, A. I. (1993). The construction of understanding in a sixth-grade bilingual class. *Linguistics and Education, 5*(3&4), 275–299.
Innocenti, R. (1985). *Rose Blanche.* Makato: Creative Education, Inc.
Innocenti, R. (1987). *Rosa Blanca.* Madrid: Lógues Ediciones.
Jennings, L.B. (1996). *Multiple contexts for learning social justice: An ethnographic and sociolinguistic study of a fifth grade bilingual class.* Unpublished doctoral dissertation, University of California, Santa Barbara.
Jennings, L. B. (2010). Challenges and possibilities of Holocaust education and critical citizenship: An ethnographic study of a fifth-grade bilingual class revisited. *Prospects, 40*(1), 35–56.
Jennings, L. B., & Da Matta, G. B. (2009). Rooted in resistance: Women teachers constructing counter-pedagogies in post-authoritarian Brazil. *Teaching Education, 20*(3), 215–228.
Jennings, L. B., & Green, J. L. (1999). Locating democratizing and transformative practices within classroom discourse. *Journal of Classroom Interaction, 34*(2), i–iv.
Jennings, L. B., & Pattenaude, I. (1998). Making meaning and beyond: Literate strategies for exploring and enacting tolerance. *The New Advocate, 11*(4), 325–343.
Jennings, L. B., & Pattenaude, I. (1999). *Oye y escucha mi voz*/Hear and see my voice: Responding to intolerance and genocide. *Multicultural Perspectives, 1*(1), 30–36.
Jennings, L. B., Parra-Medina, D. M., Messias, D. K. H., & McLoughlin, K. (2006). Toward a theory of critical social youth empowerment: An examination of youth empowerment models. *Journal of Community Practice, 14*(1/2), 31–55.
Jennings, L. B., Jewett, P., Laman, T. T., Souto-Manning, M., & Wilson, J. (Eds.) (2010). *Sites of possibility: Critical dialogue across educational contexts.* Cresskill: Hampton Press.
Kohn, A. (1997). How not to teach values: A critical look at character education. *The Phi Delta Kappan, 78*(6), 428–439.
Kristeva, J. (1986). *The Kristeva reader* (T. Moi, Ed.), New York: Columbia University Press.
Laman, T. T., Jewett, P., Jennings, L. B., Wilson, J. L., & Souto-Manning, M. V. (2012). Supporting critical dialogue across educational contexts. *Equity & Excellence in Education, 45*(1), 197–216.

Lemke, J. L. (1992). Intertextuality and educational research. *Linguistics and Education, 4*(3–4), 257–267.
Lipstadt, D. E. (1995, 6 March). Not facing history: How not to teach the Holocaust. *The New Republic*, pp. 26–29.
Lowry, L. (1989a). *Number the stars*. New York: Dell Publishing.
Lowry, L. (1989b). *Quien cuenta las estrellas?* Boston: Houghton Mifflin.
McCall, A. L. (1996). Making a difference: Integrating social problems and social action in the social studies curriculum. *Social Studies, 87*(5), 203–210.
Mitchell, J. C. (1984). Case studies. In R. F. Ellen (Ed.), *Ethnographic research: A guide to general conduct* (pp. 237–241). San Diego: Academic.
Nieto, S., & Bode, P. (2011). *Affirming diversity: The sociopolitical context of multicultural education* (6th ed.). New York: Pearson.
Power, S. (2002). *"A problem from hell": America and the age of genocide*. New York: Basic Books.
Santa Barbara Classroom Discourse Group (Dixon, C., de la Cruz, E., Green, J., Lin, L., & Brandts, L.) (1992a). Do you see what we see? The referential and intertextual nature of classroom life. *Journal of Classroom Interaction, 27*(2), 29–36.
Santa Barbara Classroom Discourse Group (Green, J., Dixon, C., Lin, L., Floriani, A., & Bradley, M.) (1992b). Constructing literacy in classrooms: Literate action as social accomplishment. In H. Marshall (Ed.), *Redefining student learning: Roots of educational change* (pp. 119–150). Norwood: Ablex.
Santa Barbara Classroom Discourse Group (Eds.) (1993). Special issue, *Linguistics in Education: An International Research Journal, 4*(3–4).
Schwag, T., & Wackerlig, O. (2010). Far away and nearby: Holocaust remembrance and human rights education in Switzerland. *Prospects, 40*(2), 223–237.
Schweber, S. (2008). "What happened to their pets?": Third graders encounter the Holocaust. *Teachers College Record, 110*(10), 2073–2115.
Shoemaker, R. (2003). Teaching the Holocaust in America's schools: Some considerations for teachers. *Intercultural Education, 14*(2), 191–199.
Short, K. (1992). Researching intertextuality within collaborative learning environments. *Linguistics and Education, 4*, 313–333.
Short, G. (1994). Teaching the Holocaust: The relevance of children's perceptions of Jewish culture and identity. *British Educational Research Journal, 20*(4), 393–405.
Short, G. (2000). Holocaust education and citizenship: A view from the United Kingdom. In M. Leicester, C. Modgil, & S. Modgil (Eds.), *Politics, education and citizenship* (pp. 2–23). London: Falmer.
Short, G., & Carrington, B. (1992). The development of children's understanding of Jewish identity and culture. *School Psychology International, 14*(1), 73–89.
Smagorinsky, P., & Coppock, J. (1994). Cultural tools and the classroom context: An exploration of an artistic response to literature. *Written Communication, 11*(3), 283–310.
Spalding, E., Savage, T. A., & Garcia, J. (2007). The march of remembrance and hope: Teaching and learning about diversity and social justice through the Holocaust. *Teachers College Record, 109*(6), 1423–1456.
Spradley, J. P. (1980). *Participant observation*. New York: Holt, Rinehart and Winston.
Stevick, E. D., & Gross, Z. (2010). Epistemology and Holocaust education: History, memory and the politics of knowledge. *Prospects, 40*(2), 189–200.
Supple, C. (1998a). *From prejudice to genocide: Learning about the Holocaust* (Rev. ed.). Stoke-on-Trent, UK: Trentham Books.
Supple, C. (1998b). Issues and problems in teaching about the Holocaust. In G. Short, C. Supple, & K. Klinger (Eds.), *The Holocaust in the school curriculum: A European perspective* (pp. 17–58). Strasbourg: Council of Europe.
Totten, S. (1998). The start is as important as the finish: Establishing a foundation for the study of the Holocaust. *Social Education, 62*(2), 70–76.

Totten, S. (1999). Should there be Holocaust education for K-4 students? The answer is no. *Social Studies and the Young Learner, 12*(1), 36–39.

Totten, S. (2002). *Holocaust education: Issues and approaches.* Boston: Allyn & Bacon.

Tuyay, S., Jennings, L., & Dixon, C. (1995). Classroom discourse and opportunities for learning: An ethnographic study of knowledge construction in a bilingual third grade classroom. *Discourse Processes, 19*(1), 75–110.

Uchida, A. (1990). Letter from a concentration camp. In A. Durell & M. Sachs (Eds.), *The big book for peace* (pp. 57–61). New York: Dutton Children's Books.

USHMM [United States Holocaust Memorial Museum] (2001). *Teaching about the Holocaust: A resource book for educators.* Washington, DC: USHMM.

USHMM (2014). *Martin Niemöller: "First they came for the Socialists".* http://www.ushmm.org/wlc/en/article.php?ModuleId=10007392

Westheimer, J., & Kahne, J. (2004). What kind of citizen? The politics of educating for democracy. *American Educational Research Journal, 41*(2), 237–269.

Whitin, P. (1994). Opening potential: Visual response to literature. *Language Arts, 71,* 101–107.

Wild, M. (1991). *Let the celebrations begin!* New York: Orchard Books.

Yeager, B., Pattenaude, I., Fránquiz, M., & Jennings, L. (1999). Rights, respect, and responsibility: Toward a theory of action in two bilingual classrooms. In J. Robertson (Ed.), *Teaching for a tolerant world, grades K–6* (pp. 196–218). Chicago: National Council of Teachers of English.

"They Think It Is Funny to Call Us Nazis": Holocaust Education and Multicultural Education in a Diverse Germany

Debora Hinderliter Ortloff

Introduction

The reunification of Germany not only marked a new political way forward, but also created a space to reassess Germany's past. The process of reunification and subsequent re-examination of identity and memory has also meant confronting the reality of multiculturalism in contemporary Germany. As the schools attempt to navigate these multicultural realities, engagement with the Holocaust may well present unexpected challenges. In this chapter I focus on one German state, and investigate the conflicts and compromises presented by the demands to have both robust Holocaust education and multicultural education.

In the decade that followed political reunification, particularly once the Social Democrats ascended to the chancellorship in 1998, the longstanding emphasis on a blood-based (*jus sanguinis*), ethnocultural (Brubaker 1992) German identity was abandoned in favor of recasting Germany as a multicultural country (Joppke 2000; Thraenhardt 2000). This effort to recast Germany as a multicultural society, represented formally by national legislation aimed at changing citizenship requirements and developing immigration policies, is a continuation of Germany's reconciliation with National Socialism. In part these laws, and the discussions which accompanied them, highlighted the fact that recognising Germany as a multicultural nation means coming to terms with how "others" were, and are, incorporated into the German state. German Jews, Roma, and German-speaking Slavs all lived in and contributed to German society, but were constructed as non-Germans prior to World War II (Brubaker 1992; Klopp 2002; Thraenhardt 2000). Even after the Holocaust, other groups were not included as Germans insofar as citizenship laws precluded them

---

D.H. Ortloff (✉)
Department of Social Sciences, Finger Lakes Community College,
3325 Marvin Sands Drive, Canandaigua, NY 14424, USA
e-mail: Debora.ortloff@flcc.edu

from attaining citizenship and immigration, according to the letter of the law, did not exist (Joppke 2000). In particular, the guestworker (*Gastarbeiter*) population recruited from Italy, Spain, Yugoslavia, and Turkey became disenfranchised from the democratic process (Ortloff 2007, 2009): even into their third generation of living in Germany they had no right to citizenship. Indeed, as Brubaker (1992) has argued, the late political unification of Germany (under Bismarck) specifically required an ethnocultural notion of Germanness to be promoted and reified. In short, the lack of political unity, what Brubaker terms "pre-political Germany", meant that some foundation for identity from outside of the political realm was necessary; the process of othering on the basis of ethnicity, race, and religion made an ethnocultural "Germanness" possible (Gosewinkel 1998; Joppke 2000). After World War II, the Cold War, and in particular the existence of ethnocultural Germans in the Soviet bloc, allowed for this ethnocultural sense of German identity to be further propagated—despite its obvious overlap with Nazi ideology (Joppke 2000; Rathel 1995). Thus, reunification has created a space where the diversity of the present German state must be reconciled with long-held notions of what it means to be German.

Ultimately this re-examination of national identity has educational implications. If future citizens are to be prepared for citizenship in a multicultural German state, then it follows that a citizenship education process must be developed, one which both recognises the implications of the past and embraces a multicultural future. In this chapter, I probe into the question of how, in the conservative German state of Bavaria, official citizenship education policy (in the form of state-approved textbooks in social studies) and teachers' reflections on their implementation of this policy, can be used to reconcile Germany's past with a new multicultural education.

In particular, I examine anti-violence education, a required part of social studies education in the *Hauptschule*, as a means of understanding how education policy and teachers are specifically addressing xenophobia and othering. The *Hauptschule* is a form of secondary school ending at the 9th grade, in which students are prepared for blue-collar apprenticeships to be completed after graduation.

This subject is critical for explicating how German schools are confronting questions of identity because, as explained above, othering has been an integral part of German identity. Further, anti-violence education has become a primary means of addressing the Holocaust in the social studies curriculum. Although education about the Holocaust and World War II occurs primarily through history classes, the anti-violence education unit, as my study reveals, allows teachers to connect to the Holocaust in ways that are relevant to examining contemporary society. Thus, understanding Holocaust education in Germany requires not just a study of Holocaust education itself, but also an examination of how future German citizens are being prepared to embrace an inclusive German identity.

Methodology

This chapter evolved out of a larger exploration of changes in multicultural education policy and practice in Bavaria (Ortloff 2007, 2009; Ortloff and McCarty 2009), based on a qualitative analysis of *Hauptschule* and *Realschule* social studies textbooks and interviews with 58 teachers at these two school levels. The *Realschule* is a school form ending in 10th grade, in which students prepare for a technical education and technical-oriented apprenticeships; in this chapter I use only data from the *Hauptschule*. The data provided a window into the twin processes of grappling with the legacy of National Socialism while conceptualising a future or present multicultural German state. This coupling, of multicultural and Holocaust education, was present in the textbooks, but emerged most strikingly as the teachers discussed their teaching practice and how they implemented the prescribed curriculum.

By coupling, as I will explain in more depth below, I mean that the curriculum, and in particular the teachers, connect the teaching of both anti-violence education and multicultural education to teaching about the Holocaust. In short, teaching about the Holocaust, an event in the past, functions as a distancing mechanism, fulfilling the prescribed discussions of present-day xenophobic violence and other challenges to multicultural living from a comfortable and familiar vantage point. At the same time, paradoxically, teachers' discussion of the Holocaust effectively excludes non-ethnic Germans. Non-ethnic Germans are therefore excluded from a multicultural education in multiple ways because of their ethnicity.

In this chapter I re-examine data from the larger study on multiculturalism in German education with the explicit intent of probing the relationship between teaching about Germany's perpetration of the Holocaust and teaching about a multicultural notion of German identity. This is significant, not only because it contributes to our broader understanding about the status of Holocaust education in Europe, but also because it contextualises the role Holocaust education plays in pushing German identity towards a more inclusive posture. Thus this chapter unites two strands of educational research, Holocaust education (cf. Becher 2008a, 2008b; Deckert-Peaceman 2002; Deckert-Peaceman and Kloesser 2002; Pingel 2000, 2002) and multicultural education (cf. Aurenheimer 2006; Himmelmann 2004, 2006; Klopp 2002; Luchtenberg and Nieke 1994). Previous studies on the German case in both of these fields either frame Holocaust education as something separate from multicultural education or have recognised, abstractly, that multicultural classrooms and rising xenophobia may require a different approach. They have failed to examine, empirically, how teachers connect these distinct curricular goals in their examination of Holocaust education. Brinkmann et al. (2000) stress the need to consider contemporary exhibitions of xenophobia and to include a moral dimension to Holocaust education. By doing so they, and others, are actually connecting multicultural education to Holocaust education. Indeed, they show that, at least in the interpretation of teachers, multicultural education and Holocaust education have strong connections.

Case Selection

In this study I specifically consider Bavaria, which is located in southern Germany, sharing a border with the Czech Republic, Switzerland, and Austria. With its consistently conservative government and anti-multicultural rhetoric and its particularly diverse population, Bavaria is useful as a case study of multicultural education, particularly when situated as a potentially more extreme case, a tool suggested as one means of purposive sampling. Educationally speaking, Bavaria also has a highly centralised compulsory schooling system in which all curricular decisions are made by the state education ministry and all materials, particularly textbooks, must come from a ministry-approved list. The ministry of education officials, whom I interviewed for this project, explained that the procedure for approval of textbooks is followed very strictly and very fastidiously because it is viewed as a means of ensuring that the teachers are not straying from state-mandated curricular guidelines. In an interview in August, 2006, one such official explained this approach:

> The textbooks provide the content that is outlined in the curricula. It is the best way we have to make sure that the content is spot-on with the curricula. This way we can make sure that the teachers are teaching what they are supposed to do. We invest time and money in approving the textbooks and making sure the teachers know them and use them. We do professional development with teachers and observe them using the textbooks. They are just as important as the curriculum because they are an extension of it.

Thus, textbooks and curricula work in tandem to create the Bavarian state practice regarding citizenship education policy. Social studies offers the most direct connection to the overall goal of examining the wide variety of outcomes associated with citizenship education, including anti-violence education and multicultural education, since citizenship education is not a subject by itself.

Data Collection

Textbooks

I used textbooks, archived through the Georg Eckert Institute for International Textbook Research (GEI), and included any general textbook for the *Hauptschule* generally available in the period from 1988 to 2006 and approved for use in Bavaria. I list the textbook series I examined in the appendix. I compared the textbooks collected to lists of approved textbooks for the time periods sought, compiled both by the GEI archivists and the Bavarian education ministry. Although in the larger study I coded the textbooks based on seven relevant state curricular guidelines, in this chapter I use only data from the textbook sections that aimed to fulfill the required anti-violence education; in Ortloff (2009) I discuss these data further. Since this theme is identified in the *Hauptschule* curricula as an overall learning outcome, it is methodologically appropriate for guiding the initial selection of material for the content analysis. This selection process follows the suggestions of both Krippendorf (2004) and Neuendorf (2001) for ensuring consistency in developing a unit of analysis.

Teacher Reflections

I interviewed Bavarian teachers from about 18 *Hauptschule*. The schools were in both urban and rural areas of the state and had student populations in which the proportions of non-native speakers of German ranged from 5 to 90%. I used this category as a designator because many of the students who are non-native German speakers have German citizenship because they are so-called repatriates (Ethnic German returnees from areas of the former Soviet Union). However, in the interviews, the participants universally refer to these students as foreigners regardless of their citizenship status. In recruiting teachers, it was important to interview a range of teachers in terms of their years of teaching experience and experience with teaching in diverse settings. In its urban areas, particularly Munich and Nuremburg, Bavaria has had a diverse population since the guest workers were first recruited to work in Germany in the 1960s. The teachers I interviewed in these areas had worked with diverse student populations for most of their careers, although in the last ten years each *Hauptschule* teacher in these urban areas explained that their classrooms had become nearly universally non-native German speaking.

In the more rural areas of the state, in particular Franken, a region in Northern Bavaria where I conducted the majority of the interviews, in a few smaller communities with factories, the majority of the non-German residents, of Turkish and Greek origin, have been residents since the 1960s. However, most of the areas have seen a dramatic rise in the number of non-native German speakers since 1990 mainly through the repatriation of ethnic Germans and their families from areas of the former Soviet Union. By seeking teachers with a wide variety of experiences, I constructed what Tagg (1985) calls a maximum variation sample, which seeks to include the widest degree of experiences within the interview participants.

Data Analysis

After identifying the section of each textbook pertaining to anti-violence education (the Bavarian curricular guideline used as the unit of analysis) I used close reading (Carspecken 1996) to initially organise the material into content sections, in this case at the paragraph level. After reading each identified section three times, I highlighted topic sentences, taken directly from the texts, and grouped them according to topic; this process is similar to conducting in-vivo coding (coding using the words of the participants) and keeps the level of inference as low as possible before proceeding to analysis. I followed a similar process for the participant interviews, identifying sections of the interviews that specifically dealt with anti-violence education, multicultural education, and Holocaust education through close reading. I further validated my choices by using the search function in NVIVO, a qualitative research software package. I then conducted in-vivo level coding, to organise the teachers' responses based on topics they named in their own words.

From this initial coding, in both data sets, I used a two-step analysis process based on Carspecken's (1996): approach: meaning field analysis and reconstructive horizon analysis on each paragraph (textbooks) or speech act (interviews) organised under the topic sentences. As an analytic tool, the meaning field reveals how meaning is bounded. The statement "Germans are punctual" cannot mean "Pillows are soft" or even "Germans like to drive fast". In brief, by using meaning field analysis, I was able to understand the full range of possible, and less possible, meanings for a statement. After the meaning field analysis, I conducted reconstructive horizon analysis on the data. This form of analysis is an extension of the meaning field analysis because it enables the researcher to view the "horizon" of possible meanings in any given statement. Gadamer developed the concept of "horizon" as part of the hermeneutic process to refer to the world affiliations of researchers. He deemed the researcher's hermeneutic acts of interpretation, specifically with regard to analysis of tests, as a "fusion of horizons" (Habermas 1984, p. 134). Carspecken (1996) draws on this concept of horizons and pairs it with Habermas' (1987) idea of validity claims, in order to develop his reconstructive horizon analysis (p. 103). Carspecken conceives of the horizon as having both vertical and horizontal axes. An example of a reconstructive horizon analysis from this study is reproduced in Table 1. The teacher said "Because we are Germans, and we will always have it [Holocaust] in our baggage". To add this item to the analysis, I chose statements that fit what Carspecken calls foregrounded (very explicit), intermediary (somewhat explicit, but requiring some inference), and backgrounded (requiring inference to understand tacit implications).

Both of these techniques are aimed at moving qualitative analysis beyond coding and categorising at the explicit level by focusing on tacit meaning. In a study such as this one, where I was probing in two data sets, looking for volatile and conceptually complex ideas such as identity, responsibility for the Holocaust, and multiculturalism, it is critical to have analysis tools aimed at implicit meaning. Likewise, these techniques allowed me to examine the implicit meaning both within and

Table 1 Example of reconstructive horizon analysis

	Foregrounded	Intermediary	Backgrounded
Objective	There was a Holocaust and millions of people died because of the actions of Germans.		Germans, then and now, are responsible for the Holocaust.
Subjective	Germans feel shame because of the Holocaust.	I feel shame because of the Holocaust.	It is hard to deal with these feelings of shame for something that happened so long ago.
Normative	Germans should feel shame and should remember this feeling of shame.	Germans should be careful to remember so that it does not happen again.	It should be okay to be proud of being German, but it is not.

Source: Ortloff (2007, 2009)

across the data sets, that is within the textbooks or within the interview transcripts, and to compare official policy from the textbooks to teacher reflections on these policies.

Findings

Textbook Analysis

German textbooks have consistent coverage of the Holocaust and World War II (Pingel 2000; Steffens 1991). In fact, some aspect of World War II is included in the curriculum of every grade in the *Hauptschule*. This fact mirrors the national discussions about Holocaust education, and recognises that one of the defining notions regarding Germanness is guilt over the Holocaust (von Thadden 1998). Contemporary rises in neo-Nazism have once again focused attention on the need for Holocaust education, including a required unit on anti-violence education in the *Hauptschule*. This section is the main focus for this analysis.

In the textbooks, within the anti-violence section, frank and open depictions of right-wing radicalism tend to focus on antisemitism and the Nazi past. This focus becomes clear when one examines older textbooks and is also confirmed in Pingel's (2000) analysis of Holocaust education. However, particularly after the anti-foreigner attacks and the arson of two asylum homes in the former East Germany in 1993 and 1998, the textbooks began to address violence in general. According to the curricula, xenophobia, with a particular emphasis on anti-foreigner sentiments as developed themes, should be included in separate chapters in the 8th grade texts. Also, anti-violence education should be a thematic development in the 7th and 9th grade texts, when possible. The 9th grade texts, in particular those published after 1998, include an emphasis on Islam and the curriculum requires a sub-chapter on "Foreigners in Germany", usually a profile of a Turkish resident's experiences, including experiences with xenophobia. One woman describes how she and her husband could not find an apartment because they would be rejected as soon as the owner heard the word "foreigner" (*Begegnungen* 9, 2003, p. 208).

Violence against others tends to be described in fictionalised accounts, which primarily include only ethnic Germans. Take, for example, the story of "Jürgen" from *Trio 8* (1999, p. 101). Using staged photos, the textbook presents Jürgen's encounter with school bullies who beat him up for his soda. The violence itself is not portrayed; rather we see a photo of Jürgen, a white, blond-haired adolescent, buying his soda and then in the next frame a picture of Jürgen on the ground in pain. The caption reads in German *Jürgen wurde niedergeschlagen* (Jürgen was struck down). The passive voice construction, with no perpetrator mentioned, emphasises the anonymous nature of violence as portrayed in the textbooks. This fictional violence is typical of the books' portrayal of violence. For example, in this chapter the only mention of xenophobia is in the title picture (*Trio 8*, 1999, p. 100) which shows anti-foreigner graffiti. The picture is not discussed, nor is any mention made of the concept of xenophobia represented by the graffiti that reads *Ausländer raus* (Foreigners out). The phrase *Auslaender raus* certainly evokes the memory of *Juden raus* (Jews out), a slogan used by the Nazis, and consequently takes on both a literal and a more historical sense of xenophobia. Both connotations present opportunities for education that are not taken up in the textbook. Instead the violence is thematised through Jürgen's story.

In contrast, chapters that deal directly with violence against foreigners approach it from the perspective of the perpetrator. Neo-Nazism is approached in each 8th grade textbook. The reasons neo-Nazis give for joining their movement are presented and criticised, and the consequences of illegal actions are explained. In one example, a neo-Nazi is arrested and writes a letter to his girlfriend; her letter to him, condemning his actions, is also printed. Much like the attention paid to the Holocaust, neo-Nazism is problematised and presented in an open fashion. Of course this perspective is important for critically approaching the topic of violence and motivation for violent acts. However, I find it curious that, as in the example above, the conversation remains between two members of the majority; even here, the minority voice, the victim's voice, is silent.

In the 8th grade texts, only one series, *Begegnungen* (Interactions), specifically addresses violence against minorities in the school setting. Yet, here again the perspective of a majority student is highlighted. Accompanying a picture of a darker-skinned student sitting alone and a group of white boys in a group, Sandra, a 12-year old student, explains how her classmates called a new student *ein Schoko* (a chocolate). She expresses shame at the boys' behavior. As with the other examples of violence, it is important that it is being directly addressed and characterised negatively, but the lack of minority perspective is noticeable.

The 9th grade books usually include a small section on xenophobia in the "Foreigners in Germany" subsection of the migration chapter. Right-wing radicalism is again addressed, but as with the 8th grade textbooks, the victims' voices are not included. Finally it bears mention that the discussion of violence, xenophobic or otherwise, never includes a non-German in the role of the perpetrator even though, in fact, Turkish and Russian youth gangs are a growing problem (Dietz 1999). One can imagine that the textbook developers chose not to address this issue from a fear of stereotyping; still, if non-ethnic Germans are to be integrated into citizenship education, that process must be true and honest. Considering this within Banks's (2001) framework, it is necessary to include the contributions of Turkish, Russian, and other non-ethnic Germans to criminality and violence, to achieve what Banks terms "structural reform". This level of transformation indicates that all previously segregated histories, such as those of guestworkers, are a part of the mainstream perspective. Leaving them out of the presentation of anti-violence education, both as victims and perpetrators, marginalises their inclusion in the larger German society.

Here we see an implicit supposition that Sandra's expression of shame and the refusal to cast a non-German in the role of a perpetrator are elements of the shared history on which Holocaust education rests. In other words, Holocaust education in Germany relies on building from the continued shame and shared responsibility of Germans, but as with anti-violence education, this fails to allow a more complex and inclusive idea of Germanness to emerge. In short, the textbooks, serving as a statement of the state's idea of who is German, are at least implicitly excluding non-ethnic Germans even in their direct discussions of xenophobia. My interviews with teachers, as I describe in the next section, show how teachers respond to this implicit claim.

Teachers' Reflections

Throughout my interviews with teachers, I probed how they enact the curricular guidelines and textbook materials discussed above. When I re-examined my results as they relate to Holocaust education and post-unification identity, the connection between Germanness and shame over the Holocaust became clear. What also became clear, however, is that the pairing of shame and Germanness creates a constraint on practising an actual multicultural education. As the data show, teachers view the Holocaust and shame as things uniquely German and do not include the many non-ethnic Germans, especially in the *Hauptschule* classroom, in discussions of the Holocaust. These constraints are further tightened by teachers' use of anti-violence and Holocaust education to "handle" or "deal" with the diversity question. Consequently, despite a new rhetoric about multiculturalism, my data show that reflections about the Holocaust and the implementation of current curricula are not achieving real change.

The teachers consistently offered the notion of shame as a reason why no one, except a German, could understand how it feels to be German. Here I noticed a tendency for the older teachers, those who had been teaching for over 15 years, to reflect on this in relation to the way they taught citizenship and diversity. However, shame was not a theme exclusive to older teachers' reflections; several younger teachers also mentioned it. In some cases these reflections were a way of explaining why there is something unique about being German. One teacher explained:

> We Germans, we are very susceptible, more susceptible than others [to nationalism and xenophobia], and we don't know how to handle it. I don't know, maybe the younger people can handle it. I would wish it for them, that we, like other countries, have finally learned.

Teachers also explained how this fear and shame affects how they teach and what they teach. One teacher said:

> One must also give them both sides. One must say: you are not guilty, you were born much later, you have not done anything. But you will forever, as long as there are Germans, have to help carry this package. We must stand by it, because otherwise the world will not recognise us. We are lucky that the people of the world even acknowledge us now, because for many years it did not look like they would and we must be careful not to destroy this accomplishment. There are two sides that belong together. When the media say that we should draw a line under this history, I say we can never do this. Because we are Germans, and we will always have it in our baggage. And the students understand this well.

In her eyes it was one of her most important jobs, in both the social studies and religion classes she taught, to convey to her students this special burden of being German.

In saying that no one except a German can feel the guilt of being German, the teachers touch upon Germanness as a notion not bound to place but to emotion, in this case the sense of shared guilt. In essence this statement is enacting the temporal nature of Germanness which is a hallmark of ethnoculturalism. Temporality, as conceived by Cornwall and Stoddard (2001), is not merely the lack of a spatial relationship, but refers to the notion of Germanness transcending place through time; Germanness is passed from generation to generation regardless of physical location. The teachers touched upon this temporality frequently as they discussed how one teaches "being German".

Likewise, the teachers explicitly named the ideas of temporality and shame as items that must be taught in order to teach about the Holocaust. They described doing so as their duty. But they see this duty differently; here I noticed another break mainly along generational lines. Although they quite often used the concept of duty itself to explain the moral obligation extending from Holocaust education and teaching about being German, older teachers linked this idea to passing on the idea of shame, whereas younger teachers connected it to coping with history and moving forward from it.

The teachers often gave this idea of shame for being German as one of the key aspects of raising good German citizens, but they also explained that non-Germans cannot understand this guilt, nor should they be expected to. One younger teacher, who was in his second year of teaching social studies and English, told me that since my last name is German perhaps I would understand it better than the Turkish students.

> They cannot get it, they think it is funny to call us Nazis, there is no way they can be German because they cannot feel what we feel. I don't know how else to explain that, so I just stick to the content in the book about voting in Germany.

He continued:

> In a lot of ways teaching about the Holocaust is much easier; there are clear items to teach the students about. They know most of it before they get to me though, because we teach about the Holocaust in every grade. But I can approach it as history. It is connecting it to being German, I don't know how to do that for someone who is not German.

This same teacher then reflected on what he can teach and discussed the Holocaust and anti-violence education:

> It is easier to say we will learn about the Holocaust so as not to repeat it. It is easier to say don't be a neo-Nazi, don't be in a gang because this is repeating it. That is all easier than getting to teaching about being German, I really don't know how one would do that, especially [in my diverse classroom].

This last exchange, typical of the way many of the younger teachers reflected thoughtfully on their practice, is particularly important because it represents a certain inability to conceive of a multicultural education, in part because of they way they interpret German history. Here we see Holocaust education becoming something easier to achieve than multicultural education. Implicitly, in a trend evident in many of the interviews, the teacher here links Holocaust education and multicultural education. But the link is incomplete: these teachers view Holocaust and multicultural education as achieving similar things without really interrogating the relationship or asking why both might need to be achieved.

Conclusions

In his now famous essay *Education after Auschwitz,* Theodore Adorno (1971) argues that all political education must be aimed towards preventing another Auschwitz. In Germany's case, some have argued that this has gone too far. Education about the Holocaust permeates every level of education. Researchers such as Becher (2007), Heyl (2001), Pingel (2000, 2002), Rathenow (2000), and Fechler (2000) report that students feel overloaded by the sheer repetition of the subject matter, which starts in elementary school and continues through each grade level and in each type of school. Still, there is a moral imperative, not just in Germany, but especially in Germany, to educate pupils about the Holocaust. Indeed, the rise of neo-Nazism and the complex reality of a multicultural Germany place new pressures on education policy and practice to educate young people with Adorno's purpose firmly in mind.

My analysis reveals, however, that in terms of both state policy, as represented by state-approved textbooks, and teacher reflections on their practice, Holocaust education and multicultural education are often intertwined to the point that a truly multicultural education is truncated. This happens in two distinct ways. First, the idea of the Holocaust and shame is put forward, especially by the teachers, but also in more subtle ways in the textbooks, as something uniquely German. Non-ethnic Germans cannot be included in this education because their ethnicity bars them from engaging in the shame discussion. Violence in the textbooks was depicted as perpetrated by Germans, but the victims' voices were, for the most part absent. Non-ethnic Germans were also absent as perpetrators. Shame and guilt over xenophobia and violence were held as uniquely the purview of ethnic Germans.

In addition to this complex means of exclusion, a second way of intertwining Holocaust education and multicultural education also brought about a de facto segregation of non-ethnic Germans. Teachers viewed the Holocaust—an historical event—as an easier way to approach the difficult topics of diversity, multiculturalism, and tolerance. In and of itself, this would not necessarily be problematic, but when coupled with the teachers' belief that non-ethnic Germans cannot really be included in Holocaust education, we have a—perhaps unintended—marginalisation.

While the case of Holocaust education and multicultural education in Germany involves particular elements that do not immediately apply to other settings, this study does offer some important and global lessons. If, as Adorno argues, education must set as its goal the prevention of another Holocaust, then it is imperative that Holocaust education be able to include a wide variety of conversations and interrogations on the question of what it means to live together in a diverse society. Holocaust education cannot continue to be just a separate educational goal, but must be an educational goal that contributes to preparing citizens to live in a multicultural society.

Acknowledgements Funding from the University of Houston Clear Lake and the Indiana University European Union Center made this study possible.

Appendix

Textbook Series used in Project Analysis (Grades 5–10 for the *Hauptschule* and Grade 10 for the *Realschule*)

1. *Begegnungen Geschichte, Sozialkunde, Erdkunde.* Karl Filser. Munchen: Oldenbourg Ambros Brucker, 1997, 1998, 1999, 2005
2. *Demokratie verpflichtet.* Andreas Mack. Munchen: Oldenbourg Verlag, 1984, 1995, 2003 (used through 1994)
3. *Durchblick/Bayern/Hauptschule.* Hanne Auer. Braunschweig: Westermann, 1997, 1998, 1999, 2001, 2004
4. *Forum: Sozialkunde, Realschule Bayern.* Christine Fischer, Jakob Pritscher, Karl Uhl. Braunschweig: Westermann, 2004
5. *Geschichte, Sozialkunde, Erdkunde.* Harald-Matthias Neumann. Stuttgart: Klett-Perthes (Terra), 1997, 1998, 1999, 2004
6. *Politik-nicht ohne mich!* Rainer Dörrfuß, Alexander Ohgke, Ulla Oppenländer, Stefan Pistner. Bamberg: Buchner, 2003.
7. *Politik-Wie? So!* Rainer Dorrfuss. Bamberg: Buchner, 1995
8. *Geschichte-Sozialkunde-Erdkunde: GSE; Hauptschule.* Helmut Heinrich, Günther Kaniber, Anton Krug. Regensburg: Wolf, 1997, 1998, 1999
9. *Sozialkunde/Bayern/Hauptschule.* Regensburg: Wolf, 1994, 1995
10. *Menschen, Zeiten, Raume/Barern/Hauptschule.* Wolfgang Von Schierl. Berlin: Cornelsen, 1997, 1998, 1999
11. *Trio/Bayern/Hauptschule: Geschichte/Sozialkunde/Erdkunde.* Norbert Autenrieth. Hannover: Schroedel, 1994, 1997, 1998, 1999, 2004
12. *ZeitRaume: entdecken, erfahren, orientieren.* Norbert Horberg. Stuttgart: Klett, 1997, 1998
13. *Burger und Politik: ein Lehrund Arbeisbuch fur Sozialkunde, politische Bildung.* Eduard Steinbugl. Darmstadt: Winklers Verl. Gebr. Grimm, 1995.
14. *bsv-Sozialkunde.* Ingrid Ziegler. Munchen: Bayer. Schulbuch-Verl., 1991, 1992
15. *Denkanstosse: Sozialkunde fur die Hauptschule.* Gunter Neumann. Kulmbach: Baumann, 1986, 1987
16. *Politisch denken, urteilen and handeln: ein Lehr- und Arbeitsbuch fur den politischen und sozialkundlichen Unterricht.* Roland Herold. Wolfenbuttel: Heckner, 1982
17. *Sozialkunde.. Schulerarbeitscheft.* Oskar Buhler. Ansbach: Ansbacher Verl., Ges., 1986
18. *Sozialkunde fur Hauptschulen in Bayern.* Dieter Grosser. Braunschweig: Westermann, 1988
19. *Burger und Politik: e. Lehr-u. Arbeisbuch fur Sozialkunde, polit. Bildung.* E. Steinbugl. Darmstadt: Winkler, 1984

References

Adorno, T. W. (1971). Erziehung nach Auschwitz. In T. W. Adorno (Ed.), *Erziehung zur Mündigkeit. Vorträge und Gespräche mit Hellmut Becker 1959–1969* [Education to responsibility: Lectures and discussions with Hellmut Becker 1959–1969] (pp. 88–104). Frankfurt am Main: Suhrkamp.

Aurenheimer, G. (2006). The German education system: Dysfunctional for an immigration society. *European Education, 37*(4), 75–89.

Banks, J. (2001). Citizenship education and diversity: Implications for teacher education. *Journal of Teacher Education, 52*(1), 5–16. http://jte.sagepub.com/content/52/1/5.abstract

Becher, A. (2007). "Ich glaube, die Nazis haben Hitler geholfen, die Welt zu erobern": Forschungen zu Kindervorstellungen zum Holocaust und Nationalsozialismus ["I believe the Nazis helped Hitler conquer the world"]. In S. Pfeiffer (Ed.), *Innovative Perspektiven auf Sachunterricht. Oldenburger Vor Drucke* (pp. 20–38). Oldenburg: Didaktisches Zentrum der Universität Oldenburg.

Becher, A. (2008a). "Der wollte die Juden ausrotten und dann hat er sie vergasen oder aushungern lassen". Kann eine "Erziehung nach Auschwitz" im Sachunterricht eine "Erziehung ohne Auschwitz" sein? ["They wanted to eradicate the Jews and then they gassed them or let them hang": Can a social studies "education after Auschwitz" be an "education without Auschwitz"?] In H. Giest & J. Wiesemann (Eds.), *Kind und Wissenschaft: Welches Wissenschaftsverständnis hat der Sachunterricht?* (pp. 121–131). Bad Heilbrunn: Klinkhardt.

Becher, A. (2008b). *Holocaust und Nationalsozialismus im Sachunterricht thematisieren: Konsequenzen aus einter qualitattiv-empirischen Studie zu Vorstellungen von Kindern* [The Holocaust and National Socialism in Social Studies' Themes: Findings from a qualitative study about children's perspectives]. http://www.widerstreit-sachunterricht.de/ebeneI/superworte/historisch/vorstell.pdf

Brinkmann, A., Ehemann, A., & Milton, S. (2000). *Learning from history: the Nazi era and the Holocaust in German Education*. Bonn: Arcult Media.

Brubaker, R. (1992). *Citizenship and nationhood in France and Germany*. Cambridge/London: Cambridge University Press.

Carspecken, P. F. (1996). *Critical ethnography in educational research: A theoretical and practical guide*. New York: Routledge.

Cornwall, G. H., & Stoddard, E. W. (Eds.) (2001). *Global multiculturalism: Comparative perspectives on ethnicity, race and nation*. Lanham: Rowman & Littlefield.

Deckert-Peaceman, H. (2002). *Holocaust als Thema für Grundschulkinder? Ethnographische Feldforschung zur Holocaust Education am Beispiel einer Fallstudie aus dem amerikanischen Grundschulunterricht und ihre Relevanz für die Grundschulpädagogik in Deutschland* [The Holocaust as a topic for elementary aged children? Ethnographic field work about Holocaust education with an example of a case study from an American elementary school and its relevance for elementary school pedagogy in Germany]. Frankfurt: Peter Lang.

Deckert-Peaceman, H., & Kloesser, G. (2002). Konfrontationen. Impulse für die Auseinandersetzung mit Geschichte und Wirkung des Holocaust im Kontext von Menschenrechtserziehung. [Confrontations: Impetus for the debate on history and the effects of the Holocaust in the context of human rights]. In C. Lenz, J. Schmidt, & O. von Wrochem (Eds.), *Erinnerungskulturen im Dialog. Europäische Perspektiven auf die NS-Vergangenheit* [Memories of culture in Dialog. European perspectives of the NS-past] (pp. 243–248). Hamburg/Münster: Unrast.

Dietz, B. (1999). Jugendliche Aussiedler in Deutschland: Risiken und Chancen [Young repatriates in Germany: Risks and opportunities]. In K. J. Bade & J. Oltmer (Eds.), *Aussiedler: deutsche Einwanderer aus Osteuropa* (pp. 153–176). Osnabrueck: Universitaetsverlag Rasch.

Fechler, B. (2000). Zwischen Tradierung und Konfliktvermittlung. Über den Umgang mit "problematischen" Aneignungsformen der NS-Geschichte in multikulturellen Schulklassen. Ein Praxisbericht [Between establishing tradition and relaying conflict: Dealing with forms of appropriation in NS-history in multicultural school classrooms. A field report]. In B. Fechler,

G. Kößler, & T. Liebertz-Groß (Eds.), *"Erziehung nach Auschwitz" in der multikulturellen Gesellschaft. Pädagogische und soziologische Annäherungen* (pp. 207–227). Weinheim/ München: Juventa.

Gosewinkel, D. (1998). Citizenship and nationhood: The historical development of the German case. In U. Preuss & F. Requejo Coll (Eds.), *European citizenship, multiculturalism and the state* (pp. 125–136). Baden Baden: Nomos Verlagsgesellschaft.

Habermas, J. (1984). *The theory of communicative action* (Vol. I, T. McCarthy, Trans.). Boston: Beacon Press.

Habermas, J. (1987). *The theory of communicative action*, Vol. II: Lifeworld and system, a critique of functionalist reason (T. McCarthy, Trans.). Boston: Beacon Press.

Heyl, M. (2001). *Erziehung nach und über Auschwitz: Dass der Unterricht sich in Soziologie verwandle*. Presentation at the 13th Onderwijssociologische Conferentie in Amsterdam. http://www.fasena.de

Himmelmann, G. (2004). *Demokratie-Lernen als Lebens-, Gesellschafts-und Herrschaftsform* [Learning democracy as forms of life, society, and domination]. Schwalbauch am Taunus: Wochenschau.

Himmelmann, G. (2006). Concepts and issues in citizenship education: A comparative study of Germany, Britain and USA. In G. Alred, M. Byram, & M. Flemming (Eds.), *Education of intercultural citizenship* (pp. 69–85). Clevedon: Multilingual Matters.

Joppke, C. (2000). Mobilization of culture and the reform of citizenship law: Germany and the United States. In R. Koopmans & P. Statham (Eds.), *Challenging the politics of ethnic relations in Europe*. Oxford: Oxford University Press.

Klopp, B. (2002). *German multiculturalism: Immigrant integration and the transformation of citizenship*. Westport: Praeger.

Krippendorf, K. (2004). *Content analysis: An introduction to its methodology* (2nd ed.). Thousand Oaks: Sage Publications.

Luchtenberg, S., & Nieke, W. (Eds.) (1994). *Interkulturelle paedagogik und Europaeische dimension: Herausforderungen fuer Bildungssystem und Erziehungswissenschaft* [Intercultural pedagogy and the European dimension: Challenges for education systems and education]. Muenster/New York: Waxmann.

Neuendorf, K. A. (2001). *The content analysis guidebook*. Thousand Oaks: Sage.

Ortloff, D. H. (2007). *Holding to tradition: Citizenship, diversity and education in post-unification Germany: A case study of Bavaria*. PhD dissertation, Indiana University, Bloomington. Dissertations & Theses: A&I. (Publication No. AAT 3283958). https://scholarworks.iu.edu/dspace/handle/2022/7327

Ortloff, D. H. (2009). Social studies teachers' reflections on citizenship education in Bavaria. *Germany Race/Ethnicity: Multidisciplinary Global Perspectives, 2*(2), 189–214.

Ortloff, D. H., & McCarty, L. P. (2009). Educating for a multicultural Germany in a global era. In G. A. Wiggan & C. Hutchinson (Eds.), *Global issues in education: Pedagogy, policy, practice and the minority experience* (pp. 81–102). Lanham: Rowman and Littlefield.

Pingel, F. (2000). National socialism and the Holocaust in West German school books. *International Textbook Research, 22*(1), 11–30.

Pingel, F. (2002). Unterrricht ueber den Holocaust: Eine kritische Bewertung der aktuellen paedagogischen Diskussion [Education about the Holocaust: A critical rating of the current pedagogical discussion]. In E. Fuchs, F. Pingel, & V. Radkaus (Eds.), *Holocaust und Nationalsozialismus* (pp. 11–23). Innsbruck: StudienVerlag.

Rathel, N. (1995). *Development of German citizenship laws*. New York: Routledge.

Rathenow, H. F. (2000). Teaching Holocaust in Germany. In I. Davies (Ed.), *Teaching the Holocaust: Educational dimensions, principles and practice* (pp. 63–76). London: Continuum.

Steffens, G. (1991). *Die nationalsozialistischen Verbrechen und der Voelkermord. Bermerkungen zur Unterrichtspraxis in der Bundesrepublik* [The National Socialist crimes and genocide: Remarks about instructional practices in Germany]. Paper presented at the Recontre

Pedagogiique Internationale. Le memoire d'Auschwitz dans l'enseignement. Problems et perspectives.

Tagg, S. K. (1985). Life story interviews and their interpretation. In M. Brenner, J. Brown, & D. Canter (Eds.), *The research interview: Uses and approaches* (pp. 163–199). London: Academic.

Thraenhardt, D. (2000). Conflict, consensus, and policy outcomes: Immigration and integration in Germany and the Netherlands. In R. Koopmans & P. Statham (Eds.), *Challenging immigration and ethnic relation politics*. Oxford: Oxford University Press.

von Thadden, R. (1998). Zusammenwachsende Zusammengehörigkeit? Deutschland in Europa [Growing togetherness: Germany in Europe]. *International Textbook Research, 20*(1), 9–18.

Genocide or Holocaust Education: Exploring Different Australian Approaches for Muslim School Children

Suzanne D. Rutland

Introduction

In recent years, anti-Jewish sentiment has increased amongst Muslims and Arabic-speaking peoples internationally. Such sentiments have also increased in Australia with the recent growth of the Muslim population there. This can be seen in the attitudes manifested in government schools that have high proportions of Muslim children, and in Muslim schools themselves. In parallel, the number of antisemitic attacks on the Jewish community has increased; the police classify the Jewish community as "terrorist target number 1 in Australia" (Rutland 2005, pp. 154–161). As attacks increase on both Jewish individuals and institutions, combating anti-Jewish prejudice is clearly an important educational challenge. Jewish community leaders in Australia believe that educational programmes on the Holocaust are ideal for combating racism, and support making such study compulsory. They argue that teaching about the genocidal policies of the Nazis illustrates the evils of targeting one group within society, as Nazi propaganda reinforced the negative stereotypes of Jews, leading to their humiliation and mass murder. But other educators argue that this approach will not effectively combat Muslim anti-Jewish feelings; they believe a focus on accepting differences and on the commonalities between the Abrahamic faiths will be more effective. Alternatively, they suggest educating through genocide studies, so that Muslim children can understand that racial stereotyping and hatred can lead to violence against any ethnic or religious group, as occurred in Bosnia.

In this chapter I explore the negative attitudes of the Muslim and Arabic-speaking school population in Sydney towards Jews and the Holocaust, and then examine four different approaches to combating these attitudes. I discuss the various

---

S.D. Rutland (✉)
Department of Hebrew, Biblical & Jewish Studies, University of Sydney,
Sydney, NSW 2006, Australia
e-mail: suzanne.rutland@sydney.edu.au

arguments about the advantages and disadvantages of using the Holocaust as a case study of racism with Muslim and Arabic-speaking children and suggest which models might be more effective in combating the hate language that can lead to violence. In considering the various points of view, I seek to disentangle the complexities of Holocaust education for this particular group, given the tensions engendered by the Palestinian-Israeli conflict.

To date no extensive research has been conducted on this topic in Australia, apart from one brief paper by Mendes (2008). Most research has focused on the Eurocentric orientation of schools (Clyne 2001, p. 125), the lack of knowledge of Muslim culture, and anti-Muslim feelings, which pose a significant threat to social cohesion. Some commentators have argued that the lack of academic analysis of Muslim antisemitism in Australia is due to the left-wing orientation of many of the scholars in the areas of cultural studies, peace studies, and social work, leading to their stress on Muslim victimhood to the exclusion of other issues (Mendes 2008, p. 5). This chapter is based on original data derived from interviews with teachers in schools in Southwestern Sydney, where a very high proportion of children have Arabic-speaking and Muslim backgrounds. I also interviewed people involved in programmes devised to counter these feelings.

Jewish and Muslim Communities in Australia

Australian Jewry is largely a post-Holocaust community. Melbourne has a larger percentage of Holocaust survivors than any other Diaspora Jewish community (Rutland 2005) and Holocaust memory is a prevalent theme within the Jewish community.

The growth of the Muslim population in Australia is a much more recent phenomenon. The desire to exclude Asian migrants was a key factor in the federation of the Australian colonies in 1901. One of the first acts of the newly-established federal parliament addressed immigration and became known as the "White Australia policy" (Yarwood 1964). After 1901, it excluded virtually all Asian immigrants, and those from the Muslim countries of Malaysia and Indonesia. Until 1945 Australian government policy decreed that the Australian population should be 95% Anglo-Celtic and the country had no separate Department of Immigration. Together with the indigenous Aboriginal population, Asian and Jewish immigrants were the main targets of abuse and degradation (Encel 1971). The ongoing Australian xenophobia reflected a dislike of something different and "a long tradition of being afraid of people who come from other parts of the world" (Clark 1949).

In December 1972, the Whitlam Labor government came to power, after 23 years of conservative Liberal government, marking a sea change in Australian immigration policies and officially ending the White Australia policy. For the first time non-Christian, non-European immigrants were allowed to enter Australia, providing the basis for Muslim immigration (Wilton and Bosworth 1984, p. 34). With this radical change in immigration policies, the Muslim community has grown remarkably since 1971, when it numbered only 20,000, a mere 0.2% of the population. In the quarter of a century to 1996, Muslims increased tenfold to 200,000, or 1.1% of the total population; according to a recent Australian census (ABS 2011), they have increased to 476,300, or 2.2%. In comparison, the Jewish community numbered only 97,300 in the 2011 census (Graham 2014).

Interestingly, both the Jewish and Muslim communities are concentrated in the two main urban centres of Melbourne and Sydney. As of 2006, the Melbourne Jewish population numbered around 50,000 compared to the Muslim population of 93,000, while the Sydney Jewish population was 40,000, compared to the Muslim population of 161,000 (ABS 2006). More recently, the Muslim population in Sydney rose to 208,149, constituting 4.7% of the Greater Sydney population (ABS 2011), while the Jewish population in Sydney rose to 43,261, based on an adjusted figure (Graham 2014, p. 40). While both groups are clustered in these two cities, their settlement patterns are very different, reflecting their different socio-economic patterns. The Jewish community is clustered in the wealthy southeastern suburbs of Melbourne, and the eastern and northern suburbs of Sydney, reflecting their concentration in the merchant and professional classes (Rutland 2005, pp. 148–150; Eckstein n.d., p. 20). The Muslims tend to be in the lower socio-economic strata of society and face problems of low educational levels (Kabir 2004, 2005), unemployment, and other issues relating to adjustment to Australian society. The 2006 census showed that the Muslim unemployment rate was 12.74% compared to 4.78% of the Australian-born population and 4.73% of the national total (Kabir 2008, p. 233). In Sydney, most Muslims live in the more working-class southern and western areas, where annual incomes are much lower (Kabir 2008, p. 233) and property is much less expensive. In Melbourne, most Muslims live in the northern and western suburbs. Thus, while Muslims and Jews live in the same cities, they have minimal social interaction in neighbourhoods and schools.

Given their low socio-economic status, most Muslim children in Australia attend government schools. Muslim schools do receive some government subsidies on the same basis as other non-government schools, but all non-government schools still have to charge fees, unlike government schools. For students not in day schools, the mosques and the home are responsible for providing in-faith religious education, whilst weekend ethnic language schools, supported by the government, teach Arabic. There can be tensions with government school curricula, which are seen as not only secular, but infused with Judeo-Christian values, creating a sense of frustration for Muslim parents (Clyne 2001, p. 120). Thus, Muslim parents are faced with a dilemma if they send their children to government schools. Since 1996, Muslim religious schools have grown rapidly, with the 2006 census showing that 21% attended non-government schools (Buckingham 2010). Clyne (2001) noted that "many of the founders of the first Islamic schools were converts to Islam and thus were aware of the values underpinning the government education system. They looked for a more Islamic education for their children and began the struggle to establish an Islamic school" (p. 127), often having to seek outside funding to do so.

Nahid Kabir (2008, 2011) undertook a study of the attitudes of Muslim immigrant youths in two government schools in Sydney and one high school in Melbourne, conducting 46 in-depth interviews. She explored whether these youth had acculturated and absorbed Australian values, including knowledge of English, adopting

Western dress, supporting the concept of a "fair go" for all, and enjoying Australian culture, including Western music and sports. She concluded that most of the students "presented as moderate Muslims whose world revolved around their schools and the society where they lived". Further, she said, "The global debate concerning jihadi Islam and the Iraq war or Palestine did not come up in their conversation" (Kabir 2008, p. 239). She found that participating in various school activities, particularly sports, facilitated their integration into Australian life; meanwhile, they retained their traditional religious and cultural values. "Arguably", she said, "their biculturalism was allowing them both to sustain self-esteem and to stretch their culture gradually to adopt Australian values and behaviours" (p. 239).

The large increase in the Muslim population in Australia has led to a rise in anti-Muslim prejudice among the general population, as evidenced in the attacks on the Muslim communities after the First Gulf War in 1991, and on September 11, 2001, and the December 2005 riots in the southern beachside Sydney suburb of Cronulla (Poynting 2006). In 1992, the Australian Arabic Council (AAC) was established in response to the racist attacks that occurred during the First Gulf War, and over the last two decades it has increased its activities, cooperating with the government on a number of issues, including racial vilification legislation, international relations and trade in the Middle East, education, welfare assistance and government funding to the Arabic-speaking communities (Batrouney 2006, p. 69). The AAC has also opposed a number of government policies, especially in relation to immigration policies that restrict Middle Eastern migration, and the government's support of the Iraqi invasion and pro-Israel policies (p. 69).

In response to anti-Muslim feelings, the government has tried to foster a better understanding of Islam in the general Australian community so that teachers can respond to the needs of their Muslim students. As part of this initiative, they have produced a lengthy document entitled *Learning from one another: Bridging Muslim perspectives into Australian schools*. This document was written by Muslim scholars at three Australian universities, but is produced from a within-faith perspective, and has avoided dealing with possible conflicts between the values of the Western democratic world and sharia law (Day 2009).

At the same time, Muslims have developed more pronounced anti-Jewish attitudes and behaviours. The social disconnection described above decreases the potential for knowledge and understanding between the groups, and exacerbates Muslim children's negative feelings towards Jews and the Holocaust, the focus of this study. The *Learning from one another* document does not touch on issues relating to Jews and Judaism.

The "New Racism" in Australia

The new kind of racism I described above has been defined as "cultural racism" and is based on "the insurmountability of cultural differences" (Dunn, Forrest, Burnley, and McDonald 2004, p. 410). Under this construct, ethnic groups are discriminated against and attacked on the basis of perceived "threats to 'social cohesion' and national unity", that is threats to the Anglo-Celtic majority (p. 411). In their study on racism in Australia, Dunn and his colleagues identified three main elements of this "new racism": out-groups, cultural diversity and nation, and issues of normalcy and privilege. They measured the level of comfort respondents felt if a member of their family married into one of seven groups. The lowest level of tolerance was for Muslims (46%), whilst the highest level was for Italians (87.3%), Christians (90.7%), and people of British ancestry (91.8%). Jews, Asians, and Aborigines were grouped together, with a range from 74.9% (Jews) to 70.5% (Aborigines). A later study, by Dunn et al. (2008), indicated that racism was still very prevalent in Australia and that 27% of respondents had been called names or similarly insulted; 23.4% felt that they were treated with less respect because of their ethnic origins. Andrew Markus (2011) found that the migrant groups that had been settled in Australia for longer experienced lower levels of racism than the more recent arrivals. These findings supported the conclusions of the Dunn et al. (2004) study, in relation to the levels of tolerance discussed above, since the Muslims are the newest migrant group in Australia.

The 2004 study also found a strong correlation between the respondents' ages and their level of tolerance towards Australians who are Muslim, indigenous, and Asian (Figure 1). Older people were the least tolerant, with the level of tolerance increasing progressively among the younger age groups. Given that older respondents grew up during the era of the White Australia policy and that indigenous Australians only became full citizens in 1967, this difference between age groups is not surprising.

Jews, however, were the exception to this trend: younger and older respondents of all religious persuasions surveyed were almost equally intolerant of the idea of a family member marrying someone Jewish. This raises the question of why younger people still view marriage to a Jew with the same level of suspicion as their parents' generation, a question the researchers did not address. Several explanations are possible. First, the anti-Jewish stereotype from the White Australia period is an enduring one (Gross and Rutland 2014). In addition, a high level of anti-Israel criticism, especially from the far left, fosters anti-Jewish feelings. The comparison of Israel's tactics with those of the Nazis has become a powerful tool for critics of Israel and legitimises violent acts against Jews. These issues become more significant given that the Australian Human Rights Commission lists Jews among the more "visible" and "newer" religious and ethnic minorities, together with Arabs, Muslims, Africans, Palestinians, and Turkish people (Szoke 2012), even though Jews have been present since the British arrived in 1788 and have never constituted more than 0.5% of the population (Rutland 2005).

Therefore, anti-racism education programmes are important. Holocaust and genocide education can be an important component of such a programme. In his seminal book, *Rethinking the Holocaust*, Yehuda Bauer (2001) stressed that people must be able to differentiate "between mass murder, genocide, and say, the amok killing of children in a Scottish village by a disturbed individual" (p. 67). He points out that all are types of murder, but that "Just as we cannot fight cholera, typhoid and cancer

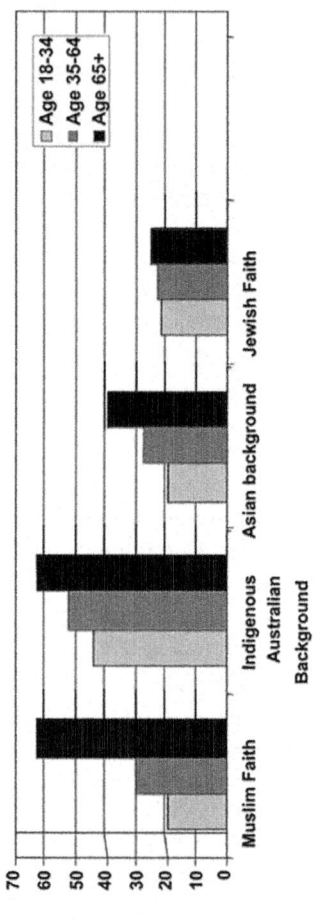

Fig. 1 Percentage stating concern about a relative marrying a member of selected "out-groups", by age
Source: Based on data from Dunn et al. 2004

with the same medicines, mass murder for political reasons has to be fought differently than genocides and Holocausts" (p. 67).

Methodology

This is a qualitative research project, which emerged from a broader study focused partly on the recent growth of anti-Jewish feeling. The broader study, on the Political Sociology of Australian Jewry, was funded through an Australian Research Council (ARC)/Linkage Grant that Professor Emeritus Sol Encel and I received for the period December 2004 to July 2008. I interviewed 8 high school teachers (6 females and 2 males, 6 Christians and 2 Jews), and one student teacher (male, Christian) from eight different government schools with a total school population of close to 7,000 students from southwest Sydney. I refer to these schools using broader geographical areas, not the actual school names; no personal names are used. Six of the teachers had participated in an intensive Holocaust education programme at Yad Vashem, the Holocaust memorial in Jerusalem. The interviews were semi-structured; the questions related to their school's student population, their own background and knowledge about the Holocaust, and their experiences teaching Muslim children, including their students' attitudes toward Hitler and the Holocaust. All had very difficult experiences, and the six who undertook the programme at Yad Vashem chose to do so because of the anti-Jewish feelings and misunderstandings of the Holocaust they encountered in their schools.

In addition, I interviewed the coordinators and facilitators of four programmes in Sydney that seek to redress the anti-Jewish feelings prevalent in school groups. I asked each of these people about their approach to teaching the Holocaust. One programme does not include Holocaust education, and I asked about the reasons behind this educational approach. My interviewees in this group also provided me with external evaluation studies of their programmes, where these had been conducted (Alba and Sztrum 2006; Nayler 2009). I also spoke with a volunteer guide at the Sydney Jewish Museum, and a presenter for the New South Wales Jewish Board of Deputies, and interviewed a Jewish mother whose children attended a government school with a high proportion of Muslim school children (Rutland 2010). In total I interviewed 15 people for this study.

The government schools across the area of southwest Sydney have a high concentration of Arabic-speaking children. Most are Australian-born Lebanese Muslims and, in the girls' schools, one in three wears a hijab to school (Cruickshank 2006). In 2005, New South Wales had 25,194 Arabic-speaking school children, the second largest group after the Chinese. Of these, 16,536 resided in the southwestern suburbs of Sydney (Table 4, NSWDET 2006). The total number of Muslim children in these schools is even higher, as it includes children from Muslim but not Arabic-speaking countries. Indeed, the Muslims in Australia are ethnically diverse, with roots in 120 countries (ABS 2006). This diversity has resulted in a variety of Muslim responses to the challenges of living in multicultural Australia, ranging from those whose primary concern is to educate their children in a subculture that stresses Islamic values and practices to those taking an assimilationist approach (Clyne 2001, pp. 117–118).

Anti-Jewish Feelings of Muslim Children in Southwest Sydney Government Schools

The narrative I present here is based on the teachers' descriptions of their personal experiences and perceptions of their students' attitudes towards Jews. The eight teachers consistently testified to a pattern of antisemitic attitudes and beliefs among their Muslim students. The various misconceptions of Jews that Muslim children hold are illustrated by a single question that a Muslim student put to a Jewish professional I interviewed: "Yes, Miss: Why do you Jews hate us, want to take over our land, and take over the world?" In contrast, Kabir (2008, 2011) did not report any of these responses in her studies of attitudes of Muslim youths in Australian schools. This may be because she was focusing on how the students acculturate into Australian society, and she does not seem to have probed her student interviewees about their attitudes toward Jews or the Holocaust, or other issues such as whether they watched Al Jazeera or which websites they accessed. She also drew her findings from a comparatively small sample of students from only three schools. In contrast, the teachers I interviewed for this study represented a wider range of government schools. They did not methodically investigate antisemitic attitudes, but were reporting on comments that their students made spontaneously in their presence in the classroom and on the playground.

In the interviews, the teachers said that the Muslim students often expressed an admiration for Nazism and Hitler; some drew swastikas on their desks and had posters of Hitler. They also made statements in class such as "Hitler did not go far enough". Many also believe that the Zionists cooperated with Hitler during the Holocaust in order to create a pretext to take Palestine from the Arabs.

According to these teachers, the students have also been indoctrinated with myths and misconceptions about Jews, including traditional world conspiracy theories propagated by the well-known forgery, *The Protocols of the Elders of Zion* (Litvak and Webman 2009, pp. 6–7). One student told a teacher that she had watched another girl on the train taking her mobile phone apart. When the teacher asked the student why her friend did this, she said, "Jews are able to listen in because they own all the communication systems". One teacher found that students had pictures of dead babies supposedly killed by Israeli soldiers that had been distributed at the local mosque. The students could not understand why it was not appropriate to have such pictures.

A number of teachers noted that many Muslim students believed the conspiracy theory that Jews were responsible for the terror attacks on September 11, 2001. One teacher noted,

> Once [the students] believe something, they are not going to hear another point of view. This is perpetuated through their homes and I wonder if also from their media. They and their parents would maintain that [Sept. 11] was a Jewish holiday—it was planned—they rang each other up on the morning saying, "Stay home".

Jewish teachers in these schools have experienced harassment from their Muslim students; one Jewish teacher had to request a transfer on compassionate grounds following ongoing harassment from the students. Teachers who are Jewish in schools with a high concentration of Muslim Arabic pupils have been counseled not to reveal that they are Jewish. One said, "I am not able to come out—I want my students to know I am a person like anyone else, just flesh and blood". Another, almost in tears, said this: "I am terrified that the students will find out that I am Jewish. I am very ashamed to say this". Another teacher who is not Jewish, but who is interested in Judaism, mentioned this interest to the principal of the school who was supportive but warned the teacher not to reveal this interest to the students.

In these interviews, the teachers said that most of the prejudicial views came from the students' homes; students reported that this is what their parents have told them. The students experience a sense of disconnection when their teachers tell them something different about the Jewish people or the Holocaust from what they have learnt at home. In addition, outside authorities, including the religious leaders in the mosques, tend to undermine Western influences so that teachers in government schools often face serious discipline problems. As one teacher put it:

> We [the teachers] have been called *sharmuta*—which means whore, prostitute in Arabic—we have made complaints.... The students are learning that there are no serious consequences for disrespect, for hatred, for racism, discrimination, verbal abuse, and even violence.
> I know that in Syria, Lebanon, Sudan, Iraq, Kuwait, they do know how to respect authority figures and teachers and even women to a certain level within their own culture. They have been allowed to use our system and disregard it at the same time because there are no consequences for their behaviour.

Studies of Muslim children and the Australian school system have found that Muslim families have different expectations of schooling because they mainly come from authoritarian cultures where schools are teacher centred and based on rote learning, to the Australian schools which are student centred and encourage questioning and analysis (Clyne 2001, pp. 122–124, 199). In her study on educating Muslim children in Australia, Clyne noted that many Muslim parents blame their children's low achievement levels on the "lack of discipline, differences in the teacher's role and lack of structured teaching and learning" (p. 122). The few Jewish children in the government schools in the southwest of Sydney have also been targeted and some Jewish parents have had to remove their children and move to another area because of ongoing harassment.

Table 1 Muslim students' beliefs about behaviors of Muslims and Jews

Behavior or attribute	Students agreeing that statement applies to Muslim people (%)	Students agreeing that statement applies to Jewish people (%)
Sell drugs	0	60
Are scary	0	60
Dislike people from other groups	0	93
Steal other people's lands	0	60
Are selfish	0	73
Have no morals	0	73
Are dangerous	13	60
Are racist	0	60

Source: Nayler (2009)

Most teachers in southwestern Sydney believe that they need to focus on the anti-Muslim feelings that are prevalent in Australian society. The teachers I interviewed commented on the fact that, on the whole, other teachers in their schools were less concerned by the phenomenon of Muslim children's hatred of Jews. One commented, "There has to be a wider appreciation that there is a problem of antisemitism in the Arab community.... It is a problem that needs to be tackled".

This information from my interviews with teachers about Muslim children's negative attitudes towards Jewish people was validated by a survey Jennifer Nayler (2009) conducted at a government high school in southwestern Sydney, where the majority of students are of Arabic-speaking backgrounds. She asked students if Muslims and Jews engaged in particular negative behaviors, as shown in Table 1. She found that far higher percentages held these beliefs about Jews than about Muslims.

Another study of antisemitism amongst Muslim youth, by Philip Mendes (2008), also supports these findings. However, Mendes argues that these sentiments "appear to be a form of male violence which is not mirrored by girls in the same cohort" (p. 2). My interviewees support Mendes' contention that antisemitism was a source of amusement among the boys socialising in the playground. One teacher reported that the boys would download "beheadings and attacks against 'infidels' onto their mobile phones" and would then "swap and show them with their friends". However, some of the teachers I interviewed teach at girls' high schools, where antisemitic attitudes were also present. A study in Canberra (Ben-Moshe 2011) found that Jewish children experience racist taunts from children of both Christian and Muslim backgrounds. However, the one physical assault reported in that study occurred in an incident with a Muslim child in connection to the Middle East conflict. Ben-Moshe commented that "this supports the contention that antisemitism takes an additional and potentially more sinister and dangerous form in high school and in relation to Israel" (p. 15).

From my survey of teachers, it is clear that Muslim school students, both male and female, hold negative perceptions of Jews. Some express this by using hate language relating to Jews; their negative attitudes are consistent with their high regard for Nazism. If Australia is to remain an ethnically harmonious country, there is clearly a need to counter these negative stereotypes and to develop more accepting attitudes towards Jews amongst Muslim and Arabic-speaking students in Australia.

Addressing the Problem of Anti-Jewish and Anti-Religious Feelings

Over the last decade, several programmes have been developed, mostly by members of the Jewish community, to combat the anti-Jewish feelings I have described above. Here I outline four of these programmes; three include the Holocaust and the fourth takes a different approach.

The first, Courage to Care (CTCNSW 2009), is a student-centred programme totally focused on those who risked their lives to save victims of the Nazis during the Holocaust: people who had the "courage to care". Its aim is to convey the message of community tolerance and living in harmony, emphasising the importance of standing up against persecution. Between 1998 and 2005 it attracted 155,000 participants, of whom 55,000 were school children (Kangisser Cohen 2005, p. 121). The programme's organisers report very positive feedback, as can be seen on the website of Courage to Care Victoria (CTCVIC 2009); these findings are supported by the study by Sharon Kangisser Cohen (2005, p. 122).

The second set of programmes was initiated in 2004, when the New South Wales Jewish Board of Deputies introduced two programmes for high school students: Youth Encounters; and Respect, Understanding and Acceptance (RUA). These programmes take an interfaith approach, bringing together students from Jewish, Christian, and Muslim schools. In Youth Encounters, the students meet three times, once at a school of each faith; this bridge-building exercise aims to develop communication and leadership skills and develop students' understanding of the commonalities of the three Abrahamic faiths. RUA is a more extensive programme; it uses an intercultural approach, consisting of three meetings, one of them at the Sydney Jewish Museum, a Holocaust museum. However, the approach is to teach about the theme of international genocide, with the Holocaust being incorporated into that theme. These programmes include elements from interfaith and intercultural programming, as well as the Holocaust (Rutland 2010, p. 85).

In a third approach, teachers who are concerned about anti-Jewish feelings in their schools are sponsored to study at the Yad Vashem Centre in Jerusalem, initially through the Blashild Fellowship Programme and later the Gandel Holocaust Studies Programme for Australian Educators. Because they allow teachers to develop their own specific study programmes to counter racism, using the Holocaust as a case study, they are particularly effective in helping teachers to develop programmes that meet the needs of Muslim children (Rutland 2010, pp. 85–86). For example, one participant, a female English teacher from a Christian background, taught at a government school with a high proportion of Muslim students. She was inspired to apply to the programme after discovering that her students had almost no knowledge of the Holocaust. Following the Yad Vashem course, she implemented an innovative programme looking at different texts relating to the Holocaust, which resulted in her students becoming deeply involved with the topic.

In contrast to the programmes described above, Together for Humanity (T4H) is an interfaith programme run in both government and non-government schools that focuses on opposing racism. It aims to show children the common moral values that inform the three Abrahamic faiths—Judaism, Christianity, and Islam—and involves a presenter from each religion, working together. Nayler (2009) conducted a professional evaluation of the programme in which she concluded that the children's attitudes towards Jews changed following the T4H programme, and that it influenced students to have a more positive attitude towards members of the other faith groups. T4H does not use the Holocaust at all in its material because it believes that doing so could be counterproductive to the programme's aims, especially for the Muslim children. However, T4H team members do try to respond openly to issues that students raise, including questions about the Holocaust.

Using the Holocaust as a Case Study: The Debate

The Muslim world holds both contradictory and inaccurate views regarding the Holocaust, views that need to be countered. On the one hand, there is a strand of Holocaust denial in the Arab/Muslim world, highlighted by the statements and activities of the previous Iranian President, Mahmoud Ahmadinejad (Achcar 2009, pp. 267–268). Teaching about the Holocaust is not common in the Muslim world and those programmes that have been introduced are limited in scope. Indeed, in a country like Morocco, the topic has been "taboo" (Polak 2010, p. 55).

On the other hand, the main Muslim/Arab narrative recognises that the Holocaust did occur but equates Zionism with Nazism and argues that the Palestinians have become "the Holocaust's true victims" because they were displaced following the creation of Israel (Litvak and Webman 2009). A narrative has emerged in the Arab and Muslim worlds that the Jewish state in Palestine was created as compensation for the murder of six million Jews in Europe during the Holocaust (see Said 1981). Recent scholarship has affirmed the prevalence of this view. For example, Sicher (2009, p. 21) has argued that "the Holocaust… is the moral standard of the injustice done to others as 'compensation' for the suffering of the Jews". Similarly, Karen Polak (2010) found in Morocco that a focus on the plight of the Palestinians and the 2008/9 Gaza conflict, together with the UN fact-finding report into this conflict, headed by Judge Richard Goldstone, known as the *Goldstone Report* (Goldstone 2009) prevented the implementation of a planned project to teach about the Holocaust in Morocco. In addition, there is a strong veneration of Hitler within the Arab world and support for the Nazi killing of Jews who are seen as "inherently malicious" and "evil" (Litvak and Webman 2009, p. 193); *Mein Kampf*, in Arabic translation, is sold widely (Sicher 2009, p. 38). My interviews revealed that these views are prevalent amongst Arabic-speaking and Muslim high school students in Sydney.

In his introduction to *Rethinking the Holocaust*, Yehuda Bauer argued that

> The Holocaust has, therefore, become the symbol for genocide, for racism, for hatred to foreigners, and of course for antisemitism, yet the existence of rescuers on the margins provides a hope that these evils are not inevitable, that they can be fought. The result is the beginning of international cooperation to educate as many people as possible—to warn them. (2001, p. xi)

Bauer's message is that the Holocaust is an extreme form of genocide. Despite its unprecedented nature, if it has happened once, it can happen again (p. 50). Thus, education about the Holocaust and genocide is an important element in preventing incitement to hate. The facilitators of the first three programmes discussed above concur with this view. They believe that educating about the Holocaust as a paradigm of genocide can help to counter racism and inspire mutual respect and cross-cultural understanding within Australian society. The Australian government has endorsed this view. The new national curriculum for history will include a compulsory section on Holocaust and genocide.

Both Jewish and non-Jewish educators and Jewish community leaders argue that it is important to teach about the Holocaust, particularly in Muslim schools, to counter their misconceptions. They believe that teaching the Holocaust is a particularly effective way to highlight the problems of genocide and the negative results of racist attitudes. However, with Muslim students, it is best to incorporate the Holocaust into a broader study of genocide. One of my interviewees commented:

> With Year 11 Modern History… I had a discussion about Israel with the girls. Because I have been friendly and I was involved in the school Eid celebration, I had enough trust from the girls to talk openly about Israel. They told me how the Arab world should join together to kick Israel off the map. I told them the same thing was said by Serbs in the Bosnian genocide. Because most knew about Bosnia, some personally so, they did see my point that saying that is wrong… I have to admit, I was a little scared talking like this, but the girls responded well…

She continued,

> All in all, I think learning about genocide as a universal topic, that includes the Holocaust, is a better way to combat intolerance and anti-Jewish feeling as it draws on the experiences that Muslim students have often personally had and shows the results of targeting a group.

This interviewee stressed that teachers need to develop strong personal relationships with their students, so that they take note of what their teachers tell them about racist attitudes.

Furthermore, using the Holocaust as a case study by itself can lead to criticisms from Muslim educators. For example, one of my interviewees reported that a fairly senior public servant had commented that Courage to Care was simply "Jewish propaganda". Such negative comments can undermine the effectiveness of the programme, especially in Muslim schools. It has been suggested that the Jewish community is also seen as so self-absorbed with its own past history of suffering that it cannot recognise or acknowledge the sufferings of others.

If Muslim children have a negative view towards the Holocaust, based on the false belief that it led to the Palestinians being dispossessed and expelled from their native homeland, making its study compulsory might only aggravate the situation. For example, a guide at the Sydney Jewish Museum noted in an interview that her only negative experience as a guide was with children from a Muslim school, who were unruly and badly behaved. When she commented on their poor behaviour, one student asked why they should want to learn about the Holocaust when it had caused the Palestinians to lose their land. Hence, teachers need to consider this context when teaching about the Holocaust, and ensure that it is carried out within the broader frame of genocide.

The more general approach to genocide is used by Facing History and Ourselves and The Memorial de la Shoah (Paris), whose travelling exhibition on the Genocide of the Tutsis in Rwanda includes panels on the Holocaust. By introducing the genocides of Rwanda and the former Yugoslavia, students can learn that "irrespective of who the victim groups are... genocide is an issue which concerns us all" (Polak 2010, p. 58)..

Another key issue is family education, particularly within the Muslim and Arabic-speaking communities. The SJM study (Alba and Sztrum 2006) found that, in Holocaust education, context is extremely important, and that the family can greatly influence students' level of interest in the subject matter. Given this, educators must take Muslim perceptions into account when preparing programmes for this particular school population.

Several other issues must be considered in teaching the Holocaust within the framework of the new national Australian curriculum. There are significant positive elements, especially when educators include the personal story of a survivor, which makes history "more real" (Alba and Sztrum 2006). Not only do students understand the evils of racism; such stories also provide hope because of the Holocaust survivors' courage and determination (Kangisser Cohen 2005, p. 128). However, there are also challenges. First, meeting with survivors can help students to value their own lives more, but the experience can also lead them to invalidate personal suffering compared with the Holocaust experience; this may prevent them from empathising with their classmates' traumatic experiences (Kangisser Cohen 2005, p. 125). Further, during the Holocaust, being a rescuer could involve risking one's own life. In Australia today, taking a positive stand against racism or bullying may be difficult, but it is not life threatening. Finally, there is the potential problem with young males who see violent images all the time and may be fascinated by them, but "this limits their ability to see them as real" (Alba and Sztrum 2006, slide 15).

Another problem in making Holocaust education compulsory is the fact that few teachers are adequately equipped to teach it. The English teacher referred to earlier, who had taken the Yad Vashem course, stressed that most of the English teachers in her school would not have the knowledge and skills to teach about the Holocaust. The SJM study found that the role of the teacher was extremely important, that "the teacher may know little about the subject or its sensitivities", and that "the enthusiasm and likeability of the teacher or subject impacts on visits" (Alba and Sztrum

2006, slide 14). That study recommended the development of kits and other material for teachers to use both before and after their visits to the SJM, to ensure that the messages given to the students are consistent.

Effective Models for Interfaith and Anti-Racism Education

Holocaust education is a paradigm study of the evils of racism and the incitement to hate. It is also needed to expose some of the myths discussed above that propagate anti-Jewish feeling in some population groups. It can be incorporated into an anti-racism curriculum with Muslim children, provided that it is adapted to the particular needs of this group. For this to occur, teacher education is an essential component of anti-racist Holocaust education and should take place at both the pre-service and professional development levels. Each principal should also ensure that the Holocaust is taught within the school's religious and ethnic context to meet the needs of their individual student bodies. The most effective form of anti-racism education occurs when an empathetic teacher integrates it into a broad curriculum area such as History or English. For Muslim students it is important to teach genocides where Muslims have suffered, such as Bosnia, in addition to using the Holocaust to illustrate the evils of racism and conveying the message that Muslims, as well as Jews, could have suffered under Nazi racial ideology. Reaching out to include the families of the Muslim students is also very important. The different programmes discussed in this chapter can also provide additional value.

Ongoing evaluation, especially of the long-term impact of anti-racism programmes that include the Holocaust, is another important component (McEntee et al. 2003). In the conclusion to her study of Courage to Care, Kangisser Cohen (2005) stressed that the programme's long-term effects on its visitors should be subject to further research. To date, the only research in Sydney into long-term effects has been the 2006 study of the Sydney Jewish Museum, reported by Alba and Sztrum. My findings in the study reported here, which are based on qualitative research using interviews with teachers and programme coordinators, highlight the importance of such evaluative research.

Holocaust and genocide education can provide an important educational framework to promote mutual understanding and facilitate more positive inter-faith and inter-ethnic relations. While the different models discussed here may not be directly relevant for other international communities, they can be adapted to suit local needs. The findings of my study are based on empirical evidence in a field that is under-researched and very relevant for contemporary global society because of the ongoing threat of genocide. Another important and related area is using anti-racist education to develop respect for the Muslim religion and culture. Further research needs to be undertaken in these fields, not only in Australia but also in other parts of the world.

References

ABS [Australian Bureau of Statistics] (2006). Census data. Melbourne: ABS. http://abs.gov.au/websitedbs/censushome.nsf/home/historicaldata2006

ABS (2011). Census data. Melbourne: ABS. http://www.abs.gov.au/websitedbs/censushome.nsf/home/CO-61

Achcar, G. (2009). *The Arabs and the Holocaust: The Arab-Israeli war of narratives* (G. M. Goshgarian, Trans.). New York: Metropolitan Books, Henry Holt and Company.

Alba, A., & Sztrum, M. (2006). *Heartbeat: Sydney Jewish Museum Holocaust education research findings*. PowerPoint presentation at the Sydney Jewish Museum, June 2006, based on a study by Natalie Kyan and Neer Korn.

Batrouney, T. (2006). Arab migration from the Middle East. In F. Mansouri (Ed.), *Australia and the Middle East: A front-line relationship* (pp. 37–62). London: Tauris Academic Studies.

Bauer, Y. (2001). *Rethinking the Holocaust*. New Haven/London: Yale University Press.

Ben-Moshe, D. (2011, December). *Antisemitism in Canberra*. Unpublished report to the ACT Jewish Community, Inc.

Buckingham, J. (2010, 1 October). The rise of religious schools in Australia. *ABC [Media] Religion and Ethics*. http://www.abc.net.au/religion/articles/2010/10/01/3027021.htm

Clark, C. M. (1949, 15 October). What are we doing to our migrants?" Broadcast on ABC radio, reported in *The New Citizen*, 4(10).

Clyne, I. D. (2001). Educating Muslim children in Australia. In S. Akbarzadeh, A. Saeed, & S. Akbarzadeh (Eds.), *Muslim communities in Australia*. Sydney: UNSW Press.

Cruickshank, K. (2006). *Teenagers, literacy and school: Researching multilingual contexts*. London/New York: Routledge.

CTCNSW [Courage to Care, New South Wales] (2009). Organisational website. http://www.couragetocare.com.au/

CTCVIC [Courage to Care, Victoria] (2009). Organisational website. http://www.couragetocare.org.au/

Day, P. (2009). Australian public policy: Examining the foundations. In D. Claydon (Ed.), *Islam, human rights and public policy* (pp. 1–25). Brunswick East: Acorn.

Dunn, K. M., Forrest, J., Burnley, I., & McDonald, A. (2004). Constructing racism in Australia. *Australian Journal of Social Issues, 39*(4), 409–430.

Dunn, K., Forrest, J., Ip, D., Babacan, H., Paradies, Y., & Pedersen, A. (2008, 30 September–3 October). *Challenging racism: The anti-racism research project, state level comparisons*. Paper presented at 4Rs Conference, University of Technology, Sydney. http://www.uws.edu.au/__data/assets/pdf_file/0020/42185/State_level_comparison_for_4Rs_conference.pdf

Eckstein, G. (n.d.). *Sydney Jewish community demographic profile, New South Wales*. Unpublished study undertaken for the New South Wales Jewish Communal Appeal [NSWJCA]. Sydney: NSWJCA.

Encel, S. (1971). The nature of race prejudice in Australia. In F. S. Stevens (Ed.), *Racism: The Australian experience* (Vol. 1, pp. 30–42). Sydney: ANZ Book Co.

Goldstone, R. (2009). *Human rights in Palestine and other Occupied Arab Territories*. Report of the United Nations Fact-Finding Mission on the Gaza Conflict. New York: UN General Assembly. http://www2.ohchr.org/english/bodies/hrcouncil/docs/12session/A-HRC-12-48.pdf

Graham, D. (2014). *The Jewish population of Australia: Key findings from the 2011 census*. Sydney: NSWJCA.

Gross, Z., & Rutland, S. D. (2014). Combatting antisemitism in the school playground: An Australian case study. *Patterns of Prejudice, 48*(3), 309–330. doi:10.1080/0031322X.2014.918703.

Kabir, N. (2004). *Muslims in Australia: Immigration, race relations and cultural history*. London: Kegan Paul.

Kabir, N.A. (2005). Nahid Kabir on Muslims in Australia. *The religion report with David Rutledge*. Radio programme, ABC radio, 30 March. http://www.abc.net.au/radionational/programs/religionreport/nahid-kabir-on-muslims-in-australia/3447566

Kabir, N. A. (2008). Are young Muslims adopting Australian values? *Australian Journal of Education, 52*(3), 229–241.

Kabir, N. A. (2011). A study of Australian Muslim youth identity: The Melbourne case. *Journal of Muslim Minority Affairs, 31*(2), 243–258. http://dx.doi.org/10.1080/13602004.2011.583518

Kangisser Cohen, S. (2005). "Courage to Care": A first encounter between the Holocaust and Australian school students. *Australian Journal of Jewish Studies, 19*, 121–133.

Litvak, M., & Webman, E. (2009). *From empathy to denial: Arab responses to the Holocaust.* New York: Columbia University Press.

Markus, A. (2011). *Mapping social cohesion 2011: The Scanlon Foundation Survey.* Executive summary. Monash, Victoria: Monash Institute for the Study of Global Movements, Monash University. http://scanlonfoundation.org.au/wp-content/uploads/2014/07/mapping-social-cohesion-summary-report-2011.pdf

McEntee, G. H., Appleby, J., Dowd, J., Grant, J., Hole, S., Silva, P., et al. (2003). *At the heart of teaching: A guide to reflective practice.* New York: Teachers College Press.

Mendes, P. (2008). *Antisemitism among Muslim youth: A Sydney teacher's perspective.* ADC special report, no. 37. Melbourne: B'nai B'rith Anti-Defamation Commission.

Nayler, J. (2009). *Students together for humanity (T4H).* Final independent evaluation report. Unpublished report for T4H. Brisbane: Jenny Nayler Learning aJeNcy.

NSWDET [New South Wales Department of Education and Training] (2006). Department website. www.det.nsw.edu.au/reports_stats/index.htm

Polak, K. (2010). Tolerance education in Morocco: "Anne Frank: A History for Today": Learning about our past, contributing to our future. *Intercultural Education, 21*(51), 51–59.

Poynting, S. (2006). What caused the Cronulla riot. *Race and Class, 48*(1), 85–92. http://state-crime.org/wp-content/uploads/2011/10/poynting2006a.pdf

Rutland, S. D. (2005). *The Jews in Australia.* Melbourne: Cambridge University Press.

Rutland, S. D. (2010). Creating effective Holocaust education programmes for government schools with large Muslim populations in Sydney. *Prospects, 40*(1), 75–91.

Said, E. W. (1981). *The question of Palestine.* London: Routledge & Kegan Paul.

Sicher, E. (2009). Multiculturalism, globalization and antisemitism: The British case. *Analysis of Current Trends in Antisemitism, 32*, 21.

Szoke, H. (2012, 16 February). *Racism exists in Australia. Are we doing enough to address it?* Keynote address, Queensland University of Technology, Brisbane. https://www.humanrights.gov.au/news/speeches/racism-exists-australia-are-we-doing-enough-address-it

Wilton, J., & Bosworth, R. (1984). *Old worlds and new Australia: The post war migrant experience.* Melbourne: Penguin Australia.

Yarwood, A. T. (1964). *Asian migration to Australia.* Melbourne: Melbourne University Press.

Part V
International Dynamics, Global Trends and Comparative Research in Holocaust Education

A Global Mapping of the Holocaust in Textbooks and Curricula

Peter Carrier, Eckhardt Fuchs, and Torben Messinger

Concept and Aims

Although most European countries—and an increasing number of countries worldwide, including the United States, Canada, South Africa, and Argentina—have made the Holocaust a mandatory or recommended topic in the teaching of history, teaching about the Holocaust differs considerably from one country to another. Within any one country, the content, support structures, and time allocated to studying the subject also vary. Several organisations and groups of researchers have conducted thorough international assessments: FRA (2010), Fracapane and Haß (2014), Lecomte (2001), OSCE (2005), and Pettigrew et al. (2009). The ITF/IHRA has also released several reports since 2009 (ITF/IHRA 2014).

In this chapter, we summarise information from the UNESCO/GEI (2014) report, which seeks to complement these reports by providing hitherto unavailable information about curricula and textbook representations of the Holocaust around the world, especially in countries whose populations were not directly involved in the event. We do not address Holocaust education in general, including teaching methods and pupils' results, but focus on the specific concepts and narratives that appear in curricula and textbooks; the aim of the report was to provide a foundation for understanding local narratives derived from contemporary local perspectives. We first present concepts and narratives with which the Holocaust is represented in curricula and textbooks in specific countries, and then assess the degrees to which concepts and narratives converge or diverge internationally.

This study addresses the historiographical status of the Holocaust as represented in the specific media of curricula and textbooks. Therefore, it conceives of the

---

P. Carrier • E. Fuchs (✉) • T. Messinger
Georg Eckert Institute for International Textbook Research,
Celler Str. 3, D-38114 Braunschweig, Germany
e-mail: fuchs@gei.de

© Springer International Publishing Switzerland 2015
Z. Gross, E.D. Stevick (Eds.), *As the Witnesses Fall Silent: 21st Century Holocaust Education in Curriculum, Policy and Practice*,
DOI 10.1007/978-3-319-15419-0_14

Holocaust not as a legal or an ethical standard, which has already been done adroitly by Isaksson (2010) and MacDonald (2008), but as an object of what Angi Buettner (2011, p. 101) calls the historical imaginary. A historical event may be classified as an object of the imaginary in two cases. The primary referent, the historical event as an object of immediate empirical experience, may be remote in time. Or, the language and imagery customarily used to recount the event may be subject to what Buettner (p. 97) calls a process of transfer; that is, they are used to depict other events in other times and places. Buettner (p. 141) uses the word tropes to refer to this language and imagery, and Schmid (2008, p. 778) calls them chiffres.

The worldwide scope of this report meant that concepts and narratives found in curricula and educational media were indeed prone to surprising semantic shifts. For example, by borrowing the language and imagery of the Holocaust and applying them to the Nanking massacres of 1937 in China, or to the devastation of Japanese cities by atomic bombs at the end of World War II, historians engage in what David MacDonald (2008, p. 161) calls identity-reinforcing techniques in order to "tragedise their respective pasts". Even more conspicuous transfers of Holocaust imaginary are practiced by Hindu nationalists, or with reference to a "Cambodian Holocaust" and an "atomic Holocaust" (Schmid 2008, p. 177).

Data and Methods

The task of documenting the status of the Holocaust in curricula and textbooks worldwide involved collecting information which reflects the specific historical understanding of the event in a given country and can, at the same time, be compared across countries whose languages and histories are very diverse. Information gathered from curricula therefore included the terminology used to refer to the event, and the contexts in which references to the Holocaust occurred, as well as the discipline in which the topic is taught and the document's date and country of publication. Similarly, the criteria for exploring textbook presentations of the Holocaust consisted of the geographical space and time period within which the event is recounted, the main protagonists involved, the major interpretive paradigms employed (historiographical archetypes, comparisons and moral or legal modes of explanation), narrative techniques, didactic methods, and national idiosyncracies. This conceptual and narrative approach provided relatively straightforward historiographical criteria with which to assess curricula and textbooks comparatively.

The study adopted an inductive approach based on insights into local perceptions of the Holocaust provided by researchers who not only are fluent in local languages, but also have first-hand experience of education systems in the countries covered in the survey. This inductive approach therefore reflects the multiplicity of concepts and narratives used to refer to the same event; this multiplicity derives either from linguistic differences or from the reasoned choices that authors of curricula and textbooks make to adopt concepts, such as Shoah, Holocaust, genocide, massacre, and extermination, and to draw on one of many narrative templates (Wertsch 2004) in order to explain the event. For example, the Holocaust is often rendered via a narrative "fall-rise" template, when presented as a catastrophe followed by the institutionalising of genocide prevention after World War II.

At the same time, the inductive approach helps us to understand how one concept may be used to signify different things in different political and historical contexts, following "the fact that the same word, or the same concept in most cases, means very different things when used by differently situated persons" (Mannheim 1985, p. 273). Thus, just as concepts have a history and change in meaning over time, they also have a geographical place and change in meaning from one place to another.

The curricula analysis is based on 272 history or social sciences curricula from 135 (out of a potential total of 195) countries which were valid at the time of the study, from 2013 to 2014. Most curricula were issued by state education ministries; federal countries provided a representative sample from provincial regions, and in other countries the curricula were not available. The primary aim of the analysis is to provide a comprehensive overview of the countries in which the Holocaust does or does not feature in history or social studies education. And since it strives to offer a broad overview in as many countries as possible and to represent all continents, the analysis is confined to general information answering four questions: Is the Holocaust stipulated? Where, in relation to other historical events, is such teaching stipulated? In what terms is it stipulated? And (where information is available) what objectives are ascribed to teaching about the Holocaust?

The textbook analysis draws on 89 textbooks published in 26 countries since 2000. We selected the 26 countries on the basis of hypotheses designed to ensure that the study would cover a wide range of different types of historical writing which lend themselves to intra- and international comparison. The selection of countries highlights a wide range of characteristic approaches to the Holocaust in various parts of the world. We used three criteria for selection. The first was *geographical*, to provide a broad overview of various regions of the world. The second was based on *historical and political issues*: were countries involved in an event of mass violence or genocide, and were they members of the Warsaw Pact or the Soviet Union? The third was *pragmatic*: How accessible were curricula and textbooks and language expertise? With this approach we sought to highlight features common to all countries, features common to certain groups of countries, and features that sometimes diverged, in order to enable educational policymakers to learn from the challenges facing other countries.

Seven questions guided our enquiry into the status of the Holocaust in textbooks:

1. On what specific textbooks is the sample based and in relation to what assumptions do they contextualise the Holocaust?
2. What spatial (or geographical) temporal scales are ascribed to the Holocaust? That is, does the textbook locate the event in a local, national, European, global or transnational context? And when is its beginning and end defined, and what major occurrences are named?

3. What characteristics are ascribed to which protagonists? Are they qualified (as individuals or groups, or as political, national, religious, ethnic, or racial types), and presented as active or passive agents? And what relationships between groups or individuals are implied?
4. What interpretive paradigms are used to explain the event? How do authors explain responsibility and causality, and is the event made banal, or distorted?
5. What narrative structures and points of view do textbook authors apply? Do one-sided or multiple authorial perspectives dominate, and are narratives progressive, regressive, or fatalistic?
6. What teaching methodologies do authors adopt?
7. What idiosyncracies do the textbooks convey in different national contexts? That is, in what ways is the local relevance of the Holocaust expressed and illustrated, either in relation to local events or memorial sites, and in relation to atrocities and genocides other than the Holocaust?

The Holocaust in Curricula

What status do currently valid national curricula designed for secondary-level schooling (for pupils aged approximately 14–18) ascribe to the Holocaust? Using a representative sample of curricula, we were able to assess the ways in which the Holocaust is presented and also explain the contexts and semantic idiosyncrasies of references to the Holocaust, even when curricula neither refer explicitly to nor entirely disregard the Holocaust. Thus, our aim when conducting this analysis was to establish whether teaching about the Holocaust is explicitly addressed in curricula, in what terms the Holocaust is defined, and in which contexts (subdisciplines, sections, and hierarchies) it is dealt with.

In broad terms, the Holocaust is stipulated in the history curricula of approximately half of the countries investigated, with varying contexts and terminologies (see Table 1). The event is presented most frequently in the context of World War II, but also features in the context of lessons about human rights violations. It is generally referred to using the term Holocaust, while fewer curricula use the term Shoah, and some use both terms in conjunction. In some cases, curricula forego both terms, preferring to describe the event with alternative terms such as extermination or genocide of the Jews, or they make indirect references to the event, with terms such as concentration camp or Final Solution, or they combine terms which clearly indicate teaching about the Holocaust, such as destruction and Jews, or genocide and National Socialism. In some curricula, only Jews are named explicitly as victims; references to Sinti and Roma, people with disabilities, political opponents, homosexuals, or other socially marginalised groups are infrequent. Most curricula do not specify the victim groups to be discussed in teaching. Moreover, while a quarter of all curricula contain no reference to the Holocaust, they instead discuss the purpose of the subject and methods to be used in its teaching, or else they explicitly refer to its historical contexts such as World War II and/or National Socialism, in such ways that one may assume that the topic is part of teaching in the subject although it is not

A Global Mapping of the Holocaust in Textbooks and Curricula 249

Table 1 Categories of curricula by status, 2013

Status	Continent	Country	Number
Direct reference	Africa	Ethiopia, Namibia, South Africa, Swaziland	57
	Asia	Israel, Kazakhstan, Philippines, Singapore	
	Australia and Oceania	Australia	
	Europe	Albania, Andorra, Armenia, Austria, Belarus, Belgium (German-speaking Community, Flanders, Wallonia), Bermuda (British Overseas Territory), Bosnia and Herzegovina (Republika Srpska), Bulgaria, Cayman Islands (British Overseas Territory), Croatia, Czech Republic, Denmark, England, Estonia, Finland, France, Germany (Lower Saxony, Saxony, Bavaria, North Rhine-Westphalia), Greece, Hungary, Ireland, Italy, Latvia, Liechtenstein, Lithuania, Luxembourg, Macedonia, Malta, Moldova, Montenegro, Netherlands, Northern Ireland, Poland, Portugal, Romania, Russia, Serbia, Slovakia, Spain, Sweden, Switzerland (Basel-Landschaft, Bern, Central Switzerland), Turkey, Wales	
	North America	Canada (British Columbia, Newfoundland and Labrador, Ontario), Guatemala, Panama, Trinidad and Tobago, United States (Arkansas, California, Texas)	
	South America	Brazil, Chile	
Partial reference	Europe	Slovenia	8
	North America	Belize, Canada (Alberta, Nova Scotia, Prince Edward Island), Mexico, United States (Maryland)	
	South America	Argentina, Colombia, Ecuador	
Context only	Africa	Algeria, Botswana, Burkina Faso, Congo (Democratic Republic), Gambia, Ivory Coast, Kenya, Lesotho, Mauritius, Morocco, Mozambique, Niger, Rwanda, Senegal, Tanzania, Tunisia, Uganda, Zimbabwe	46
	Asia	Bhutan, China, India, Indonesia, Japan, Korea (Republic of), Malaysia, Pakistan, Sri Lanka, United Arab Emirates, Yemen	
	Australia and Oceania	Cook Islands	
	Europe	Bosnia and Herzegovina (Federation of Bosnia and Herzegovina), Cyprus, Georgia, Norway, Scotland, Switzerland (Jura, Lausanne), Ukraine	
	North America	Costa Rica, Dominican Republic, El Salvador, Honduras, Nicaragua	
	South America	Paraguay, Peru, Suriname, Uruguay	

(continued)

Table 1 (continued)

Status	Continent	Country	Number
No reference	Africa	Angola, Benin, Cameroon, Egypt, Ghana, Seychelles, Zambia	28
	Asia	Bahrain, Iraq, Lebanon, Nepal, Palestinian National Authority, Thailand	
	Australia and Oceania	Fiji, Micronesia (Federted States of), New Zealand, Papua New Guinea, Samoa	
	Europe	Azerbaijan, Iceland, Kosovo	
	North America	Antigua & Barbuda, Bahamas, Dominica, Jamaica	
	South America	Bolivia, Guyana	
No data/not available	Africa	Cape Verde, Central African Republic, Chad, Comoros, Congo (Republic of the), Djibouti, Equatorial Guinea, Eritrea, Gabon, Guinea, Guinea-Bissau, Liberia, Libya, Madagascar, Malawi, Mali, Mauritania, Nigeria, Sierra Leone, São Tomé and Príncipe, Somalia, South Sudan, Sudan, Togo	64
	Asia	Afghanistan, Bangladesh, Cambodia, Iran, Jordan, Korea (Democratic People's Republic of), Kuwait, Kyrgyzstan, Lao People's Democratic Republic, Maldives, Mongolia, Myanmar, Oman, Palau, Qatar, Saudi Arabia, Syria, Tajikistan, Timor-Leste, Turkmenistan, Uzbekistan, Vietnam	
	Australia and Oceania	Kiribati, Marshall Islands, Nauru, Niue, Solomon Islands, Tonga, Tuvalu, Vanuatu	
	Europe	Monaco, San Marino	
	North America	Barbados, Cuba, Grenada, Haiti, Saint Kitts and Nevis, Saint Lucia, Saint Vincent and the Grenadines	
	South America	Venezuela	

explicitly named. We also point out semantic variations arising from the various languages whose vocabularies do not permit the direct adoption of the customary terms Holocaust or Shoah.

Overall, we found four ways in which the Holocaust is represented in curricula. We summarise them as direct or partial references, context only, or no information.

Direct References

Many countries' curricula directly stipulate teaching about the Holocaust by using the term Holocaust or Shoah or by using alternative terminologies such as 'genocide against the Jews', or 'Nazi persecution of minorities'. While most curricula employ the term Holocaust (in Albania, Australia, Denmark, Ethiopia and Poland, for example), some use Shoah (Ivory Coast, Italy, Luxembourg, and Belgium (Flanders)). Others use the two terms as synonyms: Switzerland (canton of Bern), Germany (Saxony), and Argentina. In other countries, the Holocaust is referred to directly, albeit by using alternative terms. These include "the singularity of the Jewish genocide" in Spain, the "Nazi policy of extermination" in Andorra, the "extermination of Jews" (Ecuador, Belgium (Wallonia)), "genocide of the Jews" (France, Germany (Lower Saxony)), "mass murder of… Jews" (Trinidad and Tobago), "persecution of Jews" (Singapore) and the "Final Solution" (Namibia). In Turkey the curricula make no direct reference to the Holocaust, but the way in which themes related to the Holocaust are contextualised or local terminology is used makes it clear that the Holocaust is in fact stipulated. There, *soykırım* (genocide) is the standard term used to refer to the Holocaust, and terms analogous to Holocaust or Shoah are strictly avoided in order to emphasise the uniqueness of the genocide against Jews in contradistinction to the genocide against Armenians in 1915 and 1916, which occurred at a time before the term genocide came into use (Bali 2013, p. 62).

Partial References

Eight countries' curricula stipulate teaching about the Holocaust indirectly in order to achieve a learning aim which is not primarily about the history of the Holocaust (but about responses to the Holocaust outside Europe, for example) or which illustrates a topic other than the Holocaust (where the Holocaust is mentioned as one of several aspects of human rights education). In such cases, when the Holocaust is named in the curriculum as a means to other ends, the curriculum does not address the event's historical meaning and complexity. Thus the curricula of Argentina, Belize, Columbia, Ecuador, Mexico, and Slovenia present the Holocaust as an example of violations of human rights. Similarly, in the United States (Maryland), pupils are required to "explain the events that led to the beginning of the Second World War", and to "investigate the response of the United States government to the discovery of the Holocaust and immigration policies with respect to refugees". In Canada (Prince Edward Island and Nova Scotia), pupils are required only to study responses to the Holocaust in Canada.

Context Only

In several countries, curricula refer to World War II or to National Socialism without referring explicitly to the Holocaust. The curricula of Sri Lanka and India, for example, contain references to the "Results/Impact of Nazism" or the "Consequences/Results/Impact of World War II". The curricula in Botswana, Burkina Faso, Kenya, Malaysia, Niger, Norway, Pakistan, Peru, Senegal, Uruguay, and 40 other countries contain similarly indirect contextualisations. More direct and elaborate references to the context occur in the Zimbabwean curriculum, which requires pupils to "Discuss injustices practised by the Nazis and Fascists", and refers to "human rights violation" and "atrocities against minorities and conquered nations". The Rwandan curriculum likewise requires pupils to "compare the phenomenon between [sic] Fascism and Nazism and what took place in Rwanda", and refers to "Nazi doctrines", "loss of human life", the "comparative study of various genocides", and "stages of genocide". Likewise, the curriculum of the Democratic Republic of the Congo refers to "the harmful effects of Nazism", and the Costa Rican curriculum refers to "antisemitism and racial superiority: the case of Jews, Muslims, Slavs and Gypsies".

No Reference

The curricula of 28 other countries in the study mention neither the Holocaust as a term and an event nor its context. Several do not stipulate the specific contents of history teaching; instead they merely discuss the necessity and purpose of the school subjects of history or social studies and the teaching methods to be used, as in Brunei Darussalum, Dominica, Fiji, Iceland, and Thailand.

Several curricula do not conform to the above pattern and require further explanation. In federal education systems, for example, curricular contents differ from one state, province, or canton to another. In Switzerland, education about the Holocaust is obligatory but not contained in the curricula of all regions and cantons because, as Davis and Rubinstein-Avila (2013) suggest, no constraints on how this event should be taught are imposed in the face of a complex national story. In Switzerland, Jews were partially accepted as refugees, but also partly turned away at the border, and banks collaborated with the Nazi regime. Here, a "self-reflexive approach" is taken to teaching about the Holocaust (p. 12 ff). Likewise, the Brazilian Ministry of Education issues national guidelines which stipulate teaching about the Holocaust—but these guidelines are not binding and function only as recommendations whose content can be adapted and extended locally. Curricula for the nine-year primary school level in Brazil are provided on a municipal level, whereas the provincial states determine curricula content for secondary schools: schools have the final decision over what is actually taught in classrooms. Following attacks on synagogues and Jewish cemeteries, Porto Alegre was the first municipality to introduce compulsory education about the Holocaust for all public schools in 2010 (see WJC 2010; USHMM and SGS 2013, p. 18).

In some countries, such as Finland, Hungary, Morocco, and Ukraine, curricula are in a state of transition. For example, Finland's history curriculum of 2003 prescribes the teaching of "European extremist movements, the crisis of democracy and persecution of people [in] different countries; the Second World War and its consequences", and thus contains only the context but no direct reference to the Holocaust. However, amendments made by the Ministry of Education in 2010 have led to a shift towards a more explicit stipulation to teach about the Holocaust in the context of human rights education. In the section concerning ethics for school years 7–9, the curriculum stipulates the teaching of "human rights violations such as the Holocaust"; in the section devoted to history, "human rights, human rights violations such as genocide, the Holocaust, and persecution of people in different countries" (FME 2010, p. 2). Likewise, in the section concerning ethics, the curriculum for upper secondary school levels stipulates teaching about "human rights, human rights conventions and their history, human rights violations such as the Holocaust", and in the section on history, "human rights, genocide, the Holocaust and persecution of people in different countries" (FME 2010, p. 2). This testifies to a shift towards contextualised and instrumentalised teaching about the Holocaust, with only one section of the upper-level history curriculum stipulating direct education about the history of the Holocaust.

The names of victims' groups contained in curricula are also inconsistent. Some curricula do not clearly name groups of victims: those in Australia, Bulgaria, Ethiopia, Italy, Mexico, Alberta, and Texas. In others Jews are the only group of victims named (in the curricula of the Walloon authority in Belgium, and in Hungary, Ivory Coast, Panama, and Bavaria in Germany). Some curricula merely state that the Holocaust has something to do with antisemitism (in Albania, Liechtenstein, Namibia, Ireland, Portugal, Spain, and Ontario, for example), while others explicitly mention several groups of victims such as Sinti and Roma (in France, Costa Rica, Ecuador, South Africa, Trinidad and Tobago, and USA/California), homosexuals (in USA/California, Trinidad and Tobago, and South Africa), political opponents (in South Africa, the and German *Land* of Lower Saxony) and further groups subsumed under the term other minorities (in Germany (Lower Saxony and North Rhine-Westphalia), Namibia, Singapore, and Swaziland) or summarised as "others who failed to meet the Aryan ideal" (in USA/California).

The Holocaust in Textbooks

How is the Holocaust presented in the textbooks of 26 countries? To respond to this question, we outlined the temporal and spatial scales that authors ascribed to the event, their characterisations of protagonists, the ways they interpret causes and effects of the event, and their didactic approaches and examples of national or local colour ("idiosyncracies"), albeit without assuming either global standardisation or national fragmentation. Our initial summaries or country studies of textbooks were based on answers to a questionnaire distributed to specialists who read up to five textbooks currently in use and designed for students aged 14–18 in Albania, Argentina, Belarus, Brazil, China, Egypt, El Salvador, England, France, Germany, India, Iraq, Ivory Coast, Japan, Moldova, Namibia, Poland, Russia, Rwanda, Singapore, South Africa, Spain, Syria, USA, Uruguay, and Yemen (UNESCO/GEI 2014, chapter 5.1). The national characteristics of textbook representations of the Holocaust that resulted from this process then provided a basis on which we could identify ways the representations converged and diverged internationally.

Our analysis showed that, despite certain international consistencies in textbook representations, education about the Holocaust also depends partially on local historical concepts and narrative traditions. Textbooks reflect a dual pattern, including both convergence and divergence, as documented by the dominant concepts and narrative techniques they contain. Certain regional consistencies are evident, for example, within western Europe, central and eastern Europe, the Middle East, Asia, Africa, North America and South America; however, the concepts, narratives, and thematic foci largely differ not only from one region or country to another, but even from one textbook to another in relation to the topics, events, and didactic traditions with which the Holocaust is associated locally. These findings suggest that educational media provide a foundation not for a common education about the Holocaust, but for a number of different approaches or educations about the Holocaust which render the event in very different ways.

This assessment of conceptual and narrative trends in textbooks enabled us to identify partially shared narratives of the Holocaust, based on overlaps between characteristics of textbook representations in western Europe, eastern Europe, North America, and Africa, in countries with local genocides, in Middle Eastern countries, or even in countries with no apparent historical relation to the event. An example of a partially shared depiction of the Holocaust occurs when the Holocaust is de- and recontextualised. For example, vocabulary customarily used to describe the Holocaust, including "terrible massacres", "killings", "mass murders", "atrocities", and "extermination", was adopted in Rwandan textbooks to describe the genocide of 1994, which is historically distinct though comparable in terms of its spatial and temporal scales, types of protagonists, interpretive paradigms, narrative structures, and didactic approaches. We also found that the Holocaust is domesticated, that is, conceptualised in new idiosyncratic or local ways. For example, the Chinese textbooks (in the sample) employ no derivatives of the terms Holocaust or Shoah, but rather the terms genocide (*datusha*) and kinds of crimes (*zhongzhong zuixing*). The Chinese textbooks thereby render the event understandable for local readers in a language which is familiar to them, but which does not convey the historical specificity that western scholars and teachers have traditionally ascribed to the Holocaust.

In sum, while the textbooks of nearly all these countries refer to the Holocaust, those textbooks which provide knowledge *of* the event do not necessarily provide thorough historical knowledge *about* it. Instead, the Holocaust regularly functions as a model, paradigm, or measure of representations of other atrocities in accordance with one of several processes. The first process is one of "narrative transfer", in which the event is described and explained in various languages and national contexts (Buettner 2011, p. 97). In the second, "shifting frames of reference", explanations change over time or in different places; Ebbrecht (2011, p. 324) calls this *Wechselrahmung*. The third is the duplication of "image schemata", the repetition of visual topoi in the presentations of different historical events (Taylor 2002, p. 172). Writers may construct analogies between the Holocaust and other events by adopting vocabulary and narrative tropes from the Holocaust with respect, for example, to the Ukraine Famine, the Nanjing Massacre, or apartheid in South Africa. In short, the Holocaust is not a force of international standardisation, but proof of the multiscale divergence of overlapping narratives, according to which local specificities are dominant, and where similarities occur between specific textbooks or between regions, nations, and continents without adhering to a singular pattern.

The following section summarises some general convergences and divergences between textbook representations of the Holocaust. We do not have space here for an exhaustive summary, but invite readers to read the more detailed UNESCO/GEI (2014) report. Our findings show that the Holocaust is rendered in very different ways, but also that these differences are not only regional or even national, but often the result of individual authors' forms of understanding.

Spatial and Temporal Scale

The textbooks offer insight into perceptions of where and when the Holocaust took place. The event is generally named as one which occurred in Europe and Germany, while some textbooks domesticate the event, as in Belarus, Germany, and Moldova, by providing details about the local repercussions of the Holocaust. They rarely provide details about the occupying regime and administration of the General Government and of the role of satellite states. They do evoke transnational spaces in relation to the topics of collaboration (in France and Moldova, for example), emigration (in China, Argentina, and the United States, for example) and in relation to comparable genocides in China and Rwanda. They sometimes establish transcontinental connections which pit Europe against Asia. For example, Indian authors refer to the threat of the "Europeanisation" of Asia, authors of a Russian textbook qualify National Socialism as a "European" phenomenon, and those of another Russian textbook refer to a "battle of European culture against Russian and bolshevist barbarity".

The temporal or historical context ascribed to the Holocaust is generally that of World War II; time spans given range from 1933 to 1945, with some mentions of key changes in 1938 or 1942 or the Warsaw Ghetto Uprising of 1943. References to deeper historical currents such as racial theories from the 19th century are mentioned in textbooks in Brazil, India, Germany, and Namibia; Jewish history, emigration, or pre–20th-century antisemitism are addressed in Argentinian, German, Japanese, and American textbooks. Likewise, several textbook authors in Argentina, France, Germany, Namibia, and Russia write about the aftereffects or memory of the Holocaust after 1945. No textbook in any country can be said to present an ahistorical or universal narrative of the Holocaust.

Protagonists

Perpetrators are most frequently referred to as Nazis, Germans, and fascists. Individuals commonly named include Hitler, Himmler, Heydrich, Höss, and Eichmann. Most striking is the extent to which a focus on Hitler pervades textbook narratives of the Holocaust. Hitler functions as a moral repository for the event, as embodied in portraits of him and excerpts from *Mein Kampf*. And phrases like "Hitlerian aggression" and the "policy of Hitler-Germany", found in Russian textbooks, attribute sole responsibility to him. By contrast, textbooks in France and Germany generally marginalise his role and instead explain the event as a result of plural causes.

Victims are most frequently named as Jews and "Gypsies" in textbooks from almost all countries, while other groups of victims, such as Slavs, people with disabilities, political opponents, and homosexuals, are named less frequently. Other categories of victims are named, for example, as "black victims" or "black people" in South African, Rwandan, and Indian textbooks. Generic references to an "inner enemy" (in one Russian textbook) or to "inferior" or "undesirable" "people" (in Chinese, Russian, and Uruguyan textbooks) detract from the specificity of Nazi ideology. Meanwhile, some references to Jewish victims as "opponents" (in Ivory Coast, for example) may even mislead readers into believing that all Jews resisted or posed a threat to the National Socialist regime and that they were therefore a legitimate target of repression. Few textbooks depict Jewish life immediately before 1933 or after 1945, although those in Germany do. Therefore, most textbooks largely present Jews as voiceless victims and as objects of perpetrators' volition. Textbook authors in some countries also define victims in terms of national groups (as Poles, Ukrainians, and Russians in Russian textbooks, for example) or nationalise Jewish identity in terms of Polish and European (in Chinese textbooks), or Ukrainian and Hungarian Jews (in French textbooks).

Other protagonists include members of the resistance, rescuers of the persecuted, the Allies, and local individuals who are named by their proper names in Polish textbooks, such as the acclaimed doctor, educator, and writer Janusz Korczak. Few bystanders or collaborators feature in the textbooks.

Interpretive Paradigms

The majority of textbooks in all countries name the event as the Holocaust. In the course of the presentations, paraphrases of the event are added using such terms as "discrimination against Jewish people, sent to concentration camps" (in a Japanese textbook) or, characteristically, as "systematic killings", "extermination", "systematic genocide", the "Final Solution", and "massacres" (in South African textbooks). The largely descriptive nature of history textbooks means that they generally employ inclusive definitions of the event, that is, definitions which derive from the details of the event rather than from an exclusive *a priori* definition. In a few exceptions to this general rule, the Holocaust is not named, or is alluded to euphemistically as "driving out the Jews"; for example, the Hindi term *ihudi bitaran* is used in one Indian textbook (Patra and Chakraborty 2005). Or the Holocaust may be paraphrased in partial terms, as in Egyptian and Syrian textbooks.

Textbooks in almost all countries explain the event as one stemming from the personal convictions of Adolf Hitler. The textbook currently used in Namibian schools is characteristic of this technique; in it, the Holocaust is addressed in a section entitled Antisemitism. The word Hitler appears in a box in the middle of the section's first page and from it arrows point towards party organisations; the authors describe Hitler's personal "determination to remove Jews from Germany". English textbooks also refer to Hitler's irrational hatred of the Jews and to his personal desire for revenge against Jews. It follows that the most frequently named cause of the Holocaust is ideology (racism, antisemitism, totalitarianism, authoritarianism, militarism, capitalism, fascism). Textbooks in Brazil, Germany, Ivory Coast, Japan, Moldova, and Rwanda even qualify the expansionist policy of Nazi Germany as a form of colonialism.

A small number of textbooks, for example in Argentina, Poland, Spain, and the United States, complement their presentations of the history of the Holocaust with metahistorical commentaries in the form of glossaries of historic terms. Metanarrative approaches are pedagogically effective when explaining the political expediency of commemorating the Holocaust via monuments or in international relations, as in textbooks from Argentina, Germany, India, and Russia. They also encourage a critical approach to such phenomena as the personality cult surrounding Hitler, as outlined in the Salvadorian textbook in the sample. In exceptional cases, authors not only apply historiographical paradigms, but also discuss their merits, as the authors of Argentinian texts do when sketching how Hannah Arendt, Zygmunt Bauman, and Daniel Goldhagen explain the Holocaust.

Comparisons between the Holocaust and other genocides are often alluded to but not explained. The authors of some Polish texts use the terms terror and cleansing to describe historically different events, which makes them less historically specific. Similarly, the use of the term terrorist to describe Hitler in one Brazilian textbook, terror to describe the Holocaust in one German textbook, and even the definition of Zionist forces in Palestine as Jewish "terror groups" in one Iraqi textbook lend themselves to semantic confusion if not anachronism. Similar semantic confusion arises when the term extermination is used to describe the function of the Gulag in one Brazilian textbook or when a Belarussian textbook inaccurately claims that the National Socialist regime planned the "extermination of the Soviet people", or when different regimes are described collectively as totalitarian in Brazilian, Argentinian, French, Moldovan, Polish, Spanish texts, and in passing in English and Rwandan textbooks. The use of the term fascism to describe the German and Japanese authorities during World War II and the use of the term genocide (*datusha*) in Chinese textbooks to refer to crimes committed by both the Japanese forces in Nanjing and the National Socialists in the Holocaust also detract from historical distinctions.

Authors also evoke comparisons by using images. Two different French texts juxtapose images of different events, such as the images of Auschwitz and the Nanjing Massacre, or of Dresden and Hiroshima. In an Ivorian text, the suffering during the Holocaust is associated with that caused by the atomic bomb in Hiroshima, and in a South African text, Auschwitz is associated with life under apartheid. These all obscure historical differences rather than explaining them comparatively.

Narrative Techniques

Narrative techniques found in a small number of the textbooks are "closed"; that is, the authorial perspective involves a single narrative voice without quotations or complementary documents (as in Albanian textbooks). At the other extreme, some authors apply, at least in part, an open technique: juxtaposing images of different historical events, in order to allude to meanings without explaining them. For example a South African text juxtaposes a man holding his passport during apartheid beside an image of prisoners arriving in Auschwitz. However, most texts apply a technique midway between these extremes, juxtaposing authorial texts with additional perspectives reflected in quotations and textual and visual documentation.

Often, the narrative point of view inadvertently perpetuates the perpetrators' viewpoint. One Ivorian textbook, for example, presents victims primarily as "opponents, especially the Jews and the Gypsies", then as "millions of men, women and children", then as "Jews", and thereby reinforces the idea that "the" Jews and "the" Gypsies (that is, all of them) were killed as a result of their role as "opponents", as if the killers, at least according to their own reasoning, therefore had a just reason to kill them. This conflation of members of the resistance, Jews, and Gypsies effectively reproduces the perpetrators' view that the Third Reich needed to defend itself against an alleged threat.

Most striking are the different ways in which authors lend moral value to the Holocaust. Most authors couch its history in terms of decline followed by progress. However, the object of this progression varies from one country to another. Polish textbooks notably combine stories of national resistance to the German occupation of Poland with references to the Polish underground government, Polish helpers, and Jewish resistance as exemplified by the Warsaw Ghetto Uprising. By contrast, Russian textbooks, like those from the United States, focus on progression towards military victory in World War II and thus present Allied military victory in the place of victory over the Holocaust, in particular over the camp system. The most commonly found narrative of progression ends with an allusion to the Universal Declaration of Human Rights and the Convention on the Prevention and Punishment of the Crime of Genocide, adopted by the United Nations in 1948.

Didactic Approaches

While many textbooks do not contain exercises urging pupils to question and explore materials presented in the textbooks, others feature a wide variety of exercises, including story telling, document interpretation, role play, textual or pictorial analysis, and exercises requiring pupils to either find rational explanations of the events or else to empathise with protagonists via letter writing, biographical writing, or analysis of protagonists' decisions. The textbooks testify to a trend towards stating and affirming learning objectives such as understanding human rights (in India,

Iraq, Moldova, Namibia, and Rwanda, for example) or affirming the role of the United Nations in securing human rights after 1945 (in Brazil, El Salvador, Spain, and Uruguay, for example), albeit without explaining the origins, meaning, history, implementation, and effectiveness of the principles of human rights. Many textbooks link the Holocaust to local horizons by appealing to pupils to, for example, conduct interviews with Jewish survivors in Shanghai (in a Chinese textbook), explore the rescuing of persecuted people (Albania), compare the motivations of perpetrators in Romania and Germany (Moldova), or explore local historical and commemorative sites (Germany).

Conclusions

Rather than assessing education about the Holocaust in general, as previous reports have done, the UNESCO/GEI report of 2014 focused exclusively on conceptual and narrative representations of the Holocaust and grounded them in specific examples drawn from nationally approved formal curricula and textbooks currently in use. Historians may insist quite vehemently on the accurate depiction of core information, such as dates, names of places and people, and their numbers, more than on the formal arrangement of information or causal explanation of events; however, the worldwide reach of the material covered in this study suggests that we should acknowledge the conceptual and narrative inflections underpinning the multiple Holocausts found in educational media. We rarely found, for example, that the curricula and textbooks of one country make absolutely no reference to the Holocaust while those of another country are entirely comprehensive and accurate, or that the materials of one country contain what those in another country lack, and vice versa. German textbooks are strong on issues of ideology and on documentation but weak on discussions of collaboration. While Moldovan textbooks address collaboration with the National Socialists in Romania, they understate ideology, preferring to explain the event in terms of military strategy and personal decisions. And while South African textbooks explore racism historically in a way which could provide models for European textbooks, they remain somewhat monothematic.

The inductive approach we applied in this study offers new insights into the multiple concepts and narratives used to refer to the Holocaust worldwide. We support the appeal by Davis and Rubinstein-Avila (2013) to educators to eschew "a standardised, hierarchical, global curriculum" in favour of a "rhizomatic" approach to education about the Holocaust which allows pupils to build "on their own experiences" (p. 15ff) and gain insight into multiple perspectives that allow them to learn for themselves; still, our analysis indicates that curricula and textbooks in many countries do not provide students with the educational means to develop Holocaust literacy. Curricula often allude or refer to the Holocaust in ambivalent terms (in Burkina Faso, Democratic Republic of the Congo, Costa Rica, Rwanda, and Zimbabwe, for example) or as a means to an end which deviates from historical learning (in Columbia, Mexico, and Slovenia, for example), and the formal curricula are often not congruent with the textbooks. Writers tend to confine the main timeframe to the years of intense killing from 1942 to 1944 and/or to the years of World War II, and to name the spaces in which the Holocaust took place in general terms as Europe or Germany.

Two other common features are the quantitative and qualitative imbalance of textual and visual representations of protagonists in favour of perpetrators, and the intentionalist explanation of history through personalising Adolf Hitler. In addition, various facts about the texts can be misleading: factual inaccuracies and less than comprehensive presentations of the history of the Holocaust, conceptual inconsistencies, and semantic allusions evoked by juxtaposing of images and terms. Some textbook authors also confine the narrative voice to that of a single, neutral, and authoritative point of view, while frequently using the passive voice.

In sum, our analysis provides new insights into ways the Holocaust is represented in curricula and textbooks worldwide. On the basis of these findings, the larger report includes a variety of policy recommendations, indicating ways that curricula and textbook representations of the Holocaust may, in the future, be modified and thereby merit common approval. Our analysis also suggests that one should strive not towards a one-way flow of knowledge (from "good" textbooks in some countries as reference points for shortcomings in "bad" textbooks elsewhere), but rather recognise the potential for interpretations to be complementary, such that authors in all countries may learn from one another in different ways.

References

Bali, R. (2013). Perceptions of the Holocaust in Turkey. In G. Jikeli & J. Allouche-Benayoun (Eds.), *Perceptions of the Holocaust in Europe and Muslim communities: Sources, comparisons and educational challenges* (pp. 61–69). Dordrecht/New York: Springer.

Buettner, A. (2011). *Holocaust images and picturing catastrophe: The cultural politics of seeing.* Burlington: Ashgate.

Davis, B., & Rubinstein-Avila, E. (2013). Holocaust education: Global forces shaping curricula integration and implementation. *Intercultural Education, 1–2,* 1–18.

Ebbrecht, T. (2011). *Geschichtsbilder im medialen Gedächtnis: Filmische Narrationen des Holocaust* [Perceptions of history in media memory: Filmic narratives of the Holocaust]. Bielefeld: Transcript.

FME [Finnish Ministry of Education] (2010). *Amendments to the national core curriculum for basic education of 2004.* In Regulation 41/011/2010, 18 June, 2010.

FRA [European Union Agency for Fundamental Rights] (2010). *Excursion to the past: Teaching for the future* (Handbook for teachers). Vienna: FRA.

Fracapane, K., & Haß, M. (Eds.) (2014). *Holocaust education in a global context.* Paris: UNESCO.

Isaksson, M. (2010). *The Holocaust and genocide in history and politics: A study of the discrepancy between human rights law and international politics.* Malmö: University of Gothenburg.

ITF/IHRA [Task Force for International Cooperation on Holocaust Education, Remembrance and Research/International Holocaust Remembrance Alliance] (2014). *Holocaust education reports, by country.* http://www.holocaustremembrance.com/educate/education-reports

Lecomte, J. M. (2001). *Teaching about the Holocaust in the 21st century.* Strasbourg: Council of Europe and FRA.

MacDonald, D. (2008). *Identity politics in an age of genocide: The Holocaust and historical representation*. London: Routledge.
Mannheim, K. (1985). *Ideology and utopia: An introduction to the sociology of knowledge* (L. Wirth & E. Shils, Trans.). New York: Harvest Books.
OSCE [Organisation for Security and Co-operation in Europe] (2005). *Education on the Holocaust and on antisemitism: An overview and analysis of educational approaches*. Vienna: OSCE.
Patra, M. S., & Chakraborty, N. S. (2005). *Bharater Itihas* [History of India]. Kolkata: Rajkrishna Pustakalaya.
Pettigrew, A., Foster, S., Howson, J., Salmons, P., Lenga, R. A., & Andrews, K. (2009). *Teaching about the Holocaust in English secondary schools: An empirical study of national trends, perspectives and practice*. London: University of London, Institute of Education, Holocaust Education Development Programme.
Schmid, H. (2008). Europäisierung des Auschwitzgedenkens? Zum Aufstieg des 27. Januar 1945 als "Holocaustgedenktag" in Europa [Is Auschwitz commemoration being Europeanised? The emergence of 27 January 1945 as "Holocaust Memorial Day" in Europe]. In J. Eckel & C. Moisel (Eds.), *Universalisierung des Holocaust? Erinnerungskultur und Geschichtspolitik in internationaler Perspektive* (pp. 174–202). Göttingen: Wallstein.
Taylor, C. (2002). The cultural face of terror in the Rwanda genocide of 1994. In A. Hinton (Ed.), *Annihilating difference: The anthropology of genocide* (pp. 137–178). Berkeley: California University Press.
Wertsch, J. (2004). Specific narratives and schematic narrative templates. In P. Seixas (Ed.), *Theorizing historical consciousness* (pp. 49–62). Toronto: University of Toronto Press.
WJC [World Jewish Congress] (2010). *Porto Alegre first Brazilian city to make Holocaust education mandatory in schools*. Organisational website. http://www.worldjewishcongress.org/en/news/9633
UNESCO/GEI [UNESCO/Georg Eckert Institute] (Ed.) (2014). *The international status of education about the Holocaust: A global mapping of textbooks and curricula*. Paris: UNESCO.
USHMM [United States Holocaust Memorial Museum], & SGS [Salzburg Global Seminar] (Eds.) (2013). *Global perspectives on Holocaust education: Trends, patterns and practices*. Washington, DC: USHMM/SGS.

International Organisations in the Globalisation of Holocaust Education

Karel Fracapane

Introduction

The dissemination of Holocaust education and remembrance across the globe owes much to the actions taken by intergovernmental organisations, starting with the United Nations, to ensure that this historical event becomes a key global reference. Commemoration is not the only objective and, in a global context, remembering the Holocaust is supposed to meet a global educational aim: through encounters with the darkest pages of history, to help the people of the world to uphold universal values of peace and mutual respect, and thus contribute to preventing the resurgence of events of a similar nature. Placed under the triple auspices of the Universal Declaration of Human Rights, the International Covenant on Civil and Political Rights, and the Convention for the Prevention and Punishment of the Crime of Genocide, the United Nations General Assembly (UNGA 2005) designated 27 January as an International Day of Commemoration; the declaration and urges member states "to develop programmes that will inculcate future generations with the lessons of the Holocaust in order to help to prevent future acts of genocide".

It further calls for the "mobilization of the civil society for Holocaust remembrance and education, in order to help prevent future acts of genocide". A subsequent UNESCO (2007) resolution invites member states to turn this call into action. Placing the resolution in the very heart of the organisation's key mission, it directly refers to the Constitution of UNESCO, which stipulates that

> ... the great and terrible war which has now ended was a war made possible by the denial of the democratic principles of the dignity, equality and mutual respect of men, and by the propagation, in their place, through ignorance and prejudice, of the doctrine of the inequality of men and races.

K. Fracapane (✉)
Division of Education for Peace and Sustainable Development, UNESCO,
7, Place de Fontenoy, 07 SP, 75352 Paris, France
e-mail: k.fracapane@unesco.org

Therefore, member states invite the director general to take the steps necessary to render the resolutions passed by the General Assembly concrete through education.

The question remains of how to proceed, given the challenges and obstacles such a globalisation process may entail, politically and educationally. Indeed, by these successive resolutions, Holocaust remembrance is intended to become *officially* a universal point of reference, shared by all the peoples of the earth, including those that have no relationship whatsoever with this history, or even with the broader history of the Jewish people. This leads to a double consequence: on one hand, the genocide of the Jewish people is fully recognised because of its radicalism, singularity, and unprecedented character in the history of humanity; on the other hand, the Shoah as a historical event moves away from European history to become a globalised framework of references.

Because the Holocaust is to serve as a global "lesson" for the world, the image of the Holocaust functions as a shared moral reference. In other words, the historical event that one is invited to commemorate and teach becomes an abstract object of exemplary value, far removed from the historical and geographical context in which the event took place. It becomes the seed of a broad reflection encompassing various issues related to human rights, peace, the fight against discrimination, racism, xenophobia, and ultimately, the prevention of genocide. This dialectical dimension highlights the significance of this emerging globalised, human-rights–focused culture of remembrance, to which the Holocaust would be, literally as well as figuratively, the "commonplace". From the narrower perspective of Holocaust education, it leads to a series of challenges that profoundly influence learning and teaching practices. It also brings about great opportunities for educators and for policy makers eager to disseminate a better knowledge of this subject, contribute to the promotion of human rights, and sensitise the public at large about the difficult challenge of preventing mass atrocity crimes.

Institutionalising Holocaust Education

Holocaust remembrance and education is a largely institutionalised field at the international level. Numerous public and private structures support the development of Holocaust education worldwide. Some countries, including especially the United States, Israel, and Germany, but also the Netherlands, France, and the United Kingdom, have been promoting Holocaust remembrance as a subject of public diplomacy by financing and supporting international endeavours and by being particularly active within international organisations. At the intergovernmental level, the institutionalisation of Holocaust memory stems mostly from a process, beginning with the London Conference in 1997 and ending with the 2000 International Forum of Stockholm on the Holocaust, which fixed the main trends of what a globalised politics of historical memory of the Holocaust will be for the years to come: a common set of references to help overcome divisions of the past; an opportunity to convey universalistic values of human rights, mutual understanding and peace; and a shared moral responsibility to engage in actions for a better future, in contrast with a past characterised by violence, indifference, and guilt.

These considerations also guide the actions of all the other intergovernmental organisations involved in promoting Holocaust education, remembrance, and research. In addition to the United Nations (Resolution 60/7, 2005) and UNESCO (Resolution 34C/61, 2007), these include the International Holocaust Remembrance Alliance (created in 1998 and launched in January 2000 as a Task Force for International Cooperation on Holocaust Remembrance and Research), the Council of Europe (18 October 2002 Declaration by the Ministers of Education), the European Union (27 January 2005 European Parliament Resolution on Remembrance of the Holocaust, Antisemitism, and Racism), and, to a certain extent, the Organisation for Security and Cooperation in Europe, as the 2005 Declaration of the Cordoba Conference explicitly mentions the Holocaust, while previous declarations focus on antisemitism.

This normative process reflects the instrumental role the United States played in bringing Holocaust memory to the fore of the international agenda, in part owing to the discussions on stolen Jewish assets. Indeed, the 1997 London Conference on Nazi Gold, and especially the 1998 Washington Conference on Holocaust-Era Assets, hold particular significance as regards the development of new remembrance policies which go far beyond compensation and restitution issues, and which will contribute to accelerating Europe's ongoing deconstruction of the post-war national narratives of heroism and victimisation. Secretary of State Madeleine Albright made this perfectly clear in her opening speech at the 1998 Washington Conference on Holocaust-Era Assets in Washington DC: "The struggle to reveal and deal with the full truth surrounding the handling of Holocaust-Era assets is wrenching, but also cathartic. Only by knowing and being honest about the past can we gain peace in the present and confidence in the future" (USDOS 1999, p. 32). In other words, European countries are prompted to accept their responsibilities for perpetrating the Holocaust and, by doing so, to break with national pasts characterised by guilt and silence. By the same token, they are invited to enter a new era in which the legacy of the horrors of the Holocaust will serve as a safeguard for peace and human rights:

> While turning the page on this black chapter of history, we must take from the lessons of yesterday a renewed commitment to usher in a new and brighter century. Our words must provide enduring lessons from this awful experience, guiding all our countries to act with a greater sensitivity to present and future crimes against humanity, even if on a different scale. (USDOS 1999, p. 8)

This pivotal moment constitutes a transition from international politics (negotiations over non-settled Holocaust and war issues) to cultural policy (promotion of remembrance, research, and education), from division to moral consensus, and from a discourse about the past to a vision of the future. The United States and post–Cold-War unified Europe should unite around an ensemble of universal core values, for which the genocide of the Jewish people is the negative example. This primarily American policy (Surmann 2011), assigning a moral imperative to European nations that had collaborated in the Nazi plunder and assassination of the Jewish people during World War II, will in effect reinforce Europeans' reassessment of their own past and profoundly affect their national cultures of remembrance. The 2000 Declaration of the International Forum of Stockholm on the Holocaust was a watershed moment in that regard; it has formed the basis of most international efforts in the field of Holocaust remembrance.

The Stockholm Forum was the first intergovernmental conference solely dedicated to Holocaust remembrance and education. It gathered together representatives of 38 states, including many heads of state and chiefs of government, as well as a myriad of civil society organisations. Together they declared the political and moral commitment to fight against oblivion and support research and education. Attendees produced the Declaration of the Stockholm International Forum and formalised the Task Force for International Cooperation on Holocaust Education, Remembrance, and Research, which had been launched as an informal working group two years earlier at the initiative of Sweden, the United States, and the United Kingdom. In December 2012, it became the International Holocaust Remembrance Alliance.

What makes the Alliance unique is its relatively informal structure: it is not an international organisation in the legal sense of the term, and it manages to gather in a rather flexible forum of discussion specialised NGOs and government representatives. This allows it to deploy its activity at several levels: *diplomatic* first, following a proactive approach aiming at attracting new candidates for membership; *political* also as its purpose is to formulate policy recommendations about remembrance, education, and research for member and candidate states and the community of educators and researchers involved in Holocaust-related issues; and last, *programmatic*, because it assumes the responsibility of financing multilateral projects that aim to improve the exchange of knowledge and expertise between member countries and specialising organisations.

In practice, the flexible structure of the Alliance has great advantages. First, several countries have taken advantage of the composition of delegations (representatives of several ministries, memorial museums, independent experts, NGOs) to improve local dialogue, coordinate national initiatives, and better formulate countries' interests and external action. On another level, the Alliance ensures fluidity of exchanges and direct access to expertise, partnerships, and financial sources for many NGOs and governments, for which it constitutes also a good platform for public relations. Its successes are confirmed by the number of candidate countries: membership has tripled in about 10 years, and most countries with a direct connection to the Holocaust are either full-fledged members or have candidate status (Bulgaria, the Former Yugoslav Republic of Macedonia, Portugal, and Turkey).

This maturation of the organisation also comes with new challenges: administrative growth and subsequent development of more procedures; more projects to manage and therefore an ongoing need to reassess priorities and outcomes of expenses, and what is more problematic, a growing politicisation of discussions. The Alliance was developed as a consensual and flexible organisation functioning much as a group of friends, opening the door to other club members of good will. The initial wish to build up cooperative policy in an atmosphere of almost perfect consensus now collides more and more often with very difficult unsettled sub-regional historical issues such as divergent narratives between ex-Yugoslav countries, or between Bulgaria, Greece, and the Former Yugoslav Republic of Macedonia, to which the Alliance is expected to offer a space for settlement. Or, even worse, the Alliance is now faced with conflicting national interests that may be largely irrelevant to the Holocaust and that the organisation is not set up to address (Greece and the Former Yugoslav Republic of Macedonia, Turkey and Israel, etc.).

In other words, while the Alliance forms the infrastructure of international action in the field and is a strong actor in the globalising Holocaust remembrance, important efforts are necessary to reinforce its role as an active and innovative body that can inspire— and could possibly catalyse—international policy. This holds all the more true now that most international organisations with a foot in Europe have integrated Holocaust education into their programmes and hold political and administrative capacities far more powerful than the Alliance. This should not result in the Alliance losing any of its legitimacy. On the contrary, it should reinforce its position at a time when coordination between these different prominent actors becomes particularly relevant and necessary.

The actions taken by international organisations indeed reflect the willingness of their member states to continue supporting Holocaust education, remembrance, and research and show the rather positive overall picture of a continuous development. For instance, the OSCE has been the first to provide an overview of the state of Holocaust education and remembrance on the continent with its 2006 *Education on the Holocaust and on Antisemitism* and its recently published *Holocaust Memorial Days in the OSCE Region: An Overview of Governmental Practices*, showing that most OSCE participating states support Holocaust education, including 37 that have established an official Holocaust memorial day. The Council of Europe has prepared guidelines for teachers on both the Holocaust and the genocide of the Roma, and is providing professional development opportunities for educators in partnership with several NGOs across Europe. In 2012, the Fundamental Rights Agency of the European Union conducted important research on Holocaust and human rights education at memorial sites. More importantly, for the past few years the European Commission has been contributing substantially to Holocaust education and remembrance through its Active European Remembrance programme, which contributed 1.8 million Euros in 2011 and 2.4 million Euros in 2012 to educational endeavours in support of remembrance of crimes perpetrated by the Nazi and the Communist regimes. The United Nations and UNESCO are now also quite active actors, and conduct various advocacy and educational programmes in several regions of the world.

At the same time, however, the financial means available for the programmes created and the evident lack of unified or coherent long-term strategy strongly limit the reach of these programmes and continue to impede organisations from launching more ambitious national, regional, or international programmes which would have a sustainable impact on member states' policies as well as on practices within the education communities. Challenges remain vast in Europe, the cradle of the judeocide, and, as the United Nations and UNESCO expand their programmes in the rest of world as well.

Current Priorities for International Bodies

In the course of the past two decades, Western European nations have quite consensually come to accept the idea that the Holocaust should be commemorated and information about it transmitted to new generations. The post-war narratives based on victimhood and heroism have been progressively replaced by a more self-critical vision of history, including at its core the specific fate of the Jewish minorities. This entailed the explicit recognition that local governments or groups had collaborated in perpetrating the genocide, after decades of a dominant national-oriented, monolithic paradigm focusing on resistance and the suffering of the majority population. In that regard, the movement to internationalise this work functions on two different levels: transnational first, as Holocaust remembrance arises as a preoccupation beyond the national borders in which it was confined as a relatively marginal subject; then national as the international resonance of the theme reverberates on national cultures of remembrance. The globalisation of the Holocaust is by the pendulum effect a matter of both de-contextualisation and re-nationalisation. In other words, the growing feeling of a shared history reinforces the central position that the Holocaust now occupies in national cultures of remembrance.

And indeed, dozens of specialised institutions have emerged or grown significantly in the past decade. Museums and educational and research centres can be found in every national capital, and hundreds of thousands of students visit historic sites and exhibitions. Most archives are open for researchers, and academic programmes operate in several countries in Europe and North America. Textbooks include Holocaust history, which is present and mandatory in most secondary school curricula, and even in some for primary schools. Teachers have training opportunities, and sometimes their ministries encourage them to take courses. Students and educators alike have an abundance of teaching and learning materials at their disposal, developed locally or by organisations with considerable international outreach such as Yad Vashem, the Anne Frank House, the US Holocaust Memorial Museum, and Facing History and Ourselves. Moreover, public and private funding opportunities help to develop further programmes, whether such opportunities are offered by state or regional authorities, foundations, or the European Union.

Despite this general picture of success, a lot of work remains to be done. Education about the Holocaust has still not been developed in all countries of the western part of the continent, and it keeps facing new challenges as time passes and societies change. For instance, training educators is a continued necessity; so are ensuring the financial sustainability of specialised structures devoted to it, preserving and adapting historic sites for educational activities, and supporting academic research and creating more higher education programmes. Furthermore, tensions arise on occasion as aspects of history are still debated; and in multicultural societies, the predominance of Holocaust memory in the European historical consciousness may also generate conflict or contestation, even rejection in some cases, in relation to other traumatic pasts that may not have yet been properly addressed (crimes of de/colonisation, slavery, other minorities persecuted by the Nazi regime, etc.) or over contemporary issues (Israel-Palestine conflict). The enduring presence of antisemitism may of course also constitute a serious obstacle, as well as the sustained presence of neo-Nazi groups and radical right parties in some parts of the continent. Despite these obstacles, the general picture that former Western Europe—as well as the United States, Canada, and Israel—offers is that of a shared commitment to pursue, strengthen, and improve the ongoing educational policies and to promote further actions in the field elsewhere in the world.

The introduction of the countries that were formerly in the orbit of the Soviet Union into a new "community of memory" (Assmann 2007), now that they are gaining membership in the European Union and NATO, is following a different path. Current debates about the Nazi and Stalinist crimes show that a consensus on how the Holocaust should be remembered and taught is yet to emerge. Not only was the subject obscured during decades of a communist-driven historical narrative of the war and Nazi crimes, but it was also in many cases completely neglected during the years following the collapse of the Soviet Union. In addition, the Western-type celebration of the victory over Nazi Germany must coexist with a new narrative focused on five decades of communist persecutions and slightly less enthusiasm to emphasise the liberation of Europe from the grasp of Nazi Germany. The crimes perpetrated by both the Nazis and the Communists caused the deaths of millions in this region, affected most national groups, and left several countries totally devastated.

At the same time, it is in that very region that most of the victims of the Holocaust were killed, in operations of mass shootings, in ghettos or in killing centres, sometimes before the eyes of their former neighbours. The latter, potentially victims themselves, are also thus forced to confront their simultaneous position as witnesses of other crimes, as *bystanders*, and sometimes as perpetrators. In this phase of transition from a Communist to an ethno/national-centred narrative of victimisation, the reality of the atrocious crimes perpetrated by Nazis and Communists in the general population must now coexist with another, very disturbing element: the recognition of their own responsibility in destroying the Jewish minority. This added dimension is fundamental to understanding the problematic status of Holocaust education in the region: there can be victims of victims. In other words, accepting the history of the Holocaust is also giving up a part of the innocence that was granted by the status of victim and the moral stature that seems to be attached to it (Potel 2009). In a context where the Jewish community has been largely, if not entirely, destroyed, and its voice has gone unrepresented over time or has been silenced, the emergence of new narratives in a monolithic culture of remembrance can constitute a huge breakout. The conflict induced is all the more painful because these memorial claims are legitimate, although the crimes perpetrated may be of a different nature and therefore qualify differently. As Aleida Assmann (2007) points out, in this case, the main challenge is "to turn the *entangled* memories into *shared* memories", based on "mutual acknowledgement of sufferings relating to civilian experiences of the war" (p. 14).

Other parts of Europe face slightly different issues. The countries of the former Yugoslavia are still very much struggling with a recent past of conflicts and crimes against humanity. The Holocaust is taught in the classrooms of some of the former republics (Croatia, Serbia, the Former Yugoslav Republic of Macedonia, and Slovenia), but its memory remains overshadowed by the realities of the recent Yugoslav wars, and prone to political manipulations. Furthermore, educating about the Holocaust in this former Yugoslav context also requires being able to build bridges among governments, historic sites, and academic institutions of the region, as a national approach on the history of the Holocaust can hardly be enough in this regional context. UNESCO has been coordinating an effort of all six countries of former Yugoslavia to create together a new permanent exhibition on the Holocaust within the Ex-Yugoslav Pavilion of the Auschwitz-Birkenau State Museum; this is just one example, but a considerable one, of Holocaust education in a region still torn by very divisive discourses on history.

In the eastern parts of Europe, then, the issue of dealing with the history of the Holocaust remains very much tainted with politics of memory; meanwhile, in Western Europe, the educational challenge seems to lie in managing an abundance of learning and teaching materials and relies heavily on how traditional teaching methods are being adapted to new generations of children, with very diverse religious, ethnic, or national backgrounds, who will never meet a witness of these times. Promoting Holocaust education in that regard is therefore not so much about trying to do more, but about trying to do better, and about assessing the policies and practices of the past 20 years. However, the fact remains that several countries directly affected by the Holocaust, essentially those of the former Soviet Union, but also some situated along the southern borders of the Mediterranean, have not yet started implementing nationwide policies in support of Holocaust education, research, and remembrance. This should be a priority for international bodies involved in the region.

While most international bodies committed to Holocaust remembrance have a strong European rooting, the emergence of the United Nations as a new, by definition global, actor in this field raises a new series of issues: How to introduce the Holocaust in new historical, memorial, and educational contexts? Likewise, if the memory of the Holocaust in a global context proceeds as a meta-narrative, how do we ensure that the events referred to are still understood, in other words, that Holocaust education is still teaching and learning about the Holocaust?

From Holocaust Globalisation to Holocaust Oblivion

The first question that one might ask when dealing with the globalisation of Holocaust remembrance is whether talking *more* about the Holocaust implies knowing *better* about it. This fundamentally is an educational question. It may seem paradoxical, but remembrance can indeed go hand in hand with oblivion or, at least with altering the understanding of what the history was and what it implies, as pointed out by several Holocaust scholars (Levy and Sznaider 2005; Rosenfeld 2011). For instance, common references to the Holocaust in the mass media often reflect a very superficial consciousness rather than even minimal historical knowledge of what actually occurred. As Alvin Rosenfeld (2011) explains, "the term 'historical memory' is in common usage", but

> ... for most people a sense of the Nazi crimes against the Jews is formed less by the record of events established by professional historians than by individual stories and images that reach us from more popular writers, artists, film directors, television producers, and the like. (p. 53)

In other words, the Holocaust tends to become a reference or symbol rather than a tangible reality with an everlasting impact, and is reduced to a minimal moral standard, a volatile metaphor about good and evil that fails to put forward the most uncomfortable questions it raises. Imre Kertesz writes that

> The Holocaust appears to be ever more unintelligible the more people talk about it… [It] recedes ever more into distance, into history, the more memorials to it we construct… The unbearable burden of the Holocaust has over time given forms of language that appear to talk about the Holocaust, while never even touching the reality of it. (quoted in Rosenfeld 2011, p. 12)

Not only does this paradoxical process open the door to the over-simplification of historical facts, avoiding a confrontation with the complexity of historical contexts and the most horrifying aspects of human experience in order to make them fit into the "lessons" we would like these events to convey, but it may also lead to much worse. If it is just an abstract rhetorical device without any real substance and distinctiveness, the Holocaust can be equated to any sort of events, be they atrocity crimes or anything else, and can then serve as a polemical pretext for pursuing contemporary political agendas. It is quite telling that debate continues over the 2 April 2009 vote of the European Parliament to establish on 23 August a European Day of Remembrance for Victims of Nazism and Stalinism in reference to the Ribbentrop-Molotov pact of 1939.

It is obvious that victims of communist crimes deserve full recognition and should be commemorated. In fact, much work remains to be done, in particular in Western Europe, to disseminate knowledge about those crimes, which would certainly help deepen the understanding of the Eastern and Central European war experience and subsequent cultures of remembrance. However, one can only wonder about the intention of blending victims of Nazism and communism into one and the same commemorative act. Is the aim to devalue the most radical difference between the two totalitarianisms—the invention of Treblinka—and, as a result, to silence the collaboration of local populations in the genocide? The emerging common understanding of the Holocaust as a pivotal moment in the history of humanity is therefore challenged by means of diminishing the scope and impact of crimes perpetrated by the Nazis and their collaborators against the Jewish people. This type of insidious manipulation of memory is an example of how the realities of the Holocaust can be distorted in a way that strips the event of its specifics and minimises its impact in the history of humanity.

As more time passes, as witnesses disappear, and as ritualised commemorations keep spreading around the world, this is one of the greatest didactic challenges educators must be prepared to handle when dealing with the history of the Holocaust. This history of systematic extermination and dehumanisation does not bring any simple answers, nor does it provide clear lessons and guidelines for the future. The Holocaust is not just a frame or a story providing formulas and solutions to deal with an uncertain present. Rather, it is a warning, with particular features and universal implications that can resonate in many parts of the world.

These challenges indicate that although the globalisation process of Holocaust remembrance carries standardised representations of the event conveyed by various media, educating and teaching about the Holocaust is not standardised practice. International organisations have a particular responsibility to facilitate exchanges of good practice and help interested countries and organisations find the methods best adapted to their local contexts. The diverse ways in which Europeans, Israelis, and North Americans are dealing and struggling with this daunting past cannot be generalised or transferred elsewhere. But in fact, in a globalised environment, the future orientations in Holocaust education also lie in the way non-European nations will tackle the subject, and the ways that educators will adapt methodologies and apply concepts to realities that are remote from its central, historical teaching focus.

From this point of view, the priority at this point is to assess better why and how the Holocaust is taught in countries that have no overt connections with the genocide and the history of the Jewish people. How does this history relate to the local preoccupations of policy makers in these countries? What pedagogies are being developed, and what messages conveyed in classrooms? In 2012, UNESCO launched a series of events—conferences, experts meetings and, more importantly, consultations—with member states in sub-Saharan Africa and Latin America that wish to engage further in Holocaust education. The overall impression that emerges from these discussions is that Holocaust education is seen as a meaningful starting point to address issues of both universal and local concern. These issues may be related to promoting human rights, cultural understanding, and tolerance, or, more particularly in societies struggling with a past of conflict or crimes against humanity, they may be a powerful tool to address a difficult and traumatic past. In these regions, as in European countries, Holocaust remembrance became internalised when the subject was re-appropriated. In societies not directly connected to the Holocaust, introducing issues of universal concern via Holocaust studies may actually lead to people reinvesting in local issues.

Holocaust Education as a Prism for National Memories

As we can see in the very region where it took place, the process of Holocaust education becoming internalised has not led to people holding a homogenised memory of the genocide. Indeed, the Holocaust is remembered against the historical background of the societies in which it is taught and the present challenges they face. But as a transnational subject, it may serve as a prism on the basis of which local traumatic issues can be addressed. As Assmann (2007, p. 14) explains,

...the Holocaust has not become a single universally shared memory, but it has become a paradigm or template through which other genocides and historical traumas are very often perceived and presented. The Holocaust has not thereby replaced other traumatic memories around the globe but has provided a language for their articulation.

In this respect, Holocaust education is first and foremost seen as a powerful tool of transformation in transitional periods. It is introduced as an opportunity to stimulate open debate about a history of discrimination or even crimes against humanity, and thus as an educational instrument to help reassess events of the past. Holocaust education therefore functions as a catalyst, providing a conceptual framework to refer to one's own history by interrogating contentious aspects of the past and facilitating the negotiation between conflicting narratives. Addressing the history of the Holocaust thus constitutes a method providing a safe environment to address local traumatic issues born of a conflicting past that have remained latent challenges in the society.

This dynamic appears clearly in the example of post-apartheid South Africa. Education about the Holocaust started informally in 1999 with the development of a private Holocaust Centre in Cape Town that was instrumental in raising awareness about the history of the Jewish people during World War II. This subject was integrated into the national curriculum in 2007. The South African Holocaust and Genocide Foundation, which supervises the activities of now three centres in Cape Town, Durban, and Johannesburg, is the pillar of Holocaust education in the country, providing educational materials and circulating exhibitions, and offering possibilities for professional development. According to its director, Richard Freedman (Fracapane and Haß 2014), its purpose in exploring of the history of the Holocaust is not to draw a direct comparison between the Holocaust and apartheid, which would quickly show its limitations, but to challenge local conceptions of racial prejudice inherited from the past through the exploration of a history far removed from immediate concerns in South Africa. Holocaust education in such a context is therefore seen as a tool for social transformation, both an exploration of the past, and a response to the immediate needs of the society.

In Argentina, the attention given to the history of the Holocaust was also determined by the agenda of the time. The growing awareness of this period of history corresponds to the process of democratisation in which several countries of the region engaged in the mid-1980s. Indeed, besides the fact that Argentina has hosted Nazi war criminals, and that it is home to a sizeable Jewish community including Holocaust survivors and their descendants, the authorities have looked at introducing the history of the Holocaust as a way to put Argentina's own history of oppression and crimes against humanity into perspective. Beyond the national level, this effort for remembrance has led Argentina to be the first—and only—Latin American member of the International Holocaust Remembrance Alliance and a leading actor in preventing genocide and mass atrocities in the region and beyond. In 2008, together with Switzerland and Tanzania, it launched a series of Regional Forums for the Prevention of Genocide (FDFA 2014), in order to raise awareness among United Nations member countries about the need to tackle this issue. Around the world, several other examples exist of situations in which the history of the Holocaust has been, or is being, introduced as a subject in its own right in the curriculum, with a view to it serving as a catalyst and a starting point to sensitise the audience to issues that afflict their own society.

Holocaust Education to Promote Human Rights and Contribute to Preventing Genocide

As clearly shown in a recent study performed for UNESCO's International Bureau of Education (Bromley and Garnett 2010), Holocaust education is more and more often assigned the task of sensitising students to injustice and to the need to promote and nurture human rights. The globalisation of Holocaust remembrance and education therefore comes with the idea that dealing with the Holocaust will be a tool to address local and global issues of prejudice and racism while supporting more active and responsible citizenry. This raises the question of whether educating about the Holocaust can serve the purpose of learning about human rights. The answer is mitigated: It should be hoped that educating about the Holocaust will help students make connections with their present life and the societies they live in, reflecting upon their own role as active citizens who can identify and address human rights issues. But at the same time, it is hardly possible to teach children how to uphold human rights solely on the basis of a study of the history of the Holocaust. As Monique Eckmann (2010, p. 13) puts it,

> Holocaust education can be a good starting point to confront human rights issues. But even if it seems difficult to learn *for* human rights in the context of Holocaust education, it is nevertheless crucial to learn a few things *about* human rights and learn *within a framework* of human rights.

In that regard, the learning environment is particularly important: upholding human rights through Holocaust education does not have the same signification in a western European country and a Central or Eastern African state. There is a huge discrepancy between dealing with matters of exclusion and intolerance in a peaceful, violence-free society, and dealing with issues of crimes against humanity in a post-conflict society. Furthermore, if the concept of human rights is taken in a broad sense, it may be quite difficult for educators to make the history of the Holocaust, the most extensive form of genocide, fit neatly with the everyday experience of children. In fact, if the only purpose of dealing with the Holocaust is to help children reflect on their daily life, then it might be better to just skip the subject. The Holocaust is a very distressing, unsettling topic, and will certainly not bring to pupils the sought-after answers regarding their daily experience. On the contrary, it raises mostly difficult questions about human nature and the use of power, and it questions some pillars of our modernity. It cannot be easily conveyed in the classroom as a reference or as a platform to illustrate or transmit values and to stress ethical lessons. To put it simply, a study of the Holocaust, wherever it takes place, should start with the Holocaust, without predetermined answers. Students who engage with this history should be enabled to make their own meaning out of the difficult questions and dilemmas it raises. From there, they may be able to connect with preoccupations that are closer to them and, from a larger perspective, to reflect about the causes of mass atrocities and what, in our present societies, can become sources of violence. In that regard, it is obvious that educating about the Holocaust, which is first and foremost the exploration of a complex history, cannot fulfil all the requirements of human rights education, but it certainly can serve as a primary step to raise awareness about core human rights issues and dilemmas, and to build bridges with present concerns and different histories.

This vision provides a direct and clear link with the terms of the 2005 UN resolution on Holocaust remembrance: education about the Holocaust can contribute to the prevention of genocide. Of course, such prevention relies on the multiplicity of parameters that will ensure that people create sustainable peace and inclusive and just societies based on respect for human rights and democratic practices. But according to this approach, disseminating knowledge about the Holocaust in all possible contexts, and introducing the subject of the Holocaust in education, can serve as tools, alongside, or as part of, the broader mandate of human rights education. In turn, those tools can raise awareness—globally—about the root causes of genocide and highlight the responsibilities that citizens, states, and civil societies bear to prevent it.

The Holocaust was not the first case of genocide, nor was it the last. But it does constitute a defining historical moment, first as the most extreme case of genocide ever perpetrated, and second because Nazi crimes gave rise to the definition of the concept of genocide and to the subsequent development of international legal instruments designed to prevent and punish genocide, starting with the 1948 Convention for the Prevention and the Punishment of the Crime of Genocide. In other words, it is an unavoidable starting point for studying the history of mass atrocities in a comparative fashion, so as to better understand similarities and differences between various historical cases of mass atrocities, and the legal categories that may define them. By the same token, studying the Holocaust from that perspective will help students identify the processes that may lead to the perpetration of genocidal violence. Teaching and learning about the Holocaust can thus relate strongly to the preoccupations of many policy makers across the globe who seek to promote peace and human rights through education in their countries.

References

Assmann, A. (2007). Europe: A community of memory? Twentieth annual lecture of the GHI. *Bulletin of the German Historical Institute, 40*, 11–25.
Bromley, P., & Garnett, S. R. (2010). The Holocaust as history and human rights: A cross-national analysis of Holocaust education in social science textbooks, 1970–2008. *Prospects, 40*(1), 153–173.
Eckmann, M. (2010). Exploring the relevance of Holocaust education for human rights education. *Prospects, 40*(1), 7–16.

FDFA [Federal Department of Foreign Affairs, Switzerland] (2014). *Genocide: Regional forums on the prevention of genocide*. Bern: FDFA. http://www.eda.admin.ch/eda/en/home/topics/peasec/peac/confre/genoci.html

Fracapane, K., & Haß, M. (2014). *Holocaust education in a global context*. Paris: UNESCO. http://unesdoc.unesco.org/images/0022/002259/225973e.pdf

Levy, D., & Sznaider, N. (2005). *The Holocaust and memory in the Global Age*. Philadelphia: Temple University Press.

Potel, J. -Y. (2009). *La fin de l'innocence: la Pologne face à son passé juif* [The end of innocence: Poland facing its Jewish past]. Paris: Autrement.

Rosenfeld, A. H. (2011). *The end of the Holocaust*. Bloomington: Indiana University Press.

Surmann, J. (2011). Restitution policy and the transformation of Holocaust memory: The impact of the American "crusade for justice" after 1989. *Bulletin of the German Historical Institute, 49*, 31–49.

UNESCO (2007, 1 November). *Holocaust remembrance*. General Conference resolution 34C/61. Paris: UNESCO.

UNGA [United Nations General Assembly] (2005, 1 November). *Holocaust remembrance*. UNGA resolution 60/7. New York: United Nations.

USDOS [United States Department of State] (1999). *Washington conference on Holocaust-era assets*. USDOS publication no. 10603. Washington, DC: USDOS Bureau of European Affairs.

Compliant Policy and Multiple Meanings: Conflicting Holocaust Discourses in Estonia

E. Doyle Stevick

After successfully declaring independence from Soviet rule just a decade earlier, Estonia witnessed a shift in geopolitics after September 11th, 2001, a shift that complicated its pursuit of security from its former master. The United States and its European allies began to approach Russia less as an ongoing Cold War threat to be contained than as a potential partner in what would be called the "global war on terror". This shift of focus meant that the United States and NATO's constituent countries would avoid antagonising Russia by pressuring it to confront, document, prosecute, and teach about the many crimes of the Soviet regime, of which Russia was the primary heir. After nearly a half century as its Cold War nemesis, Russia was once again an ally of the West, as it had been in defeating Nazi Germany, the lead perpetrator of the Holocaust.

Estonia was overrun by Soviet forces at the beginning of the war, and after a 3-year Nazi occupation, was ruled by the Soviet Union for nearly a half century. Estonia's incorporation into the Soviet Union is variously termed occupation and annexation on opposite sides of the border, a reflection of the continuing tensions over history and geopolitics, a pattern echoed recently in Crimea and Ukraine. Russia never did acknowledge Estonia's involuntary annexation into the USSR. Nor did it apologise for crimes committed in Estonia or against Estonians, prosecute any participants in those crimes, document the fates of many deported citizens, or provide reparations. While these outcomes would have been highly desirable for Estonia, most important for the country were long-term security in the form of NATO membership and access to European markets as part of the European Union. Indeed, as Estonia would come to understand quite profoundly, the standards demanded of a potential NATO and European Union member with marginal strategic

E.D. Stevick (✉)
College of Education, University of South Carolina,
318 Wardlaw Hall, Columbia, SC 29208, USA
e-mail: stevick@mailbox.sc.edu

© Springer International Publishing Switzerland 2015
Z. Gross, E.D. Stevick (Eds.), *As the Witnesses Fall Silent: 21st Century Holocaust Education in Curriculum, Policy and Practice*,
DOI 10.1007/978-3-319-15419-0_16

importance were significantly different from those expected from a critical superpower ally. Estonia would be pushed to confront the difficult aspects of its own history in ways that Russia would not be.

Many Estonians found it difficult to accept the conditions embedded in the accession processes for NATO and the European Union. The changes they demanded were not simply "good policy", or neutral practices to adopt, but instead reflected broader understandings of the world and of history that conflicted in profound ways with Estonians' own. Nowhere were these differences more evident than in the struggles over the meaning of the Holocaust in Europe.

This chapter is a sociocultural analysis of the ways in which education policy related to the Holocaust in Estonia was formulated and implemented. In this ongoing, normative process, creative agents navigate a policy terrain characterised by shifting power relations and continual negotiation of meanings. In the first two sections, I elaborate a sociocultural conception of policy, and then describe the research methods I used in applying this conception to Estonia's education policy on the Holocaust. In the third section, I begin to apply this conceptual framework to the unfolding of the policy, as reconstructed chronologically through the research, by addressing the goals of international engagement in domestic Holocaust issues, the ways in which power was leveraged to affect change in Estonia, and how meanings were negotiated in this context. In subsequent sections I address the multi-faceted nature of the normative discourse developed with the policy and the ways in which meanings and power were tested and contested in the implementation phase. Finally, I discuss how this policy serves as a good test case for elaborating the theory, and explore how it might be further refined.

Power, Meaning and Norms: The Sociocultural Analysis of Policy

As Guba (1984) observed, there are many different conceptions of policy, and each one has its own corresponding research focus. Some are narrowly focused on the legally ratified texts, while others are so broad as to seem almost without meaning, such as Dye's (1992) conception of policy as "what governments do or don't do" (p. 1). Guba (1984) categorised some of the common policy definitions into three domains: policy as intention, as action, and as experience (p. 65). These domains encompass everything from goals, strategies, and norms to outcomes. The field of implementation studies has, in Fowler's (2009) reckoning, worked through three generations: the first came to appreciate just how difficult implementation is, while the second sought to understand the roots of success and failure, and the third has grappled with the sheer complexity of policy, particularly in light of increasingly ambitious American policies about education (pp. 273–278).

These developments in understanding policy called attention to the need for deep, qualitative work that could make sense of the situated logic of policy within and across cultures, sites, and institutional structures. This work is essential to unravel the conundrum that is the commonplace deviation of implementation from design: anthropologists can "take on the complexity, ambiguity and messiness of policy processes" and "anthropological analysis can disentangle the outcomes and help explain how and why they often contradict the stated intentions of policymakers" (Wedel and Feldman 2005, p. 2). Indeed, this way of thinking is in direct contrast to most policy thinking, which is intrinsically "top-down". As Burawoy and Verdery (1999) explained, even though micro-level processes are often taken to be the by-products of macro-level forces, ethnographic approaches can begin to shed light on the ways that micro-level processes can transform and even constitute the macro-level forces (p. 3). Torney-Purta's (2000) insight about the political socialisation process applies equally well to policy: "scholars need to move beyond a narrow view of outcomes and inputs... taking a more complex, reciprocal, and situated view" (p. 94).

In particular, the advances in understanding education policy and implementation have created a need to fundamentally reconceptualise policy in ways that regard the broad range of implementation as normal rather than simply as aberration, deviance, or resistance. The critical ethnographic study of education policy has made important strides in the past decade, in large part due to the work of Levinson and Sutton (2001)—later joined by Theresa Winstead—in theorising policy as a sociocultural practice of power.

Levinson et al. (2009) see the study of policy unfolding from an uncritical and theory-bereft technocratic examination of whether a policy worked as designed, to an explicitly normative and critical orientation focused upon power, inequality, and domination (pp. 768–769). They introduce a sociocultural lens "to inspire democratic dialogue, and to foster and empower participatory agency in the democratic production of policy" (p. 769). Thus, in their conception, policy scholarship is both analytic and normative, a potential contributor to a broader liberatory project, a potential force for deepening democracy. While these authors are willing to entertain broader conceptions of democracy, they bypass democratic outcomes in favor of a process-centred conception focused upon broader participation by marginalised groups, with some attention as well to open dialogue.

The sociocultural lens contributes a focus upon culture and its relation to the production of norms in a context of power. The authors argue that "the most immediate product of the policy process should be understood as a normative cultural discourse" (p. 771). This discourse involves "the negotiation of meaning [which] is always a part of policy formation"; that is, "the process of normative cultural production requires an active negotiation of meaning" (p. 779).

In an era of globalisation and transnational governing entities such as the European Union, when power shifts to varying degrees beyond the boundaries of the state itself, the normative cultural discourse may be multifaceted, addressing multiple audiences. In such contexts, policy as an act of power may simultaneously contest meanings internationally while conveying different normative messages nationally and locally. When power imbalances suffuse the policy process, the normative cultural discourse must take account not only of public discourse, but also of private discourse, of the explicit as well as the implicit, and—to borrow Dye's phrase—what governments say and what they don't say.

Taken together, these varied forms of discourse constitute what Spillane, Reiser, and Reimer (2002) call "policy signals". Such signals must be interpreted, consciously and unconsciously, and those in the policy chain who are aware of the potential ambiguity of such signals may decide to test their interpretations explicitly by further contesting their meanings publicly, or implicitly by appropriating the policy, in what Levinson and Sutton (2001) termed policy as practice.

The concept of appropriation is helpful to understand how conflicts over meaning can play out in separate contexts, as the meanings shift. Levinson and Sutton (2001) define appropriation as "an active process of cultural production through borrowing, recontextualising, remolding, and thereby resignifying cultural forms". They say it "emphasizes the agency of local actors in interpreting and adapting [resources] to the situated logic in their contexts of everyday practice" (p. 17, fn. 2).

This process "gets at the way individuals… engage in situated behaviors that are both constrained and enabled by existing structures, but which allow the person to exercise agency in the emerging situation" (Levinson and Sutton 2001, p. 3). The concept is powerful in part because it helps us to understand the full range of responses not merely as failures of implementation, but rather as parts of "a complex social practice, an ongoing process of normative cultural production, constituted by diverse actors across diverse social and institutional contexts" (p. 1). To research policy effectively across different institutional contexts, appropriate research methods are needed.

Research Methods

This chapter stems from a larger research project I conducted into the policy and practice of civic education in post-Soviet Estonia. I sought to follow the flow of resources, ideas, and methods between international forums and local classroom practices, with a particular focus on the nature of international influences on education policy and classroom teaching in this area. To achieve these ends, I adopted multi-sited ethnographic research (Marcus 1995) as an approach, participating in and observing international conferences and meetings related to civic education throughout Estonia, from university conferences to teacher-training seminars and meetings of local teachers associations. To supplement these observations, I conducted interviews with key figures in the field—including textbook authors, curriculum developers, university professors, and officials of non-governmental organisations (NGOs)—in Estonia and the Baltic States more broadly. Between September 2001 and December 2004, to gain a sense of the broader context, I attended civic education and history classes regularly in five schools with six different teachers, across urban and rural, and elite and low-performing contexts, with frequent visits to other schools around the country.

During August of 2002, near the end of my first full year in Estonia, the Holocaust emerged as a controversial topic across the country, and especially in education.

Though it had not been an anticipated area of focus, it marked a fascinating case study of international attempts to influence domestic education in areas with civic implications, with the added interest and complexity that it engaged institutions beyond the education sector. Qualitative research often provides the flexibility to respond to emergent issues and trends, and the issue of Holocaust education became a focus of my work and interviews during 2003–2004. I have monitored the politics of the Holocaust and memory regularly since that time, conducting additional interviews, and reviewing newspaper coverage of the Holocaust and education from the adoption of the policy to the present. My broader research in civic education generally allowed me to locate the case of Holocaust education in Estonia within the broader contexts of foreign involvement in domestic education, contemporary geopolitics, and domestic relations between the Russian minority and the Estonian majority.

I organised the data chronologically to map out the unfolding of Estonia's adoption of a day to commemorate the Holocaust in schools. I then integrated these data with the broader coverage of the issue within Estonia's major newspapers and professional education publications in order to develop a broader picture of the policy context. Given the complexity of this policy, I distinguish between the international level, particularly the foreign pressure to adopt such a policy and the contested meanings at that level, and the national level, where the normative national discourse was constructed.

Prelude to a Holocaust Education Policy in Estonia: Foreign Goals

Estonia's 2002 decision to adopt a policy to commemorate Holocaust victims in schools must be understood in its international context, because it would never have been adopted without international pressure. Foreign groups concerned about the Holocaust in Central and Eastern Europe had six general priorities. These spanned some less challenging tasks, including acknowledgment of guilt, apology for crimes, and commemoration of the victims, and two considerably more difficult ones: restitution, and prosecuting perpetrators. The other two aims lay in between: documenting the events—rewriting the historical narrative—and education—particularly writing new textbooks (Zuroff 2009, p. 100).

From among these six goals, education about the Holocaust was one of the three prioritised goals; the other two included prosecuting Nazi war criminals and Holocaust perpetrators and commemorating Holocaust victims. Even these three were emphasised differently depending on the organisation in question. For example, in a newspaper column, the then US ambassador, Joseph Michael DeThomas (2002), proposed three "modest steps": prosecute those who had committed crimes, recognise that the Holocaust was part of Estonia's history, and teach children about it. However, Efraim Zuroff, the "Nazi hunter" of the Simon Wiesenthal Center (SWC), advocated for a Holocaust memorial day and noted that when there are no longer living Nazis to prosecute, the Wiesenthal Center would shift its efforts to education about the Holocaust (Online Intervjuud 2002).

Because the Holocaust-related efforts of the US government and Zuroff himself were occurring in the same period with some shared priorities, the public had no particular reason to see them as distinct, to distinguish between their stated priorities, or to keep as separate their different approaches to diplomacy. Three participants in an online interview with Zuroff (Online Intervjuud 2002) expressed their concern that his activism might threaten Estonia's chances to enter NATO. The first inquired, "Why have you come out with your statements against Estonia and the Baltic States this year, is it related to the fact that on this fall Estonia can be invited to NATO?" A second asked, "If the Estonian government doesn't prosecute and punish these alleged war criminals to SWC's satisfaction, will you or SWC lobby any or all NATO member countries (officially or unofficially) against Estonia's admission into NATO or the EU?" The third posed this question: "Does your organisation have an official opinion about Estonia's possible membership in the NATO and EU? What do you personally think of this matter?" These questions show a broader pattern: Estonians perceived the pressure to confront the Holocaust as a threat to their national security. Unfortunately, the Soviet Union, although condemning the Nazis as fascists, made no effort to challenge Nazi (or other) antisemitism, and anyone who had accepted the ideas of global Jewish conspiracy theories or the Judeo-Bolshevik myth could infer support for their views in the foreign effort to address the Holocaust.

Sometimes the aims of foreign advocates conflicted with one another. Zuroff noted that "restitution can go on forever, to the grandchildren and great-grandchildren. I'm very much against it because it squanders moral capital. We don't study the Holocaust because it was grand larceny; we study it because it was genocide" (Click 2010). Indeed, the pursuit of restitution and of justice can exacerbate another major concern: antisemitism in the region. Zuroff acknowledged that antisemitic "incidents themselves are very often sparked by fights over restitution and prosecution of local criminals" (Click 2010). Sensitivity to, if not fear of, this backlash of rising antisemitism sometimes put small, local Jewish communities at odds with international attempts to prosecute Holocaust perpetrators.

The ethnic majority often conflated Holocaust-related goals, and objections or obstacles to any one of them could inhibit progress on the other issues. The perception among many Estonians that both commemoration and potential prosecutions seemed to imply a hierarchy of victims was most troublesome for educational improvements regarding the Holocaust because both cases elevated what had been a small minority within the country while seemingly degrading Estonians. While deeply held national views about justice and commemoration significantly hindered a broad embrace of Estonia's Holocaust policy, Zuroff argued that, had the barriers to a successful prosecution been overcome, the educational value of a trial would have been unparalleled: "We firmly believe that one of the best ways to teach about the history of the Holocaust is to see to it that the criminals are put on trial in the countries in which they committed their crimes or in their countries of origin. These trials are the best history lesson imaginable" (Online Intervjuud 2002). Certainly, the trial of Adolph Eichmann marked a turning point in Israel's knowledge of and attitudes towards the Holocaust (Gross 2010).

Although a number of different groups and institutions made efforts in Estonia to advance issues surrounding the Holocaust, Zuroff was the first and most visible, and later efforts were often seen through the lens of his work there. He launched Operation Last Chance to identify and to prosecute individual Holocaust perpetrators before they died off. In Estonia, a public accustomed to collective accusations of fascism during the Soviet period had been quickly inflamed by misrepresentations of Zuroff's meaning and intentions in a major headline during 2001 that read "Nazi-hunter Accuses Estonian Nation of Murders" (Zuroff 2009, p. 127). Such misinterpretations and misunderstandings further complicated what was already a daunting task.

Power, Policy Signals, and What It Means to Be Democratic

Spillane et al. (2002) argued that "what a policy means for implementing agents is constituted in the interaction of their existing cognitive structures (including knowledge, beliefs, and attitudes), their situation, and the policy signals" (p. 388). While their conceptualisation made a critical contribution to domestic policy research in the United States, its application to a transnational policy arena requires a broader conception of "policy signals" to include those transmitted by foreign groups or institutions that deploy power to pursue their ends. In other words, such deployments of power, whether as carrot or stick, must be understood as policy signals not just in the implementation stage, but in the policy formation stage itself. As Levinson et al. (2009) noted, "policy formation is best conceived as a practice of wielding power" (p. 771), and if the power in question transcends the domestic arena, then it is necessary to consider the "positive and negative sanctions, that is, a set of statements about how things should or must be done, with corresponding inducements or punishments" (p. 771).

The policy signals that NATO sent to Estonia were not ambiguous. In the aftermath of September 11th, 2001, for example, the Baltic States could have reasonably expected pressure to contribute troops to Afghanistan; incidentally, many of their men had been sent to Afghanistan as involuntary conscripts among the Soviet forces beginning in 1979. Similarly, force readiness, weapons procurement, and the like might be expected to earn membership in a military alliance. When the Baltic States gathered at the Stockholm Security conference, however, Heather Conley, US Deputy Assistant Secretary of State for European and Eurasian Affairs, praised their progress, but told them that

> ... all the NATO aspirants need to do more to better prepare themselves for membership so that they are ready and able to contribute to European security in tangible ways. For the Baltic States, this means hard work—not just words but concrete action—on complex domestic issues like dealing with the history of the Holocaust. It means tackling the difficult task of fully integrating ethnic Russian-speakers into society—despite significant political cost. (Embassy of the United States in Estonia 2002)

In this statement, Conley readily acknowledged that these tasks would not be popular; in a democratic society, "significant political cost" can mean losing elections. It was a tacit acknowledgment that though the government action in these related arenas—i.e., policy—was adopted by a democratically elected government, it would run counter to the democratic will of the governed. The policy signal to the Baltic States implicitly ranked priorities: acting on the Holocaust and the Russian minority in ways favored by NATO countries, particularly the United States, was more important than either democratic policy processes or national sovereignty in domestic affairs. This was a strong claim to make on a country whose independence had been restored scarcely a decade before, after a half century of Soviet hegemony.

For Estonia, the stakes could not have been higher; many in the Baltic States felt threatened by Russia and believed that the Soviets had perpetrated genocide upon the Baltic States. Membership in NATO was the only clear safeguard against continuing Russian designs on the Baltic States and its meddling in domestic affairs on behalf of the Russian minorities there. This was not the impossibly bad choice Estonians had faced when they were trapped between the Nazi and Soviet regimes, but it was an unappealing and paradoxical one: to secure a democratic future for Estonia, the government would have to act strongly against the democratic will of its people. The message was not misconstrued, and a blogger articulated it quite clearly: "Holocaust day is the entry-ticket for NATO" (Mauri 2003).

Critical ethnographic or sociocultural approaches to education policy are explicitly normative and committed to broader participation in the policy process, along with open dialogue, yet, this case reveals both the complexity of democratisation and the problems of relying on a process-centred conception of democracy. Levinson et al. (2009) argue that "a practice of power may be more or less democratic, depending on the ways that power elites are formed and legitimated, or the ways that other social groups may participate in policy formation" (pp. 771–772). People may claim to value broader participation in general, but what if its outcomes are undemocratic? Richard Holbrooke, then a US assistant secretary of state, captured this problem well when the 1996 elections in Bosnia were imminent: "Suppose the election was declared free and fair [and that those elected are] racists, fascists, separatists, who are publicly opposed to [peace and reintegration]. That is the dilemma" (Zakaria 1997).

Can power be used to impose democratising practices against the will of the governed? In many contexts, Holocaust education can make a clear and documented contribution to civic education, and to efforts to teach anti-racism and inclusion (Stevick and Gross 2010). Civic education is imposed upon children, involuntarily, through the mandate of the state, and adults raised in subjugated societies were denied that democratically adopted opportunity. What does it mean to be democratic in a post-authoritarian context?

The problem is more acute still in the European Union, which as a transnational, democratic institution must contend with the problem of what Dennis Thompson (1999) calls "overlapping majorities". This case is a perfect illustration of the problem: "if the majority of Europeans strongly support a Holocaust Education Day policy, and a strong majority of Estonians oppose it, which majority should guide the country's policy?" (Stevick 2009, p. 44). What additional criteria would help to evaluate whether a certain policy choice better fulfilled democratic criteria in a small, post-authoritarian state in the European Union in a context of globalisation? Certainly, one such criterion would be open deliberation about a policy.

Holocaust Policy as Normative Discourse: Negotiating Meaning

The formation of policy involves not just deploying power but also negotiating meaning, ideally through open discussion or debate. In this situation, power imbalances functioned to suppress open discussion and debate over the Holocaust and its meanings, which undermined the possibilities of an open exchange of perspectives and evidence-based debates, and thus of successful and meaningful policy implementation. The high sanctions attached to engagement with the Holocaust generated a dramatic split between public and private discourse, a distinction that a robust sociocultural theory about education policy must take into account. When officials in the policy process are significantly constrained in their speech, then public discourse must be analysed not simply for its explicit statements, but for its selective silences, its deliberate ambiguity, its selectivity in medium, and "the ways in which symbolic forms intersect with relations of power" (Thompson 1990, as cited by Levinson et al. 2009, p. 775). To borrow Dye's formulation, governments construct policy as a normative discourse through what they say and don't say.

This particular public/private schism was familiar from Soviet times: Aarelaid-Tart (2003) described "The formation of ambivalent double-mindedness", which "made it possible for" Baltic peoples "to cherish the values of the oppressed private sphere while acting in accordance with the firmly restricted public sphere, thus diminishing the mental influence of the oppression of alien power" (p. 216). The assertiveness of foreign powers on domestic issues of education and commemoration thus had an unpleasant and familiar resonance. If, during the Soviet period, people had learned to pay lip service to unwelcome, official state positions, while doing what they felt appropriate whenever they perceived the latitude to do so, this adaptive practice and mentality remained available as a cultural resource for Estonians to draw upon when faced with new and unwanted foreign impositions.

In the period leading up to the announcement of a Holocaust policy, Zuroff was highly visible in Estonia. The Estonian International Commission for the Investigation of Crimes Against Humanity, which also researched both Soviet occupations, published its results on the Nazi period; hoping that any living perpetrators might still be brought to justice, Zuroff pursued its claim that evidence documented Estonian participation in a reported massacre in Belarus. His efforts went nowhere. Zuroff (2002) submitted an editorial to a leading Estonian paper for 7 August, 2002, the anniversary of the killings, and strongly criticised the lack of will to prosecute Estonian perpetrators of the Holocaust; he also advocated for a day of commemoration that would symbolically acknowledge the seriousness of the crimes and Estonians' complicity in them. Estonian officials pre-empted this publication by announcing the day before that they had "named January 27—the anniversary of the liberation of the Auschwitz-Birkenau Nazi concentration camp—as official Holocaust Day" (City Paper's Baltics Worldwide 2002). The choice of the day was quite significant symbolically in the struggle over the meaning of the Holocaust, a fact that became clear years later when Zuroff (2005) described his own involvement in lobbying the government on this issue:

> ... 27 January, which has no ostensible link whatsoever to the history of the Holocaust in Estonia since no Estonian Jews were deported to Auschwitz. In fact, Estonian officials rejected a suggestion by the Simon Wiesenthal Center that they choose either 20 January, the date of the infamous Wannsee Conference in 1942, at which the implementation of the Final Solution was discussed and Estonia was declared Judenrein [free of Jews], or 7 August, the date on which the 36th Estonian Security Battalion murdered Jews in Nowogrudok, Belarus.

Estonian officials had acceded to foreign pressure, but in a way that contested (at least some of) the meaning that the policy was intended to have. The date they selected distanced Estonia, Estonia's Jews, and Estonian perpetrators from the crimes of the Holocaust, and, by emphasising Auschwitz, downplayed the complicity of some Central Europeans.

Despite the international emphasis on the Holocaust from NATO and Zuroff's high visibility, Estonia's prime minister at the time, Siim Kallas, denied that the measure was adopted because of foreign pressure; he stated that the timing was simply a coincidence, and that the policy was adopted unanimously by the government ministers (Kalamees 2002). However incredulous Estonians might have been over such a claim, it was likely a political necessity, given their deep resentment of foreign interference in domestic matters. For example, in a June 2003 interview, a former prime minister of Estonia told me this:

> I would not support it. During my government, I would not allow it. Mostly it feels like it is coming from outside so it is not helping.... The communist terror took more lives than the Holocaust. It must be combined with crimes against humanity.

His argument pairs a claim about the relative importance of the Holocaust (using the criterion of sheer numbers killed) with the critique of its foreign imposition. He insisted, notably, that the Holocaust must not be treated independently as a subject worthy of attention in its own right: the implications of singling out the Holocaust as unique or distinct were apparently too threatening.

Those promoting Holocaust education from abroad carry with them a very specific set of meanings and intentions that are to be implicit in the programmes, policies, or materials adopted within the target country. These include the ideas that the Holocaust was an unprecedented event, worthy of study on its own, and that members of the titular majority participated in systematic killings of Jews and others in Estonia and abroad. Estonians who were willing to consider Holocaust education at all often did so while rejecting these premises, in order to advance local needs and concerns. Consider the transformation of meaning implicit in the following account from a leading education official in a November 2004 interview:

> The Swedish Institute just came to Estonia. They wanted to create a relationship and start a Holocaust program, a tolerance program and I know from Latvian colleagues that they were very successful in Latvia and I really just supported their idea because, as it worked in Latvia, it is important for us, too, because all the questions of violence in the classrooms and at school and tolerance and it's all very much related, and we know what it means to be tolerant, but how to teach it, just methods or models or something we have to learn.

In other words, Holocaust education was a means to the ends of tolerance education and of combating school violence. The Holocaust was not framed as an event of intrinsic importance to the future citizens of Estonia. This self-identified outspoken advocate for Holocaust education was interested in appropriating Holocaust education primarily to serve such national interests as reducing school violence. Local purposes guided the approach to a resource that had been promoted externally for a related, yet distinct, set of purposes, with profoundly different meanings attached.

Compliance, Discourse, and the Reconstruction of Policy Signals

The adoption of the day of Holocaust commemoration seemingly acknowledged its significance as an event worthy of focused attention, even while the officials involved sought to downplay that significance. More precisely, the government attempted to convey to the international audience its compliance with what it perceived to be the required orthodox view, while communicating a very different message domestically. In effect, Estonian officials began to construct a new set of policy signals to counter the meanings of the policy signals that had been sent by transnational institutions like the Council of Europe and NATO. The prime minister sought some cover by invoking former Minister of Education Tõnis Lukas, who had signed on to the Council of Europe convention at its October, 2000 meeting of ministers of education (Kalamees 2002).

The reference was notable because Lukas created a stir just days after signing the convention: he argued that a Holocaust day did not make any sense for Estonian schools and that he saw no reason to change the curriculum or provide special training to pay special attention to the Holocaust (Lukas 2000). He continued to note that the declaration he had signed was not binding, and so the Estonian government would be free to decide whether or not to make it mandatory. By referring to Lukas, Kallas evoked another government's similar action, deflecting criticism for the decision by citing a precedent while denying that it had been adopted under foreign pressure; he also evoked the level of commitment that Lukas had articulated without having to voice such sentiments directly. Indeed, the notion of choice that Lukas articulated would be employed as both a policy mechanism and a policy signal.

Given the high stakes for deviating from the Western European discourse on the Holocaust, the normative discourse constituted by the open, public use of language was carefully constructed. As the prime minister noted about the Holocaust, "this was one of the most horrific crimes in human history" (Kalamees 2002). This formulation does not exclude the deportations of Estonians, and other Soviet crimes; thus it implicitly permits the Holocaust to be recognised alongside Estonian suffering, but does not suggest a meaningful distinction.

This inclusive way of referring to the Holocaust using broader terms like "genocide" or "crimes against humanity" implicitly rejects the international contention that the Holocaust was unique, and Estonian officials have used it consistently in their discourse since that time. A characteristic example is Foreign Minister Urmas Paet's speech on 14 May, 2010, at the opening of Estonia's Museum of Occupation exhibit on 900 French Jews who were sent to Estonia to be killed. He emphasises Estonia's progressive interwar policies towards Jews, the fact that Estonia was occupied, and the Soviet deportation of Estonia's Jews—but did not acknowledge Estonians' participation in Holocaust atrocities. The inclusive language allows him implicitly to frame Estonians exclusively as fellow victims of atrocities:

> In 1945 this horrendous chapter of history ended, but the crimes against humanity perpetrated during World War II still require our attention. We must work together in the name of getting archives opened to everyone, increasing peoples' awareness of what happened, and making sure that these crimes against humanity are never repeated. (Paet 2010, para. 6)

While language associated with complicity seems to have changed little since 2001, terms used to identify the victims have. Indeed, while the controversy surrounding Zuroff in 2003 generated a discourse that "suggested that the titular population did not consider the Jews a part of Estonian history" (Weiss-Wendt 2008, p. 485), Paet repeatedly used terms that embrace Jews as part of Estonian society both historically and today ("the Estonian Jewish community", "Estonian citizens of Jewish faith", and "Estonian Jews") rather than as distinct from it. Jews from the Baltic States were still often framed as others.

Ambiguous language was a technique used to navigate two widely disparate worldviews or meaning systems, using the same language to convey very different messages or policy signals. Levinson et al. (2009) note that policy as a normative discourse "also crucially presupposes an implicit view of how things are—a model of the world, an operative cosmology, as it were" (p. 771). This case reveals that such discourse can simultaneously sustain multiple conflicting cosmologies.

In 2006, the foreign ministry released a statement about the Holocaust, articulating the goal that "the crimes of the last century will never be repeated" and noting further that "the Ministry of Education and Science called on all Estonian schools to explain to students the tragic events of the last century" (Estonian Ministry 2006). In one semantic field, among the audience addressed by this English-language document, the signifier of "tragic events of the last century" would lead this audience to understand those "tragic events" simply as an alternative way to reference the Holocaust. The quote from the Ministry of Education, however, was taken from an Estonian-language summons addressed to teachers, and in that semantic field the signifier is meant to include the trials that Estonians faced under Soviet hegemony. Indeed, when the time for the first Holocaust Day approached, "in a circular sent to the schools in the fall", Education Minister Mailis Rand "noted that not only the Nazi crimes against Jews but also all other victims persecuted for ethnic, racial, religious, and political reasons should be remembered" (Baltic States Report 2003).

This coded use of language for different audiences did not represent an attempt to openly contest the meanings of foreign Holocaust advocates. Instead, it constituted a rhetorical strategy that permitted the government to navigate a context of power without compromising its own views or alienating its constituencies. Thus, it enabled parallel systems of meaning to coexist by seeming to affirm foreign views while conveying policy signals consistent with broadly held domestic understandings. The government was, in effect, creating space for its citizens to operate with their own views.

Because policy is a form of normative discourse—yet the government also feels it necessary to enable incompatible worldviews to coexist, a constraint that inhibits free expression—how can it fashion policy signals that convey the necessary specific but multiple meanings? Above, we have seen the use of deliberately ambiguous language across different semantic fields, the varied deployment of broadly accessible English and the relatively impermeable Estonian language, and the careful selection of the media through which messages are conveyed. Elsewhere I have emphasised the symbolic role of anniversaries, particularly the potential meanings for Estonians—but not foreigners—of announcing the adoption of a Holocaust commemoration day on the anniversary of the Soviet Union's formal annexation of Estonia (Stevick 2007, pp. 225–226). Two additional such strategies for developing clear policy signals merit attention here: selective silences, and the design of the policy itself.

Two prominent sets of silences are notable in this policy context. While the second emerged later in the policy process as a different form of communication, the first involved the rationalisations for adopting the policy that were presented to Estonians. There was no attempt to justify the policy on the grounds that the Holocaust had any intrinsic importance worthy of attention in its own right. The prime minister spoke of adopting the view of the international community that the Holocaust merited special attention, while being careful to emphasise that such attention was confined to a single day (Kalamees 2002).

The Ministry of Education released a statement that "its observance would foster understanding of genocide"—the broad term, inclusive of Estonians' self-understanding—"and would underline 'as an important foreign policy factor, solidarity with the European and trans-Atlantic community'" (City Paper's Baltics Worldwide 2002). The justification for the policy emphasised its adoption, rather than its content, and in both cases it specifically referred to belonging to Europe and the trans-Atlantic community, phrases sure to evoke Estonia's broader goals of

European Union and NATO membership. Through its publicly offered rationales, the government made no effort to legitimise the content of the decision, but sought to shift the focus on issues of security, establishing the Holocaust policy not as a worthy end in itself, but as a justified means to much more important ends.

As noted above, policy can be understood as "a normative cultural discourse with positive and negative sanctions, that is, a set of statements about how things should or must be done, with corresponding inducements or punishments" (Levinson et al. 2009, p. 771). NATO was perceived as conveying the importance of the Holocaust by using a negative sanction of great weight: the prospect of gaining security and independence through membership. On the other hand, those designing the policy of adopting a Holocaust day used the opposite approach: they signaled its insignificance by attaching no positive or negative sanction to its implementation. In case the failure to justify the policy and to create an enforcement mechanism failed to send a clear message (or policy signal), those presenting the policy emphasised that schools and teachers would have complete discretion in how (or whether) to carry out the policy. Indeed, "the selective deployment of choice mechanisms" (Stevick 2011, p. 191) more or less undermined any possibility that the policy would amount to anything substantive in practice.

The decision to employ a choice mechanism has two salient features in this context, and both contradict the notion that expanding choice is a means of increasing freedom or agency. First, the general opposition among Estonians to the Holocaust Education Day policy was so widespread that it took little guesswork to determine what choices would be made; under such circumstances, when choice is more or less predictable, there is little distinction between providing choice and simply legislating the predictable outcome. In other words, granting choice when the outcome is more or less predictable is essentially a form of policy fiat (Stevick 2011). Second, in those rare cases when teachers or schools would go against the grain, it positions them in opposition to the majority of their peers and compels them to function as advocates for a policy whose content no one in the national government will openly endorse. Since lessons provided to classes about a tremendously controversial issue can hardly be kept secret from fellow teachers, the choice mechanism forces them to justify their decisions to a broader group that is likely to be strongly opposed. Such an approach hardly represents free choice, but rather leverages peer pressure to contain potential deviance from the norm.

The points I have discussed thus far may all be subsumed under the umbrella of policy formation, though the transnational dynamics of the process suggest a more complex process, one that requires further theorising. Indeed, an international policy context of normative discourse with overwhelming inducements and punishments coerced compliance without conviction; the national government appropriated Holocaust policy ends as the means to desired memberships, while constructing an elaborate, yet largely unspoken, discourse to create a secure space to allow the national cosmology to endure unthreatened. In so doing, they left a vacuum in the discourse about the explicit content of the policy and questions about their intent to apply governmental authority to compel implementation.

Testing the Waters: Interpreting Policy Signals on Power and Content

Because Estonia developed policies in a complex international geopolitical context while seeking membership in NATO and the European Union, both its national government and its school directors were middle links in an extended policy chain, adjusting to the tension applied on both ends. Prominent Estonian school leaders, responding to a policy for which no attempt to build consensus had been made, contributed significantly to the explicit public normative discourse about the policy, while simultaneously gauging the potential use of power in the process.

Just 3 days after the policy was announced, Lauri Leesi (2002), the Estonian principal of the prestigious French lyceum and a public intellectual, directed his concerns to other educators in a professional newsletter: schools might find themselves teaching the Holocaust to kindergartners; children are not mature enough to deal with concepts like "fascism, communism, and genocide"; and the short school calendar is already marked with enough "special days". A few days later, Leesi told a reporter that "personally I do not consider it necessary since I certainly do not know of any graduate of our school who doesn't know what the Holocaust is" (Oolo 2002). Implicit in this statement is a normative assertion about what Estonia's students should know about the Holocaust, and it is limited to a simple knowledge of what the term represents. He does not entertain the possibility that there is more to be learned from studying the Holocaust. Ott Ojaveer, the director of Hugo Treffner, Tartu's most elite public high school, extended this critique, apparently seeing a focus on the Holocaust as competing with the Estonian nation's own historical suffering:

> One should not over exaggerate some historical events and Estonia should not highlight the Holocaust over the most important events to its own people… the Estonian people should not forget… what has happened to the Estonian nation, and in particular the memory of these crimes should just be the most important to us. (Oolo 2002)

Rein Eglon, the director of the Pärnu Koidula gymnasium, went the furthest, voicing an opinion he acknowledged to be problematic. Though relatively commonplace in the Baltic States, it is nevertheless startling to the Western ear: "The Holocaust is not the kind of event that the Estonian nation should commemorate… Russia's violence against the Estonian nation—with all of their deportation and repression—was much more crazy" (Oolo 2002). Together, these three prominent school directors developed the normative discourse around the content of the policy that the prime minister and Ministry of Education had avoided.

These three leading school directors did not limit their public statements to content, however, but instead tested the ministry's willingness to enforce an unpopular policy. Leesi (2002), for example, initially noted approvingly that the ministry would not compel schools to follow any practice, but later shifted his focus: "If someone from above orders me how to do it, then my job is only to obey" (Oolo 2002). With this statement, he challenged the ministry to compel him to act, implying that the existence of the policy was insufficient on its own to spur compliance. Rhetorically, it positioned the Ministry of Education in a position akin to that of the Soviet state: able to force unwilling compliance. Put another way, he was seeking reassurance that he had correctly interpreted the policy signals providing freedom not to act. Similarly, Ojaveer praised the ministry for giving educators a free hand, while Eglon indicated that he would comply if he had to.

In the processes of co-constructing a normative discourse through negotiating meaning about the content of the Holocaust Day policy and of interpreting the policy signals sent by the ministry, the principals had created a context in which the ministry could either rebuke them for their positions and challenge their interpretations publicly, or let those views stand unchallenged as the dominant public discourse on the subject. The ministry was silent, implicitly affirming the publicly circulating meanings of the policy content as well as the intention not to enforce compliance (Stevick 2011).

Not all principals were as prominent or felt the same level of confidence to speak out on the issue. Other principals contacted by the media in the days leading up Holocaust Day indicated a range of intentions. The director of the Sõle Gymnasium, Õie Raudmägi, apparently used a more participatory, and democratic, decision-making process that was obedient to the mandated curriculum, rather than simply to the policy per se: "[The Holocaust] is a mandatory part of the history curriculum. Together with the history teachers, we decided that each one of them should talk about this theme in their own history class" (Tooming 2003). The others who were willing to go on the record indicated a range of different intentions (discussed in Stevick 2009), substantiating the emphasis on appropriation in sociocultural analyses of policy, the diverse ways in which situated local actors interpret policies across parallel social sites (Levinson et al. 2009, p. 789) as part of the individual and collective sense-making that characterises the policy implementation process (Spillane et al. 2002, p. 388; Levinson et al. 2009, p. 773).

The normative discourse surrounding the Holocaust policy, which had both international and national dimensions, developed in a context characterised at the first level by strong punishments and sanctions for deviating from so-called international norms and opinion. In their public discourse, principals in the national arena generally took a deferential stance towards the ministry and its authority while a number adamantly critiqued the policy content. Estonia was a country whose authoritarian legacy included a stark distinction between public and private discourse, and this distinction played out in the more private discourse among peers. This discourse can best be understood through the concept of community of practice, which has analytic value "as a construct that can illuminate what happens when policy is formulated and what happens when it gets appropriated" (Levinson et al. 2009, p. 780). Characterised by "mutual engagement, joint enterprise, and shared repertoire" (p. 780), the community of practice is a critical arena for negotiating meaning and establishing norms; here, it helps to illustrate the split between the public and private discourses that together shape policy appropriation and practice. In an interview, a national curriculum specialist working with 30 school directors explained how they sought to understand how the first Holocaust Day was conducted in 2003:

> We asked them to get the information from another school: to ask how it was spent and what people were thinking about the Holocaust Day. People were very bitter, most of the people in their responses were very direct and honest, saying that this is not the day that [should be] celebrated in Estonian schools, and not in a nice way. But public opinion and the opinion of teachers and head directors was that this came from outside... and among these thirty answers, we had zero responses that this was an important day that we need to have in our school system.

Not surprisingly, teachers who were comfortable speaking publicly to the media echoed the distaste for the planned Holocaust Day; several from Pärnu, quoted by Nielson (2003), concisely articulated a representative arsenal of objections:

> I think that Holocaust Day is only an activity for activity's sake, nothing more.
> The Soviet occupation interests students more, because they have more connections with this, more relatives were deported.
> You shouldn't traumatise a child with description of this, how a baby was thrown into the air as target practice, the idea of history is not to shock youth. Rather on this day we should emphasise the danger of all types of violence.
> This is foolish, I'm not going to make the students march or do something else on Holocaust Day; this could destroy the history class.
> Let every nation commemorate its own day of mourning.

The Holocaust Day activities in schools, as might be surmised, did not align with the vision of international advocates. There was no evidence of a substantial shift in general public knowledge about the Holocaust or in overall attitudes about it. Indeed, as Estonia was formally admitted to the European Union and NATO, attention to the issue gradually subsided. During my interviews on a return visit during 2006, an official noted that "Basically, Holocaust Day does not exist in Estonia". In 2007 and 2008, 27 January fell on a weekend, disrupting any significant practices that may have taken root. Since that time, the Holocaust has remained entangled with contemporary struggles between Russia and Estonia, particularly over commemorations, the politics of history, and the Russian-speaking minorities in Estonia. But with Estonia firmly ensconced in NATO and the European Union, the immediate heat of foreign pressure abated, and the gradual shifting of generations, a general recognition of the Holocaust seems to be growing.

Rather than marking an end to the policy as such, however, the successful accession processes created a significant shift in international power dynamics that initiated a new phase in the negotiation of meaning of the Holocaust across Europe. This ongoing struggle over the meanings of the Holocaust and World War II, to which I cannot do justice in this space, is most clearly articulated by the 2008 Prague Declaration (http://www.praguedeclaration.eu/). It associated the communists and Nazis as (equally) terrible authoritarian regimes and advocated successfully to commemorate the victims of both regimes in tandem on the anniversary of the Molotov-Ribbentrop pact—rather than singling out Holocaust victims—while ensuring that all of Europe's children would be educated about communist crimes. Its most alarming current manifestation is the attempted prosecution of Holocaust survivors in Lithuania for war crimes, including police visits to their homes that were conducted, likely for symbolic effect, on 27 January, the Holocaust Memorial Day and anniversary of the liberation of Auschwitz (Katz 2010).

Critics and scholars, including Shafir (2002), Katz (2009a, 2009b, 2010) and Zuroff (2005, 2009, 2010), have dissected and condemned attempts to imply that the suffering of Baltic peoples can be equated with the Holocaust or that the regimes were equally terrible in what they variously call the double-genocide theory, the Red-Brown movement, the comparative trivialisation of the Holocaust, and Holocaust obfuscation. The Holocaust in the Baltics website (http://www.holocaustinthebaltics.com) has become a hub for the opposition to this movement.

This ongoing struggle over meaning will continue to have profound implications for policies regarding Holocaust commemoration and education across Europe. The attempted imposition of one European cosmology through overwhelming sanctions and inducements has largely failed. However, the conditions for a more open and productive dialogue are in place. The divergent views are evident, in the public sphere, open for discussion, and available for examination by argument and by evidence. While any expression of Holocaust denial and even obfuscation is troubling, this shift may provide an opportunity for engagement and dialogue, which are preconditions for any deeper transformation.

In the meantime, the two underlying, distinct, and incompatible cosmologies continue to exist, and will continue to do so for as long as Europeans harbor these competing historical understandings:

> Many West Europeans saw… that the horrors of Nazi rule… had been undone… by communism. Meanwhile, many East Europeans saw… that Soviet policies, far from undoing Nazi policies, provoked them, exacerbated them, imitated them, and multiplied the damage that they caused. (Snyder 2009, p. 10)

Elaborating the Sociocultural Theory and Analysis of Education Policy

Estonia's voluntary, if unwelcome, adoption of a Holocaust Day policy provided a valuable test case for the analytical power and normative basis for a sociocultural theory of education policy. The complexity of the context, with its international layer and trans-national institutions, required an understanding of policy formation that exceeded a single moment in time, and was in fact a multi-stage process. Incorporating power into the latest iteration of this theory strengthened my analysis by allowing me to account for extra-national sources of power, while also setting the stage to understand the tremendously complex nature of the normative discourse produced by the policy in this extended policy chain.

The discourse was not free and open, as an ideal democratic situation would allow, but instead the strong sanctions against non-compliance compelled national officials to remain silent about their views, creating a discourse vacuum on the policy content that those responsible for overseeing the implementation—school directors—would seek to fill. The selective silence, however, was a form of communication in itself, as people both refused to advocate for an unpopular policy on its merits and refrained from challenging the public objections of leading school directors. Still, their objections both praised the choice mechanisms in the policy and conveyed deference to the ministry's power. Even then, the legacy of Soviet occupation seemed to find an echo in the strong split between public and private discourse.

This nuanced approach to policy—as simultaneously a form of normative discourse, an act of power, and a process of negotiating meanings—prevented these complex cultural processes of interpretation and communication from being reduced to a simple dynamic of resistance. The concept of policy signals helped to make clear that policy tools were not merely means to an end, but forms of communication in and of themselves. Further, the formation of policy at the nexus of such different cosmologies resulted in a remarkable product: a unitary discourse with divergent meanings that sustained two different world views while maintaining their separation. Because the policy crossed these incompatible worlds, stripping away one set of intended goals for another, the concept of appropriation is critical to making sense of the range of inevitable deviations from the original intent.

Finally, the various policy actors and phases are not easily parsed according to the critical, democratic orientation of sociocultural policy analysis, which valorises appropriation at the expense of policy elites. Indeed, people charged with carrying out elite-driven policies of inclusion may instead ratify exclusivist historical narratives and conceptions of citizenship. Still, democratic theorists have not themselves fully resolved the democratic criteria for overlapping majorities, and ethnographic studies are designed not to render simple judgments but to grapple with complex realities.

References

Aarelaid-Tart, A. (2003). Double mental standards in the Baltic countries: Three generations. In A. M. Kõll (Ed.), *The Baltic countries under occupation: Soviet and Nazi rule 1939–1991* (pp. 215–228). Stockholm: University of Stockholm Press.
Baltic States Report (2003, 10 February). RFE/RL Reports 4, no. 5.
Burawoy, M., & Verdery, K. (Eds.) (1999). *Uncertain transitions: Ethnographies of change in the post-socialist world*. Lanham: Rowman and Littlefield.
City Paper's Baltics Worldwide (2002, 18 November). News highlights from Lithuania, Latvia, and Estonia.
Click, C. (2010, 21 May). A Q&A with Nazi hunter Efraim Zuroff. *The State*.
DeThomas, J. M. (2002, 28 May) *Estonia is silent about the Holocaust*. http://epl.delfi.ee/news/arvamus/joseph-m-de-thomas-eesti-vaikib-holokaustist?id=50924763
Dye, T. R. (1992). *Understanding public policy* (7th ed.). Englewood Cliffs: Prentice-Hall.
Embassy of the United States in Estonia (2002, 24 April). *A continuing commitment*. Remarks by Heather Conley, US Deputy Assistant Secretary of State for European and Eurasian Affairs at Stockholm Security Conference, The United States and Northern Europe.

Estonian Ministry of Foreign Affairs (2006, 26 January). The Holocaust Day was commemorated in Estonia. *Estonian Review.* http://www.eu.estemb.be/eng/frontpage/estonian_review/newwin-middle50/aid-534

Fowler, F. C. (2009). *Policy studies for educational leaders* (3rd ed.). Boston: Allyn & Bacon.

Gross, Z. (2010). Holocaust education in Jewish schools in Israel: Goals, dilemmas, challenges. *Prospects, 40*(1), 93–113.

Guba, E. (1984, October). The effects of definitions of policy on the nature and outcomes of policy analysis. *Educational Leadership 42*, 63–70.

Kalamees, K. (2002, 7 August). Lapsed peavad natside hukatud juute mälestama [Children must remember Jews killed by the Nazis]. *Eesti Päevaleht.* http://epl.delfi.ee/news/eesti/lapsed-peavad-natside-hukatud-juute-malestama.d?id=50930606

Katz, D. (2009a, 23 June). *The Baltic project to delete the Holocaust from European history: Observations from Lithuania.* Twelfth lecture of the Eighth Herbert Berman Memorial Series, Institute for Global Jewish Affairs, Jerusalem.

Katz, D. (2009b). On three definitions: Genocide, Holocaust denial, Holocaust obfuscation. In L. Donskis (Ed.), *A litmus test case of modernity: Examining modern sensibilities and the public domain in the Baltic States at the turn of the century* (pp. 259–277). Bern: Peter Lang.

Katz, D. (2010, 3 May). The crime of surviving. *Tablet Magazine.* http://www.tabletmag.com/news-and-politics/32432/the-crime-of-surviving/print/

Leesi, L. (2002, 9 August). Millal ja kuidas võiks eesti koolides tähistada holokausti mälestuspäeva? [When and how should Holocaust Memorial Day be commemorated in Estonian schools?]. *Õppetajate leht.*

Levinson, B. A. U., & Sutton, M. (2001). Introduction: Policy as/in practice: A sociocultural approach to the study of educational policy. In M. Sutton & B. A. U. Levinson (Eds.), *Policy as practice: Toward a comparative sociocultural analysis of educational policy* (pp. 1–22). Westport: Ablex.

Levinson, B. A. U., Sutton, M., & Winstead, T. (2009). Education policy as a practice of power: Theoretical tools, ethnographic methods, democratic options. *Educational Policy, 23*(6), 767–795.

Lukas, T. (2000, 18 October). Tõnis Lukas: Eesti koolides ei ole holokaustipäeval mõtet. [In Estonian schools, no thought is given to Holocaust Day]. *Eesti Päevaleht.* http://www.epl.ee/artikkel/125725

Marcus, G. E. (1995). Ethnography in/of the world system: The emergence of multi-sited ethnography. *Annual Review of Anthropology, 24*, 95–117.

Mauri [sic] (2003, 10 April). Holokaustipäev kui NATO pileti konts [Holocaust Day as the entry ticket for NATO]. Please note: The original post is no longer available online, but a Google search in quotations for the phrase *"Holokaustipäev kui NATO pileti konts"* [Holocaust Day as the entry ticket for NATO] shows its former presence.

Nielson, I. (2003, 25 January). Holokaustipäev jätab koolid ükskõikseks [Schools remain indifferent to Holocaust Day]. *Pärnu Postimees.* http://www.epl.ee/news/eesti/holokaustipaev-jatab-koolid-ukskoikseks.d?id=50945177

Online Intervjuud [Online Interviews] (2002, 8 August). Dr. Efraim Zuroff online: Eestikeelsed vastused [Dr. Efraim Zuroff online: Answers in English]. http://www.epl.ee/artikkel_211663.html&P=1

Oolo, A. (2002, 24 August). Koolijuhid peavad holokaustipäeva tähistamist ületähtsustamiseks [School directors believe Holocaust Commemoration Day overemphasises its significance]. *Ärileht.* http://epl.delfi.ee/news/eesti/koolijuhid-peavad-holokaustipaeva-tahistamist-uletahtsustamiseks?id=50931893

Paet, U. (2010, 14 May). Speech of Foreign Minister Urmas Paet at the opening of the exhibit Convoy nr. 73—Convoy with a singular fate. http://www.holocausttaskforce.org/images/itf_data/documents/08_news/speech_of_urmas_paet_at_exhibition_opening.pdf

Shafir, M. (2002). Between denial and "comparative trivialization": Holocaust negationism in post-Communist East Central Europe. In *Analysis of current trends in antisemitism* (Vol. 19). Jerusalem: Hebrew University, Vidal Sassoon International Center for the Study of Antisemitism. http://books.google.com/books/about/Between_denial_and_comparative_trivializ. html?id=T84WAQAAIAAJ

Snyder, T. (2009). The historical reality of Eastern Europe. *East European Politics and Societies, 23*(7), 7–12.

Spillane, J., Reiser, B., & Reimer, T. (2002). Policy implementation and cognition: Reframing and refocusing policy implementation research. *Review of Educational Research, 72*, 387–431.

Stevick, E. D. (2007). The politics of the Holocaust in Estonia: Historical memory and social divisions in Estonian education. In E. D. Stevick & B. A. U. Levinson (Eds.), *Reimagining civic education: How diverse societies form democratic citizens* (pp. 217–244). Lanham: Rowman and Littlefield.

Stevick, E. D. (2009). Overlapping democracies, Europe's democratic deficit, and national education policy: Estonia's school leaders as heirs to a Soviet legacy or as agents of democracy? *European Education, 41*(3), 42–59.

Stevick, E. D. (2011). Finessing foreign pressure in education policy: Soviet legacy, European prescriptions, and democratic accountability in Estonia. In J. N. Hawkins & W. J. Jacob (Eds.), *Policy debates in comparative, international and development education* (pp. 175–197). New York: Palgrave Macmillan.

Stevick, E. D., & Gross, Z. (2010). Epistemology and Holocaust education: History, memory and the politics of knowledge. *Prospects, 40*(2), 189–200.

Thompson, D. (1999). Democratic theory and global society. *Journal of Political Philosophy, 7*(2), 114–125.

Thompson, J. B. (1990). *Ideology and modern culture*. Stanford: Stanford University.

Tooming, R. (2003, 24 January). Koolides tähistatakse holokausti päeva [Holocaust Day is commemorated in schools]. *Eesti Päevaleht*. http://epl.delfi.ee/news/eesti/koolides-tahistatakse-holokausti-paeva?id=50944977

Torney-Purta, J. (2000). Comparative perspectives on political socialization and civic education. *Comparative Education Review, 44*(1), 88–95.

Wedel, J., & Feldman, G. (2005). Why an anthropology of public policy? *Anthropology Today, 21*(1), 1–2.

Weiss-Wendt, A. (2008). Why the Holocaust does not matter to Estonians. *Journal of Baltic Studies, 39*(4), 475–497.

Zakaria, F. (1997, November/December). The rise of illiberal democracy. *Foreign Affairs*. http://www.foreignaffairs.com/articles/53577/fareed-zakaria/the-rise-of-illiberal-democracy

Zuroff, E. (2002, 7 August). Holokausti päev Eestis oleks suur samm edasi [Holocaust Day would be a big step forward]. *Eesti Päevaleht*. http://www.epl.ee/artikkel/211542

Zuroff, E. (2005, Spring). Eastern Europe: Anti-Semitism in the wake of Holocaust-related issues. *Jewish Political Studies Review, 17*(1–2). www.jcpa.org/phas/phas-zuroff-s05.htm

Zuroff, E. (2009). *Operation last chance: One man's quest to bring Nazi criminals to justice*. New York: Palgrave-Macmillan.

Zuroff, E. (2010, 1 May). No tolerance for false history. *Jerusalem Post*. http://www.jpost.com/LandedPages/PrintArticle.aspx?id=174425

The Holocaust as History and Human Rights: A Cross-National Analysis of Holocaust Education in Social Science Textbooks, 1970–2008

Patricia Bromley and Susan Garnett Russell

The historical legacy of antisemitism and the ongoing conflict in Israel and Palestine contribute to the emotionally and politically charged discussions surrounding Holocaust education worldwide. As a result, those involved in education may not feel well equipped to handle the subject and avoid it entirely, while others support the inclusion of Holocaust education in schooling. Advocates are deeply divided on their basic conceptualisation of the Holocaust. One view promotes a focus on the Holocaust as embedded historical knowledge, while a more recent alternative perspective emphasizes its importance for civic education, particularly as linked to teaching about universal human rights. Despite the potential contribution of teaching about the Holocaust for history and human rights education, few studies have analyzed the cross-national and longitudinal trends: How many countries include the Holocaust in their curriculum and do they depict it in historical or human rights terms?

Using a unique dataset constructed through a content analysis of 465 high school history, civics, and social studies textbooks from 69 countries from 1970 to 2008, we provide a macro-level overview of trends in Holocaust education. Our research addresses three inter-related questions:

1. Is the prevalence of Holocaust education increasing or decreasing over the period of our study?
2. Is Holocaust education a primarily Western phenomenon, or is it found in countries worldwide over time?

P. Bromley (✉)
Department of Political Science/Public Administration, University of Utah,
260 S. Central Campus Dr, Salt Lake City, UT 84112, USA
e-mail: p.bromley@utah.edu

S.G. Russell
Teachers College, Columbia University, 368 Grace Dodge Hall, New York, NY, USA
e-mail: sgrussell@tc.columbia.edu

3. To what extent is the Holocaust framed in terms of universal human rights in textbooks?

To address these questions we describe the trends in mentions of the Holocaust in textbooks around the world over time; we also conducted a quantitative multilevel analysis to empirically consider the properties of textbooks and countries associated with the likelihood of discussing the Holocaust.

In what follows we first discuss the rise of Holocaust education in society and describe two main conceptual understandings of the Holocaust. Next, we outline the theoretical perspective that motivates our questions and arguments, and describe our data and measures. We then report our descriptive findings and the results of our multilevel analysis. Finally, we discuss the implications of our findings for a broader sociological understanding of social science instruction and the place of the Holocaust within it.

The Rise of Holocaust Education in Society

Existing studies show that for several decades following World War II, the North American and European public had little awareness and education about the Holocaust (Short and Reed 2004). Beginning in the 1970s, however, the Holocaust emerged as a topic in school curricula in Western countries, primarily in the US, Canada, Germany, and the United Kingdom (Fallace 2008; Keren 2004; Rathenow 2000, 2004; Schweber 1998; Short and Reed 2004).

A confluence of several events has made the Holocaust increasingly visible in society and schools. For example, the apprehension and subsequent trial of Adolf Eichmann in Jerusalem in 1961 was widely reported in countries around the world. This event, along with the 1967 Six-Day War between Israel and neighbouring Arab nations, heightened awareness of Israel and led to increased visibility of Holocaust survivors. In the United States, the 1993 release of *Schindler's List*, the opening of the US Holocaust Memorial Museum in Washington, DC, and the development of a Holocaust curriculum by the non-profit group Facing History and Ourselves (FHAO) increased the prominence of the Holocaust, instituting Holocaust remembrance as an integral part of American culture (Fallace 2008). As the Holocaust became more important within mainstream culture, Holocaust education was firmly established in several Western countries by the early 1990s.

Going beyond the Western world, international organisations, both governmental and non-governmental, have launched programmes that reflect a view of the Holocaust as having global relevance. For example, the UN General Assembly designated an International Holocaust Remembrance Day starting in 1995, and FHAO works to spread Holocaust education worldwide. FHAO works globally with 1.8 million students and 25,000 educators per year, primarily in the United States, Canada, Northern Ireland, Israel, Rwanda, and South Africa. Then, in 2000, the Stockholm International Forum on the Holocaust drew representatives from 46 nations to discuss education about and remembrance of the Holocaust; they included heads of state, diplomats, NGOs, religious leaders, academics, and survivors.

Conceptions of the Holocaust

Initially, the Holocaust was conceptualised in society as a historical event central to the moral narrative of the Western world. This view is best described by Maier (2000), who argues that one account of the Holocaust is a Eurocentric story focusing "on the Holocaust and/or Stalinist Communist political killing as the culminating historical experience of the century" (p. 826). Gregory (2000, p. 52) also holds this perspective, claiming the Holocaust is "the most important single event of the twentieth century".

A contrasting perspective conceptualises the Holocaust as having universal moral relevance. Alexander (2009a, b) traces the transformation of the Holocaust into a global cultural symbol of evil. Levy and Sznaider (2002) describe this process as the formation of a "cosmopolitan memory", and argue that "memories of the Holocaust facilitate the formation of transnational memory cultures, which in turn, have the potential to become the cultural foundation for global human rights politics" (p. 88). Similarly, Dunne and Wheeler (2002) characterise the experience of the Holocaust as directly leading to the establishment of an international human rights regime. Notions of the Holocaust as an element of global human rights are intricately tied to visions of modern human society, of rational progress towards contemporary notions of progress and justice. While one could think of the Holocaust as an aberration in the modern world, Bauman (2000, 2001) argues that it is a product of modernity, a point to which we will return in our discussion. His key insight is that the Holocaust is crucial to our understanding of all modern bureaucratic societies, which we would argue includes all formal nation-states, "because it reminds us (as if we needed reminding) just how formal and ethically blind is the bureaucratic pursuit of efficiency" (Bauman 2000, p. 243). Whereas the historical view of the Holocaust is linked to (primarily Western) history, this new view is tied to the depiction of universal moral lessons, especially notions of human rights.

The question of whether it is best to conceptualise the Holocaust in embedded historical or universal human rights terms is controversial (see, for example, the debates in Alexander et al. 2009). As Maier (2000) writes, in light of growing recognition of other atrocities committed worldwide, such as in Bosnia or Rwanda, it seems increasingly parochial to emphasise the uniqueness of the atrocities committed during the Holocaust relative to other human tragedies. But he takes a critical view of linking the Holocaust to human tragedies elsewhere, arguing that it is a weak and ineffective strategy to maintain the contemporary relevance of a Eurocentric perspective. Instead, he asserts, the Western narrative, and the Holocaust, have lost their dominance as the central moral story of the 20th century, replaced by an emphasis on the legacy of global inequality left by colonisation and deepened by economic globalisation.

Debates within Education

Conflicting conceptions of the Holocaust emerge as debates over how it should be taught in schools. Some argue that the main purpose of teaching about the Holocaust should be to teach students to become historians rather than to reduce incidents of racism and to prevent future atrocities (Kinloch 2001). Similarly, others (such as Novick 1999) question the alleged civic, moral, and historical lessons learned from the Holocaust in light of the extremity of the event. In this view, the Holocaust should not be abstracted globally because it cannot be understood outside of the specific confluence of circumstances that created it.

In contrast, Short and Reed (2004) view the purpose of studying the Holocaust as preventing future human rights violations; this view assumes that through the study of atrocities like the Holocaust one can draw general lessons across space and time. According to Salmons (2003, p. 139), "a key motivation for teaching about the Holocaust is that it can sensitise young people to examples of injustice, persecution, racism, antisemitism and other forms of hatred in the world today".

Looking directly at textbooks, one finds many clear examples that show both the historical and human rights conceptions of the Holocaust. For example, a 10th-grade history textbook from India (Dev and Dev 2005) provides a map of Europe marking all the concentration camps and states, "Concentration camps were set up and anti-fascists and Jews were sent there and many of them were killed" (p. 132). Similarly, a US history textbook, *Our Land, Our Time: A History of the United States from 1865*, gives this relatively factual account of the Holocaust:

> In Germany, this belief in a "master race" led to the massive and brutal persecution of German Jews. Hitler's government stripped Jews of their civil rights and seized or destroyed their property. During World War II, the Nazis systematically murdered Jews of conquered lands, and other groups such as gypsies, handicapped people, and all dissidents and resistance fighters. (Conlin 1986, pp. 425–426)

The discourse is certainly normative, using strong language such as "murdered" and "stripped of civil rights", but the Holocaust is presented as a contextualised historical event that took place in Germany and neighbouring countries. These books contain no explicit conceptualisation of the Holocaust as a violation of universal principles of human rights, nor are there any direct connections to global implications for proper civic behaviour.

In contrast, a book for senior secondary students in Malawi, *Social and Development Studies*, explicitly links the Holocaust to global human rights principles (Fabiano and Maganga 2002). In a chapter titled "Social and ethical values for international life", the authors state:

> Closely connected to the idea of universal human rights is the idea that all people are equal, regardless of their race or ethnic group…. You have seen in this course some of the effects of racism. You have seen how it became a system of government in apartheid South Africa; you have seen how the Nazis of Germany in the 1930s and 1940s had such a strong belief in their racial superiority that they carried out a policy of genocide against the Jews. What is important to remember is international reactions to these events. South Africa was isolated from the rest of the world because of its racist policies. A war was fought throughout the world to defeat the forces of Nazism. (pp. 109–110)

In this Malawian book, the Holocaust is an example of a vicious ethnic conflict that violates the principles of the international community. It is presented as parallel to other violations of international norms: apartheid in South Africa, the caste system in India, and racism in the United States. All these negative phenomena are depicted as global aberrations for which the international community brings the perpetrators to justice.

The history textbook currently used for grade 11 in South Africa (Bottaro et al. 2009) also ties the Holocaust directly to human rights. It says, "The Holocaust and other atrocities during the war led to a reaction against 'Scientific Racism', Social Darwinism, and eugenics. After the war there was a greater awareness of the need to protect human rights" (p. 265). The authors go on to link the post-World War II reaction to international social movements against racism, including the civil rights movement and anti-apartheid movement.

In the historical examples above, the Holocaust is presented as important for students to know about because it is a central moral event in the Western story. But when linked to human rights, the Holocaust is presented as an instance of globally unacceptable behaviour, important for teaching universally-relevant lessons in tolerance and peace. Our goal is not to take sides in this debate, but rather to contribute to the discussion by providing empirical evidence of cross-national trends in Holocaust education over time.

Theory and Arguments

The conceptions of the Holocaust presented above suggest several propositions about what we may find as we examine discourse in textbooks. Our approach starts from the observation that, particularly since World War II, many of the world's key actors, especially nation-states, behave as though many aspects of social and cultural life are governed by a set of universal principles applicable worldwide (Meyer et al. 1997). This "highly rationalized and universalistic" world society results in the convergence of many features of nation-states around the world in the absence of direct coercion or obvious functionality (Meyer et al. 1997, p. 153). In education, for example, studies show that a surprisingly standard curriculum has emerged worldwide (Meyer et al. 1992a, 1992b).

Our primary argument in this chapter is that the Holocaust is emerging as a central symbol of world society. Our view is elegantly captured in the opening speech at the Stockholm Forum, given by Professor Yehuda Bauer (2000):

> An amazing thing has happened in the last decade—in fact, during the last few years: a tragedy that befell a certain people, at a certain time and certain places, has become the symbol of radical evil as such, the world over.

Hence, as Dubiel (2003) asserts, the Holocaust has become a meta-narrative of evil, pain and suffering—a "symbolic repertoire" that has been embraced globally (p. 61). Similarly, Alexander (2009a, 2009b) describes the social construction of the Holocaust as a free-floating, universal symbol of evil.

Working from a body of research that shows that education systems reflect global patterns and universal principles, over and above distinctive national histories (Meyer and Ramirez 2000; Ramirez and Meyer 2002), we expect to observe the following changes in Holocaust education:

Proposition 1 *To the extent that the Holocaust has become a central symbol of world society, we expect the following changes in education as world society expands*:

1a. Textbooks will increasingly mention the Holocaust over time.
1b. Mentions of the Holocaust will increasingly appear in a range of countries around the world.
1c. The Holocaust will be increasingly framed in terms of universal human rights.

The Holocaust as a Symbol of World Society

A second set of ideas explores the role of the Holocaust as a constitutive symbol of world society in more depth. Here, the core theme is that Holocaust education becomes a way to teach the student that he/she is a human person in a global society where certain civic rights and responsibilities are universally applicable. The opposition is with nationalist themes that stress corporate nation-states governing a culturally homogenous citizenry, and the subordination of individuals and civic behaviour to the unified nation-state. Our line of argument reflects the point that the main theme of Holocaust education, worldwide, is increasingly a universal doctrine rather than a reflection of immediate local circumstances. Thus:

Proposition 2 *Holocaust education in textbooks reflects a general set of dimensions stressing the student's individual human membership in a global society and de-emphasising the nation-state as a unitary polity. Holocaust education should be greater in books that are*:

2a. More focused on universal human rights,
2b. More focused on depictions of society as diverse,
2c. More focused on international, rather than national, society.

Holocaust Education as Contingent on National Characteristics

The propositions above focus on the expansion of global society and its associated culture. However, this line of thought is not inconsistent with classic theories of education in general and the curriculum in particular stressing the importance of national economic and political factors as well as national cultural heritages. Rather, it emphasises global linkages in addition to national characteristics. Contemporary notions of human rights stem from Western political philosophy and documents such as the Declaration of the Rights of Man and the Bill of Rights. In addition, although world society is increasingly global, it has its roots in ideologies of progress and justice stemming back to the Enlightenment (Meyer et al. 1992a, 1992b; Chabbott 2003). Further, as Maier (2000) describes, the Holocaust itself is a core feature of the Western moral narrative. As a result of this social and cultural legacy, countries with a Western cultural heritage may be more closely linked to world society and to the Holocaust and therefore more likely to discuss it in textbooks.

Proposition 3 *Holocaust education may be more prevalent in countries more closely tied to world culture.*

In sum, we argue that the Holocaust has emerged as a symbol of the principles of a world society. We hypothesise that as world society expands over time, countries and textbooks are increasingly likely to discuss the Holocaust, and a greater range of countries are likely to include the Holocaust in their curricula. We expect the increase to be most pronounced among the countries and books most closely tied to world society. Furthermore, the nature of Holocaust discussion is likely to be shifting towards human rights discourse as the human rights movement emerges as a key facet of world society. We tested these propositions using the data and methods we describe in the next section.

Data, Measures, and Analyses

Finding Books

One key reason for the dearth of cross-national, longitudinal research on Holocaust education is the difficulty of finding adequate data. Curricula are poorly tracked and recorded, particularly over time. Ministry of education reports, such as those found in the International Bureau of Education, sometimes indicate what should be in mass educational curricula (see the uses of these reports in Benavot and Amadio 2005; Benavot and Braslavsky 2006; Meyer et al. 1992a, 1992b), but data for early time points are rare and data are available for only a limited number of countries. Detailed cross-national, longitudinal information on textbooks is even more difficult to obtain. It is sometimes possible to acquire current lists of approved textbooks, but historical records are rarely kept and earlier books are hard to find. Thus, despite the valuable source of data that textbooks can provide on longitudinal, cross-national education systems, it is difficult to collect books systematically.

As the source of data for this study, we drew on a sample of history, civics, and social studies textbooks collected and analyzed as part of a multi-year study on human rights and citizenship education. These books come mainly from the library of the Georg Eckert Institute for International Textbook Research in Braunschweig, Germany. A secondary source of textbooks, particularly those from developing countries, is a network of comparative education researchers and practitioners. Appendix A provides a list of the countries and books covered by the data set over time.

Some important caveats should be mentioned. It is not possible to obtain representative samples of textbooks from many countries over time in multiple subjects. In four cases we have just a single textbook from a country and our data cover only about a third of the extant countries in the world. Further, we do not know how extensively any given book was used in classrooms. Thus, our findings cannot be generalized beyond the books and countries that actually enter into our analyses.

Measures

For our core dependent variables, we employed two measures. First, to capture whether the Holocaust was discussed we asked whether the book contained "at least a paragraph" related to the Holocaust. We examined this variable both descriptively and through quantitative analyses. Second, to capture the nature of Holocaust discourse, we asked whether the Holocaust was "discussed explicitly as a human rights violation or crime against humanity" and we examined descriptive trends in this variable. Of the books in our sample, 25% mention the Holocaust, and 12% talk about the Holocaust using human rights discourse. Appendix B provides a list of countries that have at least one textbook that discusses the Holocaust and the Holocaust in relation to human rights.

At the country level, we relied mainly on a variable for Western cultural heritage as a proxy for cultural, political, and economic characteristics of countries. We compared the likelihood that books from Eastern Europe and other non-Western, non-Eastern European countries would discuss the Holocaust, compared to countries with a Western cultural heritage (Western Europe plus the United States, Canada, Australia, and New Zealand).

As a methodological check, we also tested standard measures used in crossnational analyses: GDP per capita and secondary school enrollment from the World Development Indicators (World Bank 2008), the log of memberships in international non-governmental organisations, taken from the *Yearbook of International Organizations* (Union of International Associations 1980), ethno-linguistic fractionalisation (Montalvo and Reynal-Querol 2005), and human rights violations (Hafner-Burton and Tsutsui 2005). Our analytic model, which we describe below, requires fixed country characteristics, so values are equivalent to a country's score in 1980 (for example, GDP/capita in 1980). We used these variables primarily to check our initial proposition that linkage to the world society will explain the likelihood that a book mentions the Holocaust. Many of these predictors, such as GDP/capita, overlap substantially with our West variable; thus, we could not include them in the same model.

We used four measures to characterise books: (1) the date they were published; (2) an indicator of the degree to which the book's content is international in focus (a five-point item asking the coder to note the proportion of the book addressing international issues); (3) a measure of the amount of the book that discusses human rights (also on a five-point scale); and (4) a count of the number of diverse groups mentioned, such as children, women, minorities, indigenous groups, and the elderly. (Note that for measure 3, the book had to include the exact phrase "human rights" or a translation of it.) These measures were developed as part of a broader study aimed at explaining the rise of human rights education but here we used them to predict a parallel trend in Holocaust education; see Meyer et al. (2010) and Bromley Meyer, and Ramirez (2011) for additional discussion of the data and measures.

As control variables, we also included the length of the book in pages and the grade level. In addition, we controlled for whether a book is in history versus social studies or civics. Prior studies using this data found a difference between history and social studies or civics books in the rise of human rights (Meyer et al. 2010) and student-centred pedagogy (Bromley et al. 2011).

Analytic Model

We present descriptive findings for the data, and then shift to a hierarchical generalised linear model (Raudenbush and Bryk 2002). Hierarchical models are appropriate because we hypothesised that mentions of the Holocaust in textbooks are influenced by both textbook-level and country-level variables. In addition, the data is clustered by country, as Appendix A indicates. Modeling the outcome using ordinary least squares (OLS) regression underestimates the error that arises from the commonalities of textbooks within particular countries, violating the assumptions of OLS regression. Because hierarchical models incorporate both textbook-level and country-level error, they allowed us to use the fullest range of information available. To account for the binary nature of our outcome, we used a logit link function to transform our predicted values into the log odds of success (i.e. the odds of a textbook answering "yes" to the question of whether it discusses the Holocaust, or the Holocaust as a human rights violation). The results can be interpreted simply as a positive coefficient indicating an increase in the likelihood that a book will mention the Holocaust, and a negative coefficient indicating a decrease in that likelihood.

Our hierarchical model consists of textbook (level 1) and country (level 2) equations. The constant of the textbook-level equation and the effect of publication date are modeled as functions of country characteristics. Thus, the interpretation of the constant is of utmost importance. We constructed the variables such that the constant in the textbook-level equation should be interpreted as the estimated likelihood that a textbook that is average on all independent variables will discuss the Holocaust. We accomplished this through grand-mean centring of all textbook-level variables. The equations for our final model (Model 4) were:

1. Log odds of Mentioning Holocaust $= \beta_0 + \beta_1$ (*High Grade, 11–13*) $+ \beta_2$ (*N. Pages, log*) $+ \beta_3$ (*History*) $+ \beta_4$ (*Publication Date*) $+ \beta_5$ (*Human Rights*) $+ \beta_6$ (*Diversity*) $+ \beta_7$ (*Internationalization*) $+ r_{ij}$
2. $\beta_0 = \gamma_{00} + \mu_{0j}$
3. $\beta_4 = \gamma_{10} + \gamma_{11}$ (*Communist or Post-Communist*) $+ \gamma_{11}$ (*Non-West, Non-Communist*) $+ \mu_{0j}$

Results and Discussion

Descriptive Findings

Figure 1 presents descriptive findings on the extent of discussions of the Holocaust in textbooks and countries over time. (Note that the data lines in Figures 1, 2, and 3 have been smoothed using a 10-year running average.) We see a general increase from about 12% of books in any given year discussing the Holocaust to over 25%, with most growth taking place in the 1970s and early 1980s. Similarly, the proportion of countries with a book discussing the Holocaust in any year increases from about 11 to 25% over the period, with the rate rising early on and remaining stable beginning in the mid-1980s. Thus, we see a general increase in discussions of the Holocaust in textbooks over time, in support of our first proposition.

Figure 2 shows some support for our proposition 1b. The increase in discussion of the Holocaust in textbooks over time is not spread equally among Western, Eastern European, and other countries, but comes mainly from a rapid rise in its inclusion into books in post-Communist Eastern Europe. Surprisingly, the rate at which the Holocaust is mentioned in textbooks among Western countries and other non-Western, non-Eastern European countries appears relatively flat over time. So, although the average proportion of books mentioning the Holocaust is higher in the West, the rate does not appear to increase over time. Discussions of the Holocaust were previously rare in the Communist countries of Eastern Europe but have been increasing rapidly to a level that today is nearly on par with that of Western countries. For countries outside the West and Eastern Europe, the trend appears to be flat over time; however, as our description of the quantitative analyses will show, we found that the rate is actually increasing significantly relative to the West, once we controlled for characteristics of books and countries.

Most strikingly, Figure 3 strongly supports proposition 2c, as it shows a steep increase in the proportion of books and countries that discuss the Holocaust

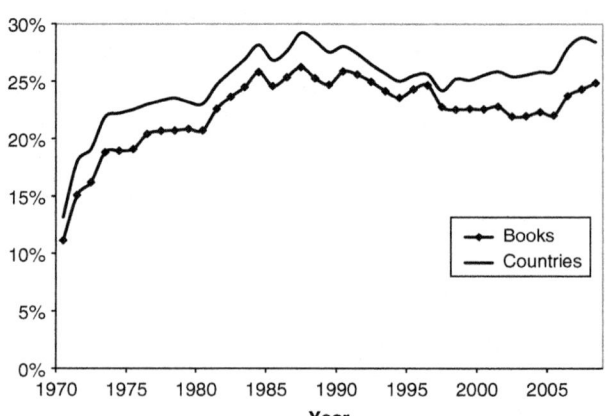

Fig. 1 Average percentage of books and countries discussing the Holocaust over time

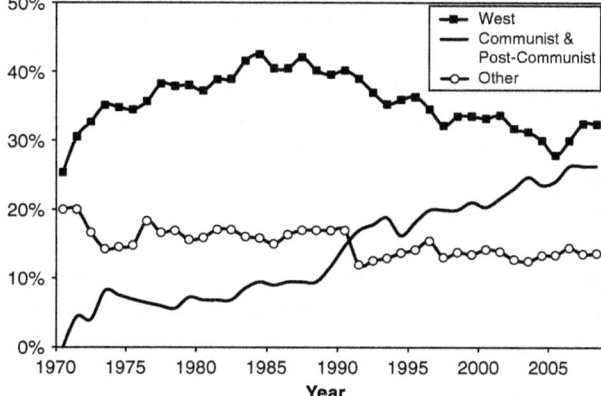

Fig. 2 Average percentage of books discussing the Holocaust over time by country type

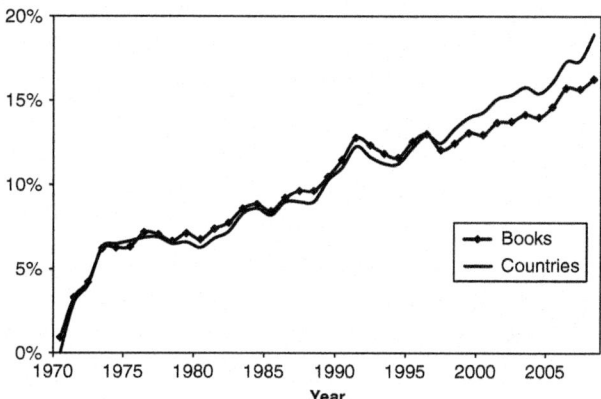

Fig. 3 Average percentage of books and countries discussing the Holocaust as a human rights violation over time

specifically as a human rights violation. In the 1970s very few books or countries used human rights language to discuss the Holocaust. But by 2008, nearly 20% of textbooks and over 15% of countries included discussion of the Holocaust using human rights language. Considered another way, in the 1970s and 1980s, few textbooks discussed the Holocaust, and, of those that did, about one third used human rights language. In contrast, by about 2000 roughly 70% of books with some discussion of the Holocaust used human rights terms. We found this increase in texts on history, civics, and social studies. If we roughly split the entire body of books into those published before and after 1995, the proportion of history books that discuss the Holocaust using human rights discourse increases from 14 to 20%; for civics and social studies the proportion increases from 2 to 11%. This strongly supports our contention that the Holocaust discourse has shifted over time, from a matter of historical fact to a violation of human rights. In the next section we move to quantitative analyses of the prevalence of Holocaust education worldwide.

Quantitative Findings

We found general support for our descriptive findings and hypotheses in a quantitative analysis of Holocaust curricula. Table 1 presents the results of our hierarchical generalised linear model for the likelihood that a book will have any mention of the Holocaust.

Model 1 is simply our control variables: number of pages, grade level, and subject. As expected, we found that history books are more likely to discuss the Holocaust than civics or social studies books. Grade level turned out to be an unimportant factor, and longer books may be slightly more likely to discuss the Holocaust. Our substantive analysis began with the textbook-level indicators in Model 2. We entered the variables individually and together and found the same results; here we present only the full models.

Our second set of propositions reflects our view of the Holocaust as a global cultural symbol. We proposed that books that de-emphasise the nation-state as a unitary, bounded polity reflect a view of society as global, and are therefore more likely to talk about the Holocaust. These are books that focus on universal human rights and diversity in society, and discuss international social and cultural organisations. In support of these hypotheses, Models 2 through 7 show a positive, significant effect for discussion of human rights, mentions of diversity, and a book's level of internationalisation.

Our third proposition considers the argument that countries more linked to world society are more likely to discuss the Holocaust. One key indicator of linkage is a Western cultural heritage. Model 2 shows that relative to those from Western countries, books from the countries of Eastern Europe are less likely to mention the Holocaust, although the difference is not significant. The lack of a significant Eastern European effect is likely due to a rapid increase since the mid-1990s, which was illustrated in Figure 3. On average, books from other non-Western, non-Eastern European countries are significantly less likely to discuss the Holocaust, compared to books from Western countries.

We also tested several other country properties using alternative measures of linkage. Model 4 uses a standard measure of linkage to world society: the log of memberships in international non-governmental organisations. This measure has a positive and significant association with the likelihood that a textbook mentions the Holocaust. Model 5 uses a measure of development, GDP per capita, and also has a positive and significant correlation with discussion of the Holocaust. We argue that the effect of GDP per capita on mentions of the Holocaust is not due directly to wealth per se. Rather, in the stratified world system, wealth and Western culture overlap substantially. We tested several other measures of development, including level of democracy, secondary enrollment, foreign investment, and aid per capita, and found that they had no significant association with the outcome.

In Model 6, as a measure of distance from world society, we tested ethnolinguistic fractionalisation. This phenomenon is commonly used as an indication of the number of corporate groups in society that could potentially come into conflict. Nations with a higher number of competing ethnic and linguistic groups may be less

Table 1 HGLM models predicting discussion of the Holocaust

	Model 1		Model 2		Model 3		Model 4		Model 5		Model 6		Model 7	
Textbook-level controls														
School grade (11–13)	0.313		0.103		0.058		0.079		0.094		0.057		0.046	
Number of pages (log)	0.510		0.544	*	0.504	*	0.452		0.511		0.542		0.604	*
History	1.458	****	1.692	****	1.637	****	1.689	****	1.696	****	1.659	****	1.796	****
Textbook-level core variables														
Year			−0.006		0.000		0.005		0.003		−0.002		−0.054	**
Human rights			0.360	***	0.363	***	0.364	**	0.364	***	0.336	**	0.385	***
Diversity			0.123	***	0.107	**	0.102	**	0.093	*	0.117	**	0.124	**
Internationalisation			0.543	****	0.540	****	0.543	****	0.545	****	0.543	****	0.558	****
Intercept	−1.233	****	−1.616	****	−1.169	***	−1.797	****	−1.685	****	−1.645	****	−1.805	****
Country level (predicting avg.)														
Eastern Europe					−0.284									
Non-West, Non-Eastern Europe					−0.979	**								
INGO memberships (log)							4.896	**						
GDP/capita									0.045	*				
Ethnolinguistic Fractionalisation											−1.708	**		
Country Level (Predicting Year)														
(Post-) Communist													0.112	*
Non-West, Non-Eastern Europe													0.088	**

****p<.001, ***p<.01, **p<.05, *p<.1, two-tailed tests
Notes: N at level 1 is 465; N at level 2 is 69. We used robust standard errors.

integrated into an overarching world culture, and thus less likely to discuss the Holocaust. From the opposite perspective, it is also plausible that the more fractionalised countries are the ones most in need of the lessons of peace and tolerance that Holocaust education could provide. In support of our first argument, we found that ethnolinguistic fractionalisation had a negative effect on mention of the Holocaust in textbooks. A parallel measure, human rights violations, had no effect; we do not discuss the results here. Together, Models 4 through 6 show that alternative measures of linkage to world society support our argument that those countries more closely connected to the world society are more likely to discuss the Holocaust.

Our final analysis, in Model 7, was designed to provide a more rigorous test of the first set of propositions regarding the expansion of Holocaust education to a broad range of countries over time. Although our descriptive data in Figure 1 show an overall increase in the proportion of books discussing the Holocaust, our quantitative analysis did not find that a book's publication date had significant effects. This finding leads us to suspect that, rather than expanding worldwide at an equal rate, mentions of the Holocaust are increasing outside the West as the Holocaust becomes a global symbol, while the number of mentions remains constant in the West. The regional differences illustrated in Figure 2 also suggest that mentions of the Holocaust may be increasing in Eastern Europe in particular, and remaining stable elsewhere.

To explore this idea, in Model 7 we tested an interaction between Year and a country's geographic location in one of three broad world regions: Eastern Europe, West, or Other. In models 2 through 6 the Year coefficient represents the rate in all countries, but in Model 7 we added controls for country type, changing the interpretation of the Year coefficient to the rate for Western countries. Surprisingly, the negative and significant effect of Year shows that, among the Western countries in our sample, the rate of Holocaust discussion is decreasing significantly over time. The magnitude of the effect is so slight, however, that given our sampling limitations, we make a conservative interpretation: the proportion of textbooks in Western countries that mention the Holocaust has been relatively flat in recent decades, following the increase in the 1970s and early 1980s that is shown in Figure 3. The positive and significant coefficients for Eastern Europe and other non-Western, non-Eastern European countries indicate that over time they are increasingly likely to discuss the Holocaust relative to Western countries. The magnitude of this effect is largest for Eastern Europe, supported by the increase we see in their rate over time in Figure 3. Finally, in Model 7, we controlled for change over time in different country types and found that it explains 45% of the variance in the likelihood that a book mentions the Holocaust; this is a larger proportion than in any of our previous models.

Discussion

Our analyses show that in earlier periods, the Holocaust was a more Western concern; increasingly, however, it is being recognised in countries worldwide. We argue that interpreting the worldwide spread of Holocaust education and the increasing tendency to frame teaching about the Holocaust in human rights terms, as linked to the emergence of a world society, helps explain why we see teaching about the Holocaust in countries as diverse as Malawi, El Salvador, and South Africa, rather than finding it only in expected countries such as Israel, Germany, the United Kingdom, and the United States.

Our interpretation of the Holocaust as increasingly adopted into curricula worldwide as a universal symbol of human rights leaves open the normative questions of whether this trend is positive or effective. An optimistic interpretation argues that understanding the Holocaust can help foster civic and democratic values in society (Lindquist 2008; Misco 2009; Stevick 2007) and can be a means to promote tolerance, peace, and justice (Misco 2009; Salmons 2003). Short and Reed (2004) argue that studying the Holocaust will "help secure the future against further violations of human rights whether based on ethnicity, religion, gender, sexual orientation or disability" (p. 2).

However, countries may have alternative, complex reasons for incorporating Holocaust education into their curricula. As a symbol of world society, the Holocaust has powerful ideological appeal as a signal of conformity with international norms. For example, Stevick (2007) finds that Estonia adopted a Holocaust Day as a way to signal solidarity with the European and transatlantic community in advance of its entry into NATO. Much research by world society scholars emphasises the decoupling between formal policies and actual practices; that is, countries adopt formal policies to conform symbolically, but such policies are unlikely to lead to actual changes (Meyer et al. 1997). Additionally, claiming the universality of any social or cultural principles is certainly open to criticism as a form of hegemony. Segesten (2008) describes Romania's experience of feeling cultural pressure to mimic European values by incorporating the Holocaust into its curriculum despite the absence of direct coercion and notes that the international norms implied by Holocaust education have yet to be institutionalised.

In other cases, references to the Holocaust may provide a way for countries to indicate that egregious human rights abuses occur beyond their borders, or to keep the principles of human rights so abstract as to delink them from reality. Tunisia, for instance, has been the target of many highly critical reports charging the government with human rights violations such as arbitrary arrest, torture and physical abuse of prisoners, and severe media restrictions (US Department of State 2008). At the same time, recently published Tunisian history textbooks include extensive discussions of human rights abuses elsewhere in the world, such as colonial occupation, or poverty in the United States. In reference to the Holocaust, a 2006 Tunisian history textbook asks students to consider why France, the country with perhaps the longest tradition of human rights, collaborated with the Nazis in exterminating Jews:

> France is the land of human rights, renowned throughout the world for its tradition of welcoming foreigners, but during the Second World War the Vichy government collaborated in the extermination of European Jews even before it received orders from her Nazi occupiers. Why and how was this policy possible? (Brisson and Martin 2006, p. 154, our translation)

Although countries' motivations for incorporating the Holocaust into high school education are complex, their rationales are tied to an understanding of the importance of the Holocaust as a global symbol. Both the desire to instill proper global civic values of respect for human rights, peace and tolerance, and the goal of signaling support for these norms (perhaps especially using an example removed from a country's own history, as in the case of Tunisia) indicate awareness of a broader world community.

Interestingly, not all human rights violations become equally recognised as global symbols in world culture. For example, just 3% of textbooks in our sample (16 books) mention the Armenian genocide, and one third of those (5 books) come from Armenia. Similarly, atrocities committed by the Japanese in Nanjing are mentioned by just 2% of books. In contrast, the Holocaust, apartheid in South Africa, slavery, the abuses of colonisation, and the mistreatment of indigenous groups are mentioned by 15 to 25% of books. Why do some events become global cultural symbols while others remain primarily national issues? This remains an open question and a valuable area for researchers to explore in the future. Obvious possible explanations include the scope and scale of the atrocity, the particular group subject to suffering, and perhaps the length of time since an abuse took place.

Bauman (2001) provides another possible explanation for why the Holocaust would become a symbol of world society over other human tragedies. For Bauman, the Holocaust is a product of the modern, rational world: "Modern civilization was not the Holocaust's *sufficient* condition; it was, however, most certainly its *necessary* condition" (p. 13). The products of modern society—institutionalised and bureaucratic forms—increased the likelihood that an event such as the Holocaust would occur; without modern industrial forms and highly rationalised thought, it would not have occurred. Hence, the Holocaust is a product of the modern rationalised world, perhaps explaining its centrality in world society.

Our findings should not be interpreted as a judgment of particular education systems or approaches to Holocaust education. A debate continues, far beyond the scope of our research, over whether the Holocaust should be taught in historical or human rights terms. We do not argue that one method of presenting the Holocaust is inherently better than the other: both perspectives cast the Holocaust in critical terms. We do, however, provide some evidence that speaks to the debate by showing that the Holocaust is increasingly discussed in human rights terms, even within history texts. In addition, although textbooks in Western countries tend to include more discussion of the Holocaust, the rate for post-Communist and other countries is increasing. We have aimed to explain why so many countries include the Holocaust in their curricula and to document a shift towards portraying the Holocaust in global human rights terms.

Conclusions

A key limitation of our study is that textbooks are only one aspect of the many factors that influence student learning. We do not know how teachers implement Holocaust education in the classroom, or the effect their teaching has on students. Studying the effects of Holocaust education, particularly cross-culturally, is an important area for future research. Considering these more specific measures will facilitate a deeper exploration of the mechanisms that promote or inhibit Holocaust education at the country level. Further, through an in-depth analysis of a very few textbooks, one could explore whether changing textbook emphases co-vary with individual-level knowledge, beliefs, and attitudes regarding the Holocaust. Such a study would, of course, require much more fine-grained data than that used in this study but could provide a more nuanced understanding of the relationship between conceptions of the Holocaust in textbooks and society more broadly.

Despite these limitations, we were able to identify broad changes in Holocaust education worldwide over time. Existing research on Holocaust education largely focuses on case studies, primarily from the United States, United Kingdom, Canada, and Germany. Our research complements these studies by providing a rare cross-national, longitudinal view of trends in Holocaust education. The Holocaust is increasingly taught about in terms of human rights, in history as well as civics and social studies, and is widely used in the curricula of non-Western countries. Books that portray society as more international and diverse, and that place more emphasis on human rights are more likely to discuss the Holocaust. At the country level, those nation-states more linked to world society are more likely to discuss the Holocaust; Eastern European countries are rapidly approaching a level on par with the West. Understanding these worldwide trends helps explain how cultural globalisation is influencing Holocaust education, why we find education about the Holocaust in countries worldwide, why it is more prevalent in some countries than others, and why we see a global shift towards teaching about the Holocaust in human rights terms.

Acknowledgements This chapter is based on Bromley and Garnett (2010). A version of the hierarchical linear model included in this chapter was developed for a related project in a seminar conducted by Anthony Bryk, whose comments were most helpful. Work on this study was funded by a grant from the Spencer Foundation (200600003). The paper benefited from the related studies of members of Stanford's Comparative Workshop. We are particularly grateful to John Meyer and Francisco Ramirez for their comments. The study was possible only because of the impressive textbook collection of the Georg Eckert Institute, in Braunschweig, and the extraordinarily helpful assistance of Brigitte Depner and her staff. In addition, we thank individual colleagues who helped us collect textbooks, including Dijana Tiplic, Suk Ying Wong, Rennie Moon, David Suárez, Marine Chitashvili, Pepka Boyadjieva, Shushanik Makaryan, Marika Korotkova, Gili Drori, Sandra Staklis, Marina Andina, Jaime Quevedo, Nii Addy, Magdalena Gross, and Rebecca Taylor.

Appendices

Appendix A: List of Textbooks by Country over Time

	1970–1984	1985–1994	1995–2006	Total
Argentina	1	2	4	7
Armenia	0	1	6	7
Australia	2	4	2	8
Austria	5	4	3	12

(continued)

	1970–1984	1985–1994	1995–2006	Total
Belarus	0	1	3	4
Belgium	2	3	2	7
Bolivia	0	5	0	5
Bosnia and Herzegovina	0	1	8	9
Bulgaria	8	4	4	16
Canada	4	4	3	11
Colombia	1	6	0	7
Costa Rica	0	0	4	4
Croatia	0	1	1	2
Czechoslovakia	3	1	0	4
Denmark	2	2	2	6
Ecuador	0	1	4	5
El Salvador	0	0	1	1
Ethiopia	0	2	0	2
Finland	2	2	0	4
France	5	5	5	15
Georgia	0	0	5	5
Germany	2	2	2	6
Ghana	0	8	6	14
Greece	1	2	2	5
Guatemala	0	0	2	2
Guyana	0	0	1	1
India	3	2	9	14
Indonesia	0	0	12	12
Iran	2	2	0	4
Ireland	3	2	4	9
Israel	1	4	0	5
Italy	1	2	2	5
Japan	2	2	3	7
Kenya	0	6	0	6
Latvia	0	0	3	3
Macedonia	0	1	1	2
Malawi	0	0	2	2
Mexico	1	3	2	6
Namibia	0	3	0	3
Nepal	0	0	7	7
Nicaragua	0	1	0	1
North Korea	0	2	4	6
Northern Ireland	0	0	2	2
Norway	2	2	2	6
PR China	0	1	1	2
Pakistan	0	0	3	3
Panama	0	1	2	3
Philippines	0	4	2	6
Portugal	2	2	2	6

(continued)

	1970–1984	1985–1994	1995–2006	Total
Puerto Rico	0	0	1	1
Romania	1	2	2	5
Russia	0	4	23	27
Serbia	0	1	2	3
Singapore	0	2	0	2
Slovenia	0	1	2	3
South Africa	2	2	0	4
South Korea	3	3	4	10
Spain	3	2	6	11
Sweden	2	2	2	6
Switzerland	2	2	1	5
Taiwan	0	1	12	13
Tanzania	0	0	8	8
Tunisia	0	0	3	3
Turkey	2	1	4	7
USA	3	6	3	12
USSR	14	12	0	26
United Kingdom	7	5	11	23
Venezuela	0	1	1	2
Yugoslavia	3	2	0	5
Total	97	150	218	465

Appendix B: Countries Discussing the Holocaust and Holocaust as Human Rights Violation

Discuss Holocaust	Discuss Holocaust as human rights violation
Argentina	Argentina
Armenia	Armenia
Australia	Australia
Austria	Belarus
Belarus	Bulgaria
Belgium	Canada
Bulgaria	Croatia
Canada	Czechoslovakia
Croatia	Denmark
Czechoslovakia	El Salvador
Denmark	France
El Salvador	Georgia
Finland	Greece
France	India

(continued)

Discuss Holocaust	Discuss Holocaust as human rights violation
Georgia	Indonesia
Germany	Ireland
Greece	Norway
India	Romania
Indonesia	Russia
Ireland	Serbia
Israel	Slovenia
Italy	Spain
Japan	Sweden
Latvia	Taiwan
Malawi	Tanzania
Mexico	Tunisia
Norway	United Kingdom
Philippines	United States
Portugal	
Romania	
Russia	
Serbia	
Slovenia	
South Africa	
Spain	
Sweden	
Switzerland	
Taiwan	
Tanzania	
Tunisia	
United Kingdom	
United States	

References

Alexander, J. (2009a). The social construction of moral universals. In J. Alexander, M. Jay, B. Giesen, R. Manne, & M. Rothberg (Eds.), *Remembering the Holocaust: A debate* (pp. 3–104). New York: Oxford University Press.

Alexander, J. (2009b). On the global and local representations of the Holocaust tragedy. In J. Alexander, M. Jay, B. Giesen, R. Manne, & M. Rothberg (Eds.), *Remembering the Holocaust: A debate* (pp. 173–192). New York: Oxford University Press.

Alexander, J., Jay, M., Gisen, B., Manne, R., & Rothberg, M. (Eds.) (2009). *Remembering the Holocaust: A debate*. New York: Oxford University Press.

Bauer, Y. (2000, 26 January). *Opening speech at Stockholm Forum*. http://www.d.dccam.org/Projects/Affinity/SIF/DATA/2000/page898.html

Bauman, Z. (2000). *Modernity and the Holocaust*. Ithaca: Cornell University Press.

Bauman, Z. (2001). Sociology after the Holocaust. In P. Beilharz (Ed.), *The Bauman reader* (pp. 230–258). Malden: Blackwell Publishers Inc.

Benavot, A., & Amadio, A. (2005). *A global study of intended instructional time and official school curricula, 1980–2000*. Background report for UNESCO EFA Global Monitoring Report 2005. Geneva: UNESCO International Bureau of Education.

Benavot, A., & Braslavsky, C. (Eds.) (2006). *School curricula for global citizenship*. Hong Kong: Comparative Education Research Centre, University of Hong Kong/Springer.

Bottaro, J., Visser, P., & Worden, N. (2009). *In search of history: Grade 11 learner's book*. Cape Town: Oxford University Press Southern Africa.

Brisson, É., & Martin, S. (2006). *Histoire géo: Course et methods*. Paris: Hatier.

Bromley, P., & Garnett, S. R. (2010). The Holocaust as history and human rights: A cross-national analysis of Holocaust education in social science textbooks, 1970–2008. *Prospects, 40*(1), 153–173.

Bromley, P., Meyer, J., & Ramirez, F. O. (2011). Student centrism in social science textbooks, 1970–2008. *Social Forces, 90*(2), 1–24.

Chabbott, C. (2003). *Constructing education for development: International organizations and Education for All*. New York: Routledge Falmer.

Conlin, J. R. (1986). *Our land, our time: A history of the United States from 1865*. San Diego: Coronado Publishers.

Dev, A., & Dev, I. A. (2005). *Contemporary world history part I: A history textbook for class XII*. New Delhi: National Council of Educational Research and Training.

Dubiel, H. (2003). The remembrance of the Holocaust as a catalyst for a transnational ethic? *New German Critique, 90*, 59–70.

Dunne, T., & Wheeler, N. (Eds.) (2002). *Human rights in global politics*. Cambridge, UK: Cambridge University Press.

Fabiano, M., & Maganga, J. (2002). *Malaŵi senior secondary social and development studies 4*. Malaysia: MacMillan Malaŵi Ltd.

Fallace, T. D. (2008). *The emergence of Holocaust education in American schools*. New York: Palgrave Macmillan.

Gregory, I. (2000). Teaching about the Holocaust: Perplexities, issues and suggestions. In I. Davies (Ed.), *Teaching the Holocaust: Educational dimensions, principles and practice* (pp. 1–8). London/New York: Continuum.

Hafner-Burton, E., & Tsutsui, K. (2005). Human rights in a globalizing world: The paradox of empty promises. *American Journal of Sociology, 110*(5), 1373–1411.

Keren, N. (2004). Teaching the Holocaust: A mission. In S. Totten, P. R. Bartrop, & S. L. Jacobs (Eds.), *Teaching about the Holocaust: Essays by college and university teachers* (pp. 123–138). Westport: Praeger.

Kinloch, N. (2001). Parallel catastrophes? Uniqueness, redemption and the Shoah. *Teaching History, 104*, 8–14.

Levy, D., & Sznaider, N. (2002). Memory unbound: The Holocaust and the formation of cosmopolitan memory. *European Journal of Social Theory, 5*(1), 87–106.

Lindquist, D. H. (2008). Five perspectives for teaching the Holocaust. *American Secondary Education, 36*(3), 4–14.

Maier, C. S. (2000). Consigning the twentieth century to history: Alternative narratives for the modern era. *The American Historical Review, 105*(3), 807–831.

Meyer, J. W., & Ramirez, F. O. (2000). The world institutionalization of education. In J. Schriewer (Ed.), *Discourse formation in comparative education* (pp. 111–132). Frankfurt: Peter Lang.

Meyer, J. W., Kamens, D., Benavot, A., Cha, Y., & Wong, S. (1992a). *School knowledge for the masses: World models and national primary curricular categories in the twentieth century*. Washington, DC: Falmer Press.

Meyer, J. W., Ramirez, F. O., & Soysal, Y. (1992b). World expansion of mass education, 1870–1980. *Sociology of Education, 65*(2), 128–149.

Meyer, J. W., Boli, J., Thomas, G. M., & Ramirez, F. O. (1997). World society and the nation-state. *American Journal of Sociology, 103*(1), 144–81.

Meyer, J. W., Bromley, P., & Ramirez, F. O. (2010). Human rights in social science textbooks: Cross-national analysis, 1975–2006. *Sociology of Education, 83*(2), 111–134.

Misco, T. (2009). Teaching the Holocaust through case study. *The Social Studies, 100*(1), 14–22.

Montalvo, J. G., & Reynal-Querol, M. (2005). Ethnic diversity and economic development. *Journal of Development Economics, 76*, 293–323.

Novick, P. (1999). *The Holocaust in American life*. New York: Houghton Mifflin.

Ramirez, F. O., & Meyer, J. W. (2002). National curricula: World models and national historical legacies. In M. Caruso & H. Tenorth (Eds.), *Internationalisation* (pp. 91–107). Frankfurt: Peter Lang.

Rathenow, H. (2000). Teaching the Holocaust in Germany. In I. Davies (Ed.), *Teaching the Holocaust: Educational dimensions, principles and practice* (pp. 63–76). London/New York: Continuum.

Rathenow, H. (2004). The past is not dead: Memories, reflections, and perspectives. In S. Totten, P. R. Bartrop, & S. L. Jacobs (Eds.), *Teaching about the Holocaust: Essays by college and university teachers* (pp. 153–174). Westport: Praeger.

Raudenbush, S., & Bryk, A. (2002). *Hierarchical linear models: Applications and data analysis methods* (2nd ed.). Thousand Oaks: Sage Publications.

Salmons, P. (2003). Teaching or preaching? The Holocaust and intercultural education in the UK. *Intercultural Education, 14*(2), 139–149.

Schweber, S. A. (1998). *Teaching history, teaching morality: Holocaust education in American public high schools*. Unpublished Ph.D. dissertation, Stanford University.

Segesten, A. D. (2008). *The Holocaust and international norm socialization: The case of Holocaust education in Romania* (Working paper no. 38). Lund: Centre for European Studies.

Short, G., & Reed, C. A. (2004). *Issues in Holocaust education*. Aldershot: Ashgate.

Stevick, E. D. (2007). The politics of the Holocaust in Estonia: Historical memory and social divisions in Estonian education. In E. D. Stevick & B. Levinson (Eds.), *Reimagining civic education: How diverse societies form democratic citizens* (pp. 217–244). Lanham: Rowman and Littlefield.

Union of International Associations (1980). *The yearbook of international associations*. Munich: K.G. Saur.

US Department of State (2008). *2008 human rights practices: Tunisia*. http://tunisia.usembassy.gov/dos_reports2/008-human-rights-practices-tunisia.html

World Bank (2008). *World development indicators*. [CD-Rom]. Washington, DC: World Bank.

Measuring Holocaust Knowledge and Its Relationship to Attitudes towards Diversity in Spain, Canada, Germany, and the United States

Jack Jedwab

Introduction

When it comes to education about the Holocaust, many are concerned that as time passes, fewer witnesses will be alive and able to carry forward the message of history. Yet, despite the growing time gap since World War II, there is much optimism about the global degree of interest in acquiring knowledge about the Holocaust.

Tony Kushner (2002) has observed that "as we cross the threshold into a new millennium, interest in the Holocaust continues to escalate at an artistic and cultural level, representations of the Holocaust, especially in film and literature have never been so intense and pervasive" (p. 57). Similarly, Yehuda Bauer (2006) notes that "more and more people show an interest in this particular tragedy" which explains the "flood of fiction, theater, films, TV series, art, music, and of course historical, sociological, philosophical, psychological, and other academic research, a flood that has rarely if ever been equaled in dealing with any other historical event" (p. 5).

Other observers seem less optimistic. Notwithstanding the increased interest in the Holocaust, the concern is that its lessons are being lost on too many people. Wiesel (2009) remarked that "if the civilized world allowed the crimes in Cambodia, Bosnia, Rwanda and Darfur to happen, it is because the lessons of Auschwitz and Treblinka have not been learned. And these lessons have not been learned quite simply because, for many reasons, the civilized world would rather not know". Still, the observations made by Bauer and Wiesel are not contradictory. A growing interest in knowledge about the Holocaust may not result in people better understanding its contemporary lessons. The gap between knowledge and understanding of the Holocaust underscores the ongoing challenge facing educators in this field. We do

---

J. Jedwab (✉)
Association for Canadian Studies, 1822a Sherbrooke West, Montreal, QC H3H 1E4, Canada
e-mail: jack.jedwab@acs-aec.ca

not acquire knowledge about the Holocaust in a vacuum, and how we comprehend its lessons is shaped by our broader learning experience.

Although opportunities to expand knowledge of the Holocaust may seem limitless, those engaged in disseminating it face important obstacles in doing so. Assessing the degree of global knowledge about the Holocaust is no simple task. The ability to reach large numbers of people with information about the Holocaust does not mean that its intended lessons—however defined—are being conveyed effectively. To this end, it would be useful to know how people interpret the knowledge that is imparted to them. However, relatively few efforts have been made to properly measure such knowledge. To do so would require some consensus around a common set of questions used to establish benchmarks to help determine what might be considered a satisfactory level of knowledge. Of the empirical studies conducted to date, observers have been surprised by just how many people report limited or no awareness of the Holocaust. Perhaps this is because leaders in the field of Holocaust education set the bar too high when it comes to the desired level of knowledge. *The World Must Know*, the title of a 1993 publication by Michael Berenbaum, former director of the United States Holocaust Memorial Museum (USHMM), likely captures the objective of many persons who promote knowledge about the Holocaust. Given this goal, one might expect to see more effort directed at some empirically-based global assessment of knowledge about the Holocaust. To assess students' knowledge of the past, I believe that establishing benchmarks is increasingly important.

Ascertaining the national level of knowledge about the Holocaust can be a formidable task. Creating a survey to measure such a sensitive topic requires that questions be carefully formulated. As Samuel Totten (1999) has remarked, "the Holocaust is one of the most tortuously complex, not to mention horrific subjects an educator can tackle" (p. 36). As I observed, the failure of past experiments using public opinion surveys to estimate knowledge about the Holocaust was related to the way that questions were formulated. Efforts to promote Holocaust knowledge in various countries are undoubtedly affected by how this historical event influences a country's national self-image, and whether there are contemporary political challenges associated with revisiting what often represents a difficult part of the past. Such conditions may also result in diverging levels of commitment to providing Holocaust education as well as varying strategies for promoting Holocaust knowledge. Given this situation, it may be difficult to achieve agreement on the best questions for testing knowledge of the Holocaust. However, benchmarking such knowledge remains vital if we are to determine where knowledge gaps persist and how and what lessons are to be drawn from them.

While opinion surveys on knowledge of the Holocaust have their limits, they nonetheless provide one of the few means to develop some baseline information. They also can help identify future avenues for the much-needed quantitative and qualitative research in this important area.

Educators and those setting education policies are interested in identifying the meanings attributed to historic events and their contemporary lessons. Indeed, many educators believe the purpose of disseminating knowledge about the Holocaust is to convey specific lessons to the population about how to prevent its reoccurrence. Among the reasons cited for teaching about the Holocaust, the United States Holocaust Memorial Museum website (USHMM 2010) points to the importance of helping others develop "an understanding of the roots and ramifications of prejudice, racism, and stereotyping"; it also hopes people will "develop an awareness of the value of pluralism and encourage acceptance of diversity in a pluralistic society". To determine whether such ends are attained one would need to establish the links between knowledge of the Holocaust and attitudes towards prejudice, as well as, openness to diversity.

In this chapter I seek to establish the degree to which the Canadian, American, German, and Spanish populations estimate their respective levels of knowledge about the Holocaust. I then explore the relationship between estimated Holocaust knowledge and attitudes towards Jews and Muslims, notably around concerns over prejudice towards the two groups. In addition, I examine the four publics' views on issues connected with immigration and newcomer integration. Finally, I test the hypotheses that a nation's proximity (in both time and geography) to the events of World War II results in greater awareness of the Holocaust (Smith 2005) against the evidence gathered in these surveys.

The results of the survey are intended to encourage reflection on the impact that Holocaust knowledge can have on multicultural, citizenship, and anti-racist education. This issue is especially important as some observers regard multiculturalism as particularly receptive to Holocaust education, as a means to help reduce discrimination and to encourage respect for cultural diversity (Short and Reed 2001). The findings are based on four national surveys conducted in September 2010, with samples ranging from 1,000 to 1,500 respondents in Canada, the United States, Spain, and Germany; further notes on methodology are contained in Appendix.

The Global Challenge of Estimating Holocaust Knowledge

Researchers have made relatively few large-scale attempts to quantify the degree of knowledge about the Holocaust and even fewer efforts to determine how such knowledge correlates with views on tolerance and openness to diversity. Undoubtedly, there are limits to the conclusions that can be drawn on the basis of public opinion surveys. Thus far, efforts to use public opinion surveys to shed light on knowledge about the Holocaust have encountered mixed success. Given the complexity of measuring knowledge about the Holocaust, the way in which questions are formulated can be crucial. Conclusions can be flawed where questions are unclear, as evidenced by the interpretation of results of a Holocaust-knowledge study that Burns Roper conducted in 1993 for the American Jewish Committee (AJC). According to Golub and Cohen (1993) the AJC survey findings suggested that more than one in five Americans believed it possible that the Holocaust had never happened. This alarming finding gave rise to much debate over the survey method that was employed to arrive at this conclusion. Further examination revealed that the survey question was constructed with a confusing double negative: "Does it seem possible or does it seem impossible to you that the Nazi extermination of the Jews never happened?" Based on their analysis of the question, Moore and Newport (1994) used a simplified version of it and found that fewer than 10% of the American population appeared to doubt that the Holocaust had occurred. In an analysis of the controversy, Bischoping (1998) noted that several survey researchers deliberating on the topic of measuring Holocaust knowledge concurred that better survey questions could produce more consistent estimates of public ignorance on this important matter.

In 2005, the AJC commissioned a survey on the topic of Holocaust knowledge, which was conducted in seven countries: Austria, France, Germany, Poland, Sweden, the United Kingdom, and the United States. In analyzing the findings, Tom Smith (2005) observed that knowledge of the Holocaust was limited and uneven across the countries surveyed. However, the survey revealed strong support across the countries for transmitting knowledge of the Holocaust to future generations. Smith assumed that since people tend to learn more about their own national histories, Holocaust knowledge would be greater in countries that were most directly involved in World War II. He thus expected that Germans and Austrians would know more about the Holocaust than Poles who, in turn, would know more than people in France, the United Kingdom, and the United States. The survey, however, did not support this assumption. Instead, it revealed that knowledge about the Holocaust was greatest in Sweden, followed by France, Germany, Austria, the United Kingdom, Poland, and the United States. Smith was surprised by the substantial degree of Holocaust knowledge in Sweden and the lower level of knowledge among Germans and Poles, given their historical proximity to the events in question.

The 2005 AJC survey asked whether respondents had heard of Auschwitz, Dachau, and Treblinka, and whether they knew how many Jews were killed during World War II. On the first question, the ability to identify these places as concentration camps or some related facility (such as death camps or extermination camps), the responses ranged from 91% in Sweden to just 44% in the United States; in Austria it was 88%, in Poland 79%, in France 78%, in Germany 77%, and in the United Kingdom 53%. The percentage indicating they did not know ranged from 46% in the United States to 5% in Sweden. Another question asked: "Approximately how many Jews in all of Europe were killed by the Nazis during the Second World War?" It generated the correct response from some 55% of respondents in Sweden and 30% of those in Poland, along with 49% in France and Germany, 41% in Austria, 39% in the United Kingdom and 33% in the United States.

The other set of questions focused on the commitment to preserve and transmit knowledge about the Holocaust. In this regard, those agreeing that it is essential or very important for all people to know about the Holocaust ranged from 89% in Austria to 70% in Poland. Respondents were asked whether it was time to put the Nazi extermination of the Jews "behind us" or to keep remembrance strong. The percentages who felt it was important to keep the memory strong ranged from 92% in Sweden to 70% in Austria. At this point, it is worth noting a significant gap among Austrians: a sizeable percentage (89%) said it was either essential or very important to have knowledge of the Holocaust. Yet, paradoxically, an important minority (27%) agreed that it was time to put the Holocaust behind us. Another question asked whether teaching about the Holocaust should be required in schools. Here, responses in support of teaching the Holocaust ranged from 92% of Austrians to 69% of Poles, along with 91% in Sweden, 86% in France, 80% in the United States, 79% in Germany, and 76% in the United Kingdom.

A large-scale survey of educators in Sweden conducted for the Living History Forum (Lange 2008) aimed to assess their knowledge about the Holocaust. The questions formulated for the survey were deemed adequate by a group of professional historians. For example, one question asked teachers "Which of the following camps were built primarily in order to murder Jews?" Seven possible responses were provided, of which six are related to places and one is an institution. Two of the names, Chelmno and Treblinka, were correct answers: places where the Nazis built camps whose principal objective was to murder Jews. Some 88% of the participating teachers answered correctly in relation to "Treblinka"; 0.9% answered incorrectly and 8.2% answered "Don't know". Nearly 17% answered correctly in relation to "Chelmno"; 7% answered incorrectly and 76.2% answered "Don't know". Almost three out of four teachers answered incorrectly in relation to the names Dachau and Bergen-Belsen. These were concentration camps, but the vast majority of teachers were unaware that they were not built with the primary objective of murdering Jews.

The report's author, Anders Lange (2008, p. 92), contends that "knowledge about the objectives associated with the Nazi's establishment of different concentration camps should constitute a part of the desirable intentional depth in teachers' awareness and understanding of German Nazism as a phenomenon and the Second World War as an historical period". He regards the teachers as having a low level of knowledge about the Holocaust, based on the questions contained in the survey. He reported that slightly over 70% of the teachers gave the wrong answer to at least 8 of the 11 knowledge questions included in the questionnaire. Only two out of just over 5,000 teachers surveyed answered all of the knowledge questions correctly, and a further 14 gave the correct answer to all but one. Yet, in the absence of another survey where the same questions have been posed to teachers or to a random sample of the whole population, it remains difficult to situate the results in a broader context.

For their part, many of the teachers felt that the questions were much too difficult and focused too much on "details". This criticism should not be dismissed, even though certain professional historians regarded the questions as valid. Indeed Lange suggests that the survey seeks to establish whether teachers possess the "desired intentional depth" when it comes to knowledge about the Holocaust. It is important to determine what the desired level of depth is about knowledge of the Holocaust.

The criteria established in the AJC and LHF surveys are highly relevant for Holocaust educators in the effort to establish some benchmark for satisfactory knowledge in this area. Contrasting the ways the two surveys approached the question of knowledge of death/concentration camps, the AJC found that knowledge among the Swedish public surveyed was very high based on their ability to identify Treblinka, Dachau, and Auschwitz. On the other hand, the LHF study concluded that the Swedish teachers have low knowledge of the Holocaust, partly because they were unaware that murdering Jews was not the primary objective at Dachau and Bergen-Belsen. Undoubtedly, the LHF survey sets the knowledge bar higher than that of the AJC.

When it comes to knowledge of the Holocaust, the two surveys reveal strong support for transmitting such knowledge among teachers, as well as among the broader population. In the case of the LHF survey, the purportedly lower knowledge of the Holocaust does not undercut the commitment to its transmission. Overall, some 80% of those responding to the AJC survey declared it essential or very important for "all people in your country to know about and understand the Nazi extermination of the Jews during the Second World War". Tom Smith (2005) described this result as reflecting the view of a strong majority. Still, depending on one's expectation, one could counter that one respondent in five did not share this view.

The AJC and LHF surveys raise important questions about the gap between knowledge of the Holocaust (as defined by the survey criteria) and the commitment to preserving its memory. The AJC survey results suggest that those with stronger knowledge of the Holocaust are more supportive of the need for transmission. In part, this can likely be attributed to the fact that those who are least aware are less capable of properly transmitting the knowledge.

Looking at the AJC survey, however, two things must be kept in mind. First, when it comes to testing the transmission of Holocaust knowledge, the questions employed in the survey assumed that a preamble would lay out the objective of the Holocaust. Hence it is necessary to provide respondents with some context to better equip them to answer questions. The second point relates to Smith's link between national proximity to the Holocaust and knowledge about it. Under certain circumstances, proximity to tragic events may result in a group wanting to create distance when such knowledge undercuts its collective sense of pride and belonging. In other words, a given collectivity's knowledge and understanding of the past may be affected by its capacity to come to terms with painful historic memories.

Assessment of Knowledge of the Holocaust in Selected Countries

For the purposes of the study I describe here, persons in Canada, the United States, Germany, and Spain were asked to assess the strength of their knowledge of the Holocaust. The challenge in employing questions that invite respondents to make such estimates lies in depending on how respondents define strong knowledge. Although we must be cautious in this regard, it is important to bear in mind that a major objective of the surveys was to look at the relationship between self-assessed knowledge of the Holocaust and concerns over antisemitism, as well as how open respondents were to diversity. In this regard, this survey made an effort to examine

Table 1 Respondents' knowledge of the Holocaust, by nationality

I have a good knowledge of the Holocaust	Strongly agree (%)	Somewhat agree (%)	Somewhat disagree (%)	Strongly disagree (%)	Don't know (%)
Canada	32.4	46.0	11.5	4.9	5.2
United States	30.1	42.7	14.0	5.6	7.6
Spain	25.4	32.0	18.1	11.6	12.9
Germany	48.5	36.2	8.0	3.9	3.4

the relationship between knowledge about the Holocaust and what is referred to as its contemporary lessons.

Survey results in the four countries (see Table 1) revealed that knowledge of the Holocaust is highest in Germany where some 48% of respondents strongly agreed and 36% somewhat agreed that they possessed a good knowledge, making a total of 84%. Following Germany, self-estimated knowledge of the Holocaust was at 78.4% for Canadians and 72.8% for Americans. It was lowest among the Spanish population at 57.4%.

Exposure to information about the Holocaust will undoubtedly have an important bearing on the assessment of knowledge. Among the younger population, the extent to which it is taught in school will likely have an important impact on the degree of self-estimated knowledge. Not surprisingly, the surveys reveal that age is an important consideration in estimated knowledge of the Holocaust. In the United States, the 18–24 cohort and those above the age of 35 offered roughly similar assessments of their knowledge. But the group aged 25–34 scored some ten points below the rest of the population in this regard. In Canada and Germany, age was not a factor in estimated knowledge of the Holocaust. However in Spain, the survey revealed a substantial gap in estimated knowledge of the Holocaust between those aged 16–24 (47.8%) and the 45–54 group at 72.9%. The lower percentage among youth in Spain is likely explained by the lack of education about the Holocaust. That members of a European country have less estimated knowledge of the Holocaust than do North Americans challenges the idea that proximity to the tragedy determines differences in levels of awareness. Research in other European countries would be useful in further testing this hypothesis.

Across the four countries the survey revealed relatively important gaps in self-estimated knowledge of the Holocaust on the basis of educational attainment. In Canada, the United States, and Germany, some seven in ten respondents with a high school diploma or less reported a good knowledge compared with over eight in ten with a university degree. In Canada, language identification played a role, with self-estimated Holocaust knowledge at 61% among the French-speaking population, at 85.1% among the English-speaking population and at 74% among those whose first language was neither English nor French (see Table 2). In the United States, the survey found differences in estimates of Holocaust knowledge on the basis of racial identification: 85% of the white population reported strong knowledge, compared with 68% of Hispanics and 63% of Blacks/African Americans.

Table 2 Canadian and US respondents' Holocaust knowledge by ethnic/language group

I have a good knowledge of the Holocaust	Canada			United States		
	French	English	Other	White	Black/African-American	Hispanic/Latino
Strongly agree (%)	21.0	36.2	34.2	31.3	20.5	27.3
Somewhat agree (%)	40.1	48.9	44.0	43.9	42.3	40.9
Somewhat disagree (%)	16.7	9.0	13.5	12.6	19.2	21.2
Strongly disagree (%)	10.8	2.7	4.6	5.6	6.4	3.0
I don't know/I prefer not to answer (%)	11.6	3.2	3.7	6.6	11.5	7.6

Table 3 Respondents' agreement that antisemitism is a problem, by Holocaust knowledge

Antisemitism is a problem in our society (% strongly and somewhat agree)	I have a good knowledge of the Holocaust (%)			
	Strongly agree (%)	Somewhat agree (%)	Somewhat disagree (%)	Strongly disagree (%)
Canada	88.0	49.7	39.8	27.1
United States	61.9	45.2	35.4	33.9
Spain	65.9	49.2	42.1	39.4
Germany	57.9	53.4	60.0	Ns

Holocaust Knowledge: Perceived Prejudice and Social Distance

In Canada, the United States, and Spain, those persons with stronger self-assessed knowledge of the Holocaust were more likely to agree that antisemitism was a problem in their society (see Table 3). Germany was an exception here, with the majority who estimated weaker knowledge of the Holocaust continuing to see antisemitism as a problem in society. A relatively small percentage of Germans estimate weak knowledge of the Holocaust.

On the question of whether prejudice towards Muslims was a serious problem, the degree of Holocaust knowledge had no significant effect on German respondents, with two thirds agreeing that it was a problem. But in the United States, the survey revealed important gaps, as some six in ten Americans with strong knowledge regarded prejudice towards Muslims as a problem, versus four in ten with the weakest assessment of their knowledge. There was a similar gap among Spanish respondents, as three quarters of those with strong knowledge about the Holocaust believed that prejudice towards Muslims was a problem, a concern shared by nearly half of those who said they had the least knowledge.

Measuring Holocaust Knowledge

Where the gaps are perhaps widest is around the intersection of two factors: degree of knowledge of the Holocaust and degree of social distance from Jews and Muslims. In this chapter, I use the term social distance to reflect the degree to which respondents believe that they share values with either Jews or Muslims. In general, across the four countries, respondents were far more likely to say that Jews share their values, compared to Muslims. In Canada, some 32% of respondents agreed that Muslims shared their values compared with 29.8% of those in the United States, 24.9% in Spain, and 23.8% in Germany. The results may reflect a wider degree of perceived social distance with Muslims in each of the four countries. As I observe below, the estimated level of knowledge about the Holocaust gives rise to substantial gaps in agreement with the statement: "Jews share our values" (see Table 4). In the United States, some 60 percentage points separate those estimating the strongest knowledge and those estimating the weakest knowledge when it comes to the belief that "Jews share our values"; in Canada the equivalent gap was over 40 points. In Germany and Spain, the gaps around social distance were also relatively significant: in Spain, over 30 points separated the most and least knowledgeable and in Germany the difference was over 20 points.

Those estimating greater Holocaust knowledge are also more likely to agree that Muslims share their values than those estimating less knowledge. In Canada, some 34% of persons reporting the strongest knowledge of the Holocaust agreed with the statement that "Muslims share our values", compared with 13% of those who estimated the weakest knowledge. In the United States, some 39% of those reporting the strongest knowledge of the Holocaust agreed with that statement, compared with 12% who placed themselves in the weakest knowledge category. Overall, the gaps are not as wide those between perceived Holocaust knowledge and shared values with Jews. In part, that finding can be attributed to the fact that majorities in the four countries disagree with the view that Muslims share our values. It would be difficult to make the case that Holocaust knowledge would reduce societies' perceived social distance with Muslims, as it does not target this objective. Nevertheless, to the extent that education around multiculturalism aims to reduce social distance, it is worth looking at the relationship in order to help make connections between areas of education that target greater openness to diversity.

Table 4 Respondents' beliefs that Jews share their values, by Holocaust knowledge

Jews share our values (% strongly and somewhat agree)	I have a good knowledge of the Holocaust			
	Strongly agree (%)	Somewhat agree (%)	Somewhat disagree (%)	Strongly disagree (%)
Canada	72.2	66.8	44.7	28.6
United States	86.8	63.6	40.8	20.3
Spain	59.6	43.0	31.6	27.9
Germany	67.3	47.2	45.0	Ns

Holocaust Knowledge and Openness to Diversity

Salmons (2003) suggests that teaching the lessons of the Holocaust might inspire youth to work harder towards a fairer, more tolerant society that sees strength in diversity, values multiculturalism, and combats racism. He points out that in the United Kingdom, education about the Holocaust is clearly linked with the objectives of intercultural education and preparing students to participate in a multicultural society. Other than issues of racism and discrimination, rarely have there been tests of the impact that Holocaust education has on views around openness to immigration and valuing multicultural diversity. Drawing on research done with Scottish secondary students, Maitles et al. (2006) offer evidence that Holocaust education can make an important contribution to human rights awareness and foster appreciation of the harmful effects of stereotyping and scapegoating. Nonetheless, they note that while Holocaust education did influence primary and secondary school children in this regard, it cannot eradicate all racist attitudes. Landau (1989, cited in Maitles et al. 2006, p. 17) asserts that Holocaust teaching "perhaps more effectively than any other subject, has the power to sensitize pupils to the dangers of indifference, intolerance and racism". Seppinwall (1999) suggests that a major purpose in teaching young children about the Holocaust is to have them learn "the importance of tolerance and respect for others who are different", along with "living together in a spirit of mutual cooperation and appreciation for the contribution of others" (p. 38). Our four country surveys found a relatively significant relationship in each of the four countries between the estimated level of Holocaust knowledge and the likelihood of agreeing with the view that "people with different ethnic and religious backgrounds than the majority make an important contribution to our national culture" (see Table 5). As I observe below, some three quarters of Canadians reporting a good knowledge of the Holocaust value the contribution from persons of diverse backgrounds, compared with approximately 40% with the weakest knowledge. Elsewhere, the survey also revealed noteworthy gaps around the degree to which those estimating stronger knowledge of the Holocaust attribute value to the societal contribution from diverse cultures.

Table 5 Respondents' beliefs that those of diverse backgrounds contribute to national culture, by Holocaust knowledge

People with different ethnic and religious backgrounds than the majority make an important contribution to our national culture (% strongly and somewhat agree)	I have a good knowledge of the Holocaust			
	Strongly agree (%)	Somewhat agree (%)	Somewhat disagree (%)	Strongly disagree (%)
Canada	75.1	76.6	66.0	39.7
United States	76.2	76.8	59.1	57.7
Spain	68.6	61.4	44.2	44.5
Germany	60.0	50.0	40.0	–

Table 6 Respondents' beliefs that immigrants should give up the customs/traditions, by Holocaust knowledge

Immigrants should be encouraged to give up their customs and traditions and become more like the rest of the population (% strongly and somewhat agree)	I have a good knowledge of the Holocaust			
	Strongly agree (%)	Somewhat agree (%)	Somewhat disagree (%)	Strongly disagree (%)
Canada	56.1	46.5	47.5	51.2
United States	40.9	36.0	44.2	44.0
Spain	52.1	51.0	45.3	45.9
Germany	52.7	57.4	60.0	58.9

On another dimension of diversity—the idea that immigrants should give up their customs and traditions and become more like the rest of the population—the level of perceived knowledge about the Holocaust had no meaningful influence (see Table 6). Hence, more of those with perceived knowledge of the Holocaust attribute value to diversity, but they show much less tendency to support the idea that immigrants should maintain their customs and traditions. Since education around multiculturalism tends to look favorably upon the preservation of culture, our survey findings raise questions about the relationship between Holocaust education and multicultural education. Yet, another survey question that may provide some insight into Holocaust knowledge and openness to diversity is the one that asked respondents whether they felt there were too many immigrants in their countries. Only in Canada was there any meaningful variation in opinion on this issue based on estimated levels of Holocaust knowledge. In effect, some 37% of those respondents who estimate the strongest knowledge agree that there are too many immigrants, a view held by 64% of those Canadians estimating the weakest knowledge.

Conclusions

Short and Reed (2004) suggest that the main purpose of Holocaust education is to inoculate the population against antisemitic and racist propaganda. Survey results in the four countries provide evidence that those with higher self-estimated Holocaust knowledge are more inclined to view antisemitism as a societal problem. Across the four countries, the more knowledgeable respondents also tend to be more concerned with prejudice towards Muslims. The four surveys also attempted to shed light on the assumption that Holocaust knowledge leads to greater openness to diversity.

That knowledge of the Holocaust may have less bearing than we would assume on responses to the debate over societal diversity may well reflect the ways that people learn about and interpret the relevant issues in a broader context. The relationship between knowledge of the Holocaust and attitudes towards multiculturalism is especially complex given the ongoing global discussion about how best to respond to such issues as integrating immigrants and retaining and transmitting minority cultures. Educators cannot be expected to offer easy answers on such matters where discussions take place both within and outside the classroom. Often, there is no societal consensus around many of the issues. As I mentioned at the outset, the lessons drawn from Holocaust education cannot be understood in a vacuum. Youth are exposed to a broad range of ideas from various sources that undoubtedly modify the impact of specific classroom lessons about the Holocaust. It is vital to look at education about the Holocaust in conjunction with each student's broader learning experience. The issue merits further inquiry, particularly where connections are made between Holocaust education, multicultural education, and citizenship education.

Following Smith's (2005) logic, the United States and Canada might not be regarded as countries with strong proximity to the events of the Holocaust; by consequence, North Americans' knowledge about it might be relatively low. On the other hand, in the post-war period, the United States and Canada became home to a relatively important number of Holocaust survivors, and the broader Jewish community to which they belong is committed to widely transmitting knowledge about the Holocaust. In short, a nation's geographic proximity to World War II does not always result in greater knowledge about the Holocaust.

Establishing the percentage that is better informed about the Holocaust may be a helpful starting point, but it does not provide the kind of in-depth analysis required to determine more detailed knowledge benchmarks. Ideally, surveys of public opinion around knowledge of the Holocaust should give rise to debate on the minimal criteria defining what it means to be properly informed on the subject.

Holocaust educators regularly test students' knowledge of the subject and a comparative analysis of the content of such tests would be valuable. The four national surveys, which form the basis of much of the discussion above, examine the degree to which individuals assess their own knowledge of the Holocaust. Undoubtedly, there are some limits in relying on such assessments, especially insofar as they can accurately reflect awareness of the specific events that occurred during the Holocaust. On the other hand, an exclusive focus on knowledge of facts and figures may not reflect a broader comprehension of the Holocaust and the lessons to which it gives rise. Ideally, cross-national comparisons of Holocaust knowledge will consider both self-assessed knowledge, as well as awareness of the specifics.

Appendix: Information on Research Methods

The Association for Canadian Studies commissioned public opinion surveys in four countries in August and September of 2010. In the United States, the survey was carried out by the firm Caravan via web panel (ACS-Caravan 2010); 1,048 people responded on 30 August and 31 August. An equivalent telephone survey would have a margin of error of 3.9 points, 19 times out of 20. In Germany, the survey was conducted by Produkt+Market Marketing ACS-Produkt Market (2010), a member of the Arbeitskreis Deutscher Markt- und Sozialforschungsinstitute (ADM/ Federation of German Market and Social Research Institutes). It contacted 1,000 respondents between 4 September and 10 September. The margin of error was between 1 and 5%.

In Spain, the survey was conducted by ACS-TNS Global (Spain 2010), and reached 1,052 respondents, between 16 September and 20 September. The margin of error statistics are: the mean was not more than 3.5%, and the error variance was 0.039. In Canada, the survey was conducted by the firm Leger Marketing via web panel (ACS-Leger 2010). The 1,707 respondents were surveyed between 4 September and 7 September, 2010. An equivalent telephone survey would have a margin of error of 2.9 points, 19 times out of 20.

References

ACS-Caravan (2010). *Survey conducted in the United States for ACS, 30 and 31 August, 2010*. Princeton: Caravan Research.
ACS-Leger (2010). *Survey conducted in Canada for ACS, 4 September to 7 September 2010*. Montreal: Leger Marketing.
ACS-Produkt Market (2010). *Survey conducted in Germany for ACS, 4 September to 10 September, 2010*. Wallenhorst: Produkt Market.
ACS-TNS Global Spain (2010). *Survey conducted in Spain for ACS, 30 and 31 August, 2010*. Madrid: TNS Global Spain.
Bauer, Y. (2006, 27 January). *On the Holocaust and its implications: In the wake of Holocaust Remembrance Day* (Discussion paper 1, Holocaust and the United Nations discussion paper series). http://www.un.org/holocaustremembrance/docs/paper1.shtml
Bischoping, K. (1998). Method and meaning in Holocaust-knowledge surveys. *Holocaust and Genocide Studies, 12*(3), 454–474.
Golub, J., & Cohen, R. (1993). *What do Americans know about the Holocaust?* New York: American Jewish Council.
Kushner, T. (2002). "Pissing in the wind"? The search for nuance in the study of Holocaust 'bystanders'. In D. Cesarani & P. A. Levine (Eds.), *Bystanders to the Holocaust: A re-evaluation* (pp. 57–76). London/Portland: Frank Cass.
Landau, R. S. (1989, 25 August). No Nazi war in British history. *Jewish Chronicle*.
Lange, A. (2008). A survey of teachers' experiences and perceptions in relation to teaching about the Holocaust. *Living History Forum*. http://www.levandehistoria.se/sites/default/files/wysiwyg_media/teachersurvey_eng_webb.pdf
Maitles, H., Cowan, P., & Butler, E. (2006). *Never again! Does Holocaust education have an effect on pupils' citizenship values and attitudes?* (Report produced for Scottish Executive Education Department). http://www.scotland.gov.uk/Publications/2006/09/06133626/0
Moore, D. W., & Newport, F. (1994). Misreading the public: The case of the Holocaust poll. *The Public Perspective, 5*, 28–39.
Salmons, P. (2003). Teaching or preaching? The Holocaust and intercultural education in the UK. *Intercultural Education, 14*(2), 139–149.
Seppinwall, H. (1999). Incorporating Holocaust education into K4 curriculum and teaching in the United States. *Social Studies and the Young Learner, 10*(3), 36–38.
Short, G., & Reed, C. A. (2001). *Holocaust education in Canada: A review and analysis of curriculum, policies, programs and teacher training*. Toronto: Bnai Brith Canada.

Short, G., & Reed, C. A. (2004). *Issues in Holocaust education*. Surrey/Burlington: Ashgate.
Smith, T. (2005). *The Holocaust and its implications: A seven-nation comparative study*. New York: American Jewish Committee. http://www.ajc.org/atf/cf/%7B42D75369-D582-4380-8395-D25925B85EAF%7D/HolocaustImplicationsNov2005.pdf
Totten, S. (1999). Should there be Holocaust education for K-4 students? The answer is no. *Social Sciences and the Young Learner, 12*(1), 36–39.
USHMM [United States Holocaust Memorial Museum] (2010). Organisation website. http://www.ushmm.org/education/foreducators/guideline/
Wiesel, E. (2009, 11 April). Holocaust survivor, Nobel Peace Prize winner Elie Wiesel warns against drugs that erase memory. *New York Daily News*. http://www.nydailynews.com/opinion/forget-holocaust-survivor-nobel-peace-prize-winner-warns-drugs-erase-memory-article-1.364875

Part VI
Holocaust Education in National and Regional Contexts

Holocaust History, Memory and Citizenship Education: The Case of Latvia

Thomas Misco

Introduction

The Nazi occupation of Latvia during World War II resulted in a series of horrific events for thousands of Jews and other minorities in Latvia. During this time, many Latvians made an array of choices in response to this occupation. Some chose to actively collaborate with the Nazis, others engaged in rescuing Jews, and the great majority chose to acquiesce and act as bystanders. But following the Soviet reoccupation of Latvia in 1945, schools rarely addressed the topic of the Holocaust, including the array of choices available and the ultimate murder of victims. After Latvia regained independence in 1991, the large number of living bystanders and collaborators, a lack of political encouragement, and a crowded public school curriculum further inhibited teaching about the Holocaust, which was already a sensitive subject. As such, this history constituted a controversy, especially within an educational context.

A Citizenship Rationale

Engaging students in controversial issues increases student civic participation, critical thinking skills, interpersonal skills, content understanding, and political activity (Harwood and Hahn 1990; Hess 2009). Judgments about normative contested issues also elevate interest in current events, social studies, and social issues,

T. Misco (✉)
College of Education, Health, and Society, Miami University,
301G McGuffey Hall, Oxford, OH 45056, USA
e-mail: miscotj@miamioh.edu

and increase the development of tolerance (Curtis and Shaver 1980; Goldenson 1978; Harwood and Hahn 1990; Hess 2009; Hess and Ganzler 2006; Hess and Posselt 2002; Remy 1972; Torney-Purta et al. 2002). Students who engage in discussions involving both controversial and multicultural issues are well positioned to become agents of change who recognise, celebrate, and embrace diversity among and within groups, as well as expand content knowledge though the consideration of other perspectives and develop understandings of justice and the common good (Crossa 2005; King 2009; Young 1996). In addition, opening heretofore closed areas and entering into polemical discussions helps to make political issues more meaningful and relevant for students (McGowan et al. 1994). Challenging assumptions and addressing prejudices fits within the aims of prejudice reduction, democratic citizenship education, and reflective pedagogy, where "right" answers are not sought (Gaughan 2001; Graseck 2009; Hunt and Metcalf 1968; Misco 2011).

In a pluralistic democracy, the means of education has exceedingly significant implications for developing skills and dispositions that perpetuate free, active, and harmonious social life. Students need to engage in judgments concerning societal values and evaluating how standards, which some perceive as established and uncontested, originate and are perpetuated (Griffin 1942). As societies continually renegotiate the degree to which students will rationally grapple with closed and gray areas, they are also shaping the larger enterprise of education as fostering democratic or totalitarian attitudes (Hunt and Metcalf 1968). In the former, students require the chance to deliberate on controversial matters (Parker 2003; Ross and Marker 2005), but an often narrow focus on content knowledge is divorced from controversial topics, leaving little room for experiences to develop that promote and contain considerations for the common good. Ultimately, the avoidance of controversial issues leaves disciplines isolated and removed from their social bearings, thereby compromising their utility (Dewey 1938).

Similar to most controversial issues, historical memory is situated and located within cultures and societies (Simon 2000) and in some societies, memory of the Holocaust constitutes a critical controversial issue. At issue in these societies is the extent or degree to which the attention of citizens is directed toward or away from examining and understanding history (LaCapra 1992). Because Holocaust memory contains an ethical responsibility, all individuals within these societies form some degree of moral relationship with the past, which involves articulating and renegotiating Holocaust representation and pedagogy (Baum 2000). Therefore, the representation of history changes over time as particular cultures recreate different relationships with their past.

One such country involved in an ongoing renegotiation of its past is the Republic of Latvia. There, the Holocaust remains a difficult event to confront for both Latvian Jews and ethnic Latvians (Misco 2007, 2010; Zisere 2005). As Latvia continues to develop its new democratic way of life after centuries of occupation, decisions are constantly being made about the historical narrative and about which historical and civic knowledge, skills, and dispositions are most worthy of privilege in the school experience. Some of these decisions naturally involve the Holocaust in general and the Holocaust, as it occurred in Latvia, in particular. Given the beneficial collateral effects of addressing closed areas, controversial topics, and Holocaust history, any efforts aimed at advancing these issues demand the attention of social studies educators and educational researchers. These effects include sensitisation to indifference, intolerance, dehumanisation of others, and racism, as well as a commitment to caring about the affairs of others, and recognising the common unity of humanity, the responsibilities that stem from that unity, and the fragile nature of democratic values (Burtonwood 2002; Shoemaker 2003; Short 2003).

Persistent Silences

Despite the largely unassailable democratic citizenship rationale for teaching the Holocaust, since 1945 many societies have chosen not to do so. For example, Holocaust education started in the United States during the 1960s and 1970s (van Driel 2003). Holocaust curricula began by covering topics such as *Kristallnacht*, the invasion of Poland, the Warsaw Ghetto, and liberation, though we know little about what is currently taught because of the decentralised system of education in the United States (Shoemaker 2003). Although the Latvian population does not publicly contest the Holocaust, public discourse remains uninformed and sometimes hostile about what took place (Zisere 2005).

In numerous European countries, the Holocaust was a "dark chapter that many wanted to forget, especially owing to issues of collaboration, bystander inaction, and the fact that many non-Jewish citizens also suffered" (van Driel 2003, p. 125). In Germany, for example, Holocaust education began in earnest during the 1960s, when a larger backlash against the participant generation occurred (Rathenow 2000). Having initially treated it as a minor part of its history, Germany later augmented its Holocaust education after the United States, with which it was closely aligned during the Cold War, began to devote significant energy and time to creating new Holocaust curricula (Deckert-Peaceman 2003). Prior to the collapse of the Soviet Union, West Germans assumed that East Germany had been "immunized against racism and xenophobia by their 'anti-fascist' education" (Rathenow 2000, p. 65), which unfortunately was not the case.

In the Czech Republic, only since the mid-1990s has the Holocaust become a "more popular issue" (Frankl 2003, p. 180). The issue of Czech collaboration still needs to be addressed, but Czech teachers and textbook writers have made considerable advances from the "almost unanimous silence about the genocide of Jews and Roma that characterised the beginning of the 1990's" (Frankl 2003, p. 186). Now that much of the Czech curriculum has resolved historical issues, the main work appears to be aligning the materials with modern pedagogical methods. The Czech situation is quite similar to that in Italy, where a lengthy period of silence was broken within the context of commemorating the 50th anniversary of the war's end (Santerini 2003). At present, Holocaust education in Italy is becoming more prevalent because teachers are creating more lessons that are simultaneously responsive to the Holocaust and to social and political contexts. To make the Italian curriculum more engaging, recent efforts have employed more documentary sources, created affective tie-ins, and built connections between intercultural education and Holocaust education in order to stymie antisemitism (Santerini 2003).

A number of former Soviet republics were not in a position to pay homage to the unique history and suffering of the Holocaust. Given the millions of other victims of World War II who required commemoration, the Soviet Union treated the murder of Jews as part of the larger attack of fascism on Soviet society. Recently, however, Holocaust workshops and curricula have emerged in the former Soviet republics of the Baltic region. In Lithuania, the Anne Frank House has held workshops for roughly 30 teachers, which has resulted in participants being more willing to teach about the Holocaust (van Driel 2003). In Latvia, in 2001, the Soros Foundation funded the development of a high school curriculum that uses cooperative learning to ameliorate status differences in classrooms by examining testimonies from survivors of the Holocaust (Gundare and Batelaan 2003). More recently, a curriculum developed in 2005 brought forth a series of modular lesson plans focused on individuals and choices unique to the Holocaust in Latvia (Hlebowitsh et al. 2006).

Because many post-Soviet states failed to experience the turn toward Holocaust education, given their date of independence and the time required to deal with national histories, a number of those countries are just now beginning to examine both the Holocaust in general and their countries' roles in particular. Totten and Feinberg (1995) noted that it is infinitely easier to turn away and forget the horrors and inhumanity; this response is exacerbated when issues of morality and politics make the Holocaust even more sensitive and controversial to large portions of the population (Gregory 2000; Schweber 2004), as has happened in several countries. The post-war teacher generation in these societies included the participants themselves and therefore the roles of bystander and collaborator were often glossed over (Rathenow 2000). Holocaust education is becoming more widespread in Europe (van Driel 2003), but much work remains to be done.

Historical Context

Prior to 1990, historiography of the Holocaust in Latvia was limited to Western sources, which contained few perspectives (Feldmanis 2005a). Often, apocryphal Soviet sources placed blame on antisemitic Latvians (Ezergailis 1996) and tended to downplay the loss of Jewish life. To recognise and memorialise Jewish suffering and murder would be to minimise or diminish the sacrifice of those fighting the Great Patriotic War of the Soviet Union (Erglis 2005). During the Soviet era, dictionaries did not even list the word Holocaust (Cimdina 2003).

Press (2000, p. 193) noted a reason why the issue of remembrance and reconciliation concerning the Holocaust in Latvia was problematic:

> Those around us had scarcely any interest in our fate. One reason for this was certainly the amount of misfortune that the people in Latvia and the USSR as a whole had themselves to bear as a result of the war's devastation.

The phenomenon of comparative trivialisation is therefore instructive for those trying to understand the history of the Holocaust in Latvia and the representation of that history. Comparative trivialisation involves not only comparing the Holocaust to other pernicious events, but frequently comparing it to contemporary events that involve violence. As a result of comparison, the uniqueness and sanctity of the Holocaust is diminished and sometimes dismissed. In the case of Latvia, comparative trivialisation minimised the Holocaust in light of the Gulag, often by insisting that the Gulag claimed more victims (Shafir 2003). Due to the uniqueness of the Holocaust, in terms of ideology, universality, and totality, comparisons can work to "negate the singularity of the Holocaust" and claim that Jews indulge in a "monopolization of suffering" (Shafir 2003, p. 7).

The annihilation of the Jews in Latvia, during Nazi German occupation, was the gravest crime and tragedy in the modern history of Latvia (Erglis 2005; Stranga 2005). The Holocaust in Latvia resulted in the death of over 70,000 Latvian Jews, as well as 20,000 Jews from other territories under Nazi German control. At first glance, a reader of history might assume that as a result of occupation, Nazi Germany alone committed these heinous acts. Or, because propaganda from that era has endured into the present day, others might assume that Latvia was a collaborationist and antisemitic country that willingly participated in genocidal acts independent of German involvement (Viksne 2005b). But the history of the Holocaust in Latvia is extremely complicated, and involved numerous responses among Latvian individuals and institutions within the context of multiple occupations. In order to understand the Holocaust in Latvia, as well as World War II in the Baltic region, in the rest of this chapter I also unpack the role of the two "paradigms of evil" (Feldmanis 2005a, p. 78): Nazi Germany and the Soviet Union.

Antecedents to the Holocaust

External forces and occupying nations largely shaped Latvia's history (Feldmanis 2005a). Throughout its history and due to its geographic location and desirability, Vikings, Teutonic knights, Russians, Swedes, Poles, Soviets, and Germans have, at times, influenced and occupied Latvia, though its history has been peppered with stints of independence (Plakans 1995). As the former member of the Hanseatic League (which Riga joined in 1282) that most recently incurred Germanic and Russian encroachment, Latvians thought, until the 1880s, that their primary threat was Germany, though they also had to fend off the Russian autocracy (Ezergailis 1996). Beginning around the middle of the 19th century, Latvians developed a consciousness based on language and culture in the form of a national awakening that inspired desires for autonomy. In addition, this consciousness highlighted the predominantly lower economic status of Latvians within their own country (Nollendorfs 2002).

During the 16th century, Jews from Poland were frequent guests in Liepāja, a large coastal city in western Latvia. A number of Jews also began to arrive from the

Ukraine, Belarus, and Russia, driven out by the repressive regime of Ivan the Terrible. This was followed by Jewish immigration from Germany in the 17th century. Because of Latvia's history of foreign control, the way that Jews were treated within Latvia was often a consequence of Polish, Russian, or German policy, though larger cities such as Riga were able to exert some autonomy. An attitude of tolerance existed during the late 18th century: Latvian folk songs characterised the Jew as "a stranger who differs in his appearance, clothing, and traditions, but who is needed, is 'a Jewish neighbor'" (Dribins 2001, p. 17).

Although antisemitic policies had existed to varying degrees in Czarist Russia, the tenures of Alexander I and Nicholas I brought forth an attempted "transformation of Jews" (Dribins 2001, p. 17), which sought to assimilate and integrate Jews en masse. Attempts to convert Jews fit within the early stages of antisemitism that Hilberg (1985) set forth; he suggested that since the 4th century, anti-Jewish policies have attempted "conversion, expulsion, and annihilation" (p. 7). For example, in the 1880s, Jews who were not working in registered professions were forced to flee cities under the czar's control. By 1881, Latvia was 77% Latvian, 11% German, 5% Jewish, and 4% Russian. This sharply contrasts with 1993, when Latvians constituted only 53% of the population, with 33% of its population Russian, 0.6% Jewish, and very few Germans (Plakans 1995). Although during the 19th century the "majority of Latvians and Baltic Germans were tolerant toward refugees" (Dribins 2001, p. 21), the growing nationalism and antisemitism of the late nineteenth and early twentieth centuries throughout Europe could also be found in Latvia, as there were boycotts of Jewish goods and limited rights. A tension of tolerance and xenophobia pervaded, resulting in Jews migrating to Palestine and the United States. At the same time, Jews moved into Latvia from Poland. By 1900, 142,000 Jews lived in Latvia (Dribins 2001).

The end of World War I brought about a unique and rare opportunity for Latvian independence. Even though Germans still occupied Latvia and contemplated plans to colonise it, Kārlis Ulmanis, head of the Agrarian Union Party, was chosen as Latvia's first Prime Minister (Plakans 1995). Following independence, the passage of the Law on Education provided minorities with educational and cultural autonomy, as well as equality (Dribins 2001). Latvia's Constitution, ratified in 1922, solidified these equal rights. As a result, from 1920 to 1935, Latvia experienced a marked increase in Jewish immigrants receiving citizenship.

The Soviet Occupation of Latvia

By 1939, the tenor within Latvia had changed dramatically. The agreements that Latvia ultimately chose to sign with the Soviet Union to demonstrate pacific desires led to the influx of Soviet troops and the *Baigais Gads* (Year of Terror) for many Latvians (Nollendorfs 2002; Sneidere 2005). On 5 October, 1939, Latvia and other Baltic countries signed a treaty of mutual assistance with the Soviet Union, which led to Soviet military bases within Latvian territory. The eventual Soviet occupation had more nefarious consequences for Latvia than the dissolution of independent Latvia, a capitulation perhaps eased by living under Ulmanis' authoritarian government (Sneidere 2005). First, the nationalisation of companies and institutions resulted in negative economic consequences for Latvians and Latvian Jews alike. Yet, simultaneously, Jews could find employment in occupations heretofore closed to them. This was significant, because Germans later presented this gain in opportunity for Jews to the Latvians in their attempt to conflate Latvian Jews and Bolsheviks (Press 2000). Second, the Soviets deported any individuals they found to be unreliable or undesirable; many of them ultimately went on to gulags. From July 1940 through June 1941, the Soviets deported hundreds of Latvian residents, with an eventual total of 35,000 deportees (Plakans 1995; Viksne 2005a). Many of those deported were political and cultural leaders (Reichelt 2004), as well as the bulk of the Latvian army leadership (Nollendorfs 2002). Third, the arrest and deportation of Ulmanis and others initiated a sense of fear within Latvia; now, anyone the Soviets saw as an enemy of the people might face punitive consequences (Senn 2005; Viksne 2005a). The pervasive fear that the Soviets brought on the Latvians helped inform the choices that would be made under German occupation in 1941. Fourth, the way the Latvians and Latvian Jews responded, or at least purportedly responded, to Soviet occupation had profound implications for the way the Holocaust unfolded in Latvia.

In order to understand this complex history, it is essential to not view any group in monolithic terms. Both Latvian Jews and non-Jews were sympathetic to the Soviet cause and both were also victims. Some Jewish communities in Latvia "reacted favorably to the new regime" (Senn 2005, p. 23) and many young Jews welcomed the Soviet army as a liberator (Senn 2005). But the myth that Latvian Jews were more ebullient than Latvians at the arrival of Soviet troops, including the "kissing of tanks", has largely been discredited (Sneidere 2005). A push-and-pull effect existed for many Latvians: they were repelled by the threat of the Nazis and attracted to the promises of communism. But for many, it was a push-and-push effect: both Nazi Germany and the Soviet Union were unattractive suitors.

The Soviets directed their deportations of 35,000 people between 1940 and 1941 at particular groups of politically and economically active Latvians and Latvian Jews which constituted a genocidal act (Riekstins 2005; Totten and Parsons 1997). If it was not genocide, as Vaira Vike-Freiberga, the former president of Latvia suggested it was (Cimdina 2003), then Soviet deportation might be classified as a crime against humanity (Sneidere 2005). Although the Soviets did not aim at destroying the "group" of Latvians through deportations, the terminology typically required for genocidal classification, one may speak of these practices as genocidal in terms of their implications (Legters 1997).

As the Soviets fled Latvia in June of 1941, they usurped any means of transport, emptied warehouses, and appropriated cash registers. After their departure, "the vast majority of the population felt relief" (Sneidere 2005, p. 42), including the thousands of individuals related to the military and government of independent Latvia, who fled to the forests to stay alive. Because Latvians were not aware that Germany had agreed to the Soviet control of Latvia in 1939, many viewed German entry as a potential return to independence and freedom (Feldmanis 2005a). After all, judging from the events and consequences of the end of World War I, this was a reasonable, though illusory, expectation. Therefore, many Latvians viewed the Germans as "liberators" (Plakans 1995, p. 149), because the "hatred and contempt for the Russians was greater than the fear of the Germans" (Press 2000, p. 38). It was not so much that Nazi Germany appealed to Latvians, though it did to some, but rather that their invasion represented freedom and release from communism, a point that did not go unnoticed by Nazi propagandists (Plakans 1995; Sneidere 2005). Soon after occupation, the Nazis produced a photo book entitled *Baigais Gads* (The Year of Horror) which attempted to implicate Jews as Soviet sympathisers and served to remind Latvians of the suffering the Soviets had caused (Dribins 2001).

The Murder of Latvian Jews

What was new in Latvia, compared to other German-occupied territories, was the murder of Jews less than a week after invasion, as well as the systematic nature of the murders compared to those in Byelorussia or Galicia (Stranga 2005). Lativan Jews in small towns and throughout the countryside were the first victims of the Holocaust, beginning on 23 June, 1941. During July of 1941, Germans murdered thousands of Latvian Jews living in Riga at Bikernieki, a forest on the periphery of the city (Dribins 2001). In other cities, Germans and Latvians burned synagogues and pushed Jews into cordons, in order to murder them later. According to an Einsatzgruppen report, by 7 July Latvians had arrested 1,125 Jews in Daugavpils and pogroms were underway in Riga, where a chief from Berlin led the police force (Yitzhak et al. 1989). On 4 July, 1941, Germans and local police ordered Jews into the cellar of the Great Choral Synagogue, where others were already seeking refuge, and proceeded to burn it and murder those inside. By 17 July, less than 1 month after the invasion, the Germans reported that they destroyed all the Riga synagogues (Press 2000). Einsatzgruppen reports from 15 October, 1941, reported that 30,025 Jews had been murdered in Latvia. In reality, over 40,000 were murdered at this point, with the majority of survivors living in designated ghettos within Riga, Daugavpils, and Liepāja (Press 2000). In other cities, automobiles with loudspeakers recruited townspeople to join Latvian defense units, which ultimately led to more manpower for murder (Ezergailis 1996).

In September of 1941, Germans forced 23,000 Jews into a section of Riga, in addition to the 6,000 Jews who lived there, and during the process Germans and Latvians engaged in rampant looting (Ezergailis 1996). The formation of the ghetto eventually became an unresolved problem partly because more Jews had been deported to Latvia; this prompted commands from Nazis to engage in mass murder. As a result, a grove of trees near the train station at Rumbula, some 10 km from Riga, soon had six pits dug by Soviet prisoners of war, each the size of a small house (Dribins 2001).

In October 1941, Germans and Latvians sealed the Riga ghetto. Late in the evening of 29 November, intoxicated Latvian executioners and police received orders to enter. They immediately murdered the infirm and elderly and at 4 a.m., Germans, Latvians, and the police drove and frightened the majority of the ghetto's residents to Rumbula, with many dying along the way (Dribins 2001). On 20 November, beginning at 8:15 a.m. and lasting until 7:45 p.m., 12 Germans murdered 15,000 Jews (Ezergailis 1996; Press 2000). A similar action occurred on 8 December, resulting in the murder of 11,000 Jews.

Frida Michelson (1979), one of the only known survivors of Rumbula, recalled "columns of armed Latvian policeman marching into the ghetto. Some looked drunk.... The Latvian policemen were shouting 'Faster! Faster!' and lashing whips over the heads of the crowd" (pp. 76–77). Once they were walking toward Rumbula, the "situation was hopeless. We were guarded on both sides by policemen and SS men. The little forest was in turn also surrounded by a ring of SS men" (p. 88). According to Michelson, some Latvians showed an interest in taking the Jews' money and other possessions that became available because of this event. Ultimately, of the roughly 85,000 Jews in Latvia during the German occupation, 84,000 were murdered (Press 2000).

Collaboration

The scope of native collaboration in Latvia was quite wide and it encompassed nebulous motivations ranging from accommodation to self-preservation (Nollendorfs 2002). The construct of collaboration is problematised by those explaining or defending their actions as "tactical collaborationists", whose ends served the Latvian people (Feldmanis 2005a). Alternatively, we might think of collaboration in terms of cooperation or treasonous cooperation (Feldmanis 2005b). Either way, it is difficult to tease out the motives and actions of individuals during the Holocaust in Latvia, particularly those who joined killing commandos (Ezergailis 1996). Both the Soviets and Nazis used propaganda, deception, and fear to suppress the national interests of Latvians and advance their own. The use of these tools of persuasion and the incompatible ideologies of fascism and communism blurred the lines surrounding collaboration (Zunda 2005). What we do know is that not all murders were of Jews and not all murderers were German. We also know that recruitment into Latvian police units was voluntary, though often influenced by propaganda (Kangeris 2005). Although it may be "absolutely absurd to call the Latvian people in general...collaborators" (Reichelt 2004, p. 5), thousands of Latvians did collaborate and many more took on the role of bystander.

Who then were the Latvian collaborators? Although an exact figure is difficult to determine, "a few thousands" took part directly or indirectly in the annihilation of the Jews (Stranga 2005, p. 167). Some individuals were not affiliated with a group. For example, the mayor of Krustpils, after arresting Jews in his town, addressed them as those who "trespassed against the Latvian people by betraying them to the Soviet authorities and had to be punished" (Erglis 2005, p. 177). In the provinces, many local residents took part in looting and appropriating the property of victims while Latvian doctors took part in sterilising Jews (Stranga 2005). Typically, the active collaborators and perpetrators were young and unemployed (Reichelt 2004). The largest group of collaborators consisted of those who enlisted in the German armed forces (Feldmanis 2005b) and those who voluntarily served in the *Schutzmannschaften*, or auxiliary police (Ezergailis 1996). Auxiliary and civilian police units registered Jews, murdered Jews, and convoyed Jews to Rumbula. Latvian units were set up explicitly to murder Jews and these men were selected on the basis of whether they had family or relatives who had been murdered or deported by Russians (Ezergailis 1996). The most common rationale for collaboration was the need for a job; no one reported joining a commando out of antisemitism and most Latvians did not commit themselves to the annihilation of the entire group (Ezergailis 1996; Niewyk 1997).

During the early phases of the Holocaust, a number of Latvians considered the theft of Jewish property to be their compensation for participating in the killings (Ezergailis 1996). Free alcohol and cigarettes, a position of privileged power, and the ability to stay within Latvia were additional motivating factors (Ezergailis 1996; Viksne 2005b). Finally, many Latvians did risk their lives trying to help Jews and other victims, yet the number of murderers far exceeded the number of rescuers (Stranga 2005). Looting was another motive that many found attractive, as a number of Latvian officers were stranded in the war with no income and little purpose (Reichelt 2004). Nazi Germany's invasion also provided Latvians with an opportunity to avenge Stalinist crimes.

Ezergailis (1996) proposed several possible reasons why the vast number of Latvian bystanders took no action. First, no public defense against Nazi Germany, or the Soviet army, was really practical. Second, hiding Jews would result in imprisonment and family suffering. Third, the Nazis penetrated Latvian society with spies in order to undermine resistance and rescue. It took "some time for the Latvians to discover that the Nazis were as dangerous to their country as were the Soviets" (Ezergailis 1996, p. 25). Fourth, many of the younger collaborators grew up under the authoritarian Ulmanis regime and were consequently not free and critical thinkers (Viksne 2005b). Latvians still followed and respected the "rule of law", albeit one Germany imposed, resulting in few interventions (Ezergailis 1996). As a result, some Latvians responded to their neighbors as Press (2000) described:

> People watched for Jews standing in line in front of shops and tried not to sell them food.... Our Latvian friends, with whom we had only yesterday caroused and celebrated, acted as though they no longer knew us. (p. 51)

Moreover, the experience of a short-lived occupation prior to the arrival of the Germans, as well as hope of escaping forced labor or some worse fate, enhanced people's motivations to either participate or stand by (Niewyk 1997).

Contemporary Renderings of the Past

One reason that discussions default to collaboration when dealing with the Holocaust in Latvia is linked to the participation of Latvians in the Waffen branch of the Nazi SS. Misperceptions have further enhanced the myth that some outsiders wish to perpetuate: that all Latvians were collaborators and antisemites. This has exacerbated the desire to focus on Soviet crimes against Latvia. The annual commemoration of veterans from the Latvian legion of the Waffen-SS is often quite visible in the media, which provides fuel for Russian criticism of Latvian society. This myth twists the historical record, as most Latvian members of the SS were conscripted and this happened after the majority of Latvian Jews had been murdered. But it ultimately serves to further divert the focus away from the Holocaust. One school in northern Latvia has attempted to bridge this chasm by inviting veterans who fought on both Soviet and German sides into classrooms. Latvians fighting for both Soviet and German armies more often than not had little choice but to fight. But students are often unaware of the complexities that informed the motives at work in the war, or of the way participation is represented today.

The international media in the Baltic States also continue to bring visibility to the relationship that thousands of Latvians had with the SS; they consistently excoriate the annual march memorialising the Latvian SS legion (Lefkovits 2008). Nazi Germany had not planned on using Latvian troops as armed units (Pavlovics 2005), but after 1942, as the war effort faltered, there was a growing demand among the Germans to recruit more Latvians into uniform (Ezergailis 1996). As a result, under Hitler's orders, a Latvian legion was formed within the Waffen-SS, the combat arm of the *Schutzstaffel* (protective squadron), though this was accomplished by draft. In total, 146,000 Latvians born between 1919 and 1929 were conscripted. Latvians who served for the Waffen-SS fought against the Soviets, who had "annihilated Latvia's independence, carried out repressions against civilians, and threatened to occupy their country for a second time" (Feldmanis 2005a, p. 86). Other countries occupied by Germany at this time experienced a similar fate of native troops conscripted into the Waffen-SS, as over half were not Germans (Feldmanis 2005b). But these sorts of troops are not the same as German Waffen-SS divisions. Natives could not simply form their own divisions nor enter the regular German army; this resulted in Himmler placing them in his organisation and assigning them a logically appropriate name (Feldmanis 2005a; Kangeris 2005). The Waffen-SS legion consisted of over 100,000 soldiers at a time when the Holocaust in Latvia had largely ended.

Latvia's history very much informs the present. At the end of the curriculum project I worked on (2006), one curriculum writer cogently noted that in normal interaction within Latvian society "almost every conversation comes back to Latvia's history". She pointed to the treatment of Russians, memories of the Holocaust, and topics relegated to closed areas as examples of a present and past that apparently time has still not distanced from daily life. Latvia's history of occupation has profoundly influenced the way of life for many, as evinced in societal tendencies to maintain bureaucracy, pervasive reticence, and passivity, as well as its visibility in current events. Other examples include the United States Congressmen who excoriated Russia for admitting to neither the occupation of Latvia after World War II nor the fact that this occupation was illegal (Eglitis 2005b). In addition, Putin's interest in abrogating the Molotov-Ribbentrop Pact of 1939 (Putin Prepared 2005) has made frequent headlines. The visit of Latvia's president to Russia was also very much informed by the occupation, for had she not attended, some felt that Russia and other countries would have declared that Latvia was a "Nazi country".

Influences on Holocaust Education

Holocaust education is a controversial topic shaped through a variety of political, educational, historical, and nationalistic forces. The deportation of Latvians during the Soviet occupation of 1940–1941 still very much influences the views of teachers, parents, politicians, and students. The focus that many Latvians have on the perceived absence of dialogue about Latvian suffering during that period is related to the problem of comparative trivialisation, which often disrupts effective Holocaust education (Shafir 2003). As a result of the decades of silence concerning the Holocaust during Soviet occupation, which is a recurring theme in a number of former Soviet countries (Frankl 2003), the absence of an accurate Holocaust education curriculum in Latvian schools resulted in ignorance and indifference to the fate of Jews. Yet now, more than 15 years after independence, the bulk of schools in Latvia teach about the Holocaust in two lessons, for a total of 80 min, without deep analysis of the Holocaust as it occurred in Latvia.

This cursory approach is reinforced by three factors: the general resistance to discussing collaborators, external pressures to address Latvian complicity, and misunderstandings foreigners have concerning Latvian legionnaires in the Nazi Waffen-SS. The lack of analytic investigations of the Holocaust after Soviet reoccupation and the perpetuation of spurious and propagandistic ideas in texts such as *Bagais Gads* have ultimately advanced uncomplicated renderings of this history as subsequent generations have inherited a distorted version of Latvia's past. Moreover, the rigorous control of collective memory and history within the Soviet Union (Wertsch 2002) helped shape the way Latvians thought about the Holocaust. Apathy, ignorance, victimisation, and antisemitism all clearly work against the willingness of teachers and citizens to engage in teaching or learning about the Holocaust in Latvia.

Similar to other European countries that experienced the Holocaust within their borders, many Latvians had avoided facing their history due to collaboration, bystander inaction, and non-Jewish suffering (van Driel 2003). One teacher I interviewed during a study on Holocaust education as practiced in schools suggested that "we just don't have different people" and that a fundamental equality permeates educational discourse concerning difference (Misco 2006). But in reality, non-Latvians are often treated quite differently. The fears associated with mixing Latvian and Russian speakers (Silova 2002), the glacial pace of granting citizenship to

Russians (Ozolins 1999; Protassova 2002), and the othering of those who are perceptibly different exemplify the incongruity of education and societal life. Yet, these contemporary societal problems represent only part of a rationale for Holocaust education. In addition, the Holocaust is an essential topic for a democracy (Brown and Davies 1998), it is effective at addressing intolerance in a society (Salmons 2003), and when it constitutes a closed area it becomes a lesson for unearthing and revaluing the beliefs, attitudes, and assumptions of that society (Schweber 2004), which is an essential component of a democratic education (Griffin 1942).

Although circumstances in Latvia are certainly unique, other societies face similar problems (Stevick 2007). Some societies experience strong restrictions on instructional time (Davies 2000; Misco 2008) and course structures (Frankl 2003), have little obligation to instruct about the Holocaust (Santerini 2003; Short 2003), and have national assessments that focus on other subjects (Brown and Davies 1998; Misco 2008). Together, these elements serve to diminish the opportunities for Holocaust education. In Latvia, many teachers cite forces related to their Ministry of Education, including a limited number of lessons, lack of time, adherence to a set curriculum, syllabi, national exams, national standards, gaps in teacher knowledge, and limited materials, all of which serve to diminish Holocaust education (Misco 2007).

Impediments to Facing History, and Consequences of Not Doing So

In the main, ethnic Latvians have a nostalgic view of the past and do not contest the Judeo-Bolshevik conflation; meanwhile they generalise about the Holocaust, often glossing over details and neglecting to separate the deportations of Latvians and murder of Jews (Zisere 2005). A number of negative consequences exist for not facing a history replete with prejudice and intolerance, including the further entrenchment of silence among teachers, students, and the milieu concerning the Holocaust in Latvia. Therefore, the factors that reduce Holocaust education also help perpetuate and entrench those influences. Although we cannot establish a causal linkage between avoiding historical topics and contemporary intolerance, being aware of the avoidance at least helps to explain how prejudices are perpetuated. Currently, Latvia faces intolerance in the form of homophobia, xenophobia, ethnocracy, antisemitism, and racism. I contend that each of these prejudices is partially rooted in the sustained silence about the Holocaust in Latvia within Latvian schools and society. One educator I spoke with noted this about Latvians:

> [We] are a little too concentrated on ourselves. We are the ones who suffered and we've gone through a specific and awful situation, and that's all true, but just let's recognize that other nations and other people in different parts of the world have suffered very similarly and with awful things as we have. Also, in this contemporary situation it would help young people and teachers to somehow become more accepting of variety and diversity, to the whole meaning of tolerance. So we are not the ones who are the best or suffered the most. But it's just common things that happen, and what to do to not allow them to happen, right?

Reducing intolerance and prejudice is a legitimate goal of any Holocaust education programme, which is even more pronounced given the challenges Latvia faces with issues of diversity.

In July 2005, *The Baltic Times* reported that Latvia's first gay pride parade, held in Riga's Old Town, resulted in a violent interchange between police and protestors (Eglitis 2005c). Protestors threw eggs and other items at the parade's participants and members of anti-gay groups attempted to physically obstruct the march. Amnesty International expressed outrage at the failure of some government officials to support the protestors. In a television interview following the parade, Prime Minister Aigars Kalvitis referred to the event as a "mistake", given the country's "Christian value roots". In an effort to stymie homophobic views, the daily paper *Diena* published an open letter that expressed concern over Latvian intolerance, citing recent racially motivated attacks, active homophobia, and visible antisemitism as examples. The lack of receptivity to parade participants prompted German tour operators to cancel tours to Latvia until there is a "better policy for minorities like gays" (Eglitis 2005d). Because Holocaust education can help bring about the reduction of intolerance and prejudice, its absence is linked to contemporary homophobia, as well as to the murder of homosexuals during the Holocaust.

Although roughly 30% of Latvian residents are Russian, they remain conspicuously distinct from ethnic Latvians. For example, the language of instruction in Latvian schools is currently a highly contentious issue (Crawford 2002). When a larger proportion of Russian parents began sending children to Latvian-speaking schools, officials responded by suggesting that "mixed" schools were not desirable because of the potential "negative effects" for Latvian students (Silova 2002, p. 466). Fearful of the "mixing" effects associated with increased enrollment of Russian students in Latvian-speaking schools, policy makers decided to step up the Latvianisation of minority schools, thereby providing Latvian language skills but maintaining separate institutions (Batelaan 2002). In addition, Russians, many of whom have lived in Latvia since independence, must endure long waits to gain citizenship (Ozolins 1999), which has resulted in a lack of political voice. As a result of these policies, Russia continually cites ill treatment of minorities in Latvia (Latvia to Appeal 2005), including discrimination and disenfranchisement.

Teachers I spoke with indicated that Latvia is "not a very tolerant society in terms of otherness" and others echoed this sentiment, suggesting that "xenophobia and antisemitism is very alive in our society" (Misco 2006, p. 138). In many ways, xenophobia, intolerance, and racism interact, with common roots in a disdain for difference and otherness. Latvia has also witnessed an increase in graffiti that includes swastikas and messages such as "white power" (Eglitis 2005a). Ilze Kehris, director of Latvia's Human Rights Centre, suggested that "there is an illusion that Latvia is a tolerant society", in spite of the polls that "have shown a tendency toward xenophobia… and growing intolerance against Africans, Chinese, Central Asians, and especially Muslims" (Eglitis 2005a). A memorial to Jews murdered in the Bikernieki forest was vandalised in September 2005–two years after vandals overturned tombstones and painted swastikas in a Jewish cemetery (Latvian Holocaust Memorial 2005).

Yet, much like the Holocaust, racism is rarely exposed to substantive discourse and reflection. Racism and antisemitism are both tied to an unwillingness to broach complicated, sensitive, and controversial issues. In response, teaching about the Holocaust can help uncover antisemitic, discriminatory, and racist beliefs (Short 2003), build tolerance and respect for diversity, develop sensitivities to injustice (Frankl 2003), and apply it to future and contemporary events (Rathenow 2000). Therefore, antisemitism and racism are not only justifications for deep and accurate Holocaust education instruction, but also crucial because the growth and perpetuation of intolerance makes it even harder for members of Latvian society to examine historical differences with an open mind, and to willingly broach Holocaust history.

Remembrance and Memorialisation

Following Latvia's independence in 1991, numerous declarations, memorials, and efforts have attempted to confront the history of the Holocaust in Latvia. Remembrance had a difficult beginning. During a 1991 ceremony memorialising the 50th anniversary of the murder of Jews at Rumbula, Parliamentary President Anatolijs Gorbunovs offered words about the death of innocent victims, and then claimed that the victims themselves were to blame because they had shown favour to Soviet rulers when Latvia was first occupied – a common but persistent bit of anachronistic propaganda. And, as recently as 2000, cross-country skiers from Riga were still riding over the mass graves in Bikernieki (Press 2000).

More recently, remembrance has moved in a positive direction. For example, after independence, the Latvian Parliament issued a declaration on the Inadmissibility of Genocide and Antisemitism in Latvia (Gūtmanis 2001, p. 89). July 4th was proclaimed as the Remembrance Day to honor the loss of life of Jews who were led into the Synagogue on Gogola Street and burned to death. On the anniversary of this event in 2000, the President of Latvia said this:

> It is important not only to research those episodes in the tragedy of the Holocaust that are not yet known to us but also to research the participation of Latvian citizens in these crimes. (Cimdina 2003, p. 164)

By 2001, Latvia had joined the Special Task Force for International Co-operation on Holocaust Education, Research, and Remembrance, which was part of the larger movement towards understanding, atonement, and acceptance in the European Union. Worldwide attempts to understand the Holocaust have served to awaken consciousness of the Holocaust as well as other genocides, with the ultimate hope that never again will pervasive indifference take hold (Charny 1997). Former President Vaira Vike-Freiberga recognised the value of introspection and understanding the past, and she has noted the "need for education about the Holocaust in Latvia's schools", continuing that "Only that way can we help ensure stable democracy in the future" (Cimdina 2003, p. 164).

Ostensibly, Latvian politicians and authorities are increasingly supporting Holocaust education (Gūtmanis 2001). In this context, teaching about the Holocaust is a process of healing, remembering, reflecting, reconciling, and reforming (Patrick 2005). In other words, much is asked of a topic that receives short shrift in a crowded curriculum. If a new social and political identity is to form in democratic and independent Latvia, it can only do so "after the contradictions in the society created by the occupation have been fully understood and overcome, including those of collaboration and resistance" (Nollendorfs 2002, p. 75). Students who study genocide need to learn not only about the causes and effects, but also about every individual's responsibility for moral action when rights are violated (Totten and Parsons 1997).

In 2002, Prime Minister Einars Repse, at the Riga Jewish Museum, said that "Latvia has to be able to openly and honestly analyze our past; unpleasant historical facts cannot be changed or hidden" (Coleman 2002). The widening and enlarging normative mandate of the public school experience is the proper venue for these discussions and considerations (Hlebowitsh 2005) and if students do not address difficult questions they will be less able to develop life skills. Because any belief that is not "subjected to rational examination is by definition a prejudice no matter how correct or incorrect it might be" (Hunt and Metcalf 1968, p. 27), schools need to provide a suitable environment and a significant amount of time for prejudice reduction. The need to reduce prejudices by opening closed areas ties into contemporary intolerances in Latvian society and the need to teach about the Holocaust.

References

Batelaan, P. (2002). Bilingual education: The case of Latvia from a comparative perspective. *International Education, 13*(4), 359–374.

Baum, R. N. (2000). Never to forget: Pedagogical memory and second-generation witness. In R. I. Simon, R. Rosenberg, & C. Eppert (Eds.), *Between hope and despair* (pp. 91–116). New York: Rowman & Littlefield.

Brown, M., & Davies, I. (1998). The Holocaust and education for citizenship: The teaching of history, religion and human rights in England. *Education Review, 50*(1), 75–83.

Burtonwood, N. (2002). Holocaust memorial day in schools – Context, process, and content: A review of research into Holocaust education. *Educational Research, 44*(1), 69–82.

Charny, I. W. (1997). Which genocide matters more? Learning to care about humanity. In S. Totten, W. S. Parsons, & I. W. Charny (Eds.), *Century of genocide: Eyewitness accounts and critical views* (pp. xiii–xix). New York: Garland.

Cimdina, A. (2003). *In the name of freedom: A biography of Vaira Vike-Freiberga* (K. Streips, Trans.). Riga: Jumava.

Coleman, N. (2002, 5 December). Memorial to 26,000 who died in Holocaust unveiled. *Baltic Times.* http://www.baltictimes.com/news/articles/7282/#.U5G8wpRdUgQ

Crawford, A. N. (2002). Bilingual education in the United States: A window on the Latvian situation. *Intercultural Education, 13*(4), 375–389.

Crossa, V. (2005). Converting the "small stories" into "big" ones: A response to Susan Smith's "States, markets and an ethic of care". *Political Geography, 24*, 29–34.

Curtis, C. K., & Shaver, J. P. (1980). Slow learners as the study of contemporary problems. *Social Education, 44*, 302–309.

Davies, I. (2000). Introduction: The challenges of teaching and learning about the Holocaust. In I. Davies (Ed.), *Teaching the Holocaust: Educational dimensions, principles and practices* (pp. 1–8). New York: Continuum.

Deckert-Peaceman, H. (2003). Teaching the Holocaust in the USA: A German perspective. *Intercultural Education, 14*(2), 215–224.

Dewey, J. (1938). What is social study? *Progressive Education, 15*(5).

Dribins, L. (2001). The history of the Jewish community in Latvia. In L. Dribins, A. Gūtmanis, & M. Vestermanis (Eds.), *Latvia's Jewish community: History, tragedy, revival* (pp. 9–86). Riga: Institute of the History of Latvia.

Eglitis, A. (2005a, 13 April). Racism rears its ugly head. *Baltic Times.* http://www.baltictimes.com/news/articles/12455/#.U5HH7ZRdUgQ

Eglitis, A. (2005b, 20 April). U.S. Congressmen: Russia should admit occupation. *Baltic Times.* http://www.baltictimes.com/news/articles/12502/#.U5HJHZRdUgQ

Eglitis, A. (2005c, 27 July). Gays march amid huge police contingent. *Baltic Times.* http://www.baltictimes.com/news/articles/13120/#.U5G7M5RdUgQ

Eglitis, A. (2005d, 3 August). Parade sours Latvia's image. *Baltic Times.* http://www.baltictimes.com/news/articles/13167/#.U5G-85RdUgQ

Erglis, D. (2005). A few episodes of the Holocaust in Krustpils: A microcosm of the Holocaust in occupied Latvia. In V. Nollendorfs & E. Oberlander (Eds.), *The hidden and forbidden history of Latvia under Soviet and Nazi occupations 1940–1991*. Riga: Institute of the History of Latvia.

Ezergailis, A. (1996). *The Holocaust in Latvia, 1941–1944: The missing center*. Riga: Model Printing House.

Feldmanis, I. (2005a). Latvia under the occupation of national socialist Germany 1941–1945. In V. Nollendorfs & E. Oberlander (Eds.), *The hidden and forbidden history of Latvia under Soviet and Nazi occupations 1940–1991* (pp. 77–91). Riga: Institute of the History of Latvia.

Feldmanis, I. (2005b). Waffen-SS units of Latvians and other non-Germanic peoples in World War II: Methods of formation, ideology and goals. In V. Nollendorfs & E. Oberlander (Eds.), *The hidden and forbidden history of Latvia under Soviet and Nazi occupations 1940–1991* (pp. 122–131). Riga: Institute of the History of Latvia.

Frankl, M. (2003). Holocaust education in the Czech Republic, 1989–2002. *Intercultural Education, 14*(2), 177–189.

Gaughan, J. (2001). *Reinventing English: Teaching in the contact zone*. Portsmouth: Boynton/Cook.

Goldenson, D. R. (1978). An alternative view about the role of the secondary school in political socialization: A field-experimental study of the development of civil liberties attitudes. *Theory and Research in Social Education, 6*(1), 44–72.

Graseck, S. (2009). Teaching with controversy: Educators awaken student voice by providing a safe place for dialogue about immigration, war, and other hot–button issues. *Educational Leadership, 67*, 45–49.

Gregory, I. (2000). Teaching about the Holocaust: Perplexities, issues and suggestions. In I. Davies (Ed.), *Teaching the Holocaust: Educational dimensions, principles and practices* (pp. 49–60). New York: Continuum.

Griffin, A. F. (1942). Teaching in authoritarian and democratic states. In W. C. Parker (Ed.), *Educating the democratic mind* (pp. 79–94). Albany: State University of New York Press.

Gundare, I., & Batelaan, P. (2003). Learning about and from the Holocaust: The development and implementation of a complex instruction unit in Latvia. *Intercultural Education, 14*(2), 151–166.

Gūtmanis, A. (2001). Holocaust education, research, and remembrance: Latvian public policy after the re-establishment of independence in 1991. In L. Dribins, A. Gūtmanis, & M. Vestermanis (Eds.), *Latvia's Jewish community: History, tragedy, revival* (pp. 89–98). Riga: Institute of the History of Latvia.

Harwood, A. M., & Hahn, C. L. (1990). *Controversial issues in the classroom*. Bloomington: Eric Clearinghouse for Social Studies Education. ERIC document no. ED327453.

Hess, D. (2009). *Controversy in the classroom: The democratic power of discussion.* New York: Routledge.

Hess, D., & Ganzler, L. (2006). Patriotism and ideological diversity in the classroom. In J. Westheimer (Ed.), *Pledging allegiance: The politics of patriotism in America's schools* (pp. 131–138). New York: Teachers College Press.

Hess, D., & Posselt, J. (2002). How high school students experience and learn from the discussion of controversial public issues. *Journal of Curriculum and Supervision, 17*(4), 283–314.

Hilberg, R. (1985). *The destruction of the European Jews.* New York: Holmes & Meier.

Hlebowitsh, P. S. (2005). *Designing the school curriculum.* Boston: Allyn & Bacon.

Hlebowitsh, P. S., Hamot, G. E., & Misco, T. (2006). *The development of Holocaust education materials for two curriculum forms in the Latvian schools: A final report.* Iowa City: The University of Iowa.

Hunt, M. P., & Metcalf, L. E. (1968). *Teaching high school social studies.* New York: Harper and Row.

Kangeris, K. (2005). "Closed" units of Latvian police – lettische schutzmannschafts-bataillone: Research issues and pre-history. In V. Nollendorfs & E. Oberlander (Eds.), *The hidden and forbidden history of Latvia under Soviet and Nazi occupations 1940–1991* (pp. 104–121). Riga: Institute of the History of Latvia.

King, J. T. (2009). Teaching and learning about controversial issues: Lessons from Northern Ireland. *Theory and Research in Social Education, 37*(2), 215–246.

LaCapra, D. (1992). Representing the Holocaust: Reflections on the historians' debate. In S. Friedlander (Ed.), *Probing the limits of representation* (pp. 108–127). Cambridge: Harvard University Press.

Latvia to Appeal European Court Ruling on Soviet Military Family (2005, 30 September). *Agence France Presse.* Retrieved 22 October, 2005, from LexisNexis Academic Database.

Latvian Holocaust Memorial Vandalized (2005, 12 September). *Deutsche Presse-Agentur.* Retrieved 22 October, 2005, from LexisNexis Academic Database.

Lefkovits, E. (2008, 17 March). Nazi hunter blasts Latvian march honoring SS unit. *Jerusalem Post.* http://www.jpost.com/Jewish-World/Jewish-News/Nazi-hunter-blasts-Latvian-march-honoring-SS-unit

Legters, L. H. (1997). Soviet deportation of whole nations: A genocidal process. In S. Totten, W. S. Parsons, & I. W. Charny (Eds.), *Century of genocide: Eyewitness accounts and critical views* (pp. 113–135). New York: Garland.

McGowan, T., McGowan, M. J., & Lombard, R. H. (1994). Empowering young citizens for social action. *Social Studies and the Young Learner, 7*(1), 21–23.

Michelson, F. (1979). *I survived Rumbuli* (W. Goodman, Trans.). New York: Holocaust Library.

Misco, T. (2006). Breaking historical silences through cross-cultural curriculum deliberation: Teaching the Holocaust in Latvian schools. Doctoral dissertation, University of Iowa, Iowa City, UMI: 3225652.

Misco, T. (2007). Holocaust curriculum development for Latvian schools: Arriving at purposes, aims, and goals through curriculum deliberation. *Theory and Research in Social Education, 35*(3), 393–426.

Misco, T. (2008). "We did also save people": A study of Holocaust education in Romania after decades of historical silence. *Theory and Research in Social Education, 36*(2), 61–94.

Misco, T. (2010). Moving beyond fidelity expectations: Rethinking curriculum reform for controversial topics in post-communist settings. *Theory and Research in Social Education, 38*(2), 182–216.

Misco, T. (2011). Teaching about controversial issues: Rationale, practice, and need for inquiry. *International Journal for Education, Law, and Policy, 7*(1), 7–18.

Niewyk, D. L. (1997). Holocaust: The genocide of the Jews. In S. Totten, W. S. Parsons, & I. W. Charny (Eds.), *Century of genocide: Eyewitness accounts and critical views* (pp. 127–160). New York: Garland.

Nollendorfs, V. (2002). *Museum of the occupation of Latvia.* Riga: Madonas Poligrāfists.

Ozolins, U. (1999). Between Russian and European hegemony: Current language policy in the Baltic states. *Current Issues in Language and Society, 6*(1), 6–47.

Parker, W. C. (2003). The deliberative approach to education for democracy: Problems and possibilities. In J. J. Patrick, G. E. Hamot, & R. S. Leming (Eds.), *Civic learning in teacher education* (pp. 99–115). Bloomington: Eric Clearinghouse.

Patrick, J. (2005, August). *Remembrance, reflection, reconciliation, and reformation: Imperatives of teaching and learning about the Holocaust within civic education for liberty and democracy.* Paper presented at From the Past to the Future: Learning about the Holocaust within the Framework of Civic Education, Riga.

Pavlovics, J. (2005). Change of occupation powers in Latvia in summer 1941: Experience of small communities. In V. Nollendorts & E. Oberlander (Eds.), *The hidden and forbidden history of Latvia under Soviet and Nazi occupations 1940–1991* (pp. 92–103). Riga: Institute of the History of Latvia.

Plakans, A. (1995). *The Latvians: A short history*. Stanford: Hoover Institution Press.

Press, B. (2000). *The murder of the Jews in Latvia*. Evanston: Northwestern University Press.

Protassova, E. (2002). Latvian bilingual education: Towards a new approach. *Intercultural Education, 13*(4), 439–449.

Putin Prepared to Annul Molotov-Ribbentrop Pact (2005, 19 January). *The Baltic Times*. http://www.baltictimes.com/news/articles/11812/#.U5HHgpRdUgQ

Rathenow, H. (2000). Teaching the Holocaust in Germany. In I. Davies (Ed.), *Teaching the Holocaust: Educational dimensions, principles and practices* (pp. 63–76). New York: Continuum.

Reichelt, K. (2004, 20 September). *The fate of the Latvian Jewry under different occupations especially under the condition of the persecution by the Nazi occupiers and the Latvian reaction to it*. Paper presented at the United States Holocaust Memorial Museum, Washington, DC.

Remy, R. C. (1972). High school seniors' attitudes toward their civics and government instruction. *Social Education, 36*, 590–597.

Riekstins, J. (2005). The 14 June 1941 deportation in Latvia. In V. Nollendorts & E. Oberlander (Eds.), *The hidden and forbidden history of Latvia under Soviet and Nazi occupations 1940–1991* (pp. 62–76). Riga: Institute of the History of Latvia.

Ross, E. W., & Marker, P. M. (2005). (If social studies is wrong) I don't want to be right. *Theory and Research in Social Education, 33*(1), 142–151.

Salmons, P. (2003). Teaching or preaching? The Holocaust and intercultural education in the UK. *Intercultural Education, 14*(2), 139–149.

Santerini, M. (2003). Holocaust education in Italy. *Intercultural Education, 14*(2), 225–232.

Schweber, S. (2004). *Making sense of the Holocaust*. New York: Teachers College Press.

Senn, A. E. (2005). Baltic battleground. In V. Nollendorts & E. Oberlander (Eds.), *The hidden and forbidden history of Latvia under Soviet and Nazi occupations 1940–1991* (pp. 17–32). Riga: Institute of the History of Latvia.

Shafir, M. (2003). *The 'comparative trivialization' of the Holocaust*. Washington, DC: Radio Free Europe/Radio Liberty.

Shoemaker, R. (2003). Teaching the Holocaust in America's schools: Some considerations for teachers. *Intercultural Education, 14*(2), 191–199.

Short, G. (2003). Lessons of the Holocaust: A response to the critics. *Educational Review, 55*(3), 277–287.

Silova, I. (2002). Bilingual education theater: Behind the scenes of Latvian minority education reform. *Intercultural Education, 13*(4), 463–476.

Simon, R. I. (2000). The paradoxical practice of zakhor: Memories of "what has never been my fault or my deed". In R. I. Simon, R. Rosenberg, & C. Eppert (Eds.), *Between hope & despair* (pp. 9–26). New York: Rowman & Littlefield.

Sneidere, I. (2005). The first Soviet occupation period in Latvia 1940–1941. In V. Nollendorfs & E. Oberlander (Eds.), *The hidden and forbidden history of Latvia under Soviet and Nazi occupations 1940–1991* (pp. 33–42). Riga: Institute of the History of Latvia.

Stevick, E. D. (2007). The politics of the Holocaust in Estonia: Historical memory and social divisions in Estonian education. In E. D. Stevick & B. A. U. Levinson (Eds.), *Reimagining civic education: How diverse societies form democratic citizens* (pp. 217–244). Lanham: Rowman and Littlefield.

Stranga, A. (2005). The Holocaust in occupied Latvia: 1941–1945. In V. Nollendorfs & E. Oberlander (Eds.), *The hidden and forbidden history of Latvia under Soviet and Nazi occupations 1940–1991* (pp. 161–174). Riga: Institute of the History of Latvia.

Torney-Purta, J., Lehman, R., Oswald, H., & Schulz, W. (2002). Citizenship and education in twenty-eight countries. Amsterdam: International Association for the Evaluation of Education Achievement. http://www.terpconnect.umd.edu/~jtpurta/

Totten, S., & Feinberg, S. (1995). Teaching about the Holocaust: Rationale, content, methodology, & resources. *Social Education, 59*(6), 323–333.

Totten, S., & Parsons, W. S. (1997). Introduction. In S. Totten, W. S. Parsons, & I. W. Charny (Eds.), *Century of genocide: Eyewitness accounts and critical views* (pp. 1–16). New York: Garland.

van Driel, B. (2003). Some reflections on the connection between Holocaust education and intercultural education. *Intercultural Education, 14*(2), 125–137.

Viksne, R. (2005a). Soviet repressions against residents of Latvia in 1940–1941: Typical trends. In V. Nollendorfs & E. Oberlander (Eds.), *The hidden and forbidden history of Latvia under Soviet and Nazi occupations 1940–1991* (pp. 53–61). Riga: Institute of the History of Latvia.

Viksne, R. (2005b). Members of the Arajs commando in Soviet court files: Social position, education, reasons for volunteering, penalty. In V. Nollendorfs & E. Oberlander (Eds.), *The hidden and forbidden history of Latvia under Soviet and Nazi occupations 1940–1991* (pp. 188–208). Riga: Institute of the History of Latvia.

Wertsch, J. V. (2002). *Voices of collective remembering*. New York: Cambridge University Press.

Yitzhak, A., Krakowski, S., & Spector, S. (1989). *The Einsatzgruppen reports*. New York: Holocaust Library.

Young, I. M. (1996). Communication and the other: Beyond deliberative democracy. In S. Benhabib (Ed.), *Democracy and difference: Contesting the boundaries of the political* (pp. 120–137). Princeton: Princeton University Press.

Zisere, B. (2005). The memory of the Shoah in the post-Soviet Latvia. *East European Jewish Affairs, 35*(2), 155–165.

Zunda, A. (2005). Resistance against Nazi German occupation in Latvia: Positions in historical literature. In V. Nollendorts & E. Oberlander (Eds.), *The hidden and forbidden history of Latvia under Soviet and Nazi occupations 1940–1991* (pp. 148–160). Riga: Institute of the History of Latvia.

Mastering the Past? Nazism and the Holocaust in West German History Textbooks of the 1960s

Brian M. Puaca

Introduction

In his 1963 textbook on modern German history for children in Bavarian secondary schools, Josef Scherl (1963) broached difficult material that may have been a revelation to some of his readers. In this revised edition of his *Geschichte unseres Volkes* (History of our People), Scherl dedicated several pages to an examination of Germany's crimes against the Jews. In a section covering the first years of the Third Reich, he discussed the many unjust measures passed against the Jews and included a discussion of *Kristallnacht*, the November 1938 pogrom orchestrated by the Nazis. Even more significantly, Scherl incorporated several pages on Nazi racism and the extermination of the Jews in a later section on the war. In these pages, young readers learned about the gas chambers and ovens used at Auschwitz, read the Nuremberg testimony of former commandant Rudolf Hoess detailing the use of Zyklon B and its effects, and encountered a map that illustrated the complex network of camps that made possible the murder of millions of Jews.

Making Scherl's textbook all the more remarkable was its use of open-ended moral questions requiring pupils to reflect on, deliberate, and discuss the difficult issues it engaged. At one point, pupils were asked to consider whether one should discuss the shameful deeds that Germans had committed before and during the war. Before answering, pupils encountered a reminder from the author that to learn from mistakes, one has to acknowledge and reflect on them. Scherl also informed his readers that even if others do evil, that is no excuse for them to commit the same transgressions. "My guilt will not be reduced", he intoned, "if I point out the mistakes of my neighbour" (p. 124). Scherl likely used this prompt as a means to have

---

B.M. Puaca (✉)
Department of History, Christopher Newport University, 1 Avenue of the Arts, Newport News, VA 23606, USA
e-mail: bpuaca@cnu.edu

his readers discuss the common post-war defense employed by many Germans who sought to divert attention from their own responsibility by drawing attention to the crimes of others or their own suffering. Perhaps more subtly, this point also relates to the popular post-war refrain that many Germans had simply followed orders. Another question prompted pupils to consider how they would respond if an American said: "All Germans are murderers! One should make them wear the symbol of the gallows on their jacket!" (p. 101). An obvious allusion to the Star of David that Jews were forced to wear during the Third Reich (explicitly mentioned in the text), the question was likely intended to spark a discussion of individual responsibility, the dangers of prejudice and hatred, and the moral hazards of remaining silent when openly confronted with the persecution of others.

Published in a textbook for pupils who were completing their education in the *Volksschulen* of Bavaria, Scherl's book began to appear in classrooms in the mid-1960s. The readers of Scherl's study would have been too young to have any personal memory of the Third Reich or World War II: these eighth graders had been born in the years after Germany's defeat and had spent their formative years living in a democratic state that had experienced a miraculous economic boom. They had also grown up in Bavaria, a strongly Catholic area that had been a Nazi stronghold only a few decades earlier. The state was now ruled by the conservative Christian Social Union (CSU) and had a Culture Ministry notorious for resisting pedagogical and curricular reforms in the schools—and equally proud of German educational practices and Bavaria's cultural traditions (Buchinger 1975, pp. 17–79; Hahn 1998, pp. 111–112; Müller 1995, pp. 111–272; Tent 1982, pp. 110–163). And yet, even here, in a state known for its historical aversion to innovative teaching methods, students aged 12 and 13 encountered a discussion of their country's recent past that was not only likely more forthright than they had heard at home, but also one that prompted them to think critically for themselves and perhaps to even ask questions of those who had witnessed these events personally. This narrative and the pedagogical strategies it employed signal a remarkable change from the textbooks published just 5–10 years earlier.

In this chapter I trace the development of history textbooks in the Federal Republic and explore the treatment of the Third Reich and, in particular, the murder of European Jewry. In doing so, I make several claims. First, the German educational system did not remain silent about Nazi crimes. Contrary to popular perceptions regarding the teaching of Germany's recent past, pupils typically began to encounter direct, frank, honest, and often explicit analysis related to the Third Reich, war, and the Holocaust in the early 1960s. Admittedly, the teaching of these traumatic events was incomplete and uneven across the schools of the Federal Republic, but it is inaccurate to characterise history instruction in West Germany during this era as completely stagnant or restorative. Second, the creation of this more open and forthright narrative required almost two decades before it truly gained traction. Were there some pioneers who sought to engage these issues before the early 1960s? There were, just as there were also those who attempted to sidestep or marginalise these important topics afterwards. That said, an analysis of the major history publications used in the schools during this period provides evidence for a significant transition in regard to the treatment of the recent German past during this pivotal decade. Indeed, these textbooks serve as a reminder that meaningful efforts to "master the past" (*Vergangenheitsbewältigung*) occurred well before the academic debates and popular controversies of the 1980s. Third, the new history textbooks of the 1960s encouraged pupils to engage actively in their study of the recent past. Unlike earlier texts, these books promoted discussion and debate among pupils, challenged them to engage the most controversial topics through group activities, and even encouraged interactions outside of class with family and community members.

In this chapter, I view the 1960s as a transitional decade in the treatment of Nazism and the Holocaust in the West German schools. Indeed, I conceive of the textbook reforms of the 1960s as constituting a distinct stage in an ongoing process. The first stage in this process—the occupation by the western Allies (1945–1949)—witnessed a variety of educational reform efforts that experienced only moderate success at best (Puaca 2009, pp. 13–55). Although the Allies attempted to confront Germans with the crimes committed in their name in the first year of the occupation, these efforts had little impact on the schools, which faced enormous physical and personnel challenges in the years following the war's end. Shortages of textbooks and an extremely limited selection of approved materials lasted throughout these years.

The second stage in this process—corresponding roughly to the 1950s—saw a number of new history textbooks begin to appear in schools. Overwhelmingly, these books failed to engage in a discussion of Nazi crimes. There were various strategies for avoiding these issues, such as focusing exclusively on political and military history, emphasizing German suffering, addressing antisemitism in the section before the war and thus failing to trace its culmination in the Holocaust, and outright silence. The huge literature on German efforts to come to terms with the past includes considerable recent scholarship on ways that West Germans remembered it selectively and inconsistently in the 1950s; see for example, Frei (1996), Herf (1997), Kansteiner (2006), Moeller (2001), Niven (2002), and Olick (2005).

In this chapter, then, I concentrate on what might be considered a third stage beginning in the 1960s. It is at this point that history textbooks increasingly began to exhibit considerable reforms in regard to not only the narrative, which became much more direct in exploring German crimes, but also in design and pedagogy. Primary sources began to feature prominently in these books, as did photos designed to complement the narrative. Questions for classroom discussion appeared at the end of chapters or main sections. Increasingly, the authors of these textbooks encouraged pupils to participate in a discussion about the past, as opposed to memorising names and dates.

Several internal reforms transpired in the West German schools following the war, which facilitated remarkable changes in discussions of the Third Reich appearing in the history textbooks of the 1960s. First, the history guidelines that were published for the states of the Federal Republic reveal that 20th-century history began to receive considerably more attention in the West German classroom at the start of the 1960s. History curricula provided to schools by the culture ministries of the federal states required ever-increasing coverage of the Nazi dictatorship, its crimes, and the war it created. Teachers do not always follow guidelines as prescribed, but greater pressure from state authorities made it more difficult to avoid this material in classroom lessons (Puaca 2009, pp. 140–143). Second, a generational shift in the teaching profession meant that by the start of the 1960s, a growing proportion of teachers had begun their careers after 1945, according to West Berlin Senator for Education Carl-Heinz Evers (1962a, 1962b), who collected an impressive amount of data related to the teaching profession for his ambitious 1962 reform proposal. These new teachers did not feel the same sense of complicity with the former regime that older teachers may have felt, nor did they share the disillusionment with what their senior colleagues often identified as the political instrumentalisation of history instruction. Third, increased emphasis on contemporary history in the training of new teachers, as well as a significant number of new continuing education courses on the Third Reich, the Holocaust, and World War II, meant that the men and women providing instruction in West German classrooms were more prepared than ever before to explore these topics with pupils. Finally, the increasing interest and involvement of new constituencies—such as parents and journalists—in educational debates meant that history instruction could not remain the private domain of teachers and historians. The narratives presented in history textbooks of the 1960s are increasingly negotiated compromises that sought to satisfy a wide audience of interested parties.

Methodology and Historiography

When evaluating the history textbooks published in the first two post-war decades, one must consider the variety of factors that affected their production. Accordingly, an examination of history textbooks in the first decades of the Federal Republic should begin with a discussion of their authorship. One significant factor that contributed to the textbooks of West Germany in the 1960s more openly engaging the Holocaust and Nazi dictatorship is the fact that these books were typically authored by secondary school teachers and not by professional historians at the university level. The pedagogues who authored these books were arguably more willing to engage Germany's difficult wartime history than their more respected colleagues for a variety of reasons. First, many of these authors were younger than those teaching at the universities. Second, by virtue of their age, the majority of these authors felt no sense of remorse or complicity for their interactions with the Nazi regime. Third, in the face of increasing attention in state history curricula in the late 1950s and early 1960s, these authors may have made the practical—and financially prudent—decision that these issues merited attention in order for their books to gain approval for use in the schools. This last point also serves as a reminder that textbooks had to be authorised by each state culture ministry for use in the classroom. Thus, it is impossible to speak of a "national textbook", since every state approved a variety of possible texts and schools then made their choices from this list.

A second consideration about production is the complicated organisational structure of the school system. West Germany's schools placed children into one of three educational tracks after they completed fourth grade in the common *Grundschule*. The *Volksschule* provided pupils with instruction through grade 9, at which point they entered vocational training. The *Realschule* lasted through grade 10 in most states and prepared pupils for careers in business and the civil service. The *Gymnasium* extended through grade 13 and served as the gateway for university admission. As a result of this multi-track system, publishers typically produced a variety of books and often had multiple publications addressing the recent German past, each targeting different class levels. For example, pupils completing their studies in a *Gymnasium* in the state of Hesse during the 1960s studied the Nazi era in the tenth grade as well as their final year (thirteenth) of coursework—probably using different textbooks each time—before departing for the university. Likewise, publishers produced multiple editions of the same textbook, with different books specifically prepared for each type of school. It is also worth noting that the more relaxed pace of study in the *Gymnasium* translated into extra time to study these difficult issues. Whereas the majority of young Hessian pupils would have had a compressed treatment of this material in the eighth (or eventually the ninth) grade, those advancing to the university had considerably more time to study Germany's recent past. These decisions are described in detail in the curricula (Bildungspläne 1957a, 1957b) published by the state culture ministries.

It is also important to acknowledge some of the methodological limitations of working with textbooks, since they are important sources but only one tool among many in the secondary school classroom. It is virtually impossible to know precisely how teachers employed textbooks in their classrooms or what topics received attention in class meetings. It is by no means safe to assume that a class vigorously debated Hitler's policies toward the Jews simply because a question on the topic appeared on the pages of a textbook. Nor do I claim that because something appeared in a textbook, it inevitably became part of class instruction. The historian needs to be mindful of the agency of teachers and their enormous role in shaping what happens in the classroom, as I have found in surveys of teachers in West Berlin (Puaca 2009, pp. 140–145). That said, the considerable reforms visible on the pages of history textbooks published in the 1960s suggest that meaningful change was underway in the schools of the Federal Republic. Put differently, it became increasingly difficult for unwilling teachers to avoid discussing these issues in their history classrooms 20 years after the war ended.

In this examination of history textbooks, I draw examples from representative books used widely in the schools of the Federal Republic. These are books that typically had long shelf lives, having undergone multiple revisions and having appeared in several editions through the post-war era. They were also approved for use in many of the federal states, thus increasing the potential impact of the narrative as it entered into a large number of schools. At the same time, I also analyse materials from states that have been viewed as exceptional or unusual by scholars, such as Bavaria, which was resistant to many American educational reforms proposed during the occupation era. In doing this, I illustrate that changes in the treatment of the German past did not occur exclusively in places deemed friendly toward reform.

Finally, I devote the majority of my analysis to books used in the *Volksschulen* (renamed *Hauptschulen* during this period) and *Realschulen*, which provided the final years of compulsory schooling for most Germans in the 1960s. Many of the history textbooks targeting pupils in the *Gymnasium*, which prepared pupils for university study, retained problematic discussions of the recent German past throughout this decade or sought to avoid difficult topics by focusing its narrative solely on political or military events.

The belief that the Third Reich and Holocaust, if not officially proscribed subjects, received only cursory treatment in German history textbooks until the 1970s—or later—has dominated historical scholarship on the post-war German educational system. Indeed, the perception that Germans failed to come to terms with the past until relatively recently has circulated among many scholars over the past few decades. The earliest research on the subject regularly reiterated claims that Nazi-era textbooks had been republished in the West after 1945 with minimal revision (Becker 1978). While Weimar-era books did reappear in an emergency capacity and for a brief time during the occupation, it would have been highly unlikely to still find these in classrooms at the close of the 1950s. Other scholars, such as Stephen Pagaard (1995), have argued that reforms in the textbooks of West Germany only began to appear in the 1970s and that instruction on the Holocaust is a "relatively recent phenomenon" (p. 544). The historian Falk Pingel (2000) offers a similar claim, noting that the revision of history textbooks in regard to the Third Reich and Holocaust came about as a result of the student protests of the late 1960s. More recently, Bodo von Borries (2003) has authored an article that, while acknowledging some minor reforms in the pages of history texts, is highly critical of books published before 1989. Unfortunately, many of these authors overgeneralise on the basis of a few texts: von Borries examined only three books, published in 1957, 1971, and 1996. Another concern is that scholars may examine one edition of a textbook and fail to analyze the many multiple new versions that typically appeared over the course of years and often decades. Sometimes these revisions were cosmetic or limited, but in other cases one can discern significant changes to the narrative presented to pupils.

Those scholars who have overlooked the educational reforms that transpired within the post-war schools, or located those changes in the 1970s or later, fit comfortably inside the larger framework of a model that depicts the educational system that developed after 1945 as a "restoration" of pre-Nazi education. The perception of the 1950s and 1960s as a time of pedagogical stagnation has dominated the literature for decades (Hearnden 1974; Herrlitz et al. 1981; Lange-Quassowski 1979; Robinsohn and Kuhlmann 1995). Interestingly, contemporary examinations of post-war history textbooks often cast doubt on this notion of non-reform; see Huebener (1962), Mattheisen (1968), and Mielcke (1961). Given this context, I investigate several of the most popular history textbooks of the late 1950s and 1960s, to illuminate subtle changes in the treatment of Germany's World War II experience. I do not want to suggest that a single, frank, and nuanced presentation of National Socialism and the Holocaust appeared before the 1970s, but I do hope to demonstrate that meaningful reform transpired before the tumultuous events of the late 1960s in regard to textbook content, design, and pedagogical approach.

The Silences of the Late 1940s and 1950s

The earliest history textbooks of the western occupation zones and Federal Republic by no means attempted to come to terms with the crimes of the Third Reich and the genocide of European Jewry. In the earliest years, as was the case with the first new post-war history textbook series *Wege der Völker* (Paths of the Peoples), these books were assembled hastily and designed to meet an immediate need for teaching materials. Perhaps shockingly, the American-approved *Wege der Völker* series fails to mention extermination camps, the crimes of the *Wehrmacht*, or any specific quantitative evidence related to the scope of atrocities committed against civilians; Wegner (1988, pp. 244–245) offers more on this series. While the authors do discuss German antisemitism, concentration camps, and German efforts to eradicate those deemed to be inferior, the narrative here is incomplete and highly problematic. There can be little dispute that other early history publications of the 1950s carried similar narratives that failed to engage in a vigorous analysis of German crimes.

There are, as many historians have amply illustrated, many examples of history textbooks published in the 1950s that sought to minimise, sidestep, or in extreme cases, completely overlook the most heinous crimes of the Nazi regime. Indeed one need not search too long for examples that highlight efforts to avoid dealing with the recent German past. For instance, the 1956 textbook *Europa und die Welt* (Europe and the World), which was prepared for the middle grades of the *Gymnasium*, offered a fragmented and misleading discussion of the persecution and murder of European Jewry. One half of a sentence is dedicated to the removal of Jews from their positions in a section entitled Internal Political Terror, which continues to employ Nazi terminology such as "non-Aryan". In a paragraph-long subsection a few pages later, The Fate of the Polish Jews, the author masterfully employs a passive voice sentence that obscures more than it explains: "Unprecedented in the history of humanity was the extermination of millions of Polish Jews" (Thierbach 1956, p. 119). The authors acknowledged that terrible crimes had occurred, but they were unwilling to assign responsibility for these actions.

Following this declaration, the tone of the textbook shifted as the narrative continued to be evasive but now became defensive as well. The textbook informed pupils that "Hitler knew that he could not expect the German Army and its officer corps to carry out such orders of mass extermination" (p. 119). And so the paragraph leaves its readers with the information that some sort of special troops carried out these orders. Who were these killers? Who should be considered as their victims? And how and where were these people murdered? These were questions that the author studiously avoided as he returned to his narrative emphasising political and military developments. Remarkably, the textbook devotes more time to the Germans who fled from the East in 1944 and 1945 than to the persecution of the Jews (pp. 127, 129). This textbook—and many others published around the same time—viewed the suffering of the war as a zero-sum game in which Germans and Jews were exclusive groups without overlap. Moreover, no mention is made of extermination camps, gas chambers, popular antisemitism, or the murder of

German Jews. The continued use of the passive voice, as Walter Renn (1993) thoughtfully notes, further removed the agency and responsibility of Germans for the crimes committed against the Jews. The narrative and methodology of this book are representative of others published in the 1950s and serve as a starting point in regard to the reforms that would come in the years that followed.

Transitioning into the 1960s

As the 1960s began, textbooks began to devote considerable attention to the Nazi period, the Holocaust, the crimes committed on the Eastern Front, and the repression of dissent at home. A number of broader political and social factors contributed to these developments in the late 1950s and early 1960s. First was a renewed public discussion about the teaching of modern history in the pages of German newspapers and periodicals. The appearance of antisemitic graffiti throughout the Federal Republic in 1959 and 1960, the capture of Adolf Eichmann in 1960 and his subsequent trial, and the Spiegel Affair of 1962, which constituted an attack on the freedom of the press, prompted many discussions about how pupils studied contemporary German history. These debates played out not only on the pages of professional journals for teachers and historians but often in the daily newspapers as well. Second, the founding of the Institut für Zeitgeschichte (the IfZ, or Institute for Contemporary History) in Munich in 1949 promoted serious scholarly research on the history of Germany under National Socialism. This, in turn, helped facilitate support, albeit limited, for the emerging sub-discipline in some universities over the next two decades (Möller 1999). Third, and partly in response to both this new public pressure and the shift in the historical profession mentioned earlier, state and federal authorities published new guidelines revitalising the teaching of contemporary history (*Zeitgeschichte*) in post-war classrooms. Most West German states proposed significant reforms to the history curriculum around 1960. For instance Hesse introduced several important new policies regarding history, social studies, and student government in the early 1960s (Zilien 1997). The fact that a new generation of teachers had entered into the teaching profession in the late 1940s and 1950s only served as further fuel for the reforms emerging in history instruction. Thus, these interrelated processes of curricular revision, social awakening, and professional renewal served as the catalyst for a more honest and complete engagement with the recent past in the history textbooks of the Federal Republic.

One of the first books to exhibit the transition taking place in the history textbooks of the new decade was Hans Heumann's (1961) *Unser Weg durch die Geschichte* (Our Path through History). While Heumann's text continued to feature the suffering of Germans under the Nazis and during World War II, his narrative devoted considerable attention to the concentration camps, widespread antisemitism before the war, and the murder of European Jewry that came with the start of the war. For instance, in a passage on the concentration camps, Heumann integrated a six-paragraph excerpt (two textbook pages in length!) from Eugen Kogon's

SS State, which offered pupils a frightening glimpse into life in a concentration camp. Although Kogon himself had been imprisoned in Buchenwald for political reasons, he also discussed Auschwitz in the passage. Heumann refused to adhere to the Nazi lexicon that had survived the demise of the Third Reich and problematised the terminology. For example, a review section at the end of the chapter asked pupils to define and discuss terms such as Aryan and master race, alongside other vocabulary such as gas chamber and *Kristallnacht* (Night of the Broken Glass) (Heumann 1961, p. 107). Despite these notable reforms, Heumann's book still exhibited some of the problems of the books that had preceded his. The persecution of the Jews—and the genocide perpetrated against them after 1939—does not appear in the chapter covering the war. Instead, this discussion is confined to the pages leading up to the conflict. Furthermore, important questions of responsibility, popular knowledge, and collaboration, among others, receive no attention here. Finally, while Heumann did break new ground by incorporating primary sources, he selected them exclusively from the perpetrator's perspective. Nevertheless, Heumann's book marked a shift in how Nazi crimes were treated in post-war textbooks and signaled a greater willingness to discuss the Holocaust.

A new text for pupils in the *Gymnasium* from the Klett publishing house was introduced in the same year as Heumann's book. Comparing the two reveals that, despite reforms in instructional materials for schools of all levels, these changes were not necessarily uniform. Authored by a married couple (Dittrich-Gallmeister and Dittrich 1961) who taught in a *Gymnasium* in Essen, this book offers more tepid revisions in its treatment of Nazi crimes and the Holocaust. As was becoming standard in books published in the new decade, a clear presentation of Nazi legal persecution of the Jews featured prominently in the chapter on the Nazi seizure of power. But the authors seem unable to formulate a coherent narrative about the extermination of European Jewry during the war. In a section entitled Reign of Terror and Resistance (a problematic formulation in its own right), pupils learned that half of Germany's Jews failed to emigrate before 1939. While the narrative does mention that Jews were gassed and shot in the "occupied areas" after 1941, the scope of these crimes and the horrors of the camps are not made clear to readers. Furthermore, the authors sought to exonerate Germans for any responsibility for these crimes, stating that "only after the war did the names of the extermination camps (Auschwitz, Chelmno, Belzec, Sobibor, Treblinka, and Maidanek) become known" (p. 188). This passage concludes with an excerpt from Kurt Gerstein's report on the operation of the gas chambers. Gerstein, a member of the SS who had personally witnessed the murder of thousands of Jews in the extermination camps, provided his written testimony to French officials after being captured in April 1945. Undoubtedly an important primary source, it received no further comment from the authors, nor were readers encouraged to consider, debate, or discuss the issue further.

One of the strongest examples of a textbook attempting a more comprehensive treatment of the crimes committed by Germans during the war is Hans Ebeling's (1964) *Die Reise in die Vergangenheit* [Journey into the Past] series. Ebeling, who had begun his career as a secondary school history teacher in Braunschweig, had by the 1960s become arguably the most prolific author of history textbooks in the Federal Republic. While his *Deutsche Geschichte* (German History) series, which was one of the most widely used books in the 1950s, provided its young readers with a fairly conventional and perhaps even mildly comforting narrative, this new series represented a very different treatment of the recent German past.

One of the most notable changes in the 1963 edition of his book was Ebeling's attention to the persecution of the Jews. He made no attempt to hide the methods used to exterminate the regime's enemies or the numbers of people murdered as a result of the concentration and extermination camps. He explicitly mentions the gas chambers, and lists 16 camps by name (1964a, p. 204). Dachau, Buchenwald, and Auschwitz might have been places already familiar to young readers, but Neuengamme, Natzweiler, Maidanek, and Treblinka might have compelled pupils to consult a map. Of the more than ten million Jews who lived in Europe before the war, only four million remained in 1945. Ebeling hedged his bets, however, on the number killed, stating that between four and six million of these Jews were murdered. For teachers interested in providing an even fuller discussion of these issues, the teacher's guide provided a Jewish survivor's personal account of *Kristallnacht* and transport to a concentration camp. Additionally, it included a list of additional works for consultation including the work of Kogon, the historian Martin Broszat, the psychoanalyst Alexander Mitscherlich, and *The Diary of Anne Frank* (1964b, pp. 84–85).

Even more remarkable than the narrative explaining the persecution of the Jews in this text are the explanations for how it happened and why it mattered. Unlike other history books that elided the question of responsibility, Ebeling made it clear that Hitler could not have achieved so much destruction on his own. These crimes were only made possible because of the support of "many thousands of supporters". As he had done more than a decade earlier, Ebeling made clear that most Germans had heard about the camps, even if they chose not to learn about what went on behind their gates. Ebeling also distanced himself from those Germans who sought to repress the Nazi period. In a dramatic appeal, he informed pupils that "even today there are many who do not want to know anything about these crimes. *But it is folly and cowardice to close oneself off from the truth*" (1964a, p. 205, emphasis in original). He concluded this section of his textbook by encouraging pupils to explore their locality and investigate graves, monuments, and buildings related to Hitler's victims. Ebeling charged his readers with keeping watch over these memories and discussing them with others. This emphasis on active engagement in exploring Germany's recent past signaled a pedagogical reform in how authors envisioned the role of the textbook in the history classroom.

Redesigning Textbooks and Engaging the Recent Past

Moving deeper into the 1960s, the history textbooks of the Federal Republic display increasing evidence of a shift toward a more comprehensive analysis of German crimes. One of the most interesting examples of this transition is Friedrich J. Lucas's (1966)

Menschen in ihrer Zeiten (People in their times). Lucas, a professor at the university in Giessen, taught courses on history didactics and brought a new design to the rather staid field of German history textbooks. Lucas's book not only constituted a further challenge to those earlier works that had remained silent about the genocide of Europe's Jews, it also marked a radical rethinking of the traditional textbook format. The teenagers who read Lucas's work in the late 1960s encountered a book that was physically divided into two main sections. The top half of every page—shaded gray and extending throughout the entire book—was an edited collection of primary source documents that complemented the main narrative. This portion of the book also included questions for pupils to consider that were likely intended to provoke discussion in the classroom. For example, following a paragraph excerpt from a 1943 Himmler speech on the people living under German occupation, pupils are asked "What kind of culture requires slaves in the 20th century?" (p. 96). The bottom half of the page contained the more traditional narrative, although it incorporated significantly more social history than many other contemporary books. Thus, Lucas provided his young readers with a recapitulation of Germany's tumultuous recent past while at the same time giving them the opportunity to read a rich variety of primary source materials and draw their own conclusions. For both of these reasons, it is worth noting that Lucas's book is a far cry from history texts that had appeared only a decade before.

Pupils reading Lucas's book may have been rather surprised by his presentation of recent German history as one plagued by hatred, persecution, greed, jealousy, and violence. The text pointed out that the Nazis had intimidated and repressed their enemies from their very first days in power, and it highlighted the construction of concentration camps, arrest of political enemies, and opportunism of those who joined the NSDAP after January 1933. It also examined the persecution of the Jews from 1933 to 1939, including an analysis of the Nuremberg Laws and *Kristallnacht*. It also noted that while many Germans did not realise that the regime was committing these crimes, many others did see the evils underway and "remained quiet, looked away, or actually assisted" (pp. 64–65). This section concludes with a challenge to pupils to answer the following claims (undoubtedly heard by some pupils even in the late 1960s): "Hitler's social measures were very good" and "Hitler ruled very well until the war, but he should have left the Jews alone" (p. 65).

A section (entitled The Final Stage of Inhumanity) in the next chapter, on World War II, devoted several pages to the extermination camps and the murder of Europe's Jews. On these pages, readers learned of intensifying persecution of the Jews after the war began, their deportation to extermination camps, and their murder in gas chambers. To reinforce his narrative, Lucas included now iconic photographs of the clearing of the Warsaw Ghetto, the "selection" of new prisoners upon arrival at Auschwitz, and an elderly woman with children on their way to the gas chambers—and captioned them in clear and descriptive language (YVPA 2011a, 2011b, 2011c). He also pointed out to his young readers that the Germans also targeted other groups for extermination, and specifically mentioned the Gypsies (Roma) as victims. Finally, Lucas pointed out that while the most horrible crimes were intentionally hidden from the population, Germans could see the brutal exploitation and mistreatment of so-called *Fremdarbeiter* (foreign workers) on a daily basis. The feigned ignorance of parents and grandparents about the crimes committed in the name of the Germans, Lucas implied to his teenaged readers, was precisely that: an act.

Complementing this narrative was the radically different design of the textbook. While Lucas was not the first to introduce primary source materials from the Nazi period into history textbooks, no other book published to this point had made them as central as his did. Pupils encountered original documents sharing roughly equal space on every page in support of the corresponding historical narrative. Lucas relied on many well-known sources, such as Nuremberg Trial records and the speeches and publications of leading Nazis, but he also included many lesser known and often more illuminating materials. For instance, in addressing the persecution of the Jews during the first years of the Third Reich, he included the 1935 letter of a pupil published in the infamous antisemitic newspaper of Julius Streicher, *Der Stürmer*. The young girl says:

> Gauleiter Streicher has told us so much about the Jews that we hate them with a vengeance. We wrote an essay in school on the topic "The Jews Are Our Misfortune".... Unfortunately many say: "The Jews are also God's creations. Therefore you must also respect them". We say, however: "Bugs are also animals and we exterminate (*vernichten*) them nonetheless". (p. 63)

The letter highlights both the influence of Nazi ideology in the classroom as well as how quickly young Germans accepted and internalised the racism they encountered. Following the document, Lucas asked readers to consider whether this pupil really knew many Jews and how she had come to hate them so intensely.

Lucas included particularly damning passages from the speeches and writings and publications of leading Nazis, but his book also provided pupils with rich documentary evidence from the perspective of those who had been their victims. In the section examining the exploitation and murder of the Jews, Lucas included passages from the diary of Anne Frank; a Polish Jew named David Rubinowicz, who recounted the arrest of his family; and Hungarian Jew Miklos Nyiszli, who provided a lengthy and chilling account of the extermination process at Auschwitz. Furthermore, Lucas highlighted the fact that Hitler had not acted alone in his efforts to murder Jews. To facilitate independent thinking and classroom discussion, this section concluded with the following questions:

> Hitler had many helpers. The majority of them today claim to have followed the orders of superiors. What do you think of this? Why do most of these trials last for such a long time? Why are the verdicts always based only on specific individual punishable acts? And why do the accused have all the opportunities and rights that the Third Reich never allowed to its victims? (p. 100)

This textbook thus invited its readers to consider some very difficult questions about what their parents and grandparents had known, why they had not done more, and how it was that so many could have hated so few with such ferocity.

Further illuminating the fact that significant reform was afoot throughout the Federal Republic—as well as the limits of those changes—was a new textbook that appeared in Bavaria during the late 1960s. Authored by Johannes Hampel and Franz

Seilnacht (1967), the second edition of *Wir erleben die Geschichte* (We Experience History) confronted readers with a detailed section devoted to the Mass Murder of the Jews. While the authors positioned this analysis apart from the coverage of the war, it nevertheless constituted a thorough (and even emotionally challenging) discussion of German crimes for seventh and eighth grade pupils. In a four-page section devoted exclusively to the persecution and murder of Europe's Jews, the authors trace the evolution of Nazi antisemitic policies and the move toward open violence.

As one would expect, the Nuremberg Laws and *Kristallnacht* receive considerable attention here, and the authors incorporate primary sources for their young readers (such as the infamous testimony from Rudolf Hoess). It is in these sources that pupils learn about the magnitude of the crimes against the Jews, however, as the authors do not discuss the nature or extent of the death camps in their own words. In their narrative, the authors do encourage pupils to think about Nazi terminology, as they pointedly remark that this process was called "the final solution of the Jewish question in the language of the Nazi henchmen" (Hampel and Seilnacht 1967, p. 197). Furthermore, each section ends with questions intended to promote more discussion. For example, one question notes that "there are people today who argue whether six million Jews were killed or 'only' four and a half million. What is your response?" (p. 197). Based on the narrative that precedes this question, it is likely that the authors intended pupils to discuss the scope of the genocide, as well as the problem of minimising or excusing these crimes. While this book still struggles to contextualise the murder of the Jews within the war after 1939 and ignores the issue of popular support for antisemitic policies and violence, these authors presented teachers and readers with a challenging narrative designed to provoke questions and spark further interest in the topic.

Changes in how history textbooks handled the crimes of the National Socialists and their persecution of the Jews were gradual and piecemeal, particularly in already established textbooks that were revised on an irregular basis. An example of the sort of substantive—if belated—revisions that could take place from one edition to the next can be found in the *Spiegel der Zeiten* (Mirror of the times) series. Here we see the evolution not only of the treatment of the National Socialism and the murder of European Jewry but a notable transition in the larger narrative as well (Stellmann 1965). In fact, this series was a revision of the old *Wege der Völker* books that first appeared in the late 1940s—which may explain why its narrative was more traditional than other contemporary texts. The 1965 edition of the book, approved in six federal states and West Berlin, relies almost solely on military, political, and diplomatic history; it pays little attention to social and cultural developments. Furthermore, it devotes only passing attention to the Holocaust, noting a few important but basic points in just over one page of coverage. Appearing 6 years later, the completely revised edition offered much more social and cultural history and a re-organised narrative on Germany's history during the Third Reich and World War II—and it was printed in color. The 1971 edition provided three pages of analysis in a new section entitled The Genocide of the Jews (Stellmann 1971, pp. 118–120). This new section on genocide specifically discussed the Wannsee Conference, and the use of gas chambers in extermination camps, and it included visual aids to reinforce the narrative, such as photos of a "selection" on the train platform at Auschwitz and the iconic image of the boy holding his hands up during the clearing of the Warsaw Ghetto. Notably, by this point in the text, pupils had already encountered significant discussion of the historical development of antisemitism in Germany before the 1930s, the influence of Social Darwinism, and passages from relevant primary sources such as early Hitler speeches.

Despite these substantive revisions, this book, like others it was competing with in the marketplace, remained problematic for several reasons. It is fair to say that the inclusion of lengthy primary source material—such as Rudolf Hoess' Nuremberg testimony, which also appears here—shielded the author from a more analytical discussion of these difficult issues. Furthermore, a five-page section on German resistance to Hitler seems disproportionate in comparison to the three-page passage on the genocide of six million Jews. The fact that these editions from the mid-1960s and early 1970s still contained such an incomplete and problematic treatment of these issues further underscores the fact that this transition took considerable time and continued to play out in the decades that followed.

Complementing the changes taking place in the history textbooks of this era are those that appeared in the pedagogical literature targeting teachers. Recognising the need to encourage instruction on the Third Reich and Holocaust and aware that those working with pupils in the schools needed to know about new research, several publishers provided specialised publications for professional educators in this field. These materials highlight the changing narrative in regard to the crimes of the Nazis and illuminate the issues, sources, and interpretations that teachers encountered as they prepared—and revised—their lessons. For example, the Otto Suhr Institute for Political Science at the Free University in West Berlin partnered with the city's Office for Political Education to publish a special edition of historian Wolfgang Scheffler's (1964) work on Nazi racial policies and the persecution of the Jews in the early 1960s. This volume, provided free of charge to the city's history teachers, offered readers a 68-page narrative on the religious and racial origins of antisemitism and traced its development into the 20th century. It then concentrated on how Nazi policies evolved, culminating in the murder of European Jewry. This resource highlights both the persecution of German Jews and the treatment of Jews in the territories Germany occupied during the war. Notably, it not only details the path that ended in the extermination camps of Poland, but also discusses medical experiences conducted on prisoners and the slave labor that German companies used. Furthermore, it includes a partial indictment of the German people, as readers learn that while very few Germans knew what happened behind the gates of Auschwitz, many knew very well about the persecution and deportation of Jews and had likely heard stories from eyewitnesses regarding the horrible violence committed in their name. So, too, Scheffler adds, did the churches remain quiet in the face of Nazi brutality. Finally, this resource also included 20 pages of primary sources that could be used in the classroom. Many sources showcased the perpetrator's perspective, but others did depict these crimes through the eyes of the victims.

Conclusions

In closing, I have argued that in the decades after 1945 the history textbooks of West Germany experienced meaningful revision and reform in regard to the crimes of the Third Reich. As we have seen, a new generation of textbooks published starting in the 1960s offered young readers a more honest and forthright explanation of the genocide committed against European Jewry. These new books increasingly challenged pupils to take a more active role in their history instruction through the inclusion of questions, primary sources, and activities that required them to engage critically with these topics. The 1960s, then, might be considered a critical stage of transition in Germans coming to terms with their recent past in the schools of the Federal Republic following the false starts of the late 1940s and the calculated omissions of the 1950s.

This is not to say, however, that these changes had reached their endpoint as the 1960s came to a close. Significant problems—especially of terminology, agency, and contextualisation—still plagued the books circulating in the schools of West Germany. Thus, I do not seek to convince the reader that this process was complete by the 1970s. Rather, I identify the origins of the reforms that reshaped history instruction in the West in an earlier era. Changes to the history curriculum more broadly—and textbooks more specifically—did not begin as a result of the student movement of the late 1960s, as is so often suggested. These reforms had already been initiated earlier in the decade, while many of the future protesters were still completing secondary school. Perhaps the fact that young Germans did encounter Nazi crimes and the murder of European Jewry in their history lessons as teenagers—albeit in an uneven and incomplete fashion—prompted them to seize on this issue in their protests. Indeed, one wonders if these history textbooks, coupled with a new generation of teachers, helped provoke the anger of those who would soon be marching on the streets of West Berlin, Frankfurt, Munich, and Stuttgart.

References

Becker, J. J. R. (1978). Textbooks and the political system in the Federal Republic of Germany, 1945–1975. *School Review, 86*, 251–270.

Bildungspläne für die allgemeinbildenden Schulen im Lande Hessen, B. Das Bildungsgut der Volksschule [Curricula for the general schools of the State of Hesse, B. The general education of the Volksschule] (1957a, February). *Amtsblatt des Hessischen Ministers für Erziehung und Volksbildung, 10*(2), 172–173.

Bildungspläne für die allgemeinbildenden Schulen im Lande Hessen, B. Das Bildungsgut des Gymnasiums [Curricula for the general schools of the State of Hesse, B. The general education of the gymnasium] (1957b, March). *Amtsblatt des Hessischen Ministers für Erziehung und Volksbildung, 10*(4), 476–481.

Buchinger, H. (1975). *Volksschule und Lehrerbildung im Spannungsfeld politischer Entscheidungen 1945–1970* [The elementary school and teacher training in the context of political decisions on education reform, 1945–1970]. Munich: Ehrenwirth.

Dittrich-Gallmeister, E., & Dittrich, J. (1961). *Von 1950 bis zur Gegenwart* [From 1950 to the present] (Vol. 3, Grundriss der Geschichte). Stuttgart: Klett.
Ebeling, H. (1964a). *Die Reise in die Vergangenheit* [A trip into the past] (4th ed., Vol. IV). Braunschweig: Westermann.
Ebeling, H. (1964b). *Die Reise in die Vergangenheit* [A trip into the past] (Vol. IV, Teacher's supplement). Braunschweig: Westermann.
Evers, C.-H. (1962a). *Denkschrift zur inneren Schulreform. Langfristige Planung* [Memorandum on internal school reform—long-term plans]. Berlin: Kulturbuch.
Evers, C.-H. (1962b). *Denkschrift zur inneren Schulreform* [draft version], Table 1, "Pädagogische Hochschulen und andere Anstalten und Einrichtungen für Ausbildung von Lehrern an Volksschulen, Sonderschulen und Mittelschulen sowie an berufsbildenden Schulen (ohne Handelslehramt) 1954 bis 1962", Lehrernachwuchs [Teacher training college and other institutions and facilities for the education of teachers in the Volksschulen, Sonderschulen, and Mittelschulen, as well as vocational schools]. In Landesarchiv Berlin, B. Rep. 015, No. 398, LAB.
Frei, N. (1996). *Adenauer's Germany and the Nazi past: The politics of amnesty and integration.* New York: Columbia University Press.
Hahn, H. J. (1998). *Education and society in Germany.* New York: Berg.
Hampel, J., & Seilnacht, F. (1967). *Wir erleben die Geschichte* [We experience history] (2nd ed.). Munich: Bayerischer Schulbuchverlag.
Hearnden, A. (1974). *Education in the two Germanies.* Boulder: Westview.
Herf, J. (1997). *Divided memory: The Nazi past in the two Germanys.* Cambridge, MA: Harvard University Press.
Herrlitz, H.-G., Hopf, W., & Titze, H. (1981). *Deutsche Schulgeschichte von 1800 bis zur Gegenwart* [A history of German schools from 1800 to the present]. Regensburg: Athenäum.
Heumann, H. (1961). *Unser Weg durch die Geschichte: Vom Wiener Kongress bis zur Gegenwart* [Our way through history: From the Vienna Congress to the present]. Frankfurt: Hirschgraben.
Huebener, T. (1962). What is German youth taught about the Nazis? *German Quarterly, 35,* 171–178.
Kansteiner, W. (2006). Losing the war, winning the memory battle: The legacy of Nazism, World War II, and the Holocaust in the Federal Republic of Germany. In R. N. Lebow, W. Kansteiner, & C. Fogu (Eds.), *The politics of memory in postwar Europe* (pp. 102–146). Durham: Duke University Press.
Lange-Quassowski, J.-B. (1979). *Neuordnung oder Restauration? Das Demokratiekonzept der amerikanischen Besatzungsmacht und die politische Sozialisation der Westdeutschen* [New order or restoration? The Democratic plan of the American occupying power and the political socialisation of the West Germans]. Opladen: Leske.
Lucas, F. J. (1966). *Menschen in ihrer Zeiten* [People in their times] (Vol. 6). Stuttgart: Klett.
Mattheisen, D. (1968). History and political education in West Germany. *History Teacher, 1*(3), 41–47.
Mielcke, K. (1961). *1917–1945 in den Geschichtsbüchern der Bundesrepublik* [The years 1917–1945 in the history books of the Federal Republic]. Hannover: Niedersächsische Landeszentrale für politische Bildung.
Moeller, M. (2001). *War stories: The search for a usable past in the Federal Republic of Germany.* Berkeley: University of California Press.
Möller, H. (1999). Das Institut für Zeitgeschichte und die Entwicklung der Zeitgeschichtsschreibung in Deutschland [The Institute for Contemporary History and the development of contemporary history writing in Germany]. In H. Möller & U. Wengst (Eds.), *50 Jahre Institut für Zeitgeschichte* (pp. 1–68). Munich: Oldenbourg.
Müller, W. (1995). *Schulpolitik in Bayern im Spannungsfeld von Kultusbürokratie und Besatzungsmacht 1945–1949* [School politics in Bavaria in the conflict between Culture Ministry and occupying power, 1945–1949]. Munich: Oldenbourg.
Niven, B. (2002). *Facing the Nazi past: United Germany and the legacy of the Third Reich.* New York: Routledge.

Olick, J. (2005). *In the house of the hangman: The agonies of German defeat, 1943–1949*. Chicago: University of Chicago Press.
Pagaard, S. A. (1995). German schools and the Holocaust: A focus on the secondary school system of Nordrhein-Westfalen. *History Teacher, 28*(4), 541–554.
Pingel, F. (2000). National Socialism and the Third Reich in West German school books. *Internationale Schulbuchforschung, 22*, 11–29.
Puaca, B. M. (2009). *Learning democracy: Education reform in West Germany, 1945–1965*. New York: Berghahn.
Renn, R. (1993). The Holocaust in the school textbooks of the Federal Republic of Germany. In S. S. Friedman (Ed.), *Holocaust literature: A handbook of critical, historical, and literary writings* (pp. 481–520). Westport: Greenwood.
Robinsohn, S. B., & Kuhlmann, J. C. (1995). Two decades of non-reform in West German education. In D. Phillips (Ed.), *Education in Germany: Tradition and reform in historical context* (pp. 15–35). New York: Routledge.
Scheffler, W. (1964). *Judenverfolgung im Dritten Reich, 1933–1945* [The persecution of the Jews in the Third Reich]. West Berlin: Otto Suhr Institut and the Landeszentrale für politische Bildungsarbeit Berlin.
Scherl, J. (1963). *Geschichte unseres Volkes, Teil IV: Von 1815 bis Heute* [History of our people, Part 4, from 1815 to today]. Munich: Oldenbourg.
Stellmann, M. (1965). *Spiegel der Zeiten* [Mirror of the times] (7th ed., Vol. 5). Frankfurt: Diesterweg.
Stellmann, M. (1971). *Spiegel der Zeiten* [Mirror of the times] (Vol. 4). Frankfurt: Diesterweg.
Tent, J. (1982). *Mission on the Rhine: Reeducation and denazification in American-occupied Germany*. Chicago: University of Chicago Press.
Thierbach, H. (1956). *Europa und die Welt, Vol. IV/B* [Europe and the world, Vol. 4/b]. Paderborn: Schöningh.
von Borries, B. (2003). The Third Reich in German history textbooks since 1945. *Journal of Contemporary History, 38*, 45–62.
Wegner, G. (1988). *The power of tradition in education: The formation of the history curriculum in the gymnasium of the American sector in Berlin, 1945–1955*. Doctoral dissertation, University of Wisconsin, Madison.
YVPA [Yad Vashem Photo Archive] (2011a). *Birkenau, Poland: An Elderly Jewish woman supervising young children on their way to the gas chambers, 05/1944*. http://collections.yadvashem.org/photosarchive/en-us/97836_31588.html
YVPA (2011b). *Birkenau, Poland, Geza Lajtos from Budapest during a selection on the ramp in front of an SS physician*. http://collections.yadvashem.org/photosarchive/en-us/97836_31900.html
YVPA (2011c). *Warsaw, Poland, Jews captured by SS and SD troops during the suppression of the Warsaw Ghetto Uprising, 1943*. http://collections.yadvashem.org/photosarchive/en-us/26655.html
Zilien, J. (1997). *Politische Bildung in Hessen von 1945 bis 1965: Gestaltung und Entwicklung der politischen Bildung als schulpolitisches Instrument der sozialen Demokratisierung* [Political education in Hesse from 1945 to 1965: Formation and development of political education as an educational policy instrument of social democratisation]. Frankfurt: Peter Lang.

Informed Pedagogy of the Holocaust: A Survey of Teachers Trained by Leading Holocaust Organisations in the United States

Corey L. Harbaugh

As executive director of the Shoah Foundation at the University of Southern California (USCSF 2014), Stephen Smith (2009) leads one of several national organisations that sit at a critical crossroads in Holocaust education; these organisations are investing resources in training teachers and developing models that will impact and update classroom practices in that field. In the last two decades the Holocaust has become ubiquitous: Paul Salmons (2010, p. 58) calls it "a ruling symbol in our culture". Yet, despite the historical, cultural, commemorative, and creative representations of the Holocaust inside the classroom and in popular media, Salmons and others point to a widening gap between real historical knowledge and understanding of the Holocaust, and the way its historic truths have become mythologised and misrepresented. As a result, programmes at organisations like Smith's, including the United States Holocaust Memorial Museum (USHMM 2014) in Washington, DC, and the Memorial Library (2014) in New York City, have worked to train teachers in Holocaust education (HE). These trainings develop knowledge of content, teaching practices, and educational resources, all of which are designed to help teachers become more proficient at teaching the Holocaust to their students in classrooms across the country.

These training efforts help to address a critical gap in preparing teachers to teach about the Holocaust. In 2004, the USHMM commissioned a study by SRI International (Donnelly 2004); it found that "Informal learning was by far the most prevalent way teachers reported acquiring knowledge about the Holocaust. The majority of teachers nationwide have not received any kind of formal professional development on the topic" (p. 25). In fact, 85% of teachers in the country who

---

C.L. Harbaugh (✉)
National Outreach for Teacher Initiatives, United States Holocaust Memorial Museum, 100 Raoul Wallenberg Place, SW Washington, DC 20024-2126, USA
e-mail: charbaugh2002@yahoo.com

taught about the Holocaust indicated that "informal learning" was the way they acquired their knowledge.

In the years since that study, opportunities have expanded for pre-service and practicing teachers to receive professional preparation and development in HE. But while programmes that prepare teachers to teach about the Holocaust can share key features, there is a great deal of variety in the content and pedagogy that is taught. Because competitive programmes at national organisations can only train a select number of teachers per year, they cannot make a significant dent in the 85% of untrained teachers; however, those who do participate in such programmes are likely to be highly influential in their schools, districts, and states. And, since so few teachers receive this advanced, intensive training in HE, it is important to understand the teaching practices of trained teachers as they work through the key influences and the wide variety of pedagogical choices open to them.

Intensifying the urgency for teacher professional development in the last decade is the reality that eye-witnesses to the Holocaust, especially survivors and liberators, are coming to the end of their natural life spans. Smith's programme at the USCSF, and other organisations that offer professional development to teachers in Holocaust content and pedagogy, are helping to prepare teachers for a time when first-hand witnesses to the Holocaust are no longer available to tell their stories in person. For many teachers and students, survivor testimony is the core formative experience in HE, and teachers and teacher-trainers know this: HE will look very different when no one is left alive to tell students "I was there, and this is what happened to me".

Teacher training programmes at the USHMM focus teachers on understanding and presenting accurate historical context and having clear rationales for their teaching practices. At the USCSF, teacher training focuses on teachers using survivor testimony through programmes like *IWitness*. At the Memorial Library, teachers are trained using best practices in literacy pedagogy, including strategies in reading, writing, dialogue, and inquiry. Because there is such diversity in teacher preparation and development programmes, and because teaching practice can vary so much from one classroom to another, it is instructive to look closely at the practices teachers are actually using across the country. This is especially true of those teachers who have participated in a selective programme offered by a national organisation; these programmes carefully select participants for their content knowledge of the Holocaust and their teaching experience, along with other attributes such as leadership and activity in professional organisations. Thus, these teachers are well-placed to help teacher educators, professional development organisations, and their colleagues in HE to understand the current trends in the field as they actually play out in the classrooms of those teachers specifically trained to teach it well.

In this chapter I focus on the principal findings from a national study of HE that I conducted in 2013 in a teacher fellowship project at the United States Holocaust Memorial Museum. I draw on the responses of 256 teachers who had been trained by one or more of three primary national HE organisations; they may have also received training from one or more additional programmes. I examine the context in which these teachers provide HE, key factors that influence the delivery of their instruction, and the pedagogical choices they make to deliver that instruction.

The three organisations each have selection criteria for their participants, criteria that limited the diversity of the teachers participating in the survey. For instance, the USHMM requires its applicants to have 5 years experience teaching about the Holocaust before they apply to its teacher fellowship programme. Despite the selective nature of the programmes, the teachers who participated in my study are diverse, both personally and professionally, given the information I collected about their personal demographics, such as age, sex, and religious affiliation, but do not include in this chapter.

Rationale for Studying the Teaching Practice of Trained Holocaust Educators

Thousands of teachers in the United States teach students about the Holocaust in classes in history and social studies, in English or language arts, in humanities electives, or in content areas that might at first be surprising, such as music or art. Lessons on the Holocaust are delivered in US classrooms for students at all grade levels, for varying amounts of instructional time, with a wide variety of instructional practices and goals. Yet, despite the ubiquity of the topic and classroom instruction about it—and despite the 2004 Donnelly study—few teachers receive formal training in best practices in HE. As a result, teachers who receive an opportunity for formal training have many questions about how to teach it. One common question is "How do I teach the Holocaust in a US History class when I only have two class periods to teach it?"

Trainers in the field of HE will recognise that teachers want answers and examples of how to deliver the complex content of the Holocaust while dealing with the reality of limited classroom time. The Holocaust is often taught as a unit within a study of the content and complexity of US history during the World War II era. For teachers of world history, who start with the Stone Age in September and are charged with getting past the 20th century by June, the challenge is equally daunting. Teachers of English raise other questions: "How much history should I teach in my unit on Anne Frank?" "Do I show photos and videos from concentration camps that include graphic content?" "How much is too much, and how young is too young?"

During professional development in HE, teacher trainers are required to answer these questions as they arise from the teachers they train, and the best answers are grounded both in theory and experienced practice (Green 2010). Concrete examples of both theory and practice can be found in the classrooms of teachers who have spent considerable time learning from content and pedagogy experts in programmes like those offered at the Memorial Library, USCSF, and the USHMM. The organisations carefully vet the teachers who participate in each of these programmes; the competitive process identifies teachers who best meet established criteria, such as established, documented experience in teaching about the Holocaust. During these competitive training programmes teachers receive intensive training in both content and pedagogy; after training they return to their classrooms and put the training to use delivering lessons about the Holocaust to students. The classrooms of these trained teachers thus become working models for the kinds of answers and examples of theory and practice that other teachers look for when beginning to study or prepare their own teaching about the Holocaust.

Research Design and Methodology

My design of this national research study was informed by a 2009 study of teachers in England conducted by the Holocaust Education Development Programme (HEDP 2009) at the University of London under the direction of Stuart Foster, and titled *Teaching about the Holocaust in English Secondary Schools: An Empirical Study of National Trends, Perspectives and Practice*. That study focused on the overall status and trends of HE in British schools as reported by teachers. Teachers participated in an online survey through an opportunity sample broadly representative of teachers in English secondary schools.

My survey differs from that of the HEDP, as I focus more on the practice and experience of teachers who have received significant training in HE from at least one of the following organisations: the USHMM, the USCSF, or the Memorial Library. The survey instrument was a 25-item online survey distributed via email to 1,386 teachers who had been trained by one or more programmes. Of those teachers, 256 completed the survey as an opportunity sample; this gives the results a confidence level of 95%. Most of the survey questions (18 out of 25) were closed questions in which I asked the teachers to select from a range of options that would establish the context of their teaching, such as content area, training, grade level, length of unit, assessments used, etc. Two questions asked teachers to rank the top three factors that influence their instruction in HE from a list of 13; they had the option of adding an open-ended response. Two more questions asked them to identify their primary and secondary pedagogical strategies, from a list of 10. The final three questions asked them how strongly they agreed with a statement about HE, on a Likert scale. Teachers returned the surveys anonymously and I had no way of knowing their identities as I reviewed the responses.

In this chapter I am concerned with two basic questions. First, what are the conditions that influence the pedagogical choices teachers make when teaching the Holocaust? Second, what choices do they make? The answers to these questions form the basis for this chapter.

The Context of Holocaust Education for the Teachers in This Study

To reach the teachers who participated in this study I used the email lists of past participants maintained by the USHMM, the USCSF, and the Memorial Library; the three organisations emailed out the anonymous survey for me. Thus, those teachers represent the diversity of American classrooms and the personal and professional demographics of classroom teachers who have been selected to participate in one of the three national HE programmes.

Their responses to the demographic questions on the survey indicate that 69.9% teach at a public school, 7.5% at a private school, 6.7% at a religious school, and an additional 6.7% at a college or university. Moreover, 31.1% teach at a suburban school, 23.2% at a rural school, 22.8% at an urban school, and 21.6% at a school that serves students from a mix of geographic areas. They average 18.3 years of experience: 4.3% report teaching for 2 years or less, and another 4.3% report more than 40 years, along with 18.8% who have 11–15 years in the classroom, 20.3% with 16–20 years, and 12.9% with 21–25 years.

While each of the 256 teachers who participated in this study completed at least one HE programme from one or more of the three organisations, many also participated in more than one programme and in programmes offered by other organisations, such as the Echoes and Reflections training offered by the Anti-Defamation League. The 256 unique individuals participated in a total of 639 programmes, for an average of 2.5 programmes each. Teachers who receive this kind of professional development tend to seek additional training on Holocaust content and pedagogy. I did not ask them whether they had also participated in local or state programmes, such those held at local colleges and universities, museums or memorial centres, community or religious organisations, or online sources, beyond those offered online by Facing History and Ourselves (FHAO 2014). My questionnaire did include a question about participation in FHAO programmes; 36.3% said they had done so, and 44% of those respondents said they participated in an HE programme delivered in an online format.

The Classroom Context of Holocaust Education

The 2003/2004 SRI survey (Donnelly 2004, p. 17) found that 61% of Holocaust education took place in English classes, and 39% in social studies classes. The Holocaust was most frequently addressed in general English/language arts courses, most often in grade 8. In social studies, the most common course in which the Holocaust was taught was US history, and most often in grade 11. That survey identified participants by reaching out to teachers of English, reading, and social studies who taught students in grades 6–12 in seven different regions of the country; a total of 1,113 teachers participated (Donnelly 2004, p. 7).

My survey differed from Donnelly's in the sample of teachers I targeted. I reached out to teachers who had both elected to seek out and been chosen to participate in HE professional development no matter their content area; therefore, my sample includes teachers from a wider cross-section of disciplines, including religion, foreign language, and art. My respondents identified 19 separate content areas, with 35 separate elective-based offerings. Still, the proportion of English and social studies teachers in my sample is very similar to that in the Donnelly survey a decade ago.

Looking at subject area, I found that English is still the subject area where the majority of Holocaust instruction takes place; 56.1% of respondents said it was the subject area in which they principally teach about the Holocaust. History was next, with 36.6%, and elective courses were third with 13.9%. General classes in social studies were fourth with 7.1%, and humanities courses completed the top five with 5.9%. My questionnaire encouraged teachers to identify all the subject areas that apply to their individual classroom teaching contexts; I recognise that many teach about the Holocaust in more than one subject area, and I wanted to account for the interdisciplinary and team teaching that is increasingly common in US schools.

Though the Holocaust was a historical event, students in the United States are much more likely to encounter Holocaust content in an English class than in a history class. The curricular outcomes, instructional design, and pedagogical norms of English classes are different from those for history classes, and all these factors can influence the content and delivery of HE.

When students do encounter Holocaust content in a history course, it is most often a general one on either United States history or world history. Of the teachers in my sample, 27.7% say they teach Holocaust content in a course on US history, and 21.9% in one on world history. The broad survey of content and the generalised curriculum of these two areas of history can greatly limit the time students have available to learn about the Holocaust. Significant proportions of the teachers in this sample also taught other history courses that included Holocaust content: history of genocide (10.6%), 20th-century history (9.2%), European history (8.5%), and Jewish history (4.9%).

Unless a teacher is teaching a history class specifically on the Holocaust, students tend to encounter it within the context of a larger history, such as that of the United States, and that larger context can influence the historical narrative and point of view of the telling of the history. For instance, when visitors to the USHMM first enter the permanent Holocaust exhibition, the image they immediately see is a floor-to-ceiling photograph from April, 1945 of American soldiers looking at a cremation pyre left by Nazis fleeing Ohrdruf, a camp within the Buchenwald system in Germany. This photo announces to visitors that the story of the Holocaust at the USHMM will begin from an American point of view in which US soldiers served as liberators in the concluding weeks of World War II. This same narrative point of view can be pervasive within a course on US history that includes World War II, and the story of the Holocaust in a history classroom that begins with the liberation of prisoners from concentration camps and the defeat of the German army creates challenges for providing students with a more comprehensive understanding of the complex history that is the Holocaust.

The 2003/2004 SRI study (Donnelly 2004) limited its focus to teachers of English, reading, and social studies, which includes history. In contrast, I found that teachers in other content areas are including HE within the study of their academic disciplines and are seeking out teacher professional development from national organisations. Of my respondents, 14% (35) reported teaching the Holocaust in elective courses with such individual titles as Genocide in the Modern World, Media and Propaganda, Literature and Film of the Holocaust, and International Relations.

In addition, a few said they are incorporating Holocaust instruction in classes on religion and modern foreign languages, and even art and music.

Grade Levels and Time Spent on Holocaust Education

The 2003/2004 SRI study (Donnelly 2004) was set up to focus specifically on teachers in grades 6–12. In my study, much of the grade-level range was also established in advance, because the participating organisations limit the registration in national-level programmes, and in almost all local or satellite programmes, to teachers who teach grades 6 and above. Even with those parameters in place, a small percentage of my participants reported teaching Holocaust content in elementary school.

As was true in the Donnelly study, 8th grade remains the most common grade for Holocaust instruction (24.1%), followed closely by 10th grade (23.6%) and 12th grade (23.6%). The total of 254 respondents who answered this question provided a total of 395 responses; this indicated that many of them teach multiple grade levels and/or incorporate HE into instruction at more than one grade level. This finding suggests that many American students are encountering HE at multiple grade levels as they move through school. Of my respondents, 53.1% are teaching Holocaust content to students who have not yet entered high school; therefore, high school teachers are more likely than not to be teaching that content to students who were introduced to it earlier.

In addition, 20.6% of my respondents reported that some of their students had already been introduced to Holocaust content before grade 7. This is true despite a clear consensus between the three major organisations on a developmentally appropriate age to begin teaching the Holocaust in schools: grades 6 and above.

Even outside these three organisations, scholars and teacher educators share a strong consensus about not teaching the Holocaust to children who are too young. For example, HE scholar and teacher educator Karen Shawn (2001) writes that "we end the childhood of the next generation when we showcase the agonies of Primo Levi and Elie Wiesel for our sixth graders, or introduce Anne Frank, now a character in glossy picture books, to primary school students, or explain death camps, no matter how gently, to kindergartners" (p. 144). She goes on to assert strongly that "there is no compelling reason to introduce [the Holocaust] as a unit of class study before grade five" (p. 144). Despite the consensus and the strong words from Shawn and others, my data suggest that Holocaust content is increasingly being taught in earlier grades.

In addition to 20.6% of my respondents saying their students were introduced to Holocaust content during elementary school, my data show that 82.9% of students are introduced to, or experience, such content during the years considered to be middle school in the United States, completing a study of the Holocaust before the end of 8th grade.

Paul Wieser (2001, p. 62) writes that the "body of knowledge concerning Holocaust education" is large enough "that we can speak of methods and materials that are recognized as 'sound' and 'powerful'"; he holds that "educators in the field should be aware of them". National organisations like the USHMM, which provide teachers with resources and professional development opportunities, are clear on the sound methods and materials, and they work to provide them to teachers, but respondents still report that Holocaust content is regularly being taught to students younger than the age these organisations recommend as developmentally appropriate. To the extent that these students are not ready, cognitively or developmentally, to experience this content, there is a real potential to distort the history and a "meaningful understanding of this human tragedy" (Wieser 2001, p. 66).

Wieser also addressed another issue: the amount of time dedicated to Holocaust education: "Since young people see a direct correlation between the importance of a subject and the amount of time devoted to it, any superficial type of study raises some rather serious ethical considerations" (p. 64). Teaching units that are planned for weeks, even months, allow for multiple instructional strategies and deep teaching, process-based and inquiry-based instruction, and time for scaffolding; in turn, these approaches allow teachers to follow up, to use innovative and/or deep assessments, and to introduce lessons, and provide closure, on challenging content. And they allow for personal reflection by the learner.

The data provided by my respondents suggests that most teachers who have participated in the kind of professional development I have described are able to devote significant class time to Holocaust content. Indeed, 87.2% reported spending more than a full week of class time on that content, and 71.6% spend more than two full weeks on it; at the other end of the scale, 5.9% do so for more than 18 weeks. Of course, if a total of 87.2% teach it for more than a full week, that means 12.8% of those in the sample have less than a full week to dedicate to it, including the 6.3% who said they taught it for 3 days or less. Note that the term I used on the survey was "class periods or days"; I did not differentiate between block class periods (such as 90-minute seminars), college classes, and the 50- to 60-minute periods traditional in secondary schools. Thus, a full week of class time would be five periods of whatever duration.

Influences on Holocaust Pedagogy

I also asked these teachers to identify, but not rank, the top three factors that influence how they teach about the Holocaust (Table 1). Of the 252 teachers who responded to this question, each made up to three choices, for a total of 756 individual choices. More than any other influence, teachers indicated that a subjective consideration most influenced their Holocaust pedagogy: 17.1% chose the factor personal objectives/commitment, while 12.6% identified content area, and 11.3% identified student needs.

Table 1 Factors that influence teacher decisions about Holocaust pedagogy

Influence	Percentage (%) of teachers indicating it as a top-3 influence
Personal objectives/commitment	17.1
Content area	12.1
Student needs	11.4
Grade level	10.6
Teaching philosophy	10.1
Time for teaching unit/lesson(s)	9.7
Teacher training	5.9
Teaching methods	5.0
State or local objectives	3.7
Available teaching materials	3.7
Available resources	3.4
Collaboration with others	2.6
Community expectations	1.5

Among the factors that apparently had little influence on Holocaust pedagogy were community expectations, identified by only 1.5% of respondents, collaboration with others (2.6%), and available resources (3.4%). Only 3.7% indicated that state/local objectives influenced their instructional choices; this low number is certainly influenced by the fact that HE is currently not compulsory or even recommended in most states, nor is Holocaust content knowledge assessed on standardised tests in most locations in the United States. Notably, only 5.9% indicated that teacher training was a significant influence on their pedagogy even though they had all received advanced training in HE from a national organisation.

Subjectivity was the most influential factor for these respondents as they chose how they teach the Holocaust; they saw their choices as stemming from both a personal commitment to the topic and the way they understand and/or perceive student needs. Content area and grade level do influence their instructional choices, but not because of established state or local objectives. Added together, 38.5% of respondents indicated a subjective reason (personal objectives/commitment, student needs, teaching philosophy) as an influence on the pedagogical decisions they make when teaching about the Holocaust.

When asked to think about how these same influences might limit their instruction, and what one they would most like to change, nearly half of these teachers (47.6%) identified the same item. They said would like to change the amount of time allocated for teaching units/lessons, to allow them to teach more effectively on the Holocaust. Meanwhile, 13.6% would change the factor collaboration with others, and 9.8% would change state/local objectives.

Teaching the Holocaust with the Goal of Arriving at a Universal Lesson, Belief, or Moral

The USHMM asks teachers to develop a rationale for teaching the Holocaust, to answer for themselves and their students *why* it is important to undertake such study; it also asks teachers to use a set of clearly defined guidelines as they plan, deliver, and assess the teaching and learning of their Holocaust instruction. The section of the USHMM website (2014) dedicated to educators suggests that "most students demonstrate a high level of interest in studying this history precisely because the subject raises questions of fairness, justice, individual identity, peer pressure, conformity, indifference, and obedience". The opportunity to engage with these issues and the other moral and human issues embedded in a study of the Holocaust influences many of these educators.

The majority of respondents (85.2%) indicated that they aim to have students acquire a universal lesson, belief, or moral as an outcome of their instruction. I asked if it is a goal of theirs to have students arrive at a universal lesson; 39.4% said *yes*, and 45.8% said *somewhat*. The other 14.8% indicated that it is not an intended goal of their instruction. Holocaust education scholars like Peter Novick (1999) and Paul Salmons caution against turning the Holocaust into a metaphor or a subjective singularity, as that can deprive students of the opportunity to arrive at their own personally articulated conclusions; they say such conclusions will only follow a disciplined study of the real history of the Holocaust. If teachers use a rationale and standard guidelines, that can help guard against the pedagogy becoming overly subjective. The USHMM website offers both a rationale and guidelines in its section for educators.

Pedagogical Choices Made by Trained Holocaust Educators

Simone Schweber (2004) studied the classroom practice of individual teachers engaged with students in HE; she stated that she was "stunned by the numerous complexities inherent in teaching about the Holocaust in particular and the precarious balancing acts involved in the teaching of history in general" (p. 167). These complexities and balancing acts make it difficult to quantify approaches to teaching the Holocaust, but, like Donnelly (2004), I also endeavor to do so.

In her study, Donnelly began to identify the choices teachers made in response to the complexities and balancing acts; she found that 88% of teachers taught the Holocaust from a perspective on human rights, and that Holocaust instruction was most often embedded in a unit on war crimes/human rights, which were then issues surrounding the United States' involvement in World War II. She also found that teachers used multiple resources to teach students, including film and memoir, photos, documentaries, survivor testimony, literature, and history textbooks.

English teachers often embedded Holocaust instruction in a literature unit, such as the reading of *The Diary of Anne Frank* or Elie Wiesel's *Night* (Donnelly 2004, pp. 19–24).

In my study, I asked teachers to identify their chief or primary instructional strategy, then their second instructional strategy, from a list of ten possible strategies teachers have used to deliver Holocaust instruction. The approaches were as follows:

- **Timeline/chronological** Refer to a timeline and start at a beginning point, then progress through events as they unfolded from that part of the timeline to an ending point, such as 1933–1945.
- **Historical events** Examine key historical events as antecedents, milestones, or turning points in the Holocaust: Kristallnacht, Warsaw Ghetto Uprising, Wannsee Conference, etc. Note: This differs from the approach above because the events may or may not be taught sequentially, and may not be limited to a specific timeline.
- **Catalyst/causal** Begin by establishing one or more events that serve as a cause; what follows is the effect(s), or a sequence of causes and effects, taught with a sense of dominoes falling in a chain of events. Note: this differs from the approach above because this one places a clear emphasis on one event's causal impacts on the next.
- **Literary or text-based** Select a text or texts (novels, films, poems, etc.) to serve as the primary medium/a and frame of reference. This can include introductory or context lessons, extensions, or outcomes in response to the text.
- **Thematic** Start with or establish a focus on one or more universal human themes (i.e. identity, bigotry, community, inhumanity, etc.) and teach elements and details of the Holocaust that explore that theme.
- **Cathartic** Teach to a predetermined conclusion that represents a specific value or understanding, often as an emotional experience or a shared social or psycho-social value, e.g., "Never again" or "Never forget".
- **Phase** Group events and time sequences (months, days, years, etc.) together as phases, as Hilberg (1961) does with his six phases of the Holocaust: definition, expropriation, concentration, mobile killing units, deportation, killing centres.
- **Narrative** Create major or archetypal character(s) to tell the Holocaust story, and explore their choices and actions as you might teach or talk about narrative in an English class. (Examples of "characters" include victims (Jews), perpetrators, bystanders, etc.).
- **Experiential** Create experiences for students, such as simulations, role plays, service projects, or a visit to a museum or historical site; those experiences serve as students' primary form of encounter with Holocaust content.
- **Inquiry/research/project** Generate individual/group questions about the Holocaust, then investigate and interact with source material or other historic or scholarly documentation including primary documents, photos, videos, survivor testimony (i.e. IWitness), textbook material, or other research on the Holocaust. Then generate a response to those questions in the form of a product: an original project, presentation, paper, or other creation.

I developed this list of approaches by considering and articulating the professional development models offered by the three national organisations participating in this study; I also considered the strategies that Totten and Feinberg (2001) offer (Table 2).

As the table shows, the top three approaches these respondents say they use are the literary or text-based approach, inquiry/research/projects, and teaching historical events.

Table 2 Teachers' primary pedagogical approach

Pedagogical approach	Primary approach used (%)
Literary or text-based	31.6%
Inquiry/research/project	16.3%
Historical events	13.5%
Timeline/chronological	11.1%
Thematic	10.3%
Catalyst/causal	4.7%
Narrative	3.8%
Phase	3.6%
Cathartic	3.2%
Experiential	1.9%

The literary or text-based approach is the main pedagogical approach of literature instruction in English classrooms, and 56.1% of the respondents indicated that they teach the Holocaust in an English/language arts classroom. Literature is recognised as a powerful, engaging, humanising way to present Holocaust content, but scholars of this methodology such as Paul Wieser (2001) warn that, without an accurate sense of the history it represents, literature is just a story, capable of blurring the distinction between learning that is essential, and learning that is ancillary (pp. 70–71). The second most often used approach—various forms of inquiry, research, and projects—represents a pedagogical shift toward student-centred learning. Over the past decade American educators have responded to many books, seminars, and strategies on methods, like those set forth by Wiggins and McTighe (2001) and in professional development seminars. This approach engages students in better understanding big ideas and personal questions, and/or working toward collaborative goals in an ongoing learning process.

Nearly all (95%) respondents chose a secondary pedagogical approach to Holocaust instruction. Again their top strategy was literary or text-based: 22.1% indicated they used this as a secondary approach. Considering that 31.6% said they used it as a primary approach, a total of 53.7% said it is either their primary or secondary approach; this nearly matches the percentage of respondents who teach about the Holocaust in an English/language arts class (56.1%). The runner-ups on this question—thematic, inquiry/research/project, and timeline-chronological—are strategies to teach historical knowledge that can be understood as means of providing context in English class for the study of a Holocaust text (Table 3).

Table 3 Teachers' secondary pedagogical approach

Pedagogical approach	Secondary approach used (%)
Literary or text-based	22.1%
Thematic	14.9%
Inquiry/research/project	14.5%
Timeline/chronological	13.3%
Historical events	11.7%
Narrative	7.6%
Catalyst/causal	6.8%
Phase	4.0%
Cathartic	1.6%
Experiential	1.6%
Not applicable	2.0%

End-of-Unit Assessment Strategies and/or Products These Teachers Require of Students

I also asked respondents to identify the different assessment strategies they used at the end of their Holocaust instruction, including tests, quizzes, essays, book reviews, media productions, or other activities (Table 4). Here they were free to check as many items as they liked and the average participant mentioned 3.63 different assessments, with 48.4% indicating they asked students to produce a personal paper or essay. In addition, 38.1% include a visit to a Holocaust museum and/or a visit from a Holocaust survivor as an end-of-unit experience, and 35.7% include class discussion as a strategy for assessing learning. Only 10.3% require a service or action project, and only 7.1% make use of IWitness for this purpose.

The prominence of creative, formal, and personal writing as assessment and end-of-unit strategies can be seen as a natural outcome of teaching and learning in an English/language arts (E/LA) class, and 56.1% of Holocaust education takes place in such classes. Educators have called for an increase in writing across the curriculum; as a result, more assessment strategies that use writing are being used outside of E/LA classrooms. Still, over half of respondents (52.8%) said they use a test-type assessment (quiz, unit test, final exam). Those who said they had experienced museums or visits with survivors as part of their training said they provide their students with the same kind of learning experience that happens when one hears from a survivor or sees the artifacts in a museum. Class discussion is a natural way to get at the questions and observations students are willing to share, and such discussions can naturally lead to inquiry-based research projects at the end of a unit.

It is notable that these teachers are employing multiple assessment strategies, and that these strategies allow them to be creative rather than standardised in their testing. Such strategies, however, can also lead students away from historical understanding and onto overly personal or artistic interpretations or representations of

Table 4 End-of-unit assessments and/or projects teachers used or required

Assessment or product	Percent using it
Personal paper or essay	48.4%
Museum or survivor visit	38.1%
Discussion	35.7%
Display/presentation	27.4%
Creative writing	25.8%
Other creative/art project	25.8%
Scholarly or formal essay or paper	24.2%
Unit test	24.2%
Other media-based project	21.0%
Book or film review	19.8%
All or part of final exam	15.5%
Quiz	13.1%
Action/service project	10.3%
Student portfolio	8.3%
Public event hosted by students	7.5%
Other	7.1%
IWitness project	7.1%
Other field trip	3.9%

their learning about the Holocaust. If disciplined historical learning is a goal of HE, it would be useful to study the various strategies for assessment and end-of-unit teaching and learning, to see if, and how, they potentially misrepresent or distort Holocaust history. Further, recall that the overwhelming majority of participants (85.2%) claim that they teach with a goal of having students arrive at learning a universal human lesson, belief, or value either firmly in mind or somewhat in mind. Given that these teachers aim at that goal, these assessments should also be scrutinised to see if they keep students from developing their own takeaway lessons from their study of the Holocaust.

Finally, a significant proportion of participants (21.0%) said they use new media and web-based applications for assessment and end-of-unit activities, only 7.1% said they use the IWitness application provided by the USCSF. Given the current trend toward rising use of technology in instruction, and the increasing availability of technology for teaching and learning, it is likely the use of these media and web-based activities will also increase in coming years.

A final question asked how comprehensive and successful these teachers felt their teaching to be; 54.5% said they believe the HE they deliver does succeed in delivering one or more key lessons about the Holocaust to students. However, 34.1% said they would add, develop, or expand the unit or lessons on the Holocaust but are limited by one or more factors, and 47.6% would choose to add more time to their teaching on the Holocaust. At present, only six states mandate HE, so very few examples exist of comprehensive standardised curricula in the field.

Participants' Professional Development Goals and Intentions

The teachers who responded to this survey have already participated in teacher professional development in Holocaust content and/or pedagogy, and many participated in selective, competitive programmes at national organisations, such as the Teacher Fellowship Programme at the USHMM, the Master Teacher Programme at the USCSF, or the national summer seminar and leadership institutes at the Memorial Library. Many participated in multiple such programmes, and several said they had participated in most of them. Thus, the teachers who responded to my survey are among the country's most trained and professionally developed teachers of Holocaust content and pedagogy. Still, I found an almost complete consensus among them that they see more training and learning ahead of them: 94.1% indicated that they are motivated to study, or still actively studying, Holocaust content and/or pedagogy.

For motivated teachers in Holocaust education, professional development in the content and pedagogy almost always leads them to continue learning. Very few said they moved away from such study after receiving training from the three organisations in this study. Given the concern of scholars like Paul Salmons (2010) and Peter Novick (1999) that teaching and learning about the Holocaust be grounded in the discipline of history, I see two ways to improve the historical quality of HE: provide English teachers with increased training and materials in methods of teaching history, and develop resources that provide context for literature and text-based instruction about the Holocaust.

If the field of Holocaust education is indeed at a crossroads, this study has offered a good look at the landscape on all sides. Teachers trained in the field are using that training to deliver their content effectively, but they must still do so within their broader teaching context, and within the parameters of a period in education that is being driven by a focus on standards and assessment.

My analysis confirms much of what the USHMM learned about HE from the Donnelly (2004) study, particularly that English/language arts remains the content area in which most HE takes place, and that literature is the key instructional strategy used in the field. Still, this study has yielded some interesting and important findings about the context and practice of educators who have received training from prominent HE organisations and programmes. A close look at the data provided by these educators trained in Holocaust content and/or pedagogy can both inform professional development programmes and teacher trainers, and also help teachers in the field to find more effective ways to teach about the Holocaust.

References

Donnelly, M. B. (2004). *National study of secondary teaching practices in Holocaust education. Final report*. Arlington: SRI International.
FHAO [Facing History and Ourselves] (2014). *Online learning*. http://www.facinghistory.org/for-educators/workshops-and-seminars/about-online-learning

Green, E. (2010, 2 March). Building a better teacher. *The New York Times*. http://www.nytimes.com/2010/03/07/magazine/07Teachers-t.html?pagewanted=all

HEDP [Holocaust Education Development Programme, Institute of Education, University of London] (2009). *Teaching about the Holocaust in English secondary schools: An empirical study of national trends, perspectives and practice*. London: University of London.

Hilberg, R. (1961). *The destruction of the European Jews*. New Haven: Yale University Press.

Memorial Library (2014). *Welcome to the Memorial Library & the Holocaust Educators Network*. http://www.thememoriallibrary.org/

Novick, P. (1999). *The Holocaust in American life*. Boston: Houghton Mifflin.

Salmons, P. (2010). Universal meaning or historical understanding? The Holocaust in history and history in the curriculum. *Teaching History, 141*, 57–63.

Schweber, S. (2004). *Making sense of the Holocaust: Lessons from classroom practice*. New York: Teachers College Press.

Shawn, K. (2001). Choosing Holocaust literature for early adolescents. In S. Totten & S. Feinberg (Eds.), *Teaching and studying the Holocaust* (pp. 139–155). Boston: Allyn & Bacon.

Smith, S. (2009). *Never again, yet again: A personal struggle with the Holocaust and genocide*. Jerusalem: Gefen.

Totten, S., & Feinberg, S. (Eds.) (2001). *Teaching and studying the Holocaust*. Boston: Allyn & Bacon.

USCSF [University of Southern California Shoah Foundation] (2014). *About us*. http://sfi.usc.edu/about

USHMM [United States Holocaust Memorial Museum] (2014). *Professional events and resources*. http://www.ushmm.org/educators/professional-events-and-resources

Wieser, P. (2001). Instructional issues/strategies in teaching the Holocaust. In S. Totten & S. Feinberg (Eds.), *Teaching and studying the Holocaust* (pp. 62–80). Boston: Allyn & Bacon.

Wiggins, G. P., & McTighe, J. (2001). *Understanding by design*. Upper Saddle River: Merrill/Prentice Hall.

"Unless They Have To": Power, Politics and Institutional Hierarchy in Lithuanian Holocaust Education

Christine Beresniova

Introduction

The Holocaust is a controversial topic in post-Soviet states (Bartov 2008; Dietsch 2012; Gross 2013; Gross and Stevick 2010; Himka 2008; Pettai 2011a; Stevick 2007; Weiss-Wendt 2009). Because of this, teachers in these countries can encounter critical reactions from peers when they suggest classroom lessons and additional school programmes on Holocaust history. The potential for conflict with colleagues makes teachers hesitant to teach about the Holocaust. As one teacher in Lithuania explained, teachers and school directors do not talk about the subject "unless they have to". The frequently spoken comment "unless they have to" highlights both how unpopular the topic is in Lithuanian society and their view of the educational system as a vertical hierarchy rather than a horizontal structure. In Lithuania, where the educational system remains highly centralised, teachers suggested that school directors could be a significant factor in developing Lithuanian Holocaust education; however, few studies address how politics and hierarchy influence teachers' levels of motivation to participate in Holocaust education.

Unsurprisingly, teachers with supportive school directors were more willing to subject themselves to peer criticism for working with Holocaust programmes than those without similar administrative support; the study I describe here reveals the dynamics that undergird this pattern. In addition, I examine how teacher attitudes toward the benefits of hierarchy changed significantly when international agencies became more outspoken about Lithuanian Holocaust education. Most supportive teachers and school directors saw the leadership of international "experts" in

---

C. Beresniova (✉)
Takiff Foundation Fellow, Jack, Joseph, and Morton Mandel Center for Advanced Holocaust Studies, United States Holocaust Memorial Museum, 100 Raoul Wallenberg Place, SW, Washington, DC 20024-2126 USA
e-mail: acberesn@indiana.edu

Holocaust education as counterproductive to their efforts because the visibility of foreign advocates exacerbated local perceptions of the Holocaust as a "western" or "Jewish" issue. The widely-held view that the Holocaust was an "outside" issue made it harder for supportive teachers to persuade colleagues that it had local significance. The desire teachers expressed for more visible participation by school directors—but less visible participation by international agencies—highlights how not all forms of hierarchical pressure were equally helpful in promoting Holocaust education in Lithuania.

In light of the politics inherent in post-Soviet Holocaust education, in this chapter I ask what a case study of Lithuania can tell us about the ways that school directors navigate political issues in their professional life. Additionally, I explore how the attitudes of school directors influence teachers' motivation to engage in Holocaust education. I seek to inform both theoretical and practical discussions. I also advocate for more detailed research on how power, politics, and hierarchy influence the development of Holocaust education.

Methodology

This chapter is informed by 24 months of anthropological fieldwork in Lithuania (2011–2013), which took place at schools in 19 different cities with over 75 key interviews. To better understand the role that hierarchy plays in Holocaust education, I used qualitative methods, including participant observation and interviews. Because I was interested in the effects of international power relationships, I employed a multi-sited research design. George Marcus (1995) explains that multi-sited ethnographic research "moves out from the single sites and local situations of conventional ethnographic research designs to examine the circulation of cultural meanings, objects, and identities in diffuse time-space" (p. 96). Multi-sited ethnography maps how relationships move across groups rather than how individuals relate to a topic in a fixed site.

I conducted and analysed my observations and interviews primarily in Lithuanian. I interpreted my data using Phil Carspecken's (1996) methods for ethnographic research in educational settings; they focus on how power relationships influence socially-negotiated meanings. To further understand the role of hierarchies in Lithuanian Holocaust education, I drew on the framework of "policy as practice", developed by Bradley Levinson and Margaret Sutton (2001), which views individual appropriation as integral to policy implementation. Appropriation is an important concept to integrate into policy studies; researchers need to ask how an individual understands policy expectations and then enacts these in her daily practices.

The majority of individuals I interviewed were teachers and school directors, a position that is similar to a school principal in the United States. I also spoke with politicians, diplomats, museum workers, and members of the Jewish community. As I report on our conversations, I refer to all of them with pseudonyms. One of the key participants in this study, Ona, was both a teacher and a political representative. Ona served as the deputy director of education at the Commission for the Evolution of the Crimes of the Nazi and Soviet Regimes in Lithuania (the Commission) and also taught history part-time at a large secondary school. Ona oversaw the daily operations of the Commission's educational division, which had several key aims. The first aim was to acquaint Lithuanian teachers with the Commission's findings on formal classroom lessons. The second aim was to train teachers to lead five nationally recognised days of commemoration in their schools. These are Lithuanian Holocaust Remembrance Day; International Tolerance Day; 13 January, the date when Soviet troops killed Lithuanians; International Holocaust Remembrance Day; and the Lithuanian Day of Mourning and Hope to commemorate Soviet exiles. The third aim was to establish Tolerance Education Centres (TECs) in schools around Lithuania. These centres used historical examples from the Nazi and Soviet periods to promote democratic values, such as tolerance. While the Commission's activities focused on supplementing regular classroom lessons, most of their programmes were offered as extracurricular activities in the TECs. Students who participated in the centres volunteered to clean Jewish cemeteries, research their town's wartime history, host Soviet exiles as guest speakers in their schools, or participate in local programmes about tolerance. Most of the teachers who oversaw school the TECs were also teachers of history or literature, or teachers responsible for classroom lessons on these topics.

Theorising School Directors, Politics and Hierarchy

Because teachers play an important role in school operations, the success of school policy reform depends on what Levinson and Sutton (2001) call teacher "buy-in". However, when teachers are involved in implementing policy, that process entails more than simply acting on personal motivations: practical considerations can also limit their professional practices. Levinson and Sutton see educational policy implementation as "constantly negotiated and reorganized in the ongoing flow of institutional life" (p. 2). As researchers examine how individuals appropriate policy, discussions move from how hierarchy is envisioned in theory, to how people understand its influence in practice.

One factor that influences individual policy appropriation is politics (Blase and Anderson 1995; Hallinger and Leithwood 1998; Leithwood 1995; Owen 2006). However, Gary Crow and Dick Weindling (2010) argue that scholars do not fully understand the impact of broader political situations on school leadership because most studies focus primarily on technical competencies and bureaucratic politics. In their study on English headmasters, Crow and Weindling found that contemporary school leaders had to develop professional skills beyond "micro-level" institutional politics to understand "how the school is a political institution both inside and outside at the global, societal, and community levels" (p. 141). An especially important point in their study was the need to train school leaders to navigate political situations because few English headmasters felt prepared for the politically fraught aspects of their job. Many headmasters explained that they figured out how to navigate political influences through "trial and error" (2010, p. 154)—not an approach they felt was effective for school leadership.

Because politics can significantly influence school policies, the authors posit that school leaders require "a different type of knowledge" to account for "interest group pressures on education, ideological differences that impinge on schools, and environmental conditions that struggle for recognition and resources" (p. 142). Thus, they see the need to pay more attention to the influence of political situations on school directors; this need is especially acute in post-Soviet states, where educational reforms took place simultaneously at the international and local levels.

Holocaust Education in Lithuania

In 1991, Lithuania achieved independence from the Soviet Union and immediately sought accession to western organisations, such as the European Union (EU). As part of its membership negotiations for such groups, the Lithuanian government adopted a wide array of reforms. During the conversations for accession to the North Atlantic Treaty Organisation (NATO), expectations for post-Soviet Holocaust education emerged. However, the idea that Holocaust knowledge could serve as a marker for an "educated person" (Short and Reed 2004, p. 1) was a considerable departure from earlier Soviet attitudes toward the subject. In the Soviet Union, events of the Holocaust had been subsumed into a broader Soviet narrative about mass atrocities perpetrated against all "Soviet citizens" during the war (Gundare and Batelaan 2003, p. 155; Gross and Stevick 2010, p. 23). Therefore, when post-Soviet countries applied for NATO and EU membership, local populations did not value knowing the details of Holocaust history. In fact, Eva-Clarita Pettai (2011a) found that international calls for Holocaust education actually "caught Baltic elites rather by surprise" (p. 159) because local historians saw the Soviet Occupation as more relevant to post-Soviet national identity.

To address outstanding Holocaust issues in post-Soviet states, members of the international community linked accession requirements to Holocaust atonement. These requirements included instituting commemorations for Holocaust-era events and returning Jewish communal property to survivor communities. Consequently, many Holocaust programmes in Lithuania were introduced by western agencies. The international introduction of Holocaust education had ramifications on the degree to which local populations internalised its importance.

Many scholars have attempted to explain teachers' post-Soviet attitudes toward Holocaust education, especially their negative attitudes (Gross 2013; Gundare and Batelaan 2003; Michaels 2013; Misco 2008; Stevick 2012; Waldman 2004). The most commonly cited reason for resistance to Holocaust education is the importance that the history of the Soviet Occupation holds in post-Soviet states. But local connections to Soviet history do not completely explain the situation. In Lithuania, many teachers explained that their participation in Holocaust education was shaped by the culture of their school community, which they saw as reflecting attitudes found in the wider society.

However, it is important to note that highly-charged discussions about the Holocaust were not taking place only in the post-Soviet states. In the 1990s, reparations cases were being pursued all over Europe—largely at the impetus of politicians and lawyers in the United States. Following especially visible reparations cases against Switzerland, Germany, and France, 41 member states from the Organisation for Security and Cooperation in Europe (OSCE) met in Stockholm in 2000 to discuss the future of Holocaust remembrance. As a result of the meeting, OSCE member countries agreed to create an international Holocaust task force based on the *Declaration of the Stockholm International Forum on the Holocaust* (IHRA 2000). The declaration was significant because it called on all member states to make Holocaust remembrance a national priority.

In response to international calls for more attention to Holocaust education, the Lithuanian Ministry of Education and Science organised several initiatives, including teacher training programmes. For political reasons too complex to discuss here, Lithuanian Holocaust education programmes were subsequently shifted from the purview of that ministry to the Commission, a small and relatively powerless governmental agency. Similar to historical commissions established in Latvia and Estonia at the same time, the Lithuanian Commission was a product of politics. According to Eva-Clarita Pettai (2011b), the Baltic commissions were created "in response to outside pressure to confront many still open questions about the recent past" (p. 265). While all three commissions were tasked with researching the histories of Nazi and Soviet Occupation in the Baltic States, the Lithuanian one also adopted a local educational component. Although pedagogical institutions were still technically responsible for preparing teachers to teach history in Lithuania, professional development for Holocaust education became largely the responsibility of the Commission. According to the Commission's records, it trained between 4,000 and 5,000 teachers in various seminars over the last 11 years; it cannot say exactly how many individuals attended, as some may have come to more than one seminar.

However, the work of the Commission has not been without controversy.

Controversy and the Commission

The Lithuanian government has heralded the Commission's programmes as demonstrating Lithuania's commitment to Holocaust education. But they have also sparked debate. First, some question whether its educational programmes are effective, given that they lack significant financial resources. Second, some have asked why the Commission is charged with educational programmes when it is not part of the Ministry of Education or affiliated with any pedagogical universities. Third, many educators argue that the Commission has established a monopoly on Holocaust education programmes, shutting out other potential programme partners: the OSCE,

B'nai Brith, the Anne Frank House, and Centropa have offered Holocaust education programmes in Lithuania. Finally, concerns exist about the decision to situate the Holocaust with the Soviet Occupation in historical conversations. Many western politicians questioned such a twofold approach to historical investigation because they worried that local people would conflate the suffering from the Soviet era and from the Holocaust as morally equivalent.

In conversations in the West, people discuss the Holocaust as a distinct subject, but many Lithuanians teach about the Holocaust and the Soviet Occupation as overlapping genocides. Because Lithuanians call that occupation a "genocide", some groups accuse them of trying to equalise the suffering caused by the two events; Zilinskas (2009) reviews these debates. In fact, some engage in what the historian Antony Polonsky (in Cohen 2012, p. 1) calls a "Suffering Olympics" as they discuss the motivations of Lithuanians who want to teach the Soviet Occupation as genocide. In response to such accusations, many Lithuanians criticise western politicians for neglecting the Soviet Occupation in their schools; they think this reveals an acute power imbalance in international politics of memory.

Given this context of debates over how to interpret this Nazi and Soviet history, the international origins of the Commission had a serious impact on the way local communities viewed its work. Dovilė Budrytė (2005) suggests that many local populations accepted European pressure to engage in Holocaust education because it was necessary for EU and NATO accession; thus, their "acceptance" of these policies did not significantly influence the way they viewed the Holocaust. Lithuanians generally countenanced the policies on Holocaust education to achieve political ends, but few actually internalised the Holocaust as a nationally relevant event.

Researchers have discovered a similar lack of interest in Holocaust history in many post-Soviet States. In Estonia, Doyle Stevick (2007) found that when the Estonian Ministry of Education implemented new guidelines for Holocaust education, politicians continued to refer to "multiple" tragedies in public discussions about World War II. Therefore, policies for Holocaust education were implemented in Estonia to meet EU and NATO guidelines, but politicians undermined their importance when they spoke about them publicly. Stevick also found that the Estonian government allowed teachers to "choose" when and how to interpret the Holocaust, a policy that subjected willing teachers to pressure from resistant peers.

The Estonian case highlights controversies also present in Lithuania. Many Lithuanian teachers said they experienced few professional rewards for spending more than the required lesson time on Holocaust history. More importantly, they reported that there were no professional sanctions for those who spent less time than was specified by curricular guidelines—or did not teach it at all. In fact, most said that working with Holocaust education had some personal cost. Some were nicknamed "the Holocaust teacher" as others publicly questioned their loyalty to ethnic Lithuanians, calling out a perceived allegiance to "the Jews" in their work. Given how unpopular it is to teach about the Holocaust in Lithuania, teachers saw the authority of school directors as integral to the development of Holocaust education. In the next section I describe Lithuanian school directors in more detail.

The Role of Hierarchy in Lithuanian Holocaust Education

Given the legacy of the Soviet system, hierarchical relationships still have an effect on individual motivations in Lithuanian schools. Therefore, teachers frequently articulated the need for school directors to leverage their professional authority in the face of political controversy. Ona, the deputy director for education at the Commission, said on many occasions, "It depends on the school directors. If they don't care then nothing will happen" in the schools. This statement was not wholly accurate, because some teachers did work on Holocaust education even when they were not forced to. Moreover, though teaching about the Holocaust is technically required in Lithuania, teachers reported that most of these requirements are either ineffective or unenforced. Still, Ona's comment echoed a sentiment I frequently heard in Lithuanian schools: that educational change was driven from the top down. Ona saw school directors as key to changing school culture because they could enforce reforms more expediently than grassroots initiatives working from the bottom up. Thus, Ona wanted to develop a training programme for school directors, but she struggled to find financial support because most local agencies did not see the Holocaust as an educational priority.

In turn, the need to search for external resources for Holocaust education influenced how people perceived its importance in Lithuania. Before the country was granted accession to the EU and NATO in 2004, the Lithuanian government was more willing to provide support for Holocaust programmes to facilitate that accession. Government investment in Holocaust programmes gave teachers the impression it was a nationally relevant topic. After accession, however, teachers said that financial support for those programmes dwindled, and so did concern about the topic. In order to fund school programmes, educators had to seek funding from international agencies, such as those connected with the EU, or from the US Embassy in Vilnius. This reliance on external sources of funding left many teachers feeling that Lithuanian politicians were mostly "talking to talk", as one teacher put it, when it came to the importance of Holocaust education. A teacher I will call Aronas, who had worked on Holocaust education programmes with the Lithuanian Ministry, said that politicians rarely backed political support with funds:

> We never had any problem with those [Holocaust] seminars, except one: We never received any money. So, all levels of officials are either not interested, or quite "pro" the idea. But of course, "pro" as in many other projects. Lithuanian politicians, as far as they can remember, are very "pro-Jewish". Why? You can get everything from them... except money. (Laughs)

The need to support local projects with outside funding meant that educators had to develop the political acumen to navigate international grant requirements. However, a colleague who worked at the US Embassy in Vilnius said that few Lithuanians were skilled at writing successful applications for international grants; this put them at a double disadvantage when it came to promoting Holocaust education in Lithuania.

Ona explained that she learned to navigate the international bureaucracy by paying attention to institutional politics. Her political sensitivity was visible in the way she responded to situations around her. Although she was known for her gregarious nature, she usually dissolved into the background whenever she was around her boss, the director of the Commission. She always referred to him as "director" in public, rarely calling him by name. And when other people were present, she always deferred to his decisions, even if she disagreed with them. Her deference was particularly visible to those who knew her at a 2012 ceremony with the Lithuanian prime minister, Andrius Kubilius.

At the ceremony, Kubilius recognised a dozen TEC teachers for their work. All of them worked closely with Ona, but Ona's only role during the official event was to stand in the back and bring up certificates when asked to. People who did not already know her would have had no indication that she was the educational lynchpin of the Commission. In her work, she designed training seminars, built community relationships, and stayed abreast of relevant pedagogy. In fact, not a single educational planning detail at the Commission escaped her attention. Yet, she was careful not to call attention to herself in certain circles, as hierarchy, status, and position were still central to the way the educational system operated. Petras, a secondary school teacher in a large city, expressed the importance of hierarchy most succinctly: "Without the permission of my boss, I am nothing". In light of such institutional expectations for deference to hierarchy, Ona felt that influencing school directors would be the most effective way to bolster teacher involvement in Holocaust education.

School Directors

Deference to educational hierarchy was visible in many of my conversations with Lithuanian school directors. Most of them explained that their administrative practices were guided by expectations from the ministry. While some cited a personal interest in Holocaust education, the majority said they had to temper personal interests with professional expectations. A major factor for them was whether programmes would make their school more attractive to students, given the competition between schools. Attracting students was important because each student came with an annual student funding "basket" that bolstered the bottom line of the school they attended. Given that the Holocaust was a sensitive topic for many Lithuanians, few school directors were interested in programmes that would stoke controversy.

On the other hand, that same competitiveness between schools sometimes influenced directors to open a TEC in their school. Gediminas, the director of a secondary school in a large city, explained, "The first programme came into my school when one teacher came to work here". After that teacher came, "Our goal became essentially that we would have the same [centre] in our school". In this way, competition between schools to offer various programmes could sometimes serve as a motivating factor in the directors' decision making. Still, several directors explained that even if they wanted to implement more comprehensive Holocaust education programmes, they were cautious about doing so given that the ministry had not provided a clear "path" for how to proceed.

When I talked to Ramunė, a school director in a large city, I mentioned the more than 200 local massacre sites and asked why more Lithuanian teachers did not use some of them as part of Holocaust education. She answered by pointing to the lack of professional guidelines on the topic: "The thing is, how could Lithuania use these places? First, this topic has to be prepared by someone else in a certain way". The "way" she was suggesting was through formal curriculum programmes outlined by ministry officials. While ministry approval is certainly a normal concern for school directors, it is important to note that directors did not always seek ministry guidance for every programme they undertook. What was significant about Holocaust education was that it was contested in society, so directors could cite a lack of reinforcement from above as an excuse for not engaging with it. Therefore, they sometimes pointed to hierarchy to avoid responsibility for a topic even though they could have navigated past that issue if they wanted to do so. Thus, they acted strategically when they faced conflicting social pressures about running their schools: they appropriated policy selectively, sometimes choosing to ignore it or adopt it only partially.

In addition to concerns over curricular guidelines, some directors did not want to reveal their lack of education on a topic. The directors I worked with started their professional careers during the Soviet Occupation, so many were learning about the Holocaust for the first time through Commission programmes. As school directors, they did not want to institute programmes that would expose their own unfamiliarity with a subject. Orinta, a school director who worked in an area famous for its anti-Soviet partisans, told me that her school focused minimally on the Holocaust because she knew "only a little" about it herself.

School directors frequently said that they needed more training on Holocaust history, but when I asked Ona if Commission programmes should be required for all teachers, she adamantly rejected the idea. She preferred to see teachers and school directors come to the topic on their own. She explained that the Commission's programmes remained voluntary because it was not productive to mandate seminars for attitudinal change. In fact, researchers have found that governmental mandates have only limited ability to prompt teacher involvement. For example, in a study on Holocaust education in American schools, Thomas Fallace (2008) found "not a single example of a teacher who became interested in the topic" of the Holocaust "as a result of a mandate" (p. 155). This is important to note because Holocaust education is officially mandated in the Lithuanian curriculum, but still remains a source of contention for many teachers in practice.

The few school directors who were active in Holocaust education usually worked closely with the Commission. At Commission events, it was common to hear them speak about the importance of Holocaust education. However, Fausta, a school director in a village, spoke about her responsibility differently than most: she explained that she made all the teachers in her school participate in Holocaust commemorations even if they didn't want to. In an interview, she explained:

> I am the director. As the director, I am pressing [the teachers] to do this thing [Holocaust education] (laughs)... I am not going to let [teachers] make excuses that "I will participate", or "No, I will not participate". That's the fundamental difference in our school. We are doing school commemorations... and every teacher who is in the school on that day participates. It's clear not everyone wants to do it, but they have to participate because it's their job.

Fausta saw her role as one of enforcement and she did not wait for a teacher's interest to be piqued on its own. Fausta used her position in the hierarchy to frame Holocaust education as a job-related activity for all teachers who worked in her school.

But her approach—of requiring teacher participation—was not common. However, several teachers in her school explained that her approach worked because it had gotten them interested in participating in other seminars. One of them, Ina, said that at first she had shown up at events only because Fausta required it. However, over time, she found the history interesting. When an optional programme on Holocaust history was presented in her town, Ina attended: "I realised I didn't know about it, so I thought, why not? [The Holocaust happened] here in my own town, and I didn't know what was here". Several months later, Ina called me to say she was organising a field trip to a local museum for other teachers who also didn't know the history. She went from being a required participant to a self-motivated programme organiser. In this instance, the authority of the school director resulted in a positive outcome, but that happened because an active school director leveraged her professional position to create a school culture around Holocaust education.

School Directors' Influence on Teachers

Teachers often said that they were motivated by the attitudes that their school directors held about Holocaust education—whether positive or negative. Many teachers saw school directors as central to defining their duties as a teacher; those who worked in one of Lithuania's 97 schools with a TEC said that they especially needed the directors' support. For a school to become a TEC, the director had to sign a memorandum of understanding with the Commission guaranteeing that the school administration would support the centre. Petras explained that he participated in a Commission training programme in Auschwitz in April 2012 because his director told him, "Petras, you are not going [to Auschwitz] just to travel.... we are planning that you will create a tolerance centre in our school". Because his director had instructed him to do so, Petras said that he came back from Poland with "many ideas about what to do" to start his school's centre. Uršulė, a teacher in a small town, remarked that her school director had participated in a training seminar at Yad Vashem hosted by the Commission and had similarly come back with "promises" for activities in the school's TEC.

Yet, while some directors were supportive in theory, they were not always active participants in practice. Kargauda, a teacher in a large city, said that even though the director at her school started the centre there, she still had to figure out ways "to circumvent" him because he was not always supportive of her work on Holocaust history. She appealed to her assistant director, who told her discreetly, "Don't you pay attention to the director. Pay attention to me, and I will take care of everything". Barbora, a teacher in a medium-sized town in the southern part of Lithuania, said her director tolerated their TEC but showed no real enthusiasm for it:

> He's still a little cold with that kind of thing. That he would be fired up, like those other directors from [another town], those two directors who said, "Wow. We are doing, doing,

doing everything!" That? No. [pause] He's not sitting there clapping his hands and saying, "Oh, good, good! Do it! Do it!" But he lets us work and he's not angry about it when he does.

The various ways that school directors participated in TEC activities had a direct influence on teacher interactions. Several teachers said that when their directors withheld support from centre activities, they felt especially vulnerable to peer criticism.

When the directors did not participate in TEC programmes, many teachers felt they had to defend their motivations to colleagues. Many said their peers had asked why anyone would voluntarily work on an unpopular topic when it wasn't required. Deividas, a teacher in a large city, said that some teachers made fun of his attachment to "the Jews" because of his class section on Holocaust literature. He explained that a fellow teacher had even accused him of "using" his work on the Holocaust to become the next school director. Deividas said he laughed at the suggestion: "If I was going to try and get ahead in Lithuania, I certainly wouldn't do it by talking about the Jews! That's what you talk about if you don't want to get ahead". He laughed again at the very idea. His example represents the kind of interrogations from colleagues that many teachers faced when working in schools with unsupportive directors.

Dorotėja, a teacher in a large city, said support from the director was "a necessity" in navigating relationships with other teachers. She explained, "If you are alone, and you don't have support from the administration—and if you have colleagues who are also saying, 'Aha! Again with the Jews? What's that about?' [Well,] that's it. What can you do by yourself?" Dorotėja felt that school directors could help temper criticism from peers, as well as make a stronger place for Holocaust education in the national curriculum. When I asked Ramunė, a director I mentioned earlier, how she got teachers involved at her school, she responded:

> You know how? Because I myself was involved, and I got pulled into this topic by [another teacher], and after I got pulled into this Holocaust theme then one more teacher got pulled into it like I was, and she herself wanted to participate that year.

Teachers who led by example seemed to have a positive effect on teacher involvement.

Not all teachers were motivated by oversight from their directors. Some sought more top-down support from directors as they implemented Holocaust education, but they did not want to be told what to do. Kargauda, mentioned earlier, who has three decades of experience, said she sometimes found herself forced to attend seminars run by international "experts" who "have never in their life worked in a school, and don't even know what a school is". Her reply to such seminars on teaching methods was "Whatever it is that they do, I don't want to see it". She said that when she encounters such "experts" at programme seminars, she wants to say to them, "It's best just to let me be and to try to perfect and to do my work on my own". This sentiment highlights the complicated navigations that both teachers and school directors faced in their professional decision making.

Ivan, a university professor, said that the Lithuanian educational system had become too reliant on experts, which resulted in a lack of respect for teacher expertise.

The technocratic infrastructure of the Soviet Union had remained largely intact after Lithuania gained independence in 1991, and Ivan said that the bureaucracy of the Lithuanian system did not value the input of teachers. He explained:

> Decisions are made not in the communities, in the teachers' communities, or in the universities' communities. Much more, decisions are made in the ministry by saying, "Well you will do this, and you will do that, and we are experts, and if we are not experts, we have hired an expert". And then one group of educators is saying, "Maybe we need some broader discussion; maybe you should listen to our opinion as well". And the reply is that "We have experts, and this is the suggestion of experts".

Ivan believed that few people understood the complicated ways that teachers and school directors had to navigate around various issues in their professional practices. The tension between educators wanting support, but not wanting to be told what to do, resulted in teachers only valuing the authority of certain hierarchies.

Teachers further disliked the political hierarchies that had developed between international agencies and the Lithuanian government on the topic of Holocaust education. Most teachers saw international involvement in Holocaust education in Lithuania as resulting from a patronising power imbalance between Lithuania and "the west". In this context, even the most dedicated Holocaust educators saw the international political hierarchies as lowering their motivation; they felt that international involvement prompted peer scrutiny of their efforts, when it was in fact intended to quell it. Additionally, many said the topic of the Holocaust was becoming overrepresented in their communities because of international political agendas. Three individuals used the same sentence to explain the backlash to the topic: "It's just Holocaust, Holocaust, Holocaust all the time". Thus, international attention to the Holocaust without corollary discussions of the Soviet Occupation left many Lithuanians unable—or unwilling—to see Holocaust history as connected to their identity or culture. In the next section I discuss negative reactions to the development of international hierarchies in Lithuanian Holocaust education.

International Power Politics and Holocaust Education

Since the end of the communist era, post-Soviet Holocaust education has had considerable political significance in the international community. While the international politics of Holocaust education are too complex to fully discuss here, it is understood as a "given" that the international community will play a role in post-Soviet Holocaust education programmes. From ambassadors, to politicians, to children of survivors, many Holocaust education programmes in Lithuania arose at the impetus of non-local populations, entrenching an international community dedicated to preserving the Holocaust memory, a community that linked culturally diverse educational initiatives. The role the international community played in local educational programmes has seriously affected how teachers view Holocaust education. Values education programmes are especially suspect in Lithuania because of the Soviet-era requirement that schools engage in state-sponsored character building, or *vospitanie*.

When the Soviet Union occupied Lithuania a half century earlier, the government used formal schooling to build the "New Soviet Man". The top-down bureaucracy of the Soviet Union meant that no alternatives were allowed in describing what it meant to be a Soviet citizen. Therefore, when communism ended, freedom was an important concept for many Lithuanians as they embraced ideas of national and personal self-determination. Over time, many Lithuanians started to feel that the international programmes for the promotion of "western values" were no different from the Soviet-era system of *vospitanie*. Thus, Lithuanians who were familiar with governments using educational programmes for political ends grew resistant to western policies for remaking people's political beliefs—even if the values they espoused were supposedly "universal".

In a study on the promotion of tolerance, Wendy Brown (2006) found that discourses about "universal" values gave western politicians an "acceptable" way to elevate their values over those of non-western countries. In this vein, many Lithuanians felt that western policies were openly ethnocentric, and they challenged the idea that the United States could "bring" values to Lithuania that they could not achieve on their own. As a result, conversations about policy reform in Lithuania have shifted from debates about the content of reforms to how reforms were presented in local communities. Generally, Lithuanian teachers saw programmes associated with western democratic values as unidirectional policy conversations that did not consider the experiences of local populations. Falk Pingel (2014) found that, in some countries, Holocaust education was "interpreted as a new kind of cultural hegemony of western experience" (p. 83). This is not to imply that people cannot understand values outside their original cultural context. The issue is that it is often inaccurate to perceive or promote particular values or educational programmes as universal, and that local populations are often skeptical about efforts to do so.

Many Lithuanians wanted to become part of the EU: 63% turned out to vote on accession to the EU and 93% voted in favour of it. Still, some of the accession guidelines alienated individual Lithuanians, because once again they felt that government bureaucrats were telling them how to raise their children. Nomedas, a professor of pedagogy at a Lithuanian University, described the sentiments of many:

> During Soviet times it was necessary to raise your child as an atheist so that they would not go to church, that they would not believe, that there was no God... Now people are thinking, "Don't talk to me. I will not be doing anything about this [tolerance]". Some are even thinking, "I will do something *against* this idea, in principle, because you are ordering me..." [Or they are thinking,] "You cannot order me in general to come and do it like, 'Now you will raise your children with this tolerant way of being!'" Half of the auditorium will say, "No. Oh no. You think that I will do it whether I want to or not? That's too much. No thank you".

Professor Nomedas' comment highlights the complications that arise when concepts firmly entrenched in one society are introduced into another as "universal" values. As a result, a common perception in Lithuania was that western values were supposed to change Eastern European culture but meanwhile the western states had nothing to learn from post-Soviet experiences. The impact of such perceptions was a clear differentiation in the kinds of hierarchies valued in Lithuanian Holocaust education. The issue was not simply that many Lithuanian teachers did not want to discuss the Holocaust; what they wanted was to see a shift in who was discussing it in their communities.

In light of the negative attitudes toward international involvement in Holocaust education, teachers wanted more direct involvement by school directors to help counter the perception that the Holocaust was not relevant at the local level. Therefore, many teachers saw that two factors were fundamental to forward movement in future Holocaust education programmes: more local support, and less international political pressure.

Conclusions

In Lithuania, top-down decision making continues to be an important element of the educational system, although teachers sometimes try to negotiate around this hierarchy in practice. Overall, teachers working on Holocaust education wanted to see more institutional support for their efforts, but their own support for a top-down hierarchy depended on the source. Programmes introduced into Lithuania by western agencies were viewed as hindering rather than helping teacher efforts because they drew attention to the Holocaust as an "outside" political issue. Therefore, they saw international political pressure on Lithuania as a reason to avoid talking about the Holocaust because such conversations made it harder to recruit local colleagues for school programmes. The negative perceptions that Lithuanians held about international involvement in Holocaust education meant that teachers saw school directors as being even more important to motivating teachers to participate. Responding to a school culture that allowed peers to criticise their efforts on Holocaust education, many teachers wanted school directors to hold their colleagues accountable for creating a more supportive environment. However, school directors revealed that they were also subject to broader political pressures, and therefore many blamed the politics of institutional hierarchy as a reason not to develop Holocaust education. Overall, the Lithuanian case demonstrates the need for further study on the role of power and politics in Holocaust education in post-Soviet states.

References

Bartov, O. (2008). Eastern Europe as the site of genocide. *The Journal of Modern History, 80*(3), 557–593.
Blase, J. J., & Anderson, G. L. (1995). *The micropolitics of educational leadership: From control to empowerment*. New York: Teachers College Press.
Brown, W. (2006). *Regulating aversion: Tolerance in the age of identity and empire*. Princeton: Princeton University Press.
Budrytė, D. (2005). *Taming nationalism: Political community building in the post-Soviet Baltic States*. Hampshire: Ashgate.

Carspecken, P. F. (1996). *Critical ethnography in educational research: A theoretical and practical guide*. New York: Routledge.
Cohen, R. (2012, January). The suffering Olympics. *The New York Times*. http://www.nytimes.com/2012/01/31/opinion/the-suffering-olympics.html?_r=0
Crow, G., & Weindling, D. (2010). Learning to be political: New English headteachers' roles. *Educational Policy, 24*(1), 137–158.
Dietsch, J. (2012). Textbooks and the Holocaust in independent Ukraine: An uneasy past. *European Education, 44*(3), 67–94.
Fallace, T. (2008). *The emergence of Holocaust education in American schools*. New York: Palgrave Macmillan.
Gross, M. H. (2013). To teach the Holocaust in Poland: Understanding teachers' motivations to engage the painful past. *Intercultural Education, 24*(1–2), 103–120.
Gross, Z., & Stevick, D. (2010). Introduction to the open file: Holocaust education—international perspectives: Challenges, opportunities and research. *Prospects, 40*(1), 17–33.
Gundare, I., & Batelaan, P. (2003). Learning about and from the Holocaust: The development and implementation of a complex instruction unit in Latvia. *Intercultural Education, 14*(2), 152–166.
Hallinger, P., & Leithwood, K. (1998). Unforeseen forces: The impact of social culture on school leadership. *Peabody Journal of Education, 73*(2), 126–151.
Himka, J. P. (2008). Obstacles to the integration of the Holocaust into post-communist East European historical narratives. *Canadian Slavonic Papers/Revue Canadienne des Slavistes, 50*(3/4), 359–372.
IHRA [International Holocaust Remembrance Alliance] (2000). *Declaration of the Stockholm International Forum on the Holocaust*. http://www.holocaustremembrance.com/about-us/stockholm-declaration
Leithwood, K. (1995). Introduction: Transforming politics into education. In K. Leithwood (Ed.), *Effective school leadership. Transforming politics into education* (pp. 1–12). Albany: State University of New York Press.
Levinson, B. A. U., & Sutton, M. (2001). Introduction: Policy as/in practice—A sociocultural approach to the study of educational policy. In M. Sutton & B. A. U. Levinson (Eds.), *Policy as practice: Toward a comparative sociocultural analysis of educational policy* (pp. 1–22). Westport: Ablex.
Marcus, G. (1995). Ethnography in/of the world: The emergence of multi-sited ethnography. *Annual Review of Anthropology, 24*, 95–117.
Michaels, D. L. (2013). Holocaust education in the 'black hole of Europe': Slovakia's identity politics and history textbooks pre- and post-1989. *Intercultural Education, 24*(1–2), 19–40. doi:10.1080/14675986.2013.790209.
Misco, T. (2008). No one told us what happened: The current state of Holocaust education in Romania. *International Education, 38*(1), 6–20.
Owen, J. C. (2006). *The impact of politics in local education: Navigating white water*. Lanham: Rowman & Littlefield.
Pettai, E.-C. (2011a). The convergence of two worlds: Historians and emerging histories of the Baltic States. In M. Housden & D. J. Smith (Eds.), *Forgotten pages in Baltic history. Inclusion and exclusion in history: A festscrift for John Hiden* (pp. 263–279). Amsterdam/New York: Rodopi.
Pettai, E.-C. (2011b). Establishing "Holocaust memory": A comparison of Estonia and Latvia. In O. Rathkolb & I. Sooman (Eds.), *Historical memory culture in the enlarged Baltic Sea Region and its symptoms today* (pp. 159–174). Vienna: V&R Unipress/University of Vienna Press.
Pingel, F. (2014). The Holocaust in textbooks: From a European to a global event. In K. Fracapane & M. Haß (Eds.), *Holocaust education in a global context* (pp. 77–86). Paris: UNESCO.
Short, G., & Reed, C. (2004). *Issues in Holocaust education*. Burlington: Ashgate.
Stevick, D. (2007). The politics of the Holocaust in Estonia: Historical memory and social divisions in Estonian education. In B. A. U. Levinson & D. Stevick (Eds.), *Reimagining civic*

education: How diverse societies form democratic citizens (pp. 217–244). Lanham: Rowan & Littlefield.

Stevick, D. (2012). The Holocaust in the contemporary Baltic states: International relations, politics, and education. *Holocaust: Study and Research* [Holocaust Studii şi cercetări], *1*(5), 87–103.

Waldman, F. (2004). Holocaust education in Romania. *Studia Hebraica, 4*, 88–102.

Weiss-Wendt, A. (2009). *Murder without hatred: Estonians and the Holocaust*. Syracuse: Syracuse University Press.

Zilinskas, J. (2009). Broadening the concept of genocide in Lithuania's criminal law and the principle of *nullum crimen sine lege. Jurisprudence, 4*(118), 333–348.

Holocaust Education in Austria: A (Hi)story of Complexity and Prospects for the Future

Heribert Bastel, Christian Matzka, and Helene Miklas

Introduction

Over the last few years, a number of right-wing neo-Nazi offenses directed at persons with immigration backgrounds have been registered in Austria, and these crimes seem to be on the increase throughout the country. Police documented 791 crimes against people with immigrant backgrounds in 2009, and 1,040 such crimes in 2010 (Der Standard 2011). These right-wing offenses are especially prevalent in Upper Austria. In 2010 and 2011, authorities in Upper Austria recorded 171 offenses related to right-wing groups, but only 22 crimes traced back to the left-wing extremist scene (Der Standard 2012).

The right-wing populist party, the Austrian Freedom Party (FPÖ), also agitates against immigration, especially from Muslim states, and strongly opposes the presence of Muslims in Austria. In the spring of 2012, an election poster in Innsbruck caused a scandal with the slogan *Heimatliebe statt Marokkanerdiebe*, which translates roughly as "we love our homeland, so we don't want those thieves from Morocco" (Die Welt 2012). The FPÖ Innsbruck had to take down the poster after angry protests and charges. The right-wing populists have also for years questioned Turkey's application for membership in the European Union (EU). "We have always objected to the negotiations on the grounds of Turkey belonging to Europe neither historically nor geographically nor culturally", said the party's head H.C. Strache,

---

H. Bastel • C. Matzka (✉) • H. Miklas
Christian Churches' University of Education in Vienna/Krems,
Mayerweckstr. 1, 1210 Vienna, Austria
e-mails: heribert.bastel@kphvie.at; christian.matzka@kphvie.at;
helene.miklas@kphvie.at

in a speech in 2011 (www.hcstrache.at). Even the identity the FPÖ is asserting for itself with the description "social homeland party" seems to consciously echo nationalistic and racist rhetoric of the past.

Do these incidents reflect the general atmosphere in Austria? Why have these transgressions become possible? Why are right-wing parties succeeding in drawing on history and its supposed connection to current social problems to create a mix of xenophobic and anti-European slogans for their election campaigns? With an eye on election results, the traditional mainstream parties, the Christian Democrats (ÖVP) and Social Democrats (SPÖ), are trying to find a balance between taking account of public sentiments and expressing their support for democratic principles, with sometimes unhappy results. Democracy in Austria seems to be composed of a mentality of *"Na-geh-wird-schon-nicht-so-schlimm sein"* ("Well, so what? Things just can't be that bad!"). This attitude of political indifference is the actual source of danger, according to Rohrer (2010). Looking back at history, especially at the memorials at the Heldenplatz in Vienna and at Austrian politics and society around 1900, may help to explain this specifically Austrian situation, which is intricately interwoven with nationalistic history and the present challenges.

The Heldenplatz: An Ambivalent Symbol of Austrian History

The Heldenplatz, in Vienna, is the republic's main square (Stachel 2002); since the 19th century it has been used as a political stage by different groups, including the Austrian Faschists and National Socialists (Matzka 2007a). Hitler's announcement of the *Anschluss* turned the location into a politically shunned place. Only after Pope John Paul II visited in 1983 was it rediscovered by various groups. Today the Heldenplatz is a symbol of resistance against right-wing radicalism and xenophobia as the manifestations against FPÖ in 1993, and against the ÖVP-FPÖ coalition in 2000 (Kargl and Lehmann 1994) clearly prove. The physical layout of the square and its monuments are intertwined with powerful issues in Austrian history. Two large equestrian memorials symbolise its atmosphere. They are expressions of two significant courses of events fixed in the collective and cultural memory of Austrian history and historiography, which can be traced to present discussions of daily politics (Stachel 2002, p. 109; O'Reilly and Matzka 2009).

They also symbolise two historical, but still current, topics in Austrian politics: German-Austrian nationalism, and the fear of strangers arriving from the East. Based on these topics, politicians have constructed a new German-speaking Austrian nationalism ("Austria first", "German instead of non-understanding") mixed with xenophobic, anti-Islamic, and anti-Turkish attitudes. The historical roots are worth examining.

The First Equestrian Memorial: German-Austrian Nationalism

The first monument is that of Archduke Karl, commemorating the 1809 victory over Napoleon in the battle of Aspern, with its inscription, "The fighter for the honour of Germany". Built between the wars that Austria lost to Italy in 1859 and to Prussia in 1866, it seeks to remind the Austrians of the final victory over Napoleon and of the power of the Habsburgs after 1815. At the same time it reflects German nationalism, which quickly became a major issue in Austrian politics in the second half of the 19th century and was linked to anti-Slavic and anti-Jewish attitudes.

Before World War I, the political situation in Austria included national conflicts and anti-Jewish and anti-Slavic attitudes. By the second half of the 19th century, many people from rural regions in the southern and eastern parts of the Austro-Hungarian Empire had migrated to Vienna and the industrial regions near it. Most of them were Czechs, Slovaks, Poles, and Jews from Galicia. After 1867, they had the same rights as the rest of Vienna's population, were emancipated, and could engage in any profession. The Jewish people in particular became an important part of Viennese society (Matzka 2007b; Vocelka 2002).

Austrian society, however, was strictly differentiated according to national, ethnic, religious, and political groupings (Bruckmüller 2001). Each grouping founded its own clubs and organisations and separated itself from the others. The word "German" in the name of an organisation often signalled anti-Slavic and antisemitic attitudes and programmes (e.g., German Nationalist Organisation, German Alpine Club, German School Club). Jews were not allowed to become members of such clubs. Only the social democratic clubs were open and had set up no religious, national, or racist boundaries. Especially in the regions of the monarchy close to the boundaries between regions speaking German and other languages (like Lower Styria, Carinthia, Carniola, Bohemia, and Tyrol), conflicts erupted over schools, inscriptions, and the language used in government agencies (Bogataj 1989).

In this context, German protection associations (*Schutzvereine*) supported the paranoia of Germans in Austria, who felt increasingly threatened by a rise in birth rates among the Slavic population. German-speaking schools were funded, businesses established, and farmers and craftsmen supported; tourism was also exploited, and alpine huts and paths were constructed to mark national boundaries and positions. In Vienna and its surroundings, all these groups came together and formed the foundation for the populist propaganda of Mayor Karl Lueger (Hamann 1996). Heated political discussions, anti-Czech and anti-Jewish activities, demonstrations and assaults occurred regularly in Vienna and in mixed-language regions (Glettler 1972; Judson 2001; Matzka 2007b; Vocelka 2002). Racism, especially against Jews, became a widely accepted part of Austrian politics, as a formula for what Sreeruwitz (2009, 5 June) called the construction of a "quasi civic male consciousness".

From this time on, German nationalism was a permanent political principle in Austria, and all the political parties, including the social democrats, followed it quite naturally. In 1918, so much nationalist feeling had built up that Parliament decided Austria would be part of the German Reich; only the 1919 peace treaty of

St. Germain prohibited an *Anschluss*, an "annexation" of Austria to the German Reich. This explains why many people welcomed the *Anschluss* in 1938 and perceived Hitler's dominance as a lesser evil than being a small country outside of Germany, after centuries as part of the large and important Habsburg empire.[1] As the war took its course, the social democrats distanced themselves from the *Anschluss* to Germany, but even Austrians who were opposed to it still saw themselves as Germans. The Austrian fascists followed the concept of a better German state and wanted to generate a German national Austrian identity (Heinisch 1988; Vocelka 2002).

Although the Austrians immediately distanced themselves from Germany after World War II, the question of German identity continued to arise. In 1956, 46% of Austrians still called themselves German (Vocelka 2002). Earlier German nationalistic attitudes were visible, especially in the debate about the nuclear plant at Temelin in the Czech Republic. The Austrian government's threat to veto the entry of the Czech Republic into the EU, the blockade of border crossings, and the use of anti-Czech resentments in election campaigns all show that these attitudes can be evoked at any time (Pelinka 2007; Suppan 2009).

The Second Equestrian Memorial: Anti-Turkish Attitudes

The second monument is that of Prince Eugene of Savoy, the famous general and fighter against the Turks between 1683 und 1718. The inscription, "The victor over Austria's enemies", reflects Austrian society's traditional fear of danger from the East, and reflects public opinion at the time the monument was erected in 1865.

After the wars with the Turks in 1529 and 1683, people in central Europe developed a negative image of the Ottomans, based on religious issues as well as the Ottomans' efforts to promote social discipline through increased religious activities, and their need to raise taxes to finance their wars. The clichéd images of Turkish people as enemies that had developed in the Early Modern Era had effects on the 19th and 20th century (Vocelka 2002).

The current discussion in Austria about Turkey's EU membership mirrors the two countries' long history of interaction. The battle of Vienna in 1683 is regarded as so important that it is still the subject of a question on the exam for Austrian citizenship. According to polls, Austria has been suffering from a phobia about

---

[1] The enthusiastic support was organised by the Nazis, who had not won more than 5% of the vote in any election before 1938 (3% in 1930). Many Austrians were German-Austrian nationalists, and German nationalism was a major political issue. For example, Karl Renner, the famous Austrian social democrat and chancellor in 1920, voted for Hitler because in 1918, like many Austrians, he had wanted Austria to be a part of Germany. The greater evil was to be a small country outside Germany after being part of such a large and important monarchy. Still, many people closed their eyes to politics and support for the Nazis was less enthusiastic than some hoped. This is a typical Austrian "unpolitical" attitude. Many people were German nationalists and had much in common with the Nazis, but did not support the Nazi Party.

Turks since the Turkish sieges of 1529 and 1683. In Austria, it forms an essential emotional argument in the debate about Turkey's EU membership (Kritzinger and Steinbauer 2005; Matzka 2009).

In Austria, with few exceptions, there seems to be an unwritten societal consensus (Assmann 2007) on many questions about relationships with neighbouring states and minorities, and the question of Turkey. Many of these attitudes are historically determined and are built on the passing on of mentalities (Daniel 2001; Raphael 2003) over generations. They are visible in a wide range of political activities, including the debates about the nuclear plant at Temelin, the Benes decrees, place name signs in Carinthia, the implementation of human rights, and the way Islamic organisations and their beliefs are treated in connection with Turkey's EU membership. In the 2009 election campaigns for the EU Parliament, only the Green Party did not issue any anti-Turkish statements. Polls show, as mentioned earlier, that Austria had the lowest rate of support for Turkey's EU membership (O'Reilly and Matzka 2009).

Forms of Populism and Consequences for Holocaust Education

Many of these attitudes seem to be normal in Austria and are rooted in the mostly unspoken collective consciousness, mentioned above. This is probably why the populist parties draw on them (Decker 2006). Some scholars see a direct line from the 19th century's nationalism and racism to the barbarism of the Holocaust (Pollack 2004). The Austrian public, however, prefers to discuss persecution and annihilation during the Nazi era in isolation from events that took place before or after, as there is no consensual view of history, for example concerning the era of Austrian fascism. Thus, the Holocaust seems to be regarded as an operational accident in history, unrelated to Austrian reality.

In Austria, many people who were born decades after 1945 still use the old patterns of arguments unscrupulously. A particularly high proportion of first-time voters and young people vote for right-wing populist parties. In 2006, one party even found success using the evocative election slogan, "Do you want a final solution to the question of place name signs?" in Carinthia (Matzka 2008).

The opportunities in Europe after 1989, and especially after Austria joined the EU, led to a fundamental change in the self-presentation of the FPÖ. It aimed to break open Austrian structures and habits starting in the mid-1980s, in an effort Pelinka (1995) called the "De-Austrianising of Austria", and then discovered the topic of foreigners and the homeland (*Heimat*) with a vengeance in 1990 and 1995. This had a lasting effect on Austrian political culture (Fröhlich-Steffen 2006). The FPÖ's present party line is strongly reminiscent of the attempts by Karl Lueger and Engelbert Dollfuss, both Christian democrats and antisemitic politicians, to develop a new kind of Austrian-German nationalism. Lueger was the Lord Mayor of Vienna around 1900 and Dollfuss was chancellor from 1932 to 1934.

The significance of the German language for election propaganda in Vienna, the stressing of the *Heimat*, and the seemingly conscious connotations with historical, easily evoked attitudes are all indicators of the FPÖ's current party line. This could be called a new German-speaking Austrian nationalism.

German-speaking Austrian nationalism, however, is linked to antisemitism and therefore to the Holocaust. Adorno (1997, p. 49) pointed out the danger: "genocide has its roots in this resurrection of aggressive nationalism that has developed in many countries since the end of the 19th century". Many people do not reflect on their nationalistic Austrian history either widely or explicitly, and do not know—or do not want to know—about it as a context and a condition for the Holocaust. For example, historians like Brigitte Hamann (1996) say that Hitler learned his politics in Austria, and after moving to Germany, combined political ideas from Austria with Prussian militarism. In this sense, current nationalistic attitudes can easily echo the old patterns. A contributor to the 2008 yearbook of the Documentation Centre of Austrian Resistance criticises today's history books: "In most books, antisemitism is only mentioned, if it is mentioned at all, in the context of National Socialism (or its German national predecessors), not as a wide intellectual and ideological movement that started long before National Socialism and found an overwhelming societal resonance from the end of the 19th century on" (Dreier 2008, p. 171, our translation).

Thus, Austria has an important—and new—task concerning Holocaust education. Meanwhile, the Holocaust should be seen both as a unique event and in the wider context of unreflected-upon nationalism if we want to fulfil Adorno's 1966 admonition: "The premier demand upon all education is that Auschwitz not happen again" (Adorno 1997, p. 49).

Holocaust Education in Austria: Making Up for Lost Time

After 1945, Austrians consistently pursued the persecution of war criminals (Halbrainer 2003), but other developments, including the post-war economic boom in the 1950s and 1960s (*Wirtschaftswunder*) and the construction of an Austrian identity, especially after the agreement of the Austrian State Treaty (*Staatsvertrag*) in 1955, left little room for individuals to experience co-responsibility and sense themselves as perpetrators. "By emphasizing themes of *Heimat* (homeland), *Landschaft* (landscape), culture, Catholicism and work, school materials emphasised the uniqueness of Austria. This supported the 'Austria-as-victim' myth and gave school officials the means they needed to make sense of those turbulent years" (Utgaard 2003, p. 27).

Until the 1980s, Holocaust education did not play an important role in Austrian schools. The paradigm that Austria was the first Nazi victim, and innocent of war crimes, was the main topic in teachings on World War II. The Holocaust was subsumed under World War II in Austrian curricula and schoolbooks and not treated as a unique part of history, leading to what Utgaard (2003, p. 123) calls a "one-basket-of-suffering" theory.

In 1963, an important first step was taken with the foundation of the Dokumentationsarchiv des Österreichischen Widerstandes (DÖW, Documentation Centre of Austrian Resistance). The work of the DÖW is based on the private initiative of survivors of the resistance, who were supported financially by the state and the city of Vienna, but did much of their work in an honorary capacity. Their initial goal was to gather all the available documents and tell the stories of the victims. They were key players in the research about, and the struggle against, efforts to downplay and deny the atrocities committed by the National Socialist regime (Bailer 2009, pp. 42–51).

Adorno's famous speech in 1966, "Education after Auschwitz", did not lead to a watershed in Austria, as it did in Germany. However, after the student revolts of 1968, which were quite mild in Austria, the climate changed and many younger teachers were inspired to discuss the Holocaust in their lessons as a singular and unique event. The first few fundamental analyses of Austrian antisemitism were written and published by critical researchers like Bunzl and Marin (1983) and Fuchs (1986).

But it was only after the anti-Waldheim campaign in 1985 that the perpetrator paradigm was officially created for Austria. This led to a "true watershed, which marked a fundamental re-examination of Austria's past. Austria's old myth of victimization was crumbling" (Utgaard 2003, p. 188). In his speech at the Nationalrat (Parliament) in 1991, Chancellor Franz Vranitzky was the first member of the Austrian government to mention the moral co-responsibility of Austrians in Nazi war crimes. In 1993, in a speech at Jerusalem University, he officially asked forgiveness from the victims of Austrian perpetrators:

> We have always felt and still feel that the connotation of "collective guilt" does not apply to Austria. But we do acknowledge collective responsibility, the responsibility of each and every one of us to remember and seek justice. We share moral responsibility, because many Austrians welcomed the Anschluss, supported the Nazi regime and helped it to function… (cited in Botz and Sprengnagel 1994, p. 579)

Since 1991, an impressive package of directives and initiatives for teaching about the Holocaust has been established, making up for lost time. The Task Force for International Cooperation on Holocaust Education, Remembrance, and Research (2006) prepares reports on efforts in various countries. Its most recent country report on Austria mentions some of them:

1. Holocaust Education is part of the curricula of History and Social Studies in all school types, from grade 8 onwards.
2. In-service seminars for teachers and university lecturers are a fixed part of the programme, as is a service to schedule guest appearances by witnesses and survivors, paid for by the Federal Ministry of Education.
3. The Documentation Centre has become an important centre of research and learning with a long-term exhibition.

Many activities supported by the Federal Ministry of Education are helping to implement Holocaust education in Austrian schools (Konstanian 2008; Kroh 2008; Pingel 2002; Uhl 2001). A special publication, addressing the *Anschluss* and the dangers of National Socialism, was sponsored to commemorate the 50th anniversary of the *Anschluss* in 1988 (Malina and Spann 1988). A list of impressive school projects, launched in the same year, was compiled by Ratzenböck et al. (1989).

In 1991, the Gedenkdienst (Austrian Holocaust Memorial Service) was founded (www.gedenkdienst.org). Since 1992, it has been possible for young Austrians to work at Holocaust memorials like Yad Vashem, the Anne Frank House, and the Auschwitz-Birkenau memorial instead of serving in the national military. This organisation initiates discussions with witnesses and visits to Holocaust memorials. Many Austrian pupils visit the Mauthausen concentration camp in Upper Austria during their years in secondary school. The Federal Ministry of Education is currently considering how to make a visit to this memorial obligatory for all pupils, while at the same time intensifying the courses on political education. The Mauthausen Komitee Österreich (Mauthausen Committee of Austria) organises the excursions; it has developed an educational approach that focuses on the effects of the excursions as a joint project with the ministries of the interior and education, together with experts on Holocaust education.

The Ministry for Education offers another project for teachers in Austrian schools called Nationalsozialismus und Holocaust: Gedächtnis und Gegenwart (Remembrance and Presence, www.erinnern.at). It aims to intensify and structure the discussion about Holocaust education, while at the same time reflecting on its significance for today. One of its projects, a DVD with 13 thematically-oriented interviews with Holocaust witnesses (*Das Vermächtnis*), was issued in 2008; it comes with materials that support teachers in working with the concentrated text of the interviews. Courses for teachers, called Pedagogy at Memorial Places, are being offered for all subjects and school types in cooperation with the teacher training university in Upper Austria, the Pädagogische Hochschule Oberösterreich in Linz.

A Letter to the Stars has also been very successful; children researched the lives of Holocaust victims and wrote letters which were released in May of 2003 (Worm et al. 2003, section 2; see also www.lettertothestars.at). This project encourages students and pupils to reconstruct the lives of the Jews from their hometowns who were murdered by the Nazis (Matzka 2003). The state assists schools in inviting Holocaust witnesses (*Zeitzeugen*) to come to schools and to teacher training colleges to give lectures and lead discussions (OSCE 2006). These meetings seem to be highly effective and significant as pupils and students can ask questions freely; indeed, they sometimes shock their teachers with their spontaneity and openness.

Many more innovative projects have been highly successful; here we can present only a small sample. Increasingly, they are based on regional and local initiatives where experts work together with the local population and schools, doing research on traces of Jewish life, and thus transforming pupils into "actors and actresses" (Stifter 2009).

Holocaust Education in Austria: Drawbacks and Problems

Despite this success, on closer inspection, some drawbacks can be seen.

First, Holocaust education is not explicitly included in the concept and principles of democratic learning stated in the Decree on Civics Education, a programme of citizenship and political education established in 1978, and implemented in all types of schools and all subjects. The Holocaust is only one part of democratic education, and not a major or specific topic. In history courses, it is included in the curricula under World War II and often under the heading of totalitarianism, combined with communism, etc. Teachers are responsible for addressing the subject in their lessons, but no common consensus exists on how to do it. Moreover, teaching on remembrance only began in the mid-1980s. Consequently, the Holocaust is not addressed as a unique and significant topic (Pingel 2002).

In the new curricula and schoolbooks, National Socialism has become only one example of totalitarian systems, included with other totalitarian systems like fascism and communism. Topics like persecution, resistance, and organised mass murder are well-represented in the curricula, but no distinction is made between National Socialism and the other phenomena; it no longer figures as a unique historical occurrence. Although students are given a solid account of the facts, the Holocaust is portrayed as one of the many horrible things that happened during World War II. Jewish culture and life in Austria before and after the Holocaust are remembered, and changes in ways of remembering are mentioned, but they are still subsumed under the topic of World War II (Lemberger 2003; Tscherne and Krampl 1997).

Second, the highly sensitive field of religious education needs to be explored further, as the murder of God allegation (*Gottesmordvorwurf*) still reigns implicitly and forms the basis for the stereotype that Jews were responsible for Christ's death. A study commissioned by the Anti-Defamation League (2005) found that 16% of Austrians still believe that allegation.

Third, some of the impressive activities for remembering the Holocaust, like the famous concert by the Vienna Philharmonic Orchestra called *Mauthausen 2000*, and *A Letter to the Stars*, mentioned earlier, are suffering from heavy media attention (Perz 2006, pp. 254ff). Thus, they are slowly being degraded into events and subject to event culture—and failing to avoid the critical warning by Abba Eban (cited in Blimlinger 2009, p. 18), that "there's no business like Shoah-business".

Fourth, Holocaust education in Austria suffers from a lack of empirical research. The people responsible claim—without valid evidence—that pupils and students do not show the desired attitudes towards the work. Nor is it easy to investigate the most important aspect: how feelings and emotions are affected by Holocaust education and how attitudes can be changed. The vulnerability, special needs, and age-related perceptions of young learners have probably not been considered sufficiently. Also, as a topic, Holocaust education can too easily take on layers of guilt and shame (Bar-On et al. 1997); thus, Holocaust educators need to develop a special conception for this work, one that avoids shame, exaggeration, provocation, and coldness.

Finally, again referring to the beginning of this article, there is little reflection on the roots and conditions of nationalism and antisemitism in schools and in public life. Thus, this chapter of Austrian history still remains in the dark.

The State of Research in Austria on Memorials in Comparison to Germany

A research team at the University of Education of the Christian Churches in Austria (KPH Wien/Krems), to which we belong, has been involved in a research project starting in 2009 about secondary school students' perceptions of visits to Austrian memorial places.

Among the research questions are these: What do pupils really perceive when they visit memorial places? Do they perceive what the organisers want them to? How long do the effects of such visits last, and to what extent do they facilitate the construction of the value orientation that is one of their generally accepted aims?

The point of departure for this project was that several empirical studies conducted in Germany arrived at a rather sceptical conclusion about the value of school visits to memorial places. Summarising studies from the last 25 years, Pampel (2007, 2011, pp. 28–57) asserts that visitors arrive at memorial places with a mix of highly individual images already formed in their minds. They are often disappointed in their expectation that events will be truly illustrated, giving them a chance to develop a sense of the place and its history in a tangible, vivid way that brings past experiences and suffering to life. Moreover, the visits do not necessarily develop empathy or concern and can even prevent commitment. The historical events in question are not perceived in relation to experiences in the present. Lastly, the organisers' claim that such visits will immunise visitors against right-wing extremism cannot be met.

German academics have pursued many memorial research projects. Learning from History (*Lernen aus der Geschichte*, www.holocaust-education.de) has compiled a list of projects up to 1995, and Eberle (2008), Kiesel et al. (1997), and Pampel (2007, 2011) describe more recent research. They teach us that all pedagogy of memorial places is shaped by complex and contradictory factors. Every memorial place elicits conflicting expectations; on the one hand, it is a place for the surviving families of the victims and a place of remembrance for survivors, and on the other hand, it is a historical site with a message of remembrance, a memorial for the future, and a place of learning for the present.

In a large-scale study, Eberle (2008, pp. 110ff) differentiated between three types of perceptions that teenage visitors have at memorial places:

1. Some develop an emotional defence against events which makes it impossible to articulate any other potential emotions and observations.
2. Some form an "encapsulated" terror symbolism that becomes a projection screen for subjective emotions and, during the tour, is enlarged by details of horror. This pattern evokes a defensive attitude that hinders reflection and intensifies paralysing emotions.
3. Some teenagers let themselves be guided by the question of how the terror might have played itself out from the detainees' point of view; they express negative, self-centred emotions, as well as empathy with the detainees' suffering.

Pampel (2007, pp. 191ff) points out five elements that are important for a successful visit. The first three are pre-understanding and motivation for the visit, and the perception of the memorial place that is shaped by them. The fourth is the experiences during the visit. The fifth, reflecting on the visit, is particularly important if the visit is to be sustainable. Moreover, in his most recent publication he stresses the importance of the after-effects in the families, about which hardly anything is known (Pampel 2011, p. 55).

The Austrian situation regarding memorial places differs greatly from that in Germany. First, the focus is almost exclusively on Mauthausen as *the* Austrian memorial place, although many other memorials and initiatives exist, as shown in the list at www.erinnern.at. Second, only in the past few years have initiatives been implemented, as suggested by the Germans studying memorial places. A visitor centre was set up, with improved explanations and audio guides, and research and documentation projects (interviews with over 800 survivors of Mauthausen) were funded. Through these measures the government expressed its support of Mauthausen as a memorial place, but it failed to take other necessary steps, such as funding more personnel (Perz 2006).

Werner Dreier (2008) voices his concern about an overly optimistic view of Holocaust education especially in Austrian schools: "In school, you learn to behave 'conventionally', meaning what to say at which point" (p. 170). This is diametrically opposed to the aim of Holocaust education, which places great value on self-confident and critical thinking with full self-ownership, and aims to evoke the courage in students to stand up for their own beliefs. Moreover he is concerned with the question of adolescence and its "fragile identity", when he writes:

> If young people, who are in the process of grappling with their identities, are confronted thoughtlessly with these abysses at school or even at memorial places, it becomes entirely possible that these pieces of information, which form a threat to their identity, are either remembered and labelled as "book learning", or are redrafted as a "history story" which is easier to reconcile with their own personality. (Dreier 2008, p. 178, our translation)

The absence of research on the effects of pupils' visits of memorials is notorious.

Holocaust Education: The Design of the 2009–2012 Research Project

Since May 2009, the research team at our university (KPH Wien/Krems) has evaluated excursions to the Mauthausen concentration camp by six schools with pupils aged 13–15, working in cooperation with the Institute of Conflict Research in Vienna. In the first pilot study the aim was to establish an appropriate research proposal for the study itself and to avoid repeating the methodological mistakes made in similar studies; we also wanted to consider how research can capture such complex emotional experiences in teenagers (Pampel 2007, pp. 116ff). Thus, in our pilot test, we explored how teenagers can verbalise their perceptions at a memorial place and how these are connected to their (cognitive) images of this time, but also to the moral concept, given the current context of problematic situations concerning human rights. The pilot focused on three research questions:

1. What knowledge do teenagers have of the Holocaust, and where do they get it from?
2. Do they establish a relationship between the Holocaust and present experiences of xenophobia and violations of human rights? Does visiting Mauthausen change their emotional attitudes to their own self-consciousness and to Austria and Europe?
3. What do youngsters really perceive when they visit the memorial at Mauthausen? How do they handle their experiences?

This first investigation, mainly quantitative and questionnaire-based, with some open questions, was carried out both before and after the visit to Mauthausen. University students observed the pupils during the various stages of the excursion. The following day, after a quiet and meditative session using a time-travel approach, the pupils were asked to write essays exploring their emotions and perceptions. We found that the work with the questionnaire did not give us the in-depth results we needed for our goals. The open questions, which mainly explored connections between the Holocaust, human rights, xenophobia, and religion, did not yield valid results. Several factors may have contributed to the pupils not completing these questions, including their ages (13–15 years), the type of secondary modern school (*Hauptschule*), and their resulting linguistic insecurity over putting complex thought processes into writing. The work on the essays was enlightening, however.

Therefore, in January 2010 we started with a different didactic approach, varying the concept of the guided tours. Some school classes were doing their usual tour; other classes were equipped with voice recorders. At specified spots, pupils talked into the voice recorder about their observations ("I see, I feel, I know…"). After listening to the guide's explanations, they used the voice recorder again to provide short responses: "Now I know…", "The explanations have made it clear that….", "I am specifically moved by …". And finally some school classes were divided into small groups (four to five pupils), which were given a special guided tour in which guides (trained by the research team) showed the sites, provided the information, and discussed the impressions and the facts with the group. The guided tour and the discussion were recorded.

In the first week after the excursion, the pupils wrote essays. Three weeks later, the guides and one member of the research team visited the classes and had a 1-h recorded discussion with the group about the experiences at the memorial place. Finally, the guides interviewed the accompanying teachers.

Results of the Research Project

We finished our research in January of 2013 (Bastel and Halbmayr 2013). What are our most important results?

One clear finding is that history classes at school are the most important sources of historical knowledge for young people aged 13–15. Moreover, families rarely discuss historical events. Few of the parents and even grandparents of this young generation had any direct experiences with World War II, so their historical connection to the time of National Socialism is rather vague. And, as we have described earlier (Bastel, Matzka, and Miklas 2010), looking back and reappraising the past was not a favourite pastime in Austria. Shame, repression, and glorification were the poles of this process and they were not discussed in families. Moreover, history is not necessarily the most popular subject in school. Many conceptions of this time are communicated by the media, and some such media had been used in class at the school these students attend. Pupils know the names of concentration camps and films about this time, complete with titles. It is evident, however, that they are not prepared for the psychological impact of the real visit. They see the excursion as an extended arm of the school, which a lot of them meet with a certain feeling of indifference. They arrive at Mauthausen with a bit of an attitude, as if to say, "OK, let's see what's going to happen here". As a result, their museum experience is a quasi visit.

The essays show, however, that they come with many images in their heads, which they later comment upon quite openly. But then they are faced with the particularity of the location and they have to try to find bridges in their mental processing or create parallels to their lives in order to make the unconceivable somehow understandable. They are especially affected by the biographical accounts of the guides about life in the camp and they are very much concerned with subjects like the loss of freedom, loss of dignity, humiliation, and the perpetrator's haphazard or arbitrary handling of victims. The part of the guided tour concerning the "Steps of Death" (*Todesstiege*) seems to be very realistic. They fervently discuss the height of the steps, the loads of stones and the inhumane conditions. About 40% of the pupils show strong emotional concern and empathy. We hear and read statements like "I am so glad that these things are over", "this is unbelievable", and "inconceivable".

At the barracks pupils also talk freely about what they see, linking this to their home experiences. Boys and girls alike seem to notice everyday aspects, such as "I really wonder how they could sleep together in such small beds", and "Imagine! We sleep on thick mattresses, with warm cushions and blankets"—comments that are reminiscent of Eberle's third type of perception. They also compare this with their experiences of youth camps, which they already see as a reduction of their normal life.

In the showers and in the gas chamber pupils grow silent. They are hardly able to voice their observations. They draw on their primary feelings and construct their reality: "It is so cold here", "so dark", "I can still smell what happened", "look at the brown walls", "I could really cry". Most of them are horrified at the large number of people killed, and also at the cruelty people can show.

The interaction between pupils and guides is strongly influenced by the pupils' prior knowledge, but mostly embedded in a simple scheme of communication. Even though Mauthausen is an extracurricular site, the style of communication used during the guided tours is quite similar to the one in class. Student questions elicit longer explanations by the guides, but the guides' questions dominate. During a 90-min tour, they pose between 300 and 500 questions; most of them are rather closed.

The pupils rarely name the historical actors, either as Nazi or as SS. Nor do they have names for the persecuted. In many cases they speak of "people", then also of "Jews", less frequently of "prisoners"; also the actors involved are not named as the perpetrators they are. There seems to be the risk that the principle of a concentration camp—the de-personalisation of prisoners—is also being repeated by the visit. The definite and singular assignment of blame to Hitler and his party for the atrocities is also evident here.

We also see some differences based on gender. The boys have more detailed knowledge and a significantly higher interest in history lessons. They know the names of more concentration camps, and films about this time, with titles, and can explain terms correctly. They seem to be able to cope with the facts; the emotional impact is less important to them. Girls express their emotions in a more elaborate manner than the boys and they use more clearly emotional terms like "shocked", "uprooted", "cruel", and "sad". Some of them cry or they state their reactions even more strongly: "I want to get out", "Air, please". In their study of gender differences in such visits, Frohwein and Wagner (2004) also established that girls identify with the victims more strongly than boys do. Both genders, however, see this time as "past"; when answering these questions they show no correlation to questions about current violations of human rights, especially not to questions about xenophobia. After the visit to the concentration camp, many of the pupils were happy to be able to put this special chapter of history behind them. Some of them see the need to apply oneself to prevent this from happening again, but they do not see any concrete options for action.

Thus, our findings support the German results. That is, a visit to a memorial place does not directly cause changes in thoughts or behaviour; it can, as Pampel (2007, 2011) assumes, initiate processes of learning, but those processes need an accompanying phase of reflection. Impacts on personal attitudes and attitudes towards foreigners and xenophobia could not be substantiated. The guides link the past events with the present; the essays of the pupils, however, show that this, at best, constitutes a thought-provoking impulse, though they hardly see it that way in this context. In group discussions, they also say that they consider the visit to the memorial necessary, but it does not lead to any attitude change or concrete ideas. Only where the visit to Mauthausen is part of a project within the framework of a particular school focus (e.g., against racism or National Socialism) is an update and transfer successful; the pupils relate historical events with current social developments.

A new research-based concept for Holocaust education should therefore be one of the main projects for the future. It must take into account the complexity of the subject, as we have described here, and must be linked with the roots and conditions of nationalism and antisemitism in Austria. It is crucial that pupils grasp the political and economic background of the events. And, importantly, it must focus on the pupils' ability to link the historical situation, the present, and the future, so that the issues are "connected with their understanding of national identity and their perception of recent European history and the current challenges of human rights and migration" (Schlag and Wäckerlig 2010, p. 232).

The question arises of how to work with a new generation of migrants who do not share in the history of the Holocaust, but often have their own history of trauma (OSCE 2006, 156ff). Interviews with school teachers show us that their concept of Holocaust education is still based on homogeneous classes. They often do not realise that many of their pupils do not share the same history.

We must establish a way to take advantage of some of the pupils' statements like, "I want to stand up for the fact that it should never happen again". How can we prepare them to participate actively in a democratic society, where citizenship is becoming more and more important? It will be necessary to stress other roles than that of the victim and the perpetrator, like the impassive and negative part of the bystander and the active part of "silent heroes" (www.gedenkstaette-stille-helden.de). On these, the chance of freedom and scope of action can be developed more extensively. According to Kölbl (2004, p. 347), teenagers need a "tangible past" to reconstruct history, but they must bring this element into the discourse themselves. They have to see that discrimination and intolerance are attitudes that they can experience in their schools, on their streets, and in their houses.

This task entails hard work for teachers. Most of them see an excursion to Mauthausen as an important part of teaching contemporary history and Holocaust education. They see the memorial site as an authentic place with a special energy, which allows special experiences in both cognitive and emotional learning. Although they see good preparation as an important precondition for a successful excursion, their preparation is often not very elaborate, focused, or adjusted to the cognitive and emotional needs of the pupils. And they often do not follow up with discussions of the excursions.

We had the good fortune to witness an example of good practice when the leader of the Lower Austria group of www.erinnern.at, who also works as a teacher, made an excursion to Mauthausen with his pupils just before their exams. It was their third visit there, and the teacher prepared for it carefully. After the guided tour, he asked them to photograph the sights they thought important. For their homework they had to choose three themes, describe the reasons for their choices, and combine them with their former experiences on the subject, with their family narratives, and with their perspectives about Holocaust education and human rights. The pictures and the texts were stunning in their honesty and openness. The work was so significant that we decided to analyse them carefully and publish them as a book (Miklas and Amesberger 2012).

Conclusions and Prospects for the Future

While the Holocaust and nationalism are different phenomena, in Austria, they are intricately interwoven. The Holocaust is unique in its barbarism and defeat of humanity, which cannot and must not be repeated. But "the glory of the Babenburgs and the Habsburgs, the Turkish wars, the grandeur of Austrian architecture and the Austrian landscape" (Utgaard 2003, p. 30) are deeply rooted as collective memories, forming a national identity that tends to respond to unconsidered areas of populism, antisemitism, and xenophobia. If remembrance is to be a key concept for human rights learning, we will need an honest and courageous approach to personal, national, and collective memories. We believe that one of the most necessary, and difficult, tasks for the future is to create what Adorno (1997, p. 51) envisioned: "general enlightenment that provides an intellectual, cultural, and social climate in which a recurrence would no longer be possible, a climate, therefore, in which the motives that led to the horror would become relatively conscious". And a very important part of this work will have to be done in school.

Note This chapter draws on Bastel, Matzka, and Miklas (2010).

References

Adorno, T. W. [1966] 1997. Erziehung nach Auschwitz [Education after Auschwitz]. Speech delivered on Hessischen Rundfunk [Hessian radio], Frankfurt am Main. Cited in R. von Tiedemann, *Th. Adorno: Ob nach Auschwitz noch sich leben lässt: Ein philosophisches Lesebuch*. Frankfurt: Suhrkamp Verlag. Translations from http://www.scribd.com/doc/16692127/theodor-adorno-education-after-auschwitz

Anti-Defamation League (2005). *Antisemitism international*. http://www.adl.org/main_Anti_Semitism_International/as_survey_2005.htm

Assmann, A. (2007). *Der lange Schatten der Vergangenheit* [The long shadow of the past]. Bonn: Bundeszentrale für politische Bildung.

Bailer, B. (2009). Unverzichtbar für die Erinnerung: Das Dokumentationsarchiv des österreichischen Widerstandes (DÖW) [Essential for remembrance. The Documentation Centre of Austrian Resistance]. In C. Stifter (Ed.), *Spurensuche: Hinter den Mauern des Vergessens... Erinnerungskulturen und Gedenkprojekte in Österreich*, 18/9 (pp. 1–4). Vienna: Verein zur Geschichte der Volkshochschulen.

Bar-On, D., Brendler, K., & Hare, A. P. (Eds.) (1997). *Da ist etwas kaputt gegangen an den Wurzeln: Identitätsformen deutscher und israelischer Jugendlicher im Schatten des Holocaust* [Something has broken down at the roots]. Frankfurt am Main/New York: Campus.

Bastel, H., & Halbmayr, B. (2013). *Mauthausen im Unterricht. Ein Gedenkstättenbuch und seine vielfältigen Herausforderungen* [Mauthausen in class: A book on a memorial and its manifold challenges]. Wien: LIT Verlag.

Bastel, H., Matzka, C., & Miklas, H. (2010). Holocaust education in Austria: A (hi)story of complexity and ambivalence. *Prospects, 40*(1), 57–73.

Blimlinger, E. (2009). Luftballons und Briefe in den Himmel—Gedenken und Feiern als Event [Letters and balloons to the stars—Remembrance and celebration as an event]. In C. Stifter (Ed.), *Spurensuche—Hinter den Mauern des Vergessens... Erinnerungskulturen und Gedenkprojekte in Österreich*, 18/9, 1-4/2009 (pp. 17–22). Vienna: Verein zur Geschichte der Volkshochschulen.

Bogataj, M. (1989). *Die Kärntner Slowenen* [Slovenes in Carinthia]. Vienna/Klagenfurt: Hermagoras Verlag.

Botz, G., & Sprengnagel, G. (1994). Kontroversen um Österreichs Zeitgeschichte. Verdrängte Vergangenheit. Österreich-Identität, Waldheim und die Historiker [Disputes about Austria's contemporary history. Suppressed past. Austrian identity, Waldheim and the historians]. In G. Botz, A. Müller, & G. Sprengnagel (Eds.), *Studien zur Historischen Sozialwissenschaft* (Vol. 13, pp. 571–576, 577–580). Frankfurt: Campus Verlag.

Bruckmüller, E. (2001). *Sozialgeschichte Österreichs* [Austria's social history]. Munich: Oldenbourg.

Bunzl, J., & Marin, B. (1983). Antisemitismus in Österreich: Sozialhistorische und soziologische Studien [Antisemitism in Austria: Sociohistorical and sociological studies]. In A. Pelinka & H. Reinalter (Eds.), *Vergleichende Gesellschaftsgeschichte und Politische Ideengeschichte der Neuzeit* (Vol. 3). Innsbruck: Inn-Verlag.

Daniel, U. (2001). *Kompendium Kulturgeschichte* [Compendium of cultural history]. Frankfurt am Main: Suhrkamp.

Decker, F. (2006). Die populistische Herausforderung. Theoretische und ländervergleichende Perspektiven [The challenge of populism: Theoretical and country-comparative perspectives]. In F. Decker (Ed.), *Populismus in Europa* (pp. 9–32). Bonn: Bundeszentrale für Politische Bildung.

Der Standard (2011, 5 August). *Extremismus-Delikte in Österreich ansteigend*. http://derstandard.at/1311802787220/Verfassungsschutzbericht-Extremismus-Delikte-in-Oesterreich-ansteigend

Der Standard (2012, 15 June). *Mehr Beratung am rechten Rand*. p. 10.

Die Welt (2012, 18 June). *FPÖ wirbt mit "Heimatliebe statt Marokkaner-Diebe"*. http://www.welt.de/politik/ausland/article106148765/FPOe-wirbt-mit-Heimatliebe-statt-Marokkaner-Diebe.html

Dreier, W. (2008). Ach ging's nur zu wie in der Judenschul! Anregungen für eine Auseinandersetzung mit Antisemitismus in der Schule [Oh, why can't it work like the Jewish schools! Suggestions for discussions concerning antisemitism in schools]. In Dokumentationsarchiv des österreichischen Widerstandes (Ed.), *Schwerpunkt Antisemitismus* (pp. 166–184). Vienna/Berlin: LIT Verlag.

Eberle, A. (2008). *Pädagogik und Gedenkkultur: Bildungsarbeit an NS-Gedenkorten zwischen Wissensvermittlung, Opfergedenken und Menschenrechtserziehung. Praxisfelder, Konzepte und Methoden in Bayern* [Education and culture of remembrance] (Pädagogik und Ethik, Vol. 1). Würzburg: Ergon Verlag.

Fröhlich-Steffen, S. (2006). Rechtspopulistische Herausforderer in Konkordanzdemokratien: Erfahrungen aus Österreich, der Schweiz und den Niederlanden [Right-wing populist challengers in concordance democracies]. In F. Decker (Ed.), *Populismus in Europa* (pp. 144–164). Bonn: Bundeszentrale für Politische Bildung.

Frohwein, P., & Wagner L. (2004). Geschlechterspezifische Aspekte in der Gedenkstättenpadagogik [Gender-specific aspects of education in memorial places]. *Gedenkstättenrundbrief, 120*. http://www.gedenkstaettenforum.de

Fuchs, E. (1986). Schule und Zeitgeschichte: Oder wie kommen Jugendliche zu politischen Klischeevorstellungen [School and contemporary history: How do adolescents develop political stereotypes?]. In *Veröffentlichungen zur Zeitgeschichte* (Vol. 5). Vienna/Salzburg: Geyer Edition.

Glettler, M. (1972). *Die Wiener Tschechen um 1900* [The Viennese Czechs around 1900]. Munich/Vienna: Böhlau.

Halbrainer, H. (Ed.) (2003). *Kriegsverbrecherprozesse in Österreich: Eine Bestandsaufnahme* [Trials of war criminals in Austria: A stock-taking]. Graz: Clio, Verein für Geschichts- und Bildungsarbeit.

Hamann, B. (1996). *Hitlers Wien: Lehrjahre eines Diktators* [Hitler's Vienna: Apprenticeship years of a dictator]. Munich: Piper.

Heinisch, S. (1988). SPÖ und Österreichische Nation [Social Democrats and the Austrian nation]. In H. Maimann (Ed.), *Die Ersten 100 Jahre* (pp. 100–101). Vienna: Christian Brandstätter Verlag.

Judson, P. M. (2001). Tourism, travel, and national activism in the Böhmerwald, South Tyrol and South Styria around 1900. In H. Heiss (Ed.), *Reisen im sozialen Raum* (pp. 59–90). Innsbruck/Vienna/Munich/Bozen: StudienVerlag.

Kargl, M., & Lehmann, S. (Ed.) (1994). *Land im Lichtermeer* [Austria in a sea of lights]. Vienna: Picus Verlag.

Kiesel, D., Kößler, G., Nickolai, W., & Wittmeier, M. (Eds.) (1997). *Pädagogik der Erinnerung: Didaktische Aspekte der Gedenkstättenarbeit Education of Remembrance* [The pedagogy of remembrance: Didactic aspects of education work at memorials] (Arnoldsheiner Texts, Vol. 96). Opladen: Haag & Herchen.

Kölbl, C. (2004). *Geschichtsbewusstsein im Jugendalter: Grundzüge einer Entwicklungspsychologie historischer Sinnbildung* [Historical consciousness at a young age]. Bielefeld: Transcript Verlag.

Konstanian, R. (Ed.) (2008). *Austria's unique approach to cooperation in Holocaust research in education*. Vilnius: Zara.

Kritzinger, S., & Steinbauer, F. (2005). Österreich und die Türken: Im Minenfeld zwischen rationalen Argumenten und historisch-kulturellen Vorbehalten [Austria and the Turks: The minefield between rational arguments and historical-cultural reservations]. In A. Giannakopoulos (Ed.), *Die Türkei-Debatte in Europa* (pp. 107–122). Wiesbaden: Verlag für Sozialwissenschaften.

Kroh, J. (2008). Erinnerungskultureller Akteur und geschichtspolitisches Netzwerk: Die "Task Force" for International Cooperation on Holocaust Education, Remembrance and Research [Culture of remembrance and network of history and politics]. In J. Eckel & C. Moisel (Eds.), *Universalisierung des Holocaust? Erinnerungskultur und Geschichtspolitik in internationaler Perspektive* (pp. 156–173). Göttingen: Wallenstein Verlag.

Lemberger, M. (2003). *Durch die Vergangenheit zur Gegenwart, 4* [Through history to the present, Vol. 4]. Linz: Veritas-Verlag.

Malina, P., & Spann, G. (1988). Der Nationalsozialismus im österreichischen Geschichtslehrbuch [National socialism in Austrian schoolbooks]. In E. Hanisch & E. Talos (Eds.), *NS Herrschaft in Österreich 1938–1945* (pp. 577–599). Vienna: Verlag für Gesellschaftskritik.

Matzka, V. (2003). Deine Wohnung war NS-Luftschutzschule, später SPÖ-Lokal, heute ist die ÖVP drin [Your apartment was the Nazi air raid protection school, later the office of the Social Democrats, today it is the office of the Conservatives]. In A. Worm et al. (Eds.), *A letter to the stars, Briefe in den Himmel, Schüler schreiben Geschichte* (pp. 26–27). Vienna: Verlag Verein Lernen aus der Zeitgeschichte.

Matzka, C. (2007a). Vienna's Heldenplatz, the Czech Republic and Carinthian problem: Education in geography-historically determined problems. In S. Catling & L. Taylor (Eds.), *Changing geographies: Innovative curricula. Conference proceedings*. Oxford: International Geographical Union Commission on Geographical Education/HERODOT.

Matzka, C. (2007b). *Tourismus im Wienerwald (1850–1914): Die Entstehung einer Freizeitregion vor den Toren der Großstadt, vom Bau der Eisenbahnen bis zum Ersten Weltkrieg* [Tourism in the Vienna woods (1850–1914)] (Studien und Forschungen aus dem Niederösterreichischen Institut für Landeskunde, 42). St. Pölten: Institut für Landeskunde.

Matzka, C. (2008). Politische Bildung im schulischen Alltag: Beiträge zu einem politisch orientierten Unterricht [Political education in the daily routine in schools]. In *Informationen zur Deutschdidaktik, Zeitschrift für den Deutschunterricht in Wissenschaft und Schule* (Vol. 4, pp. 47–55). Klagenfurt: Studienverlag. Publication of the Arbeitsgemeinschaft für Deutschdidaktik am Institut für Germanistik der Universität Klagenfurt.

Matzka, C. (2009). Austria and Turkey: Their burden of histories. In K. Donert, Y. Ari, M. Attard, G. O'Reilly, & D. Schmeinck (Eds.), *Geographical diversity* (pp. 163–169). Berlin: Mensch und Buch Verlag.

Miklas, H., & Amesberger, H. (2012). *Mauthausen revisited*. Wien: LIT-Verlag.

O'Reilly, G., & Matzka, C. (2009). Contested spaces of memory and identity. In M. Keane & M. Villanueva (Eds.), *Thinking European(s): New geographies of place, cultures and identities* (pp. 160–187). Newcastle upon Tyne: Cambridge Scholars Publishing.

OSCE [Organisation for Security and Co-operation in Europe] (2006). *Education on the Holocaust and on antisemitism: An overview and analysis of educational approaches*. Warsaw: OSCE Office for Democratic Institutions and Human Rights (ODIHR).

Pampel, B. (2007). *Mit eigenen Augen sehen, wozu der Mensch fähig ist: Zur Wirkung von Gedenkstätten auf ihre Besucher* [To see with one's own eyes what human beings are capable of]. Frankfurt am Main: Campus.
Pampel, B. (2011). *Erschrecken – Mitgefühl – Distanz. Empirische Befunde über Schülerinnen und Schüler in Gedenkstätten und zeitgeschichtlichen Ausstellungen* [Shock – empathy – distance]. Leipzig: Universitätsverlag.
Pelinka, A. (1995). Die Entaustrifizierung Österreichs: Zum Wandel des politischen Systems 1945–1995 [The de-Austrianizing of Austria: Change of the political system 1945–1995]. *Österreichische Zeitschrift für Politikwissenschaft, 24*(1), 5–16.
Pelinka, A. (2007). Narretei ob der Enns [Folly in upper Austria]. *Die Zeit, 24*(7), 6.
Perz, B. (2006). *Die KZ-Gedenkstätte Mauthausen 1954 bis zur Gegenwart* [The Mauthausen Memorial from 1954 to the present]. Innsbruck: Studienverlag.
Pingel, F. (2002). Unterricht über den Holocaust: Eine kritische Bewertung der aktuellen pädagogischen Diskussion [Education on the Holocaust: A critical evaluation of the current pedagogical discussion]. In E. Fuchs, F. Pingel, & V. Radkan (Eds.), *Holocaust und Nationalsozialismus* (pp. 11–23). Innsbruck/Vienna/Munich/Bozen: StudienVerlag.
Pollack, M. (2004). *Der Tote im Bunker* [The dead in the bunker]. Vienna: Paul Zsolnay Verlag.
Raphael, L. (2003). *Geschichtswissenschaft im Zeitalter der Extreme* [Historical science in the age of extremes]. Munich: Verlag C. H. Beck.
Ratzenböck, V., Morawek, E., & Amann, S. (Eds.) (1989). *Die zwei Wahrheiten: Eine Dokumentation von Projekten an Schulen zur Zeitgeschichte im Jahr 1988* [The two truths: A documentation of projects in schools about contemporary history in 1988]. Vienna: Löcker Verlag.
Rohrer, A. (2010, 5 November). Was bei uns alles passieren kann. *Die Presse.* http://diepresse.com/home/spectrum/zeichenderzeit/607958/Was-bei-uns-alles-passieren-kann?from=suche.intern.portal
Schlag, T., & Wäckerlig, O. (2010). Far away and nearby: Holocaust remembrance and human rights education in Switzerland. *Prospects, 40*(2), 223–237.
Sreeruwitz, M. (2009, 5 June). Kreuz. Kultur. Kalkül. *Die Presse.* http://diepresse.com/home/spectrum/zeichenderzeit/485008/Kreuz-Kultur-Kalkul?from=suche.intern.portal
Stachel, P. (2002). *Mythos Heldenplatz* [The myth of the Heroes Square]. Vienna: Pichler Verlag.
Stifter, C. (2009). Spurensuche—Hinter den Mauern des Vergessens... [Looking for traces— Behind the walls of oblivion…]. In *Erinnerungskulturen und Gedenkprojekte in Österreich.* 18/9, 1–4. Vienna: Verein zur Geschichte der Volkshochschulen.
Suppan, A. (2009). Österreicher und Tschechen: Missgünstige Nachbarn? [Austrians and Czechs: Begrudging neighbours?]. In S. Karner & M. Stehlik (Eds.), *Österreich, Tschechien, geteiltgetrennt-vereint* (pp. 36–47). Schallaburg: Schallaburg Kulturbetriebs.
Task Force for International Cooperation on Holocaust Education, Remembrance and Research (2006). *Country report on Austria.* Berlin: Task Force.
Tscherne, H., & Krampl, S. (1997). *Spuren der Zeit 4* [Traces of period 4]. Vienna: Verlag Dorner.
Uhl, H. (2001). Das "erste Opfer": Das österreichische Gedächtnis und seine Transformationen in der Zweiten Republik [The first victim: The Austrian memory and its transformation in the Second Republic]. In E. Lappin & B. Schneider (Eds.), *Die Lebendigkeit der Geschichte, (Dis-) Kontinuitäten in Diskussion über den Nationalsozialismus* (Österreich und internationale Literaturprozesse, Vol. 13, pp. 30–46). St. Ingbert: Röhrig Universitätsverlag.
Utgaard, P. (2003). *Remembering and forgetting Nazism: Education, national identity and the victim myth in postwar Austria.* Oxford/New York: Berghahn.
Vocelka, K. (2002). *Geschichte Österreichs* [Austria's history]. Munich: Wilhelm Heyne Verlag.
Worm, A., Krassnitzer, H., Kuba, A., Lang, M., Muskens, R., & Neumayr, J. (Eds.) (2003). *A letter to the stars. Briefe in den Himmel, Schüler schreiben Geschichte.* Vienna: Verlag Verein Lernen aus der Zeitgeschichte.

"Thanks to Scandinavia" and Beyond: Nordic Holocaust Education in the 21st Century

Fred Dervin

Introduction

In this chapter I provide an overview of the way that Holocaust education has been developed and implemented around Scandinavia and the Nordic countries. Having been involved in researching Holocaust education in the Finnish context for the last two years, I offer a review of literature and draw on my experience researching it.

People often confuse the terms Scandinavia and the Nordic countries. In terms of geography, history, culture, and language, Scandinavia includes three countries: Denmark, Norway, and Sweden. The Nordic countries include the three Scandinavian countries as well as Finland, Iceland, and associated territories (the Faroe Islands, Greenland, Svalbard, and Åland). The total population covered by the Nordic countries is approximately 30 million people. In this chapter I consider the three Scandinavian countries as well as Finland and Iceland.

For Holocaust educators the Nordic countries resonate with the important Declaration of the Stockholm International Forum on the Holocaust, a conference on education, remembrance, and research that took place from 26 to 28 January, 2000. For the signatories, the fifth point of the declaration made this statement official: "We share a commitment to encourage the study of the Holocaust in all its dimensions. We will promote education about the Holocaust in our schools and universities, in our communities and encourage it in other institutions".

According to Holmila and Kvist Geberts (2011, p. 520), researchers and educators in the Scandinavian countries—and certainly also in Finland and Iceland—have only recently taken an interest in the Holocaust. For some of these countries, including

---

F. Dervin (✉)
Department of Teacher Education, Faculty of Behavioural Sciences, University of Helsinki, Helsinki, Finland
e-mail: fred.dervin@helsinki.fi

© Springer International Publishing Switzerland 2015
Z. Gross, E.D. Stevick (Eds.), *As the Witnesses Fall Silent: 21st Century Holocaust Education in Curriculum, Policy and Practice*,
DOI 10.1007/978-3-319-15419-0_24

Norway, public discussions around the Holocaust started directly after World War II. Tellingly, in his 1996 volume entitled *The World Reacts to the Holocaust,* David Wyman (1996) did not include any single Nordic country. For Holmila and Kvist Geberts, "This new upsurge of interest in the Holocaust more broadly reflects the dynamics and the contested nature of collective memories of wartime Scandinavia" (2011, p. 520).

Historical Perspectives on Nordic Countries and the Holocaust: Thanks to Scandinavia?

The title of this chapter, "Thanks to Scandinavia", is inspired by an institution of the American Jewish Committee of the same name (http://thankstoscandinavia.org/). According to its website, the institution was founded in 1963 by the Danish entertainer Victor Borge and the New York attorney Richard Netter to provide dozens of scholarships for Scandinavian and Bulgarian students "in gratitude for the heroic rescue and protection of Jews in Europe during the Second World War".

As is true of other places, there are master narratives and counter-narratives about the relations that the Nordic countries hold in relation to the history of the Holocaust. Two of the Nordic countries—Norway and Denmark—were invaded by the Nazis in 1940. According to Lammers (2011, p. 573), Norway was ruled by the Germans while Denmark was "independent" under the "peaceful occupation", and Sweden was a non-belligerent country and was never occupied. Finland, Lammers says, held a special position between 1941 and 1944: it was the only Nordic country that was an ally with Nazi Germany, but it maintained its full sovereignty. This history is still problematic today. Iceland, which had a union with Denmark and the Danish monarchy, was neutral until 1940 and was then defended by the United Kingdom and the United States.

Though occupied by the Nazis, Denmark is well known for an amazing event in October 1943: Danish fishermen rescued 7,000 Jews, almost all of the country's Jewish population, from deportation (Lammers 2011, p. 572). They were sent to Sweden but also to a small village in the South of France. The fishermen did not receive the Righteous Among the Nations honorific that Israel has given to Christian Europeans who helped to save Jews (חסידי אומות העולם) because they had been paid to help them (Novick 1999, pp. 189–190). Approximately 500 Jews were sent to the concentration camp of Theresienstadt, in today's Czech Republic, where 53 died. The others were rescued in another act of bravery by a Swedish-Danish rescue action in 1945, the so-called white busses led by the Swedish diplomat Folke Bernadotte (Lammers 2011). In April 1945, 450 Danish Jews were saved from Theresienstadt.

For Hannah Arendt, Denmark was one of the most "stubborn" of the countries occupied by Nazi Germany. In *Eichmann in Jerusalem: A Report on the Banality of Evil* (1963, p. 171), she wrote, "The story of the Danish Jews is *sui generis*, and the behavior of the Danish people and their government was unique among all the countries of Europe... One is tempted to recommend the story as required reading in political science for all students who wish to learn something about the enormous power potential inherent in nonviolent action and in resistance to an opponent possessing vastly superior means of violence".

The situation was quite different in Norway. According to Abrahamsen (1983, p. 109), "None of the Scandinavian Jewish communities suffered such staggering losses during World War II as did the Jews of Norway". He added that Norway was the only Nordic country to be part of the Nazi final solution; more than 700 Jews were deported from Norway, and 49% of its Jewish population was murdered. Yet, the fact that Norway shares more than 1,500 km of borders with Sweden made the rescue of some Jews possible. In her book *"We Are Going to Pick Potatoes": Norway and the Holocaust, the Untold Story*, Irene Levin Berman (2010) tells the story of her escape from Norway to Sweden in order to avoid deportation to a Nazi camp.

Sweden was neutral during World War II. However it sometimes supported Germany, especially at the beginning of the war, for example, by exporting iron ore and allowing troops to transit through the country. At other times, it supported the Allies, especially after 1943 (Selling 2011). The country tightly restricted Jewish refugees who wished to enter the country, and only granted temporary stays. But in 1942, when the Swedes learnt about the treatment of Norwegian Jews, they decided to change their bystander role (Lammers 2011, p. 572). From 1942 onwards, the Swedish foreign minister admitted Jews and non-Jews who had families in Sweden (Selling 2011). Swedish diplomats multiplied such actions by, for example, granting passports. Most famously, in 1944, Raoul Wallenberg, a Swedish diplomat based in Budapest, helped thousands of Hungarian Jews, as did other notable Swedes, including another diplomat named Per Anger and the publisher Valdemar Langlet. After the war, Sweden welcomed many Jewish refugees.

Finland sided with Germany against the Soviet Union, which had invaded Finland unsuccessfully during November, 1939 in the so-called Winter War. Finland, which had been part of the Russian empire, was also the Soviet Union's route to Sweden's iron ore. That invasion, ended by the Moscow Peace Treaty of 13 March, 1940, influenced the Nazis' decision to invade Denmark and Norway just weeks later, on 9 April, 1940, in an operation named Operation *Weserübung*.

Despite Finland's allegiance with Nazi Germany, Hitler never forced it to create antisemitic laws or to deport Jews: "Finland was an important ally on the northern wing of the Eastern front, not causing any serious problems for Hitler's war" (Holmila and Kvist Geberts 2011, p. 525). Yet, at least 12 Jewish refugees were sent away from Finland in 1942 and at least eight of them were executed in the Baltic country of Estonia, across the Baltic Sea from Finland (Weiss-Wendt 2008).

Finally the Icelandic case is interesting. "Invaded" by the United Kingdom and the United States in 1940, Iceland also experienced its first Yom Kippur observance that year: its first non-Christian service since the year 1000 (Vilhjálmsson 2004). The participants were mostly Jewish servicemen from the British armed forces and some refugees from Austria and Germany. After the war Iceland had two Jewish congregations (Vilhjálmsson 2004).

Holocaust Education in the Nordic Countries

> *There is always a choice. Not to choose is also a choice.*
> —Former Swedish Prime Minister Göran Persson,
> announcing Sweden's official Remembrance Day in 2000

Sweden has been actively engaged in Holocaust education for over 10 years and is well known for the Declaration of the Stockholm International Forum on the Holocaust of 2000. In 1998, the Swedish Prime Minister, Göran Persson, set up the important Task Force for International Cooperation on Holocaust Education, Remembrance and Research. In January 2013, the Task Force was renamed the International Holocaust Remembrance Alliance (IHRA). Persson's motivation was based on at least two facts: he visited a Nazi concentration camp, and he was disturbed to learn that the majority of Swedish school children knew very little about the Holocaust or had a very distorted image of it (Mithander 2013, pp. 184–187).

The turn of the century saw a new phenomenon in the Nordic countries: the "cosmopolitanisation" of Holocaust Remembrance. In 2001, the Norwegian Research Centre for Holocaust and Religious Minorities (*Senter for studier av Holocaust og livssynsminoriteter*) was set up; it was Europe's first nationally-financed research centre dedicated to the Holocaust and genocides. The Uppsala Programme for Holocaust and Genocide Studies (*Programmet för studier kring Förintelsen och folkmord*) was established in Sweden in 1998. In Denmark, the Danish Centre for Holocaust and Genocide Studies (*Holocaust og folkedrab*) has been serving the same purposes since the early 2000s. According to Lammers (2011, p. 580), "These centres have the important didactic assignment of informing the public, and above all the youth, about the Holocaust and genocide in general, and thereby preserving the Holocaust as a vital part of the collective memory". As of early in 2014, a Finnish Network for Holocaust and Genocide Studies was being set up at the University of Helsinki.

Based on this background, I now review the formal and informal activities related to Holocaust education in the Nordic countries.

Sweden

Sweden's interest in Holocaust education became official in 1997 with the *Levande Historia Forum* (Living History Forum, LHF) project, which was launched as a permanent government institution by former Prime Minister Persson. Its website (LHF 2014b) states that its goal is "History as reflection and lesson for the future", and that the LHF is "a Swedish public authority which, using the Holocaust and other crimes against humanity as a starting point, works with issues on tolerance, democracy and human rights". The forum proposes many examples of educational projects in both Swedish and English (LHF 2014a). One of its most influential activities was publishing *Tell Ye Your Children,* by Stéphane Bruchfeld and Paul

Levine (1998). The book has been distributed for free to all school children in Sweden and translated into most of the minority languages for immigrant children. In 2001, it was translated into Finnish under the title *Kertokaa siitä lapsillenne: Kirja juutalaisten joukkotuhosta Euroopassa 1933–1945* and was distributed by the Finnish National Board of Education. The forum has also collected data concerning teaching as well as the perceptions of the Holocaust of 10,000 teachers in Swedish schools (Lange 2008).

The Holocaust is an important part of the teaching of history in Swedish schools and it can also be included in courses such as the German language, religion, social sciences, and Swedish language. Swedish schools spend an annual average of 15 hours on Holocaust education according to the IHRA (2014c). The IHRA website also says that programmes in teacher education and professional development courses should provide educators with more skills for systematically including Holocaust education in their teaching.

Many informal initiatives have been taken in Sweden to support Holocaust education; among them are trips to Holocaust memorial sites, yearly classroom visits by members of the Association of Holocaust Survivors, educational seminars for teachers organised by the Swedish Committee against antisemitism, and the marking of Holocaust Memorial Day on 27 January.

At a more local level, a journalist for *The Times of Israel* reported in January 2013 that a young Swedish Muslim, Siavosh Derakhti, received an award from the Swedish Committee against antisemitism. Derakhti founded an organisation in Malmö, in Southern Sweden, called Young Muslims against antisemitism, through which he educates others about the Holocaust. He also invites survivors to speak to students and takes them to former camps. Derakhti explains that "When we were there, several, if not most people in our class cried. The trip touched many people, the majority of whom were Muslims, including several Palestinians. They learned a lot, and now they are all encouraging people to go" (Dolsten 2013).

Norway

Norway has been a member of the IHRA since 2003. Holocaust education can be integrated into the teaching of different school subjects but the national curriculum of 2006 provides no specific guidelines—although a new curriculum is being prepared as of early 2014. Every year, up to 40,000 Norwegian school pupils travel to former concentration camps. The Centre for Studies of Holocaust and Religious Minorities in Oslo proposes a permanent exhibition on the Holocaust with images, sounds, film, items, and texts that "document the genocide on the European Jews, as well as the Nazi State's mass murder and persecution of other peoples and minorities" (HL-SENTERET 2013). Every year approximately 10,000 students visit the exhibition for a full-day programme. The centre also organises teacher training sessions.

The Falstad Centre in Levanger (also called the Norwegian Memorial and Human Rights Centre) has similar goals as a national education, exhibition, and documentation centre. It is located in a building that was used as a prison camp (*SS Strafgefangenenlager*). Finally, each year on Holocaust Memorial Day, 27 January (www.holocaustdagen.no), a Norwegian school is awarded the Benjamin Prize, after Benjamin Hermansen who was killed by neo-Nazis in 2001, for its work against racism and discrimination (IHRA 2014b).

Denmark

Denmark joined the IHRA one year after Norway did. The Holocaust is not a compulsory subject there, although it is very much present in the teaching about World War II and in courses on civics, religion, and German. There is increasing interest in teaching it; Danish teachers are in charge of the contents of their lessons. In the 1990s, a group of secondary teachers set up a network of teachers interested in Holocaust education, through which they offer professional development (IHRA 2014a).

Holocaust education has also been promoted through the 2000 creation of the Danish Centre for Holocaust and Genocide Studies, which is now part of the Danish Institute for International Studies (DIIS) in Copenhagen. The centre works on many and varied research and educational projects; one of the most noted projects is on the influence that some immigrant children's antisemitism has on Holocaust education in Danish schools (DIIS 2014). Other providers of pedagogical support in Holocaust education include the Jewish Pedagogical Centre at the Caroline School in Copenhagen and Thanks to Scandinavia (TTS). Auschwitz Day is commemorated under the auspices of the Danish Ministry of Education, which allocates around 2 million Danish Crowns (€300,000) for the events (ODIHR 2005, p. 126). Seminars, workshops, survivor testimonies, role-plays, and educational websites such as www.folkedrab.dk or www.holocaust.dk are used to raise awareness about the Holocaust.

The web-based teaching resource www.holocaust-education.dk was developed by Brian Larsen and Peter Vogelsang under the auspices of the Danish Centre for Holocaust and Genocide Studies, to provide educators with an interactive tool for Holocaust education. Its audience is teachers in Denmark and from around the world, as it is also available in English. Finally in 2011 a nationwide educational tour was organised to teach Danish high school students about the Holocaust and other genocides (IHRA 2014a).

Finland

According to Holmila and Silvennoinen (2011, p. 605), "Finland has been one of the last countries in Europe to recognise that it cannot assume a total immunity or innocence in this Europe-wide event". For a long time, the Holocaust was considered to be unrelated to Finnish history, and the rhetoric of separation—that Finland was fighting its own war against the Russians—was used to justify this argument. In the 2010s this view is being debunked (Holmila and Silvennoinen 2011). Worthen and Muir (2013, p. 14) define separation in their volume *Finland's Holocaust: Silences of History*, as the view that "Finnish society and culture were insulated from the racial antisemitism of the Third Reich". Yet, the authors argue that more recent work has demonstrated that antisemitism was an issue in Finland both before and during the war.

In her book *Luovutetut* (Extradited), Elina Sana (2003) argues that Finland deported many more Jews to the German security apparatus than previously believed. The book was strongly criticised and blamed for not being scientific enough. Its publication led the Simon Wiesenthal Center to submit an official request to then President Tarja Halonen to investigate the deportations from Finland to Nazi Germany. The investigation, led by an independent scholar, found no concrete evidence that Finland was responsible. On the same day in November 2013 that British newspapers were reporting with disgust that people were selling death camp relics on eBay, the English version of the national broadcasting company in Finland, YLE, reported that a hidden memorial of Hitler's visit to Finland in 1943 had been discovered in Imatra, in eastern Finland. Hitler was in Finland to celebrate the birthday of his ally, Carl Mannerheim, commander-in-chief of Finland's armed forces. According to the news report, "Locals now organise an official ceremony every year, when the story of the memorial is told" (Yle Uutiset 2013).

Less controversial is a memorial created in 2000 by Nils Haukelund and Rafael Wardi on Helsinki's Observatory Hill (*Tähtitorninmäki*), which recalls the handover of Jewish refugees by Finnish authorities. The same year, former Prime Minister Paavo Lipponen officially apologised to Finland's Jewish community for the incident.

Finland joined the IHRA in 2010, 12 years after its creation. It showed an interest in becoming a member in 2008 and served as an observer country from 2008 to 2010. In 2010, the National Board of Education (*Opetushallitus*) provided instructions for the compulsory integration of the Holocaust into the teaching of history and philosophy in secondary education, along with life stance education (*elämänkatsomustiedo*), which means teaching various religions and worldviews in a way that is fair to all. For example in high school the third compulsory course in history is entitled "international relations" and focuses on the Holocaust. A description of the contents is available in Finnish at EDU.fi (2010).

Sirpa Bagman (2012) analysed the way this announcement was reported in the national newspaper *Helsingin Sanomat* and the tabloid *Ilta Lehti* in August 2010. She noted that the comments left by readers on the newspaper website were rather negative. Out of the total of 400 comments on the *Ilta Lehti* website, "only 35 or so could be regarded as clearly positive toward this news or in some manner providing factual information about the Holocaust and related matters to other discussion participants" (p. 572). Even history teachers were surprised that the National Board of Education was imposing its views on how to teach the Holocaust (Liiten 2010). In 2011, the Association of Religion Teachers in Finland organised a free professional development course on the teaching of the Holocaust, and offered it in Suomenlinna, in eastern Finland, and also in Tallinn in Estonia.

Since 2001 Finland has observed 27 January as the Memorial Day for the Victims of the Holocaust. A few weeks before this date, the National Board of Education reminds schoolteachers about it and on its website offers them a list of ideas for remembering the victims, such as placing the Finnish flag at half-mast at school, observing a 2-min silence, or reciting poems.

In 2010, Antero Holmila, of the University of Jyväskylä, published the first original Finnish-language textbook on the Holocaust, under the name *Holokausti: Tapahtumat ja tulkinnat* (The Holocaust: Events and Interpretations). In 2012 a travelling exhibition about Anne Frank was set up in ten Finnish cities. Called *A History for Today* (Anne Frank Stichting 2014), it tells the story of Anne Frank in relation to the Holocaust. The exhibition material, directed at young people, was also translated into Finnish and Swedish. Finnish young people served as guides to the exhibition. In addition, educators at the Department of World Cultures at the University of Helsinki organised panels about the history of antisemitism in Finland. Finnish school students also have the opportunity to travel abroad, at the initiative of their teachers, to visit former concentration camps such as Klooga in Northern Estonia, which was a Nazi labour camp.

In 2012 and 2013, a 3-week introductory course on Holocaust and Genocide Studies was offered at the Helsinki Summer School (2014) at the University of Helsinki. Conducted in English, it has attracted students from over 60 countries. The course website says it will "include a unit on the Finnish experience during World War II, as well as an excursion to Estonia to visit Holocaust-related sites in Tallinn and the Klooga concentration camp".

Iceland

Icelandic authorities took part in the 2000 Holocaust conference in Stockholm and signed the Declaration of the European Council on Holocaust Education. Yet, the state has not organised any event connected to the commemoration of the Holocaust. School students learn about the Holocaust (*helför* in Icelandic) when they are aged 16–20. History textbooks contain one to three pages on the Holocaust (ODIHR 2005, p. 89). The country made an official connection with Jews in 2003 when Ólafur Ragnar Grímsson, the country's fifth president, married an Israeli citizen, Dorrit Mussaieff. She became an Icelandic citizen in 2006.

To conclude this section, let us not forget the role that Yad Vashem can play in training teachers from Nordic countries. The world centre for documentation, research, education, and commemoration of the Holocaust, it was created in 1953. Its database of courses for educators includes several seminars and courses organised for Nordic educators and decision-makers, including a seminar for Danish teachers in October 2013, one for Finnish educators (through the Finnish National Board of Education) in November 2012, and one for Swedish Jewish educators in

June and July of 2010. Most of the feedback from Nordic participants, reproduced on Yad Vashem's (2014) website, is positive. Two examples provide a taste of their reactions:

> Interesting, educational, emotional but too much to take in and handle. This week has given me a lot to think about, both concerning my teaching but also a reminder of how precious and wonderful life is. Thank you. (Swedish participant)

> The course surpassed my expectations and aims. All this has absolutely changed my attitudes and relations within the multicultural issues. Thanks to you and your colleagues, this seminar has given me new skills and methods to fulfill my task as a teacher… to educate the pupils toward a better future, better world! My deepest thanks. (Finnish participant)

Yad Vashem also organises online courses open to anyone in the world.

Challenges for the Future of Holocaust Education in the Nordic Countries

> We continue living, we go forward, while inside our heart there is a wound. But at the same time this wound commands us to continue the eternal struggle for a better and more beautiful life. (Chavka Folman Raban, an Auschwitz survivor and refugee, in a letter from Sweden just after the war, quoted in *The Local, Sweden's News in English*, 2007)

To conclude, I return to the phrase "Thanks to Scandinavia". In this chapter I hope I have made it clear that the concept applies both to certain important events such as the Danish fishermen, and to the Swedish role in providing leadership in Holocaust education, but that this story is also incomplete, and must incorporate more problematic parts of history. Doing so will involve not just knowledge about the Holocaust itself, but adjustments to the wider narratives surrounding the war.

Like other countries involved in Holocaust education, the Nordic countries face a few challenges. The most obvious one is related to the quasi-absence of Holocaust education in Nordic teacher education: How can Nordic teachers be prepared to teach the Holocaust and under what circumstances? Are they equipped to answer questions related, for example, to the counter-narratives of the Nordic countries' relationships to the Holocaust? At the moment few departments of teacher education seem to be offering much such preparation, except for a few short-term courses organised by individual teacher educators. Another question: Could the teaching of the Holocaust fall under the teaching of either multicultural or intercultural education, which are quite popular in the Nordic countries as they become more heterogeneous? Another important issue is that of professional development: How can teachers of different subjects be coherently and systematically supported in teaching about the Holocaust? Finally, a dialogue with textbook publishers is essential: How should the Holocaust be represented in textbooks and in which subjects? Can links between the Holocaust and other atrocities be made in teaching materials?

These questions all call for more research on the development and implementation of Holocaust education in this part of the world. The efforts I have presented in this chapter are new and manifold, but it is not clear what they add up to. A collection of disparate projects, activities, and events is important, but piecemeal, and it is not yet clear what collective contribution they make. Thus, the absence of systemic action also needs to be addressed.

References

Abrahamsen, S. (1983). The Holocaust in Norway. In R. L. Braham (Ed.), *Contemporary views on the Holocaust* (pp. 109–141). Dordrecht: Kluwer.

Anne Frank Stichting (2014). *Anne Frank: A history for today*. Amsterdam: Anne Frank House. http://www.annefrank.org/en/Education/Travelling-exhibition/Introduction-international-exhibition/

Arendt, H. (1963). *Eichmann in Jerusalem: A report on the banality of evil*. New York: Viking.

Bagman, S. (2012). Finnish reactions to the Holocaust. *The Journal for the Study of Antisemitism, 4*(2), 571–581.

Berman, I. L. (2010). *'We are going to pick potatoes': Norway and the Holocaust, the untold story*. New York: Hamilton Books.

Bruchfeld, S., & Levine, P. (1998). *Tell ye your children*. Stockholm: Living History Forum. http://www.levandehistoria.se/sites/default/files/wysiwyg_media/om-detta-ma-ni-beratta-engelska_1.pdf

DIIS [Danish Institute for International Studies] (2014). *Homepage of the Research Centre on Holocaust and Genocide*. Copenhagen: DIIS. http://www.holocaust.dk/sw160.asp

Dolsten, J. (2013, 8 January). In tense Swedish city, young Muslim crusades against antisemitism. *Times of Israel*. http://www.timesofisrael.com/topic/siavosh-derakhti/#ixzz30VtOygDd

EDU.fi (2010). *Finnish curriculum: The Holocaust*. Helsinki: Ministry of Education. http://www.edu.fi/lukiokoulutus/historia_ja_yhteiskuntaoppi/historian_kurssit/kansainvaliset_suhteet_hi3/holokausti

Helsinki Summer School (2014). Organisational website. http://www.helsinkisummerschool.fi/home/introduction_to_holocaust_and_genocide_studies

HL-SENTERET [Centre for Studies of Holocaust and Religious Minorities] (2013). *The permanent exhibition*. http://www.hlsenteret.no/english/exhibition/

Holmila, A., & Kvist Geberts, K. (2011). On forgetting and rediscovering the Holocaust in Scandinavia: Introduction to the special issue on the histories and memories of the Holocaust in Scandinavia. *Scandinavian Journal of History, 36*(5), 520–535.

Holmila, A., & Silvennoinen, O. (2011). The Holocaust historiography in Finland. *Scandinavian Journal of History, 36*(5), 605–619.

IHRA [International Holocaust Remembrance Alliance] (2014a). *Holocaust education, remembrance, and research in Denmark*. Stockholm: IHRA. http://www.holocaustremembrance.com/node/112

IHRA (2014b). *Holocaust education, remembrance, and research in Norway*. Stockholm. http://www.holocaustremembrance.com/member-countries/holocaust-education-remembrance-and-research-norway

IHRA (2014c). *Holocaust education, remembrance, and research in Sweden*. Stockholm: IHRA. http://www.holocaustremembrance.com/member-countries/holocaust-education-remembrance-and-research-sweden

Lammers, K. C. (2011). The Holocaust and collective memory in Scandinavia: The Danish case. *Scandinavian Journal of History, 36*(5), 570–586.

Lange, A. (2008). *A survey of teachers' experiences and perceptions in relation to teaching about the Holocaust*. Stockholm: Living History Forum. http://www.levandehistoria.se/sites/default/files/wysiwyg_media/teachersurvey_eng_webb.pdf

LHF [Levande Historia Forum] (2014a). *Educational projects*. Stockholm: LHF. http://www.levandehistoria.se/english/educational-projects

LHF (2014b). *The living history forum*. Stockholm: LHF. http://www.levandehistoria.se/english/

Liiten, M. (2010, 14 August). Holokaustin opetuksesta tuli määräys opetussuunnitelmiin [The teaching of the Holocaust is now part of the curriculum]. *Helsingin Sanomat*.

Mithander, C. (2013). From the Holocaust to the Gulag: The crimes of Nazism and communism in Swedish post-89 memory politics. *European Studies, 30*, 177–207.

Novick, P. (1999). *The Holocaust in American life*. New York: Houghton Mifflin.

ODIHR [Office for Democratic Institutions and Human Rights] (2005). *Education on the Holocaust and on anti-semitism: An overview and analysis of educational approaches*. Warsaw: ODIHR.

Sana, E. (2003). *Luovutetut. Suomen ihmisluovutukset Gestapolle* [The extradited: Finland's deportations to the Gestapo]. Helsinki: WSOY.

Selling, J. (2011). Between history and politics: The Swedish Living History project as discursive formation. *Scandinavian Journal of History, 36*(5), 555–569.

Vilhjálmsson, V. O. (2004). Iceland, the Jews, and anti-semitism, 1625–2004. *Jewish Political Studies Review, 16*(3–4), 131–156.

Weiss-Wendt, A. (2008). Why the Holocaust does not matter to Estonians. *Journal of Baltic Studies, 39*(4), 475–497.

Worthen, H., & Muir, S. (2013). Introduction: Contesting the silences of history. In S. Muir & H. Worthen (Eds.), *Finland's Holocaust: Silences of history* (pp. 1–30). London: Palgrave Macmillan.

Wyman, D. (Ed.) (1996). *The world reacts to the Holocaust*. Baltimore/London: Johns Hopkins University Press.

Yad Vashem (2014). Museum website. http://www.yadvashem.org/yv/en/about/index.asp

Yle Uutiset (2013, 2 November). Hidden memorial of rare Hitler visit to Finland. *Yle Uutiset*. http://yle.fi/uutiset/hidden_memorial_of_rare_hitler_visit_to_finland/6914509

Holocaust Education in Scotland: Taking the Lead or Falling Behind?

Paula Cowan and Henry Maitles

Introduction

Scotland is one of the four countries that make up the United Kingdom (UK). In 1999 the Scottish Parliament was established with responsibility for a wide range of devolved powers while the UK Parliament remained responsible for reserved matters in Scotland (HMSO 1998). As education is a devolved issue, the Scottish Parliament has full legislative responsibility for the education system in Scotland, although funding is a reserved matter. This means that all matters related to school-based education are discussed and decided by the Scottish Parliament. In addition, the Scottish education system is distinct from the education systems of the rest of the United Kingdom in that it has its own curriculum and qualification frameworks.

Scotland is a multicultural country with a population of five million and a school population of approximately 673,500 students (Scottish Government 2013) and 72,000 registered teachers (GTCS 2014); 96% of Scottish schools are publicly funded, and the remaining 4% are independent private schools. Schools are either non-denominational (publicly funded and open to children of all faiths or of no faith) or denominational. Of the 2,560 schools in Scotland, 370 are publicly-funded faith schools; 366 of these are Catholic schools.

Unlike England, which houses several major Holocaust exhibitions at prominent museums, there are no such centres in Scotland. During a debate about Holocaust education in the Scottish Parliament (2008), reference was made to establishing a national Holocaust museum in Scotland, but this has not been developed further. Therefore, people in Scotland have less opportunity to engage in this type of informal learning about the Holocaust than their English peers. Focusing on the Scottish context, in this chapter we will discuss the extent to which key Holocaust educational initiatives in Scotland lead the way in Holocaust education, and the extent to which they follow the practice elsewhere, with comparisons to neighbouring England.

The Relevance of the Holocaust in Scotland

We wrote elsewhere that "Although the impact of the Holocaust on Scotland and the Scots was not as great as elsewhere in Europe, Scotland has historical connections with the Holocaust, some of which are closely linked with values education" (Cowan and Maitles 2010, p. 258). These connections include Scotland being the birthplace of Church of Scotland missionary Jane Haining (1897–1944), the only Scottish "Righteous (Person) Amongst the Nations"; she was awarded this title in recognition of her saving Jewish children in Hungary during the Holocaust. And Scotland became home for refugees, Holocaust camp survivors, and *kinder*, children from Germany, Austria, and Czechoslovakia who came to the UK on the *kindertransports* between 1938 and 1939.

The Gathering the Voices (2012) initiative is a website that aims "to gather, contextualise and digitise oral testimony from men and women who came to Scotland to escape the racism of Nazi-dominated Europe". This archival resource is distinctive in that its data collection involves collaboration between professionals and university students, with volunteer students of history transcribing data, graphic design students contributing to the website design, and audio technology students preparing or "cleaning up" the interviews (Shapiro et al. 2014), Holocaust education, therefore, occurs in the process of making this website as well as from the final product. This resource focuses on the contribution these people who came to Scotland made, and in some cases, still make, to society, as well as their experiences. It is hoped that the archive will contain 40 testimonies and that they will encourage asylum seekers in Scotland who are currently living in poor circumstances, as they show that it is possible to make a life in Scotland (Lipman 2012). This link between Scotland's past and present was highlighted in a short film, *Courage*, made by the Scottish Refugee Council in 2011 to mark the 60th anniversary of the UN Refugee Convention. It featured octogenarian Rosa Sacharin, one of the Scottish *kinder* refugees from Berlin, and Christian Kasuban, a young refugee who had recently fled the Democratic Republic of Congo to safety in Scotland.

Statistical data show that race crime charges and religiously aggravated charges in Scotland during 2012–2013 decreased by 12% and 24% respectively (COPFS 2013). Two hate crimes directed towards Jews in Scotland were reported in the media during this period. The first was the charge of racist breach of the peace by an 18-year-old university student towards a Jewish student (The Scotsman 2011). This was a landmark ruling with the judge deciding that attacking someone's Jewish identity based on their identification was racist. The second concerns five individuals who were charged in connection with antisemitic comments on Facebook

(Campsie 2012). Its heading reads "Welcome to Israel, only kidding you're in Giffnock", referring to a residential area outside Glasgow with Scotland's largest Jewish community, largest synagogue, and other communal Jewish amenities. It includes a profile picture of the late Rev. Ernest Levy, a Holocaust survivor who came to Scotland after surviving Auschwitz-Birkenau and Bergen-Belsen, and the recipient of an OBE for his contribution to Holocaust education (Cowan 2011). Of the five charged, one was acquitted, three were convicted and fined and one, a juvenile, was referred to the children's reporter as a matter of principle. These incidents, together with the anti-Catholic bigotry directed towards Celtic football manager Neil Lennon, suggests that lessons on tolerance and discrimination are relevant to people in Scotland today, and that such lessons include Holocaust education. The organisation Sense over Sectarianism (SOS), has provided financial support to the Gathering the Voices website. Set up in partnership with the Scottish Executive, SOS awards grants to individuals and community groups in the wider Glasgow area, who set up projects that challenge sectarianism and bigotry.

The Scottish Curriculum

Unlike in England and Wales, where Holocaust education is included in the school curriculum at Key Stage 3 (for pupils aged 13–14), there is no requirement to teach the Holocaust in schools in Scotland. However, there is scope for teaching it, as Holocaust education can help to develop "responsible citizenship", which is one of the key aims of the Scottish curriculum (Cowan and Maitles 2010, p. 259). Research evidence, from a 2009 study carried out for the Holocaust Educational Trust (HET 2010), shows that of the 105 students who participated in the Lessons from Auschwitz Project in Scotland in 2007 and in the subsequent study, approximately 70% had received some form of Holocaust education at school. The HET works in schools and the wider community to raise awareness and understanding of the Holocaust and its modern-day lessons; it also organises the Lessons from Auschwitz Project (LFAP).

While the omission of the Holocaust in the Scottish curriculum has inevitably led to a limited amount of Holocaust teaching, it has not prevented teachers who wish to teach it from doing so, or head teachers from encouraging its teaching in their schools. It is possible that one consequence of Holocaust education not being mandatory is that primary and secondary teachers who teach the Holocaust in Scotland do so willingly and with a genuine interest in this topic. They may choose to integrate it into a school's history or citizenship programme which may or may not contribute to wider events such as national Holocaust Memorial Day. However, its teaching depends on local authorities, schools, and teachers who are committed to it. Worryingly, some secondary schools in Scotland have taken the subject of history off the curriculum and this potentially will lead to less Holocaust teaching. On a more positive note, the Scottish curriculum (Scottish Executive 2004), with its emphasis on teachers and students choosing their subjects, opens the possibility of more Holocaust education in the classroom.

The placement of the Holocaust in the national curriculum for secondary students in England and Wales reflects the traditional notion that the Holocaust is too difficult, or inappropriate, for younger students. This view is conveyed by Landau (2008) and Totten (1999) who hold that the Holocaust is inappropriate and too complex for this age group to study, and Kochan (1989) who objects to its teaching to the "immature and unsophisticated", claiming that such teaching can have deleterious consequences for pupils. In contrast, Burtonwood (2002, p. 70) cites research and commentaries on Holocaust education that emphasise its relevance in the primary sector. So too do our case studies of a local educational initiative in Scotland where Holocaust teaching was the norm for the upper primary classes, i.e. for students aged 10–12 years (Cowan and Maitles 2002) and of changing practices of Holocaust teaching in primary schools in one local authority (Cowan and Maitles 2014). It is further challenged by the research which suggests that teaching the Holocaust in the primary school has developed young students' understanding of justice, stereotyping and discrimination (Cowan and Maitles 2007; Maitles and Cowan 1999; Short and Carrington 1991).

The Education for Citizenship policy (LTS 2002a) has added impetus to the development of teaching about the Holocaust in primary and secondary schools. Scotland has adopted a cross-curricular approach to teaching citizenship in that all subject areas in the school have an input into its teaching. Despite some fears that the responsibility of all can become the responsibility of none, case studies (Deuchar 2007; Maitles 2005; Maitles and Gilchrist 2006) have shown that, in the limited cases where it is attempted, education for citizenship can be effective, particularly if senior management in the school is openly positive and encouraging about it. Lessons on the Holocaust share a strong focus on the areas of knowledge and understanding relevant to the development of active and responsible citizenship. "Values and Citizenship", which involves teaching pupils the "duties and responsibilities of citizenship in democratic society" and "respect for self and one another", has been a national priority in Scotland since the *Standards in Scotland's Schools Act* (Scottish Parliament 2000).

Teaching about the Holocaust provides a suitable context for attainment in many key areas which are specified in proposals for Education for Citizenship in Scotland, e.g., human rights, the need for mutual respect, tolerance, and understanding of a diverse and multicultural Scotland (LTS 2002b). This is particularly important as two reports in 2007 commissioned by the British Government (Ajegbo et al. 2007; Singh 2007) found that issues relating to diversity and race are often neglected in citizenship programmes. Indeed, many schools use human rights as a starting point for an understanding of citizenship rights; the UNESCO (2008) *Plan of Action* can be a starting point for a discussion and activities in the classroom as to what should be done.

Further, in Scotland there is an emphasis on a cross-curricular or inter-disciplinary focus wherever possible, involving the traditional curricular areas of Religious and Moral Education, Environmental Studies, History, Modern Studies and Personal and Social Development, along with wider subjects where feasible. The General Teaching Council for Scotland (GTCS) is the world's first independent regulatory body which maintains and enhances teaching standards and promotes and regulates the teaching profession in Scotland. It has recognised this cross-curricular practice in its award of Professional Recognition to registered teachers who focus their continuing professional development (CPD) in one particular area of interest. Teachers are required to demonstrate professional reading related to the area of expertise, professional expertise in one particular area, professional action, collaborative practice with teachers, and impact on professional practice on learners. They also provide a summary of their professional discussion with their head teacher.

Two secondary teachers have received this award for their work in Holocaust education. The first was an English teacher who used the Holocaust to provide a context for learning in classes in art, drama, maths, German, and technology, as well as in history and English, for Holocaust Memorial Day. When one of the Scottish *kinder* agreed to speak to pupils, this teacher arranged for another teacher to sign for the students with hearing impairments. Excepting senior classes who were involved in preliminary examinations for external assessments, every year group in this school engaged in learning about the Holocaust and teachers of different subject areas worked in each other's classrooms (Cowan 2010). The second teacher was a drama teacher who taught an 8-week course to every S.2 student (13–14 years), provided a series of CPD sessions in Holocaust education for primary and secondary teachers in his local authority, and organised a community event for his authority for Holocaust Memorial Day, which involved the participation of local primary and schools. This suggests that in addition to teaching pupils about the Holocaust, committed teachers have the potential to educate and encourage other teachers to teach the Holocaust. That the national professional body has acknowledged the good practice of Holocaust education in schools contributes to the Holocaust being accepted into mainstream education and to Holocaust educators being developed across Scotland.

Evaluating the Impact of Holocaust Teaching

Although teaching the Holocaust is mandatory in primary schools in several European countries, including the Netherlands and France, there is little research on its teaching in the primary context. In Scotland, in 2004, the Scottish Executive (now called the Scottish Government) sponsored a study we conducted to evaluate the impact of teaching the Holocaust in the primary school; we published the findings in 2006 (Scottish Executive 2006). We used a longitudinal strategy to examine whether such teaching produces "immediate" and "lasting" effects on the attitudes and dispositions of students; further, we compared the values of the group of primary students who studied the Holocaust to their primary peers who had not studied the Holocaust in primary school. We conducted the study in an area that was overwhelmingly white, with no Jewish students in the schools' sample.

The first part of this study involved a core group of 99 students from two schools, in their last year at primary school (aged 11–12 years) completing the same questionnaire immediately before and after they had learned about the Holocaust. We found that students' attitudes towards minority groups such as Jews, Blacks, Chinese, Asians, Gypsies/Travellers, refugees and the disabled, improved immediately after they learned about the Holocaust, with significant positive trends in attitudes towards Gypsies/Travellers and refugees (Maitles et al. 2006). Further, while students perceived gains in knowledge of human rights, Gypsies/Travellers, and refugees, they reflected a lack of understanding of antisemitism. This may be due to primary teachers explaining the genocide of the Jews as a matter of racism and not of antisemitism.

Responses to the question "Do you know what antisemitism is?" varied significantly between the two schools; 3.7% of students in School A answered yes, compared to 39% in School B. Feedback from the class teachers showed that School B had regularly used and displayed flashcards of the key terms of the Holocaust, which included antisemitism, while the teacher in School A had not used this term in the classroom (Cowan and Maitles 2005). Teacher feedback also showed that these schools had used different general teaching approaches and materials. School A had integrated the Holocaust into a topic on World War II; School B had taught the Holocaust as a separate topic. Time spent on the topic varied from 2 h a week for 5 weeks (School A) to 4 h a week for 3 weeks (School B). School A's core approach was using the Story of Anne Frank (Dring 1992) and engaging students in a great deal of individual research (Cowan and Maitles 2007). Though we focused on impact, this study provides some insight into teaching pedagogy in the primary classroom. It follows that further research in this area would be beneficial.

This cohort then completed the same questionnaire in their first year at secondary school, to let us compare their attitudes with earlier findings. This involved 238 students, as we also gave it to secondary students in the core group's school who had not previously studied the Holocaust, in order to compare their attitudes with those of the core group. We found both a short-term and a long-term improvement in the citizenship values of students who had studied the Holocaust, compared to those who had not (Cowan and Maitles 2007). The core group had stronger positive values and was more disposed to active citizenship by their perceived understanding of individual responsibility towards racism.

We acknowledged that many other factors could have influenced the students' values and attitudes during this time, but because we had guaranteed anonymity to the school and the local authority and to the students, it was not possible to conduct in-depth interviews to clarify students' understanding, or track individual students to follow up particular responses. While this part of the research could not be definitive about the impact of Holocaust teaching in the schools, the fact that the core group continued to hold more positive attitudes towards minorities in Scotland suggests that their learning about the Holocaust had had an impact on their general outlook towards key citizenship areas. This supports previous research in secondary schools (Ben-Peretz 2003; Brown and Davies 1998; Carrington and Short 1997; Davies 2000; Hector 2000; Schweber 2003; Short and Reed 2004; Short et al. 1998; Totten 2000) demonstrating the contribution that Holocaust education can make to citizenship in developing students' awareness of human rights issues including genocide, the concepts of stereotyping and scapegoating, and the exercise of power in local, national, and global contexts.

Professional Development for Teachers

Holocaust education has been included in the Scottish Continuing International Professional Development Programme (SCIPD) which is organised by Education Scotland, a key national body, funded by the (Scottish) government, which is at the centre of all developments in Scottish education. The inclusion of Holocaust education in SCIPD has enabled small numbers of teachers across Scotland to participate in group study outside the United Kingdom focusing on the Holocaust and Holocaust-related issues. Aimed at developing a global perspective, visits to Amsterdam (2008) and Berlin (2009) and Oslo (2010) have focused on approaches to teaching the Holocaust and human rights education. Compared to England, where the Holocaust Education Development Programme (HEDP 2009) provides free professional development to secondary teachers from state-maintained schools, CPD in Scotland is far less frequent. It can thus be argued that in the area of CPD in Holocaust education, Scotland has fallen behind. This is highlighted by the HEDP extending its services to providing free professional development to student teachers; student teachers in Scotland have no such opportunity.

One way in which Scotland is taking the lead is in its use of Glow, the world's first national intranet for education, and the online community for schools in Scotland. It currently has categories, known as Glow Groups, for Education for Citizenship, Holocaust Education, and Holocaust Memorial Day. The Holocaust Education site focuses on learning and teaching about the Holocaust and includes more recent genocides. Glow incorporates the web conferencing tool, Glow Meet, which is a part of Glow Groups that allows teachers and students to interact using video, audio, and a shared whiteboard space. When schools register for a Glow Meet activity, that activity becomes visible on their computer(s) and/or the classroom interactive whiteboard(s) and students are active participants.. This innovative tool was used when international guest speakers spoke to primary school students in Dundee about *Hana's Suitcase* (Levine 2003) at one of Scotland's Holocaust Memorial Day events in 2012. Schools across Scotland who logged onto this Glow Meet were (virtual) members of the audience and as such were able to join in with their Dundee peers. Glow Meet, therefore, facilitates the participation of a larger and wider audience and is being effectively used in Holocaust education in Scotland.

Holocaust Memorial Day

In 2001, the national UK Holocaust Memorial Day (HMD) was introduced and Scotland has since held its separate national commemorative event every year, except in 2003 when the national UK event was held in Scotland's capital city, Edinburgh. Although these events have been organised by a variety of different local authorities, they have been criticised for having little impact outside the densely populated area in southern Scotland known as the "central belt". There has been less interest in Scotland in hosting a large-scale national event, compared to England, where authorities initially competed to host this event (Cowan 2009). One possible reason for this is the finance involved: authorities that host a (Scottish) national event are required to organise activities and events for their wider community on the Holocaust and its related themes, in addition to a major commemorative event. This requires significant funding and human resources and its success depends on financial support from the Scottish Government. Another possible reason is the timing of this event, as 27 January falls 2 days after an important date on the Scottish calendar: the annual celebration of the life and works of Scotland's national poet, Robert Burns. Still, in addition to hosting a national HMD event, many areas across Scotland organise a smaller-scale commemorative event for their local communities each year.

Initially, the event commemorating HMD in England was a movable one, with authorities across the country being invited to express their interest in hosting it. This led to HMD being held in Newcastle (2007), Liverpool (2008), and Coventry (2009). While it has been held in London since 2010, in Scotland, it continues to be a moveable event. This has several advantages: it is easier to maintain a fresh approach each year and it achieves a focus on Holocaust education in different geographical areas. In addition, the venues have contributed to conveying an ethos of inclusion as they have varied from grand theatres to local secondary schools. One possible disadvantage is that the experience gained from organising one event may not be passed on the following year. In Scotland, this has been addressed by the national organisation Interfaith Scotland, working collaboratively with the named authority, the Scottish Government, Education Scotland, and the Holocaust Memorial Day Trust (HMDT).

The Scottish national HMD events have been diverse and imaginative. In 2007, for example, Fife Council (2007) organised a 3-week festival, entitled the Anne Frank and You Festival, which culminated with the national HMD event which was attended by about 500 people. This authority had not previously engaged with HMD and was inspired by school students who had visited the Auschwitz–Birkenau Memorial and Museum (ABMM) in 2005 (Cowan 2008a). This festival involved students aged 16 and 17 in planning, organising, and implementing workshops, presentations, and a range of activities that included a school community debate and a creative workshop programme; in total nearly 3,000 school students participated. For more than a year, students worked collaboratively with their peers, teachers, and professionals from the community sector on planning this project and created a dynamic synergy.

Other national events were equally engaging. For the 2011 national event, held in Craigroyston High School, Edinburgh, school students designed and presented the programme and interviewed the guest speakers immediately after the event. In 2012, leading up to HMD, Dundee Council arranged for hundreds of school pupils to watch the film *Inside Hana's Suitcase*, based on the book *Hana's Suitcase* (Levine 2003), a biography of a young Jewish girl in Czechoslovakia who died in the Holocaust. The pupils got to meet the film's director and the actress who played the central character, and several international guest speakers participated in the national event.

In addition to partially funding the Scottish national HMD event, the Scottish Government funded Holocaust teaching resources in preparation for this commemoration. The Scottish Executive first commissioned an education pack for teaching the Holocaust to primary students aged 10–12 years (LTS 2000). This resource was based on the testimony of the late Rev. Ernest Levy, whom we mentioned earlier, and was distributed to every primary school in Scotland. The Scottish Executive later commissioned an education pack for secondary schools that built on the knowledge students had gained from the primary resource; it complemented the principles of the Scottish curriculum and was based on the experiences of Marianne Grant, another Holocaust survivor who had lived in Scotland (LTS 2002b). It has since funded additional teaching materials (Morley and Nunn 2005; Scottish Executive 2006).

As mentioned above, we (Cowan and Maitles 2002) found that HMD was an important stimulus that led to Holocaust teaching being the norm in upper primary classes; this supports Burtonwood's (2002) view that HMD can facilitate school-based Holocaust education. However, we conducted that study a decade ago, and it is not known whether this reflects current practice of Holocaust teaching in Scotland. HMDT records show that the numbers engaging with commemorative events in Scotland continue to grow, "from 18 events held in 2006, 40 in 2008, to nearly 60 in 2009" (Cowan 2009, p. 37), and over 100 in 2011, according to internal documents.

School Visits to Auschwitz

In 2005, the former Secretary of State for Scotland, Jim Murphy, organised the first 1-day Scottish visit to Auschwitz for students and teachers after a BBC survey revealed that 60% of those under 35 had not heard of Auschwitz (Cowan 2012). Since then, Scottish senior secondary students have participated in educational day visits to the camp and museum in several ways: with a school or community group as part of a longer educational trip to Europe or Poland, as participants in the above first Scottish visit, and, since 2007, as participants in the Lessons From Auschwitz Project.

One advantage that a school or community group visit has over the other two types is that participants know each other and, as some will already be friends, can provide support to each other. In contrast, in the other types, although students may be from the same school, they may not be acquainted with each other and may not be able to provide this support. An example of the first type of visit is that by the Scout Group 102, a group of 20 boys aged between 11 and 21 who visited the Auschwitz memorial site as part of a trip to Poland. The senior scout leader who accompanied the group commented that in his opinion the younger participants did not get as much out of the visit as the older ones, but he emphasised the value of doing so with a group of people who knew each other, as the scouts talked to each other, asked each other questions, and gave each other emotional support (Cowan 2008b).

Focussing on the other two types of participation, the 2005 trip was organised independently by local politicians with the support and assistance of the Holocaust Educational Trust. These latter two types of school visits aim to have students learn universal and contemporary lessons *from* the Holocaust and/or Auschwitz, in addition to learning *about* it. They shared other common aspects: participants were aged 16–18, each school was allowed to send one teacher to accompany student participants, and students were required to carry out a Next Steps activity as a means of passing on their learning.

The Lessons from Auschwitz Project

Since 1999, school visits to the ABMM have been organised and subsidised by the Holocaust Educational Trust (HET) (2006) and comprise one of the four components of the Lessons From Auschwitz Project (LFAP). Since 2007, the governments of Britain (UK) and Scotland have sponsored two students per secondary school/ further education college to participate in this project. In 2012 the project achieved a high profile in Scotland when the Scottish Government increased its funding for the scheme and when students who had participated in the LFAP addressed the Scottish Parliament about the impact the visit had had on them. Between 2007 and 2011, a total of more than 1,600 students and 260 teachers from Scotland participated in the project.

Research commissioned by the HET in 2009 (HET 2010; Cowan and Maitles 2011; Maitles and Cowan 2012) examined the LFAP in Scotland as of 2007; it involved an online questionnaire to the cohort (236 students) to which we were allowed access, and received a 54% response; we also conducted nine follow-up interviews. We found that student and teacher participants perceived gains in their knowledge of World War II as a result of the LFAP. Interview data suggested that some students had developed their learning about wider social issues as shown in these comments from two students:

> It [the visit to ABMM] has made me more aware of other things that are going on in the world. It has changed my attitude towards genocide… it helped me a lot to understand how it must have felt to have been Jewish at the time and what it would have been like not to be Jewish, and either be at risk of supporting Jewish people or just going along with the crowd.
>
> It definitely made me think that things like separation on racial grounds are not acceptable and things like sectarianism…. You hear a lot of jokes about it…. It definitely made me less accepting towards things of this nature.

This research data shows that students discussed the LFAP experience on their return to school. Of the cohort of 105 students, 85% indicated in an online survey that they had the opportunity to talk about the visit to the ABMM on their return to school. In the survey, these percentages of students reported that discussions took place on the following topics: 98% on the Holocaust, 63% on discrimination, 57% on antisemitism, and 52% each on racism and other genocides. These discussions occurred in a variety of subject areas ranging from History and Modern Studies to French and English. Student feedback shows that such discussions focused on the Holocaust and its broader lessons such as racial inequality within world communities, global responses to the violation of human rights, and the responsibility for the Holocaust. Students also talked informally to their friends about their experience and this is likely to have stimulated more interest in Holocaust education.

Data from the 2007 investigation of the LFAP in Scotland provides evidence that students took their responsibilities on return from the ABMM visit very seriously and organised a wide range of Next Steps events for both their schools and communities. Assemblies and year-group sessions were the most common school activities; some were particularly innovative. Among the school activities, students wrote articles for the school magazine and worked cooperatively with teachers to draw up a lesson plan for younger students on the Holocaust and its lessons for today. Community activities included an HMD service which community members were invited to attend, and students giving presentations to a range of audiences, including their local Member of Parliament and Member of the Scottish Parliament, along with local community groups, college students, and primary school teachers. The quality of these activities is unknown and evidence on this relies heavily on student perceptions which are largely determined by what they remember. Student comments on the questions they received from their teachers and school peers and the praise they received suggest that the activities were interesting and of good quality. The above activities strongly suggest that the LFAP had an impact on students' participatory role as citizens as they made a significant contribution to the social and cultural life of their schools and communities and became Holocaust educators.

Conclusions

The evidence outlined in this chapter is that schools and wider communities in Scotland are becoming increasingly engaged with Holocaust education, through the curriculum, the commemoration of national Holocaust Memorial Day, and the participation and impact of the Lessons from Auschwitz Project. The research evidence we have outlined suggests that these lessons, and their subsequent activities, are powerful, whether delivered by teachers, students, or other professionals. Further, Scotland is taking the lead by involving students in the process of compiling a public archive of oral testimonies about the Holocaust; by using GLOW in Holocaust education, which involves large numbers of students across a wide geographical area, in a range of activities; and by GTCS recognition rewarding innovative Holocaust teaching. Another positive factor is that those teachers who are involved in learning and teaching about the Holocaust are doing so out of a conviction that teaching about the Holocaust is a valuable way of developing citizenship values. One point that is worthy of consideration is whether primary and secondary teachers in Scotland (and primary teachers in England and Wales), who volunteer to provide Holocaust education, are more committed and enthusiastic in their approach to and delivery of Holocaust education than those who are required to teach it according to a prescribed curriculum.

However, we see a number of areas relating to the ongoing development of Holocaust education in Scotland that suggest that Scotland is at risk of falling behind. At present there is no systematic knowledge of teaching programmes in place. Few opportunities exist for Scottish teachers and educators to develop their skills and knowledge in teaching the Holocaust through CPD, particularly as CPD budgets are being reduced. Finally, not every student in Scotland has access to Holocaust education or indeed any discussion of genocide, as it is not prescribed in any curricular area. Hence, it is vital to make Holocaust Memorial Day and the Lessons from Auschwitz Project sustainable, and to encourage innovative practices such as the use of GLOW, in order to maintain the impact of Holocaust education in Scotland. Without these initiatives accompanied by government financial support, this aspect of education may become even more vulnerable than it is at present.

References

Ajegbo, K., Kiwan, D., & Sharma, S. (2007). *Curriculum review: Diversity and citizenship*. London: Department for Education and Skills.
Ben-Peretz, M. (2003). Identifying with horror: Teaching about the Holocaust. *Curriculum Inquiry, 33*(2), 189–198.
Brown, M., & Davies, I. (1998). The Holocaust and education for citizenship. *Educational Review, 50*, 75–83.
Burtonwood, N. (2002). Holocaust Memorial Day in schools—Context, process and content: A review of research into Holocaust education. *Educational Research, 44*(1), 69–82.
Campsie, A. (2012, 17 May). Six arrests in anti-Semitic raids. *The Herald*. http://www.heraldscotland.com/mobile/news/crime-courts/six-arrests-in-anti-semitic-raids.17611503
Carrington, B., & Short, G. (1997). Holocaust education, anti-racism and citizenship. *Educational Review, 47*, 271–282.
COPFS [Crown Office and Procurator Fiscal Service] (2013). *Hate crime in Scotland 2012–13*. Edinburgh: COPFS. http://www.copfs.gov.uk/images/Documents/Equality_Diversity/Hate%20Crime%20in%20Scotland%202012-13.pdf

Cowan, P. (2008a). Seeing, hearing and feeling—How can a visit to Auschwitz encourage young people to practise citizenship? In A. Ross & P. Cunningham (Eds.), *Reflecting on identities: Research, practice and innovation* (pp. 511–520). London: London Metropolitan University.

Cowan, P. (2008b). Learning about the Holocaust and responsible citizenship in Scotland. *Race Equality Teaching, 26*(2), 36–39.

Cowan, P. (2009). Remembering the Holocaust: UK initiatives associated with Holocaust Memorial Day. *Canadian Diversity, 7*(2), 35–38.

Cowan, P. (2010, November/December). Holocaust studies in schools. *St. Andrews in focus.*

Cowan, P. (2011, 13 October). The Scots who still think it's acceptable to mock the Jews. *Scottish Review.* http://www.scottishreview.net/PaulaCowan184.shtml

Cowan, P. (2012). Visiting Auschwitz: Valuable lessons or Holocaust tourism? In P. Cowan & H. Maitles (Eds.), *Teaching controversial issues in the classroom* (pp. 144–151). London: Continuum.

Cowan, P., & Maitles, H. (2002). Developing positive values: A case study of Holocaust Memorial Day in the primary schools of one local authority in Scotland. *Educational Review, 54*(3), 219–229.

Cowan, P., & Maitles, H. (2005). Values and attitudes—Positive and negative: A study of the impact of teaching the Holocaust on citizenship among Scottish 11–12 year olds. *Scottish Education Review, 37*(2), 104–115.

Cowan, P., & Maitles, H. (2007). Does addressing prejudice and discrimination through Holocaust education produce better citizens? *Educational Review, 59*(2), 115–130.

Cowan, P., & Maitles, H. (2010). Policy and practice of Holocaust education in Scotland. *Prospects, 40*(2), 257–272.

Cowan, P., & Maitles, H. (2011). 'We Saw Inhumanity Close Up'. What is gained by school students from Scotland visiting Auschwitz? *Journal of Curriculum Studies, 43*(2), 163–185.

Cowan, P., & Maitles, H. (2014, 12–14 June). *Are changing practices of Holocaust teaching good for citizenship education?* Paper presented at conference, Children's Identity and Citizenship in Europe, Olsztyn, Poland.

Davies, I. (2000). *Teaching the Holocaust.* London: Continuum.

Deuchar, R. (2007). *Citizenship, enterprise and learning.* Stoke on Trent: Trentham.

Dring, J. (1992). *Fast forward.* Cambridge: LDA Publishers.

Fife Council (2007). *Anne Frank and you: The festival.* Fife: Fife Council.

Gathering the Voices (2012). Organisational website. http://www.gatheringthevoices.com

GTCS [General Teaching Council for Scotland] (2014). Organisational website. http://www.gtcs.org.uk/about-gtcs/statistics.aspx

Hector, S. (2000). Teaching the Holocaust in England. In I. Davies (Ed.), *Teaching the Holocaust* (pp. 105–115). London: Continuum.

HEDP [Holocaust Education Development Programme] (2009). *Teaching about the Holocaust in English secondary schools.* London: Institute of London.

HET [Holocaust Educational Trust] (2006). *Lessons from Auschwitz student course.* London: HET.

HET (2010). *Never again: How the lessons from Auschwitz project impacts on schools in Scotland* (Final Report). Ayr: University of the West of Scotland.

HMSO [Her Majesty's Stationery Office] (1998). *Scotland Act.* http://www.opsi.gov.uk/acts/acts1998/ukpga_19980046_en_1

Kochan, L. (1989, 22 December). Life over death. *Jewish Chronicle.*

Landau, R. (2008, 12 September). Teaching the Shoah. *Jewish Chronicle.*

Levine, K. (2003). *Hana's suitcase.* London: Evans Brothers Ltd.

Lipman, J. (2012, 12 January). Voices designed to speak to the new generation. *Jewish Chronicle.* http://www.thejc.com/community/community-life/62646/voices-designed-speak-next-generation

LTS [Learning and Teaching Scotland] (2000). *The Holocaust: A teaching pack for primary schools.* Dundee: LTS.

LTS (2002a). *Education for citizenship in Scotland.* Dundee: LTS.

LTS (2002b). *The Holocaust: A teaching pack for secondary schools*. Dundee: LTS.
Maitles, H. (2005). *Values in education: We're citizens now*. Edinburgh: Dunedin Press.
Maitles, H., & Cowan, P. (1999). Teaching the Holocaust in primary schools in Scotland: Modes, methodology and content. *Educational Review, 51*(3), 263–271.
Maitles, H., & Cowan, P. (2012). "It reminded me of what really matters": Teacher responses to the lessons from Auschwitz project. *Educational Review, 64*(2), 131–143.
Maitles, H., & Gilchrist, I. (2006). Never too young to learn democracy!: A case study of a democratic approach to learning in a religious and moral education (RME) secondary class in the West of Scotland. *Educational Review, 58*(1), 67–86.
Maitles, H., Cowan, P., & Butler, E. (2006). *Never again: Does Holocaust education have an impact on pupils' citizenship values and attitudes?* Report produced for Scottish Executive Education Department. Edinburgh: Scottish Government. http://www.scotland.gov.uk/resource/doc/147037/0038530.pdf
Morley, K., & Nunn, T. (2005). *The arts and the Holocaust: Lessons from the past for citizens of today*. Barrhead: East Renfrewshire Council.
Schweber, S. (2003). Simulating survival. *Curriculum Inquiry, 33*(2), 139–188.
Scottish Executive (2004). *A curriculum for excellence*. Edinburgh: Scottish Executive/Learning and Teaching Scotland.
Scottish Executive (2006). *Opening of new Holocaust exhibition*. http://www.scotland.gov.uk/News/Releases/2006/01/25165820
Scottish Government (2013). *Frequently asked questions*. http://www.scotland.gov.uk/topics/education/schools/faqs
Scottish Parliament (2000). *Standards in Scotland's Schools Act (2000)*. Edinburgh: The Stationery Office.
Scottish Parliament (2008, 5 June). *Minutes of chamber proceedings* (Vol. 2, No. 8, Session 3, Item 7). http://www.scottish.parliament.uk/parliamentarybusiness/16510.aspx
Shapiro, A., McDonald, B., & Johnston, A. (2014). Gathering the voices: Disseminating the message of the Holocaust for the digital generation by applying an interdisciplinary approach. *Social Sciences, 3*, 499–513. http://www.mdpi.com/2076-0760/3/3/499
Short, G., & Carrington, B. (1991). Unfair discrimination: Teaching the principles to children of primary school age. *Journal of Moral Education, 20*(2), 157–177.
Short, G., & Reed, C. (2004). *Issues in Holocaust education*. Hampshire: Ashgate.
Short, G., Supple, C., & Klinger, K. (1998). *The Holocaust in the school curriculum: A European perspective*. Strasbourg: Council of Europe.
Singh, D. (2007). *Our shared future: Final report of the Commission on Integration and Cohesion*. London: Commission on Integration and Cohesion.
The Scotsman (2011, 13 September). *Court protest as student found guilty of racism*. http://www.scotsman.com/news/scotland/top-stories/court-protest-as-student-found-guilty-of-racism-1-1847224
Totten, S. (1999). Should there be Holocaust education for K-4 students? The answer is no. *Social Studies and the Young Learner, 12*, 36–39.
Totten, S. (2000). Diminishing the complexity and horror of the Holocaust: Using simulations in an attempt to convey historical experience. *Social Education, 64*(3), 165–171.
UNESCO (2008). *UNESCO's plan of action*. Paris: UNESCO. http://www.unesco.org/new/en/social-and-human-sciences/themes/human-rights-based-approach/60th-anniversary-of-udhr/unescos-plan-of-action/

Part VII
To Know, to Remember, to Act

Failing to Learn from the Holocaust

Geoffrey Short

Introduction

A number of scholars, including Kinloch (2001), Kochan (1989), and Novick (1999), have cast doubt on whether the Holocaust contains any useful lessons. My own view is that we have much to learn from the Holocaust, particularly with regard to the nature of racism and the measures necessary to prevent genocide (Short 2003). Holocaust education can be said to fail insofar as these lessons are not learnt. It also fails if, for whatever reason, students learn inappropriate ones. In the course of this chapter I attempt to explain, with reference to empirical research, how such unsatisfactory outcomes can arise. I begin with the commonsense assumption that, other things being equal, students are more likely to learn useful lessons from the Holocaust the longer they are exposed to it. In a study conducted in the UK in the mid-1990s (Short 1995), I found that most teachers devoted between two and four hours to the subject with a substantial minority spending in excess of five hours. The time allotted included any preliminary activity undertaken as background to the history of the Jews in Europe between 1933 and 1945.

However, one respondent, teaching in a Catholic school, allowed a total of just 50 minutes, despite admitting that "an awful lot of our children are extremely antisemitic and this has to be countered by teachers looking at the Holocaust". Another objected to the government insisting that the Holocaust be taught to an age group that he considered too young. When asked how long he spent teaching the Holocaust, he said, "I don't teach it at all. I just tell them to read the section in the textbook". Superficiality of this kind is problematic, not just because of the missed opportunity to learn significant lessons, but because of the danger that students will, instead, imbibe the implicit and malign message that racism, even in its most

G. Short (✉)
School of Education, University of Hertfordshire, Hertfordshire AL10 9AB, UK
e-mail: G.A.Short2@herts.ac.uk

extreme form, is not something that need greatly concern them. In a replication of the study, which I conducted in Toronto (Short 2000a), teachers assigned an average of 5 hours to the Holocaust, although this figure again masked a wide variation.

Lessons Relating to the Nature of Racism

Arguably, the single most important lesson to extract from the Holocaust is that Nazism, in respect of its racial policies, is an unmitigated evil. If students are to regard it as such, they have to see the overwhelming majority of Jewish victims as wholly innocent of the charges laid against them. They may fail do so, however, partly because of what psychologists refer to as the just world theory: the belief that we all have a natural inclination to perceive the world as fundamentally fair (Lerner 1977). In regard to young children, Piaget (1932) suggested something similar with his notion of "immanent justice". If people suffer, we assume that they must have done something to deserve it. When learning about the Holocaust, students in the West are particularly likely to make this inference if they subscribe to antisemitic stereotypes, a strong possibility given their ubiquity in Christian or nominally Christian societies, and the fact that that they are absorbed at an early age (Allport 1954).

Taken together, the belief in an equitable world and acceptance of antisemitic stereotypes not only help to explain the Holocaust but also to justify it, for the Jews are seen as getting what they deserve. To lessen the chances of students interpreting the Holocaust in this way—as the triumph of good over evil—it is essential that before they commence work on the topic, teachers set out to explore and, if necessary, to challenge their pupils' perceptions of Jews and Jewish culture. Not to do so is to invite the failure of all subsequent teaching.

That said, it appears that teachers rarely carry out this critically important task. In the British study cited above, only 2 out of the 34 teachers in the sample actively investigated the way their pupils perceived Jews before teaching about the Holocaust. In neither case, though, was it clear whether they focused on religious as well as on secular myths. Some religious misconceptions, notably that the Jews killed Christ, can have lethal consequences. Others may be less harmful but, insofar as they suggest that Jews are an alien presence in the country, they lessen sympathy for them and thereby increase understanding for their persecutors. Rejection of "the other" as not legitimately belonging to the nation is the essence of what Barker (1981) terms "the new racism".

Many of the teachers said they did nothing to undermine any misconceptions either because their pupils had none, or because they were dealt with elsewhere in the curriculum, either in religious education (RE) or in personal and social education. The following comments are illustrative.

> We do not analyse any of the stereotypes before studying the Holocaust. I am not aware of any stereotypes. I would hope that with the work they do in RE, with visits to the synagogue etc., that's all been dispelled.

We have the advantage that virtually all our pupils come from respectable middle-class homes where such prejudices aren't likely to exist. I don't set out deliberately to remove any pre-set ideas because I assume they don't have them.

In Toronto the results were almost identical. None of the 23 teachers I interviewed examined their students' beliefs about Jews and Judaism before starting work on the Holocaust with a view to deconstructing them if need be. The reasons for non-intervention were familiar.

I've never run into those misconceptions... In my experience, the students here don't have any particularly strong feelings about Jews or any other ethnic group.

We really don't have to [explore their views on Judaism] because the Catholic church and its teaching right now see the Jews as the chosen people and their religion is deeply connected to ours.

The just world theory is not only relevant to perceptions of the Holocaust; it applies equally to the way Jewish suffering is seen throughout the ages. Awareness of this history is likely to reinforce students' tendency to assume that there is no smoke without fire and, for this reason, teachers should stress that the Jewish past is, in reality, far from a litany of unremitting torment. Whether or not they do so is currently unknown.

If we want students to reject antisemitism as morally repugnant, they have to learn more about the nature of racism in general than that it relies heavily on false or misleading stereotypes. In particular, they should know that racists rarely have a single target in their sights. As Gordon Allport (1954), the leading authority on the nature of prejudice put it, "One of the facts of which we are most certain is that people who reject one out-group will tend to reject other out-groups. If a person is anti-Jewish, he is likely to be anti-Catholic, anti-Negro, anti-any out-group" (p. 68). To get this point across, teachers need to address *the full range* of victims of Nazi persecution and do so in a non-tokenistic manner. In the British study, comparatively few teachers were asked if they talk about victims of the Nazis other than Jews. In every case they answered in the affirmative, but some admitted to doing so superficially. In Toronto, the entire sample was asked the question and a similar picture emerged. There were many references to "Gypsies", homosexuals, and Slavs, but only one teacher mentioned Germans with disabilities and none spoke about Jehovah's Witnesses.

Another lesson that students should learn about the nature of racism is that it does not arise in a vacuum. Its roots are deeply embedded in a culture and it thus poses a potential threat even when dormant. For students to understand this aspect of racism, teachers of the Holocaust ought to spend some time looking at the tradition of antisemitism in the western world and the role of Christianity in perpetuating it. More than half the British sample, however, either made no reference to the historical background or covered it quite inadequately. One teacher, when asked how long he spent discussing the history of antisemitism said, "almost [no time] at all. It doesn't figure on the course", whilst another admitted to spending "about five minutes". Although many stated that they would mention that antisemitism was not just a 20th-century phenomenon, they nonetheless tended to restrict discussion of its form and development to Nazi Germany. They often insisted that this was not a matter of choice, but rather the result of time constraints. The data from Toronto were similar. Nearly half the sample said they just "touch[ed] on the role of the Church" and most of the others did nothing. The reasons were varied. One teacher cited the need to prioritise: "I don't have time to do that. If there's one thing I have to cut back on it's that". Another attributed it to the religious ethos of the school: "It's difficult being in a Catholic school to make the association". For a couple of teachers the problem was one of ignorance, not of church teachings, but of Jewish history. To compound this relative neglect, none of the textbooks used in the schools made any mention of the historic link between the Church and antisemitism.

Examining the link is important not just to illustrate a critical feature of racism, but to highlight the distinctive nature of antisemitism. The late Lucy Dawidowicz (1992) was among the first to argue that the specificity of antisemitism was often lost when students learnt about the Holocaust because the latter was seen only in terms of racism or prejudice. When I questioned British teachers about the advantages of teaching the Holocaust (Short 1995), the most frequent response (given by 20 out of the 34 teachers) was the need to alert students to the dangers of racism. Not a single teacher suggested its value in helping students understand the specific nature of antisemitism. Indeed, one teacher said, "we learn about the death camps, but we do it through the viewpoint of racism and not antisemitism" (pp. 172–173).

Dawidowicz wrote that "the trouble with this kind of universalization is that it... ignores the particular religious and historical roots that nurture specific prejudices" (p. 74). This is an important dimension of racism that students should know about. They should also know that racism, by its nature, is not restricted to any one group of people or to a particular place or time. While discussion of antisemitism over the centuries helps to drive this point home, reference should also be made to events immediately prior to the Holocaust, such as the Evian Conference of 1938 and the fruitless journey of the SS St. Louis, both of which showed that antisemitism *in other countries* was a major obstacle to the emigration of German and Austrian Jews. In neither my British nor my Canadian study were teachers asked if they mentioned these portentous events. However, in subsequent research (Short 2000b) that sought to discover what a group of 14- to 16-year-olds learnt about citizenship as a result of studying the Holocaust as history, I asked respondents to explain why the rest of the world was reluctant to accept Jewish refugees in large numbers. Significantly, only around a quarter of them attributed the reluctance to antisemitism. Their comments included the following:

> They might have felt that their jobs and economies would have been taken over by the Jews if they came in large numbers.
>
> Deep down they must have been scared that Hitler believed the Jews were responsible for ruining the economy and it was because of them that they lost the war and many countries wouldn't want to take the gamble just [in case] he was right and then suffer the consequences.

That just a minority spoke in these terms is a concern if Germans are not to be stereotyped as singularly lacking in humanitarianism and uniquely evil in respect of racism and antisemitism. In the study, one girl said spontaneously of her experience of learning about the Holocaust that it had made her "more against the Germans". This is precisely the sort of inappropriate lesson I alluded to earlier which can be said to constitute a failure of Holocaust education.

Finally, with regard to racism, students should understand that the Holocaust is not just an event of historical interest, but one that has a striking contemporary resonance. Stressing the latter is essential, partly for motivational reasons—students may be more likely to take the past seriously if they see it as connected in some way to their own lives—but mainly because far-right political parties retain a seductive appeal to those unfamiliar with where their underlying racist ideology can lead. The vast majority of teachers in the British study (Short 1995) did relate the Holocaust to current events, sometimes in respect to ethnic cleansing in the former Yugoslavia (usefully undermining the myth that crimes against humanity only happen when Germans are involved), but more often in respect of a resurgent racism across Europe. One respondent observed that,

> When you start talking about Hitler and the Nazis, the low-ability children say oh, is it like the National Front? I say yes and we talk about that and the rise of neo-Nazis in Germany and elsewhere in Europe and the fact that foreigners often get blamed for a country's problems. At this point the children sometimes express their own racist views about immigrants coming over and taking our jobs and I try to question that.

In my Canadian study, the majority of teachers drew their students' attention to atrocities committed in Rwanda as well as in the former Yugoslavia, but comparatively few referred to what was happening in Canada itself. Textbooks too, tended to eschew discussion of present-day racism in the country.

Lessons Unrelated to the Nature of Racism

Important lessons derive from the Holocaust independently of those relating to the nature of racism. They include the realisation that ordinary people are not necessarily reduced to the role of impotent bystanders in the face of evil. This lesson can be taught or inferred in the context of those who rescued Jews. I have in mind the well-known examples of Miep Gies, who cared for the Frank family and others in Amsterdam, and the Danish fishermen, who, in September 1943, ferried most of their nation's Jewish community to safety in neutral Sweden. However, when teachers in the UK and Canada were asked if they talk to their students about rescuers, the topic seemed to have a low priority. In Britain, Oskar Schindler was often the only one mentioned by name, while in Canada barely a handful of respondents referred to Miep Gies and just a couple mentioned the people of Denmark (Short 1995, 2000a).

There are other lessons unrelated to racism that might prove valuable in preventing genocide and which we could reasonably expect students to learn The first concerns the role of commemoration and particularly the need for schools to teach and explain the Holocaust to future generations. This need arises from the suspicion that Hitler was prompted to give vent to his apocalyptic fantasies by a belief that the international community had forgotten about an earlier attempt at genocide. In a speech delivered to high-ranking army officers on the eve of Germany's invasion of Poland, he is reputed to have said:

> Ghengis Khan had millions of women and men killed by his own will and with a gay heart. History sees in him only a great state builder... and I have sent to the east... my "Death's Head Units", with the order to kill without mercy men, women and children of Polish race or language. Only in such a way will we win the Lebensraum that we need. Who, after all, talks nowadays of the extermination of the Armenians? (cited in Fein 1979, p. 4)

The notorious final sentence of this quotation suggests that a *sine qua non* of reducing the chances of a second Holocaust (or its equivalent) is that the subject be taught in schools. George Santayana (1905) might have overstated the case when he wrote that those who do not remember the past are condemned to repeat it, but there is surely a greater probability of a catastrophe recurring if it is subsequently forgotten. Certainly, Holocaust deniers appear to be in no doubt that public awareness of the Nazis' extermination policy is detrimental to their electoral prospects (Dalrymple 1992).

Reflecting on the Holocaust should also enable students to appreciate that the threat of genocide diminishes if powerful organisations such as the church condemn the persecution of potential victims. After the Nazis came to power, both Protestant and Catholic churches in Germany were remiss in this respect, although they were quite prepared to criticise the government openly on other matters. I refer to the 1941 campaign mounted by Count von Galen, Bishop of Münster, against the euthanasia programme and to the less well known opposition to the removal of crucifixes from Bavarian schools. Possibly fearing the consequences for his own church, the Pope condemned Nazi persecution, but did not mention the Jews by name and he said nothing at all when, in the autumn of 1943, the Jews of Rome were being deported.

We might also expect students who are familiar with the Holocaust to question whether overtly racist political parties have any role in a democracy, whether religious traditions other than Christianity might contain the seeds of hatred, and whether the Westphalia doctrine, whereby one country is denied the right to interfere in the internal affairs of another, ought to govern the conduct of international relations.

Learning from Genocide?

I turn now to a study I conducted in Britain (Short 2005) that focused explicitly on whether lessons unrelated to racism are, in fact, learnt by students participating in a Holocaust education programme. The research was undertaken in 2004 and originated in a week-long event organised by the Jewish community of an outer London borough to mark that year's Holocaust Memorial Day (HMD), a national commemoration that takes place each year on 27 January, the anniversary of the liberation of Auschwitz. In 2004, the theme for HMD was "Lessons learned; lessons still to be learned". Students from eight secondary schools in the borough attended one of two local synagogues for half a day. They were given an introductory talk on the Holocaust, heard a survivor speak, and watched a video about the Rwandan genocide before splitting into small groups to reflect on what they had learnt. Discussion within the groups centred around the issue of intervention, as it affects both the politics of international relations and the conduct of individual lives.

The sample comprised 16 boys and 15 girls drawn from four of the schools involved, each having a culturally diverse catchment area. The students from one school (for Catholic girls) were aged 14–15; the others were a year older. All of them had previously engaged with the Holocaust. The questions they were asked included the following:

Do you think there are any lessons to be learned from the Holocaust?

Does the Holocaust have any lessons for (a) the international community; (b) for British society (including schools); (c) for your religion or for others; (d) for you as an individual?

Has the Holocaust affected your daily life in any way?

Do you think the Holocaust will affect your life as an adult?

The data analysis indicated that for many students, the benefits of participating in the day were largely restricted to developing their knowledge of the Holocaust and acquainting themselves with what had happened in Rwanda. I do not wish to imply that furthering their education in this way was anything other than worthwhile, but their greater familiarity with the genocides should not be allowed to obscure the fact that, overall, the students failed to learn lessons from the Holocaust and the events leading up to it.

It is not known whether teachers discussed these lessons with their students prior to the visit. The organisers of the day made plans for a discussion but only, as I have pointed out, in the context of intervention. That some important lessons of the Holocaust were mentioned by no more than a handful of students, while others were not mentioned at all, suggests that, for the most part, they were overlooked by both teachers and organisers. If this is so, it might well reflect a general lack of awareness in the country of the value of Holocaust education, for the textbooks and other instructional materials currently available there tend to contain little guidance on lessons. Typifying the dearth is the popular teaching pack *Lessons of the Holocaust* jointly produced in 1997 by the Spiro Institute and the Holocaust Educational Trust

(SI and HET 1997). Despite the title, the section of the pack dealing with how students might benefit from reflecting on the Holocaust is limited to rather trite observations such as the following:

> The Holocaust reminds us that hatred of others who are different from ourselves and whom we place beyond the pale of humanity can lead only to group violence and atrocity. It tells us that any society, however culturally, scientifically, and technically advanced, can become totally criminal once it loses the ability and the will to distinguish between right and wrong. (p. 22)

It was clear from the study that *some* students were able to distil meaningful lessons from what they had been taught. For example, there was a recognition of the need for bodies such as the United Nations to assume a more proactive and interventionist role in international relations, for the church to condemn serious wrongdoing, and for schools to promote tolerance. When asked whether they thought the Holocaust held any lessons for themselves, one girl commented on the morality of bystander behaviour. For her, the lesson was "not to ignore situations like they did in the Holocaust. We shouldn't just ignore it when people are in trouble". Likewise, a single student referred to the equally important value of thinking for oneself: "Just because someone says that something is right, it doesn't mean that it is. I need to think for myself instead of following other people".

Nearly two thirds of the sample maintained that studying the Holocaust had had no discernible impact on their daily lives. The rest had been affected in diverse ways. Two of the boys had become less inclined to tell antisemitic jokes while a couple of girls were generally less willing to stereotype. As to whether knowledge of the Holocaust would affect their lives as adults, the largest response category, once again, was students who said that it probably would not. A few, however, believed that as adults they would make a point of talking about the Holocaust, especially to their own children.

The fact that these lessons were referred to by so few students suggests that the majority cannot be relied upon to work them out for themselves. On the contrary, it seems that such learning requires an explicit focus. This conclusion is reinforced by the finding that some critical lessons were not alluded to by any of the students. There was no mention, for example, of the implications that the Holocaust might have for domestic politics on issues such as free speech or the proscription of overtly racist organisations. Nor was there any comment on lessons related to the key role played by Christian antisemitism in preparing the groundwork for the Holocaust. Consequently, no student pointed out that social cohesion might be fostered (and the likelihood of genocide lessened) by different faith communities examining their own sacred texts and liturgy in search of offensive references to "the other".

As well as showing that lessons of the Holocaust will not emerge automatically as students assimilate new knowledge, the study indicated that organised events taking place outside the classroom will not necessarily facilitate the process despite the provision of ostensibly relevant activities such as listening to a survivor. It is hard to escape the conclusion that students need help not just in learning about the Holocaust, but also in learning from it. To this end, teachers might usefully consult the widely acclaimed American Holocaust education programme Facing History and Ourselves, renowned both for its comprehensive historical analysis and its commitment to explicating the lessons of the Holocaust (Shoemaker 2003).

Sins of Commission

Thus far, I have been principally concerned with students' inability to learn lessons from the Holocaust as a result of teachers and textbooks neglecting particular issues. I now want to consider the danger of students learning inappropriate lessons as a result of teachers, textbooks, and other resources providing a misleading account of the Holocaust. In other words, I want to turn from the sins of omission to those of commission.

There is clearly greater scope for distorting students' understanding of the Holocaust in countries where the subject is taught not just in history, but also in religious education. In the UK, teachers have discretion as to whether to include the Holocaust in the RE syllabus, but the obvious problem in deciding to do so is the implicit message that the Nazi persecution of the Jews was essentially an expression of religious oppression. In addition to this fundamental misconception, some RE teachers have been shown to tackle the Holocaust in a way that gives the impression that all the victims were committed to Judaism. In a study that I carried out in the London area several years ago (Short 2001), one teacher, when asked how she introduced the subject to 13- and 14-year-olds, said:

> It begins with a study of the use of symbols in religions and it widens into how those symbols might be used in a religious [context] to show that someone belongs to a faith community. This leads to the area of prejudice, that sometimes belonging to a faith community might mean that you suffer from the prejudice of others and, as one example of this, we look at the story of Anne Frank and of the experience of the Jews in the Holocaust.

Another teacher, responding to a question on the role of religious education in respect of the Holocaust, insisted that:

> What we want to do in RE is inform students in terms of giving them knowledge and understanding about what religion is. We also want to look at what religious belief is and what religious experience actually means to people. So, by dealing with an issue like the Holocaust, what we're looking at is the experience that people had *which was a direct result of being a particular member of a religion*. (emphasis added)

As part of the study, I examined seven textbooks used by the RE teachers. They too tended to depict Jews as necessarily religious. One text actually begins its coverage by stating that "this section tells you about how Jews have been punished for their faith", while another maintains that "Jews are brought together by their belief in God..." In fact, only one of the seven texts recognised that Jews are an ethnic group, pointing out that "some [of them] are religious; many are not". Incidentally, the misconception that Jews are a monolithic entity loyal to the precepts of Judaism is also to be found in works of fiction recommended for young adolescents learning about the Holocaust (Goldberg 1996). For example, in Hans Peter Richter's (1987) popular novella, *Friedrich*, all the Jewish characters are observant. Readers learn about the preparations for a Friday night (Sabbath) meal and are given a detailed description of Friedrich's bar mitzvah. They also encounter a doctor described as "a middle-aged man in a dark suit" wearing a skullcap.

Holocaust museums cannot be relied upon to correct this misconception. At Beth Shalom, the first such museum in Britain, and one that attracts many school parties, a gallery dedicated to the history of the Jews contains a brief reference to Judaism. The importance of the Torah and Talmud is highlighted together with Judaism's "emphasis on moral values and social justice [which] have provided a basis for others to emulate". However, visitors are also told that "the lighting of the Shabbat [Sabbath] candles is very special to Jews wherever they may be". This statement is not only far from the truth, but unfortunate, in that it once again encourages a perception of Jews as necessarily committed, in some degree, to Judaism.

History textbooks too can be guilty of sins of commission. As part of my research into British teachers' attitudes and practices (Short 1995), I subjected seven books in widespread use at the time to a content analysis. Among other things, I found that a couple could be faulted for reinforcing antisemitic stereotypes, or at least for presenting misinformation. The most widely used, for instance, states that "prejudice against the Jews grew during the economic depression.... Many Germans were poor and unemployed and wanted someone to blame. They turned on the Jews, many of whom were rich..." Now this assertion, whilst not contrary to fact, hardly gives an accurate account of the state of German Jewry at the time, for it makes no mention of the *Ostjuden*: the Jews from eastern Europe who, according to Landau (1992, p. 92), "frequently fell victim to unemployment and economic distress". Another book claims that "Hitler's attempt to exterminate a race of people was only discovered once the Allies entered Germany and Poland". This is a regrettable statement, not only because it is historically incorrect, but because, by concealing the fact that the British and American governments knew what was going on from the middle of 1942, it effectively denies students an opportunity to assess the Allies' culpability for the extent of the devastation wrought by the Holocaust. Other instances of misleading text include the tendency for some books to talk about Jews *and* Germans, implying that Jews were an alien presence in the country rather than fully fledged citizens (as was the case prior to 1935) whose human rights were subsequently violated by their compatriots. There is also the matter of *Kristallnacht* (the night of broken glass), referred to in all seven books in the context of the shooting in Paris of the German diplomat, Ernst vom Rath. However, all but one of the books provide a misleading narrative in that they fail to explain why the diplomat was shot— essential information if students are not to be left with the impression that *Kristallnacht* was a justified response to an unprovoked attack.

Intellectual Immaturity as an Explanation of Failure to Learn from the Holocaust

The reasons discussed so far to explain why students might not learn from the Holocaust relate to the allocation of insufficient time, the provision of inadequate or misleading content, the neglect by teachers of critical subject matter, and their failure to engage with students' perceptions of Jews and Jewish culture before embarking on the Holocaust. In this penultimate section of the chapter I want to consider another factor, that of age-appropriateness, for I contend that Holocaust education can also fail if it is delivered to students who, because of their age, are unlikely to possess the conceptual sophistication necessary to understand its essence. The issue is not just a theoretical one, for some Holocaust curricula (such as that of the American state of New Jersey) begin in kindergarten (Sepinwall 1999), and the subject is not infrequently taught in primary or elementary schools. In Scotland, for example, Maitles and Cowan (1999) looked at how teachers of 9- and 10-year-olds tackled the Holocaust. Their overall assessment was positive, but they did not interview any of the pupils and so it is not possible to ascertain, with any degree of confidence, what they learnt and how, if at all, they might have benefited from their experience.

There has long been a school of thought within developmental psychology that emphasises the intellectual limitations of young children. It is most often associated with the work of Jean Piaget, yet, over the past 30 years or so, his account of cognitive development has often been tested and found wanting (e.g., Donaldson 1978) and the more optimistic views of the Russian psychologist, Lev Vygotsky, on the value of adult instruction, are now in vogue. Teachers have consequently been urged to raise their expectations of children's abilities in all areas of the curriculum and it would seem that some Holocaust educators have been affected by the prevailing mood. However, this newfound confidence in young children's intellectual reach is not supported by research that is relevant to Holocaust education. Specifically, children aged 8 and 9 have been shown to possess no real concept of a Jew (Short 1991). The findings come from a study based on a class of 28 children (7 girls and 21 boys) all of whom attended a non-denominational and virtually "all-white" school adjacent to a substantial Jewish community in southeast England. At an early stage in the interview the children were asked if they had ever heard the word "Jew" or "Jewish". Among those answering in the affirmative, some clearly had no idea what either word referred to.

Claire:	(8 years, 6 months) I think so, once. I heard someone say it.
Michael:	(8:7) Yes. Is it a language?
Pamela:	(9:1) Yes. In a book I think. Was Jews a name?
Paul:	(8:6) I heard it in Assembly once.
Interviewer:	Can you remember what was said?
Paul:	No.

Those who did possess a rudimentary concept of a Jew still demonstrated a fair amount of confusion. A number of them, for instance, saw Jews as necessarily alien and viewed the notion of a British Jew as incomprehensible.

Interviewer: Have you ever heard the word "Jewish"?
Peter: (9:2) Yes.
Interviewer: What have you heard?
Peter: People from Jerusalem. They're Jewish.
Interviewer: So, if you are born in England, can you be Jewish?
Peter: Yes, if you go to Jerusalem for a long time.

Thinking along similar lines, Matthew (9:2) maintained that we do have Jewish people in England because "they could come here for a holiday". Asked if it was possible for someone Jewish to be born in England, he said it was not.

It would appear from these comments that many 8- and 9-year-olds have no concept, or virtually no concept, of a Jew. One wonders, therefore, what the children in Maitles and Cowan's study learnt from their lessons on the Holocaust, for they were only a year older. The same question arises in relation to some of the resources used to teach the Holocaust to young children such as the well-known teaching pack produced by the Anne Frank Educational Trust (AFET 1996). Most of its suggested activities are directed at teachers of 7- to 11-year-olds and have the twin purpose of providing information about Anne's life and assisting children to become more tolerant and more appreciative of the benefits of living in a democratic society. I will focus on the one activity recommended for 5- to 7-year-olds. It is suggested that schools hold an assembly for children in this age group with the aim of introducing them "to Anne Frank as someone who was special and to explore and celebrate friendship as a special relationship". A story is to be read to the children which starts as follows:

There once lived a girl called Anne Frank. She was born in the city of Frankfurt in Germany on 12 June, 1929. In that country there were people who hated Jews. They were called Nazis. Four years after Anne Frank was born, the Nazis and their leader Adolf Hitler became the most powerful people in the land. Anne Frank and her family were Jews and so they knew that soon their lives would be in danger. They moved to another country called Holland where they could feel safer.

In view of the evidence indicating that 8- and 9-year-olds have almost no conception of a Jew, one wonders what 5- and 6-year-olds will make of this story. One wonders too, how a teacher would respond if a child, quite reasonably, were to ask, "What is a Jew and why did the Nazis not like them?" There can be no meaningful engagement with the Holocaust if students lack the concepts necessary to understand it.

Concluding Thoughts

In this chapter I have outlined some of the ways in which Holocaust education can be said to fail. Initially, I noted the importance of the time factor, arguing that other things being equal, there is likely to be a direct correlation between the benefits students derive from engaging with the Holocaust and the length of time schools devote to it. After considering a range of lessons that should be learnt, particularly in respect of racism and the reasons why they might not be, I focused on the learning of inappropriate lessons—the sins of commission. Finally, I looked at why children in primary or elementary school are unlikely to gain much from studying the Holocaust. However, in seeking a full explanation of students' failure to learn from the Holocaust, it may be necessary to move beyond the issues I have examined thus far. For example, the fact that teachers in more or less the same situation have been shown to vary widely in the amount of time they assign to the Holocaust suggests the importance of teachers' personal commitment in determining what is learnt from the subject. If this speculation is well-founded, timetabling the Holocaust (in secondary schools) across a range of subjects, rather than just in history, might help to obviate the problem. As I pointed out earlier, it is also possible that teachers fail to address certain lessons simply because they are unaware of them. If this is the case, the answer would appear to lie in better teacher training, an aspect of Holocaust education that has been ignored for too long.

References

AFET [Anne Frank Educational Trust] (1996). *Anne Frank*. London: AFET.
Allport, G. W. (1954). *The nature of prejudice*. Cambridge, MA: Addison-Wesley.
Barker, M. (1981). *The new racism*. London: Junction Books.
Dalrymple, J. (1992). Holocaust lies of the new Nazis. *British Journal of Holocaust Education, 1*, 202–212.
Dawidowicz, L. (1992). How they teach the Holocaust. In L. Dawidowicz (Ed.), *What's the use of Jewish history?* New York: Shocken Books.
Donaldson, M. (1978). *Children's minds*. Glasgow: Fontana/Collins.
Fein, H. (1979). *Accounting for genocide: National responses and Jewish victimization during the Holocaust*. London: Free Press.
Goldberg, M. (1996). Children's autobiographies and diaries of the Holocaust. *Teaching History, 83*, 8–12.
Kinloch, N. (2001). Parallel catastrophes? Uniqueness, redemption and the Shoah. *Teaching History, 104*, 8–14.
Kochan, L. (1989, 22 December). Life over death. *Jewish Chronicle*, p. 25.
Landau, R. (1992). *The Nazi Holocaust*. London: I. B. Taurus.
Lerner, M. J. (1977). The justice motive: Some hypotheses as to its origins and forms. *Journal of Personality, 45*, 1–52.
Maitles, H., & Cowan, P. (1999). Teaching the Holocaust in primary schools in Scotland: Modes, methodology and content. *Educational Review, 51*(3), 263–272.
Novick, P. (1999). *The Holocaust in American life*. New York: Houghton Mifflin.
Piaget, J. (1932). *The moral judgment of the child*. London: Routledge and Kegan Paul.

Richter, H. P. (1987). *Friedrich*. New York: Puffin Books.
Santayana, G. (1905). *The life of reason* (Vol. 1). New York: Charles Scribner's Sons.
Sepinwall, H. (1999). Incorporating Holocaust education into K–4 curriculum and teaching in the United States. *Social Studies and the Young Learner, 10*, 5–8.
Shoemaker, R. (2003). Teaching the Holocaust in America's schools: Some considerations for teachers. *Intercultural Education, 14*(2), 191–200.
Short, G. (1991). Teaching the Holocaust: Some reflections on a problematic area. *British Journal of Religious Education, 14*(1), 28–34.
Short, G. (1995). The Holocaust in the national curriculum: A survey of teachers' attitudes and practices. *The Journal of Holocaust Education, 4*(2), 167–188.
Short, G. (2000a). Holocaust education in Ontario high schools: An antidote to racism? *Cambridge Journal of Education, 30*(2), 291–306.
Short, G. (2000b). Holocaust education and citizenship: A view from the United Kingdom. In M. Leicester, C. Modgil, & S. Modgil (Eds.), *Politics, education and citizenship*. London: Falmer Press.
Short, G. (2001). Confronting the Holocaust in religious education. *Journal of Beliefs and Values, 22*(1), 41–54.
Short, G. (2003). Lessons of the Holocaust: A response to the critics. *Educational Review, 55*(3), 277–287.
Short, G. (2005). Learning from genocide? A study in the failure of Holocaust Education. *Intercultural Education, 16*(4), 367–380.
SI & HET [Spiro Institute & Holocaust Educational Trust] (1997). *Lessons of the Holocaust*. London: SI & HET.

Towards a New Theory of Holocaust Remembrance in Germany: Education, Preventing Antisemitism, and Advancing Human Rights

Reinhold Boschki, Bettina Reichmann, and Wilhelm Schwendemann

Introduction

In Germany today, very few people who were directly involved in the National Socialism (NS) system are still alive. Those still living may be killers, perpetrators, decision makers, members of the NS party, helpers, bystanders, spectators, and frenetic or silent supporters. Even members of the second generation (those who were children at the end of World War II), have already retired. Society is run by the third and fourth generation after the Shoah. In this situation, it is clear that Holocaust remembrance is undergoing a radical shift. The generations now living and acting cannot be blamed for what happened in the past and what was carried out by their ancestors. As Elie Wiesel (1997, p. 12) has put it, "The children of killers are not killers but children".

The issue that has to be raised today is that of *responsibility*. Germans today are *responsible* for the remembrance of the Holocaust, and for preserving the memory of defamation, discrimination, exclusion, concentration, deportation, and murder of each single Jewish family and individual who perished or suffered, as well as those of other minorities. For this reason, Holocaust education is one of the most valuable

---

R. Boschki (✉)
Seminar für Religionspädagogik, religiöse Erwachsenenbildung und Homiletik,
Universität Bonn, Am Hof 1, 53113 Bonn, Germany
e-mail: reinhold.boschki@uni-bonn.de

B. Reichmann
Institut für Katholische Theologie, Universität Koblenz · Landau,
Bürgerstraße 23, 76829 Landau, Germany
e-mail: reichmann@uni-landau.de

W. Schwendemann
Evangelische Hochschule Freiburg, Buggingerstr. 38, 79114 Freiburg, Germany
e-mail: schwendemann@eh-freiburg.de

duties of the educational system on all levels: primary schools, high schools, professional training, universities, adult education, and civic education (Boschki et al. 2010). People living in Germany, be they natives or migrants, ask about what happened on the territory and in the history of this country because past events and their impact are always part of the social identity of groups, be it positive or negative. None of the democratic forces in Germany would ever question that this task is a mandatory part of public and political lives (e.g., Holocaust Remembrance Day), and also of school curricula. Remembrance of mass murder of European Jews by the hands of the German Nazis is part of the democratic culture in this country.

The first and most important reason to engage in remembrance of a historical catastrophe is respect for the victims. Those who have been victimised in the past by totalitarian regimes have the fundamental human right to be remembered by democratic systems today and in the future. Democracy is always the successor of totalitarianism. For this reason remembering the victims is a democratic act. At the same time, remembrance implies a special function or duty: to never forget what happened in the past helps us to never repeat it in the present and future.

Empirical Research on Antisemitism in Germany Today

Recent studies on the growing antisemitic tendencies in Germany show that antisemitism has not disappeared with the end of the Holocaust; Rosenfeld (2013) describes this in a global perspective. Shockingly, it is returning in forms that are not unimportant. Two incidents from 2012 illustrate this tendency. First, a Berlin rabbi was attacked and injured by neo-Nazis because he wore his *kippah*, the traditional religious head cover, in public. Second, a German court decided to outlaw the circumcision of boys, which is rooted in religious traditions for both Jews and Muslims; the decision caused an intense public debate in the press and media on religious practices. These emotional discussions brought to the surface many antisemitic feelings and attitudes within the German population. For example, circumcision was denounced as an "archaic ritual" (Heil and Kramer 2012, p. 225) that would emphasise the otherness and strangeness of Jews as well as Muslims.

Incidents like these give rise to pressing questions: Has Germany not learned the lessons of the Nazi past? Has Holocaust education failed? Does the teaching of history in schools have little or no effect on the democratic vision and attitude of learners? Is Germany in danger of forgetting what happened and repeating the faults of the past?

The special focus of the following empirical insights is the life-world of concrete persons today. Life-world, a philosophical term created by Edmund Husserl and reformulated in social-empirical terms by Alfred Schütz, means the subjective interpretation of life and world by concrete individuals, the subjective theories facing their own experiences, or the meaning they give to their experiences (Srubar and Vaitkus 2003). For this reason life-world is always a form of interpretation and mental construction of world and reality, a private and personal way of conceptualising one's biography, society, social life, and personal and social experiences. It is clear that the concept is deeply connected with both the personal identity of individuals and the social conditions of society, meaning the social belonging and identification with a special social, ethnic, cultural, or religious group.

What is the life-world of people, especially of young people, in Germany today concerning the issue of remembrance of the Holocaust and antisemitism? The European Forum on Antisemitism (AJC 2012) defines antisemitism as "a certain perception of Jews, which may be expressed as hatred toward Jews. Rhetorical and physical manifestations of antisemitism are directed toward Jewish or non-Jewish individuals and/or their property, toward Jewish community institutions and religious facilities". Whereas various phenomena of antisemitism today seem like an update of old and classical forms of hate against the Jews as described in the definition above, the social shape of antisemitism has changed in recent decades. Still we find group-focused antisemitism, religious, racist, and nationalistic forms, and also new forms like "antisemitism without Jews" (prejudices by people who have never met a single Jew), anti-Zionism (directed against the state of Israel), and/or the so called "secondary antisemitism". According to Knothe (2009, p. 7), characteristics of secondary antisemitic thinking are the tendencies to refuse the remembrance of the Holocaust, to understand the world in a dualistic way, to resort to world conspiracy theories, and to personalise the structures of power in a capitalist economic system, especially in relation to the Holocaust perpetrators and exchange of victims.

The social secondary antisemitism can enter into dialogue with, for example, the criticism of transnational financial markets, in the political perception of the United States and Israel and in the uncritical solidarity with some Islamist-oriented movements in the European civil societies. According to Knothe, secondary antisemitism belongs to pragmatic antisemitism and has replaced manifest antisemitism in certain parts of the population. Below, we consider the connection between antisemitism and new research into what Heitmeyer (2012) calls "group-focused enmity".

In December 2011, an independent group of researchers published a government-funded report on antisemitism in Germany. It is an official report of the German Ministry of the Interior (BdI 2011), but it was written by independent university professors and members of research institutes such as the Institute for Antisemitism Research at the University of Berlin. In this report, we get a clear picture of the situation concerning anti-Jewish attitudes in the country that created the Holocaust. The rates of antisemitic attitudes have decreased in the last few decades, although empirically the rates fluctuate quite a bit (p. 58). According to the study, today, approximately 20% of the German population holds antisemitic attitudes; that is, every fifth person has an implicit, latent, or explicit tendency toward antisemitic prejudices or behaviour.

The report (p. 11) lists various forms of antisemitism that can be evaluated empirically:

- latent or implicit negative attitudes that are not expressed publicly, i.e., resentments, stereotypes, or prejudices carried along in privacy;

- publicly verbalised dislike and defamation of Jews (e.g., in ascription of negative characteristics to Jews);
- political demands to discriminate against Jews;
- acts of discrimination;
- violence against Jews and Jewish institutions;
- the persistence of secondary antisemitism that arose from either defending against blame, refusing to discuss NS, or trying to relieve itself through anti-Zionist agitation;
- a transnational "European" antisemitism, which operates mainly in the media (Internet);
- the traditional hatred of Jews, among others, through migrants from Eastern Europe;
- a Muslim antisemitism, among some Muslims in Germany; and
- an extended antisemitism of the radical right-wing youth scenes, radical right-wing music, groups, and parties.

In addition to this list, Stender (2010, p. 26ff) provides more.

In German society today, we find all of these forms of antisemitism (BdI 2011, p. 14ff), but fortunately not all at the same level of intensity. The spread of antisemitic attitudes in the extreme-right youth culture is alarming (Bergich and Raabe 2010). We have too many right- wing rock music bands, concerts, and CDs available in certain scenes.

Today, we also have right-wing and anti-Jewish internet activities in the German language. Furthermore, we have classical forms of antisemitism, as well as new forms, such as anti-Zionist and anti-Israel attitudes that are not only located within the right-wing scene but also popular in left-wing and even mainstream parties.

Concerning the young generation, a recent found that "the truth is that antisemitism subsists in many of the young people" (Scherr and Schäuble 2007, p. 4). However, it is just as important to note that "the social constellations of antisemitism are changing" (Stender 2010, p. 7). Since the 1960s, a new form of antisemitism has developed in Germany, which represents a problematic way of overcoming the past. The defense against German guilt, the need for normalisation, and the unspoken persistence of broad anti-Jewish sentiments in everyday life have generated a latent, secondary antisemitism. At the beginning of the 21st century, the form of antisemitism changed again, a change which must be understood in the context of social transformation. As lifestyles become transnationalised, that trend increases the risk of secondary antisemitism. The global process of modernisation leads to a sense of crisis among the losers of modernisation. This is how a "European antisemitism" was born (Bergmann 2008, 2009). In Germany, the political opportunities to articulate antisemitism have increased significantly (Bergmann 2006, p. 35). It is not legitimate to see this tendency as only a matter of a "Muslim antisemitism", resulting from the increasing presence of Islam in Europe and in Germany. "In fact", Stender (2010) holds, "Antisemitism does not come from without but from within the society, in all its forms" (p. 26).

Almost 20% of the German population agreed to the statement that "Jews have too much influence in Germany", agreeing, for example, that "they have too much power in the business world" or "in international financial markets" (BdI 2011, p. 55). In another study on right-wing extremism in Germany, 25% of the total population agreed partly with the statement that "the influence of the Jews is still too high today", while another 17% largely agreed to it (Decker et al. 2010, p. 73). Meanwhile 21% of those respondents partly believed and another 15% largely believed that the Jews use "dirty tricks" to achieve their goals. Compared with other European countries Germany finds itself in a middle position on these issues. An international survey on people who agree to the sentence "Jews have too much power in our country" shows the following figures, as reported by BdI (2011, p. 63). In Europe as a whole, 24.5% agreed. Moving from highest to lowest, the percentages for various countries are as follows: Hungary 69.2%, Poland 49.9%, Italy 21.2%, Portugal 19.9%, Germany 19.6%, Great Britain 13.9%, and the Netherlands 5.6%.

An important point for our topic of Holocaust remembrance is the fact that antisemitism is not only found in right-wing activities or at the borders of society. The 2011 report (pp 66 ff) makes it crystal clear that antisemitic attitudes are present in political discourses, in the media, in culture, and in everyday life, for example in family gatherings, on school yards, in peer group conversations, in youth clubs, restaurants, at football and soccer events, in Internet blogs, social networks and emails, and even in churches and mosques within their parish meeting centres. "Negative stereotypes about Jews are deeply rooted in the history and culture of the so called Christian Occident" (p. 70). These stereotypes are passed down from generation to generation even in today's democratic societies.

We could say, with Radvan (2010, p. 9) that "Antisemitism is not an abstract phenomenon, but a social practice". This practice is reflected in everyday communication among young people. Most students know the negative expression "You Jew!" and what it means: a sneaky, lying, greedy fellow student, lacking in solidarity (Stender 2010, p. 19). Young people in Germany are affected with antisemitic ideology or at least stereotypes and prejudices against Jews, although many of them have never personally met Jews. The rates among the younger generations are lower than the rest of the population, but large differences are related to the level of education: lower levels of education or training correlate with higher rates of antisemitism (Bergmann 2011, p. 8).

Let us make one more point: Antisemitic attitudes are still present in Christian settings and the "life world" of members of churches. Alongside the general antisemitism report, the German Ministry of the Interior published two expert reports on antisemitism in both the Roman-Catholic and Protestant Churches in Germany (Blum 2011; Scherr 2011; see also BdI 2011, pp. 92–94). The disturbing finding of these studies is that Christians do not differ from the rest of the population concerning antisemitic attitudes and behaviour; Christian religiosity does not necessarily protect against these prejudices. To see these statistics is alarming, almost 50 years after the proclamation of the Vatican II document *Nostra Aetate*, in which the Roman Catholic church fundamentally revisited its relation to Jews and Judaism and which rejected all forms of antisemitism. Similar statements were delivered by Protestant churches throughout the world. Obviously, Christian institutions have at least partially failed to educate people in these new understandings of Jews and Judaism in religious education settings, in preaching, and teaching.

The Broader Scope: Group-Focused Enmity

Other studies provide more empirical findings on the life-world of people in Germany today. First, as in all European countries, we find not only ideologies of antisemitism but also of Islamophobia, and in some cases even to a higher extent. Anti-Muslim attitudes, anti-immigrant attitudes, xenophobia, different forms of racism, sexism, and homophobia: these are all aspects of a common phenomenon that was investigated by the Institute of Interdisciplinary Research Group on Conflict and Violence (IIRGCV) at the University of Bielefeld. This research group conducted a long-term empirical study on intolerance, prejudice, and discrimination in Germany and Europe. It has just released the final results from a 10-year survey spanning 2002 to 2012 (Heitmeyer 2012). The group focused on antisemitism and its relationship to negative attitudes toward other minorities, whether they be ethnic, social, sexual, or religious groups.

The attitudes towards immigrants were particularly notable. Overall, 45.1% of respondents across Europe agreed with the statement "There are too many immigrants in our country". The rates for various other countries were as follows: Italy 62.5%, Great Britain 62.2%, Portugal 59.6%, Hungary 58.7%, Germany 50.0%, the Netherlands 46.0%, France 40.3%, and Poland, 27.1% (Zick et al. 2011, p. 54).

When considered in the context of the latest violence against immigrants in Germany, these figures are quite alarming. Over the last 10 years, the terror group called the National-Socialist Underground (NSU) killed ten immigrants in Germany. They operated underground and shot innocent immigrants from Turkey and other countries who had their own small businesses selling food or providing other services. One of the basic ideologies of the NSU was antisemitism and anti-immigrant attitudes "There are too many immigrants in our country".

In its study, the IIRGCV worked with a central research term it called "group-focused enmity" (Heitmeyer 2012); they say it "describes a generalised devaluation of out-groups. At its core is an ideology of unequal status" (Zick et al. 2011, p. 37). Group-focused enmity is a multifaceted phenomenon, they tell us, a syndrome of different elements that can be evaluated empirically. They continue:

> We speak of a syndrome of group-focused enmity in order to make it clear that prejudices directed towards different target groups are linked to one another and share the common core of an ideology of unequal status. Individuals who share this ideology look down upon out-groups regardless of these groups' specific identity. (p. 37)

Figure 1 shows some of the connected elements of this syndrome.

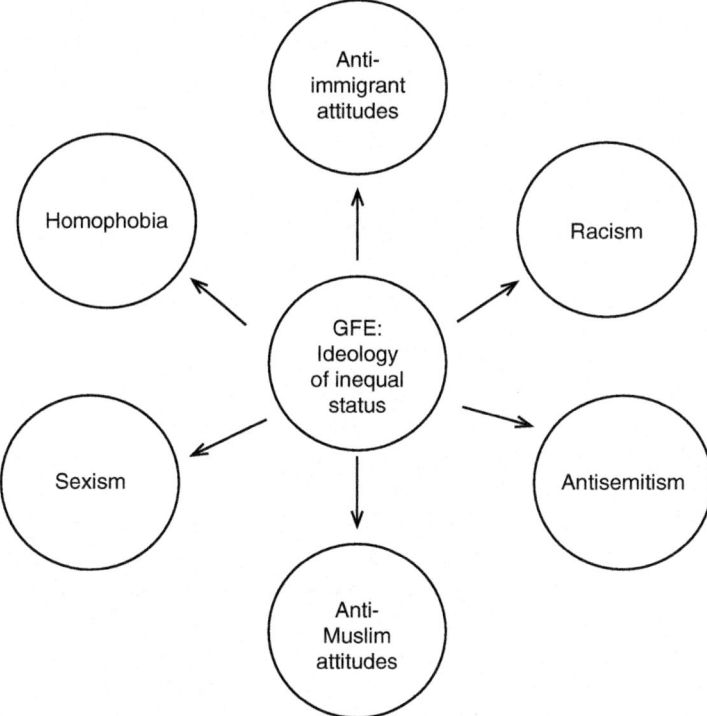

Fig. 1 Group-focused enmity: GFE
Source: Heitmeyer 2012, p. 69

All of these elements are significantly related to one another. That is, if someone has an antisemitic attitude, he or she also tends to be anti-Muslim and anti-immigrant as well (Zick et al. 2011, p. 70). Again, we have alarming results not only from Germany but also from other European countries. Group-focused enmity at the level of attitudes correlates with greater willingness to discriminate against minority groups and even to use violence against them (p. 122).

All of these findings call for intensified efforts on both the political and educational levels to set up programmes and concepts in order to prevent inhuman attitudes and behaviour.

Empirical Research on the Historical Consciousness of Young People

Coming back to our focus on Holocaust remembrance, we would like to introduce one last are of empirical research, that on so-called "historical consciousness", especially among young people. Historical consciousness means much more than knowing mere facts about history. Researchers can investigate people's knowledge

of facts using quantitative studies on knowledge concerning history, for example—
in our case in Germany—on the Nazi period. Disturbingly, such studies show a deep
lack of information and a small base of concrete knowledge (Silbermann and
Stoffers 2000; Zülsdorf-Kersting 2008, p. 83). Moreover, history lessons at school
are relatively ineffective in promoting students' long-term historical knowledge
(Zülsdorf-Kersting 2008, pp. 85, 467); one reason is that virtually all such teaching
is irrelevant to students' identity construction (pp. 113ff).

Against these trends, researchers in historical didactics speak of historical consciousness as a goal for educational efforts. According to Zülsdorf-Kersting (pp. 13–32), it can be defined as the ability to combine historical events with present challenges. A person who is conscious of historical terms can remember past events, know at least some important historical facts, and analyze the mechanisms behind historical events. At the same time he or she is able to interpret present events while keeping in mind the events of history. The competence to discover the presence of history within the presence of our time could be described as historical consciousness or historical awareness.

Empirical studies show that few young people have any idea how relevant examining the Holocaust is for understanding the present (Zülsdorf-Kersting 2008, p. 470). For those in the fourth and fifth generations after the Nazi period in Germany, the Holocaust is far removed. Few see its relevance for the present.

These and other empirical data (e.g., Schäuble 2011) show that the threat from antisemitism and other inhumane ideologies in Germany did not disappear so easily with the end of National Socialism. On the contrary, in times of crisis, antisemitic, racist, xenophobic, and anti-democratic tendencies amplify quickly. This requires a large, permanent effort in politics and education to combat antisemitism, especially among the young, and to raise their sensitivity to history. Only then can human rights in Germany be permanently ensured.

Theoretical Reflections on Antisemitism and the Devaluing of Minorities

The group of philosophers and thinkers about a social philosophy called Critical Theory or the Frankfurt School has been leading the way in the analysis of antisemitism (see Adorno 2003; Horkheimer 1988; Horkheimer and Adorno 2006). According to Knothe (2009), at the epistemological level, it is possible to identify an analogy between antisemitic worldviews and a dualistic understanding of the world ("good and evil"; see Knothe 2009, pp. 7 ff). These trends are perceptible, says Knothe, especially in secondary antisemitism.

Knothe points out that the social manifestations of Antisemitism have changed. Conducting a study in Germany, Heyder et al. (2005) found that people had blocked their memories in relation to National Socialism and the Holocaust; 62% of the Germans responding to the survey said they wanted to hear no more of the crimes of the Nazi regime against the Jews (pp. 151ff). More than a half agreed to the comparison between the Nazi regime's polices towards the Jews and Israel's policies towards the Palestinians today (see Diner 2004, pp. 310–328). Knothe discusses in detail the various theories on the social function of antisemitism, including theories of economic crises theories and social-psychological models. Critical theorists would hold that in antisemitism, the National-Socialist ideology leads people to rationalise their repressed and taboo feelings:

> This constitution of the subject is thus distinguished primarily by the fact that the innermost and most secret, and hence the most undesirable and forbidden wishes and desires of the other are dedicated to the enemy, and in this case, to the Jews.... In the Nazi era, however, this individual paranoia is transferred into the greater reference of the collective paranoia, it is the law of action, and the madness is legitimised. (Knothe 2009, p. 67)

The core element of NS antisemitic ideology was the devaluing of other groups of people, especially the Jews. Within the dualistic anthropology of the Nazis, the Jews, as the out-group, did not have the same status as the in-group. This devaluation follows the same mechanism as the syndrome of today's group-focused enmity which we described above. Thus, we see both the historical and current forms of negative ways to construct the relationship between "us" and "them"; these both represent an ideology of unequal status. This is the very heart of inhumane thinking and behaviour. To look down upon others leads directly to actions of humiliation, discrimination, and contempt against these people. The behaviour represents the opposite of that what was called the "decent society" (Margalit 1996), which is built on respect for the dignity of all, no matter their origin or where they belong.

In the life-world, prejudices against Jews and other groups have a clear function. The most important function is bonding: differentiating oneself from the other helps the individual create a social identity and a sense of belonging within the in-group. This is why political propaganda so often tends to incorporate prejudice and racism, because devaluing minorities like the Jews heightens the importance of the in-group (Zick et al. 2011, p. 32). Prejudices and stereotypes supply knowledge and orientation; they show who can be trusted and who cannot. For some (young) people, antisemitic ideology is part of their social identity.

If we think about Holocaust remembrance in Germany, we must take into account these recent developments and research studies on antisemitism as well as group-focused enmity, as today's antisemitic and anti-minority tendencies in Germany must always be seen in relation to the Holocaust. They represent a particular interpretation of the catastrophe of Auschwitz, either conscious or unconscious, since they either deny, downplay, or minimise the attempted elimination of all Jews, or reinterpret the history in a revanchist way.

Implications for "Education after and about Auschwitz": Holocaust Remembrance and Education in Times of Transformation

The future of remembrance of the Holocaust is at stake more than ever before (Hartman and Assmann 2012). Society is changing rapidly; this means traditions lose ground, social structures become "liquid" (Bauman 2000), group relationships dissolve, postmodern living conditions spread, and the media and markets are dominating life. And at the same time the last witnesses and survivors of the Holocaust die. In this situation, Holocaust remembrance and education need to be profoundly reshaped. A short historical flashback, as well as some aspects of current issues, will help to highlight the challenges for our time; for more detail see Boschki et al. 2010.

In 1966, Theodor Adorno delivered his famous radio speech titled "Education after Auschwitz"; in his opening statement he insisted that "the very first demand on education is that there not be another Auschwitz" (Adorno 1997 [1966], p. 13). Adorno did not refer merely to isolated formation processes, but addressed the entirety of person and society:

> When I speak of education after Auschwitz, I mean two areas: (1) education in childhood, especially early childhood, and (2) general enlightenment that creates a spiritual, cultural and social climate that permits no repetition of such monstrous action, thus a climate in which motives that have led to the horror become conscious to some degree. (p. 13)

This speech hit German society at a point when it was not really dealing with its past to the extent that the Holocaust was being taught in classrooms or other educational institutions. The mood of most Germans was of shame, suppressed guilt feelings, oppression of memory, and refusal to deal with the past.

From the mid-1980s to the present, the discourse about Holocaust education in Germany has been marked by an ever-increasing intensity of academic, pedagogic, and public interest. Indeed, Adorno's speech has intensified the discourse on the subject of Holocaust education amongst educators up to the present (Boschki and Konrad 1997; Fechler et al. 2001; Rathenow and Weber 1988; Schreier and Heyl 1992, 1995; Schwendemann and Boschki 2009; Wagensommer 2009). Aside from the development of instructional concepts, over the last 20 years this emphasis has driven the educational and sociological sciences to increasingly employ empirical approaches to study historic awareness, the level of knowledge of the Holocaust, and young peoples' approaches to the memory of Auschwitz (for an overview from the 1960s to the present, see Zülsdorf-Kersting 2008, pp. 35–121).

In Germany today, the frame of education about and after Auschwitz includes a wide range of methods and approaches: classes in schools, memorial days, memorial sites, education programmes for adults, education on these topics as part of religious education, and last but not least, films, the Internet, and instructional media. Each of these fields has its own positive elements but also its own difficulties, ambivalences—and dead ends and bewilderment. In the next few paragraphs we review some of their limitations.

Although teaching about NS and the Holocaust is an obligatory part of German school curricula, some experts in the teaching of history have argued that history teaching in schools is relatively unimportant; they highlight the "inadequate role of schools", and "the subject of History and teachers" (von Borries 2009, p. 46; for a summary of research, see Zülsdorf-Kersting 2008, pp. 63ff, 120). Family ties are very powerful, particularly around issues concerning NS, and the media have immense power to confront issues via films, discussions, and documentaries. Also, discussion about NS and the Holocaust enters school curricula quite late, when students are already 15 or 16 years old.

The official Holocaust Memorial Day in Germany is 27 January, the day when the concentration camp at Auschwitz was liberated. A wide range of initiatives are carried out on that day, by the government in official memory ceremonies and speeches, by the media in special programmes that focus on Holocaust-related topics, by memory ceremonies in towns and cities, and by schools. The inherent problem is that many of these actions are driven by political correctness and remain isolated from experiences of everyday life. Ever since the liberation from the Nazi regime, sites of NS injustice such as concentration camps, prisons, Gestapo cellars, and SS headquarters have systematically been turned into memorial sites or museums, using federal funds. One challenge arises when school classes come for a mandatory visit and students are unwilling to deal with the Holocaust, especially if they have not been well prepared; then visits to memorial places can have the opposite effect of what the teachers intended.

Educational discourse on and about the Holocaust is not limited to children and adolescents. Adults in Germany are just as much a target audience for memorial sites, remembrance events, various types of related activities, and academic research (Theile 2009), but few adults are ready to get involved in educational programmes concerning the Holocaust.

Education about and after Auschwitz in Germany is also part of religious education in schools and Christian communities. Churches, both Protestant and Catholic, often feel responsible for continuing cultures of memory, but how intensely to address the topic, if at all, depends on the specific persons in the given educational setting or parish.

Finally, a variety of films, Internet sites, and teaching media on the Holocaust are widely used. All the major empirical studies on Holocaust education highlight the influence the media have on historical consciousness, especially that of young people (Krings 2006; Schwendemann 2009). Some media products are very effective in creating historical awareness, but some are rather dangerous depending on the way they are used in educational settings, as the case study below will illustrate.

German society is undergoing an essential change: migration in particular is changing it into a multicultural society. This has increasingly led educational researchers to search for conditions and methods that make education after and about Auschwitz possible in a heterogeneous society (Fechler et al. 2001), but how can educators address the Holocaust in multicultural groups? This remain an almost insoluble challenge.

Since the 1990s right-wing extremist violence has continued to increase (Globisch 2008). "The anti-democratic attitude in Germany is strongly marked" (Decker et al. 2010, p. 75). Against the background of all these points, in the next two sections we describe some the difficulties of Holocaust education that can end up in frustration, puzzlement or worse—exactly what teachers do not intend.

Some Less Effective Forms of Holocaust Education

As we have described earlier (Boschki et al. 2010), empirical studies on Holocaust education in German schools have revealed ineffective forms of teaching or even failure. For example, in the course of a 9th grade school project, students were interviewed before and after a teaching block on National Socialism and an associated project week (Schwendemann and Marks 2003). Analysis of the data gathered before the teaching block, which therefore reflected the students' general level of knowledge and awareness of the topic, showed that most of them tended towards "Hitlerism": they saw him as more or less as the sole person responsible for National Socialism. Somewhat worryingly, this attitude appeared not to have changed after 11 full weeks of teaching on the subject. The students were still convinced that Hitler himself—and he alone—was responsible for all atrocities in the NS period.

An important result of this study was the observation that every student had some prior knowledge of the Nazi period, primarily provided by grandparents, parents, or the media. Frequently, however, the researchers found significant discrepancies between the information taught at school and that provided through the family (Schwendemann and Marks 2003, pp. 189–210). Family socialisation always tends to embellish the Nazi experiences, leaving the young generation with the conviction that "Grandpa wasn't a Nazi" (Welzer et al. 2002).

A further reason why Holocaust education often fails, or is not very effective, is that often neither teachers nor learners are familiar with the psychology behind Nazi ideology. Thus, well-intended teaching approaches frequently result in misjudgments about the classroom setting (Marks 2007) that include traces of Nazi ideology. The frightening conclusion is that the process of learning from history is only just beginning. Fragments of Nazi ideology still appear to be present in German society, which essentially follows similar patterns as in the Nazi era, such as dualistic thinking in terms of good and evil with respect to certain groups of people, or group-focused enmity and devaluation of others. Nazi ideology used forms of oppression, humiliation, and terror systematically against minorities and all groups of dissenters. The psychodynamic structures of these forms are still present in the German language (Klemperer 2006) and in structures of behaviour in group dynamics (Knothe 2009). It is these patterns that may block understanding during attempts to teach memory and remembrance.

Towards a New Concept for Holocaust Remembrance and Education

Our work in this chapter to place Holocaust remembrance in context and our review of the reasons why education after Auschwitz has been only partly effective, at best, reveal the urgent need to develop a new theory of Holocaust remembrance and Holocaust education. From a theory of remembrance, a new concept for learning memory can be developed, and not just in and for Germany; it must be expanded to a European (Boschki 2005) and indeed global context (Gross and Stevick 2010).

Now, against the background of the empirical data we provided above and our educational reflections, we suggest six elements that are essential to a theory of Holocaust remembrance.

Holocaust Remembrance Is Antisemitism Prevention

If Holocaust remembrance and education do not help learners to become more sensitive towards the phenomena of antisemitism and group behaviour, then it has failed to achieve two of its most critical aims. Educators do not deal with the Holocaust simply to create students who are well educated with respect to a certain historical time period. To increase knowledge in terms of knowing about the past is good, but if it does not intensify sensitivity, change attitudes, or provoke commitment, it is relatively useless. Therefore, we support a competence-oriented approach to education (Müller-Ruckwitt 2008); that is, we believe the goal of educational intervention can be expressed in concrete competencies that learners should develop.

With respect to Holocaust remembrance, learners should gain the competence to understand motifs and mechanisms that led to inhumane actions in the past and to transfer these insights to the present. This competence is implicit in the terms historical consciousness and historical awareness that we discussed above: the competence to combine historical events with present challenges, in this case to be attentive to any form of upsurge of antisemitism in today's Germany and Europe.

Antisemitism prevention should therefore be present in all educational settings. Responsibility for Holocaust remembrance in Germany primarily means educating people to never be indifferent when Jews are devalued or discriminated against, let alone attacked. To centres in Berlin, the Centre for Antisemitism Research and the Anne Frank Centre, provide excellent didactic material for classroom courses in various school subjects alongside comprehensive background information for teachers on their websites.

Holocaust remembrance means fighting all forms of devaluation and discrimination.

Holocaust remembrance and education should not focus on antisemitism alone. Although Jews have been the first and central target of Nazi persecution, and racist antisemitism has been the core element of Nazi ideology, the whole political and social system of National Socialism was that of unequal status of humans. Fascists thought themselves and the "Aryan race" to be more valuable and of higher status than other "races". The consequence was a systematic devaluation and humiliation of, and discrimination against, other human beings: members of other nations, religions, and social and ethnic groups. "Humiliation is any sort of behaviour or condition that constitutes a sound reason for a person to consider his or her self-respect injured" (Margalit 1996, p. 9).

Again, historical understanding can trigger sensitivity and attentiveness toward present challenges. Democratic societies built on fundamental human rights and dignity for everyone must strengthen the values of freedom, equality, and democracy in their educational systems and teach younger generations to combat antisemitism, racism, and discrimination in all of its forms.

Holocaust Remembrance Is Learning about Human Rights

Education about and after Auschwitz is not merely a history lesson; it must also be a lesson promoting humanity and tolerance. The human concept of self is practically steered by memory and remembrance. A fundamental and unavoidable, if somewhat uncomfortable, insight that results from the study of Auschwitz is that "a return to barbarism will always remain a possibility" (Zimmermann 2005, p. 15). In historic terms, Auschwitz is "without precedent" (Bauer 2001, p. 42), but this does not mean that it cannot repeat itself.

It is crucial, therefore, that learning processes enable a "moral contemporariness" in the learner, based on the ability to successfully "negate inhumanity" (Zimmermann 2005, pp. 87, 92ff). Thus, students primarily learn humanity as the negation of inhumanity. It is crucial, therefore, to extend approaches in the pedagogy of human rights (Benedek 2006) to include the dimension of historic and religious learning and, consequently, the dimension of care and mindfulness.

Holocaust Remembrance Focuses on the Victims

A decisive point of Holocaust remembrance is its orientation towards the testimonies of victims. Remembrance can never be general; it is bound to a specific group of victims. The catastrophe of Auschwitz cannot be measured through historical facts only, no matter how important historiography is for the understanding of National Socialism. The accounts of the victims must be understood in a dialectical relation to the results of the historiography.

In the educational work of remembrance with (young) people, the perspective of the victims facilitates access to historical events, which is much more effective than a mere historical lesson (Schwendemann and Boschki 2009). Because today only a few witnesses can be present "live" during lessons, media presentation forms are brought to the fore: video interviews with the witnesses, films, books, etc. In this respect, however, two aspects are important. On the one hand, those in charge must not indulge themselves with the students' emotional consternation, nor should they leave the learners alone with their feelings. A crucial step in this educational work is reflexively processing emotional inputs. The memories of the victims have to be put in the context of the historical events; they must be discussed and understood contextually.

On the other hand, the perspective of the victim must be supplemented by a focus on the world of the perpetrator, especially in Germany and Austria, the countries of the perpetrators. We need to inquire about them historically. Who was actively or passively involved in the Nazi crimes? And where, when, and for what reasons? The students must find out to what extent their ancestors belonged to the group of perpetrators. As people transfer feelings across the generations—guilt, defense, and denial of guilt—this process can lead to blockages in the emotional lives of families, to the third and fourth generation, which can prevent them from contending openly with the history (Welzer 2007).

Holocaust Remembrance Operates in an Interdisciplinary Perspective

Research on the Holocaust is conducted by a great variety of academic disciplines in order to gain as many insights as possible into the mechanisms of inhumane behaviour. The same should be true for Holocaust education. It cannot only be the task of a simple history lesson at school. In Germany, many school subjects include for Holocaust remembrance, but they are too often not connected and interdisciplinary cooperation is rare—and lessons on the Holocaust are often separated among different subjects. That is why students get the feeling that they are hearing about the NS over and over again during their school career and sometimes feel oversaturated with information about the Holocaust.

The important task of future Holocaust education in Germany is to create internal school curricula where teachers of history, ethics, religion, social science, language, art, and even music sit together to plan a curriculum from the first class level to the last in order to teach the various aspects according to the students' ages, social conditions, and levels of understanding. In addition, interdisciplinary school projects can significantly improve the teaching about National Socialism. A particular feature of this approach to teaching is hands-on teaching events such as carefully prepared visits to memorial sites and the creation of exhibitions, archival research, theatre projects, etc.

Holocaust Remembrance Is a Core Element of a Culture of Remembrance

The field of remembrance research has grown in recent years. But the boom of works in the context of so-called Cultural Memory Studies (e.g., Erll and Nünning 2010) must be critically examined. Only a few works are devoted to the Holocaust as a central remembrance date for Europe (Assmann 2006). Many studies remain in an uncertain zone. For example, one can point out all the special places of remembrance (*lieux de mémoire*) around the world: the Rhine Valley, the castles of the Loire, the papal encyclical, and many more. A Culture of Remembrance does not follow a universal memory of historically significant events, but places the Holocaust in the heart of European memory. The breach of civilisation with the attempted elimination of all European Jews leads to a specific hermeneutics for interpreting the past and present.

In addition, a Culture of Remembrance can be adequately understood only if we take into account the religious lines of development, from which the term remembrance stems. Examples are "*Zachor!*" ("Remember!") as a central category of the Jewish holy scriptures and the *Memoria Passionis* of the Christian tradition (see Metz 2006). In the aftermath of the Holocaust, remembrance is newly being discovered as a key religious term in Judaism and in Christianity, and is filled with new content from historical experiences. Amongst many others, Yerushalmi (1982) reflects on the relationship between history and memory in the long tradition of Judaism and advocates a dialectic relationship between historiography and the tradition of remembrance.

Johann Baptist Metz (1992), one of the most important representatives of a Christian theology after Auschwitz, was the first to develop the contours of what he calls an "anamnestic culture", drawing on Jewish and Christian traditions as well as on the philosophical theories of remembrance of Adorno and Walter Benjamin. He lists several elements of such a culture: it implies the remembrance of foreign suffering and the suffering of others, and it needs close contact with literature and art and an intensive educational effort.

These implications could be aggregated into what is recently being called a culture of remembrance of the Holocaust (Gross and Boschki 2014). The theoretical framework of this culture, particularly for educational settings, integrates the work of Auschwitz survivor Elie Wiesel (Boschki 1995, 1998) and represents Wiesel's (1956/2006) whole work. In Wiesel's sense, history is never just facts and figures that lie far away in the past but is deeply connected to the present. A culture of remembrance, in the way he represents it in his works, calls for a relational approach which focuses on the interrelations between remembrance and education, remembrance and human rights, remembrance and hope. For him, education and remembrance are closely related concepts: "the two are the same: education occurs through remembrance, and remembrance through education. Education implies remembrance" (Wiesel 1989, p. 80).

References

Adorno, T. W. (1997). Education after Auschwitz [1966]. In H. Schreier & M. Heyl (Eds.), *Never again! The Holocaust's challenge for educators* (pp. 11–20). Hamburg: Kraemer.
Adorno, T. W. (2003). *Gesammelte Schriften* [Collected writings]. Berlin: Directmedia Publishers.
AJC [European Forum on Antisemitism] (2012). *Working definition of antisemitism*. Berlin: AJC. http://www.european-forum-on-antisemitism.org/
Assmann, A. (2006). *Der lange Schatten der Vergangenheit: Erinnerungskultur und Geschichtspolitik* [The long shadow of the past: Culture of remembrance and politics of history]. Munich: Beck.
Bauer, Y. (2001). *Die dunkle Seite der Geschichte: Die Shoah in historischer Sicht. Interpretationen und Re-Interpretationen* [The dark side of history: An historical view of the Shoah. Interpretation and re-interpretation]. Frankfurt am Main: Jüdischer Verlag im Suhrkamp-Verlag.
Bauman, Z. (2000). *Liquid modernity*. Cambridge: Polity Press.
BdI [Bundesministerium des Innern] (Ed.) (2011). *Report 2011: Antisemitismus in Deutschland. Erscheinungsformen, Bedingungen, Präventionsansätze* [Antisemitism in Germany: Phenomena, conditions, concepts for prevention]. Berlin: Media Consulta.
Benedek, W. (Ed.) (2006). *Understanding human rights: Manual on human rights education*. Vienna/Graz: Neuer Wissenschaftlicher Verlag.
Bergich, D., & Raabe, J. (2010). Antisemitismus in extrem rechten jugendkulturellen Szenen [Antisemitism in extreme-right youth cultural scenes]. In W. Stender et al. *Konstellationen des Antisemitismus* [Constellations of antisemitism] (pp. 225–242) Wiesbaden: Verlag für Sozialwissenschaften.
Bergmann, W. (2006). *Geschichte des Antisemitismus* [History of antisemitism]. Munich: Beck.
Bergmann, W. (2008). Vergleichende Meinungsforschung zum Antisemitismus in Europa und die Frage nach einem "neuen europäischen Antisemitismus" [Comparative opinion research on antisemitism in Europe and the question of a "new European Antisemitism"]. In L. Rensmann & J. H. Schoeps (Eds.), *Feindbild Judentum. Antisemitismus in Europa* [Concept of the enemy: Antisemitism in Europe] (pp. 473–507). Potsdam: Moses-Mendelsohn-Zentrums für Europäisch-Jüdische Studien.
Bergmann, W. (Ed.) (2009). *Antisemitische Geschichtsbilder* [Antisemitic images of history]. Essen: Klartext-Verlag.
Bergmann, W. (2011). *Vortrag zu Ergebnissen der Einstellungsforschung zum "Antisemitismus in Deutschland"* [Antisemitism in Germany]. Berlin: Bundesministerium des Innern. http://www.bmi.bund.de/SharedDocs/Downloads/DE/Themen/Politik_Gesellschaft/EXpertenkreis_Antisemmitismus/bergmann.pdf;jsessionid=EDDD39502479D2CD49DEFF41AE5D5
3FE.2_cid373?__blob=publicationFile
Blum, M. (2011). Expertise "Katholische Kirche und Antisemitismus" [The Roman Catholic church and antisemitism]. Berlin: Bundesministerium des Innern. http://www.bmi.bund.de/SharedDocs/Downloads/DE/Themen/Politik_Gesellschaft/EXpertenkreis_Antisemmitismus/blum.pdf?__blob=publicationFile
Boschki, R. (1995). *Der Schrei. Gott und Mensch im Werk von Elie Wiesel* [The cry: God and man in Elie Wiesel's work]. Mainz: Grünewald-Verlag.
Boschki, R. (1998). Towards an ethics of remembrance after the Shoah. In A. Rosen (Ed.), *Celebrating Elie Wiesel: Stories, essays, reflections* (pp. 203–222). Notre Dame: Notre Dame Press.
Boschki, R. (2005). Bedingungen und Möglichkeiten einer anamnetischen Kultur in Europa: Individuelle, gesellschaftliche und religionspädagogische Aspekte des Gedenkens [Conditions and possibilities of an anamnetic culture in Europe: Individual, societal, and religious educational aspects of memories]. *Religionspädagogische Beiträge, 55*, 99–112.
Boschki, R., & Konrad, F.-M. (Eds.) (1997). *Ist die Vergangenheit noch ein Argument? Aspekte einer Erziehung nach Auschwitz* [Is the past still an argument? Aspects of an education after Auschwitz]. Tubingen: Attempto.

Boschki, R., Reichmann, B., & Schwendemann, W. (2010). Education after and about Auschwitz in Germany: Towards a theory of remembrance in the European context. *Prospects, 40*(1), 133–152.
Decker, O., Weißmann, M., Kiess, J., & Brähler, E. (2010). *Rechtsextreme Einstellung in Deutschland* [The extreme-right attitude in Germany]. Bonn: Friedrich-Ebert-Stiftung.
Diner, D. (2004). Der Sarkophag zeigt Risse. Über Israel, Palästina und die Frage eines "neuen Antisemitismus" [The sarcophagus shows some cracks: About Israel, Palestine and the question of a "new antisemitism"]. In D. Rabinovici et al. (Eds.), *Neuer Antisemitismus? Eine globale Debatte* (pp. 310–328). Frankfurt: Suhrkamp.
Erll, A., & Nünning, A. (Eds.) (2010). *A companion to cultural memory studies*. Berlin/New York: De Gruyter.
Fechler, B., Kößler, G., & Liebertz-Groß, T. (Eds.) (2001). *"Erziehung nach Auschwitz" in der multi-kulturellen Gesellschaft: Pädagogische und soziologische Annäherungen* ["Education after Auschwitz" in the multi-cultural society: Educational and social approximations]. Weinheim: Juventa.
Globisch, C. (2008). Warum fordert die NPD "die Türkei den Türkei"? [Why does the NPD say, "Turkey for the Turks?"]. In F. Virchow & C. X. Dornbusch (Eds.), *88 Fragen und Antworten zur NPD. Weltanschaung, Strategie und Auftreten einer Rechtspartei—und was Demokraten dagegen tun können* (pp. 65–67). Schwalbach am Taunus: Wochenschau Verlag.
Gross, Z., & Boschki, R. (2014). *Culture of remembrance: Theoretical framework*. Bonn: Bonn University Press.
Gross, Z., & Stevick, D. (Eds.) (2010). Special issue on Policies and Practices of Holocaust Education: International Perspectives. *Prospects, 40*(1).
Hartman, G., & Assmann, A. (2012). *Die Zukunft der Erinnerung und der Holocaust* [The future of remembrance and the Holocaust]. Paderborn: Konstanz University Press.
Heil, J., & Kramer, S. J. (2012). *Beschneidung: Das Zeichen des Bundes in der Kritik. Zur Debatte um das Kölner Urteil* [Circumcision; The sign of the covenant under criticism. Debate on the Cologne abjudication] Berlin: Metropol Verlag.
Heitmeyer, W. (Ed.) (2012). *Deutsche Zustände* [German conditions] (Vol. 10). Frankfurt: Suhrkamp.
Heyder, A., Iser, J., & Schmidt, P. (2005). Israelkritik oder Antisemitismus? Meinungsbildung zwischen Öffentlichkeit, Medien und Tabus [Criticism of Israel or antisemitism? The formation of opinions between the public, media and taboos]. In W. Heitmeyer (Ed.), *Deutsche Zustände* [German conditions], (Vol. 3, pp. 144–165) Frankfurt: Suhrkamp.
Horkheimer, M. (1988). *Gesammelte Schriften. Autorität und Familie* [Collected writings: Authority and family]. Frankfurt: Fischer.
Horkheimer, M., & Adorno, T. W. (2006). *Dialektik der Aufklärung. Philosophische Fragmente* [The dialectic of enlightenment: Philosophical fragments]. Frankfurt: Fischer.
Klemperer, V. (2006). *The language of the third Reich: LTI—Lingua Tertii Imperi, a philologist's notebook*. London/New York: Continuum.
Knothe, H. (2009). *Eine andere Welt ist möglich: Ohne Antisemitismus?* [Another world is possible: One without antisemitism?]. Bielefeld: Transcript-Verlag.
Krings, A. (2006). *Die Macht der Bilder* [The power of images]. Münster: LIT.
Margalit, A. (1996). *The decent society*. Cambridge: Harvard University Press.
Marks, S. (2007). *Warum folgten sie Hitler? Die Psychologie des Nationalsozialismus* [Why did they follow Hitler? The psychology of National Socialism]. Düsseldorf: Patmos.
Metz, J. B. (1992). Für eine anamnetische Kultur [For an anamnetic culture]. In H. Loewy (Ed.), *Holocaust: Die Grenzen des Verstehens. Eine Debatte über die Besetzung der Geschichte* (pp. 35–41). Reinbek bei Hamburg: Rowohlt.
Metz, J. B. (2006). *Memoria passionis: Ein provozierendes Gedächtnis in pluralistischer Gesellschaft* [Memoria passionis: A provocative memory in a pluralistic society]. Freiburg/Basel/Vienna: Herder.

Müller-Ruckwitt, A. (2008). *"Kompetenz". Bildungstheoretische Untersuchungen zu einem aktuellen Begriff* [Competence: Investigation of a current term from the perspective of educational theory]. Würzburg: Ergon-Verlag.
Radvan, H. (2010). *Pädagogisches Handeln und Antisemitismus* [Educational action and antisemitism]. Bad Heilbrunn: Klinkhardt.
Rathenow, H., & Weber, N. (Eds.) (1988). *Erziehung nach Auschwitz* [Education after Auschwitz]. Pfaffenweiler: Centaurus-Verlag.
Rosenfeld, A. H. (Ed.) (2013). *Resurgent antisemitism: Global perspectives*. Bloomington: Indiana University Press.
Schäuble, B. (2011). *Jugend und Antisemitismus* [Youth and antisemitism]. Weinheim: Beltz.
Scherr, A. (2011). Expertise "Verbreitung von Stereotypen über Juden und antisemitischer Vorurteile in der evangelischen Kirche" [Stereotypes of Jews and antisemitic prejudices in the Protestant church in Germany]. Berlin: Bundesministerium des Innern http://www.bmi.bund. de/SharedDocs/Downloads/DE/Themen/Politik_Gesellschaft/EXpertenkreis_ Antisemmitismus/scherr.pdf?__blob=publicationFile
Scherr, A., & Schäuble, B. (2007). *"Ich habe nichts gegen Juden, aber..." Ausgangsbedingungen und Perspektiven gesellschaftspolitischer Bildungsarbeit gegen Antisemitismus* ["I have nothing against Jews, but..." Basic conditions and perspectives of socio-political educational work against antisemitism]. Berlin: Amadeu Antonio Stiftung.
Schreier, H., & Heyl, M. (Eds.) (1992). *Das Echo des Holocaust: Pädagogische Aspekte des Erinnerns* [The echo of the Holocaust: Educational aspects of remembrance]. Hamburg: Kraemer.
Schreier, H., & Heyl, M. (Eds.) (1995). *"Dass Auschwitz nicht noch einmal sei": Zur Erziehung nach Auschwitz* ["So that Auschwitz cannot happen again": Education after Auschwitz]. Hamburg: Kraemer.
Schwendemann, W. (2009). Gedenkstättenpädagogik in der vierten Generation nach Auschwitz als eine Form von Menschenrechtspädagogik [Remembrance education with the fourth generation after Auschwitz as a form of human rights education]. In T. Oeftering (Ed.), *Texte zur Menschenrechtspädagogik* [Textbook on human rights education] (pp. 49–64). Münster: LIT.
Schwendemann, W., & Boschki, R. (Eds.) (2009). *Vier Generationen nach Auschwitz: Wie ist Erinnerungslernen heute noch möglich?* [Four generations after Auschwitz: How is learning to remember possible today?]. Münster: LIT.
Schwendemann, W., & Marks, S. (Eds.) (2003). *Aus der Geschichte lernen?* [Can we learn from history?]. *Vol. 1: Nationalsozialismus und Antisemitismus als Unterrichtsthema* [National Socialism and Antisemitism as subjects in school instruction]. Grundsätzliche Überlegungen. Münster: LIT.
Silbermann, A., & Stoffers, M. (2000). *Auschwitz: Nie davon gehört? Erinnern und Vergessen in Deutschland* [Auschwitz. Never heard of it? Remembering and forgetting in Germany]. Berlin: Rowohlt.
Srubar, I., & Vaitkus, S. (Eds.) (2003). *Phänomenologie und soziale Wirklichkeit.* [Phenomenology and social reality]. Opladen: Leske+Budrich.
Stender, W. (2010). *Konstellationen des Antisemitismus* [Constellations of antisemitism]. Wiesbaden: Verlag für Sozialwissenschaften.
Theile, E. E. (2009). *Erinnerungskultur und Erwachsenenbildung* [Culture of remembrance and adult education]. Schwalbach am Taunus: Wochenschau Verlag.
von Borries, B. (2009). Geschichtsbewusstsein Jugendlicher vier Generationen nach Auschwitz: Zwischen Illusionen und Irritationen [Historical consciousness of young people four generations after Auschwitz: Between illusions and irritations]. In W. Schwendemann & R. Boschki (Eds.), *Vier Generationen nach Auschwitz: Wie ist Erinnerungslernen heute noch möglich?* (pp. 41–75). Münster: LIT.
Wagensommer, G. (2009). *How to teach the Holocaust: Didaktische Leitlinien und empirische Forschung zur Religionspädagogik nach Auschwitz* [How to teach the Holocaust: Teaching

guidelines and empirical research for religious education after Auschwitz]. Frankfurt am Main: Lang.

Welzer, H. (2007). *Täter: Wie aus ganz normalen Menschen Massenmörder werden* [Perpetrators: How normal people become mass murderers]. Frankfurt: Fischer.

Welzer, H., Moller, S., & Tschuggnall, K. (2002). *"Opa war kein Nazi": Nationalsozialismus und Holocaust im Familiengedächtnis* ["Grandpa wasn't a Nazi": National socialism and the Holocaust in family memories]. Frankfurt am Main: Fischer.

Wiesel, E. (1956/2006). *Night* (M. Wiesel, trans.). New York: Hill and Wang.

Wiesel, E. (1989). *Silence et mémoire d'hommes* [Silence and the memory of man]. Paris: Édition du Seuil.

Wiesel, E. (1997). *Ethics and memory*. Berlin/New York: de Gruyter.

Yerushalmi, Y. H. (1982). *Zakhor: Jewish history and Jewish memory*. Seattle: University of Washington Press.

Zick, A., Küpper, B., & Hövermann, A. (Eds.) (2011). *Intolerance, prejudice and discrimination: A European report*. Berlin: Friedrich-Ebert-Stiftung.

Zimmermann, R. (2005). *Philosophie nach Auschwitz: Eine Neubestimmung von Moral in Politik und Gesellschaft* [Philosophy after Auschwitz: A redefinition of morals in politics and society]. Reinbek bei Hamburg: Rowolth.

Zülsdorf-Kersting, M. (2008). *Sechzig Jahre danach: Jugendliche und Holocaust. Eine Studie zur geschichtskulturellen Sozialisation* [Sixty years later: Youth and the Holocaust. A study in historical cultural socialisation]. Münster: LIT.

Epistemological Aspects of Holocaust Education: Between Ideologies and Interpretations

Zehavit Gross and E. Doyle Stevick

The Politics of Knowledge

That the Holocaust should be taught is beyond dispute; deciding what should be taught about the Holocaust, however, is a more complex issue. Questions abound concerning content, methods, and context: what knowledge should be transmitted in the socialisation process? When should it be taught, to which age group, and how? Within the formal curriculum in the classroom only, or also with outside activities? In museums? Through trips to Poland? Normative answers to what should be taught vary extensively by purpose and by context, and are urgent considerations for practitioners; empirical questions about what is taught, for what reasons, and with what effects, in different contexts, are pressing for researchers.

Despite the profound importance of these issues (Gross 2008), other critical and related questions have not been yet addressed; these concern epistemology and the politics of knowledge. Apple (2010, p. 152) argues that the school is "a mechanism for selecting, preserving and passing on conceptions of competence, ideological norms and values, and often only certain groups' 'knowledge'". Such issues are particularly pertinent for Holocaust education: "Whose knowledge is distributed or ignored, and how is Holocaust education constructed and used in different settings by teachers and students?" (Gross 2008).

In the early 1970s, scholars including Foucault, Bourdieu, and Bernstein made important contributions to understanding the role that knowledge plays within the

Z. Gross (✉)
School of Education, Bar-Ilan University, Ramat-Gan, Israel
e-mail: grossz@mail.biu.ac.il

E.D. Stevick
College of Education, University of South Carolina,
318 Wardlaw Hall, Columbia, SC 29208, USA
e-mail: stevick@mailbox.sc.edu

educational arena. Young (1971) extended their work in his landmark *Knowledge and Control: New Directions in Educational Sociology.* Young addressed four aspects of school knowledge: the curriculum, teachers' knowledge, subject matter and pedagogical knowledge, and knowledge about students. He worked from the premise that every educational act or presentation of a text before pupils is a social activity of selection and organisation, deliberately or unconsciously constructed out of available knowledge in a specific time. The selection and organisation of knowledge is conducted by powerful people who decide whose knowledge counts and what knowledge is valuable, thus strengthening and empowering their social status and particularistic needs. What knowledge is presented and how requires a sociological inquiry.

Knowledge is not neutral, and the distribution of knowledge is not a neutral process. The value of a fact, a piece of knowledge, is not absolute and its meaning, derived from a socially dominant or marginal ideology, is reconstructed in the dynamic interaction of people within the school. Those who select this knowledge believe that it can serve their interests and strengthen their social status. Every educational decision is inherently ideological, rooted in a specific ideology (Apple 2004). For this reason, schools should be wary of the notion that knowledge is objective or neutral. Knowledge has meaning, and depends on context. The way knowledge is presented and the way people interpret knowledge is relational and contingent upon a wide range of personal and social factors that reflect definite interests and intentions. As Apple (2010) argues, education should be seen and examined as a political act. He claims that "we need to think relationally.... understanding education requires that we situate it in the unequal relations of power in the larger society and in the realities of dominance and subordination—and the conflicts that are generated by these relations" (p. 152). Given this charge, we may ask, what is the nature of the knowledge to which students are exposed? Is it objective knowledge, or is it subjective knowledge that we construct through our personal lenses? Apple (2010) broadens the scope of this question beyond "whose knowledge is this?" by asking how it became official:

> What is the relationship between this knowledge and the ways in which it is taught and evaluated, and who has cultural, social and economic capital in this society? Who benefits from these definitions of legitimated knowledge and from the way schooling and this society are organized, and who does not? How do what are usually seen as reforms actually work? What can we do as critical educators, researchers, and activists to change existing educational and social inequalities and to create curricula and teaching that are more socially just? (p. 152)

Apple's questions about whose knowledge is included and legitimated are particularly important for Holocaust education, in which the complex interrelationships between history and memory are compounded by the fact that not only the many millions of victims, but also those survivors behind the Iron Curtain, were rendered unable to share their stories.

The construction, legitimation, and selection of knowledge in textbooks and curricula help to create the context within which teachers further select and interpret materials in their dialogic relations with the children in the class, a sociocultural process in which they co-construct and negotiate the meaning. This relational process of creating meaning must be understood in its complex interrelationship with the context in which they meet, a construct shaped in important ways by the processes discussed above. The relational process of co-constructing meaning must be understand as involving culture, and thus inevitably must include a consideration of ideology, but not stop at that.

Alon Confino (2005) makes this point with regard to the Holocaust itself, noting that "the current dominant interpretative framework of the extermination of the Jews [is] the emphasis on Nazi racial ideology that motivated Germans in the brutal circumstances of World War II" (p. 297). We must "examine more closely the cultural making of Nazi values and beliefs" because "the central explanatory problem of the Nazi persecution and extermination of the Jews is… how the Nazis created a world of cultural representations and societal practices in which their beliefs made some sense" (p. 298).

To narrow this conceptual focus to contemporary issues of education about the Holocaust—rather than about the Holocaust itself—we must move beyond ideology to culture and consider how cultural processes shape the contexts within which students derive meaning from their interactions with legitimated ideologies in their relational interactions in classrooms and other educational settings. A central area of focus in these cultural investigations and considerations must be the role of memory itself.

Memory and History

A critical challenge for Holocaust education is the tendency to simplify history. Primo Levi (1988), a Holocaust survivor, asserts that our main difficulty in the history of the Holocaust is the attempt to understand what he calls "the grey zone". In an essay dedicated to the analysis of the grey zone, he argues that "we… tend to simplify history; but the pattern within which events are ordered is not always identifiable in a single unequivocal fashion, and it may therefore happen that different historians understand and construe history in ways that are incompatible with one another" (p. 22).

The tendency towards oversimplification is a fundamental issue in Holocaust education that reflects our inability to cope with the nature of knowledge and how we handle and conceptualise it. We cannot speak simply about one memory or one truth through which memory is inculcated. We must instead grapple with the difference between history (the so-called official and objective historical account) and memory (the personal and collective interpretation and transmission of experience), and particularly, the complex interrelationships between them. The experience of Belarus illustrates some of the complexity of history and memory:

> By starving Soviet prisoners of war, shooting and gassing Jews, and shooting civilians in anti-partisan actions, German forces made Belarus the deadliest place in the world between 1941 and 1944. Half of the population of Soviet Belarus was either killed or forcibly

displaced during World War II; nothing of the kind can be said of any other European country.

> Belarusian memories of this experience, cultivated by the current dictatorial regime, help to explain suspicions of initiatives coming from the West. Yet West Europeans would generally be surprised to learn that Belarus was both the epicenter of European mass killing and the base of operations of anti-Nazi partisans who actually contributed to the victory of the Allies. It is striking that such a country can be entirely displaced from European remembrance. The absence of Belarus from discussions of the past is the clearest sign of the difference between memory and history. (Snyder 2009, para. 28–29)

Some aspects of the memory/history challenge have relatively clear explanations, particularly in societies that were not free. The Soviet bloc, generally, suppressed free historical inquiry. Knowledge of the Holocaust, publications about it, and even acknowledgments of local complicity (for example, in the Baltic states) existed in the Soviet Union, but publications were generally in Yiddish (Rohdewald 2008, p. 173), with one notable exception in Estonian (Gitelman 1990, p. 28). In addition to suppressing historical inquiry, the Soviets propagandised the war, generally claiming Jewish victims of the Holocaust as Soviet citizens who were victims of fascism. (The Soviets also counted peoples in Eastern Europe who were first conquered by the Soviet Union before the Germans later took over.)

Moreover, the Soviets shut off free interaction with the West, which had two obvious consequences for their subsequent knowledge of the Holocaust. First, countries under Soviet hegemony did not typically have access to the historical understanding of the Holocaust that was evolving in Western Europe, Israel, the United States, and beyond. Second, survivors of the Holocaust from the East were not free to share their experiences, limiting the West's understanding of the Holocaust to accounts of Anne Frank or survivors from countries outside the block (Snyder 2009). Snyder argues that the real geographic centre of the Holocaust is further to the east, with the largely Yiddish-speaking, Orthodox unassimilated Jews of Eastern Europe; the countries gaining freedom between 1989 and 1991 have struggled to write themselves back into Europe (Michaels and Stevick 2009), whose imaginary boundaries had shrunk as a result of post-war geopolitics.

In many of these contexts, the broader understanding of the war was confined to private familial memories, framed by a limited national perspective, which functioned as a bulwark against the propaganda of the (illegitimate) state. The illegitimacy of Soviet spin and corruption has hampered efforts to deal with local histories of the Holocaust for many reasons. Perhaps the most important is the fact that the Soviets liberated many camps, documented many of the atrocities, and prosecuted a number of the most egregious offenders in the Holocaust; however, their abuse of the criminal justice system for political ends leads many who lived under Soviet occupation or hegemony—and were aware of its coerced confessions or incentivised denunciations (Weiss-Wendt 2008)—to doubt any evidence that they did gather. This obstacle to progress in reconciling memory and history was compounded by the continued refusal of Russian authorities to provide researchers with free access to work in Soviet archives.

These dynamics created a situation in which history, mediated through schools, and memory worked very much in opposition. And yet, the distinct histories of different cultures play a critical role in the direction that memory takes. For example, Rohdewald (2008) compared the trajectories of remembrance in Russia, Ukraine, and Lithuania and found three distinct approaches, which are connected to the fact that "Lithuania totally condemns its communist past (East-Central Europe), Ukraine is split on this question, and Russia does not ask questions about it (Eastern Europe in its narrow sense)" (p. 174). Further, he says, Russia latches onto victory against the Nazis as one of the few positives it can take from the Soviet period, a commemoration not challenged by the Holocaust, which remains secondary in its consideration, although conspiracy theorists too often hold Jews responsible for a Russian Holocaust (p. 175). Years earlier, Ukraine suffered a Soviet-induced famine, and in a new twist, "L. Deshchynskyi described the 'Holodomor' famine and the Holocaust as a single 'Genocide of the peoples of Ukraine', with the population of Ukraine as victims of 'Russian Bolshevism' and 'German Fascism', omitting Ukrainian collaboration in both contexts" (p. 177). Rohdewald also explains that Lithuania generally avoids the subject of collaboration, yet, while "the Lithuanian genocide is being conceptualised by example of the Holocaust", it is also true that "the (Jewish) Holocaust is seen neither as a unique tragedy, nor as a catastrophe for Jews as citizens of Lithuania, i.e. as Lithuanians. Here, it simply stands in a sequence alongside the Holocausts against ethnic Lithuanians and other nations" (p. 180).

These differences have profound implications for the educators of the region, who grow up immersed in these ways of thinking, and for outsiders who hope to engage productively with local educators about the Holocaust. If nothing else, it seems that people remain committed to choosing sides between the Soviets and the Nazis, almost inevitably against the regime that inflicted the most suffering on the group to which they most identify, rather than recognising each for their distinctive horrors. After all, the people trapped between the Soviets and the Nazis had little opportunity to choose a positive side to support unequivocally; rather than a simple, attractive black and white portrait, there is instead mostly darkness, and such realities require a recognition of grey.

Mace (2004, following Ebbinghaus, 1885/1964) distinguishes between voluntary and involuntary memories. He posits that voluntary memories are normally well intended and relate to a search for memories, whereas involuntary memories come to mind spontaneously, unintentionally and automatically, without effort. Whereas voluntary memory is a conscious action, involuntary memory does not result from a conscious effort. Both types of memory are important for people to internalise educational messages. Researchers have found that most involuntary memories might be triggered by sensory cues.

Whereas the research on voluntary memory is well established, the role of involuntary memory remains largely uncharted. The investigation of involuntary memory in relation to Holocaust education can expose some new layers of this subject matter that were previously unknown. Mace (2004) argues that involuntary memories can effectively evoke autobiographical memories. Involuntary memories are evoked by sensory experiences, thoughts, perceptual experiences, and psychological states.

Mace (2004) found that involuntary memories were more likely to be elicited by abstract types of cues (all thoughts of linguistic referents to the original episode) than by sensory/perceptual cues. This finding means that memory can be invoked not only by experiential learning but also by systematic verbal experiences or linguistically based cues. Moreover, "direct retrieval of recollective information" is more likely to occur with cues that are more cognitively elaborated (Mace 2008, p. 7). Involuntary memories, in addition to being difficult to research, have not received sufficient attention in education because it was assumed that they are triggered by sensory, transitory cues. Mace's findings, however, present a different point of view. He explains that they should be considered effective because they are more likely to be incongruent with current cognitive activity. This finding might have an important implication for education as the congruence with the cognitive aspects can help to systemise the educational process. This insight can bring about a shift in teachers' epistemic beliefs about how different forms of memories serve as sources of history, essentially a form of critical history, in order to better instill students with the skills in historical literacy for Holocaust education. Memories have a multi-layered function that should be taken into account.

European adolescents are confronted with contested memories (Gross 2009). On the one hand, Europe is the centre of liberalism and freedom. On the other hand, during the 20th century, Europe was the most brutal place in the world. How can an adolescent cope simultaneously with shadows and glory (Van der Tuin 2009)? Judt (2005) argues that the act of forgetting was the main strategy the Europeans used in their attempt to reconstruct Europe after World War II. It was necessary because, during the Nazi regime, many Europeans collaborated in the atrocity. At the beginning of the 1960s, they began to construct a "purified" memory in order to rebuild a new European identity and culture. Europe is full of museums, monuments, and artifacts, all efforts to cope with those bitter and destructive memories. In order for Europe to survive and rebuild its unique identity, it was necessary to remember and forget certain things. Who controls these processes of collective or personal forgetting and remembrance? Whose interests do they serve and what mechanisms of socialisation do people use to reach these ends?

Scholars and educators involved with Holocaust education should understand the legacy of European forgetting. As Tony Judt put it,

> Were it not for the long period of forgetting… many countries in Europe—east and west—would have had trouble putting themselves back together as politically stable units. But living a lie can be useful that way…. It allowed time for divisions to heal…. The fact that most European history textbooks pre–1980 are skimpy or even outright disingenuous about WWII should not simply provoke scorn or irony: there was a reason. (Judt, personal communication)

Every memory is a product of social interaction. As educators and researchers we seek to understand how education shapes our awareness of the past. Each lesson may seem to consist of exposure to a collection of historical texts, but how do we read those documents? In particular, what do we bring into the text while reading it? Each reader brings into the text her own personal history and culture. History lessons reconstruct historical consciousness. The lesson itself influences the way the historical information is constructed. The question is not simply "what really happened?" but especially, "how is the event presented in the historical discourse?"

Primo Levi (1988) explains that perhaps the origins of simplification stem from what happens if we "go back to our origins as social animals". Then, he says,

> ... the need to divide the field into 'we' and 'they' is so strong that this pattern, this bi-partition-friend-enemy prevails over all others. Popular history, and also the history taught in schools, is influenced by this Manichean tendency which shuns half-tints and complexities; it is prone to reduce the river of human occurrences to conflicts, and the conflicts to duels—we and they, Athenians and Spartans, Romans and Carthaginians. (p. 22)

People often think in categories rooted in clear dichotomies. They see not the whole continuum but rather its edges and polarities. Levi continues:

> This is certainly the reason for the enormous popularity of spectator sports such as soccer, baseball and boxing, in which the contenders are two teams or two individuals, clearly distinct and identifiable, and at the end of the match there will be vanished and victors. If the result is a draw, the spectator feels defrauded and disappointed: at the more or less unconscious level, he wanted winners and losers and he identified them respectively with the good guys and the bad guys, because the good must prevail, otherwise the world would be subverted. (pp. 22–23)

Holocaust education is particularly vulnerable to such simple narratives and dichotomies, and can be used in ways that reinforce such dichotomous thinking, strengthening categories and determining who can impose them rather than challenging the categories, and the categorisation itself.

Apple (2010) argues that education is "a process of repositioning" (p. 152). But can Holocaust educators reposition themselves in the grey zone? Who creates and defines grey zones? For what purpose? What benefit do they get from it? Is there a possibility of grey zones in Holocaust education? Whose knowledge is used to create them? And how are they constructed or deconstructed? How do we redistribute knowledge in order to reposition our perceptions within those grey zones?

The attempt to contain the bad and good within the arena of the grey zone is complicated and sometimes deluding. Even Michael Apple (2010), the critical analyst, falls into this pit of dividing the bad and good and the weak and strong, saying "we need to see the world through the eyes of the dispossessed and act against the ideological and institutional processes and forms that reproduce oppressive conditions" (p. 152). Though this perspective is generally true, who is oppressed and who is the oppressor, and from what perspective? Whose knowledge constructs someone, or some group, as the oppressed or the oppressor? Is there an absolute way to determine this or is it a matter of the cultural and political interpretations that people bring into the process of repositioning?

Addressing this problem is extremely important in Holocaust education because we must wrestle with whether we can explain things only through the prism of good and bad. On the other hand, is it permissible—or even possible—to remain only descriptive? Can we describe things objectively? Every event that we experience undergoes a process of construction. The way people construct knowledge is inevitably shaped through cultural and political lenses. Bar-On (1995) distinguishes between two modes of biases: the enlisted bias that uses knowledge instrumentally for specific ends, and the existential bias that analyses historical events from particularistic angles. Ram (1996, p. 17), looking at Holocaust research, distinguishes between what he calls the level of knowledge—the way historians perceive the knowledge as old, new, apologetic, or critical—and the nature of their perception, the way historians perceive the essence of knowledge as objective or relativist. Hence, some historians or teachers will present the Holocaust in an apologetic or critical way, yet believe that they base it on objective knowledge, whereas other teachers might present it in an equally apologetic or critical way, but base it on an epistemological foundation that is relativist. These approaches result in different history lessons and the conclusions pupils will draw from these varying experiences will be different.

Do teachers consider one text or multiple sub-texts, or one historical narrative, or multiple narratives and sub-narratives? Two different teachers who use the same documents will develop different lessons as they interact with the texts based on their own personalities, and their different social and cultural backgrounds. This question is connected not only to the way that Holocaust education is taught or researched, but especially to whether it can be generalised or measured at all, when it involves diverse epistemologies. Can teachers, for example, differentiate between opinions and facts? Ram (1996, p. 19) distinguishes between homogenous and heterogeneous historical consciousness and consensual and conflictual historical consciousness. Is it legitimate to teach from a conflictual consciousness, one that does not drive towards a resolution and that leaves certain discussions open?

Beyond these questions, another fundamental one undergirds the teaching of the Holocaust: is the Holocaust a historical event like others, or is it a unique case? Therefore, can we analyse the Holocaust using the conventional historical terminology, or do we need a new framework and concepts in order to comprehend it? Can we equate the oppression under Stalin's regime with Hitler's "final solution"? Should Soviet and Nazi victims be examined together in the same light or separately, from a purely historical perspective? In turn, the answers to these questions lead researchers and educators to ask whose interests are served by constructing the Holocaust as a unique or conventional historical event. And what impact does this interpretation have on individual identity?

Memory and Identity

Memory is one of the basic constituents of identity (Erikson 1950). A change in memory, therefore, might also entail a change in identity. Scholarship distinguishes between personal and collective memories, and each has a meaningful impact on the construction of the "self". John Locke (1979 [1689]), in *An Essay Concerning Human Understanding,* argues:

> For since consciousness always accompanies thinking, and 'tis that, that makes every one to be, what he calls *self*; and thereby distinguishes himself from all other thinking things, in this alone consists *personal Identity, i.e.* the sameness of a rational Being: And as far as this

consciousness can be extended backwards to any past Action or Thought, so far reaches the Identity of that *Person*. (p. 335)

Locke implies that memory of past experience is an essential component of one's being. Forgetting, then, must also be considered. What happens to those events that we forget or that socialisation wants us to forget? What impact does this selective mechanism have upon us? And, of course, in whose interest is it that we forget or remember certain events?

Collective memory is a socially constructed understanding and an integral part of the personal identity of the individual. "While the collective memory endures and draws strength from its base in a coherent body of people, it is individuals as group members who remember" (Halbwachs 1950, p. 48). There is thus a close interrelationship between personal and collective memory. Halbwachs argues that the individual can function only within a collective context. Memory is selective and context dependent. An individual who is situated in a specific group constructs his memories in relation to this specific collection of people. The group becomes his context and through its lenses he constructs the past in relation to them. The realm of memory is thus a relational arena: "every collective memory requires the support of a group delineated in space and time" (p. 84).

Memory has historically been constructed in relation to a group that is located within a specific time frame and space. The interrelationships between the group, time, and space intensify the memory and make it more unique and concrete. This constructive process is a substantial action that defines the individual and the group. Though memory is connected to the past, it is experienced in the present and acquires its meanings in its present context. The process of memory, therefore, makes the past an eternal present.

Which Approaches to Teaching?

This question is connected to the presence of the teacher within the "history" that is being inculcated. Varying descriptions of the teacher's role derive from different epistemological paradigms and approaches to the transmission of knowledge (Gross 2010). Pedagogical literature distinguishes between *instrumental teachers*, who consider their principal function to be the transmission of knowledge (Keiny 1993, 1998), and *reflective teachers*, who examine knowledge critically and inquisitively, thereby conceptualising practical knowledge and transforming it into theories of action (Schon 1987, 1988; Zeichner 1994). Teachers who employ the instrumental approach function according to the basic assumption that the corpus of knowledge they are charged with imparting to their students is objective, structured, and organised. Consequently, the learning process involves the passive reception of messages, and the teacher's role is to systematically transmit the requisite knowledge.

The reflective approach, in contrast, maintains that the curriculum is neither fixed nor predictable, but is part of a dynamic process of interaction between the learner and knowledge. It perceives the goal of teaching as the structuring of socialisation to yield proactive learners whose humanistic commitment is both part of their personal structuring and the result of the internalisation of knowledge. Such knowledge emerges and evolves as a result of interaction with the environment and constitutes an integral part of cognition (Rogoff 2003).

Holocaust Education and Citizenship

Holocaust education has the potential to get students to ponder the consequences of systematic racism. Short and Reed (2004) clarify its connection to citizenship education: "the contribution that a knowledge of the Holocaust can make to citizenship education is self-evident, for one of the latter's principal purposes in a multi-ethnic society must be to expose racism as an anti-democratic force" (p. 73). It can teach how a systematic process of stereotyping and scapegoating is the basis of atrocity and can lead to catastrophe. The basis for this understanding is knowledge. Roth and Burbules (2007) argue that "the notion of citizenship education is linked to concepts such as knowledge, values, aims, purposes" (p. 1). Further, those terms are relational and context dependent: "The meaning of the concept of citizenship education is dependent upon the conceptual schemes or web of beliefs of which it is part, and since these schemas or web of beliefs vary, the meaning of the concept also varies" (p. 1).

These issues have clear links to epistemology. Indeed, Banks (1997) perceives epistemology as the main foundation of citizenship education. Hence he argues that educators should select pedagogical knowledge and content that empower students from diverse racial, ethnic, cultural, and social-class groups. To make students "effective citizens", teachers should help them "to understand and critically examine all types of knowledge and to become knowledge producers themselves" (p. 33).

Engaging civic education and Holocaust education through the lenses of epistemology can raise a few very important concerns, which must be addressed. To discuss the ideological nature of knowledge is not to claim that there is no reality at all. Teaching Holocaust education within the framework of civic education requires us to distinguish clearly between the extreme relativism that denies any reality (e.g., the Holocaust), and our real need to examine the power dynamics that are implicit in interrogating knowledge about the Holocaust that is distributed in mass media and in schools. We consider separately the historical process of constructing knowledge about the Holocaust by professional historians, and the politics of knowledge that explores how people select and use particular aspects of that knowledge for specific purposes.

Thus, Holocaust education can serve as a case study within the scholarship of civic education on how to cope with over-politicised issues—and meanwhile still be able to distinguish fact from fiction, and stereotypical and racist standpoints, as opposed to sound historical judgments and reasoning, and an oversimplified approach compared to a more profound and complicated mode of teaching. This might be the future direction for thinking about Holocaust education while making use of new lenses.

The Relational Process of Meaning Making in Holocaust Education: Grappling with Culture, Context, and Ideology

When we ask why Holocaust education has spread around the globe, an important element seems to be its potential as a tool for anti-racist education (Gross and Stevick 2010). Certainly, this is a consideration in, for example, UNESCO's promotion of Holocaust education around the globe (Fracapane and Haß 2014). It seems that the relational process of meaning making in Holocaust education—namely the dynamics of culture, context, and ideology—makes this journey profound and challenging for teachers. This perspective seems especially relevant because genocides have continued to occur since the end of World War II.

Teaching the Holocaust involves navigating between ideologies and interpretations. It is clear that Holocaust education is often used as a means to enhance human rights education and cope with xenophobia. There are documented incidents (for example in Germany, Austria, and Australia) in which teachers who raise the issue of the Holocaust in their classes encounter antisemitic reactions. For example, Rutland (2010) documents the reactions in some Australian neighborhoods with a substantial Muslim immigrant population, where some students sometimes expressed an admiration for Nazism and Hitler. Some drew swastikas on their desks and had posters of Hitler. They also made statements in the class such as: "Hitler did the right thing" and "Hitler did not go far enough". One teacher reported that a student asked him: "Sir, why do all teachers hate Hitler? After all, he only killed Jews". The students accuse Jews of being responsible for the September 11 bombing and teachers have reported overhearing students asking each other: "Why is it that no Jews were killed in September 11… Obviously they [the Jews] did it" (p. 81). (Also see Rutland, this volume.) Naturally, these are students in whom we would hope to foster a more enlightened and tolerant view. Can Holocaust education inflame such attitudes rather than undermining them? Certainly Holocaust education is highly politicised and is often connected to the Israeli-Arab conflict.

It is notable that discussions of Armenia or Rwanda may not produce the same reaction: most students in the world have never met someone from Armenia or from Rwanda. For them, these countries are abstract entities, without any real substance that can invite a serious reaction. Images of "Jews" seem to be more pervasive around the world: though many have never met a Jewish person, they have a more distinct image in mind. Certainly the Anti-Defamation League (ADL 2014) study asserting that more than a billion people harbored antisemitic attitudes speaks to the ostensible familiarity of the idea of a Jew. This pervasiveness supports the notion that the history of discrimination and racial hatred towards Jews, including the Holocaust, can serve as a good starting point for anti-racist education.

Considering individual cognitive processes as an element of individual epistemology, we can explore educational psychology and its theories of knowing. Since people all over the world know and recognise Jews as "others", they become an integral part of what Piaget calls their "cognitive schemes". According to Piaget, as children develop cognitively, they adapt external stimuli and fit them into their personal schemas—the basic sets of experiences that each person constructs through personal experience and learning processes. During our life spans, we all modify those schemas to make sense of the new knowledge and new experiences that we encounter when interacting with the world. When a teacher mentions the words Holocaust or Jews, this new information interacts with the student's pre-existing knowledge (for example the knowledge that Jews are involved in the Israel-Arab conflict) and the information they have absorbed from their society and culture representing their social repertoire and approach to them (such as religious beliefs or ethnic culture). As Bar-Tal and Teichman (2005, p. 13), explain, children usually absorb the contents and the affective tone of the social repertoire and environment where they are raised. First they learn and acquire the features that characterise their specific ethnic or religious group and then they learn about "the prevailing mental representations of" other groups and their own group's approach to them.

Further, when a teacher mentions in the class the words Jew and Holocaust, this mention can, according to Piaget's theory, undergo three cognitive processes: assimilation, accommodation, and equilibration. This mention can raise the child's level of compassion but it can also fuel the psychological intergroup repertoire that might reinforce a cycle of intolerance. This kind of information processing and categorising is part of the conscious and unconscious meaning making that shape our perceptions and attitudes.

Despite the concerns raised above, we would argue that teachers who are irritated or think that it is better to avoid this problematic moment can lose a key educational opportunity. Anti-racist education must be connected with a concrete example, something that is tangible and can be perceived and grasped (Bar-Tal and Teichman 2005, p. 35). The concrete example of antisemitism leading to the murder of six million innocent men, women, and children needs to be raised in the classroom. It becomes a "teachable moment" when real and concrete feelings of disdain and prejudice fill the classroom. Here is where the real, authentic educational process can begin. The relational process of meaning making in Holocaust education is a crucial constituting moment. It has to do with the ethnic and religious cultural tradition, the dominant ideology, the unique atmosphere created in the classroom, and the teacher's personality. Such encounters can serve as "texts" that students need "to read" and comprehend. The teacher's role in those difficult moments is to equip the students with strategies to handle the prejudices that they bring from their homes and digest from the mass media, particularly the new social media.

Advocacy versus Research

Holocaust education often attracts researchers with strong moral views and commitments about the Holocaust, which can complicate the academic responsibility to maintain a critical approach. Although no researcher can be entirely unbiased, it is critical to distinguish normative views from empirical theories and to subject any beliefs and assumptions to the evidence. And certainly normative concerns shape the curriculum, policy, and practice of Holocaust education. For these reasons, it is all the more critical to bring advocacy into dialogue with research (Stevick and Michaels 2013), examining moral commitments and normative views against empirical realities whenever possible.

There are many ways to approach every problem. The researcher has to produce knowledge while considering multiple perspectives on a given research question. From an epistemological point of view, she needs to investigate the research questions by examining the phenomenon in all of its complexity, considering the various lines of argument. This task includes investigating the main scholarship on the topic and understanding its main debates. While the researcher may support one side of the debate, she must look at other sides before explaining the reasons for her own point of view.

For example, someone writing an academic article can argue that antisemitism is the key factor to consider when analysing the Holocaust. Yet, there can be many other lines of argument. It is also possible to present Nazi ideology as a form of racism from the broader, structural point of view rather than taking the more narrow approach of antisemitism. Thus, the scholar should introduce the broader concept of racism. Another key question in Holocaust studies is "was it unique?" In the past, many scholars argued that it was a unique phenomenon, but this view has been challenged more recently. Other social groups were targeted, including those the Germans considered to be second-class people, such as the Slavs and other East Europeans, and homosexuals and the Roma-Sinti.

This knowledge highlights the debate about whether the Holocaust was just one form of genocide, rather than being unique. Yehuda Bauer, the well-known Holocaust historian, underwent a shift in his own perspective. In his early writings, he claimed that the Holocaust was a unique case that cannot be compared to any other event. After the events in Rwanda and Bosnia, Bauer (2001) wrote a new book, *Rethinking the Holocaust*. In it, he claimed that the Holocaust is a paradigm of genocide—the supreme example of genocide—rather than a unique event. He argued that if something occurs once in human experience, it can occur again. But the fact that it was a systematic form of industrialised murder made it the "paradigm of genocide". From an epistemological point of view, Bauer opened a new continuum, moving from a one-dimensional analysis to a multi-layered paradigm, situating the Holocaust at the top.

Though Bauer for many years was a passionate advocate of one line of argument, as a scholar he was able to be open to another interpretation. Were his research approach one of advocacy, he would probably not have changed his mind. When faced with conflicting evidence, advocates find it harder to change their views than do evidence-driven researchers. Bauer saw the need for a theoretical framework to analyse both the Holocaust and genocide.

Denial is often a feature of advocacy. During the period of Soviet rule, few people in Eastern Europe or the Soviet Union acknowledged the Jewish Holocaust. The Soviet leadership acknowledged the general murder of civilians during the Nazi rule, and neglected to refer to the murder of six million Jews. Equally, if we acknowledge only Jewish suffering, and not the murder of all the other social groups, we lose sight of the broader picture. This broader picture, which considers different perspectives, enables a deeper and more complex analysis.

Knowing is a complex, contextual and cultural process, one that spans individual cognitive and collective/intersubjective processes. It engages not just the transmission of facts but perception and interpretation, the construction of meaning. This is never a neutral process. What we do know, what we should know, how we choose and who has the power to decide, what it all means and how we make sense of it: all these questions invite us to incorporate epistemology into the practice and study of Holocaust education.

Note This chapter draws on Stevick and Gross (2010).

References

ADL [Anti-Defamation League] (2014). The ADL global 100: An index of antisemitism. http://global100.adl.org/
Apple, M. W. (2004). *Ideology and curriculum* (3rd ed.). New York: RoutledgeFalmer.
Apple, M. W. (2010). Theory, research and the critical scholar activist. *Educational Researcher, 39*(2), 152–155.
Banks, J. A. (1997). *Educating citizens in a multicultural society*. New York: Teachers College Press.
Bar-On, M. (1995). Lo larutz lazad hasheni [Not to run to the other side]. *Haaretz, 6*(1), 95.
Bar-Tal, D., & Teichman, Y. (2005). *Stereotypes and prejudice in conflict: Representations of Arabs in Israeli Jewish society*. Cambridge: Cambridge University Press.
Bauer, Y. (2001). *Rethinking the Holocaust*. New Haven: Yale University Press.
Confino, A. (2005). Fantasies about the Jews: Cultural reflections on the Holocaust. *History & Memory, 17*(1/2), 296–322.
Erikson, E. H. (1950). *Childhood and society*. New York: Norton.
Fracapane, K., & Haß, M. (2014). Holocaust education in a global context. Paris. http://unesdoc.unesco.org/images/0022/002259/225973e.pdf
Gitelman, Z. (1990). History, memory and politics: The Holocaust in the Soviet Union. *Holocaust and Genocide Studies, 5*(1), 23–37.
Gross, Z. (2008, 11–12 December). *The culture of remembrance and its significance*. Paper presented at the European Research Consortium, Vienna, Austria.
Gross, Z. (2009, 22–23 September). *Contesting memories among European adolescents*. Paper presented at the European Research Consortium, Zurich, Switzerland.
Gross, Z. (2010). Reflective teaching as a path to religious meaning-making and growth. *Religious Education, 105*(3), 265–282.

Gross, Z., & Stevick, E. D. (2010). Holocaust education: International perspectives, challenges, opportunities, and research. *Prospects, 40*(1), 17–33.
Halbwachs, M. (1950). *The collective memory*. New York: Harper-Colophon.
Judt, T. (2005). *Postwar: A history of Europe since 1945*. New York: Penguin.
Keiny, S. (1993). Teachers' professional development as a process of conceptual change. In I. Carlgren, G. Handal, & S. Vaage (Eds.), *Teachers' minds and actions: Research in teachers' thinking and practice* (pp. 323–337). London: Falmer.
Keiny, S. (1998). Dialogue between school and academy as a strategy for developing reflective teachers and new ways of thinking about education. In M. Ben-Peretz, M. Silberstein, & S. Ziv (Eds.), *Reflection in teaching: A central pivot in the teacher's development*. Tel Aviv: Mofet Institute. (in Hebrew).
Levi, P. (1988). *The drowned and the saved* (R. Rosenthal, Trans.). New York: Summit.
Locke. J. (1979 [1689]). *An essay concerning human understanding* (P. H. Nidditch, Ed.). Oxford: Clarendon Press.
Mace, J. H. (2004). Involuntary autobiographical memories are highly dependent on abstract cuing: The Proustian view is incorrect. *Applied Cognitive Psychology, 18*(7), 893–899.
Mace, J. H. (2008). Involuntary memory: Concept and theory. In J. H. Mace (Ed.), *Involuntary memory* (pp. 1–19). Oxford: Blackwell.
Michaels, D. L., & Stevick, E. D. (2009). Europeanization in the "other" Europe: Writing the nation into "Europe" education in Slovakia and Estonia. *Journal of Curriculum Studies, 41*(2), 225–245.
Ram, U. (1996). Memory and identity: The sociology of the Israeli historians' debate. *Theory and Criticism, 8*, 9–32.
Rogoff, B. (2003). *The cultural nature of human development*. New York: Oxford University Press.
Rohdewald, S. (2008). Post-Soviet remembrance of the Holocaust and national memories of the Second World War in Russia, Ukraine, and Lithuania. *Forum for Modern Language Studies, 44*(2), 173–84.
Roth, K., & Burbules, N. C. (2007). Introduction: Understanding the meaning of citizenship education. In K. Roth & N. C. Burbules (Eds.), *Changing notions of citizenship education in contemporary nation-states* (pp. 1–9). Rotterdam: Sense Publishers.
Rutland, S. D. (2010). Creating effective Holocaust education programmes for government schools with large Muslim populations in Sydney. *Prospects, 40*(1), 75–91.
Schon, D. A. (1987). *Educating the reflective practitioner: Toward a new design for teaching and learning in the professions*. San Francisco: Jossey-Bass.
Schon, D. A. (1988). Coaching reflective teaching. In P. P. Grimmett & G. L. Erickson (Eds.), *Reflection in teacher education* (pp. 19–30). New York: Teachers College Press.
Short, G., & Reed, C. A. (2004). *Issues in Holocaust education*. Aldershot: Ashgate.
Snyder, T. (2009, 16 July). The Holocaust: The ignored reality. *The New York Review of Books, 56*(12), 14–16. http://www.nybooks.com/articles/archives/2009/jul/16/holocaust-the-ignored-reality/
Stevick, E. D., & Gross, Z. (2010). Epistemology and Holocaust education: History, memory and the politics of knowledge. *Prospects, 40*(2), 189–200.
Stevick, E. D., & Michaels, D. L. (2013). Empirical and normative foundations of Holocaust education: Bringing research and advocacy into dialogue. *Intercultural Education, 24*(1–2), 1–18.
Van der Tuin. (2009). Europe through the religious eye of young people. In H. G. Ziebertz, W. K. Kay, & U. Riegel (Eds.), *Youth in Europe III: An international empirical study about the impact of religion on life orientation* (pp. 213–228). Munster: Lit.
Weiss-Wendt, A. (2008). Why the Holocaust does not matter to Estonians. *Journal of Baltic Studies, 39*(4), 475–497.
Young, M. F. D. (1971). An approach to the study of curricula as socially organised knowledge. In M. F. D. Young (Ed.), *Knowledge and control: New directions for the sociology of education* (pp. 19–46). London: Collier-Macmillan.
Zeichner, K. M. (1994). Research on teacher thinking and different views of reflective practice in teaching and teacher education. In I. Carlgren, G. Handal, & S. Vaage (Eds.), *Teachers' minds and actions: Research in teachers' thinking and practice* (pp. 9–27). London: Falmer.

Notes on Contributors

Heribert Bastel (Austria) heads the department of secondary education at the University of Education in Linz. Until 2012 he headed the department of religious education at the Christian Churches' University of Education in Vienna/Krems, was a member of the university's centre for training in human rights education, and was a lecturer in the Faculty of Theology at the University of Vienna. For many years, he taught religious education in higher secondary schools. In this role he organised and evaluated the excursions to the memorial at Mauthausen, developing programmes for human rights education, thus combining educational theory with strong elements of reflective practice. He is currently working on a research project with the Mauthausen memorial.

Yehuda Bauer (Israel) is professor emeritus of Holocaust Studies at the Hebrew University in Jerusalem, and is currently the academic adviser to Yad Vashem, and a member of the Israeli Academy of Science. He is the honorary chairman of the International Holocaust Remembrance Alliance, and recipient of the Israel Prize (1998). His publications include 15 books, mainly on the Holocaust, antisemitism and genocide, chapters in a number of books, and some 100 articles.

Christine Beresniova (United States) is a Takiff Foundation Fellow at the Mandel Center for Advanced Holocaust Studies, at the US Holocaust Memorial Museum. She graduated from Indiana University with a doctorate in Educational Policy Studies. She has published her work in numerous edited volumes, including *(Re)Constructing Memory: School Textbooks, Identities, and the Pedagogies and Politics of Imagining Community,* and *Post-socialism is Not Dead: (Re)reading the Global in Comparative Education*. Her research has been supported by grants and fellowships from the Fulbright Foundation, the Woodrow Wilson International Center for Scholars, and the US Department of State. In 2013, she won the Nevada Press Association Gold Medal for an article about Lithuania published in *David Magazine*.

Reinhold Boschki (Germany) is a professor of religious education at the Roman Catholic Theological Department of Bonn University. After studies in theology and education at Tübingen University, Münster University, and Boston University, he taught religious education at public schools for several years. His PhD thesis focused on the work and the message of Nobel peace laureate and Holocaust survivor Elie Wiesel. Committed to improving Christian-Jewish relations, he serves as an official advisor to the German Bishops' Conference on religious relationships with Jews in Germany. He is a member of the International Seminar on Religious Education and Values, a worldwide association. Special fields of research are Christian-Jewish relations, Holocaust remembrance, theology after Auschwitz, interreligious and intercultural education, early childhood education, and adult education. He has published more than 20 books and more than 150 articles in these fields.

Patricia Bromley (United States) is an assistant professor of political science/ public administration at the University of Utah. Her research interests include cross-national, longitudinal comparisons of citizenship education, especially as related to rights education, and professionalisation of the human rights movement and non-governmental organisations. She has recently published articles in *Sociology of Education, Compare,* and *Current Issues in Comparative Education.*

Peter Carrier (Germany) is a research fellow at the Georg Eckert Institute for International Textbook Research in Braunschweig. He has taught at the universities of Tübingen, Paris VII, and Berlin, and at the Central European University in Budapest and Queen's University in Canada. His current research focuses on the historiography of the Holocaust, on history textbooks, and on theories of memory. He has published widely on Holocaust monuments, on historiography, and on national memory in France and Germany, and is also a member of the editorial committees of *National Identities* (London), *Studies in Contemporary History* (Potsdam), and *Journal for Educational Media, Memory and Society* (Braunschweig).

Paula Cowan (United Kingdom) is a senior lecturer in the School of Education, University of the West of Scotland. Her research concerns citizenship education (political literacy, Holocaust education and values education) in middle and elementary school contexts. She is the author of two curricular resources, *The Holocaust: A Teaching Pack for Primary Schools* (2000), and *The Holocaust: A Teaching Pack for Secondary Schools* (2002), which were distributed to every school in Scotland. She is a contributor to *The Chambers Dictionary of Beliefs and Religions* (2009) and co-edited *Teaching Controversial Issues in the Classroom* in 2012. She is a former trustee of the Holocaust Memorial Day Trust, and a UK delegate to the International Holocaust Remembrance Alliance.

Fred Dervin (Finland) is professor of Multicultural Education at the University of Helsinki, Finland. He specialises in multicultural teacher education, intercultural communication and education, and the sociology of multiculturalism. He has published widely in international journals on identity, the 'intercultural', and mobility/ migration. He has also published over 20 books, including: *Politics of Interculturality* (co-edited with Anne Lavanchy and Anahy Gajardo, Newcastle: CSP, 2011),

Impostures Interculturelles (Paris: L'Harmattan, 2012) and *Linguistics for Intercultural Education* (co-edited with Tony Liddicoat, New York: Benjamins, 2013).

Monique Eckmann (Switzerland), a sociologist, is professor emerita at the School for Social Work at the University of Applied Sciences Western Switzerland, in Geneva. Her work focuses on inter-group relations, on identity and memory, and on dialogue between groups in conflict. She has developed concepts and interventions in the fields of education against racism, antisemitism and right-wing extremism, human rights education, peace building, and history and memory of the Holocaust and other genocides. She is advising projects in schools, memorial sites, and museums, and cooperates with various local, national, and international organisations. She is a member of the Swiss delegation to the International Holocaust Remembrance Alliance (IHRA) and a member of the IHRA's Education Working Group. She is currently leading the IHRA's education research project. She has published widely in these fields.

Karel Fracapane (France) is a senior officer in the Education Sector of UNESCO, where he is in charge of Holocaust issues. He holds degrees in literature from the University of Angers and in political science from the Institutes of Political Studies of Bordeaux and of Paris. He previously served as policy officer at the French Ministry of Foreign Affairs, as executive secretary of the Task Force for International Cooperation on Holocaust Education, Remembrance and Research (now the International Holocaust Remembrance Alliance), and as the head of International Relations for the Shoah Memorial in Paris. He recently edited, with Matthias Haß, *Holocaust Education in a Global Context* (UNESCO 2014).

Eckhardt Fuchs (Germany) is deputy director of the Georg Eckert Institute for International Textbook Research and professor of history of education/comparative education at the Technical University Braunschweig. He has been awarded scholarships by a variety of organisations and foundations and served as a visiting professor in Sydney, Umeå, Tokyo, and Seoul. His research interests include the global history of modern education, international education policies, curriculum and textbook development, world history, and the history of science. He has published ten books and more than 100 articles and chapters on these issues. He is the editor of two educational journals and currently president of ISCHE.

Magdalena H. Gross (United States) is a fellow at the Stanford Center for International Conflict and Negotiation. She is also a lecturer in Stanford's Introductory Studies programme where she teaches about war. Her work on the teaching and learning of World War II history in contemporary Poland can be found in *Intercultural Education, Journal of Curriculum Studies, History of Education Quarterly* and other journals.

Zehavit Gross (Israel) is an associate professor at Bar-Ilan University in Israel, where she holds the UNESCO Chair for Values Education, Tolerance and Peace and heads the graduate programme of Management and Development of Informal Educational Systems. Her main area of specialisation is socialisation processes (religious, secular, feminine and civic) among adolescents. Currently she is actively participating in four international projects in Europe, North America, and Australia.

Corey L. Harbaugh (United States) is a high school English teacher in Gobles, Michigan, and a teacher fellow and member of the Regional Educator Corps at the United States Holocaust Memorial Museum. He is also a master teacher with the USC Shoah Foundation, and a teacher satellite leader in the Memorial Library's Holocaust Educator Network. He directs a summer seminar professional development programme for teachers on Holocaust Education in Michigan.

Dienke Hondius (The Netherlands) is assistant professor of history at VU University Amsterdam, and a staff member at the Anne Frank House, Amsterdam. She has been directly involved in scholarship about the Holocaust through the Anne Frank House in international exhibitions and projects, and in higher education, for three decades. Her latest book is on the history and impact of the concept of 'race' in Europe, from 1600 onwards: *Blackness in Western Europe: Racial Patterns of Paternalism and Exclusion* (Edison, NJ: Transaction Books, 2014). A new digital source is an online database, *Bystander Memories*, on the memories of non-Jewish eyewitnesses of the Holocaust in the Netherlands, in cooperation with the Oral History Department of the USHMM. Her current research projects include "Mapping Slavery", a series of digital maps and guides; *Slavery Heritage and History,* an oral history of Afro-Surinamese teachers in the Netherlands; and "Mapping Histories of Hiding", a new history of Jews in hiding in European cities, using digital maps of hiding places.

Jack Jedwab (Canada) is the executive vice president of the Association for Canadian Studies and the Canadian Institute for Identities and Migration. He taught in the Department of Sociology at McGill University (1989–1998) and at the McGill Institute for the Study of Canada (2000–2008). He is the founding editor of the publication *Canadian Diversity*. From 2013 to 2014 he was the national chair of the Metropolis Conference on Immigration and Integration. In 2009, he edited a special edition of *Canadian Diversity,* entitled Holocaust Education and Genocide Awareness in Diverse Societies.

Louise B. Jennings (United States) is a professor in the School of Education at Colorado State University. Her scholarship examines the cultural and discursive work of educational practice around issues of equity, diversity, and social justice. She engages in collaborative research that focuses on the social construction of youth empowerment and critical citizenship across educational contexts, democratic educational practices in the United States and Brazil, critical multicultural education in K-12 and teacher education settings, and inquiry-based pedagogies and inquiry-driven professional development.

Henry Maitles (United Kingdom) is a professor and assistant dean in the School of Education, University of the West of Scotland. He was part of the Learning and Teaching Scotland Review Group on Education for Citizenship in Scotland, which drew up the proposals that were accepted by the Scottish Executive/Government and are now implemented in every school in Scotland. He researches the impact of citizenship and related initiatives in schools in terms of the impact on young people's values and attitudes. His books include *Values in Education: We're Citizens Now*, published by Dunedin Press in 2005 and by Discovery Publishing House, New Delhi, in 2007; he edited *Exploring Cultural Perspectives in Education* in 2008 and co-edited *Teaching Controversial Issues in the Classroom* in 2012. He is on the editorial boards of *Citizenship Teaching and Learning*, *Genocide Studies and Prevention*, and the e-journal *Journal for Critical Education Policy Studies* (http://www.jceps.com/), and is president of the Children's Identity and Citizenship in Europe Association.

Christian Matzka (Austria) is a professor of geography and history at the Christian Churches' University of Education in Vienna/Krems, and is a lecturer at the University of Vienna in the departments of history and education. He is a member of the Herodot Network for Geography in Higher Education, and heads the City Museum of Purkersdorf in Lower Austria. His research interests are in cultural tourism, history of tourism, local history, the teaching of geography and economics, and political and civic education. His research in local and regional history and his political activities combine the facts of historical research with political science and teaching, enabling him to develop citizenship education programmes.

Wolfgang Meseth (Germany) is a professor of primary and secondary education and diversity at the Department of School Education at the Philipps-Universität Marburg. He studied education, psychology, and sociology at the Goethe University of Frankfurt from 1994 to 1999. His principal research interests are in educational theory and theory of teaching, Holocaust education, civic education, and empirical social research. Recent publications focus on how education can confront the Nazi past, and education after Auschwitz in a united Germany.

Torben Messinger (Germany) studied political science and history at the Leibniz University in Hanover and at Saint Mary's University in Halifax, Canada, and later carried out research in Turkey and Bahrain. As a student and research assistant at the Georg Eckert Institute, he has been involved in various academic projects including, since July 2012, the joint UNESCO/GEI project presented in this volume.

Helene Miklas (Austria) is a professor of pedagogy and research at the Christian Churches' University of Education in Vienna/Krems and a lecturer at the University of Vienna in the department of education. She has studied educational science and philosophy, organisational development, and systemic consulting, and is an accredited consultant in EOS (Entwicklung [development], Organisation and Systems) with a primary focus on school development and personal coaching. For many years she has taught educational science, microteaching, philosophy, personal coaching, and religion, and conducted probing research on questions of diversity. She is also involved in the research project with the Mauthausen memorial.

Thomas Misco (United States) is an associate professor of social studies education at Miami University in Ohio. His research focuses on how curriculum design, pedagogical strategies, sociocultural contexts, and other factors inhibit and encourage the discussion of controversial issues.

Debora Hinderliter Ortloff (United States) is director of assessment and assistant professor of social sciences at Finger Lakes Community College in Canandaigua, New York. After living for several years in Germany, including a year as a Fulbright Scholar in Cottbus, Germany, she returned to the United States to pursue her doctorate at Indiana University. While there she combined her interests in global studies, education policy, and research methodology, receiving a PhD in History, Philosophy and Policy Studies of Education, as well as joint master's degrees in Comparative Education and Educational Psychology. These interests still drive her professionally and she is widely published in the area of global citizenship and diversity education in Europe and the United States. She has also co-edited a volume on methodology in educational research and focuses much of her current work on applied research techniques for improving educational policy and practice.

Matthias Proske (Germany) is a professor of educational sciences at the Department of Didactics and Teaching Research at the University of Cologne. He studied education, theology, and philosophy at the universities of Frankfurt am Main and San Salvador. His research interests are in teaching research, teacher education, the philosophy of education, and Holocaust education. His recent publications focus on navigating moral expectations in classroom conversations on these topics, dealing with the Nazi past, and moral education in history classes.

Brian M. Puaca (United States) is an associate professor of history at Christopher Newport University, in Virginia. His book, *Learning Democracy: Education Reform in West Germany, 1945–1965*, received the 2011 New Scholar's Award from the American Educational Research Association (AERA). Most recently, his work on the West German schools has appeared in the *History of Education Quarterly* and *New German Critique*.

Bettina Reichmann (Germany) has been a research assistant in the Roman Catholic Theological Department at Tübingen University. She is also affiliated with the University of Koblenz-Landau, where she is involved in a research project on human rights education and religious education. After earning diplomas at Tübingen University and Boston University, she worked on the special research project *Kriegserfahrungen: Krieg und Gesellschaft in der Neuzeit* (Experience of war: War and society in modern times) at the University of Tübingen. Her PhD thesis focused on church-fostered antisemitism and nationalism in Hungary under the Catholic bishop Ottokár Prohászka (1858–1927). Special fields of research are the Catholic Church and antisemitism, religion and war, Jewish-Christian relations, Holocaust remembrance, and theology after Auschwitz.

Theodore Rosengarten (United States) holds the Zucker-Goldberg Chair in Holocaust Studies at the College of Charleston, and is an associate scholar in Jewish Studies at the University of South Carolina. His special interests include modern Jewish history and the history of the American South. He is the author of *All God's*

Dangers: The Life of Nate Shaw and *Tombee: Portrait of a Cotton Planter*, as well as numerous essays on Holocaust topics. A MacArthur Fellow and recipient of the National Book Award, Rosengarten regularly leads studies abroad to East Europe. Ted and his wife Dale have collaborated on two award-winning books that accompanied national traveling exhibitions curated by Dale: *A Portion of the People: Three Hundred Years of Southern Jewish Life*, and *Grass Roots: African Origins of an American Art*.

Susan Garnett Russell (United States) is an assistant professor of International and Comparative Education at Teachers College, Columbia University. She earned her doctorate in International and Comparative Education from Stanford University; additionally, she holds an MA in International Development from the Johns Hopkins School of Advanced International Studies (SAIS) and a BA in International Relations from Stanford University. She was a recipient of the National Science Foundation Doctoral Dissertation Fellowship and was a fellow at the Clayman Institute for Gender Research at Stanford. Additionally, she has worked as a policy analyst for UNESCO and a consultant for other non-profit organisations, including Save the Children and SRI International. Her research focuses on education and conflict, human rights, citizenship, and gender, particularly in sub-Saharan Africa, and has been published in *International Studies Quarterly, Compare, Prospects*, and *Multicultural Education Review*.

Suzanne D. Rutland (Australia) is a professor in the Department of Hebrew, Biblical, and Jewish Studies at the University of Sydney. She has published widely on Australian Jewish history, edits the Sydney edition of the *Australian Jewish Historical Society Journal*, and writes on issues relating to the Shoah, Israel, and Jewish education. She has written a book called *"Let My People Go": The Untold Story of Australia and the Soviet Jews, 1959–1989*, with Sam Lipski, to be published by Hybrid Press in 2015. In January 2008 she received the Medal of the Order of Australia for services to Higher Jewish Education and interfaith dialogue.

Wilhelm Schwendemann (Germany) is a professor of religious education and education management in the Department of Theology and Education at the Protestant University in Freiburg. After studies in theology, philosophy, orientalism, Jewish history and literature, and sociology of religion at Bethel College/University and the universities of Bielefeld, Zurich, Göttingen, and Amsterdam, he served as a Protestant pastor and then as a public school teacher. His PhD thesis focused on Calvin's theology and Platonism. He is deputy director of the Freiburg Institute of Human Rights Education. Special fields of research are Christian-Jewish relations, Holocaust remembrance, interreligious and intercultural education, and empirical studies in the theology of children and youth. He has published more than 40 books and more than 360 articles in these fields.

Geoffrey Short (United Kingdom) retired several years ago from the University of Hertfordshire, where he was a reader in Educational Research. Although much of his career has been devoted to researching and writing about 'race', ethnicity and education, his interests over the past 20 years have shifted increasingly towards antisemitism and the Holocaust. In the late 1990s he was an advisor to the Council of Europe on its Holocaust education programme and in 2004 he co-authored with Carole Ann Reed *Issues in Holocaust Education,* published by Ashgate.

E. Doyle Stevick (United States) is an associate professor in educational leadership and policies at the University of South Carolina, where he founded the Office of International and Comparative Education. Twice a Fulbright fellow in Estonia, he spent much of the period between September of 2001 and December of 2004 studying education for democracy in Estonia, where the politics surrounding Holocaust education emerged as a critical issue. He edited *Reimagining Civic Education: How Diverse Societies Form Democratic Citizens* and *Advancing Democracy Through Education? U.S. Influence Abroad and Domestic Practices,* both with Bradley A.U. Levinson.

Barry van Driel (The Netherlands) was educated at universities in the Netherlands and the United States. He holds a graduate degree in the Psychology of Culture and Religion, with a specialisation in education. In 1992, he joined the staff of the Anne Frank House, where he is now international director for teacher training and curriculum development. He has been the editor-in-chief of the international academic journal *Intercultural Education* since 2000 and is currently vice president of the International Association for Intercultural Education (IAIE). He has served as senior education consultant to the Office for Democratic Institutions and Human Rights (ODIHR) in Warsaw and consultant to UNESCO and the FRA (Fundamental Rights Agency). Since 2010 he has been a jury member of the United Nations-BMW Intercultural Innovation awards and was recently appointed chair of the jury. He recently edited books entitled *Confronting Islamophobia in Educational Practice* (2005) and *Challenging Homophobia* (with Lutz van Dijk, 2007).

Elie Wiesel (United States) is a novelist, essayist and professor. A Holocaust survivor, born in Sighet, Romania, he won the Nobel Peace Prize in 1986. In 1958, he published his first book, *La Nuit,* a memoir of his experiences in the concentration camps. He has since authored more than forty books, some of which use these events as their basic material, and he became a tireless spokesman for human rights. He was a visiting scholar at Yale University, and a Distinguished Professor of Judaic Studies at the City College of New York, and since 1976 has been Andrew W. Mellon Professor in the Humanities at Boston University. He has also been awarded the Presidential Medal of Freedom, the United States Congressional Gold Medal, and the Grand Croix of the French Legion of Honor.

Printed by Printforce, the Netherlands